SECOND EDITION

MANAGING
IN THE LEGAL
ENVIRONMENT

SECOND EDITION

Managing in the Legal Environment

Al H. Ringleb
Roger E. Meiners
Frances L. Edwards
Department of Legal Studies
College of Commerce and Industry
Clemson University

West Publishing Company

Minneapolis/St. Paul ■ New York ■ Los Angeles ■ San Francisco

Production, Prepress, Printing and Binding by West Publishing Company.

Copyediting: *Deborah Cady*
Text Design: *John Edeen*
Art: *Accurate Art*
Composition: *Carlisle Communications*
Cover Art: *Ivan Pinheiro Machado/The Image Bank*
Cover Design: *Lois Stanfield/Light Source Images*

COPYRIGHT © 1990   By WEST PUBLISHING COMPANY
COPYRIGHT © 1993   By WEST PUBLISHING COMPANY
                             610 Opperman Drive
                             P.O. Box 64526
                             St. Paul, MN 55164-0526

Library of Congress Cataloging in Publication Data

Ringleb, Al H.
   Managing in the legal environment / Al H. Ringleb, Roger E.
Meiners, Frances L. Edwards. —2nd ed.
     p. cm.
    Includes index.
    ISBN 0-314-01165-X (hard)
    1. Industrial laws and legislation—United States. 2. Trade
regulation—United States. 3. Business ethics—United States.
I. Meiners, Roger E. II. Edwards, Frances L. III. Title.
KF1600.R55 1993
343.73'07—dc20
[347.3037]
                                                                     92-30982
         CIP

CONTENTS IN BRIEF

TABLE OF CASES   xxi

PREFACE   xxiv

PART I

BUSINESS AND THE LEGAL ENVIRONMENT   1

CHAPTER 1   Business and the Legal Environment   3
CHAPTER 2   Ethics, the Law, and the Managerial Process   25
CHAPTER 3   Business and the Judicial Process   51
CHAPTER 4   Business and the Resolution of Disputes   87
CHAPTER 5   Business and the Constitution   115
CHAPTER 6   Government Agencies and the Administrative Process   141

PART II

BUSINESS AND THE COMMON LAW   169

CHAPTER 7   Business and the Law of Torts   171
CHAPTER 8   Products Liability and Intellectual Property   199
CHAPTER 9   Business and the Law of Contracts   227
CHAPTER 10   Sales and the UCC   259
CHAPTER 11   Business Organizations and the Law of Agency   295

PART III

BUSINESS AND THE REGULATORY ENVIRONMENT   329

CHAPTER 12   Labor Relations Law   331
CHAPTER 13   Employment Discrimination   367
CHAPTER 14   Environmental Regulation   397
CHAPTER 15   Consumer Protection   431
CHAPTER 16   Antitrust Law   463
CHAPTER 17   Securities Regulation   499
CHAPTER 18   International Legal Environment of Business   535

APPENDIX A   Finding the Law   574
APPENDIX B   The Constitution of the United States of America   578
APPENDIX C   The Antitrust Statutes   595
APPENDIX D   National Labor Relations Act   600
APPENDIX E   Title VII of the Civil Rights Act of 1964   605
APPENDIX F   Americans with Disabilities Act of 1990   609
APPENDIX G   Securities Statutes   612

GLOSSARY   617

INDEX   635

CONTENTS

TABLE OF CASES   xxi

PREFACE   xxiv

PART I

BUSINESS AND THE LEGAL ENVIRONMENT   1

CHAPTER 1

BUSINESS AND THE LEGAL ENVIRONMENT   3

THE AMERICAN BUSINESS CULTURE   5
Comparative Economic Statistics 6

MANAGERIAL FUNCTIONS, DEFINITIONS, AND PROCESSES   7
The Internal Environment 8   The External Environment 10

INTERNATIONAL ASPECTS:
CONSIDERING THE EXTERNAL ENVIRONMENT IN EUROPE   14

CHARACTERISTICS OF THE LEGAL ENVIRONMENT   15
Industry 16   Business Organization 16   Size of the Business 16
Business Location 17   Markets the Business Serves 17   Legal
Environment Within a Business 18

THE MANAGEMENT PROCESS AND THE LEGAL ENVIRONMENT   18
Strategic Planning and the Legal Environment 20

INTERNATIONAL ASPECTS:
CONSIDERING THE JAPANESE MANAGEMENT STYLE   20

Lost Opportunities as Threats 21

SUMMARY: A GUIDE FOR MANAGERS   22

MANAGER'S ETHICAL DILEMMA:
HOW SHOULD MANAGERS RESPOND TO DIFFICULT
DECISIONS?   23

REVIEW AND DISCUSSION QUESTIONS   23

CHAPTER 2

ETHICS, THE LAW, AND THE MANAGERIAL PROCESS   25

PERSONAL AND CORPORATE ETHICS: SURVEYS AND
PERCEPTIONS   26

ETHICS AND MORALS: DEFINITIONS, THEORIES, AND
APPLICATIONS   29
Ethics and Etiquette Compared 29   Ethics and the Law Compared 29
Conceptual Tools for Moral Thinking 30   Moral Theories 33

THE NOTION OF CORPORATE SOCIAL RESPONSIBILITY   38
Corporate Social Responsibility: Conceptual Issue Debate 39   The
Scope of Corporate Responsibility: The Narrow View 41   The Scope of
Corporate Responsibility: The Broad View 42   The RP Perspective 43
The Utilitarian Perspective 43   Making Corporations More Morally
Responsive 44

SUMMARY: A GUIDE FOR MANAGERS   45

MANAGER'S ETHICAL DILEMMA:
TAKING ETHICS SERIOUSLY   46

REVIEW AND DISCUSSION QUESTIONS   47

CHAPTER 3

BUSINESS AND THE JUDICIAL PROCESS   51

WHAT IS LAW?   52

FUNCTIONS OF LAW AND THE LEGAL SYSTEM   53
Assuring Social Control by Influencing Behavior 53   Conflict
Resolution 54   Social Maintenance 55   Social Change 55

ORIGIN OF LAW IN THE UNITED STATES: THE COMMON LAW   56
Common Law 56   Doctrine of Stare Decisis 56

SOURCES OF LAW MORE RECENT IN ORIGIN   57
Constitutions 57

INTERNATIONAL ASPECTS:
GREAT BRITAIN'S UNWRITTEN CONSTITUTION   58

Legislatures 60   Administrative Agencies 60   The Judiciary 61
The Executive 61

CLASSIFICATIONS OF LAW   61
Public or Private Law 62   Civil or Criminal Law 62   Substantive or
Procedural Law 64

THE LITIGATION PROCESS   65
Rules of Civil Procedure 65   Functions of Litigation 65

SUBJECT-MATTER JURISDICTION   65
General Organization of the American Court System 67   Subject-
Matter Jurisdiction and the State Court Systems 67   Subject-Matter
Jurisdiction and the Federal Court System 69   Federal Court System 69

INTERNATIONAL ASPECTS:
FRENCH COURT SYSTEM   72

TERRITORIAL JURISDICTION   72
Jurisdiction Over the Person 72   Jurisdiction Over Out-of-State
Defendants 74   Jurisdiction Over Out-of-State Corporate
Defendants 74   Jurisdiction Based Upon Power Over Property 76
Venue 77

APPLYING THE APPROPRIATE SUBSTANTIVE LAW   78
The Erie Doctrine: The Rule in Federal Courts 78   Substantive Law in
State Court 79

REMEDIES IN CIVIL LITIGATION   79
Monetary Damages 80   Equitable Remedies 80

SUMMARY: A GUIDE FOR MANAGERS   82

MANAGER'S ETHICAL DILEMMA:
BUILD WHERE, SUE WHERE?   83

REVIEW AND DISCUSSION QUESTIONS   84

CHAPTER 4
BUSINESS AND THE RESOLUTION OF DISPUTES   87

THE NATURE OF OUR ADVERSARY SYSTEM   88
Is the Disagreement One for Which the Law Furnishes Relief? 89
What is the Probability of Winning the Lawsuit? 89   Will the Relief the
Court Provides Make the Lawsuit Worthwhile? 89

BUSINESS AS A DEFENDANT   90
How Will Litigation Affect the Company's Goodwill? 90   How
Important Is the Underlying Relationship? 90   Is Settlement an
Economically Viable Alternative? 91   Are We Encouraging Spurious
Lawsuits? 91   Is the Lawsuit an Integral Part of the Company's
Strategic Plan? 91

RESOLVING A BUSINESS DISPUTE THROUGH THE COURTS   92
The Complexity in Resolving a Business Dispute 92   The Growing
Significance of Business Litigation 94   Size of Judgments Against
Businesses 94

BASIC TRIAL PROCEDURES   95
Pleadings Stage 95   Discovery Stage: Obtaining Information Before
Trial 99   Discovery: Impacts on Business 100   Pretrial Stage 101
Trial Stage 102   Appellate Stage 106   Enforcement Stage 107

INTERNATIONAL ASPECTS:
BASIC TRIAL PROCEDURES   107

DISPUTE RESOLUTION: ALTERNATIVES TO THE COURT
SYSTEM   107
Arbitration 108   Minitrials 109   Negotiation 109   Advantages of
ADR Processes to Businesses 110

SUMMARY: A GUIDE FOR MANAGERS   110

MANAGER'S ETHICAL DILEMMA:
HEADING OFF LEGAL TROUBLES   111

REVIEW AND DISCUSSION QUESTIONS   112

CHAPTER 5
BUSINESS AND THE CONSTITUTION   115

BACKGROUND ON THE CONSTITUTION   116

CONSTITUTIONAL BASIS OF REGULATION   117

The Commerce Clause 117   The Necessary and Proper Clause 118
Limits on Congressional Powers to Regulate Commerce 118
Federal/State Regulatory Relations 120   The Contract Clause 121
The Taxing Power 122

BUSINESS AND FREE SPEECH   124
Political Speech by Corporations 124   Commercial Speech 126

UNREASONABLE SEARCH AND SEIZURE   128
Limitations on Business Searches and Inspections 128   Restrictions on
the Use of Evidence Collected 129

INTERNATIONAL ASPECTS:
CONSTITUTIONAL LAW IN FOREIGN JURISDICTIONS   129

SELF-INCRIMINATION   130

JUST COMPENSATION   130

RIGHT TO TRIAL   132

EXCESSIVE FINES   133

DUE PROCESS   133

EQUAL PROTECTION   135

SUMMARY: A GUIDE FOR MANAGERS   136

MANAGER'S ETHICAL DILEMMA:
VALUES, RIGHTS, OR PROFITS?   137

REVIEW AND DISCUSSION QUESTIONS   137

CHAPTER 6

GOVERNMENT AGENCIES AND THE ADMINISTRATIVE
PROCESS   141

ADMINISTRATIVE AGENCIES AND ADMINISTRATIVE LAW   142
Creating an Administrative Agency 142   Administrative Law 143

DEVELOPMENT OF REGULATORY AGENCIES   144
New Deal Agencies 144   Social Reform and the Agencies of the 1960s
and 1970s 145

REGULATORY POWERS OF ADMINISTRATIVE AGENCIES   145
Legislative or Rulemaking Power 145   Investigative Powers 148
Adjudicatory Powers 150   Enforcement Power 150

ADMINISTRATIVE PROCESS AND PROCEDURES   151
Informal Agency Procedures 151   Formal Agency Procedures 152

INTERNATIONAL ASPECTS:
ADMINISTRATIVE AGENCIES IN JAPAN   156

JUDICIAL REVIEW: CONSTRAINT ON AGENCY POWERS   157
Procedural Requirements: The Right to Judicial Review 157   Scope of
Judicial Review 159

CONGRESSIONAL RESTRICTIONS ON AGENCY POWER   160
Direct Congressional Checks on Agency Power 160   Indirect
Congressional Checks on Agency Power 162

SUMMARY: A GUIDE FOR MANAGERS   163

MANAGER'S ETHICAL DILEMMA:
MY FRIEND, THE POLITICIAN   164

REVIEW AND DISCUSSION QUESTIONS   165

PART II

BUSINESS AND THE COMMON LAW   169

CHAPTER 7

BUSINESS AND THE LAW OF TORTS   171

THE SCOPE OF TORT LAW   172
Purposes of Tort Law 172   Business and the Law of Torts 173
Costs of Tort Litigation 173

INTENTIONAL TORTS   173
Interference with Personal Rights 174

INTERNATIONAL ASPECTS:
LIBEL IN FOREIGN COURTS   178

Interference with Property Rights 180

INTERNATIONAL ASPECTS:
IS JAPAN REALLY DIFFERENT?   182

NEGLIGENCE   183
The Reasonable Person Standard 183   Causation 184   Defenses to a
Negligence Action 186

INTERNATIONAL ASPECTS:
TORT LIABILITY IN FRANCE   188

STRICT LIABILITY IN TORT   189
Abnormally Dangerous Activities 189   Products Liability 190

BUSINESS TORTS   190
Disparagement 191   Interference with Contractual Relations 192
Interference with a Business Relationship 193

SUMMARY: A GUIDE FOR MANAGERS   194

MANAGER'S ETHICAL DILEMMA:
HOW DO YOU MAKE THINGS RIGHT
WHEN YOU WERE WRONG?   195

REVIEW AND DISCUSSION QUESTIONS   196

CHAPTER 8

PRODUCTS LIABILITY AND INTELLECTUAL PROPERTY   199

CONSUMER PRODUCTS AND NEGLIGENCE   200
Rule of *Caveat Emptor* 201   Rise of Negligence in Tort 201   The
Negligence Standard 202   Current Applications of Negligence 202

STRICT LIABILITY   204
Strict Liability Under Contract Law 204   Strict Liability in Tort 206
Extensions of Strict Liability 207   Market Share Liability 211
Defenses 212   Does Products Liability Need Reform? 213

INTERNATIONAL ASPECTS:
PRODUCTS LIABILITY IN EUROPE   213

INTELLECTUAL PROPERTY   214
Trademarks 215   Trade Names 216   Copyrights 217   Patents 219

INTERNATIONAL ASPECTS:
JAPANESE AND AMERICAN PATENTS   219

Trade Secrets 220

SUMMARY: A GUIDE FOR MANAGERS   221

MANAGER'S ETHICAL DILEMMA:
SHOULD LOCAL FOLKS PAY THEIR OWN TORT BILLS?   222

REVIEW AND DISCUSSION QUESTIONS   223

CHAPTER 9
BUSINESS AND THE LAW OF CONTRACTS   227

THE NOTION OF FREEDOM OF CONTRACT   228
Sources of Contract Law 229

DEFINITION AND CLASSIFICATIONS OF CONTRACTS   229
Definitions of a Contract 230   Classifications of Contracts 230

INTERNATIONAL ASPECTS:
DEVELOPING CONTRACT RIGHTS IN CENTRAL AND EASTERN
EUROPE   232

ELEMENTS OF A CONTRACT   233
The Agreement 233   Consideration 237   Capacity to Contract 241
Legality 243   Reality and Genuineness of Consent 244   Contracts in
Writing and the Statute of Frauds 244

INTERNATIONAL ASPECTS:
CONTRACTING WITH THE JAPANESE   245

DISCHARGE OF CONTRACTS   246
Discharge by Performance 246   Anticipatory Breach 247   Discharge
by Failure of Condition Precedent and by Occurence of Express
Condition Subsequent 247   Discharge by Impossibility 248
Discharge by Operation of Law 249   Discharge by Agreement of the
Parties 249

REMEDIES   250
Monetary Damages 251   Mitigation of Damages 252   Equitable
Remedies 253

SUMMARY: A GUIDE FOR MANAGERS   254

MANAGER'S ETHICAL DILEMMA:
IS IT CHEATING OR IS IT BUSINESS?   255

REVIEW AND DISCUSSION QUESTIONS   256

CHAPTER 10
SALES AND THE UCC   259

THE ORIGIN OF THE UNIFORM COMMERCIAL CODE   260
The Movement Toward Unification 261   Relationship Between Article
2 and the Common Law 261

SALES CONTRACTS UNDER THE UCC: SCOPE OF
COVERAGE   262
Sale Under the UCC 262   Goods Under the UCC 263   Sales By and
Between Merchants 263

THE FORMATION OF A SALES CONTRACT   263
Intent to Contract 264   An Indefinite Offer 265   Merchant's Firm
Offer 266   Acceptance 267   Contract Modification and Consideration
Requirements 267

INTERNATIONAL ASPECTS:
INTERNATIONAL SALES OF GOODS   268

TITLE TO GOODS   268
Identification 268   Passage of Title 269   Special Problems Regarding
Title 270   Statute of Frauds 272

PERFORMANCE AND OBLIGATIONS   272
Seller's Obligations 272   Buyer's Obligations 275

SALES WARRANTIES   276
Warranties of Title 276   Express Warranties of Quality 277   Implied
Warranties of Quality 278   Conflicting Warranties 280   Warranty
Disclaimers 281   Third-Party Beneficiaries of Warranties 282

RIGHTS AND REMEDIES   282
Seller's Rights and Remedies 282   Seller's Incidental Damages 284
Buyer's Rights and Remedies 284   Buyer's Incidental and
Consequential Damages 287

SUMMARY: A GUIDE FOR MANAGERS   288

MANAGER'S ETHICAL DILEMMA:
MEETING THE REQUIRED SPECIFICATIONS   290

REVIEW AND DISCUSSION QUESTIONS   290

CHAPTER 11
BUSINESS ORGANIZATIONS AND THE LAW OF AGENCY   295

THE AGENCY RELATIONSHIP   297
Creating an Agency 298   Principal's Duties to an Agent 298   Agent's
Duties to the Principal 298

AGENT'S AUTHORITY TO ACT FOR THE PRINCIPAL   300
Actual Authority 300   Apparent Authority 300

LIABILITY FOR CONTRACTS AND TORTS   300
Contract Liability of Disclosed and Partially Disclosed Principals 301
Liability for Torts of the Agent 301

TERMINATION OF AN AGENCY   303

MAJOR FORMS OF BUSINESS ORGANIZATION   304
A Statistical Overview 304   Sole Proprietorships 305   General
Partnerships 305   Limited Partnership 309   Corporations 311

FACTORS IN THE CHOICE OF BUSINESS ORGANIZATION   316
Liability 318   Transferability of Ownership Interests 319
Duration 320   Capital Requirements 320   Taxation
Considerations 321

OTHER FORMS OF BUSINESS ORGANIZATION   321
Joint Ventures 322   Joint Stock Companies 322   Cooperatives 322
Syndicates 323

SUMMARY: A GUIDE FOR MANAGERS   323

MANAGER'S ETHICAL DILEMMA:
ARE WE OUR EMPLOYEES' KEEPERS?   324

REVIEW AND DISCUSSION QUESTIONS   324

PART III

BUSINESS AND THE REGULATORY
ENVIRONMENT   329

CHAPTER 12
LABOR RELATIONS LAW   331

FEDERAL LABOR LEGISLATION   332
Norris-La Guardia Act 333   Wagner Act of 1935 334   The Taft-Hartley
Act of 1947 335   The Landrum-Griffin Act of 1959 335

THE NATIONAL LABOR RELATIONS BOARD   336
Jurisdication of the NLRB 336   NLRB Complaint Procedure 336

UNIONIZATION   337
Movement to Unionization 337   Agency Shops 338   Employer
Responses to Union Organizing 339

COLLECTIVE BARGAINING   341
Good Faith Bargaining 341   Mandatory Subjects of Bargaining 342
Collective Bargaining and Arbitration 343   Concerted Activities 343
Employer Economic Responses 344

UNLAWFUL LABOR ACTIVITIES   345
Secondary Boycotts 345

INTERNATIONAL ASPECTS:
LABOR RELATIONS IN JAPAN   347

EMPLOYMENT-AT-WILL   347
Public Policy Exceptions 348

EMPLOYEE HANDBOOKS   348

SUBSTANCE ABUSE   349
Practical Problems for Business 349   Legal Issues in Drug Testing 350
Employer Substance Abuse Policy 352

PROTECTION OF WORKER SAFETY AND HEALTH   353
Occupational Safety and Health Act 354   Workers and Toxic
Substances 355

WORKERS' COMPENSATION   357
Compensation Provided 357   Incentives for Safety 358   Basis for a
Claim 358   A Flawed System? 359

GENERAL REGULATION OF LABOR MARKETS   359
Restrictions on Immigration 359   Federal Minimum Wage
Requirements 360   Occupational Licensure and Regulation 360   The
Regulation of Private Employee Retirement Plans 361

SUMMARY: A GUIDE FOR MANAGERS   362

MANAGER'S ETHICAL DILEMMA:
SHOULD EMPLOYERS DICTATE EMPLOYEE LIFESTYLE?   364

REVIEW AND DISCUSSION QUESTIONS   364

CHAPTER 13

EMPLOYMENT DISCRIMINATION   367

BACKGROUND TO DISCRIMINATION LAW   368
The Civil Rights Movement 369   Equal Pay Act of 1963 369

TITLE VII OF THE 1964 CIVIL RIGHTS ACT   370
Coverage and Enforcement 370   Protected Classes Under Title VII 372
Theories of Discrimination Under Title VII 376   Defenses Under
Title VII 378   Discrimination and Remedies 380

INTERNATIONAL ASPECTS:
EMPLOYMENT DISCRIMINATION IN EUROPE AND JAPAN   382

AFFIRMATIVE ACTION PROGRAMS   383
Executive Order 11246 383   Affirmative Action as a Remedy 384
Voluntary Affirmative Action Programs 384

AGE DISCRIMINATION IN EMPLOYMENT ACT   385
BFOQ on the Basis of Age 386

DISCRIMINATION AGAINST THE DISABLED   388
Definition of Disabled 388   Compliance with the Statutes 389

SUMMARY: A GUIDE FOR MANAGERS   391

MANAGER'S ETHICAL DILEMMA:
WILL ACCESS REQUIREMENTS ACCOMMODATE BUSINESS
REQUIREMENTS?   392

REVIEW AND DISCUSSION QUESTIONS   393

CHAPTER 14

ENVIRONMENTAL REGULATION   397

POLLUTION AND THE COMMON LAW   398
Nuisance Law and Pollution 399   Trespass and Pollution 401
Negligence, Strict Liability, and Pollution 401   Common Law
Remedies 402

FEDERAL REGULATION   402
National Environmental Policy Act 403   Environmental Protection
Agency 403

AIR POLLUTION   404
Clean Air Act of 1970 405   Clean Air Act of 1977 405   Clean Air Act
of 1990 409

WATER POLLUTION   411
The Clean Water Act 411   Point Source Pollution 413   Nonpoint
Source Pollution 415   Wetlands 416

LAND POLLUTION   416
Toxic Substances Control Act 417   Pesticides 418   Resource
Conservation and Recovery Act 418   Superfund 419

WILDLIFE PROTECTION   421

GLOBAL ENVIRONMENTAL ISSUES   423
The Ozone Layer 424   International Cooperation 424

POLLUTION PREVENTION   425

SUMMARY: A GUIDE FOR MANAGERS   426

MANAGER'S ETHICAL DILEMMA:
TREES OR PEOPLE?   427

REVIEW AND DISCUSSION QUESTIONS   427

CHAPTER 15
CONSUMER PROTECTION   431

THE FDA: FOOD AND DRUG REGULATION   432
Food Safety 433   Nutrition Labeling 434   Drug Safety 435
Enforcement Activities 437

INTERNATIONAL ASPECTS:
INTERNATIONAL DRUG REGULATION   438

THE FTC AND CONSUMER PROTECTION   439
Consumer Protection Procedures 439   Regulating Unfair and Deceptive
Acts or Practices 439   Regulating Advertising Claims 440

INTERNATIONAL ASPECTS:
FOREIGN ADVERTISING REGULATION   442

FTC Enforcement Activities 442   Telemarketing Fraud 443   Trade
Regulation Rules 444   Magnuson-Moss Warranty Act 446

CONSUMER CREDIT PROTECTION ACT   447
Truth-in-Lending Act 447   Consumer Leasing Act 449   Fair Credit
Billing Act 450   Fair Credit Reporting Act 451   Equal Credit
Opportunity Act 451

INTERNATIONAL ASPECTS:
CONSUMER CREDIT PROTECTION ABROAD   453

Fair Debt Collection Practices Act 454   Electronic Fund
Transfer Act 456

SUMMARY: A GUIDE FOR MANAGERS   457

MANAGER'S ETHICAL DILEMMA:
SHOULD ADS AVOID MINORITIES AND YOUNG PEOPLE?   459

REVIEW AND DISCUSSION QUESTIONS   459

CHAPTER 16
ANTITRUST LAW   463

ANTITRUST COMMON LAW   464

THE ANTITRUST STATUTES   465
The Sherman Act 465   The Clayton Act 466   The Federal Trade
Commission Act 466

EXEMPTIONS FROM AND ENFORCEMENT OF THE ANTITRUST
LAWS   467
Exemptions 467   Enforcement 468   Remedies Available 469

INTERNATIONAL ASPECTS:
ANTITRUST ENFORCEMENT   470

THE COURTS AND ANTITRUST ANALYSIS   470
Per se Rule 470   Rule of Reason 471   Horizontal Restraints
of Trade 471   Vertical Restraints of Trade 472

INTERNATIONAL ASPECTS:
FOREIGN COMPETITORS FACE JAPANESE *DANGO* SYSTEM   473

MERGERS   473
The Supreme Court's Approach to Mergers 473   Determining a Firm's
Market Power 474   Defenses: When Mergers are Allowed 476

HORIZONTAL PRICE FIXING   477
Per se Rule in Price Fixing 477   The Rule of Reason in Price-Fixing
Cases 477

EXCHANGES OF INFORMATION   479
Purpose of Price Information Considered 479   Conspiracy to Restrain
Information 481

HORIZONTAL MARKET DIVISIONS   481

VERTICAL PRICE FIXING   482
Resale Price Maintenance 483   Vertical Maximum Price Fixing 483

VERTICAL NONPRICE RESTRAINTS   484
Are Territorial Restraints Generally Legal? 484

INTERNATIONAL ASPECTS:
INTERNATIONAL DISTRIBUTORSHIPS   486

VERTICAL EXCLUSIONARY PRACTICES   486
Tying Arrangements 487   Exclusive Dealing 489   Boycotts 489

THE ROBINSON-PATMAN ACT   491
Price Discrimination 491   Defenses 492

SUMMARY: A GUIDE FOR MANAGERS   493

MANAGER'S ETHICAL DILEMMA:
BULLYING SMALL COMPETITORS   495

REVIEW AND DISCUSSION QUESTIONS   495

CHAPTER 17
SECURITIES REGULATION   499

CORPORATE FINANCE AND EARLY REGULATION   500
Securities and Corporate Finance 500   Origins of Securities
Regulation 501

INTERNATIONAL ASPECTS:
INTERNATIONAL STOCK MARKETS   502

DEFINING A SECURITY   503
Supreme Court's *Howey* Test 504   Application of the Securities
Definition 505

DISCLOSURE REQUIREMENTS   507
Disclosure Requirements Under the 1933 Act 507   Exemptions
from Registration 509   Disclosure Requirements Under the 1934
Act 510

SECURITIES FRAUD   511
Securities Fraud Under the Common Law 511   Statutory Securities
Fraud 511   Penalties for Securities Fraud 512   Liability for
Misstatements 513   Liability for Insider Trading 515   Insider Trading
Sanctions Act 517   Major Insider Trading Cases 517

INTERNATIONAL ASPECTS:
INSIDER TRADING IN EUROPE   519

PROXIES, TENDER OFFERS, AND TAKEOVERS   519
Proxies 519   Tender Offers 520

THE INVESTMENT COMPANY ACT   521
Investment Companies 521   Regulation of Investment Companies 522
Arbitration of Disputes 522

THE INVESTMENT ADVISERS ACT   523
Brokers and Dealers 523   Professional Responsibility to Clients 524
Investment Newsletters 524

STOCK MARKET REGULATION   525
Self-Regulation of Securities Markets 525   Regulation of Securities
Transactions 526   Margin Requirements 526

FRANCHISE REGULATION   527
FTC Franchise Rule 527

INTERNATIONAL ASPECTS:
AMERICAN FRANCHISES IN EUROPE   528

SUMMARY: A GUIDE FOR MANAGERS   529

MANAGER'S ETHICAL DILEMMA:
SHOULD BROKERS DEAL WITH "INCOMPETENT"
CUSTOMERS?   531

REVIEW AND DISCUSSION QUESTIONS   531

CHAPTER 18
INTERNATIONAL LEGAL ENVIRONMENT OF BUSINESS   535

THE NATURE OF INTERNATIONAL BUSINESS   537
The International Business Environment 537   Risks in International
Business Transactions 538   Current U.S. Involvement in International
Business 538

INTERNATIONAL LAW AND THE REGULATION OF
INTERNATIONAL COMMERCE   541
History of International Law 541   Overview of Current International
Law 541

INTERNATIONAL BUSINESS IN THE 1990s   542
The Emerging Eastern European Economies 542   Europe 1992 543
A North American Unified Market 544   The Changing U.S.–Japan
Trade Relationship 544

INTERNATIONAL ORGANIZATIONS   545
The United Nations 545   The World Bank 546   International
Monetary Fund 546   General Agreement on Tariffs and Trade
(GATT) 547   Regional Organizations 548

U.S. INTERNATIONAL TRADE RESTRICTIONS AND
PROMOTIONS   548
Import Regulation and Prohibitions 548   Export Regulation and
Promotion 552

INTERNATIONAL ASPECTS:
CONTROLLING INTERNATIONAL PIRATES   554

ENTERING FOREIGN MARKETS: BUSINESS
ORGANIZATIONS   555
Exporting Manufactured Products 555   Foreign Manufacturing of
Products 555

INTERNATIONAL CONTRACTS   557
Cultural Aspects of International Contracts 557

INTERNATIONAL ASPECTS:
CULTURE AND THE EURO DISNEY INVASION   558

Financial Aspects of International Contracts 559   Selected Clauses in
International Contracts 562

LOSS OF INVESTMENT   564
Nationalization 564   Expropriation and Confiscation 564   Insuring
Against Risk of Loss 564

INTERNATIONAL DISPUTE RESOLUTION   565
The International Court of Justice 565   Judicial Litigation 566
Arbitration 567   Doctrine of Sovereign Immunity 567   Doctrine of
Act of State 568

SUMMARY: A GUIDE FOR MANAGERS   569

MANAGER'S ETHICAL DILEMMA:
SHOULD ITALIAN TAXPAYERS SUBSIDIZE
AMERICAN IMPORTERS?   571

REVIEW AND DISCUSSION QUESTIONS   572

APPENDICES

APPENDIX A   FINDING THE LAW   574

APPENDIX B   THE CONSTITUTION OF THE UNITED STATES OF
                        AMERICA   578

APPENDIX C   THE ANTITRUST STATUTES   595
Sherman Act 595   Clayton Act 595   Federal Trade
Commission Act 599

APPENDIX D   NATIONAL LABOR RELATIONS ACT   600

APPENDIX E   TITLE VII OF THE CIVIL RIGHTS ACT OF 1964   605

APPENDIX F   AMERICANS WITH DISABILITIES ACT OF 1990   609

APPENDIX G   SECURITIES STATUTES   612
Securities Act of 1933 612   Securities Exchange Act of 1934 614

GLOSSARY   617
INDEX   635

TABLE OF CASES

Principal cases are in italic type.
Non-principal cases are in roman type.
References are to pages.

Abel v. Eli Lilly Co., 212
Albrecht v. Herald Co., 483, 484
Allegheny Pittsburgh Coal Co. v. County Com'n of
    Webster County, W. Va., 136
American Textile Mfrs. Institute, Inc. v. Donovan, 162, 356
Arizona v. Maricopa County Medical Soc., 477, 484
Arkansas v. Oklahoma, 414
*Asahi Metal Industry Co., Ltd. v. Superior Court of California,
    Solano County, 134*
Aspen Skiing Co. v. Aspen Highlands Skiing Corp., 496
*Atlas Roofing Co., Inc. v. Occupational Safety and Health
    Review Com'n, 153*
Austin v. Michigan Chamber of Commerce, 126
Azar v. Lehigh Corp., 197

Banco Nacional de Cuba v. Sabbatino, 568
Bank of America Nat. Trust & Sav. Ass'n v. Liberty Nat.
    Bank & Trust Co. of Okl. City, 573
Barcellona v. Tiffany English Pub, Inc., 12
Basic Inc. v. Levinson, 513
Baughn v. Honda Motor Co., Ltd., 48
Baxter v. Ford Motor Co., 205, 206
Bigelow v. Virginia, 127
Biggs v. Surrey Broadcasting Co., 303
Blankenship v. General Motors Corp., 203
Board of Airport Com'rs of City of Los Angeles v. Jews for
    Jesus, Inc., 126
Board of Trade of City of Chicago v. United States, 471
Bodnar v. Synpol, Inc., 37
Borel v. Fibreboard Paper Products Corp., 51, 210
Bose Corp. v. Consumers Union of United States, Inc.,
    127
Boston Athletic Ass'n v. International Marathons, Inc., 326
Branch v. Western Petroleum, Inc., 401
Braswell v. United States, 138
Broadcast Music, Inc. v. CBS, 478
Brooks v. City of Baton Rouge/Parish of East Baton Rouge, 187

Browning -Ferris Industries of Vermont, Inc. v. Kelco
    Disposal, Inc., 133
Brown Shoe Co. v. United States, 474 475
Business Electronics Corp. v. Sharp Electronics Corp., 485

Cady, Roberts & Co., 515
California v. American Stores Co., 469
California v. ARC America Corp., 469, 470
California Federal Sav. and Loan Ass'n v. Guerra, 139
Caterpillar Tractor Co. v. Hulvey, 105
Central Adjustment Bureau, Inc., United States v., 455
*Central Hudson Gas & Elec. Corp. v. Public Service Com'n of
    New York, 126*
Chadha v. Immigration and Naturalization Service, 161
Chemical Waste Management, Inc. v. Hunt, 121
*Chevron, U.S.A., Inc. v. Natural Resources Defense Council,
    Inc., 408*
Chiarella v. United States, 516
Chisholm & Co. v. Bank of Jamaica, 573
Cipollone v. Liggettt Group, Inc., 47
City of (see name of city)
Coca-Cola Co. v. Koke Co. of America, 217
Cohen v. Cowles Media Co., 128
Collins v. Eli Lilly Co., 211, 212
*Consolidated Edison Co. of New York, Inc. v. Public Service
    Com'n of New York, 125*
Continental T. V., Inc. v. GTE Sylvania Inc., 485
Copenhaver v. Berryman, 252, 253
Copperweld Corp. v. Independence Tube Corp., 482
Costello v. Capital Cities Communications, Inc., 197
Craft v. McConoughy, 465
CTS Corp. v. Dynamics Corp. of America, 520, 532
Cushing v. Thomson, 237

Denney v. Reppert, 258
Dirks v. S.E.C., 516
Dow Chemical Co. v. United States, 149
Dr. Miles Medical Co. v. John D. Park & Sons Co., 483
Dun & Bradstreet, Inc. v. Greenmoss Builders, Inc., 197
duPont deNemours & Co. v. Christopher, 224

Eastern States Retail Lumber Dealers' Ass'n v. United States, 489
Edward J. DeBartolo Corp. v. Florida Gulf Coast Bldg. and Const. Trades Council, 346
El Paso Natural Gas. Co., United States v., 475
Elsner v. Albrecht, 460
Erie R. Co. v. Tompkins, 78, 78
Estate of (see name of party)

Federal Deposit Ins. Corp. v. Mallen, 135
Federal Trade Commission v. Ruberoid Co., 142
Feist Publications, Inc. v. Rural Telephone Service Co., Inc., 218
First English Evangelical Lutheran Church of Glendale v. Los Angeles County, 131
First Nat. Bank of Boston v. Bellotti, 124
F. J. Busse, Inc. v. Department of General Services, 249
Folsom v. Great Atlantic & Pacific Tea Co., 112
Fort Gratiot Sanitary Landfill, Inc. v. Michigan Dept. of Natural Resources, 121
Frank B. Hall & CO., Inc. v. Buck, 191
F.T.C. v. Indiana Federation of Dentists, 481
F.T.C. v. Procter & Gamble Co., 497
F.T.C. v. Superior Court Trial Lawyers Ass'n, 490

General Dynamics Corp., United States v., 476
Gibbons v. Ogden, 118
Goldberg v. Sweet, 123
Golden State Transit Corp. v. City of Los Angeles, 346
Goldfarb v. Virginia State Bar, 479, 480
Greenman v. Yuba Power Products, Inc., 206, 207, 208
Griggs v. Duke Power Co., 377, 378
Grimshaw v. Ford Motor Co., 40

Hamer v. Sidway, 238
Hard Rock Cafe Licensing Corp. v. Concession Services, Inc., 215
H. E. Butt Grocery Co. v. Hawkins, 224
Henningsen v. Bloomfield Motors, Inc., 205
Hoffman v. Red Owl Stores, Inc., 240
Huntington Beach Union High School Dist. v. Continental Information Systems Corp., 286

Industrial Union Dept., AFL-CIO v. American Petroleum Institute, 356
International Broth. of Teamsters, Chauffeurs, Warehousemen and Helpers of America v. Daniel, 505
International Business Machines Corp. v. United States, 487
International Shoe Co. v. Federal Trade Commission, 476

Jacques v. Sears, Roebuck & Co., Inc., 177
James S. Kemper & Co. Southeast, Inc. v. Cox & Associates, Inc., 193
Japan Line, Ltd. v. Los Angeles County, 122
Jefferson v. Jones, 277
Jefferson Parish Hosp. Dist. No. 2 v. Hyde, 488, 489
John Doe v. United States, 130
Johnson v. Transportation Agency, Santa Clara County, Cal., 385

Kahriger, United States v., 122
Katz v. United States, 128
Katzenbach v. McClung, 119
Kenrich Petrochemicals, Inc. v. N.L.R.B., 365
Kidd v. Thomas A. Edison, Inc., 326

Lechmere, Inc. v. N.L.R.B., 340
Lehnert v. Ferris Faculty Ass'n, 338, 339
Lowe v. S.E.C., 524
Lujan v. Defenders of Wildlife, 159
Lujan v. National Wildlife Federation, 159
Luxuray of New York, Div. of Beaunit Corp. v. N.L.R.B., 365

MacPherson v. Buick Motor Co., 201 202
Maine v. Taylor, 138
Marshall v. Barlow's Inc., 128, 354
Martin v. Hunter's Lessee, 117
Matsushita Elec. Indus. Co., Ltd. v. Zenith Radio Corp., 479
May v. Hall County Livestock Imp. Ass'n, 103
Mazetti v. Armour & Co., 204, 205
McDaniel v. McNeil Laboratories, Inc., 436, 437
McDonald v. Sante Fe Trail Transportation Company, 373
McDonnell-Douglas Corp. v. Green, 371
Meritor Sav. Bank, FSB v. Vinson, 374, 375
Metromedia, Inc. v. City of San Diego, 139
Mickle v. Blackmon, 203
Mildovich v. Lorain Journal Co., 128
Miller Chemical Co., Inc. v. Tams, 194
Mississippi Power & Light Co. v. Mississippi, 121
Mitchell v. Gonzales, 185
Morales v. Trans World Airlines, Inc., 121
Motor Vehicle Mfrs. Ass'n of United States, Inc. v. State Farm Mut. Auto. Ins. Co., 166
Mount Sinai Hospital of Greater Miami, Inc. v. Jordan, 257
M/S Bremen v. Zapata Off-Shore Co., 572
Mullane v. Central Hanover Bank & Trust Co., 77

National Collegiate Athletic Ass'n v. Board of Regents of University of Oklahoma, 478
National Soc. of Professional Engineers v. United States, 496
National Treasury Employees Union v. Von Raab, 352
Natural Resources Defense Council, Inc. v. E.P.A., 428
Nederlandse Draadindustrie Ndi B.V. v. Grand Pre-Stressed Corp., 292
New York City v. Federal Communications Commission, 121
New York City Transit Authority v. Beazer, 394
N. L. R. B. v. Golub Corp., 341
N.L.R.B. v. Katz, 342
N.L.R.B. v. Jones & Laughlin Steel Corp., 118
N.L.R.B. v. Washington Aluminum Co., 344
Nollan v. California Coastal Com'n, 131
Northampton Valley Constructors, Inc. v. Horne-Lang Associates, 326
Northern Pacific Railway Company v. United States, 471, 487
Northwestern States Portland Cement Co. v. Minnesota, 123

Orange & Rockland Utilities, Inc. v. Amerada Hess Corp., 265
Orkin Exterminating Co., Inc. v. F.T.C., 444

Pacific Mut. Life Ins. Co. v. Haslip, 133
Palsgraf v. Long Island R. Co., 185
Paradise, United States v., 384
Park, United States v., 434
Patterson v. Rohm Gesellschaft, 223
Pennell v. City of San Jose, 135
Perez v. United States, 119
Price Waterhouse v. Hopkins, 372

Quivira Min. Co. v. United States E.P.A., 412

Ramirez v. Autosport, 274
Reeves v. Pillsbury Co., 269, 270
Reid v. Eckerds Drugs, Inc., 279
Remenchik v. Whittington, 311
Reves v. Ernst & Young, 505, 506
Revlon, Inc. v. MacAndrews & Forbes Holdings, Inc., 315, 514
Risdon Enterprises, Inc. v. Colemill Enterprises, Inc., 85
Robertson v. King, 242
Rose v. Sheehan Buick, Inc., 257
Roseman v. Retail Credit Co., Inc., 461
Roth v. Ray-Stel's Hair Stylists, Inc., 291
Russell-Vaughn Ford, Inc. v. Rouse, 196

Rutherford, United States v., 460
Rylands v. Fletcher, 189

Santa Fe Industries, Inc. v. Green, 514
Schneidewind v. ANR Pipeline Co., 120
School Bd. of Nassau County, Fla. v. Arline, 390
Sealy, Inc., United States v., 482
Seattle Audubon Society v. Evans, 423
Securities and Exchange Com'n v. W. J. Howey Co., 504, **505,** 532
Seeger, United States v., 373
Servbest Foods, Inc. v. Emessee Industries, Inc., 292
Shaffer v. Heitner, 77
Shapero v. Kentucky Bar Ass'n, 127
Sheet Metal Workers' Intern. Ass'n v. Lynn, 336
Sierra Club v. Costle, 166
Sindell v. Abbott Laboratories, 211, 212
Skinner v. Railway Labor Executives' Ass'n, 351, 352
Smith v. Gibson, 84
Soldano v. O'Daniels, 30
Sony Corp. of America v. Universal City Studios, Inc., **218**
Sonzinsky v. United States, 122
South Carolina Recycling and Disposal, Inc., United States v., 295, 428
Southern Pacific Co. v. Arizona, 120
Southland Corp. v. Keating, 112
STandard Brands Paint Co. v. United States, 550
Standard Oil Co. of New Jersey v. United States, **473, 475**
State, Dept. of Environmental Protection v. Ventron Corp., 189
Sterling v. Velsicol Chemical Corp., 428
Swift v. Tyson, 78

Templeton v. Creative Loafing Tampa, Inc., 220
Texaco, Inc. v. Hasbrouck, 492
Texas Gulf Sulphur, 515
Tigrett v. Pointer, 318
Trans World Airlines, Inc. v. Independent Federation of Flight Attendants, 345
Trans World Airlines, Inc. v. Thurston, 386
Travelers Rental Co., Inc. v. Ford Motor Co., 101
Trenton Potteries Co., United States v., 477
Tull v. United States, 132
T.W. Oil, Inc. v. Consolidated Edison Co. of New York, Inc., 292
Two Pessos, Inc. v. Taco Cabana, Inc., 216

United Housing Foundation, Inc. v. Forman, 503
United Auto. Workers v. Johnson Controls, Inc., 48
United Paperworkers Intern. Union, AFL-CIO v. Misco, Inc., 112

United States v. _____ (see opposing party)
United States Steel Corp. v. Fortner Enterprises, Inc., 487, 488
United States Trust Co. of New York v. New Jersey, 121
United Technologies Corp. v. United States E.P.A., 147
U.S. Gypsum Co., United States v., 480

Versailles Borough v. McKeesport Coal & Coke Co., 400
Virginia Beach, City of v. Murphy, 181
Virginia State Bd. of Pharmacy v. Virginia Citizens
   Consumer Council, Inc., 127

Warner-Lambert Co. v. F. T. C., 441
Webster v. Reproductive Health Services, 32
Western Union Tel. Co. v. Hill, 175

Weyerhaeuser Co. v. Costle, 160
Whirlpool Corp. v. Marshall, 355
White Motor Co. v. United States, 484
Wickard v. Filburn, 119
Wise v. Mead Corp., 393
Witlin, Estate of, 326
Woolley v. Hoffmann-LaRoche, Inc., 366
World-Wide Volkswagen Corp. v. Woodson, 76
Wygant v. Jackson Bd. of Educ., 379
Wyoming v. Oklahoma, 124

Yommer v. McKenzie, 197

Zimmerman v. D.C.A. at Welleby, Inc., 197

PREFACE

Courses on the legal and regulatory environment of business provide important background for students preparing for a variety of careers. One faces legal and ethical issues on a daily basis in any profession. Usually these are simple situations that can be handled with common sense, but, when complex situations arise, ignorance of the principles of business and law can result in serious problems.

This textbook presents the legal environment from the perspective of the professional non-lawyer. Very few students who take this course will become lawyers and most will not take more courses in law. This course is their opportunity to gain knowledge of the law from the standpoint of a working professional. This book is aimed at those students.

The authors of any new book learn a lot from the first edition. We received excellent feedback from professors and students who pointed out the shortcomings (and some strong points) of the first text. We took these comments into account in preparing the second edition.

BASIC ORGANIZATION

Anyone teaching a one semester course in this area faces the task of determining what to cover in such a short time. It is like a medical doctor giving a one semester course to teach students all they need to know about medicine—what can be done in so little time? There is general agreement that the key elements of the legal system and ethical concerns must be covered. This is done in Part I of the book, Business and the Legal Environment, which covers six chapters. Part II, Business and the Common Law, reviews the major areas of the common law that apply to business. Part III, Business and the Regulatory Environment, covers the major regulatory law that managers are likely to face, and reviews major points of international business law.

KEY FEATURES IN EVERY CHAPTER

Manager's Legal Challenge.   Each chapter begins with a page-long discussion of an actual problem that managers faced involving legal problems related to the subject of the chapter. These make clear the importance of law in the managerial process and show how problems were headed-off, how the damage was minimized, or whether a failure to deal with the problem caused major damage to the business. These demonstrate the importance of the points of law to be covered in the chapter that follows.

Briefed Cases.   All cases are summarized. Since the students will not be lawyers, they are not concerned as much with the legal process as with the elements of the process and, more importantly, what managers should know and how they should respond. Cases begin with the "Case Background" that introduces the parties, the facts behind the dispute, and (for most cases) the findings of the lower courts. The "Case Decision" section that follows presents the (appellate) court's findings and a summary of the rationale behind the decision. Finally, each case ends with "Managerial Considerations" which focus on the shortcomings or oversights of management that may have created the dispute. Most importantly, the cases provide insights on how managers can respond strategically to the demands of the legal environment—how to avoid similar disputes or reduce the negative impact of such disputes.

International Aspects.   Short discussions are provided in each chapter of how similar aspects of the law covered in the chapter are handled in other countries. As globalization reaches more and more businesses, managers must be prepared to deal with different legal systems and cultures. This feature makes clear that the rules of the game are different elsewhere and that managers must be prepared to resolve problems under different legal regimes.

Summary: A Guide for Managers.   The discussion of the law in each chapter ends with this summary, which gives a "bullet" list of the major points of law and major rules covered in the chapter that managers will want to remember. The list serves as well as a good self-test to see if the main points of the chapter have been retained for exams.

Manager's Ethical Dilemma.   In addition to ethical considerations made throughout the text, this end-of-chapter feature allows the student to distinguish ethical issues from the legal issues covered in each chapter. Ethics mean much more than obeying the law; ethics mean having rules to live by that go beyond the legal requirements. Some of the issues are real-world examples discussed in a general context, others are based on specific instances. Class discussion can include circumstances in which following the law produces ethical problems. In many cases there is no clear answer, but there is plenty of food for thought.

Review and Discussion Questions.   Each chapter ends with a list of major new terms to be reviewed. The questions that follow ask straight questions about the law covered to review some major points. "Case Questions" are based on real cases or stylized cases that apply the law of the chapter. "Business Policy Questions" then allow discussion of public policy toward business and about the justification for the law. Finally, "Ethics Questions" pose situations related to the law of the chapter that are overshadowed by ethical issues. Discussion about these questions is provided in the *Instructor's Manual*.

CHANGES FROM FIRST EDITION

What is different in this book from the first edition of three years ago? Obviously the law has been updated to focus on legal issues that have become more important and so deserve more discussion. And, where appropriate, new cases have been used. New cases are not included just because they are new; they are used when they give the latest holdings on a major point of law or are particularly good at showing modern applications of a legal principle.

In response to users' and reviewers' comments we have condensed the book a bit to make it more manageable in a one semester course. Antitrust law and securities law have each been reduced from two chapters to one. The chapter on credit protection was deleted, but the key points were moved to Chapter 15, Consumer Protection. A new chapter, Sales and the UCC, has been added to follow the chapter on contract law. The final result is that the book is a more manageable 18 chapters instead of 20.

In addition to the revisions in the remaining chapters, the order of presentation has been changed some. The chapter on ethics has been moved up to be second, to make clear that ethical issues are background to discussion of all law. Environmental law has been substantially revised and moved up earlier due to high student interest in the topic.

ANCILLARIES

- Professor Lynda S. Hamilton of Georgia Southern University has completely revised the *Student Study Guide* to provide a variety of knowledge-testing to reinforce key material learned in the text and to help prepare for examinations.

- The *Instructor's Manual with Test Bank* has case notes, discussion of the Manager's Legal Challenge and Manager's Ethical Dilemma, and answers and background discussion for each chapter's "Review and Discussion Questions" and other material useful for classroom preparation. The test bank has over 2,000 test questions and is available in computerized form for users of IBM or Apple systems in WESTEST software.

- A set of 50, two-color *Transparency Acetates* for classroom projectors is keyed to the text.

- *Legal CLERK Software* allows students to search and review court decisions. The cases and "Case Questions" in the book that are on Legal CLERK are identified with an icon next to them. CLERK runs on IBM and compatibles; an annual site license is provided and an *Instructor's Guide*. A *Student User's Guide* is available for purchase.

- Many other West Publishing Company ancillaries are available: *Legal REVIEW Software, Contracts: An Interactive Guide, You Be the Judge, West's Business Law Video Disc, West's Video Library, PC WESTrain,* and others your West representative can explain.

ACKNOWLEDGMENTS

We would like to thank the users of the first edition who sent us helpful comments and materials. The manuscript reviewers for this edition include: Robert L. Cherry, Jr., Appalachian State University; F. Keith Griggs, Gardner-Webb College; Lynda S. Hamilton, Georgia Southern University; Nancy H. Kratzke, Memphis State University; Paul Lansing, University of Illinois; J. David Lofton, University of Southwestern Louisiana; Nancy R.

Mansfield, Georgia State University; Robert D. McMahan, Indiana State University; Laura Palmer Noone, University of Phoenix; Terry R. Schaaf, University of Nebraska–Lincoln; David Silverstein, Suffolk University; Larry D. Strate, University of Nevada–Las Vegas; and Harold E. Tepool, Vincennes University.

Special thanks to Prof. Charles E. Harris of Texas A&M University, a specialist in ethics, who made sure the ethics chapter is comprehensive and consistent. Finally, thanks to the many fine people at West Publishing Company who make it possible to get a quality book published quickly. In particular, thanks to Esther Craig at West, who has guided us for many years.

SECOND EDITION

MANAGING IN THE LEGAL ENVIRONMENT

BUSINESS AND THE LEGAL ENVIRONMENT

The first part of this book provides an overview of the main elements of the American legal system, especially as they relate to the business world. To understand how specific areas of the law covered later in the book operate in practice, it is important to know the sources of law, the structure of the legal system, and how the system functions. To build our framework for the study of the legal environment faced by managers today, we begin with these chapters:

- *Chapter 1—Business and the Legal Environment* gives an overview of the essential elements of the law and legal system as they relate to business.
- *Chapter 2—Ethics* provides background for understanding the ethical issues managers face. Law essentially tells us what is legally permissible; ethics provides a moral framework for decisions that go beyond legal considerations.
- *Chapter 3—Business and the Judicial Process* reviews the structure of the American court system and its relationship to the operation of business.
- *Chapter 4—Business and the Resolution of Disputes* explains basic litigation procedure—the main steps that occur in the court system when lawsuits arise and in private settlement of disputes.
- *Chapter 5—Business and the Constitution* discusses the key parts of the U.S. Constitution as they relate to business—the legal basis for regulation of business and the rights of managers when legal matters arise.
- *Chapter 6—Government Agencies and the Administrative Process* tells how business interacts with government regulatory agencies and the procedures that are involved.

BUSINESS AND THE LEGAL ENVIRONMENT

CHAPTER 1

MANAGER'S LEGAL CHALLENGE

Electro-Wire Products Inc. provides wiring harnesses and similar products to the U.S. auto industry. Before the 1980s and the rapid growth in Japanese autos sales in the United States, all of the company's production facilities were located in the United States. The company's legal environment was limited to the laws of the United States. Management was confronted with the same basic strategic questions as most other domestic firms: Are we meeting the legal requirements regarding our labor force, the workplace, and the environment? Could our products cause an injury to our customers? Have we entered into contracts that protect us in the event the economy worsens and people buy fewer automobiles? Foreign competition in the wire harness business was present in the United States but was typically regarded as providing a lower quality product. Thus, the managerial environment of the company was quite comfortable and predictable.

However, beginning in the 1980s, the managerial environment of the company—and particularly the company's external environment—began to change. The Japanese began to provide a variety of high-quality, low-cost automobiles to the U.S. market. The Japanese automobile industry captured one-third of the U.S. market.

In response, the U.S. automobile industry began to push automobile part suppliers like Electro-Wire for dramatic quality and price improvements. Part suppliers unable to provide improvements saw their supply contracts awarded to foreign companies who provided lower cost and often higher quality products. The management of Electro-Wire was faced with new challenges—survival, international, and ethical. It had to assess its strengths and weaknesses and reevaluate its opportunities. The company had to make difficult choices and adopt strategies to assure that the company could meet the foreign competition. The necessity of making such choices became even more clear when General Motors and the other U.S. automakers incurred losses of several billion dollars in the late 1980s and early 1990s. GM announced that more than twenty-one plants in the United States were to be closed as a consequence of the losses.

In confronting its challenges, the management of Electro-Wire decided to develop overseas operations where labor costs would be lower. By operating only in the United States, the company would have higher costs than the competition and would not be able to survive. After examining several possible countries, Electro-Wire selected Mexico. In the auto industry, Mexican workers are emerging as a low-cost, high-quality work force. In contrast to the average U.S. manufacturing worker who makes more than $15 per hour, a typical Mexican worker makes about $1 per hour.

By moving into Mexico, management had to expand its legal environment to include Mexican laws and regulations and had to become better informed about international laws in general. The company is now learning to monitor its new legal environment. Management is particularly concerned about possible changes in its future legal environment. The governments of Canada, Mexico, and the United States are negotiating a North American Free Trade Agreement, which would make the North American continent one large market rather than three separate markets. The agreement would allow goods and services to move freely (and thus more cheaply) between Mexico, the United States, and Canada. Just ten years ago, the announcement of such an agreement would not have been considered an important part of a company's legal environment. It may now dictate the central company strategy in the 1990s.

In addition to dealing with important legal environment issues, Electro-Wire faced a series of difficult ethical issues. Management clearly had to make choices to live in the global economy. However, by moving its operations to Mexico, the company would eliminate many U.S. jobs. Does the company have an ethical responsibility to the U.S. workers it leaves behind? By moving to Mexico, the company closed its Owosso, Michigan, plant, leaving 150 workers unemployed. Would it be ethically justifiable to the owners of the business to remain in the United States if to do so meant eventually losing the business to foreign suppliers? Increasingly, companies are being asked to consider these important questions. As the management of Electro-Wire discovered, an understanding of ethical issues and their resolution is becoming an important aspect of the managerial process.

Perhaps one of the most dramatic changes in the legal environment of business over the past decade has been the development of the international legal environment. With the challenges created by the move to globalization, managers now face important legal questions that may affect their survival. Much more than in the past, managers must now be prepared to make decisions that involve the strategic use of the legal environment, which plays a vital role in plant location decisions, marketing decisions, product design decisions, and other decisions where management has been able to use knowledge of the legal environment to its competitive advantage. As the *Manager's Legal Challenge* feature has implied, the strategic use of the legal environment will likely become even more important to managers in the 1990s.

Strategic responses to competition will force managers to make difficult ethical decisions. Competition will make it difficult for some companies to survive. Should companies lay off older workers to reduce labor costs? Like the management of Electro-Wire, does management move its manufacturing operations to foreign countries at the cost of U.S. jobs? Do companies make cutbacks in the safety of the workplace to save money? Do they bribe foreign officials to get things done? Do they withhold information from the public about the effectiveness or safety of their products? The resolution of these issues will not always be easy for today's managers.

This chapter provides an overview of the managerial decision-making process and how the legal environment of business affects the process. It begins with a general discussion of the American economic system, examining its basic attributes relative to other systems. The chapter then examines the managerial process and the important relationship between that process and the internal and external business environments. Finally, the chapter examines the effect of the legal environment—a key element in a company's external environment—on the managerial process.

THE AMERICAN BUSINESS CULTURE

The American economic system can be classified as a *mixed economic system*—largely a *capitalistic economic system* but significantly influenced by federal and state government. In *socialist economic systems*, the government owns the country's major industries and is responsible for most economic decisions. The American system is characterized by private decision making and entrepreneurship. Within this private enterprise system, privately owned and operated businesses attempt to make decisions to best satisfy consumer demands and thereby make *profits*.

A business's ability to make profits, however, is constrained somewhat by the system. The American system is based on the notion of *competition:* each business attempts to capture a share of the market while trying to make as much profit as possible. In maximizing profits, managers are concerned about selling the right product—products of appropriate variety and quality at the right price—at the price most attractive to consumers. In meeting their profit objectives, managers will be pushed by competitive forces to continuously improve their product or service and to lower costs and prices to attract more customers. A business that does not respond to these competitive forces will eventually fail as its customers are attracted to the higher quality, lower priced products of its competitors. This is the managerial challenge faced by Electro-Wire.

Ideally, a capitalistic economic system would provide managers and consumers with the independence to make economic decisions in their self-interest. In a mixed system, however, the government provides several important restrictions on such independent behavior. For a variety of reasons, the government imposes laws and regulations on businesses concerning such business behavior as pollution (discussed in Chapter 14), safety in the workplace (Chapter 12), employment practices (Chapter 13), the ability to monopolize markets (Chapter 16), activities in raising capital (Chapter 17), interaction with consumers (Chapter 15), and operations in international markets (Chapter 18). Clearly, the legal environment has a pronounced role in the American economic system.

■ COMPARATIVE ECONOMIC STATISTICS

As Figure 1–1 shows, the U.S. market for goods and services is by far the world's largest. The U.S. *gross domestic product* (GDP)—the market value of a nation's business output—now exceeds $5 trillion. In contrast to U.S. businesses, however, Japanese businesses rely much more heavily on international business activity. International business is very likely to be the principal source of growth for the world's major industrial economies in the 1990s and beyond.

The relative size of the U.S. economy is also reflected in the data presented in Table 1–1. Consumers in the United States generally own more durable goods—televisions, refrigerators, and automobiles, for example—than do consumers in any other country.

The salaries and bonuses paid to successful managers can be very significant in the American economic system. The president and chief executive officer of the Walt Disney Company, for example, made more than $40 million in salary and bonuses in 1988. The average salary for chief executive officers in the largest U.S. companies was nearly $2 million in 1991. Markets for managerial talent in the United States, however, are becoming increasingly more competitive—both for social responsiveness as well as for an ability to generate profits. The challenges for managers in the U.S. market are clearly increasing to reflect the demands of this new level of competition.

FIGURE 1–1

Comparative Economic Statistics: Gross Domestic Product, 1991
SOURCE: European Economic Community Data, 1992.
*Excludes what was formerly East Germany.

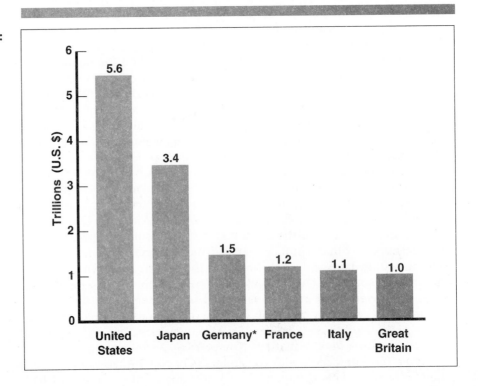

TABLE 1–1
COMPARATIVE INTERNATIONAL STATISTICS, CONSUMER GOODS, 1988

	Televisions per 1,000 Persons	Daily Newspapers per 1,000 Persons	Telephones per 100 Persons	Persons per Automobile
United States	812	259	76.0	1.8
Brazil	194	48	9.3	15.8
Canada	586	225	78.0	2.2
China	24	29	0.7	1,093.3
France	399	193	60.8	2.5
Italy	419	105	48.8	2.5
Japan	589	566	55.5	4.2
Nigeria	6	6	0.3	144.8
Russia	319	474	11.3	22.8
Switzerland	408	504	85.6	2.4
United Kingdom	435	421	52.4	2.8
(West) Germany	379	347	65.0	2.2

SOURCE: *U.S. Statistical Abstract*, 1991, and *The Economist*.

MANAGERIAL FUNCTIONS, DEFINITIONS, AND PROCESSES

The dictionary defines the term *management* as

> the act or art of managing; the conducting or supervising of something such as a business.

In more specific terms, management is the achievement of *organizational objectives*. It requires the coordination and control of people, machines, materials, and money. For a company to be successful, its managers must have several skills. Managers must be able to provide competent leadership, delegate responsibility, communicate with co-workers, and undertake responsible financial planning.

As Figure 1–2 shows, the *managerial environment* consists of the company's internal and external environments. The *internal environment* is defined by the company's structure, culture, and resources. In assessing the company's internal environment, the manager works to identify the company's strengths and weaknesses. The company's *external environment* generally includes those factors beyond the manager's control. The most significant components of the external environment are the economic, legal, social, and competitive environments. By assessing the influence of the external environment, the manager is able to determine the company's opportunities for growth and profitability on the one hand and the potential threats to the company's survival on the other. The supervision of the relationship between these environments is the essence of the *managerial process*.

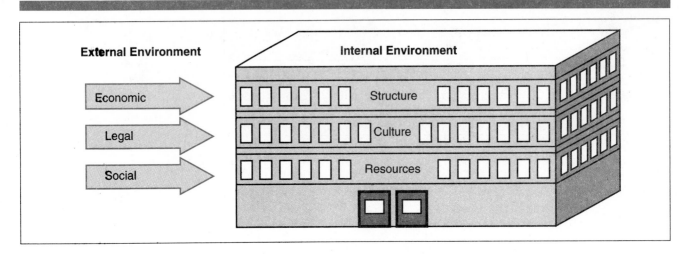

FIGURE 1–2

The Managerial Environment

■ THE INTERNAL ENVIRONMENT

As mentioned, a company's internal environment includes the company's structure, culture, and resources. The company *structure* is the way in which the company is organized. It defines the company's lines of communication, authority, responsibility, and work flow. Structure within a typical company can be illustrated by an organizational chart, such as that in Figure 1–3.

A company's *culture* is the beliefs, expectations, and values shared by the employees, managers, and shareholders of the company. Typically, culture is defined by top management. Managers use culture to attract certain types of employees and to reinforce certain kinds of behavior. It will also in large part dictate the company's *image*—the company's reputation among employees, customers, potential customers, and the general public. The company's culture is critical to long-term successful performance. Japanese automakers, for example, adopted a long-term strategy for enhancing their image and reputation for quality and performance first in the small and then in the medium-sized car market. After establishing an image as a high-quality manufacturer, the Japanese successfully entered the luxury car market in the United States.

The company's *resources* include the skills and abilities of the company's employees and managers as well as the company's financial and physical assets. This aspect of the company's internal environment generally demands the greatest amount of a manager's skill and attention. Management must know the company's financial strengths and weaknesses relative to its competitors. Sales, advertising, promotions, production levels, and prices must be coordinated closely by management. Employees must be properly motivated and compensated to assure productivity and to reduce employee turnover. The operations of the company must be watched closely to ensure that the equipment is up-to-date and well-maintained, quality is controlled, inventories are minimized, and costs are competitive. Finally, managers must constantly monitor the profit contribution of each of its products to assure long-term successful performance.

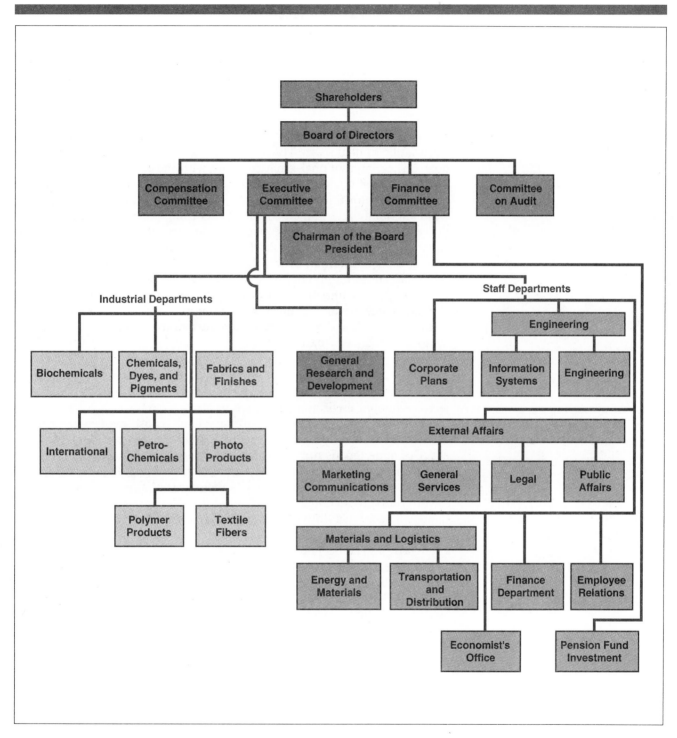

FIGURE 1–3
DuPont's Organization Chart

▓ THE EXTERNAL ENVIRONMENT

By the term *external environment*, managers mean those factors and conditions that may affect the performance of the company but are outside management's control. A business's external environment would include the company's competition, the state of the economy, the social environment, and the legal environment.

Competition.   Management must be keenly aware of the activities of its rivals and potential rivals. The term *competitors* includes all organizations— domestic or international—that compete with the company for resources. While the most obvious resource is customer dollars, companies will also be competing for financing and qualified personnel. Successful managers will continually assess the activities of its competitors in an effort to improve its relative competitive position. To meet its foreign competition, Kmart, for example, sought Pacific Basin apparel suppliers to provide it with low-cost clothing. Dow Chemical's assessment of its competitors' activities caused it to undertake a different strategy. Dow's managers tried to convince its competitors to raise safety standards in the handling of chemicals used in the manufacture of paint products. After its competitors refused, Dow elected to withdraw from the market rather than lower safety standards and risk worker injuries.

Economic Environment.   Management's decisions on present production and new product development will be influenced by the current and projected economic environment. Concerns about a *recession*—a downswing in a country's economic activity—will very likely cause management to be conservative in its decision making. Consumers often postpone the purchase of many goods during such times. Managers will likely reduce purchases of new plants and equipment necessary to implement growth and expansion strategies. They will also anticipate that a recession will lead to lower profits, reductions in hiring, and increased borrowing. On the other hand, an economic downturn can provide incentives for managers to reduce unnecessary expenses within the company.

If projections and current economic events indicate the likelihood of strong economic growth in an economic upturn, management may be willing to develop and implement more aggressive strategies. Management may seek to expand the company's market share and profitability by enlarging operations, increasing existing product lines, and introducing new products. New and more risky opportunities can be considered and undertaken because their chances of success are likely to be higher in times of strong economic growth.

Social Environment.   The social environment of the business includes the customs, traditions, and values of the society in which the business operates. The social environment influences how society views the business community and the attitudes of both employees and consumers. Consequently, product and pricing strategies, employment practices, working conditions, and managerial styles are all influenced directly by the elements that make up the social environment. *Demographic factors*—such as the size and distribution of the population, education, birth and death rates, mobility, and women in the work force—are also an important aspect of the social environment. Few would question the impact that baby boomers—that demographic group born in the decade following World War II—have had on the social environment of the United States. Managers who have anticipated the needs of the baby boomers as they have grown older have been very successful.

Over the past decade, the demands imposed on the U.S. business community by the social environment have increased significantly. Society is now demanding that businesses actively participate in developing and maintaining the social environment. Society's demands have been generated in large part by concerns about the honesty and integrity of the business community, which has responded by developing occupational, professional, and business codes of ethical conduct.

At the same time, managers have had to respond to changes in society's perception of customer, shareholder, and employee rights and responsibilities. Concerns for social responsibility have become an important factor in the managerial decision-making process. The management of Federal Express, for example, provides several full-time staff members and administrative support to assist employees who are involved in voluntary community service work. These services are unrelated to Federal Express's overnight delivery business. However, management believes that the services play an important and fundamental role in the company's social relationship with the community.

Legal Environment.   The legal environment of business can be defined as that collection of laws that influence the behavior and conduct of commercial activity. The legal environment dictates the appropriate code of conduct within which all businesses must operate. It can constrain the selection of alternative courses of action. The legal environment establishes the legal boundaries of all relationships between a business and its governing authority, competitors, consumers, investors, employees, and the community.

Businesses must operate within the code of conduct established by the legal environment of business, or *sanctions* will be imposed. Those sanctions may include liability for damages if the conduct involves a wrongful act (is tortious). They may involve fines or even imprisonment if the business's conduct is found to be a crime. Furthermore, sanctions may be used either to prevent the business from undertaking certain activities or to assure that the business undertakes certain activities. As illustrated in Table 1–2, severe penalties can be imposed on managers who violate federal statutes.

Managers in all business organizations—sole proprietorships, partnerships, corporations, and multinationals—are expected to be fully aware of the legal environment. As the following case illustrates, ignorance of a law will not excuse a manager from sanctions if the law is violated.

BARCELLONA v. TIFFANY ENGLISH PUB

United States Court of Appeals, Fifth Circuit
597 F.2d 464 (1979)

Case Background
The former waiters of Tiffany English Pub, Inc., a restaurant doing business under the name of TGI Friday's, brought suit against the restaurant. The waiters thought that the restaurant's policy of using tips to satisfy its obligations to pay a minimum wage violated the law. The restaurant contended that the tips were withheld according to a valid agreement with the waiters. Under the agreement, tips were to be the property of the restaurant and were to be used toward satisfying the minimum wage requirement.

The district court, however, found no such agreement. It found that the evidence showed a major violation of the Fair Labor Standards Act (FLSA). The statute allows an employee to sue for back wages, attorney's fees, and damages in the event of a minimum wage violation. The damages may be equal in amount to the unpaid wages recovered. The district court found the restaurant liable for $34,141.50 in actual damages and awarded $17,000 in attorney's fees. The court refused to allow damages, however, on the grounds that "the [restaurant]. . . . simply did not know and did not understand exactly what it was to do with respect to these records on these waiters." The statute does allow the court to deny damages if an employer proves he or she had a reasonable basis for believing he or she was not in violation of the statute. The restaurant appealed to the U.S. Court of Appeals.

Case Decision
The court of appeals agreed with the lower court's decisions regarding the restaurant's liability and the awards for damages and attorney's fees. The court, however, disagreed with the lower court's decision not to award dam-ages. The court stated that for a business to avoid the payment of damages, it must prove that it reasonably believed that its actions were legal. The evidence did not establish this reasonable belief. At trial, the owners of the restaurant had stated that they were farmers and that this was their first experience as employers. Ignorance, however, is not a valid defense of actions that may lead to violations of a statute. The court said, "Even inexperienced businessmen cannot claim good faith when they blindly operate a business without making any investigation as to their responsibilities under the labor laws. Apathetic ignorance is never the basis of a reasonable belief."

Managerial Considerations
The old adage "Ignorance of the law is no excuse" seems to be the basis of the court's rationale in this case. Even the most inexperienced businessperson has a duty to investigate the legal requirements surrounding the type of business he or she is conducting. This requirement may place a heavy burden on the first-time business owner. However, to allow ignorance of the law to be an excuse would allow a number of illegalities by first-time businesses to go unpunished. Such an attitude by the courts would lend a form of paternal protection to new businesses and essentially encourage ignorance. Such an attitude would not promote either compliance with the laws or business competitiveness.

Information and the use of information are cornerstones of successful business ventures. The requirements of the legal environment are important business information. Since the courts will require it and the marketplace will recognize its strategic value, a business will likely gain a competitive advantage from knowing and understanding the legal environment.

Figure 1–4 shows the number of lawsuits filed in the U.S. state court systems from 1984 to 1992. In just eight years, the number of lawsuits filed increased about 50 percent. American executives are concerned that the U.S. legal system is making it difficult for American companies to compete in the global marketplace. A *Business Week* poll in 1992 found that 62 percent of top managers believed that the U.S. civil justice system significantly constrains the ability of U.S. companies to compete with the Japanese and the Europeans. As the *International Aspects* features throughout this book will show, the Japanese and the Europeans have legal systems that in some respects are quite different from the American system. Japan and Europe have fewer lawyers (see Figure 1–5), fewer lawsuits, and a much different legal environment.

TABLE 1-2

CRIMINAL LIABILITY PENALTIES FOR MANAGERS IN VIOLATION OF SELECTED FEDERAL STATUTES

Federal Statute	Maximum Criminal Penalty (per Violation)
Food, Drug, and Cosmetic Act	$1000 fine or imprisonment for up to one year or both
Foreign Corrupt Practices Act	$10,000 fine or imprisonment for up to five years or both
Occupational Health and Safety Act	$100,000 fine or imprisonment for up to six months or both
Resource Conservation and Recovery Act	$1,000,000 fine or imprisonment for up to five years or both
Securities Act of 1934	$100,000 fine or imprisonment for up to five years or both
Sherman and Clayton Antitrust Acts	$100,000 fine or imprisonment for up to three years or both

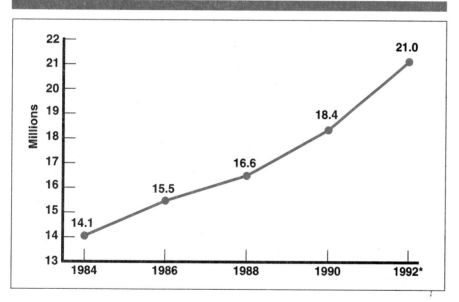

FIGURE 1-4

Lawsuits Filed in U.S. State Courts, 1984-1992
SOURCE: American Bar Association.
*Preliminary estimate.

A striking 83 percent of top managers in the *Business Week* poll stated that the fear of lawsuits has more impact on their decision making than it did just ten years ago. Dow Chemical alone estimates that it spends more than $100 million a year on legal services and liability insurance. Some companies are responding by using such alternatives to the court system as arbitration and mediation (discussed in Chapter 4). The top management of such companies as General Motors, General Mills, and Motorola have made alternatives to the court system a major part of their legal strategies. Other companies are simply avoiding the American market

FIGURE 1–5

Lawyers: An International Perspective
SOURCE: Institute for Legal Studies, University of Wisconsin.

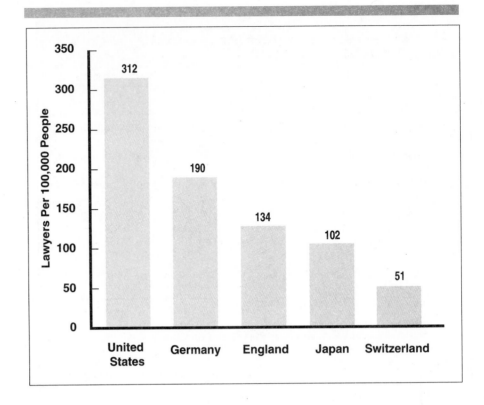

altogether. For example, Biomet refuses to sell its spinal implants (used to relieve major back problems and sold throughout the world) in the United States because of the structure of the American legal system. In this way, the legal environment can have significant effects on the competitive, economic, and social environments of the United States. The *International Aspects* feature that follows discusses how the European legal environment is having significant effects on Europe's competitive, economic, and social environments.

INTERNATIONAL ASPECTS	CONSIDERING THE EXTERNAL ENVIRONMENT IN EUROPE

The external environment often seems to be in conflict. Consider the changes that have been taking place in Europe. The countries of Europe are now undertaking significant economic changes as a group (discussed in Chapter 18 on the international legal environment). In part, these changes involve direct changes to the legal environment. Laws are taking effect that provide for more open trade among the countries of Europe and between Europe and the rest of the world. These changes will provide significant improvements in the economic environment of Europe.

(continued)

The changes under consideration, however, have caused great concern about possible impacts on the competitive environment. The European business community is particularly concerned about the effect that Japanese automobile manufacturers could have on European countries. It is estimated that with free trade, Japan's share of the automobile market in Europe will increase from about 10 percent to more than 30 percent by the year 2000. Several European automakers would likely be forced to merge or close. This could affect the economic and social environments by causing such economic hardships as unemployment.

The response from the legal environment to such hardships could be the development of laws that place restrictions on Japanese cars exported to Europe. Japan's share of the market in the year 2000 would then be much less than estimated under free trade. Although European consumers would pay more for their cars, the European automobile industry would be saved.

In contrast to free trade, the use of restrictions within the legal environment to protect local industry is called *protectionism.* If protectionist changes in the legal environment against the Japanese take place, they may be caused by pressures from the social environment. Consider the thoughts of leading French businessman Jacques Calvet, chief executive officer of PSA (which makes Peugeot and Citroen automobiles in France), as reported in *Fortune:*

> The Japanese can destroy a large part of our industrial fabric and destroy us socially and economically. If we want to compete, it's not a question of technology or technique. We're looking at a change in living standards and in our kind of civilization. Either Europeans work like the Japanese — more than 2,000 hours a year instead of 1,700 and with a two-week [vacation per year], not the five[-week vacation currently enjoyed by European workers]—or else the Japanese will have to change. It could be said that this is the shameful position of protectionism, but we are running an enormous risk of breaking up a social fabric it has taken a long time to create. If our politicians don't realize that, then in the near future there will be violence and civil strife in Europe.

CHARACTERISTICS OF THE LEGAL ENVIRONMENT

It is helpful to consider some of the general characteristics of a business that might influence the business's specific legal environment. The more important characteristics that will influence a business's legal environment include the type of industry the business is in, the kind of organization the business has selected, the size and location of the business, the markets in which the business's products are sold, and the markets the business relies upon for its raw materials. Within the business, the legal environment that a particular manager may face depends upon which department the manager is in.

◼ INDUSTRY

The legal environment of business differs significantly from one industry to another. Some industries, such as public utilities, are subject to heavy regulation by the government. According to Professor F. M. Scherer:

> . . . For industries that are regarded as public utilities, control by a regulatory authority often extends not only to prices, but also to entry [into] and exit [from the industry], service standards, financial structure, accounting methods, and a host of other elements.

The public utility industry is clearly very heavily regulated. However, other industries are not free from government regulation. The government may still impose regulations to control the product quality, disclosure of information, degree of pollution, labor-management relations, and workplace safety standards of those industries. As a consequence, the legal environments of business may also differ between industries. If one is more heavily unionized, management must have greater concerns about labor law; if one pollutes more than most, it requires greater managerial emphasis on environmental law; or if one engages in more credit relations with the public, it requires greater awareness of the laws governing creditor/debtor relationships. In addition, an industry that operates extensively in international markets will require a greater knowledge of international law by its managers than an industry that operates primarily in the domestic market.

◼ BUSINESS ORGANIZATION

The form of organization a business selects has significant consequences for the business's legal environment. Of the several forms of business organizations available, the most prominent are sole proprietorships, partnerships, limited partnerships, and corporations. Among these organizations, the form selected can influence the business's income tax rate, the owners' liability for the expenses of the business, the lifespan of the business, and the degree of managerial control enjoyed by the business's owners. In addition, the choice of business organization can influence the regulatory requirements with which the business must comply.

◼ SIZE OF THE BUSINESS

The size of a business can have a significant impact on the business's legal environment. As Table 1–3 shows, the vast majority of businesses are small, having fewer than fifty employees. The smallest category—those businesses with fewer than ten employees—makes up more than 50 percent of all businesses in the United States. These smaller businesses tend to be involved in the production of one product, contracting for the majority of their supplies and other necessary inputs from other businesses. In contrast to larger businesses, which may have production facilities throughout the world, smaller firms tend to concentrate on local markets. As a consequence, their legal and regulatory obligations and responsibilities are considerably fewer in number than those of larger businesses.

TABLE 1–3
DISTRIBUTION OF BUSINESSES IN UNITED STATES BY EMPLOYMENT SIZE CLASS

Size Category by Number of Employees	Percent of All Businesses
1 to 9 employees	50.7
10 to 49 employees	29.6
50 to 99 employees	8.7
100 to 249 employees	6.7
250 to 499 employees	2.6
500 to 999 employees	1.1
1,000 employees or more	0.6

SOURCE: U.S. Dept. of Commerce, Bureau of Census, *Survey of Manufacturers.*

Many federal laws regulating business activities specify the minimum size of business subject to the law. The Civil Rights Act of 1964, for example, specifies that for purposes of employment discrimination, the law applies only to those businesses with fifteen or more employees. Most *businesses* have fewer than fifteen employees and are not immediately affected by that law. Most *employees*, however, are covered by the law, since the majority work for larger businesses.

■ BUSINESS LOCATION

Laws on various subjects differ dramatically from state to state and therefore vary considerably in their impact on business. Some states apply particular legal rules more rigidly than other states and have regulatory requirements that go beyond federal standards. The legal environment in a state where certain rules are less rigidly applied may be more attractive to some businesses because the cost of doing business there will be lower.

In product liability cases, for example, some states apply a negligence standard in some instances, which places a duty of care on both the business and the consumers of its products to avoid accidents. Other states apply a strict liability standard, which places that responsibility almost entirely on the business. The costs of doing business in a negligence state will likely be lower, since the amount of company resources spent on product testing, the size of adverse legal judgments, and liability insurance premiums will all likely be lower.

■ MARKETS THE BUSINESS SERVES

A business's legal environment also will be affected by both the markets it serves and the markets it relies upon for its raw materials. The legal environments of two businesses will differ as those markets differ. A business that primarily sells locally, for example, has a different legal environment than a firm that sells its product abroad. A business operating in international markets must be concerned about the laws and regulations of the foreign countries in which it operates as well as the laws and regulations of the United States and the individual states in which it does business.

FIGURE 1–6

Overview of a Business's Legal Environment

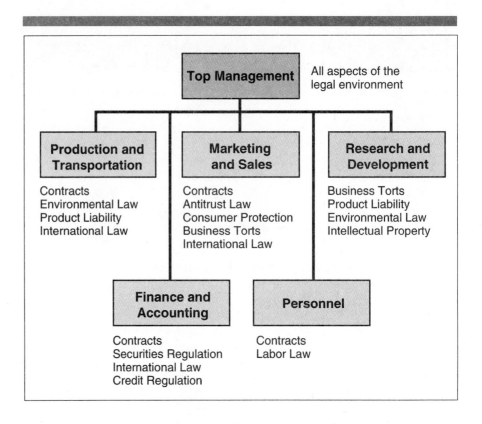

Top Management — All aspects of the legal environment

Production and Transportation

Contracts
Environmental Law
Product Liability
International Law

Marketing and Sales

Contracts
Antitrust Law
Consumer Protection
Business Torts
International Law

Research and Development

Business Torts
Product Liability
Environmental Law
Intellectual Property

Finance and Accounting

Contracts
Securities Regulation
International Law
Credit Regulation

Personnel

Contracts
Labor Law

■ LEGAL ENVIRONMENT WITHIN A BUSINESS

Besides varying among businesses, the legal environment can vary significantly from department to department within a business. The larger an organization becomes, the more specialized each department's legal environment will become. As illustrated in Figure 1–6, a business may consist of departments in charge of production and transportation, finance and accounting, marketing and sales, personnel, and research and development. While the legal environment of each department overlaps that of other departments to a degree, there are legal considerations unique to each department. A manager in personnel, for example, will have different concerns than a manager in marketing. Both must be concerned, however, with meeting the requirements of the legal environment that might affect their performance and that of the business.

THE MANAGEMENT PROCESS AND THE LEGAL ENVIRONMENT

Management involves a series of interrelated activities intended to achieve organizational objectives. In determining organizational objectives, a manager will consider both the strengths and the weaknesses of the internal environment and the opportunities and the threats posed by the external environment. The combination of these considerations, assessments, and evaluations and their effects on managerial decision making is the essence of the *management process*. This process, illustrated in Figure 1–7, will require a manager to consider three fundamental questions:

1. Where is the company now with regard to its internal environment? That is, what are the strengths and weaknesses of the organization?

2. What opportunities and threats are presented by the external environment? That is, what are the organization's goals and objectives, and what aspects of the external environment could work to hinder or promote the achievement of those objectives? (This book is most concerned about the effects of the legal environment.)

3. How is the organization going to achieve its objectives? That is, how will the employees and managers work to attain the organization's objectives?

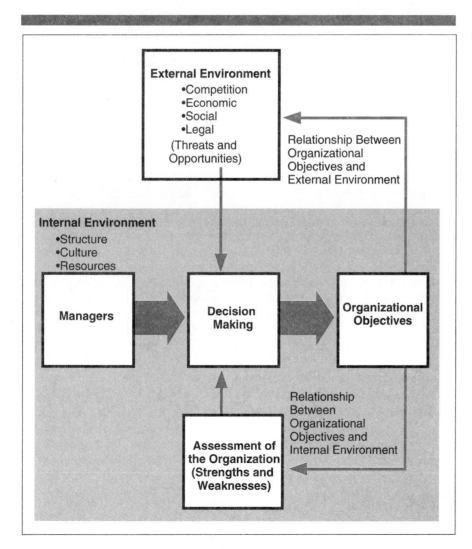

FIGURE 1–7

The Management Process

■ STRATEGIC PLANNING AND THE LEGAL ENVIRONMENT

In reacting to the legal environment, management is generally concerned with strategic planning. A *strategic decision* is a decision that affects what an organization does and how it does it. A strategic decision would involve changes in the following: the organization's fundamental concept, its societal role, the markets in which it competes, the choice of products and services it offers within those markets, or the manner in which the organization competes within its markets. Strategic decisions can be complex and wide in their coverage and impact: Do companies litigate all legal actions brought against them? Do they use alternatives to the court system? Do they settle to preserve company goodwill?

A manager will attempt through the strategic process to achieve a productive fit between the organization's external and internal environments. The concept of *environmental fit* implies that there are objectives the organization may want to accomplish but may not be able to because of the size of the risks that the legal environment may pose. A manager may be considering a merger with a competitor, for example, but the risk of a costly antitrust action may be too great. Or a manager may be considering producing a new agricultural chemical, but the environmental and health risks may raise serious concerns about potential tort liability.

In reaching a decision, managers will consider many things. They will be influenced by their social, economic, and competitive environments. As the *International Aspects* feature relates, the social environment will play an important role in how decisions are made.

INTERNATIONAL ASPECTS	CONSIDERING THE JAPANESE MANAGEMENT STYLE

The Japanese business community has enjoyed considerable economic success in the past decade. In that time, Japan's merchandise trade surplus with the United States has increased to more than $40 billion annually. That is, the Japanese are selling $40 billion more to the United States than the United States is selling to Japan.

Japan's success has raised concerns about the U.S. international competitiveness. Several factors have been cited as potential causes of the decline in U.S. competitiveness. Those factors include a decreased rate of technological development, labor costs, and an emphasis on finance and marketing rather than on production by senior management. Several commentators, however, point to differences in the Japanese and American managerial philosophies.

As Figure 1–8 illustrates, there are substantial and fundamental differences in Japanese and American managerial philosophies, organizations, and environments. In contrast to the American management style, for example, Japanese managers place greater emphasis on human resources. Japanese managers generally enjoy lifetime employment with the same company. American managers may work for several companies throughout their career. Promotions and compensation in a Japanese company are generally based on seniority. For managers in American companies, compensation and promotions are usually based on merit, with performance appraisals occurring regularly and frequently. Managerial decision making—largely the responsibility of the manager to whom

(continued)

that task is delegated in a typical American company—is generally accomplished through teamwork and cooperation in Japan. Finally, the legal environment in the United States tends to be adversarial in nature. The legal environment of business in Japan is characterized by more cooperation between government and industry. In addition, legal disputes tend to be litigated in the United States but negotiated in Japan.

FIGURE 1–8
Comparing Japanese and American Management Philosophies, Organizations, and Environments

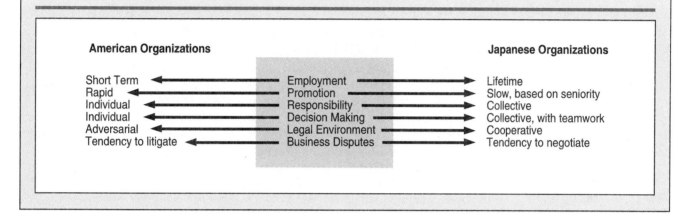

American Organizations		Japanese Organizations
Short Term	Employment	Lifetime
Rapid	Promotion	Slow, based on seniority
Individual	Responsibility	Collective
Individual	Decision Making	Collective, with teamwork
Adversarial	Legal Environment	Cooperative
Tendency to litigate	Business Disputes	Tendency to negotiate

▣ LOST OPPORTUNITIES AS THREATS

The strategic manager must carefully assess the laws and regulations to determine the most favorable opportunities for the organization. No opportunity, however, is risk free. The strategic manager must compare the risks with the rewards of any possible opportunity. In addition, the strategic manager must take note that any opportunity not undertaken by his or her company may be undertaken by competitors. The opportunity then becomes a threat. Suppose the manager mentioned above rejects the idea of merging with a competitor because of the litigation risk and another competitor undertakes the merger. The new company created by the merger may present a significant competitive threat. The new company would not exist had the first company responded to the merger opportunity itself.

Ideally, through planning, the strategic manager will try to cause changes to occur that will put the organization in a better position relative to its competition. By seizing or creating opportunities, the manager also creates a threat for the competition, forcing the competition to react. On the other hand, if the competition brings about the change, management should work to *react* effectively through advanced planning. In either case, the ability of the organization to seize opportunities or to respond to threats will depend on the company's internal strengths and weaknesses.

Management must *realistically* assess its resources to determine what it can or cannot do. To illustrate, the federal government in 1978 decided to deregulate the airline industry. The new law significantly changed the legal environment for companies in that industry. The management of Braniff Airlines assessed its resources and chose to rapidly expand its operations after deregulation. It overestimated Braniff's internal strengths. The accompanying increases in fixed and operating costs eventually forced the company into bankruptcy.

SUMMARY:
A GUIDE FOR MANAGERS

- The American economic system can be classified as a mixed economic system. It is basically a capitalistic system in that it allows for private decision making. However, in contrast to pure capitalism, the American system is strongly influenced by state and federal government.

- The U.S. market is the largest economy in the world. It produced more than $5.6 trillion in goods and services in 1992. Japan was the second largest economy, producing about $3.4 trillion in goods and services.

- Management is defined as the conducting or supervising of a business. It is the achievement of organizational objectives through the coordination and control of people, machines, materials, and money.

- The managerial environment includes the internal and external environments. The internal environment includes the company's structure, culture, and resources. Within the internal environment, management can make decisions about prices, production levels, advertising, the hiring of personnel, and other factors within the direct control of the company. The external environment includes those factors beyond the control of management.

- Managers are responsible for examining the company's internal environment to determine the company's strengths and weaknesses. In implementing strategic plans, management will want to take advantage of the company's strengths while improving upon its weaknesses.

- Managers are responsible for assessing and evaluating the company's external environment. The legal environment is an important part of the external environment. The social, competitive, and economic environments are the other components of the external environment. The social environment includes customs, traditions, and the values of the society. The economic environment includes the current and projected economic conditions that exist in the marketplace. The competitive environment includes the condition of rivals in the company's marketplace. In assessing the external environment, management will want to determine the company's best opportunities and the most significant threats to its survival.

- The legal environment can be defined as a collection of laws that affect business behavior and conduct. Changes in the legal environment can have important consequences on the social, economic, and competitive environments. The legal environment can be affected by the industry in which the business operates, the size and location of the business, and the markets the business serves.

- Managers are expected to know and understand the laws making up the legal environment that affects their business. Ignorance of the law is not considered to be justifiable defense to a violation of a law.

- Because of the rapid growth in litigation in the United States over the past decade, U.S. executives are concerned about how the U.S. legal environment is impacting U.S. international competitiveness. Many companies are looking for alternatives to the court system as a means for solving disputes.

- The effects of the legal environment are important to managers and the managerial process. Through the strategic planning process, management must assess the opportunities and threats to the company. The legal environment can constrain or encourage business behavior. Management must be well-informed about its legal environment to make good strategic decisions.

MANAGER'S ETHICAL DILEMMA

HOW SHOULD MANAGERS RESPOND TO DIFFICULT DECISIONS?

The Hardcore Manufacturing Company has been a family-operated business for nearly forty years. Its primary product line is specialty furniture. It has earned a reputation for quality and handcraftmanship. At its peak, the company employed more than 3,500 workers in what was considered to be a near perfect example of a "company town."

Beginning in the early 1980s, however, the company began to fall on hard times. International competition in the form of imports from Hong Kong and Korea were the principal source of competition. Earnings fell dramatically, employees with years of faithful service were laid off, morale among the managerial ranks declined, and several of the company's plants fell into disrepair.

Suppose that you have been hired as the top executive by Hardcore's board of directors. Your long-term assignment is to return the company to "viability for the shareholders, the employees, and the community." The board has given you free rein to undertake the necessary short-term and long-term changes—subject to the company's guiding principle to be "a large company with a small company atmosphere."

Before you undertake a detailed review of the company, the board has asked you for a general discussion about how you might proceed. You inform the board of the need to assess the company's strengths and weaknesses and to evaluate the company's opportunities and the threats to its survival. After hearing your general discussion, the board has asked your opinion on the following subjects it believes are crucial to your success.

QUESTIONS

If you considered a merger with another company, would the headquarters be in a different city? Would those managerial personnel who had been faithful to the company for many years be released? If they were not released, would their salaries be reduced? What about those employees who are related to the company's founders and whose relatives are shareholders in the company? Would the merger involve the use of automated production facilities to reduce costs, or would Hardcore's reputation for handcrafting be maintained? Would the chain of command still allow employees to take their complaints directly to the head of the company?

There has been speculation that one of the plants could be converted to produce a specialty brand of paper. Such production, however, would result in the discharge of toxic pollutants into the air. While the board understands the profitability of such a conversion, it wants to know how you would come to a decision on whether to open such an operation.

If costs were to be cut, would the company's contributions to the community be affected? Would the contributions to the city's hospital—which depends upon Hardcore for its survival—be affected? What about the contributions to the Little League baseball team that was state champion last year in large part due to Hardcore's generous support?

REVIEW AND DISCUSSION QUESTIONS

1. Define the following terms:

   mixed economic system   company resources
   management   management process
   managerial environment   strategic decision

2. Compare and contrast the following:
   a. Socialism and capitalism
   b. External and internal environments
   c. Company structure and company culture
   d. Competitive environment and the economic environment
   e. Legal environment within a company and the company's legal environment

3. How could the legal environment pose a threat to an organization? An opportunity?

CASE QUESTION

4. Suppose that after a detailed discussion over lunch, two businessmen, Mr. Held and Mr. Bird, decide to enter into an employment contract. In writing the contract, Mr. Bird asks Mr. Held about a particular point of law. Mr. Held states the law as he believes it to be. Later, however, it is determined that the law is considerably different from what Mr. Held believed it to be. As a consequence, Mr. Bird would like the contract to be declared void. Based on the *Barcellona* decision, how might a court rule in this case?

BUSINESS POLICY QUESTIONS

5. Could the Japanese managerial philosophy be implemented in an American company?

6. A large food and beverage company has organized itself along functional lines. It has marketing, finance and accounting, personnel, production, and legal departments. The legal department is a new department, the consequence of top management's strategic decision to reduce costs by doing more in-house legal work. The personnel manager is concerned about how to motivate the legal staff and has asked you for suggestions. She is concerned whether monetary compensation will be adequate. If salaries get too high, however, the cost-reduction incentive for having in-house lawyers may be lost. Should the legal staff have avenues for promotion to top-level managerial jobs within the company? Should lawyers who also manage be compensated differently than lawyers who only handle legal work? Should the other departments be charged for the use of the in-house legal counsel? Or will that discourage them from using the service and result in the regulatory fines and damage suits when they act on their own without the necessary advice?

ETHICS QUESTIONS

7. Should managers be allowed to use the legal environment strategically? Should management, for example, be allowed to implement a decision that is legal but may be difficult to justify morally? Should a company be allowed to use a particular form of business if the strategic purpose is to avoid liability?

8. Should the managers of profit-oriented companies be concerned about stress in the workplace, day care, and drug rehabilitation for workers? Would such concerns detract from managers' duties to company shareholders?

ETHICS, THE LAW, AND THE MANAGERIAL PROCESS

CHAPTER 2

MANAGER'S LEGAL CHALLENGE

Beginning in the 1970s, the management of Dow Corning sought to create a corporate culture that emphasized high ethical standards. Like several other U.S. companies, Dow Corning had become concerned with its corporate image. The company began by creating a Business Conduct Committee made up of company executives, each of whom was to serve for up to six weeks a year. The company adopted a code of ethics to serve as the framework for the new corporate culture. The company also informed its employees about ethics through training programs and encouraged employees to raise ethical issues.

The Conduct Committee began with a series of company audits to monitor compliance with legal requirements within the company. Every business operation was to be audited once every three years. The committee was to review up to thirty-five locations a year. These audits provided several successes, including an audit that uncovered a major overseas Dow Corning distributor who was bribing customs officials to obtain a lower customs tax rate.

Beginning in 1983, Dow Corning's Conduct Committee conducted four audits of the Arlington, Tennessee, facility of Dow Corning Wright, which manufactured silicon breast implants. Despite the fact that each audit involved nine employees and lasted three hours, the safety of the silicon implants was never once raised by employees in any of those audits.

Dow Corning discontinued production of silicon breast implants in 1992, after a Food and Drug Administration investigation revealed potential problems and ordered the use of implants to be restricted. The company now faces hundreds of lawsuits from women who claim that the implants have seriously damaged their health. In some cases, the implants rupture and the fluid may suppress a person's immune system.

The company's image was severely damaged by the discovery of nearly one hundred internal memos indicating that the company had been aware of the health risks for more than fifteen years but had never acted and had withheld the information from the public. Even though implants accounted for only one percent of Dow Corning's income, the scandal caused the stock of its parent company, Corning, to fall 15 percent. More than 600,000 women have Dow Corning implants. Analysts are predicting that the company will face thousands of lawsuits and millions of dollars in liabilities.

Ethicists are now beginning to question the level of importance that Dow Corning actually placed on its ethics program. Others argue that managers in Dow Corning and other companies are not properly trained to solve ethical and moral business problems. On the other hand, the general public believes simply that the corporate community is becoming less concerned about honesty and ethical standards. According to a Harris Poll conducted in 1966, 55 percent of the American people had a "great deal of confidence" in American business executives. By 1976, however, that percentage had dropped to just 16 percent. More recent polls by both Harris and Gallup continue to indicate that confidence in American business leaders remains low—especially with regard to honesty and ethical standards.

One possible explanation of this is that the ethical standards of American business have plummeted and that business is indeed operating at a lower level of personal and corporate ethics. Stories of individual and corporate misconduct such as insider trading, product-content deceptions, bribery, and industrial pollution could be seen as confirmation of this interpretation. It is more likely, however, that at least some of the decline in the image of business has been due to the increased concern with ethical issues on the part of the American public generally. Morally speaking, the public simply expects more from business now than it did in the past.

This chapter surveys some of the moral problems that are raised by this new level of ethical awareness. It begins by considering the nature of ethics and some conceptual tools that may be useful in thinking about moral problems. Within this discussion, the text comments on ethical problems that often arise in the conduct of business, such as the morality of preferential hiring, proper treatment of employees, obligations with respect to the environment, the ethics of advertising, and moral obligations in international business.

The chapter then examines the ethical responsibilities of corporations and their managements. It considers whether corporations should be morally responsible or whether moral responsibility should be given only to the management of the corporation. Finally, the growing emphasis on corporate social responsibility and the tools being used to influence corporations are discussed.

PERSONAL AND CORPORATE ETHICS: SURVEYS AND PERCEPTIONS

In response to their declining public image, corporations are developing written codes of ethics. Despite this and other efforts, however, there is growing concern that today's business climate—as reflected in the *corporate culture*—may be at least partially to blame. An article in the *Wall Street Journal* that examined corporate goals and ethics stated the following:

> [A] fresh look at data [taken] from 10 academic studies suggests that [corporate codes of ethics] merely pay lip service to a larger—and clearly unmet—problem: a business climate that condones [misbehavior]. Indeed, the studies indicate that even the most upright people are apt to become dishonest and unmindful of their civic responsibilities when placed in a typical corporate environment.

Several studies have found that the recent development of corporate codes of ethics by the business community has done little to improve corporate culture. Professor William Frederick of the University of Pittsburgh found that corporations with codes of ethics were cited for legal infractions by federal regulatory agencies more frequently than corporations without codes. In those corporations making a special effort to improve corporate ethics by placing more individuals with a socially conscious perspective on their boards of directors, relatively little change in the corporate culture was found. The Manager's Legal Challenge feature would tend to support Dr. Frederick's findings that codes of ethics alone do not do the job.

Table 2–1 presents the results of a codes-of-ethics survey of 202 *Fortune 500* companies. As the table illustrates, the provisions most commonly included in company codes emphasized improving the bottom line—customer/supplier relations, relations with the government, and conflicts of interest. Surprisingly, more than 75 percent of the codes of ethics surveyed failed to mention product quality, product safety, and environmental concerns.

Does the pressure for employees to conform to corporate organizational standards come at the expense of their personal principles? Table 2–2 presents the results of a survey of 220 managers. Not surprisingly, the managers listed self-respect as the most important personal value and honesty as the most important personal attribute. Yet when these same employees are asked to write company codes of ethics, company honesty and integrity fail to make even the top five among corporate values and

TABLE 2–1
A SURVEY OF COMPANY CODES OF ETHICS

Provisions Included in 75 Percent of Codes	Frequency	Provisions Excluded in 75 Percent of Codes	Frequency
Relations with government	86.6%	Personal characteristics	93.6%
Customer/supplier relations	86.1	Product safety	91.0
Political contributions	84.7	Environmental affairs	87.1
Conflicts of interest	75.3	Product quality	78.7
Honest records	75.3	Civic affairs	75.2

SOURCE: Marilynn Cash Mathews, Washington State University, *Wall Street Journal*, October 9, 1987, p. 2.

TABLE 2–2

SURVEY OF MANAGERS' PERSONAL VALUES AND CHARACTERISTICS

Personal Values		Personal Attributes	
Ranked Highest	*Ranked Lowest*	*Ranked Highest*	*Ranked Lowest*
Self-respect	Pleasure seeking	Honesty	Obedience
Family security	World of beauty	Responsibility	Cleanliness
Freedom	Salvation	Capability	Cheerfulness
Accomplishment	Social recognition	Ambition	Politeness
Happiness	Equality	Independence	Helpfulness

SOURCE: William Frederick and James Webber, University of Pittsburgh, *Wall Street Journal,* October 9, 1987, p. 2.

attributes. Furthermore, a congressional subcommittee has estimated that one out of three corporate employees is hired with educational or career credentials that have been altered—and thus falsified—in some way. What motivates people with strong personal beliefs in the importance of honesty and integrity to disregard those values and attributes once they enter the workplace? Has it become more important to do whatever is necessary to beat the competition—even if it means being dishonest?

A *U.S. News*-CNN poll found that the majority of Americans believe that dishonesty is significantly greater than it was just ten years ago. This growing belief by Americans that dishonesty has increased is reflected in their perceptions about activities in the workplace. The survey results presented in Table 2–3 show that 70 percent of employers believe that many or most of their coworkers steal office supplies from the company. Nearly 60 percent believe that most or many of their fellow workers pad their expense accounts, thus increasing their incomes at the expense of the employer.

TABLE 2–3

SURVEY OF EMPLOYERS REGARDING THE PERCEIVED ACTIVITIES OF COWORKERS

	Most	Many	Not Many	Very Few
Employees take office supplies or small tools home	35%	34%	18%	12%
Businesspeople pad expense accounts	28%	32%	21%	10%
Labor leaders use union funds for personal expenses	18%	29%	28%	14%
Employees take time off pretending to be ill	17%	32%	33%	15%
Job applicants exaggerate their past achievements	17%	27%	31%	17%

Adapted from *U.S. News & World Report,* Feb. 23, 1987; a *U.S. News*-CNN poll by Roper Organization.

Many companies are now hiring ethics specialists in an effort to improve their business practices and thus the perceptions about them held by the general public. Managers are increasingly being provided with incentives to be more concerned about ethics and to comply with company codes of conduct. To better screen their employees, companies are administering lie-detector and drug tests and devoting more resources to checking out prospective employees. Still, many executives believe that the answer lies in educating and informing business students on basic ethical concepts and issues.

ETHICS AND MORALS: DEFINITIONS, THEORIES, AND APPLICATIONS

In debating standards of behavior, a distinction is sometimes made between morals and ethics. The term *morals* refers to accepted standards of right and wrong in a society. The term *ethics* refers to more abstract concepts that might be encountered in the study of the standards of right and wrong in philosophy. For the purposes of this discussion, the terms *morals* and *ethics* are interchangeable.

A clear and concise definition of morals and ethics is difficult. To better understand the concept, let's compare the terms with two other terms they are likely to be confused with: etiquette and the law.

ETHICS AND ETIQUETTE COMPARED

Moral and ethical statements must not be confused with statements about etiquette or good manners. Since both kinds of statements can use terms such as *should* or *ought*, this confusion is tempting. A person may say, "You should not slurp your soup" or "You ought to introduce yourself when you enter a home for a party." These statements prescribe conduct just as ethical statements do. However, they should be considered part of good taste, not moral or ethical behavior.

Moral and ethical statements differ from etiquette in at least two important ways. First, moral and ethical statements have greater importance than etiquette statements. Most of us would take a violation of a rule such as "You should not lie to your father" as being much more serious than a violation of a rule such as "You should compliment your hostess after a good dinner." Second, moral and ethical rules cannot be established or changed by decisions of authoritative bodies or by majority vote. However, the rules for the placement of knives, forks, and spoons on a table can be changed.

ETHICS AND THE LAW COMPARED

Moral and ethical statements should not be confused with rules of law. The fact that an action is legally permissible does not establish that it is also morally and ethically permissible. Suppose management discovers that its company is emitting a toxic pollutant into the atmosphere and that the pollutant is not currently regulated by the Environmental Protection

Agency (EPA). Suppose further that the company's internal studies show that the pollutant may cause serious health problems. Should management voluntarily decide to stop emitting the pollutant? Should it wait until the EPA makes the pollution illegal? Whatever your view on this matter, it is clear that although emitting the toxic pollutant is legally permissible, it may not be morally and ethically permissible for management to do so.

Questions about legality and morality thus are not necessarily the same. In the *Soldano* case, the court faces this very issue. The plaintiff asserts that if the defendant had acted, a life could have been saved. Although the defendant's refusal to act may have been unethical or immoral, the court is asked to decide whether it was illegal.

SOLDANO v. O'DANIELS

California Court of Appeals
141 Cal.App.3d 443, 190 Cal.Rptr. 310 (1983)

Case Background
In August of 1977, a man named Villanueva entered Happy Jack's Saloon, pulled a gun, and threatened to kill Soldano. A patron of Happy Jack's quickly crossed the street to another bar called the Circle Inn and told O'Daniels, the bartender there, what was going on at Happy Jack's. He requested that O'Daniels either call the police or allow the patron to make the call. O'Daniels refused to do either. Soldano was subsequently fatally shot by Villanueva. Soldano's child brought a wrongful death action against the bartender.

On the grounds that an individual cannot be liable for his or her nonactions, the trial court granted the defendant's motion for summary judgment and dismissed the plaintiff's action. The plaintiff appealed to the court of appeals, arguing that the case should have been allowed to go to trial.

Case Decision
The appellate court reversed the trial court and concluded that there were issues that should allow the case to go to trial. The court stated that the difference between action and inaction in the law is rooted in an "attitude of extreme individualism so typical of Anglo-Saxon legal thought." The court noted that the rule had resulted in a series of cases holding that an individual is under no legal obligation to assist another individual in danger—despite moral and eth-ical reasons for providing assistance. The court stated that under the existing law, "[an individual] may sit on the dock, smoke his cigar, and watch the other drown."

In assessing past decisions, the court found them to be "revolting to any moral sense" under the current social environment. The court of appeals then held that the bartender at Circle Inn owed a duty to Soldano's child to allow the patron to call the police or make the call himself.

Managerial Considerations
As stated in the introduction to this chapter, the public has developed an increased concern over business ethics. As a consequence, managers should expect changes in the law to formally address those public concerns. Practices considered legal but morally questionable are very likely to be examined much more closely by legislatures and the courts. In California prior to this case, for example, a company policy restricting the public's use of a company telephone—even in an emergency—would have been morally questionable yet legal.

Managers should assess their current operations for policies or activities that may be legal but are nonetheless morally and ethically questionable. While nonliability may have been assured in the past, the public's new concerns raise the probability that the company will be confronted with liability. In addition, the loss of goodwill in the community if an unethical business practice is exposed can be quite costly to a company and its management.

■ CONCEPTUAL TOOLS FOR MORAL THINKING

Generally speaking, three basic kinds of disagreements can arise in a discussion of so-called moral issues. Distinguishing these disagreements is important because they are resolved in very different ways. The three kinds of disagreements can be illustrated using the Foreign Corrupt Practices Act as an example.

Congress passed the Foreign Corrupt Practices Act (FCPA) in 1977. The statute makes it unlawful to "corruptly" pay or authorize to pay money, gifts, or anything of value to any official of a foreign government, candidate for office in a foreign government, foreign political party, or official in a foreign political party. The Act was passed after it was discovered that nearly 400 American companies had paid approximately $300 million over a five-year period to foreign officials for business favors. Lockheed, for example, had paid $22 million to foreign politicians to ensure that it would receive aircraft contracts. In the same time period, Gulf Oil had secretly paid $4 million to foreign politicians to protect its oil interests.

Let's suppose that two people disagree over whether the FCPA is *morally and ethically justifiable*. While their disagreement could be over genuine moral principles, it could also be over the facts or conceptual issues.

Disagreements Over the Facts.   One major source of disagreement in determining whether a law or practice is morally and ethically justifiable is, simply, the facts. If two people disagree about the facts in a given situation, they will probably disagree about what ought to be done—even if they agree on the conceptual issues and moral principles. Many international managers have argued, for example, that the FCPA causes U.S. firms to lose business to foreign firms legally permitted to pay foreign officials. But is this argument true? If it is, the welfare of many American workers would be adversely affected. If it is not, it will have no effect on American workers. Until the argument can be determined to be true or false, the parties will disagree on this point and not on the moral and ethical justifiability of the FCPA.

Disagreements Over Conceptual Issues.   A second source of disagreement can be over conceptual issues—the proper definition of the concepts that are important to the issue in question. The FCPA, for example, permits payments made in response to *extortion demands*. A payment to an official to keep an oil rig from being blown up is permitted by the FCPA because it is in response to extortion. On the other hand, the word *extortion* has been defined narrowly by the courts to rule out "economic extortion." If a foreign official tells a company that its product will not be considered by his government unless a "side payment" is made—economic extortion—the payment would be illegal under the FCPA. It would be considered a bribe rather than an extortion payment. But when does an extortion payment actually become a bribe? Is the difference always clear? Obviously, the way that the terms *bribery* and *extortion* are defined can be important in determining the moral and ethical acceptability of the FCPA.

A good example of the important role played by conceptual issues is provided by the abortion debate. Since most people consider it immoral to kill another individual, the debate over abortion depends upon whether a fetus is a person. If one group reaches the conclusion that the fetus is a person, it will argue that abortion is immoral. On the other hand, if the fetus is not considered to be a person, abortion will be considered to be as moral as the removal of an appendix. The determination of whether the fetus is in fact a person is not a simple one. The abortion debate thus remains the classical conceptual controversy. In the following case, the Supreme Court is asked to make a decision on abortion. The Court termed the abortion issue "the most politically divisive domestic legal issue of our time."

WEBSTER v. REPRODUCTIVE HEALTH SERVICES

United States Supreme Court
492 U.S. 490, 109 S.Ct. 3040 (1989)

Case Background

In 1986, Missouri enacted a statute concerning abortions and unborn children. The statute states that "(t)he life of each human being begins at conception" and that "unborn children have protectable interests in life, health, and well-being." Among other things, the statute prohibits using public facilities or employees to perform or assist in abortions unless the abortion is necessary to save the mother's life. Two nonprofit corporations and five state health professionals brought a class-action suit against William L. Webster, the Attorney General for the state of Missouri. The lawsuit challenged the constitutionality of the Missouri statute. The federal district court ruled that several provisions of the statute were unconstitutional and issued an injunction against their enforcement. The court of appeals affirmed, holding that the statute's statement that life begins at conception was not permissible. The court ruled that states do not have the right to adopt a theory of when life begins to justify the regulation of abortion. The court of appeals relied on *Roe* v. *Wade,* a 1973 Supreme Court decision giving women a constitutional right to have abortions. Webster and the state of Missouri appealed to the U.S. Supreme Court.

Case Decision

The Court reversed the lower court's ruling and held that the Missouri statute does not create constitutional violations. The Supreme Court stated that *Roe* v. *Wade* and other precedents do not limit a state's authority to favor childbirth over abortion. The statute expresses a viewpoint about life that is not a regulation. Rather, it is just a value judgment. Further, state laws have previously given protections to unborn children that have been found to be constitutionally permissible. The Court further stated that the Constitution does not impose a duty on the state to subsidize or fund childbirth or abortions. The use of public funds is a decision made by the democratic process, and the Constitution does not forbid such processes.

Managerial Considerations

Shortly after the Supreme Court's ruling, a *USA Today* poll found that 50 percent of the public opposed the Court's decision, 40 percent supported it, and 10 percent were un-

decided. Nearly 40 percent of the respondents stated that they would vote for a candidate solely on the basis of his or her abortion stand. Clearly, the moral and ethic beliefs of the public on this subject are deep-seated. Yet, because the question of when life actually begins is very difficult to resolve, the moral disagreement surrounding the rightness or wrongness of abortion is far from being resolved.

With regard to conceptual difficulties, several ethical issues confronting the business community are similar to the abortion issue. It is has become a concern, for example, that hundreds of thousands of jobs involve a degree of risk of injury. If the risk involves losing a finger in a saw blade, precautions can be undertaken to reduce the risk. If the risk is due to an exposure to a carcinogenic substance, however, the degree of risk is not easily determined. In making that determination, scientists rely on laboratory animal tests. Laboratory animals are fed enormous quantities of a substance and are then tested for cancers. If the tests are positive, scientists then attempt to estimate the impact on humans. The estimates will involve making guesses about the effect of very small doses—parts per million for humans versus possibly gallons a day for the animals. The estimates are simply not very reliable. On the basis of the positive animal tests, however, society could adopt two very different positions: (1) a "zero tolerance" rule under which it is morally and ethically unjustifiable to expose workers to *any* increased risk or suspected risk of cancer in the workplace or (2) a rule providing that workers are to be given the best information on the risks involved and then are allowed to make the moral decision for themselves.

Consider human exposures to radiation. It is understood that exposure to large amounts of radiation can cause death. Exposure to lesser amounts can cause cancer. Under a "zero tolerance rule," no one could be hired to work where an exposure to radiation would be possible. In an application of the alternative rule, the EPA has set daily exposure limits considered to be safe. Workers must use their own judgment. Workers hired to clean the reactors in nuclear power plants—who are fully informed of the risks—are paid a full day's pay to absorb the EPA's daily "safe" limit of radiation. Generally, that limit is reached after just ten minutes of work. The rightness or wrongness of this practice, however, is no closer than the abortion issue is to being resolved.

Conceptual disagreements can be settled by agreeing on the proper definition of a concept. However, it is important to understand that arguments can often be made for differing definitions. Many so-called moral disagreements are actually disagreements over definitions. Two individuals, for example, might agree that suicide is immoral. They may disagree, however, over whether asking someone to disconnect a life-support system is a genuine case of suicide.

Disagreements Over Genuine Moral Principles.   Some moral disagreements involve genuine debates over moral principles. Moral disagreements are generally settled by appealing to moral principles. Two individuals can agree about the relevant facts and conceptual issues and still disagree over moral principles. Is bribery immoral? Is suicide immoral? These are genuine moral disagreements and must be settled by appealing to moral principles. How these moral principles are determined is discussed in the following section.

■ MORAL THEORIES

The previous section raised questions about the obligation not to contribute to the corruption of others and the morality of abortion and suicide. The evaluation of these questions could be difficult because of conflicting moral claims that can be offered in support of one view over another. Moral philosophers, however, have found that most moral claims fall into two broad categories or moral theories, termed *utilitarianism* and *ethics of respect for persons*. Before discussing these theories, it will be beneficial to examine more closely the concept of a moral theory.

The Nature of a Moral Theory.   A *moral theory* is a system of moral principles that can be divided into three parts. First, there is a *moral standard*, a criterion or test of what is right or wrong. It has the following general form:

> Those actions are right that possess characteristic X.

Thus, those and only those actions are right that possess some characteristic X. An example of a moral standard would be, "Those actions are right that produce the greatest total amount of happiness."

Second, there are *moral principles* that serve to categorize different types of actions as right or wrong. Moral principles have the following form:

> Those actions of type Y are right (or wrong).

Such actions are right because they conform to the moral standard by possessing characteristic X or wrong because they fail to conform. An example of a moral principle would be, "Discrimination is wrong." Here, the general practice of discrimination would be wrong because it fails to promote happiness.

Third, there are *moral judgments* that are statements about the rightness or wrongness of particular actions. Moral judgments have the following form:

> This action is right (or wrong).

The action is right because it is of type Y or wrong because it is not of type Y. Type Y actions must possess characteristic X. An example would be,

"ABC Widget Company was wrong when it practiced discrimination in refusing to employ John Roe." Here, the action of ABC Widget is declared wrong because it involved discrimination, and discrimination does not promote happiness.

Utilitarianism.   The moral standard of utilitarianism is "Those actions are right that produce the greatest total amount of happiness." Utilitarianism appeals to many people because human happiness seems to be a reasonable purpose of morality. There is, however, a problem with defining the term *happiness.*

What provides happiness for one individual may not provide happiness for another. If utilitarianism requires that society arrange its activities to produce the greatest overall happiness, does it mean that society must define happiness as it is generally understood? May society then impose this definition on those society members who do not agree with it?

Suppose the generally accepted definition within the society is that happiness is the greatest amount of physical pleasure. Some society members, however, may not be as interested in pleasure as they are in wealth or power. Does society as a whole then have a right to select one definition of happiness over another by majority vote?

Preference Utilitarianism.   In responding to this problem, utilitarians have proposed *preference utilitarianism.* Under preference utilitarianism, each individual within the society is allowed to pursue happiness as he or she defines it. Every individual may use his or her own preferences as a guide. One individual does not decide whether another individual should prefer the happiness produced by physical pleasure over the happiness produced by money or power. Rather, each individual tries to promote those general conditions in society that allow most individuals to realize their preferences, whatever they may be.

Necessary Conditions for the Implementation of Utilitarianism.   It seems reasonable to assume that at least two conditions must be met if an individual is to pursue his or her preferences: freedom and well-being. *Freedom* involves the individual's ability to make choices in following his or her preferences. It refers primarily to an individual's freedom from interference by others in making those choices. *Well-being* refers to the conditions necessary for an individual to make effective use of his or her freedom. Individuals who are poor, sick, and uneducated will not be able to realize their freedom—even if no one else is actively trying to inhibit them. Well-being, therefore, includes a minimal amount of wealth, physical health, and education necessary to allow an individual to pursue his or her own preferences.

Applying the Utilitarian Theory.   A utilitarian analysis involves three steps. First, the analyst must determine the audience of the action or policy—those people whose freedom or well-being would be affected. Second, the positive and negative effects imposed on members of the audience by several different courses of action need to be determined. Third, the analyst must decide which course of action produces the greatest overall utility.

Shortcomings in Utilitarianism.   The moral ideal of the utilitarian is to promote a society in which as many people as possible can pursue their own preferences. In undertaking their affairs in this fashion, society members achieve their own versions of happiness. It is an appealing ideal. However, it has two major drawbacks in its application.

First, its implementation requires extensive knowledge of facts, especially the probable future negative and positive consequences of actions. An individual has to know which actions and policies will produce the greatest total amount of freedom and well-being. This knowledge may sometimes be difficult to obtain. For example, are freedom and well-being promoted more by policies that impose strict controls on pollution but are expensive to use and reduce U.S. international competitiveness? Or are they promoted more by policies that allow greater pollution but promote international competitiveness? In resolving this dilemma, the analyst must balance considerations of health against considerations of employment and wealth in a "utilitarian arithmetic" that is difficult to calculate. Often the analyst simply has to make an educated guess.

The second problem with utilitarianism is that it can lead to injustice for certain individuals. Suppose the management of a company is considering closing a plant in an economically depressed region. The closing may make good sense from an economic—and a utilitarian—standpoint. The plant is so inefficient that its production is simply not competitive in the marketplace. Shifting the production to more modern plants would result in more efficient production, better prices for consumers, and greater returns for the company's shareholders. Although the closing will produce a real hardship on workers in the depressed region, preference utilitarianism dictates that the plant should be closed: the workers' happiness if the plant remains open is outweighed by the happiness of those who will benefit from the closing. It is this injustice that has led some philosophers to argue for the second moral theory: ethics of respect for persons.

Ethics of Respect for Persons.   The second major moral theory is called *ethic of respect for persons,* or RP morality. It attempts to resolve the utilitarian problem of injustice. The moral standard of RP morality can be stated as follows: "Those actions are right that equally respect each human person as a moral agent." A *moral agent* is an individual capable of both developing and pursuing actions of his or her own and being responsible for those actions. Thus, moral agents must be distinguished from things, such as a knives or automobiles, that can only fulfill actions imposed by agents.

The Golden Rule.   This emphasis on respect for each individual (as contrasted with concern for the greatest overall utility) is expressed in the Golden Rule: "Do unto others as you would have them do unto you." This moral maxim is found in one form or another in most major religious traditions. It forces members of society to consider other members by placing themselves in the position of other members who could be affected by their actions.

The Golden Rule is an excellent rule of thumb in many practical moral deliberations. However, it can lead to seemingly contradictory results in some applications. In the business world, for example, it can be too narrow and restrictive. To illustrate, suppose that a manager must terminate an employee. Although the manager might not want to be dismissed herself, this does not imply that her dismissal of the employee is morally unjustified.

On the other hand, there are applications of the rule in the business world where it may be too permissive. Suppose, for example, that an insensitive manager treats his employees in a way they consider to be too rough and abusive. Suppose further that the manager would be perfectly happy to be treated in the same way by his superiors. Although he may be fulfilling the requirements of the Golden Rule, the moral justifiability of his actions could still be questioned.

Doctrine of Rights. Clearly, a more precise and objective guideline than the Golden Rule is needed for respecting the moral agency of individuals. Several moral philosophers have concluded that a *doctrine of rights* answers this need. A *right* may be defined as the authority to act or to have another individual act in a certain way. Rights serve as a protective barrier, shielding individuals from the unjustified intrusions of others. Not surprisingly, these rights are essentially the rights to freedom and well-being—the same rights prized under utilitarianism.

In RP morality, however, these basic rights may not be sacrificed for the greater overall utility. More specifically, one individual's (or group's) rights may be overridden to protect another individual's (or group's) rights that are considered to be more *basic*. However, those rights to be overridden cannot be sacrificed merely to provide greater freedom or well-being for the other individual (or group).

Hierarchy of Rights. If an individual's rights may be overridden only to protect a more fundamental or basic right of another individual, those rights that are most fundamental must be known. This requirement calls for a *hierarchy of rights*. Philosopher Alan Gewirth has proposed a three-tiered hierarchy of rights. The first tier includes the most basic rights, the essential preconditions of action: life, physical integrity, and mental health. The second tier includes the right not to be deceived or cheated, to have one's possessions stolen, to be defamed, or to suffer broken promises. The third tier includes the right to such things as property, self-respect, and nondiscrimination.

According to this hierarchy, the government could tax one individual—and thus partially infringe upon his or her right to own property—for the purpose of providing a survival income to another individual who cannot provide for himself or herself. The government could not, however, make some individuals be the servants of others, even if the total utility of the society were thereby promoted. The basic rights of those individuals made slaves would be sacrificed in the process.

Applying RP Morality Theory. To apply RP morality, the audience of the action or policy must be determined. The audience whose rights are affected would ordinarily be the same as the audience under the utilitarian analysis. The analyst must evaluate the seriousness of the rights intrusions each action will impose. Then, the alternative course of action that produces the least serious rights intrusion must be chosen.

Rights intrusions can be measured in three dimensions. First, some rights are more basic than others. A right to life, for example, is more basic than the right to property. Second, an action that cancels a right altogether is more serious than one that merely limits it. Taking away all of an individual's property, for example, is a more serious rights intrusion than taking away only some of it. Third, there is a difference between an actual and a merely potential rights intrusion. An action that actually produces a disease, for example, is a more serious rights intrusion than one that merely increases the risk of having it.

Shortcomings in RP Morality.   RP morality has two principal difficulties. First, it is sometimes difficult to apply. In some cases, any alternative open to one individual involves interference with another individual's rights. In an affirmative action case, for example, management may hire a minority and violate the rights of a nonminority who may be more qualified. Alternatively, management could hire a nonminority and violate the rights of a minority who may claim a right to compensation for past discrimination. Since both rights cannot be honored, management must determine which rights are most deserving. In looking for guidance, management will find that Gewirth's hierarchy of rights is difficult to apply or simply not applicable in such cases.

A second problem with RP morality is that the moral judgments implied by it sometimes appear unworkable because they conflict so strongly with overall welfare or utility. Suppose that because of a company's severe financial problems, the company's management is considering an early retirement program. The program will effectively end the working career of many older employees. It is, however, necessary for the firm's economic survival. While the program will promote more overall utility, it involves an injustice to a few—an injustice given considerable importance under the RP morality theory. In this instance, utilitarianism seems to be a better guide to action than RP morality. In the following case, management is attempting to implement such an early retirement program.

BODNAR v. SYNPOL, INC.

United States Court of Appeals, Fifth Circuit
843 F.2d 190 (1988)

Case Background
Three employees (the plaintiffs) of Synpol, Inc. sued the company for age discrimination. Because of a serious decline in the market for its products, Synpol began a program to cut operating costs. Part of the program involved the implementation of a Special Early Retirement Incentive Program (SERIP). Under the SERIP, salaried employees who had reached age fifty-five and had been with the company for ten years were eligible for early retirement.

On September 27 and 28, 1983, twenty-eight employees were offered early retirement under the SERIP, with an effective retirement date of no later than November 1, 1983. They were given fifteen days to reject or accept the company's offer. Twenty-one employees accepted the plan. The three employees who brought this suit were among the seven employees who rejected the program and remained with the company.

The employees argued that they were effectively discharged through the threats of the company's urging early retirement. They stated the company told them that if they did not take part in the SERIP, they may be released later without severance pay or benefits. Further, the presentations of the SERIP program were made in a "threatening" manner. The U.S. District Court rejected the employees'

(continued)

arguments by granting the company's motion for a summary judgment. The employees appealed.

Case Decision

The lower court's decision in favor of the company was affirmed. The fact that an employer has an early retirement program does not necessarily violate the Age Discrimination in Employment Act. The court of appeals stated that if the employee may choose to decline the early retirement program and continue working, there is no age discrimination by such an offer.

Managerial Considerations

Human resources management involves planning, controlling, and coordinating the work force. Personnel managers are responsible for making sure that employees function to the best of their abilities and that the firm has the proper number and type of people to get the job done. In the past, personnel managers could simply perform this task with whip in hand. As ethical and moral concerns for employees increased, companies started programs to improve employee welfare. Companies became increasingly concerned about the morale and motivation of their work forces.

In their efforts to improve employee welfare, many companies are trying to give employees advance warning of a termination. Some companies allow employees who are being terminated to look for a new job while they are still employed. Companies are training retiring employees to deal with the end of their working lives. Such policies not only benefit the employees involved but also promote good morale among the other employees.

Still, a reduction in the number of employees to cut company costs poses a difficult dilemma for the personnel manager. Older employees confronting retirement face a difficult decision, and a personnel manager should be sympathetic toward those employees. On the other hand, as the company's agent, the personnel manager has the responsibility to present the company's program in a manner most beneficial to the business. The personnel manager's dilemma arises when he or she must decide how far the relationship to the company goes if he or she has to persuade employees to accept a program in which they do not wish to participate.

A Manager's Ethics Analysis.   With most complex moral problems, it is usually helpful to apply both moral theories together. In resolving some problems, the utilitarian and RP morality analyses will agree and the ethical conclusion will be clear. When the two analyses disagree, as in the case of the early retirement program, management must balance the severity of rights violations against the severity of the threat to overall utility. There is, however, no general formula for establishing such a balance. Clearly, a manager's own ethical sensitivities and commitments will play a critical role in resolving this dilemma.

THE NOTION OF CORPORATE SOCIAL RESPONSIBILITY

The law requires corporations to perform many duties and activities. The notion of corporate social responsibility involves consideration of corporate activities not required by law. For example, should corporations be confined to making a profit for their shareholders, or should they enter into the political arena, contribute to charities, and help revitalize inner cities? Should they install expensive antipollution devices that are not required by law? Should ethical considerations ever restrain their efforts to expand into new markets, increase sales, and earn profits? With sales of cigarettes declining in this country, should tobacco companies mount an intensive advertising campaign to sell cigarettes in Third World countries, even though the health hazards of smoking are well-known?

■ CORPORATE SOCIAL RESPONSIBILITY: CONCEPTUAL ISSUE DEBATE

The debate over corporate social responsibility involves a major conceptual issue. Are corporations the kinds of entities that can be praised or blamed for their actions in a way that is similar to the way individuals are praised or blamed? Corporations exhibit many types of "behavior" that resemble those of people: they pay taxes, enter into legal arrangements, exercise certain rights such as freedom of speech, and own property. On the other hand, unlike individuals, they are strictly liable for the injuries caused by their products, do not have the right to vote, are not obligated to register for the draft, and have an indefinite life. So while corporations are not full-fledged persons, are they moral agents in the sense of being entities that can be held morally accountable for their actions?

Corporations are Not Moral Agents.   One leading philosopher, John Ladd, argues that corporations are not moral agents that can be held morally accountable for their actions. Ladd holds that corporations are controlled by their structures. Corporations can act only in accordance with specified organizational goals. In the case of business corporations, those goals will include the company's survival and growth.

According to Ladd, an organization is "rational" when it works to achieve its goals. Moral principles are relevant only insofar as they relate directly to the organization's goals. Thus, if the public finds a television commercial sponsored by a corporation morally offensive, the corporation might well decide to stop showing the commercial. The reason, however, would be that the commercial might result in a boycott of the corporation's products and a reduction in profits—not that the corporation agrees with any moral ideals.

Ladd's conclusion is that organizations with "formal structures" (such as corporations) cannot have moral obligations and hence "cannot have moral responsibilities in the sense of having obligations towards those affected by their actions or subject to their actions. . . . Organizations have tremendous power, but no responsibilities." Thus, Ladd argues that corporations cannot govern themselves by moral principles but must be controlled by government. The government must see to it that corporations do not act in a way that is detrimental to society.

Corporations are Moral Agents.   Many writers do not accept the view that corporate organizational structure makes moral responsibility impossible. Ladd has not established by any convincing argument that moral principles cannot be corporate goals. Why cannot the goal of acting ethically be included in corporate objectives, along with those of self-preservation and profit? In fact, many corporate policy statements include moral objectives. It is possible to argue that these statements are only window dressing and do not express operating policy. It is not evident, however, that this is always the case. At any rate, the presence of such statements strongly suggests that corporations can be morally responsible.

The philosopher Kenneth Goodpaster provides positive support for the view that it makes sense to give moral responsibility to corporations.

Goodpaster isolates four elements of moral responsibility and finds similarities to each of them in corporate life.

1. **Perception:** All rational decision making must begin with a moral agent's perception of his or her environment. Corporations exhibit this characteristic when they gather information before making a decision. As indicated earlier, there is no reason why a corporation cannot take into account the moral as well as the economic and legal dimensions of a decision. For example, a corporation can take into account the effects of plant closings and the discharge of pollution on the community.

2. **Moral Reasoning:** A moral agent must be able to move from assumptions to conclusions about what ought to be done. Similarly, a corporation can certainly weigh alternative decisions with attention to possible injustices to employees or the community.

3. **Coordination:** A moral agent must be able to integrate the moral evaluation with various nonmoral considerations, such as self-interest, the law, economics, and politics. A corporation can make similar deliberations. Goodpaster believes that this is where much moral failure occurs in corporate life. Corporations often trade off moral for nonmoral considerations and end up in undesirable moral compromises. As the following case illustrates, the management of Ford Motor Company traded off safety for the demands imposed by fuel-efficient imports in its inexpensive Pinto.

GRIMSHAW v. FORD MOTOR COMPANY

California Court of Appeals, Fourth District, Division 2
119 Cal.App.3d 757, 174 Cal. Rptr. 348 (1981)

Case Background
The plaintiffs, thirteen-year-old Richard Grimshaw and the heirs of Lilly Gray, brought a product liability action against Ford Motor Company. The Grays had purchased an automobile manufactured by Ford Motor Company—the Ford Pinto hatchback. The auto had stalled unexpectedly on a freeway. It was struck in the rear by another auto and burst into flames. Gray, the driver, died as a result of burns from the accident. Richard Grimshaw, a passenger in Gray's car, suffered permanent and disfiguring burns over his entire body and face. At the time of the accident, the Grays' Pinto was six months old and had been driven approximately 3,000 miles.

When the Pinto was being designed, Ford engineers decided to locate the fuel tank behind the rear axle for styling purposes. Other manufacturers had placed the fuel tank over the rear axle for safety reasons. Ford crash tests proved later that the fuel tank could rupture and ignite upon a 20-mph impact or less to the auto's rear end. Although an inexpensive means was available to the management of Ford to fix the fuel tank problem, they elected not to do so. It was alleged that the management of Ford engaged in a cost-benefit analysis before marketing the Pinto. Management had balanced the costs of redesigning the fuel tank against the possible liability to the company if the design remained unchanged. Management had decided that the cost of the change in design would far exceed the liability costs resulting from accidents. On that basis, the Pinto was marketed without incorporating safety features that the plaintiffs argue could have prevented their injuries.

The jury awarded $2.5 million in compensatory and $125 million in punitive damages to Grimshaw and $559,680 in compensatory damages to the Grays. (The Grays did not seek punitive damages in their complaint and were not allowed to amend it by the trial court.) Ford appealed on several issues, including what it asserted were excessive punitive damages awarded by the jury.

Case Decision
The court of appeals affirmed the trial court's ruling, finding, among other things, that the trial court's assessment of punitive damages was proper and not excessive.

Managerial Considerations
Sound business practices require the use of a cost-benefit analysis—either explicitly or implicitly. In the vast majority of
(continued)

cases, the analysis involves some assessment of the number and costs of injuries to users. Knives, power tools, lawnmowers, airplanes, fishing tackle, guns, electrical appliances, and many other products all have the potential to inflict great bodily harm on their users. Management will compare the costs of those injuries—both the costs of compensating injured parties and the costs associated with repairing the company's reputation—with the costs of making the products safer. In essence, this decision-making process was used by Ford's management in examining changes proposed in the Pinto.

In this decision-making process, management must resolve the ethical and moral dilemma of the cost that is to be placed on human life and human suffering. Extremes clearly can be reached in resolving this dilemma. On one hand, it could be stated that the cost of human life is infinite and that products should be redesigned at any cost to prevent such a loss. On the other hand, even a redesign of the Pinto fuel tank to withstand a 30-mph crash might not aid the occupants if the auto is hit from the rear at 60-mph. In addition, redesigning the automobile to withstand a 60-mph impact would dramatically increase the price of the car, which would become too expensive for many consumers, thereby making the car safer for those who could afford it but depriving others of its benefits. Would those consumers who are deprived be willing to pay a lower price and accept more of the risk of accidents? Should that be considered in the decision making? The resolution of those ethical decisions rests in part in assigning a value to human life and human suffering.

4. **Implementation:** A moral agent must be able to carry out a strategic decision in the "real world" by understanding the environment, implementing the strategy, and guiding it towards realization. A corporation must be able to implement its decisions in a similar way.

Since the decision-making process used by corporations is very similar to that of morally responsible agents, Goodpaster concludes that there is no reason not to hold corporations morally responsible. The question that now arises is, What should corporate moral responsibilities include?

■ THE SCOPE OF CORPORATE RESPONSIBILITY: THE NARROW VIEW

The scope of corporate responsibility has two views. The first view is called the *narrow* or the *agents-of-capital view*. According to Nobel Laureate Milton Friedman, the social responsibility of a business executive (and hence of a corporation) is "to make as much money as possible while conforming to the basic rules of the society, both those embodied in law and those embodied in ethical custom."

The Corporation's Self-Interest Motivation. In examining Friedman's viewpoint, "negative" and "positive" moral obligations must be distinguished. *Negative moral obligations* include obligations *not* to undertake actions that might be highly offensive to the general public. Examples would include engaging in deception or committing fraud. Because its public image would be harmed, a corporation clearly would have self-interested motivations for not participating in offensive activities. *Positive moral obligations* include the kinds of "social obligations" that the broad view of social responsibility argues for—considerations for the quality of life and the environment, among other things. Friedman seems to view corporate responsibility in terms of negative moral obligations. Thus, a corporation should not reduce pollution below the level required by law merely to improve the environment or hire the hard-core unemployed merely to reduce poverty.

Friedman does believe that under certain circumstances, it may be in the corporation's self-interest to do things that have the *appearance* of being positive moral obligations. A corporation might institute a day-care center to improve the morale of employees or to attract a higher quality work force. It might improve safety in a factory beyond that required by law for a similar reason. Friedman asserts, however, that management should never do these things for any other motive than to promote the economic self-interest of shareholders.

RP Morality and Utilitarian Justifications for the Narrow View. Friedman provides both RP morality and utilitarian justifications for his position. From an RP standpoint, Friedman argues that business executives are agents of their principals—the shareholders. Since the corporate goal is to increase profits, a management decision to spend shareholders' money for purposes other than meeting that goal will not likely meet with shareholder approval. If management uses funds for such other purposes, it is intruding on the rights of shareholders. If individual shareholders want to promote a social cause, they can make contributions out of the profits they receive from the corporation. In this way, a shareholder will be able to honor his or her own moral agency without intruding on the rights of other shareholders. Those other shareholders either may not want to contribute to social causes or may want to contribute in a different way.

Friedman also gives some utilitarian justifications for his view of corporate social responsibility. First, Friedman points out that corporate managers are not trained in social policy. They are not necessarily the best people, either by training or desire, to deal with such social problems as pollution, unemployment, and urban decay. Second, the general social well-being can be better served if business is allowed to do what it does best—provide goods and services and make a profit for its shareholders.

■ THE SCOPE OF CORPORATE RESPONSIBILITY: THE BROAD VIEW

In contrast to Friedman, Melvin Anshen maintains that there has always been a kind of social contract between business and society. This contract represents an understanding of the proper goals and responsibilities of business. In the nineteenth century, the major social goal was rapid economic growth. Accordingly, the function of business was to promote that growth in an atmosphere of free competition and minimal government regulation. Today, our society has concerns beyond economic growth, particularly regarding the quality of life and the environment. Anshen asserts that the social contract between business and society has changed and the narrow view of corporate responsibility is no longer appropriate.

Keith Davis, a professor of business administration, agrees. "One basic proposition," he says, "is that social responsibility arises from social power." The immense economic and political power of corporations means that the actions of corporations "affect the interests of others." In a speech to the Harvard Business School in 1969, Henry Ford II stated a similar idea:

> The terms of the contract between industry and society are changing. . . . Now we are being asked to serve a wider range of human values and to accept an obligation to members of the public with whom we have no commercial transactions.

■ THE RP PERSPECTIVE

How can the seemingly contradictory claims of Friedman and Anshen be justified? The RP argument given by Friedman was based on the rights of shareholders. The argument against Friedman is based on the observation that rights can conflict. While it is true that shareholders have rights to have their corporations promote their economic well-being, it is also true that doing so can interfere with the rights of others. According to advocates of the broad view of corporate social responsibility, Friedman's position does not balance rights in the proper way. When a firm continues to sell tires that are a safety hazard, its pursuit of its own right to make a profit constitutes a violation or potential violation of a more basic right—namely consumer rights to health and safety.

Not all of the corporate policies advocated by proponents of the broad view, however, can be justified on the basis that corporations are intruding on the rights of individuals. It is reasonably clear that when a corporation emits a pollutant that causes serious health risks, it is intruding on community members' rights to life and health. However, it is considerably less clear how a corporation's failure to introduce a program to employ the hard-core unemployed intrudes on anyone's rights. Whether corporations have such obligations is much more controversial.

The basis of such positive moral obligations may be found in an equal respect for the rights of persons. If an individual in society is obligated to respect equally the rights of both himself or herself and others, it might seem that the individual should consent to have his or her less basic rights infringed to protect the more basic rights of others. It would seem that others should agree to do the same. An example of this notion can be found in the *Soldano* case presented earlier in the chapter. Most of us would say that the defendant had an obligation to assist the plaintiff at least to the extent of calling the police. The defendant's obligation grows out of the fact that he could have saved a life with relatively little risk to himself. Similarly, perhaps corporations have positive moral obligations to assist the hard-core unemployed—if they can do so with relatively little intrusion on their own general well-being.

But even on an individual level, the extent of such positive moral obligations to "rescue" others is controversial. Would the bartender in the *Soldano* case have been obligated to run out in the street and attempt to restrain the attacker physically? Similarly, would corporations be obligated to help the unemployed if doing so seriously endangered their own efficiency or profit-making potential?

■ THE UTILITARIAN PERSPECTIVE

Under a utilitarian argument against the broad view of social responsibility, Friedman asserted that managers were unqualified to wage war against social evils, such as urban decay, unemployment, and pollution. In some instances, however, managers do possess expertise that can be useful in solving larger social problems. Therefore, the utilitarian case for corporate positive moral obligations to help solve such problems as unemployment may be somewhat stronger than the RP case. But again, this would depend on whether business efficiency and profitability would be diminished.

Another aspect of the utilitarian argument seemingly against the broad view was a version of Adam Smith's "invisible hand" argument. According to Smith, corporations can contribute more to the public good if left to do what they do best, that is, to make a profit within the bounds of the law and the most basic moral guidelines prohibiting fraud and deception. A counter to this argument has been called the "invisible foot" argument. According to this argument, corporations also can cause a great deal of public harm if they operate only under the view suggested by Friedman. While being helped by the invisible hand, society can also be kicked by the invisible foot. Critics of Friedman cite a number of examples.

First, the free market, if left to itself, allows business to pass off some of the costs of its more detrimental activities to the general public. These costs (called externalities by economists) are especially evident in the area of pollution and other environmental concerns. Environmental pollution can have negative consequences for the well-being of our own and future generations. A counterargument is that managers are themselves consumers of the environment and the extent to which they may be willing to pollute it to improve shareholder well-being will be limited.

Second, it is argued that the general quality of life for both employees and the larger community can be eroded if the narrow view is embraced. For example, operating under the narrow view of corporate responsibility, a corporation will improve working conditions for its employees only when it is in the corporation's self-interest to do so. The corporation will be concerned with such issues as product safety and advertising to children only when the law requires it or when competitive conditions force it to do so. However, management will go to great lengths to maintain the company image. A reputation for shoddy workmanship, difficult working conditions, and poor product safety will quickly lead to lower profits and then to losses. Managers will have a difficult time finding employment after leaving a company in such a condition.

▪ MAKING CORPORATIONS MORE MORALLY RESPONSIVE

The debate about the extent of corporate responsibility is still open. Regardless of the outcome of the debate, businesses worldwide are being asked to be more active in carrying out social responsibilities and to be more assertive in seeking changes in the political and social environments. Shareholders are seeking more activity from corporations through shareholder resolutions and other devices. "Public interest" representatives are being placed on corporate boards of directors to review management decisions. Codes of conduct and corporate policy statements are being developed and promoted to clarify what is to be considered ethical activity within the corporation.

It is generally agreed that improving corporate social responsibility ultimately depends upon changing something much more vague. This factor usually goes under the title of "corporate culture," which refers to the values and attitudes of the corporate workplace. It is further agreed that corporate culture is set by top management. Thus, the support for corporate social responsibility by top management is crucial. Encouraging students who will be the future managers to think clearly about ethical issues is one way to ensure this support.

SUMMARY:
A GUIDE FOR MANAGERS

- Over the past two decades, the public image of business and business executives has been declining. In addition, the general public believes that dishonesty in general is greater than it was just ten years ago. In an effort to overcome these image problems, the business community is encouraging companies to write codes of ethics, screen its prospective employees, and teach business ethics and principles.

- The terms *ethics* and *morals* generally mean the same thing. These terms, should not, however, be confused with statements about etiquette or good manners or with rules of law.

- A major source of confusion in discussing and evaluating ethics is the failure to distinguish three basic kinds of disagreements: disagreements over the facts, disagreements over conceptual issues, and disagreements over genuine moral principles. Moral disagreements are generally settled by appealing to moral principles.

- According to moral philosophers, moral principles fall within two moral theories: utilitarianism and ethics of respect for persons (or RP morality). The moral standard of utilitarianism is "Those actions are right that produce the most happiness." The application of utilitarianism by individuals requires two conditions: freedom and well-being. In applying the theory, the analyst must first determine the audience of the action. The analyst must then determine the positive and negative effects imposed on members. Finally, the analyst must decide which course of action produces the most happiness or utility. The utilitarianism theory is criticized because it requires a great deal of information and can lead to injustice for certain individuals.

- The RP morality theory can be stated as "Those actions are right that equally respect each human person as a moral agent." The Golden Rule has been characterized as representative of RP morality. However, because the Golden Rule may be too permissive in its application in the business world, moral philosophers have developed a doctrine of rights under which an individual's rights may be overridden only to protect a more fundamental or basic right of another individual. In defining basic rights, moral philosophers have proposed a hierarchy of rights. At the top of the hierarchy is life, while at the third tier are such rights as the right to property and self-respect. In applying the theory, the analyst must determine the audience, the policy alternatives, and which course of action produces the least serious rights intrusions. The principal shortcomings of the theory are that it is difficult to apply and that its outcomes can appear to be implausible because they conflict with overall welfare.

- The responsibilities of corporations beyond those required by the law have been heavily debated. Some scholars assert that corporations are not moral agents and thus cannot have moral responsibilities. Others assert that corporate life has all the elements of moral responsibility and therefore corporations should be considered as moral agents.

■ The two competing theories of social responsibility include the agents-of-capital view and the social contract view. The agents-of-capital view asserts that the corporation has the responsibility to make as much money as possible while conforming to the basic rules of society. Under the social contract theory, philosophers assert that our society has moved beyond an emphasis on economic growth. Corporations should now focus more on quality of life and environmental concerns.

MANAGER'S ETHICAL DILEMMA

TAKING ETHICS SERIOUSLY

Many companies adopted codes of ethics in the past twenty years that contain clear statements of corporate commitment to ethical action. But these codes are often little more than fine sentiments because, when it comes to the bottom line, they are ignored.

The problem arises at all levels of operations. Individual instances of bad judgment are quite often reported. Citicorp fired the president and senior executives of a credit card processing operation for allegedly overstating expenses. Before Christmas in 1991, Toys "R" Us sent employees to rival stores around the country to buy their stocks of toys being sold on sale and then resold the toys at Toys "R" Us. Although that action was not illegal, it strikes some people as unethical competition.

Individual instances of unethical behavior are not surprising. The concern is that it is widespread. *Fortune* reported in 1992 that one-quarter of middle managers admit to having written deceptive internal reports. These managers make their performance look better than it is by telling their boss that things are better than they are. Compensation of top executives has come under fire as unethical. How can a high salary and a giant bonus be justified for a president whose company is losing money and laying off workers?

Firms that consistently engage in unethical behavior are more likely to cross the line into illegal activities and are more likely to alienate customers, employees, and suppliers. A company's ethics are a bottom-line issue. For an ethics program to work, the commitment by management must be serious and consistent.

Hewlett-Packard makes sure that all employees know about the company's business conduct standards, which cover such details as conflict of interest, accounting practices, and the appropriate acceptance of gifts. Sales personnel are instructed not to degrade competitors' business practices, even if there is public knowledge of problems. Northrup uses anonymous questionnaires to have managers' ethical behavior rated by their peers and their employees.

The ethics officer at Nynex notes that since the best program in the world will not prevent unethical behavior by employees who do not care, incentives must be in place. About half of all college students admit to cheating, and about one-fifth say they put false information on their resumes when looking for a job. If some employees do not think that ethics matter, for a company program to work, those who cross the ethics line must be disciplined or fired, just as if they had broken the law or failed to properly perform their job.

QUESTIONS

Should violations of ethics policy be treated more lightly than failure to perform required tasks or meet sales goals or other clearly defined bottom-line activities? Should companies use psychological profile exams when hiring workers to try to weed out those who appear to be more likely to be unethical?

REVIEW AND DISCUSSION QUESTIONS

1. Define the following terms:

morals	corporate social responsibility
ethics	agents-of-capital view of corporate social
moral principles	responsibility
moral agent	

2. Compare and contrast the following terms and phrases:
   a. Ethics and etiquette.
   b. Ethics and the law.
   c. Moral theory and moral judgment.
   d. Utilitarianism and RP morality.
   e. Freedom and well-being.
   f. The Golden Rule and a moral standard.
   g. Negative moral obligation and positive moral obligation.

3. Suppose upper management decides to adopt a corporate ethics code. The company is a manufacturer, distributor, and wholesaler of consumer products—primarily consumer pain medicines, cold remedies, and other similar nonprescription medicines. Who are the company's constituencies? Which of those constituencies should the company ethics code address? To what punishments, if any, should employees be subjected if they violate the code?

4. The engineers at your company estimate that by making certain quality improvements in the production process, the risk of death from using your product will drop from one in two million to one in four million per year. Given the current use rate of the product, one death occurs every other year and costs the firm an average of $1 million in settlements. The quality improvements would cost $30 million to make—more than the expected settlement savings. How do you resolve this issue?

■ CASE QUESTIONS

5. The evidence is continuing to mount implicating smoking as a serious health hazard. Consumer groups are arguing that tobacco manufacturers and growers are well aware of the health hazards associated with smoking but are failing to adequately inform consumers. Should cigarette manufacturers be liable for the serious illnesses and untimely deaths caused by their products—even though they have posted a warning on the package and consumers have voluntarily assumed the health risks by smoking? Wouldn't a truly responsible company not manufacture cigarettes at all? [*Cipollone v. Liggett Group, Inc.*, 644 F. Supp. 283 (D.N.J. 1986)]

6. Through the mid-1980s, Corona, a Mexican beer, became very popular in the United States. Several domestic beers were seriously hurt by Corona's sudden success. In 1988, Corona experienced a surprising slump in sales. Through the diligence of the company's management, the decline was eventually attributed to rumors about the quality of Corona—particularly, that it had traces of urine in it. The company traced the rumors to several southwestern domestic beer distributors. How should the domestic brewers who supply those distributors react to such practices? If one brewery responds by severing its relationship with the offending distributor, will the other breweries likely follow suit and sever their relationships?

7. Two eight-year-old boys were seriously injured when riding Honda mini-trail bikes provided by their parents. The boys were riding on public streets and ran a stop sign when they were hit by a truck. One boy was not wearing a helmet. The bikes had clear warning labels on the front stating that they were only for offroad use. The owner's manual was clear that the bikes were not to be used on public streets and that riders should wear helmets. The parents sued Honda. The Supreme Court of Washington said that there was one basic issue. "Is a manufacturer liable when children are injured while riding one of its mini-trail bikes on a public road in violation of manufacturer and parental warnings?" What do you think the court held? Is it unethical to make products like minibikes that will be used by children? [*Baughn* v. *Honda Motor Co.*, 107 Wash. 127, 727 P.2d 655 (1986)]

8. In 1982, Johnson Controls adopted a "fetal protection policy" that women of childbearing age could not work in the battery-making division of the company. There was evidence that exposure to the lead in the battery operation could cause harm to unborn babies. The company was concerned about possible legal liability for injury suffered by babies of mothers who had worked in the battery division. In 1991, the Supreme Court held that the company policy was illegal. It was an "excuse for denying women equal employment opportunities." Is the Court forcing the company to be unethical by allowing pregnant women who ignore the warnings to expose their babies to the lead? [*United Auto Workers* v. *Johnson Controls*, ____ U.S. ____ , 111 S.Ct. 1196 (1991)]

■ ETHICS QUESTIONS

9. The United States has more stringent restrictions on toxic substance disposal than do many poor countries that have no regulations regarding such matters. Firms can move their operations to such countries, not spend millions on expensive pollution controls required in the United States, and thus produce their products for less. Should we effectively extend our pollution laws to other countries by not allowing the import of products made in countries or at plants that do not meet American pollution standards? If we do, it will retard the development of poor countries, which may gladly trade some pollution for higher incomes. Should that make a difference?

10. The local opera company visits your company's headquarters. It asks for a donation of $10,000, claiming that without such corporate support the opera will close. What factors do you consider in making a recommendation to your company about such a donation?

11. Migrant farm workers are at about the bottom of our employment force and quality of life standards. They work very hard, do not make much money, and live with their families in what are often miserable conditions. You run a large vegetable farm operation that hires migrant workers an average of four weeks per year. You pay the going wage rate for the workers, who rent dumps to live in while they work in your area before moving north. Do you have an ethical responsibility to pay more than the market wage so that these workers can live in better conditions? Do you have a responsibility to provide housing to the workers you employ? If you pay above-market rates, your neighbor farmers will be mad at you and point out that—as you know—most of the farm operations run on thin margins as it is, so that much higher wages could drive you all out of business. Assuming these to be facts, what responsibilities do you think you have? Closing the Mexican border will reduce the number of migrant workers which will drive up the wage rate. The migrant workers in the United

States will be better off, but those who used to cross from Mexico will be worse off. Is it ethical to close the border?

12. The ABC Company has been supplying widgets to your XYZ Company for many years. The widgets are needed in the production of gidgets. ABC has always been a fair company to deal with. When problems have arisen, ABC has usually resolved them to your satisfaction. Now the LMN firm from Singapore has approached you, saying it will provide widgets to you for 10 percent less than you were paying ABC. ABC tells you there is no way it can cut its prices and if you cut the company off, it will have to pare back production so that fifty people will be fired. Should you stick with ABC to protect American jobs? What other considerations may be involved?

13. In the 1970s, the Justice Department looked into allegations of price fixing in the folding-carton industry. The department was having difficulty establishing its case when it discovered two boxes of personal notes in the home of a retired Weyerhaeuser Company executive. In the notes, the Justice Department found details of years of illegal price-fixing agreements with officials from other companies. The material helped lead to the price-fixing convictions of twenty-three companies. The case made it clear that in the event of a lawsuit, nearly any corporate document can be obtained and used by the opposing party. Companies are now shredding company documents to avoid future liabilities arising from such lawsuits. Is it ethical to shred documents if the purpose is to avoid potential liability for wrongdoing?

BUSINESS AND THE JUDICIAL PROCESS

CHAPTER 3

MANAGER'S LEGAL CHALLENGE

The Manville Corporation is a 130-year-old company that makes quality insulation, roofing products, wood and paper products, and a variety of industrial building products. Headquartered in Denver, the company employed more than 25,500 people in more than 100 plants, mines, and sales offices worldwide in 1982.

One of the products in which Manville specialized was asbestos. In the 1930s, medical knowledge of the health effects of asbestos was in its infancy. Asbestosis (a crippling, irreversible disease of the lungs) was associated only with those workers who handled 100 percent raw asbestos fiber. Concerned about those workers, the U.S. Public Health Service set an exposure limit in 1938. That limit remained the standard in the United States until the late 1960s.

In 1964, a medical study established a causal link between lung disease and exposure to asbestos at any level. In that year, the management of Manville adopted a strategy to minimize potential liabilities that could arise from workers injured by exposure to asbestos. Management began by discontinuing the company's asbestos operations and selling its asbestos-related assets. Management also litigated aggressively any asbestos injury claim made against the company.

Management's strategic response to the company's asbestos problem was based on its perception of the legal environment. Under law existing at that time, it was difficult for injured workers to litigate an asbestos case successfully. According to the law, because Manville had taken *reasonable* actions to protect employees, it was not liable for worker injuries.

The legal environment changed dramatically in the 1970s. In 1972, the U.S. Court of Appeals for the Fifth Circuit agreed with a lower court decision in *Borel* v. *Fiberboard Paper Products Corporation* (presented in Chapter 8). The case applied stricter legal standard than had previously been applied in asbestos cases. Attitudes about worker and consumer injuries from industrial products was changing. The court placed greater responsibility on asbestos manufacturers, finding them strictly liable for worker injuries due to exposure to asbestos. In effect, the court found that with the new social consciousness of the seventies, reasonable efforts on the part of asbestos manufacturers to protect workers would not be enough to relieve them of liability for injury to workers.

Like other asbestos manufacturers, the management of Manville was strategically unprepared for the decision. The failure of management to monitor and anticipate the legal environment, and thus be able to prepare viable strategic alternatives, led to thousands of asbestos claims being filed against Manville. Insurance companies refused to cover the claims.

Manville was forced to declare bankruptcy in 1982, as its potential liability far exceeded its one-billion-dollar net worth. To move the company out of bankruptcy court supervision, a trust was established by the company in 1988 to pay claims. The fund was quickly exhausted, and another $500 million had to be added in 1990.

Since tens of thousands of claims against Manville and other asbestos makers still existed in 1992, with potential liability of $50 billion, the company faces a near eternity of managing legal claims.

The *Borel* case clearly surprised the management of Manville. The consequences clearly illustrate the importance of monitoring the legal environment, understanding how law is made, and anticipating factors that affect changes in the law. As the Manville situation reflects, failure by management to consider the dynamics of the legal environment in developing a strategic plan can have severe and unexpected consequences.

The study of the legal environment of business requires an overview of the law and the legal system. Made up of law from several sources, the legal environment of business has been influenced by the business community, consumers, and government. It is not surprising, then, that the laws that make up the legal environment reflect many different perspectives, viewpoints, and legal philosophies. This chapter provides a general understanding of the fundamental objectives of law, the creation of law, the role of law in an orderly society, the classifications of law, and the important major sources of law.

The chapter then defines the litigation process. It describes the procedural rules that govern this process and considers the important functions it provides society. By discussing the means through which injured parties gain access to the court system, the procedural requirement of jurisdiction is examined. The chapter then looks at the two main systems that make up our American court system: the federal court system and the basic system of courts that exists in each state.

WHAT IS LAW?

In the study of the legal environment of business, *law* refers to a general code of conduct that defines the boundaries for all business and managerial behavior. However, because "law" is necessarily an abstract term, a more precise definition is somewhat difficult. Consider, for example, the following definitions offered by leading legal authorities. *Black's Law Dictionary*, regarded by attorneys as the best legal dictionary, defines law as follows:

> **1.** Law, in its generic sense, is a body of rules of action or conduct pre-scribed by controlling authority, and having binding legal force.
> **2.** That which must be obeyed and followed by [members of a society] subject to sanctions or legal consequences is a law.

Writing just before the turn of the century, the legal scholar Justice Oliver Wendell Holmes offered the following famous definition of law:

> Law is a statement of the circumstances, in which the public force is brought to bear . . . through the courts.

In his famous book, *Growth of Law,* the jurist Benjamin Nathan Cardozo defined law as follows:

> A principle of rule of conduct so established as to justify a prediction with reasonable certainty that it will be enforced by the courts if its authority is challenged.

Writing from an entirely different perspective, the anthropologist Bronis-law Malinowski, in his classic study of primitive law, defined law in this way:

> [T]he specific result of the configuration of obligations, which makes it impossible for [any society member] to shirk his responsibility without suffering for it in the future.

From these definitions law may be viewed as a collection of rules intended to control human behavior. Through their enforcement, those rules are intended to provide predictability and uniformity to the bound-aries of acceptable conduct within a society. It is also clear that this collec-tion of rules will include both the *formal rules* of the society as established by the government or other authority and the *informal rules* of a society as set forth by the society's history, values, customs, traditions, commercial aspirations, and ethics.

FUNCTIONS OF LAW AND THE LEGAL SYSTEM

Law and the legal system serve several important functions in an orderly society. Several of the most important are considered in this section, in-cluding influencing the behavior of the members of a society, resolving the society's disputes, maintaining the important values of the society, and providing a means for social changes deemed important.

ASSURING SOCIAL CONTROL BY INFLUENCING BEHAVIOR

It is important for the law and the legal system to both define acceptable human behavior and provide a means to control unacceptable behavior. Law and the legal system must function to instruct members of the society on what to do and what not to do in a variety of circumstances. The law thus imposes a structure on society by limiting activities determined to be harmful to the public interest and encouraging activities determined to be beneficial. Within the legal environment of business, the law will work to prohibit business practices that are viewed as being dishonest or unethical. At the same time, the law works to encourage those practices that further society's goals.

The legal system must be backed up, however, by some measure of "force" to encourage or discourage certain activities. Managers, like other members of a society, will quickly readjust their behavior when they learn that a law is being inadequately enforced by the government or other authority. The behavior of society in such circumstances will not differ from society's behavior if there were no law governing the matter.

This force requirement may involve fines, imprisonment, or other penalties. For example, a business that pollutes a river may be fined by the federal government to encourage it to comply with laws prohibiting such pollution. The force may also involve a social stigma. For example, a business that gains a reputation for overworking its employees will eventually find it difficult to hire new workers. The force in such a situation is the cost associated with the stigma of being considered a difficult company to work for. Although no formal law directs this part of the business's operations, society demands that the business behave in an acceptable way. Unacceptable behavior will often result in reactions by society members to punish the business. Society may demand, for example, that the business pay higher wages. The business can then choose to either pay the higher wage or change its unreasonable behavior.

In either case, the force employed is intended to provide incentives for acceptable behavior as dictated by society. Management should pay attention to the company's conduct to avoid damaging the company's reputation or goodwill or having to pay large fines.

■ CONFLICT RESOLUTION

The next important function of the law is to settle society's disputes. Disagreements are an expected part of a technological society made up of individuals with differing viewpoints and material desires. To ensure order, the law and the legal system must provide a formal means to settle conflicts and disputes. According to Karl N. Llewellyn, a legal theorist:

> What, then, is this law business about? It is about the fact that our society is honeycombed with disputes. Disputes actual and potential, disputes to be settled and disputes to be prevented; both appealing to law, both making up the business of law. . . . This doing of something about disputes . . . is the business of law.

Society's formal mechanism for the resolution of disputes will involve both an institution and a set of procedural rules setting forth how to function within the institution. This mechanism is used for resolving *private disputes* between society members and *public disputes* arising between a society member and the government or other authority. Within our society, that institution is the court system, and the procedural rules are the codes of civil and criminal procedure. This court system forms the *structure* of our legal system. Within that structure, society enjoys an objective, unbiased mechanism for resolving disputes.

In the absence of a formal mechanism, society members would be compelled to provide their own means of resolving disputes. If that were the case, an important function of the resolution process would be lost. In resolving disputes, the court system establishes rules of conduct to be followed by others who may become involved in similar disputes in the future. These rules of conduct form an important body of law called the common law (discussed in the following section). The common law and other rules of behavior form the *substance* of law and the legal environment of business.

■ SOCIAL MAINTENANCE

The norms of a society are molded by society's values, customs, and traditions. The laws of society work to preserve those norms. In this way, law plays an important role in maintaining the social environment of society. The values of honesty and integrity are reflected, for example, by the legality and enforceability of agreements; a genuine respect for the property of others is reflected in laws protecting private property rights; and society's measure of acceptable behavior is reflected in laws requiring wrongdoers to compensate parties they injure.

The effectiveness of the social maintenance function of law and the legal system is strongly influenced by the *legal culture* of the society. The legal culture is defined by the attitudes of society members toward law and the legal system. The legal culture of the society determines whether law will be enforced, obeyed, avoided, or abused.

■ SOCIAL CHANGE

Law and the legal system provide a means through which the government or other authority can bring about important changes in "acceptable" behavior. Behavior that was considered acceptable in the past may not serve society well in the future. Consider, for example, the changes that must have been brought about in the legal environment of business when the horse and buggy was replaced by the automobile.

Laws that serve to promote or discourage specific managerial behavior can be enacted and enforced by the government or other authority. For example, laws can be enacted to prohibit racial discrimination in management decisions to hire, promote, or discharge a worker. In the past, racial discrimination may have been an accepted—or at least a tolerated—standard of business behavior for which no fines or other penalties were imposed. Such behavior, however, is no longer considered acceptable to society. As the Manager's Legal Challenge feature at the beginning of this chapter showed, it is important for management to anticipate such changes in the legal environment—or risk serious legal consequences.

A business activity can be discouraged by the threat of a fine or penalty. Laws can be enacted and enforced that impose substantial penalties when a business pollutes the environment. Without the threat of such a penalty, businesses may be tempted to act in ways that might harm other society members.

ORIGIN OF LAW IN THE UNITED STATES: THE COMMON LAW

The original source of law in this country is *judge-made* or *common law*—law made by judges as they resolve disputes between private parties. Under the common law, the judge's resolution of current dispute will generally be consistent with past judicial decisions.

The common law in this country is traced to the colonial period. Because most of America was a British colony, English common law was adopted. The principal feature of the English law and legal system was its reliance on judge-made or common law. English cases may still be referred to today in American courts.

COMMON LAW

The origin of our law and legal system can be more easily understood by examining English common law. In 1066, the Normans conquered England. William the Conqueror and his successors began to unify the country under their rule. An important element in that unification process was the establishment of King's Courts—called *Curia Regis*—which were to develop and apply a common or uniform set of rules for the entire country. The set of rules that developed marked the beginning of English common law.

The decisions in more important cases were gathered and recorded in books. To settle disputes that were similar to past disputes, judges used cases recorded in those books as the basis for their decisions. A previously decided case that is similar in legal principle or in facts to a case under consideration is referred to as *precedent*. To settle new or unique disputes, judges created new laws, which then became precedents for deciding future cases.

DOCTRINE OF STARE DECISIS

The practice of deciding new cases by looking to past decisions is the foundation of the English and American judicial processes. The use of precedent in deciding present cases forms a doctrine called *stare decisis*, meaning "to stand on decided cases." Under this doctrine, judges are encouraged to stand by precedents. According to Judge Posner:

> Judge-made rules are the outcome of the practice of decision according to precedent (stare decisis). When a case is decided, the decision is thereafter a precedent, i.e., a reason for deciding a similar case the same way. While a single precedent is a fragile thing . . . [many] precedents dealing with the same question will create a rule of law having virtually the force of an explicit statutory rule.

The doctrine of stare decisis promotes several useful functions in our legal system. First, there is more uniformity in the decisions of the courts. As a rule is applied in more and more disputes involving the same (or similar) set of facts, managers and attorneys will be increasingly confident that the rule will be followed in the future. Second, clarity and consistency in the legal system enhances the ability of managers to plan business transactions. Under the doctrine of stare decisis, managers have reasonable expectations about the future enforcement of their agreements and the legal standards that will be applied.

One of the major advantages of dispute resolution through the common law is the law's ability to change with the times. As changes in society occur, the common law can also change and provide new rules that better fit the new environment. Although most cases are decided on the basis of stare decisis, judges may decide to change legal principles if conditions support the change. Normally, such a decision will be appealed to a higher court for review.

The higher court will agree or disagree with the change, depending upon how strong the judge's arguments for the change are. For example, in the past decade, the business community has experienced rapid changes in the way it communicates information and documents. Computers connected by modems and FAX machines make it possible to transmit documents quickly anywhere in the world. These communication devices have made it easier to establish that a document is genuine. As a result, in-person contact has become less necessary—substantially reducing business travel costs. In response to these changes in business practices, the legal system has also changed. Years ago, it was necessary for the parties to a business deal to sign agreements in person to avoid the potential for fraud. Now, courts generally accept as genuine "signatures" transmitted by telegram, FAX, and electronic mail.

SOURCES OF LAW MORE RECENT IN ORIGIN

In addition to the judge-made common law, there are several other important sources of law of more recent origin. Most fundamental of these sources are the state and federal constitutions. Through these constitutions, other important sources of law are created. The U.S. Constitution, for example, creates the executive, legislative, and judicial branches of government—each of which has the ability to make law. In addition, Congress—the legislative branch of government—has used its constitutionally granted powers to create what is often referred to as the fourth branch of government—the administrative agencies, a source of law of increasing importance to business.

CONSTITUTIONS

A *constitution* is the fundamental law of a nation. It will establish both the powers of the government and the limits of that power. The U.S. Constitution allocates the powers of government to the states on the one hand and the federal government on the other. Powers not explicitly granted to the federal government by the U.S. Constitution are retained by the state governments. With the exception of Great Britain, the major Western economies have written constitutions. As discussed in the *International Aspects* feature, there is a movement within Great Britain to establish a written constitution.

INTERNATIONAL ASPECTS | GREAT BRITAIN'S UNWRITTEN CONSTITUTION

Great Britain is governed by the oldest unwritten constitution in the world. The rights were established by the Magna Charta (signed by King John of England in 1215) and the common law that has evolved since that time. The Magna Charta provided the basis for Britain's constitutional monarchy and many individual liberties including the right of trial by jury and the principle of no taxation without representation.

Several political groups in Great Britain are proposing a written constitution. Britain is the only member of the Council of Europe that does not have a written constitution. The Council of Europe is an organization of twenty-five nations that work to promote human rights and democracy. Many of the constitutional issues being considered by the Council of Europe and by other European organizations are difficult for Britain to manage under its current unwritten constitution.

Because there is no written constitution, Parliament is sovereign to do what it likes. While Parliament has not been abusive, the judiciary exists at its whim, unlike the judiciary under constitutions that guarantee judicial independence. Judges are appointed by the Lord Chancellor, who is appointed by the Prime Minister. Hence, all judges are subject to political control.

The groups proposing a written constitution have several issues in common. Each of the proposals calls for a British *bill of rights* that would provide for individual rights and liberties. In addition, a number of proposals would include a freedom of information act, require that the upper house of the British Parliament (the House of Lords) be elected instead of appointed, abolish the monarchy, and provide for judicial independence.

The U.S. Constitution.   The U.S. Constitution is by far the oldest written constitution still in force in the world. It sets forth the general organization, powers, and limits of the federal government. Specifically, the U.S. Constitution creates the legislative, executive, and judicial branches of the U.S. government. This division in governmental power as established by the Constitution is referred to as the doctrine of *separation of powers*. This separation of powers arose out of a fear by the founders of this country that too much power might become concentrated in one governmental branch. The doctrine provides that each of the three branches of government has a separate function to perform that can be checked by the other two branches. The government structure that has developed from these constitutional provisions is illustrated in Figure 3–1.

The U.S. Constitution clearly establishes itself as the supreme law of this country. According to Article VI:

> This Constitution, and the Laws of the United States which shall be made in Pursuance thereof; and all Treaties made, or which shall be made, under the Authority of the United States, shall be the supreme Law of the Land; and the Judges in every State shall be bound thereby, any Thing in the Constitution or Laws of any State to the Contrary notwithstanding.

Thus, a state or federal law found to be in violation of the U.S. Constitution will be declared unconstitutional and will not be enforced.

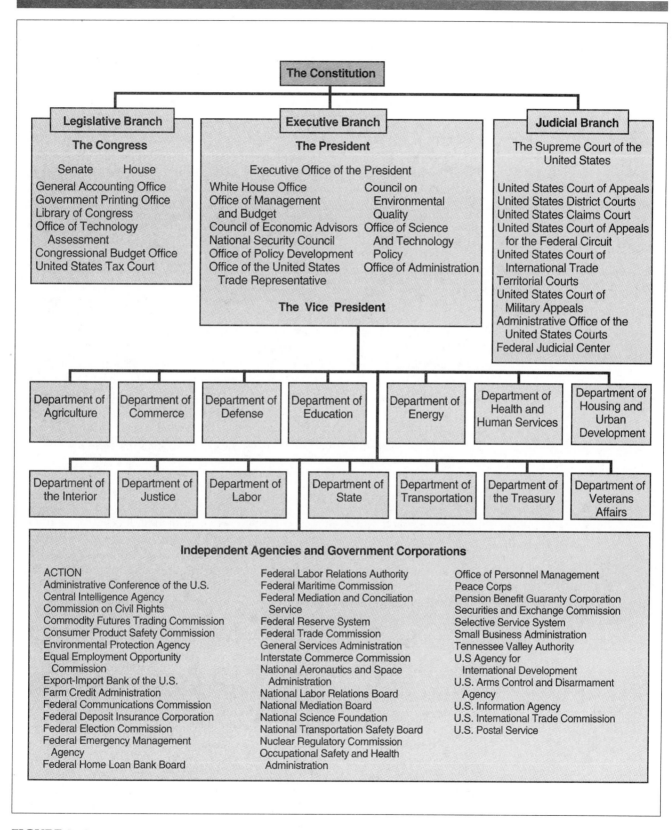

FIGURE 3–1

The Government of the United States

NOTE: This chart seeks to show only the more important agencies of the government.

State Constitutions.   All powers not granted to the federal government are retained by the state governments. According to the Tenth Amendment to the Constitution:

> The powers not delegated to the United States by the Constitution . . . are reserved to the states respectively. . . .

The powers and structures of all fifty state governments are based on written constitutions. Like the federal government, the state governments are divided into legislative, judicial, and executive branches. The constitutions specify how state officials shall be chosen and removed, how laws are passed, how the court system will be run, and how finances and revenues will be paid and collected. Each state constitution is the highest form of law in that state.

■ LEGISLATURES

The Congress and the various state legislative bodies are an important source of law called *statutory law.* Statutory law includes much of the law that affects business behavior. The most important constraint on this body of law is that it cannot violate the U.S. Constitution or the relevant state constitutions. Article I, Section 1, of the U.S. Constitution provides that all power to make laws for the federal government shall be given to Congress. (The specific powers given to the Congress that affect business are discussed in Chapter 5.) Each state has a lawmaking body similar to Congress in its functions and procedures. In recent years, state statutory law has become an important source of regulatory law affecting the legal environment of business.

■ ADMINISTRATIVE AGENCIES

An administrative agency is created when either the legislative or the executive branch of the government assigns or delegates some of its authority to an appropriate agency or group. Through Congress (or the state legislature), that delegation usually takes the form of an enactment of a law that lists the duties and responsibilities of the agency. Consider the following delegation of authority by Congress under the Clean Water Act:

> . . . [T]he Administrator of the Environmental Protection Agency . . . shall administer this [act]. . . . The Administrator is authorized to prescribe such regulations as are necessary to carry out his functions under this [act].

With congressional delegation, administrative agencies are able to apply broad legislative, judicial, and executive powers. By passing regulations, an agency uses its statutory powers to implement the act that assigns authority to it. In supervising businesses to make sure they are complying with those regulations, an agency uses its executive powers. Finally, in the adjudication of violations of those regulations, administrative agencies use their judicial powers. The regulations, agency opinions, and agency orders flowing from administrative agencies are perhaps the most important source of law affecting the legal environment of business. The practices and procedures of administrative agencies are discussed in Chapter 6.

■ THE JUDICIARY

As previously discussed, judge-made common law is a major source of law affecting the legal environment of business. The judiciary also serves to interpret and enforce laws enacted by legislative bodies. In addition, the judiciary reviews actions taken by the executive branch.

The legal environment of business is significantly affected by the judicial review of the actions and activities of the administrative agencies. According to professors Robinson and Gellhorn:

> The function of judicial review is to assure that the administrator's action is authorized (within his delegated authority) and not an abuse of discretion (an unreasonable choice not supported by available evidence). It assures that, when challenged, the administrative action has not encroached excessively on private rights. . . . [J]udicial review tests whether the agency (a) has exceeded its constitutional or statutory authority, (b) has properly interpreted the applicable law, (c) has conducted a fair proceeding, and (d) has not acted capriciously and unreasonably.

Generally speaking, statutes enacted by Congress are very broad. The agency will interpret the broad statute to determine how it will apply to a specific business. When asked to do so, the courts will review those interpretations. Thus, the combination of the statute enacted by Congress, the agency's interpretation of the statute, and the court's review of the agency's interpretation all form the law on the subject in question.

■ THE EXECUTIVE

In addition to approving (or disapproving) bills passed by Congress, the President is a major source of law affecting the legal environment of business. The lawmaking authority of the President is limited by the Constitution. However, the President can create law by issuing *executive orders.*

The President can also indirectly influence the degree to which administrative agencies undertake their duties and responsibilities. A pro-business administration, for example, may not pursue environmental, antitrust, or international trade issues as strongly as a less business-oriented administration. Thus, business may face a seemingly hostile legal environment under one administration and a much more permissive one under another.

CLASSIFICATIONS OF LAW ▰▰▰▰▰▰▰▰▰▰▰

Law can be grouped or classified in several ways. As the previous section has illustrated, law could be classified according to its source. That is, it could be classified according to whether it originated with a constitution, a legislative body, the judiciary, or the executive branch of government. It could be further classified according to whether the source was a state body—a state constitution, court, legislature, or governor—or a federal body—the federal Constitution, courts, Congress, or the President. The more common classification systems, however, classify law on the basis of whether it is public or private, civil or criminal, or procedural or substantive. It is important to note that a law may be placed in more than one category. A particular law, for example, could be not only public but also criminal and procedural.

■ PUBLIC OR PRIVATE LAW

Some examples of public and private law are provided in Table 3–1. *Public law* is concerned with the legal relationship between society members— including businesses as well as individuals—and the government or other authority. Public law includes the statutory laws enacted by Congress and the state legislatures. It serves to influence the behavior of society members and to provide a means for bringing about social change.

Private law sets forth rules governing the legal relationships among society members. It serves to resolve disputes among society members and to provide a means through which the important values, customs, and traditions of the society can influence law. Private law includes the common or judge-made law and is enforced primarily through the state court systems.

■ CIVIL OR CRIMINAL LAW

When a legislative body enacts a law, it generally decides whether the law is to be civil, criminal, or both. Unless a law is specifically designated as being criminal, it is considered civil law. Examples of civil and criminal law are provided in Table 3–2.

Civil law is concerned with the rights and duties that exist among individual society members or between individual society members and the government or other authority in noncriminal matters. A society member found *liable* for a *civil wrong* may be required to pay money damages to the injured party, stop doing a specific act, or both. In finding the wrong-doer liable, the jury (or the judge in a nonjury trial) must find that the *preponderance* (majority) *of the evidence* favored the injured party.

Criminal law concerns legal wrongs, or crimes, committed against all of society. As determined by the appropriate federal or state statute or local *ordinance*, a crime is classified as treason, a felony, or a misdemeanor.

TABLE 3–1
EXAMPLES OF PUBLIC AND PRIVATE LAW

Public Law	Private Law
Administrative law	Agency law
Antitrust law	Contract law
Constitutional law	Corporation law
Criminal law	Partnership law
Criminal procedure	Personal property
Environmental law	Real property
Labor law	Torts
Securities regulation	

TABLE 3-2
EXAMPLES OF CIVIL AND CRIMINAL LAW

Civil Law	Criminal Law
Contract Law	**Misdemeanor Offenses**
Business formation	Assault and battery (simple)
Insurance	Disturbing the peace
Real estate	Larceny (petit)
Sales	Prostitution
Services	Public intoxication
	Trespass
Tort Law	
Assault and battery	**Felony Offenses**
Defamation	Arson
Fraud	Bribery
Invasion of privacy	Burglary
Negligence	Homicide
Strict liability	Larceny (grand)
Trespass	Manslaughter
	Robbery

The crime of treason, established by the U.S. Constitution, is committed by an individual who brings war against the United States or joins with or gives aid or comfort to enemies of the United States.

The goal of criminal law is to punish the wrongdoer for violating the rules of society. Although the victim may have been killed, injured, or otherwise wronged because of the criminal act of the wrongdoer, criminal law will not give direct compensation to the victim. Victim compensation is a matter for civil law.

An individual found guilty of a criminal offense is usually fined, imprisoned, or both. In finding an individual *guilty* of a crime, the jury (or the judge in a nonjury trial) must find that the evidence presented at the trial demonstrated *beyond a reasonable doubt* that the individual committed the crime. The harshness of the punishment depends upon whether the offense was a felony or a misdemeanor. Generally only those offenses punishable by death or by imprisonment for more than one year are classified as felonies. Misdemeanors are less serious crimes, punishable by a fine and/or imprisonment for less than one year.

One category of criminal law currently receiving considerable attention is white-collar crime. This category includes crimes committed by business or by persons who manage the business. The traditional white-collar crimes include embezzlement and larceny. Both crimes involve taking the property of a business. A rapidly growing area of white-collar crime is computer crime. The computer provides white-collar criminals with access to important and valuable business assets in the form of information that can be sold by the computer criminal. As Figure 3-2 shows, law enforcement agencies are becoming more successful at catching white-collar criminals.

FIGURE 3–2

White-Collar Crime: Money Recovered by the FBI
SOURCE: Federal Bureau of Investigation

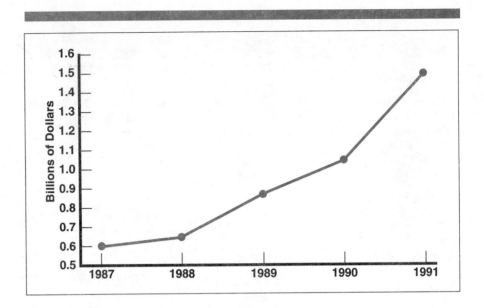

◼ SUBSTANTIVE OR PROCEDURAL LAW

Substantive law includes common law and statutory law that define and establish legal rights and regulate behavior. For example, a law restricting pollution is a substantive law. Under such a law, an individual has a legal right to an environment free of most pollution. A business would need to regulate its behavior so that it did not pollute as defined by the law.

Procedural law determines how substantive law will be enforced through the courts. For example, suppose that a case is brought to the courts involving pollution. The substantive law will decide whether one party is polluting. Procedural law will tell the parties how to question witnesses and present evidence, and a decision will be made by the court. Examples of substantive and procedural laws are provided in Table 3–3.

TABLE 3–3
EXAMPLES OF SUBSTANTIVE AND PROCEDURAL LAW

Substantive Law	Procedural Law
Administrative law	Administrative procedure
Agency law	Appellate procedure
Antitrust law	Civil procedure
Constitutional law	Court orders
Contract law	Criminal procedure
Corporation law	Rules of evidence
Criminal law	
Environmental law	
Labor law	
Property law	
Securities regulation	
Tort law	

THE LITIGATION PROCESS

Civil litigation involves the use of the law and the legal process to resolve disputes among individuals, businesses, and governments. It is a formal process, involving a mechanism provided by the government—the court system—to allow for impartial dispute resolution. Litigation is intended to provide a means of resolving disputes without the need to use violence or other illegal activities.

RULES OF CIVIL PROCEDURE

From the moment the *plaintiff*—the injured party bringing the action—decides to initiate it, a lawsuit is governed by a detailed set of procedural rules. Those rules are intended to define the issues forming the dispute. The rules are also intended to control the manner in which the parties to the dispute—the plaintiff and the *defendant* (the party who allegedly injured the plaintiff)—present evidence and arguments in support of their positions.

Although the states are free to develop their own procedural rules, most have adopted the *Federal Rules of Civil Procedure*. The Federal Rules were developed by an advisory committee appointed by the U.S. Supreme Court and became effective in 1938. The Federal Rules govern all procedural aspects of litigation. It is the avowed purpose of the Federal Rules to facilitate the litigatory process:

> These rules . . . shall be construed to secure the just, speedy, and inexpensive determination of every action.

Note that these rules govern only civil litigation; slightly different procedures are used in criminal and administrative litigation.

FUNCTIONS OF LITIGATION

In serving society, the civil litigation process has three principal functions. First, civil litigation is designed to bring a peaceful resolution to disputes between society members. No orderly society could exist without a formal dispute resolution process. Second, the civil litigation process not only decides who is right and wrong but also provides a way for enforcing its decisions. This ensures that corrective measures will be undertaken to remedy wrongs. Finally, the courts not only apply the law of the society but also develop it. As our society changes, the courts develop new laws in response to those changes.

SUBJECT-MATTER JURISDICTION

The meaning of the term *jurisdiction* is the power to speak of the law. A court's jurisdiction defines its limits to apply the law. The basic limitations imposed upon a court establish the court's subject-matter and territorial jurisdictions.

TABLE 3–4
AN OVERVIEW OF THE CONCEPT OF JURISDICTION

Type of Jurisdiction	Definition
Original jurisdiction	Power to take a lawsuit at its beginning, try it, and pass judgment upon the law and facts.
Appellate jurisdiction	Power to revise or correct the proceedings in a cause already acted upon by an inferior court.
General jurisdiction	Power to hear all controversies that may be brought before a court.
Jurisdiction over the subject matter	Power to affect the thing or issue in dispute.
Jurisdiction over the person	Power to bind a party to a dispute.
Concurrent jurisdiction	Situation where at least two different courts are each empowered to deal with the subject matter at issue in the dispute.
Exclusive jurisdiction	Power over particular subject matter is provided by statute to a specific court or court system, and all other courts are excluded.
Limited or special jurisdiction	Power to hear particular causes or power that can be exercised only under circumstances set forth by a statute.

It is the initial responsibility of the plaintiff to decide in which court the dispute is to be resolved. The plaintiff's choices will be limited to those courts having appropriate jurisdiction. In bringing the lawsuit, the plaintiff must select a court that has both of the following:

1. Jurisdiction over the subject matter of the dispute.
2. Jurisdiction over either the person of the defendant or the property of the defendant.

If a court should decide a case and it is later determined that the court did not have jurisdiction, the judgment of that court will be declared null and void upon appeal. Without appropriate jurisdiction, then, a court cannot exercise its authority. The various types of jurisdiction to be discussed in this chapter are listed in Table 3–4.

Subject-matter jurisdiction is a limitation on the type of disputes a particular court can resolve. It is established by statute or by a constitution. Subject-matter limitations imposed on a court may include minimum requirements on the dollar amount in controversy and restrictions on the type of disputes the court can hear. A state statute, for example, may restrict the disputes its district courts can hear to civil disputes where the *amount in controversy* is $2,000 or more.

■ GENERAL ORGANIZATION OF THE AMERICAN COURT SYSTEM

The state and federal court systems both have lower courts of *original jurisdiction,* where disputes are first brought and tried, and courts of *appellate jurisdiction,* where the decisions of a lower court can be taken for review. The courts of original jurisdiction are trial courts in both systems. Generally, one judge will preside over the proceeding. The courts' principal function is to determine the true facts in the dispute and to apply the appropriate law to those facts in reaching a decision. The jury has the responsibility for determining the facts in a dispute; if a jury is not requested, that responsibility is placed on the judge.

Appellate courts are concerned with errors in the application of the law and in the procedural rules applied during the trial court proceeding. Normally three judges review decisions at the intermediate appellate court level. Seven or more judges may be used in the highest appellate courts. The structure of the American court system is illustrated in Figure 3–3.

■ SUBJECT-MATTER JURISDICTION AND THE STATE COURT SYSTEMS

Although the names and organization differ somewhat from state to state, the state court systems are quite similar in general framework and jurisdictional authorities. Like the federal system, the state court system is basically a three-level court system. In addition, the state court system has several important local courts of special or limited jurisdiction.

State Courts of Original Jurisdiction.   Each state court system will have courts of *original jurisdiction,* or trial courts, where disputes are first brought and tried. These courts usually consist of one set of courts of *general jurisdiction* and several courts of *limited* or *special jurisdiction.* The courts of general jurisdiction have authority to decide almost any kind of dispute. The amount in controversy, however, must generally exceed a specific amount, typically two thousand to five thousand dollars.

The state courts of general jurisdiction are usually organized into districts. These courts have different names in different states, although their jurisdictional limitations are very similar. In many states, the courts of general jurisdiction are called superior courts. However, the same courts in Ohio and Pennsylvania are called courts of common pleas; and in Florida, Kentucky, Oregon and some other states, they are known as circuit courts. In Kansas, Louisiana, Maine, and other states, the courts of general jurisdiction are called district courts.

The state courts of limited or special jurisdiction include municipal courts, justice of the peace courts, and other more specialized courts (such as probate courts, which handle only those matters related to wills and trusts). The jurisdiction of the municipal courts is similar to that of the district courts—except the claims they hear are often less than the minimum amount in controversy necessary to fall within the jurisdiction of the district court. A party who is not satisfied with the decision of the

FIGURE 3–3

The American Court System

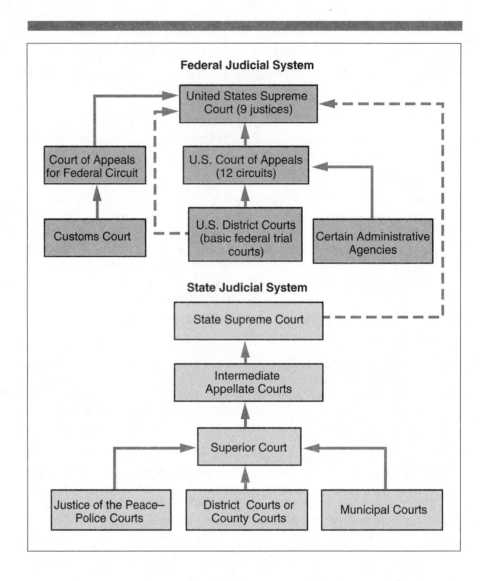

municipal court can appeal to the superior court within the area. On appeal, the parties will get a whole new trial or, in legal terminology, a *trial de novo*.

In addition, many states allow for local *small claims courts*. These courts have very limited jurisdiction, with restrictions on both the subject matter they can hear and the amount in controversy. In California, for example, the amount in controversy cannot exceed $2,000. Small claims courts are particularly useful for small debts: the procedure requirements are much less formal, and representation by a lawyer is not necessary and usually not permitted. In addition, small claims courts are a much faster forum for deciding disputes than the district courts. Although the majority of business disputes involve amounts in excess of that allowed, businesses do use small claims courts to collect smaller unpaid accounts.

State Courts of Appellate Jurisdiction.   Every judicial system provides for the review of trial court decisions by a court with *appellate jurisdiction.* Generally, a party has the right to appeal any judgment to at least one higher court. When the system has two levels of appellate courts, a party may usually appeal as a matter of right to the first level and at the discretion of the court at the second. The higher appellate court's discretion is generally used to review only those cases having legal issues of broad importance. The most common issues reaching the highest court in the state typically involve the validity of a state law, the state constitution, or a federal law as it is affected by a state law. A party who then seeks review from the highest state court may seek review from the U.S. Supreme Court.

SUBJECT-MATTER JURISDICTION AND THE FEDERAL COURT SYSTEM

As dictated by the Constitution, the federal courts have limited jurisdiction and are empowered to hear only those cases within the judicial power of the United States. According to the Constitution, federal courts have the judicial power to hear cases involving a *federal question:*

> The judicial Power shall extend to all Cases . . . arising under this Constitution, the Laws of the United States, and Treaties made, or which shall be made, under their Authority. . . .

Federal courts may also hear cases based on the relationship of the parties involved:

> [The judicial Power shall extend] to all Cases affecting Ambassadors, other public Ministers and Consuls . . . to Controversies between two or more States;—between a State and Citizens of another State;—between Citizens of different States . . . and between a State, or the Citizens thereof, and foreign States, Citizens or Subjects.

Where federal jurisdiction is based on the parties involved, most of the litigation is generated by cases involving (1) the United States as a party or (2) citizens of different states. The original purpose for allowing federal jurisdiction when a legal dispute arises between citizens of different states— commonly referred to as federal *diversity of citizenship* jurisdiction—was to provide a neutral forum for handling such disputes. State courts might be biased in favor of their own citizens and against "strangers" from other states. In addition to showing that the parties are from different states, to establish federal jurisdiction, the plaintiff must also show that the claim against the defendant—that is, the *amount in controversy*—is more than $50,000.

FEDERAL COURT SYSTEM

The federal court system was created in response to the following declaration in the U.S. Constitution:

> The judicial Power of the United States, shall be vested in one supreme Court and in such inferior Courts [Courts subordinate to the Supreme Court] as the Congress may from time to time ordain and establish.

The federal court system has developed into a three-level system. As illustrated in Figure 3–3 it currently consists of the U.S. district courts, the U.S. courts of appeals, and the U.S. Supreme Court. Each court has its own distinct role within the federal court system.

Federal District Courts.   The U.S. district courts are the courts of original jurisdiction in the federal system. As the trial court of the federal system, the U.S. district courts are the only courts in the system that use juries. Most federal question cases originate in these courts. The geographical boundaries of a district court's jurisdiction will not extend across state lines. Thus, each state has at least one federal district court, and the more populated states are divided into two, three, or—as in California, New York, and Texas—four districts. In addition, there are federal district courts in the District of Columbia, Puerto Rico, Guam, and the Virgin Islands.

Federal Appellate Courts.   Federal district court decisions are reviewable in the U.S. courts of appeals. The U.S. courts of appeals are the intermediate-level appellate courts in the federal system. There are twelve courts of appeals, one for each of the eleven circuits into which the United States is divided and one for the District of Columbia. The division of the states into circuits and the location of the U.S. courts of appeals are presented in Figure 3–4.

As appellate courts, the U.S. courts of appeals can exercise only appellate jurisdiction. If either party to the litigation is not satisfied with a federal district court's decision, it has the *right* to appeal to the court of appeals for the circuit in which that district court is located.

The U.S. courts of appeals assign three-judge panels to review decisions of the district courts within their circuits. They also review orders of federal administrative agencies when a party believes he or she has been adversely affected by an action of a regulatory agency. As a practical matter, because it is so difficult to obtain review by the U.S. Supreme Court, the decision of the court of appeals represents the court of final review for most litigants.

Specialized Federal Courts.   There are a few courts with limited or special jurisdiction of importance within the federal court system. These courts differ from other federal courts because their jurisdictions are defined in terms of subject matter rather than by geography.

The most prominent of these courts is the Court of Appeals for the Federal Circuit, created in 1982. Although its territorial jurisdiction is nationwide, its subject-matter jurisdiction is limited to the review of certain appeals from the U.S. district courts, appeals from the U.S. Claims Court and U.S. Court of International Trade, and administrative rulings of the U.S. Patent and Trademark Office. Like cases heard in the U.S. courts of appeals, cases before the Court of Appeals for the Federal Circuit are heard by three-judge panels.

U.S. Supreme Court.   The U.S. Supreme Court is the highest court in both the federal system and the country. Created by the Constitution, the U.S. Supreme Court is primarily an appellate review court. Cases reaching

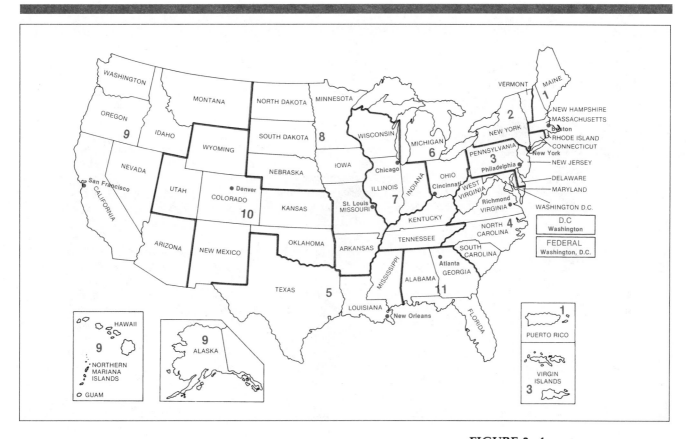

FIGURE 3–4

The Thirteen Federal Judicial Circuits

this court are generally heard by nine justices, one of whom is the Chief Justice. The term of the Court begins, by law, on the first Monday in October and continues as long as the business of the Court requires. The Court sits in Washington, D.C.

The Supreme Court may in its discretion review appeals from the U.S. district courts, the U.S. courts of appeals, and the highest courts of the states. In rare instances, such as in the case of a dispute between two state governments, the U.S. Supreme Court has *original and exclusive jurisdiction.* Although the Congress may change the court's appellate jurisdiction, it cannot change the Court's original jurisdiction as conferred upon it by the Constitution.

Appellate review is normally obtained by petitioning the Court for a *writ of certiorari.* Under the Supreme Court Selections Act of 1988, nearly all appeals to the Supreme Court are at the court's discretion. The members of the Court determine which cases they wish to review. In the event the Court does not grant *certiorari,* the decision of the lower court becomes final. If *certiorari* is granted, the Supreme Court issues the writ directing the lower court to send up for review its record in the case.

Despite differences in substantive law, foreign court systems are similar in basic structure to those in the United States. The *International Aspects* feature compares the court system in France with the U.S. court system.

INTERNATIONAL ASPECTS | FRENCH COURT SYSTEM

Like most European countries, France is a civil law country—its legal system is based on written law rather than on judge-made common law. However, the structure of the French court system is very similar to the U.S. federal court system. The French court system consists of a supreme court (*cour de cessation*), a court of appeals (*cour d'appel*), and a lower court of general jurisdiction (*tribunal d'instance*).

The appellate process in France, however, is considerably different from that in the United States. In contrast to the powers held by the U.S. Supreme Court, the *cour de cessation* does not have the authority to pronounce judgment. Rather, it has power to either reject an appeal or invalidate the decision and return the case to the court of appeal for reconsideration. The court's power to impose a judgment is limited because the intent of the post-Revolutionary founders was to give the high court far less power than the royal pre-Revolutionary courts had held.

In the event the appeal is rejected, the proceedings are finished. If, on the other hand, the decision of the *cour d'appel* is invalidated, that court then reconsiders the case before a five-judge panel. However, the judges are not bound by the higher court's determination of the law as they would be in the United States. They may either accept or reject it. They may also consider new facts.

If the case is then appealed a second time to the *cour de cessation*, the case is heard by a panel of twenty-five judges consisting of the senior and leading members of the court. If this appeal is rejected, the proceedings end; if the *cour d'appel* decision is invalidated, the case is returned to the panel for reconsideration. On the second appeal, however, the judges of the *cour d'appel* must follow the higher court's decisions on points of law.

TERRITORIAL JURISDICTION

Once the plaintiff has established that the court of his or her preference has subject-matter jurisdiction, the plaintiff must meet the court's territorial jurisdiction requirements. A court's jurisdictional authority is generally limited to the territorial boundaries of the state in which the court is located. Territorial jurisdiction usually does not become an issue unless the defendant is not a permanent resident of the state in which the plaintiff wishes to bring the lawsuit. In such a case, the plaintiff must determine how to bring the defendant—or his or her property—before the court.

■ JURISDICTION OVER THE PERSON

The court's power over the person of the defendant—referred to as *in personam jurisdiction*—is usually established by serving the defendant with a *summons*—a notice of the lawsuit. After having selected the court, the plaintiff must officially notify the defendant of the lawsuit against him or her by *service of process*, consisting of this summons. The summons will tell the defendant to appear before the court and defend himself or herself against the plaintiff's allegations. If the defendant fails to appear, the court

EXHIBIT 3–1 ▮▮▮▮▮▮▮▮▮▮▮▮▮▮▮▮▮▮▮▮▮▮▮▮

A Typical Summons

UNITED STATES DISTRICT COURT
FOR THE
SOUTHERN DISTRICT OF NEW YORK

Civil Action, File Number **80151**

Franco Gori
Plaintiff

vs.   SUMMONS

Tom Eyestone
Defendant

To the above-named Defendant:

You are hereby summoned and required to serve upon *Ronald Johnson,* plaintiff's attorney, whose address is *5450 Trump Tower, New York, New York,* and answer to the complaint which is herewith served upon you, within 20 days after service of this summons upon you, exclusive of the day of service. If you fail to do so, judgment by default will be taken against you for the relief demanded in the complaint.

Frank Hough
Clerk of Court

[Seal of the U.S. District Court]

Dated: 5/8/93

---

will order that a *default judgment* be entered against him or her. An example of a summons is presented in Exhibit 3–1.

Service of process is normally achieved by *personal service*. The summons is delivered to the defendant (or left at the defendant's home with a responsible adult) by either the plaintiff, the plaintiff's attorney, a private process server, or a public official such as a sheriff or a U.S. marshal.

If the defendant cannot be located, courts will allow the limited use of *substituted service,* such as publication of the pending lawsuit in a newspaper for a certain period of time.

■ JURISDICTION OVER OUT-OF-STATE DEFENDANTS

The most obvious method for obtaining in personam jurisdiction over nonresident defendants is to serve them with process while they are within the state. The nonresident defendant need only be passing through the state to be legally served with a summons. The defendant does not have to have intended to enter the state. A business executive, for example, could be on an airplane with no intent of landing in the state. In the event that foul weather or mechanical difficulties forces the plane to land in that state, the executive could be served with summons when departing the plane. Note that nonresident defendants may not be tricked into coming into the area for the purpose of being served.

It is much more difficult to obtain jurisdiction over nonresident defendants when they have no need to return to the state. The difficulties of obtaining in personam jurisdiction over a nonresident business are made more difficult by the fact that a substantial amount of business can be transacted solely by mail or telephone communications across state lines. A business, then, would have no need to have a physical presence in that state.

While it would seem that businesses could avoid lawsuits under such circumstances, there are still several means by which the court can have jurisdiction. If the defendant has committed a wrong (such as being involved in an automobile accident) or has done business within the state, the court will have jurisdiction under the authority of the state's *long-arm statute.* A long-arm statute is a state law that permits the state's courts to reach beyond the state's boundaries and obtain jurisdiction over nonresident defendants. An example of a long-arm statute is presented in Exhibit 3–2.

■ JURISDICTION OVER OUT-OF-STATE CORPORATE DEFENDANTS

When compared to individuals and other businesses, corporations are treated much more poorly under the law of jurisdiction. This treatment of corporations is the result of the hostility that developed towards corporations in their early history. As a consequence, several requirements are imposed upon corporations that could not be imposed on individuals. A court can exercise jurisdiction over a corporation in any of three situations:

1. The court is located in the state where the corporation was legally incorporated.
2. The court is located in the state where the corporation has its headquarters or its main plant.
3. The court is located in a state where the corporation is doing business.

The first situation is the consequence of the corporation's being created by the state as an "artificial person." One of the requirements for

EXHIBIT 3-2 ▰▰▰▰▰▰▰▰▰▰▰▰▰▰▰

Long-Arm Statute: Revised Statutes of Missouri

Sec. 506.500 Actions in which out-of-state service is authorized—jurisdiction of Missouri Courts is applicable, when:

1. Any person or firm, whether or not a citizen or resident to this state, or any corporations, who in person or through an agent does any of the acts enumerated in this section, thereby submits such person, firm, or corporation, and, if an individual, (his/her) personal representative, to the jurisdiction of the courts of this state as to any cause of action arising from the doing of any such acts:

(1) The transaction of any business within this state;

(2) The making of any contract within this state;

(3) The commission of a tortious act within this state;

(4) The ownership, use, or possession of any real estate situated in this state;

* * *

[2]. Only cases of action arising from acts enumerated in this section may be asserted against a defendant in an action in which jurisdiction over him is based upon this section.

obtaining a corporate charter from a state—that is, to become incorporated in that state—is the designation of a registered office within the state. This office is similar to an individual's residence and is a place where the corporation can always be served with process in the state.

In the second situation, the corporation is a resident of the state. Because the corporation is physically located there, the plaintiff can serve the corporation with process without having to use extraordinary measures. Like an individual's residence, the plant or corporate headquarters is effectively the residence or domicile of the corporation within the state.

The third requirement—doing business in the state—has been subjected to close constitutional scrutiny by the U.S. Supreme Court. In attempting to reach out-of-state corporate defendants, states have relied heavily upon long-arm statutes. As Exhibit 3–2 shows, those statutes often list "doing business" within the state as a basis for jurisdiction. According to the Court, the state's long-arm statutes must identify certain *minimum contacts* between the corporation and the state where the suit is being filed to qualify as doing business. The case that follows illustrates the extent of constitutional limitations placed on modern long-arm statutes in their efforts to establish jurisdiction over out-of-state corporations.

WORLD-WIDE VOLKSWAGEN CORP. v. WOODSON

United States Supreme Court
444 U.S. 286, 100 S.Ct. 559 (1980)

Case Background
The Robinsons purchased a new Audi in 1976 from Seaway Volkswagen, Inc., a dealer near their home in New York. The next year the Robinsons, who had lived in New York, left for a new home in Arizona. As they drove through Oklahoma, their Audi was struck in the rear by another car. The accident caused a fire that severely burned Mrs. Robinson. The Robinsons subsequently brought a product liability action in an Oklahoma state court. Judge Charles Woodson was the judge at the trial. He is also the defendant in this case.

The Robinsons claimed their injuries were the result of a defective design in the Audi's fuel system. They named as defendants Audi, Volkswagen of America (Audi's importer), World-Wide Volkswagen Corporation (Volkswagen's regional distributor), and Seaway (a New York retail dealer). World-Wide (the plaintiff in this case) was incorporated in New York and distributed vehicles and parts for Volkswagen to retailers like Seaway in New York, New Jersey, and Connecticut—but did no business in Oklahoma.

World-Wide made a special appearance to argue that the Oklahoma court did not have jurisdiction over it. After the court rejected World-Wide's claim, World-Wide appealed to the Supreme Court of Oklahoma to keep Judge Woodson from exercising the court's *in personam* jurisdiction. World-Wide argued that it did not have sufficient minimum contacts with the state of Oklahoma for there to be jurisdiction. The Supreme Court of Oklahoma affirmed Woodson's decision, holding that personal jurisdiction was authorized by the Oklahoma long-arm statute. World-Wide then appealed to the U.S. Supreme Court.

Case Decision
The Supreme Court reversed the decision, holding that World-Wide had no contacts, ties, or other relations with the state of Oklahoma. The Court held that a state court may exercise personal jurisdiction over a nonresident defendant only if the defendant's activities are sufficient to establish "minimum contacts" with the state. In determining whether World-Wide's activities established minimum contacts, the Court noted that World-Wide did not close sales, perform services, or solicit business through sales personnel or advertisements calculated to reach consumers in the state. Further, there was no record of car sales (wholesale or retail) by World-Wide to Oklahoma customers or residents.

Managerial Considerations
Corporations, like individuals, do not like to defend themselves against lawsuits in distant and often unfriendly forums. Not only will the costs of litigation be greater when the forum is far from the company offices, but the probability of being successful may be lower. Managers of national companies understand that their operations will establish the minimum contacts in every state. Managers of small companies, however, are often surprised by distant lawsuits.

For smaller companies, lawsuits in unexpected forums generally arise when management decides to increase sales by expanding its sales market or by selling different types of products. The company will undertake an advertising or promotional campaign in the new market with no immediate intention of locating a physical facility or establishing a residence in that market. If a consumer is injured by the product in a distant state, the consumer will very likely be able to establish that the company has minimum contacts with the state. Thus, in considering strategies to increase sales and profitability, management must consider the legal implications and be prepared to defend the company against lawsuits in other states.

◼ JURISDICTION BASED UPON POWER OVER PROPERTY

The court still has limited authority if it is unable to obtain jurisdiction over the person of the defendant. It has authority to establish jurisdiction based on the existence of the defendant's property within the state's territorial boundaries. Jurisdiction is established by directing the lawsuit against the defendant's property, either *in rem* or *quasi in rem*.

Jurisdiction *in Rem*.   In disputes where property is the matter in controversy, a court in the area where the property is located will have jurisdiction to resolve all claims against that property—whether the defendant is there or not. In such situations, the court is said to have *in rem* jurisdiction. The basis of *in rem* jurisdiction is the presence of the property within the territorial jurisdiction of the court.

Property in an *in rem* proceeding can include tangible property—real estate and personal property—or intangible property—bank accounts and stocks. To satisfy the minimum contacts requirement, however, a court cannot properly gain jurisdiction over property that has been forcibly removed from another state where it is usually kept.

Quasi in Rem **Jurisdiction.**   A court gains *quasi in rem* jurisdiction when the defendant's property within the state is attached (or seized) to secure payment for an unrelated matter. For example, Dr. Roth may owe Jefferson AutoBody for painting her automobile. Unable to collect payment for that service from Roth, AutoBody decides to bring a lawsuit against her. AutoBody, however, is unable to serve Dr. Roth personally with process to establish personal jurisdiction because Dr. Roth is a resident of another state. AutoBody then discovers that Dr. Roth has real estate within the state where it does business. To gain jurisdiction, AutoBody attaches (or seizes) the property of Dr. Roth to satisfy the debt. The basis of the court's jurisdiction is the existence of the property owned by the defendant, Dr. Roth, within the state. In such a situation, the court is said to have *quasi in rem* jurisdiction, and the decision it renders will bind the parties. As in an *in rem* proceeding, the property involved can be either tangible or intangible.

In most states, *quasi in rem* jurisdiction is granted by statute. Usually the statutes permit plaintiffs to reach any assets located in the state. Under the U.S. Supreme Court's ruling in *Shaffer* v. *Heitner* (1977), however, the assets must satisfy the minimum contacts standard. There must be a reasonable connection between the assets being attached and the state in which they are attached. In the preceding example, there is no doubt that Roth's real estate satisfies the minimum contacts standard. However, assets that are only moving through the state would not meet the minimum contacts standard and could not be attached in a *quasi in rem* proceeding.

Notification Limitations.   In using the defendant's property as a basis for jurisdiction, notice must be given in a manner that actually notifies either the defendant or someone who can represent the defendant. In the past, *constructive notice*—such as by publication in a newspaper for a specified time period—had been enough. Because it has become so easy for people and businesses to move from state to state in the past several decades, constructive notice alone has been held to be unconstitutional by the U.S. Supreme Court (*Mullane* v. *Central Hanover Bank & Trust*, 1950). Many states have now enacted statutes providing for mail or personal service in cases where jurisdiction is to be based on the property of the defendant.

■ VENUE

Not every court that has jurisdiction over the subject matter and the person of the defendant will hear a case. It is also necessary that the lawsuit be brought in a court having proper *venue*. On the basis of fairness, state statutes typically provide that the lawsuit be brought in a court located in the county where either the plaintiff or the defendant lives. Similarly, the defendant can be sued in a *federal* court only in a district where either the defendant or the plaintiff lives or where the dispute actually arose. Once this additional fairness requirement is met, the court selected will have jurisdiction and venue.

APPLYING THE APPROPRIATE SUBSTANTIVE LAW

In civil disputes involving citizens of the same state, the court system to be chosen and the proper body of law to be applied are clear. The citizens go to the state court system with proper jurisdiction and venue, and the state common and statutory law are applied. If the dispute involves citizens from more than one state, however, the parties may be confronted with a choice of bringing the suit in a state or in a federal court.

■ THE ERIE DOCTRINE: THE RULE IN FEDERAL COURTS

If a federal court is chosen, the central question becomes, Which body of substantive law does the court apply to resolve the dispute—federal law or the law of the state?

In its decision in *Swift* v. *Tyson* (1842), the U.S. Supreme Court held that federal courts need apply only the statutory law of the state; the federal courts were free to follow their own common law. As a consequence, a state court and a federal court could reach different conclusions in resolving the same dispute. In the landmark decision *Erie* v. *Tompkins*, the U.S. Supreme Court overturned *Swift* v. *Tyson* and held that except in matters governed by the federal Constitution or by acts of Congress, the law to be applied in federal courts is the law of the state. Thus, federal judges must apply both a state's common law and its statutory law when deciding diversity of citizenship cases. The federal court, however, will follow federal procedural law.

ERIE RAILROAD CO. v. TOMPKINS

United States Supreme Court
304 U.S. 64, 58 S.Ct. 817 (1938)

Case Background
Tompkins (the plaintiff) was standing next to some railroad tracks on "a dark night" and was injured by something protruding from a passing freight train in Pennsylvania. The train was owned by Erie Railroad Company (the defendant). Tompkins claimed the accident occurred because Erie was negligent in the operation of the train.

Tompkins was a citizen of Pennsylvania. Erie was incorporated in New York. Tompkins brought suit in the federal district court for southern New York, with the court's jurisdiction based on diversity of citizenship. The principal issue in the case became which law should be applied—the common law of Pennsylvania or that of the federal court system. Erie argued that the court should apply the law of Pennsylvania. Under Pennsylvania common law, Tompkins would be a trespasser and therefore Erie would not be liable for his injuries. Tompkins argued that federal common law
(continued)

should apply, under which Erie would be liable for Tompkins's injuries.

The federal district court (applying the U.S. Supreme Court's precedent established in *Swift* v. *Tyson*) agreed with Tompkins, found Erie liable for the injuries, and awarded Tompkins $30,000 in damages. The decision was affirmed by the circuit court of appeals. Erie sought review by the U.S. Supreme Court, arguing that federal courts must apply the appropriate state law in diversity of citizenship cases.

Case Decision

The U.S. Supreme Court reversed the decisions of the federal district court and the circuit court of appeals, thereby overthrowing the precedent set by *Swift* v. *Tyson*. The Court held that in diversity of citizenship cases, federal courts are to apply the appropriate state substantive law. Applying Pennsylvania common law in this case, Tompkins was a trespasser, and therefore Erie was not liable for the injuries. The Court found that the intended purpose of *Swift* to create uniformity in the administration of the law was not being met. Federal and state courts often differed in the resolution of similar disputes.

Managerial Considerations

In considering litigation, the attorney will examine the possible forums where the action could be brought. This common practice is referred to as *forum shopping*. Traditionally, businesses have received more favorable treatment in the federal than in the state court system. Thus, management generally will try to have a case tried in federal court. On specific issues, however, a particular state forum may be more favorable to businesses than the federal courts. The more favorable forum may, for example, have a history of ruling for management on labor issues, making it attractive to management but unattractive to labor.

In deciding on the forum, the attorney will compare the likely costs and benefits of bringing the action in different forums. In determining the benefits, the attorney will be most influenced by the likelihood of being successful in one forum rather than another. In assessing the costs, the attorney will be concerned with the increased costs associated with bringing the action in a distant forum. The attorney will consider the additional time executives will need to spend away from more productive activities to be involved in the litigation.

In many of the company's activities that may bring about litigation, management will have little control over the forum where the action is brought. In other activities, however, management will have a direct say in selecting the forum in advance of any disputes. In entering into contracts, for example, management will generally be able to dictate the forum where disputes generated by the contract will be resolved. This specification of the forum is particularly important in international contracts. The company is likely to find it more attractive and considerably less expensive to litigate in this country rather than in a foreign country.

■ SUBSTANTIVE LAW IN STATE COURT

When a case is brought in a state court involving incidents that took place in more than one state or entirely in a different state, a conflict-of-law problem may arise. The state court will have to determine whether its own substantive law or that of another state is to apply. To aid courts in such situations, states have developed *conflict-of-law* rules. Some general conflict-of-law rules most affecting businesses are presented in Table 3–5.

The conflict-of-law rules vary according to the nature of the dispute. In contracts cases, for example, the general rule is that the law of the state where the contract was made determines the interpretation of the contract. In tort cases, the traditional rule is that the substantive law of the state where the tort occurred is to apply.

REMEDIES IN CIVIL LITIGATION ■■■■■■

Most civil disputes are settled outside the court system. The expense of a lawsuit, the long delays before a case actually goes before the court, and concerns about how the dispute will be resolved by the court encourage litigants to settle before trial. If the dispute does go to trial, the individuals

TABLE 3–5
CONFLICT-OF-LAW PRINCIPLES MOST FREQUENTLY AFFECTING BUSINESS

Substantive Law Issue	State Whose Law Is to Apply
1. Contract disagreement	State in which contract was formed or State in which contract was to be performed or State designated in the contract
2. Liability issues arising from injury	State in which injury occurred or State having most relationship to the case
3. Workers' compensation	State of employment or State in which injury occurred

involved are seeking resolution of the dispute in the form of a specific remedy provided by the court. Within the American court system, the remedies awarded by courts in civil disputes are classified as either *equitable remedies* or *monetary damages*. The remedies available in civil litigation are summarized in Figure 3–5.

■ MONETARY DAMAGES

A monetary damage remedy is provided when the court finds that some specific legal right has been violated and has resulted in an injury. Most commonly, the monetary damages awarded are in the form of *compensatory damages*—damages awarded to the injured party to compensate for losses resulting from the other party's wrongdoing. Compensatory damages may be awarded for the loss of time and money, pain and suffering, injury to reputation, and mental anguish.

In cases where the wrongdoer's actions are particularly reprehensible, the court may award the injured party *punitive or exemplary damages*. The court's intent in awarding punitive damages is to punish the wrongdoer for having acted in a particularly offensive manner to discourage such behavior in the future. *Nominal damages,* a trivial payment, are sometimes awarded when the wrongdoer's actions violated the other party's rights but no actual injuries to person or property were incurred.

■ EQUITABLE REMEDIES

Equitable remedies are not necessarily based on any clearly established legal right. The dispute will generally involve some question of morality, justice, or conscience, where monetary damages either will not provide the injured party with adequate relief or simply cannot be determined.

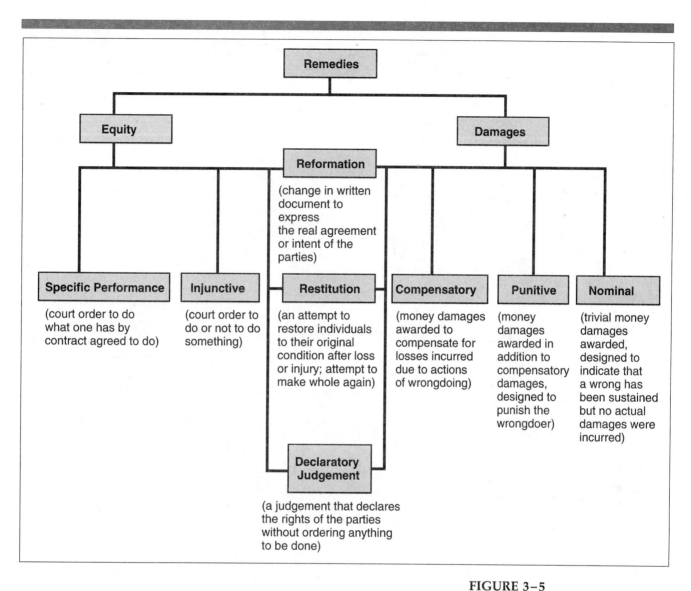

FIGURE 3–5

Equitable Remedies and Monetary Damages

In resolving such a dispute, the courts are allowed to be more creative in granting relief than they are in resolving disputes calling for monetary damages. The courts can order *specific performance* as the remedy and require the offending party to do what he or she had originally promised to do. Another important equitable remedy is the *injunction*—a court order directing a person to do something, to not do something, or to stop doing something.

SUMMARY:
A GUIDE FOR MANAGERS

- The legal environment of business is dynamic, constantly changing to conform to the public consciousness. To avoid surprise, it is important that management monitor the legal environment, understand how law is made, and anticipate the factors that effect change in the law.

- Fines and other explicit sanctions imposed against businesses found in violation of society's formal law are intended to influence behavior. In addition, if management earns a reputation for ignoring society's informal laws, society may impose "penalties" against the business. Society may, for example, refuse to buy the company's products until management adjusts its behavior. Management cannot afford to jeopardize the company's reputation any more than it can afford to pay large fines and penalties.

- The American legal system arises from common law, or judge-made law, and from the authority granted to various governments by the U.S. Constitution and the state constitutions to exercise authority over various matters.

- Law can be classified as public law—the legal relationships between citizens and government—and private law—the legal relationships among members of society. Criminal law—legal wrongs against society—must be distinguished from civil law, which covers noncriminal matters and disputes among members of society that are resolved by fines, money damages, or equitable remedies. Substantive law, which concerns legal rights and obligations, differs from procedural law, the steps that must be taken for substantive legal issues to be resolved in the judicial system.

- For a case to be resolved, the court must have jurisdiction—the power to hear and decide the case—over the subject matter (the legal issues) of the dispute, over the persons who are defendants in an action, and over the property involved in the dispute.

- Federal courts have jurisdiction over cases involving federal law and over cases involving state law when there is diversity of citizenship—citizens from different states—if the amount in controversy is over $50,000.

- State court systems are set up much like the federal court system. In the federal system, trial courts are the courts of original jurisdiction, called district courts. Decisions of those courts may be appealed to courts of appeals, where a panel of three or more judges reviews the case. Judgments of those courts may be appealed to the Supreme Court, which generally can decide what cases it wishes to accept for review.

- Businesses, particularly smaller businesses, should consider the legal implications of decisions to expand sales territories beyond state boundaries. As a business begins to provide service and sales in new territory, it establishes the minimum contacts necessary for other states' courts to exercise personal jurisdiction. Management must be prepared to defend itself against lawsuits in other states.

■ Civil litigation, which covers most actions involving businesses, is generally resolved by monetary damages—such as compensatory damages to cover the losses incurred and punitive damages to punish the losing party for having behaved badly—and by equitable remedies—such as injunctions.

MANAGER'S ETHICAL DILEMMA

BUILD WHERE, SUE WHERE?

Affiliated Chemical Company is a large chemical conglomerate with headquarters in the southwestern United States. Recently, management determined that there is going to be a good market for XDESMIC, a specialty chemical used in the production of consumer goods. The production of XDESMIC involves mixing chemicals in a process that could be dangerous or even lethal in the event of an industrial accident. The management of Affiliated is concerned about the liabilities that could arise in the event of such an accident if it produced XDESMIC. The managers are considering several alternatives:

Purchasing Insurance. Management has investigated building the plant in the United States and purchasing accident insurance. Despite a good safety record, the company can secure insurance only at a substantial cost. The insurance company would also require the installation of certain safety equipment. It is estimated that the insurance and safety equipment costs would make the price of the product uncompetitive with foreign manufacturers.

Installation of Specially Designed Manufacturing Equipment. Management hired a reputable engineering consulting company to investigate the possibility of designing a factory that relied less on human labor. By replacing much of the work force with an automated system, management reasoned that such a factory could reduce the chance of human error leading to an industrial accident. The engineering company, however, found it likely that the costs would again make the price of the product uncompetitive with XDESMIC produced by foreign manufacturers.

Offshore Manufacturing. In examining the manufacturing practices of its competitors, the management of Affiliated discovered that most XDESMIC production takes place in countries in the lower Pacific Rim. Wages are lower, and the court systems there have a history of being very favorable to business (when an industrial accident kills a worker, for example, judgments against a company rarely exceed $2,000). Furthermore, it was unlikely that an injured party would be able to establish jurisdiction in the United States. If the company chose to establish a factory there, it could expect enormous profits.

Rejecting the Project. Although the profit potential is enormous, management could reject the project. If a competitor were to enter into production of XDESMIC under an offshore strategy, that company could offer XDESMIC at prices well below what Affiliated would have to charge if it built in the United States. Affiliated is concerned that it would not be able to match such prices and would lose customers, revenues, profits, and market share.

The company has hired you as a management consultant. It would like your response to the following inquiries:

1. Which strategic alternative should the company implement?

2. It is not uncommon for companies to move operations offshore in an effort to reduce costs. However, is it ethical to move an operation offshore to avoid or reduce liability costs? Should environmental costs, such as water pollution, influence the decision?

3. Should foreigners who are injured by U.S. companies or their affiliates offshore be allowed to gain jurisdiction in the United States? If they were allowed and the Japanese do not allow foreigners who are injured by Japanese companies to gain jurisdiction in Japanese courts, will U.S. international competitiveness be hurt?

REVIEW AND DISCUSSION QUESTIONS

1. Define the following terms:

   law   jurisdiction
   common law   service of process
   stare decisis   constructive notice
   constitution   conflict of law
   substantive law   equitable remedies

2. Compare and contrast the following:
   a. Civil law and criminal law.
   b. Felony and misdemeanor.
   c. Judge-made law and law enacted by a legislature.
   d. Social maintenance and conflict resolution functions of law.
   e. Service of process and substituted service.
   f. Appellate jurisdiction and original jurisdiction.
   g. Federal question jurisdiction and diversity of citizenship jurisdiction.
   h. Jurisdiction over the person and jurisdiction over property.

3. What is the difference between a *preponderance of the evidence* and *beyond a reasonable doubt?*

4. The crime rate in Japan is less than one-quarter of the per-person crime rate in the United States. Without any more information than that presented in the chapter, on what basis could you explain this difference in crime rates?

5. Suppose Rosi Nordin and Jack Emerson are in a dispute that involves the interpretation of a federal statute. They have elected to bring the dispute to the state district court for resolution. Which substantive and procedural law will that court apply?

■ CASE QUESTIONS

6. According to the court in *Smith* v. *Gibson* (1987):

   > The general rule is, that every country has jurisdiction over all persons found within its territorial limits. . . . [A]n action may be maintained in any jurisdiction in which the defendant may be found, and is legally served with process. [For whatever reason] the defendant may have been in the State, the summons having been legally served upon him, the jurisdiction of the person was complete, in the absence of a fraudulent inducement to come.

   Suppose John Adams, president of Mieller Company, is served with process in an airplane while the plane is flying over a state with this territorial concept of jurisdiction. Is the service of process valid? Would the altitude of the airplane at the time of the service affect your answer?

7. BurgerQueen is a Florida corporation whose principal office is in Miami. It conducts most of its restaurant business through a franchise operation. Those who franchise with the company—the franchisees—are licensed to use BurgerQueen's trademark for a period of twenty years. BurgerQueen then leases the franchisee a standardized restaurant facility. The contract between BurgerQueen and its franchisees provides that the franchise relationship is established in Miami and is governed by Florida law. It requires that all monthly payments be made to the Miami headquarters. The Miami office sets policy and works directly with the franchisee to resolve major difficulties. District offices,

however, monitor the day-to-day functions. Those district offices are located throughout the country.

Jim Skivington, a Michigan resident, entered into a twenty-year franchise to operate a restaurant in Michigan. After several good months, the restaurant fell on hard times. Skivington eventually fell behind in his monthly payments. Despite negotiations with the Michigan district office and with the Miami headquarters, the franchise was terminated and Skivington was ordered to vacate the premises. Skivington refused. BurgerQueen then brought suit in federal district court in Florida. Skivington claimed because he was a Michigan resident and because the dispute did not arise under Florida law, the district court lacked jurisdiction over him. BurgerQueen argued that Florida's long-arm statute provided the court with jurisdiction. Assuming the long-arm statute reads like the Missouri statute in Exhibit 3–2, how would this jurisdictional issue likely be resolved?

8. Colemill Enterprises, a South Carolina company, purchased an airplane from Southeastern Flight Services, a Georgia company. The purchase price included a maintenance package that required Southeastern to keep the airplane in top operating condition. Shortly after the purchase, and while carrying Colemill's top executive, the airplane crashed and all passengers and crew were killed. There was evidence that the aircraft had been defectively manufactured and improperly maintained. The airplane was manufactured in Michigan and maintained in Georgia; the crash occurred in South Carolina. In a subsequent wrongful death action brought in Georgia, which state's law will apply? [*Risdon Enterprises, Inc.* v. *Colemill Enterprises, Inc.*, 172 Ga.App. 902, 324 S.E.2d 738 (1984)]

■ BUSINESS POLICY QUESTIONS

9. Does the common law produce ''better'' law than that which would exist if only the Congress or the state legislatures were allowed to enact law?

10. Are the jurisdictional limitations on the courts intended to benefit either the plaintiff or the defendant? Can you determine any detrimental impacts if they were eliminated?

11. What incentives do judges have to follow precedent?

■ ETHICS QUESTIONS

12. Should judges consider the social consequences of their decisions? What if the case involves an individual who has committed a hideous crime and the judge is being asked to release him or her on a technicality?

13. Tom Eyestone, a California resident, was invited to Utah by the West States Refining Company to negotiate a dispute. When discussions proved fruitless, West had process served on Eyestone before he could leave the state. Should the service be allowed to stand? Is it a sound business decision to serve process in such circumstances?

14. You are the president of a large airline. Competition has increased dramatically, forcing you to consider a variety of cost-cutting alternatives. One such alternative is to declare bankruptcy. Although the company is not in serious financial condition, you know that the court will invalidate your union labor contract. The company could then hire workers at much lower wages and save a considerable amount of money. Should you make strategic use of the law and the legal system in this fashion? Is this within the societal functions discussed in the chapter?

BUSINESS AND THE RESOLUTION OF DISPUTES

CHAPTER 4

MANAGER'S LEGAL CHALLENGE

General Motors Corporation (GM) is one of the largest automobile manufacturers in the world. Like all companies, it has important legal concerns that affect its day-to-day operations. When the legal environment's impact becomes large, management has incentives to react strategically to minimize the cost of that impact. An example of such a strategic reaction is the search for alternative dispute resolution processes to avoid the expenses and delays associated with the U.S. court system.

In the early 1980s, GM management discovered that about 20 million of its cars built in the late 1970s and early 1980s had potentially serious defects in their engines and transmissions. In light of the success of Japanese automakers in this country, GM was concerned that these defects would hurt future sales as consumers decided they could not rely on GM. GM management could have decided to resolve consumer complaints in traditional fashion through the court system. However, since the defects involved thousands of cars of the same make and model, this approach would have been time-consuming and expensive and would likely have further injured the company's public image.

To reduce legal expenses significantly and protect GM's public image, GM management decided to develop a Mediation/Arbitration Program in cooperation with the Council of Better Business Bureaus. Under the program, the local Better Business Bureau acted as a mediator between the customer and the company in helping the parties to reach a settlement. If a mediated settlement could not be reached, the Better Business Bureau appointed an arbiter to hear the dispute and resolve it. GM was bound by the arbiter's decision, but the consumer was not.

Within the first few years of the program, more than 100,000 consumers received over $40 million to repair defects. Nearly 97 percent of consumers completing the program received compensation. By approaching the problem strategically and deciding to avoid litigation, GM management saved the company millions of dollars in litigation expenses, lost productivity, and damage to its business image.

In response to the success of the program, GM management decided to include this alternative dispute resolution process in its new car warranties. Subsequently, Nissan, Volkswagen, Porsche-Audi, Honda, American Motors, Jeep, Renault, Volvo, Rolls Royce, and Jaguar instituted similar alternative dispute resolution programs in the United States.

The decisions GM management faced in attempting to resolve disputes with its consumers illustrate the difficulties facing business managers as they attempt to control legal expenses. Although most serious business disputes are still resolved through the court system, managers are turning more and more to alternative dispute resolution (often referred to as ADR) processes to reduce the impacts of a rapidly changing legal environment. As the reaction of GM management demonstrates, a strategic view of the legal environment can result in more cost-effective compliance with the law and preservation of the company's public image.

This chapter discusses the basic formal procedures for the resolution of disputes. It begins with a discussion of the adversarial nature of our judicial system. It also discusses the fact that most business lawsuits differ from nonbusiness lawsuits, particularly in their complexity, their evidentiary requirements, and the average size of damages awarded. The basic procedures involved in litigating a dispute are then considered. The important stages in the litigation process, including the pleadings, discovery, trial, and appellate stages, are described. Finally, alternative methods of dispute resolution, including arbitration, minitrials, and mediation, are examined. The delays and rising costs associated with litigation are making such alternatives more attractive to businesses.

THE NATURE OF OUR ADVERSARY SYSTEM

A distinctive element of our judicial system is that it is an *adversary system of justice.* It requires both parties to contest the position of the other before a court in a true case or controversy and not in a hypothetical question or inquiry. The responsibility for bringing a lawsuit, shaping its issues, and presenting convincing evidence rests almost entirely upon the parties to the dispute. The adversary system reflects the American belief that truth is best discovered through the presentation of competing ideas.

In resolving the dispute, the court will take almost no active role in establishing the facts. It will not undertake its own investigation of the parties, the basis of the dispute, or the issues. Rather, the function of the court is to apply the relevant rules of law to the true facts of the dispute. The court's intent is to bring the dispute to a peaceful resolution. Under this system of justice, then, a business considering a lawsuit must weigh several important factors before bringing the lawsuit.

■ IS THE DISAGREEMENT ONE FOR WHICH THE LAW FURNISHES RELIEF?

The management of the business obviously feels injured or it would not be considering a lawsuit. However, management must determine whether the grievance is one for which the law provides some form of relief. There are a substantial number of "injuries" a business may sustain for which the law simply will not or cannot provide a remedy.

A business may be injured, for example, when the marketing department works for weeks to persuade a major account to buy its product, only to see the sale go to a competitor. Similarly, the finance department may go to great effort and expense in attempting to hire a new finance graduate, only to see her accept a job with another company. If, as in these situations, the grievance is not redressable by a court of law, management's decision to pursue a lawsuit would be a useless and wasteful undertaking.

■ WHAT IS THE PROBABILITY OF WINNING THE LAWSUIT?

Even if management decides that a grievance can be redressed in court, it must consider the probability of winning the lawsuit. In making this estimation, management must consider several important factors. It must consider whether it can find and bring the defendant into court. It must ask whether it can produce the necessary witnesses and documents that will prove its case.

It must consider whether the *finder of fact*—the jury or, if there is no jury, the judge—will believe the evidence presented. Management must also decide whether the defendant will be able to justify its conduct or prove the existence of a *defense*—a legal excuse—for its conduct. Finally, management must consider whether its attorney is correct in estimating that the law governing the dispute is in its favor.

■ WILL THE RELIEF THE COURT PROVIDES MAKE THE LAWSUIT WORTHWHILE?

Perhaps most important of all, management must consider whether the relief the court may provide is worth the time, effort, and monetary expense. In making this determination, management must weigh the costs against alternative procedures of settlement, arbitration, self-help, or simply letting matters rest. To the extent the court's award is to be limited to monetary damages, management must also consider whether the defendant will be able to pay. If the defendant could pay, management must be concerned about its financial position after paying attorney's fees, court costs, and other litigation expenses.

Management must also consider the risks to its operations not directly connected to the lawsuit. Management must take into account the likely impact on the company's reputation and goodwill as a consequence of bringing the action. In some circumstances, management may decide to ignore the injury because a lawsuit would open up its operations to close inspection by the public. The necessary evidence at the trial, for example, may require the disclosure of a company trade secret. Management may decide that in such circumstances, close inspection is not in its long-term interest.

BUSINESS AS A DEFENDANT

The questions and concerns confronting a business as defendant are not so different from those confronting a business considering a lawsuit. Management will request that its legal counsel determine the suit's likelihood of success and estimate the costs. After accounting for its available insurance coverage, management will then begin to establish its strategic response to the lawsuit. In developing its strategy, management will consider several important questions.

■ HOW WILL LITIGATION AFFECT THE COMPANY'S GOODWILL?

In reaching a decision regarding the suit, management must be concerned about the impact the lawsuit will have on the company's reputation and goodwill. Under some circumstances, the impact will be such that it will be in the company's interest to avoid litigation. As the Manager's Legal Challenge feature at the beginning of this chapter illustrated in the case of General Motors, the costs of litigation and the likely negative impact on consumers can make alternatives to litigation an important strategic option to the company.

Under other circumstances, however, the lawsuit may seriously threaten the company's survival. Thus, the company may have no creditable option other than litigation. The cigarette industry, for example, has taken a very aggressive position with regard to lawsuits where the plaintiff alleges that smoking cigarettes led to the death of a family member or serious incapacity in the plaintiff. Responding strategically, the industry litigates each such lawsuit vigorously. It recognizes that even a single judicial decision imposing liability upon it on the basis of a causal link between lung disease and smoking will likely invite more lawsuits, reduce sales, and encourage government regulation.

■ HOW IMPORTANT IS THE UNDERLYING RELATIONSHIP?

Management must also consider the importance of the relationship between the company and the plaintiff. If the plaintiff has a business relationship with the company—for example, is an important supplier or wholesale customer—management may decide that continuation of that relationship is more important than winning in a court of law. Management may then find it in its best interest to pursue a settlement, despite the fact that it believes it would prevail if the dispute were to go to court.

When natural gas and other energy prices fell sharply in the 1980s, Natural Gas Pipeline Company of America found that it was unable to fulfill contractual commitments to natural gas producers. Numerous gas producers filed suit against Natural Gas Pipeline, alleging breach of contract. Management believed it could demonstrate through litigation that provisions in many of the contracts were against public policy. Rather than litigate, however, management worked diligently to renegotiate those contracts to preserve the valuable underlying business relationship. Had management chosen to litigate, it would have taken years to reestablish the trust and confidence needed to form the basis for a long-term, profitable business relationship with producers.

■ IS SETTLEMENT AN ECONOMICALLY VIABLE ALTERNATIVE?

In some cases, management may decide that the best course of action is to settle the lawsuit with the plaintiff. That is, the company will pay the plaintiff some amount of money in return for the plaintiff's agreement to drop the lawsuit. In such cases, management will consider settlement a viable strategic response to the plaintiff's lawsuit. Management will evaluate the direct costs—attorney's and expert witness fees—of the lawsuit as well as the important indirect costs—including the lost productivity of the company's executives as they prepare for the trial and the potentially negative impacts on the company's reputation. If these costs are larger than the costs of settling, management will seriously consider settlement a viable strategic response.

■ ARE WE ENCOURAGING SPURIOUS LAWSUITS?

Management will also need to watch for so-called nuisance actions, in which the plaintiff files an essentially baseless claim in hopes of gaining a settlement payment from the company. The company, for example, may desire to settle rather than incur either unwanted media attention or litigation expenses. Depending on the nature of the claim, it costs major corporations between $10,000 and $50,000 to defend against a single nuisance action.

A company's strategic plan to avoid publicity or litigation expenses provides plaintiffs with incentives to bring spurious lawsuits. Such plaintiffs hope that the company will consider paying a settlement of some amount of money that is less than the expected litigation expenses. To discourage nuisance actions, many companies have implemented a strategic policy to litigate all such actions. Their intent is to force the plaintiff to pay all litigation costs if the court finds the plaintiff's case to be baseless.

■ IS THE LAWSUIT AN INTEGRAL PART OF THE COMPANY'S STRATEGIC PLAN?

There are times when management may actually encourage a lawsuit. Thus, several of the questions management will typically ask itself when faced with a lawsuit will be unnecessary. The lawsuit itself is now part of management's strategic plan. Suppose, for example, that Richland Foods entered into a long-term contract with Scharmato Vegetables for the purchase of tomato paste. As the world price of tomato paste declined, Richland management decided that the terms of the contract were no longer acceptable and could hurt the company financially. Despite efforts by Richland management, Scharmato management refused to renegotiate the contract. Richland management then decided to breach the contract strategically. The company waited until the harvest season when supplies were abundant. It then informed Scharmato that it was not accepting any further shipments of tomato paste. Scharmato sued Richland for breach of contract (to the relief of Richland management). Richland management had decided that a breach of contract suit was likely to be less expensive (strategically) than purchasing tomato paste under the terms of the contract. While such a practice raises difficult ethical questions, it is nonetheless a fairly common practice within the business community.

RESOLVING A BUSINESS DISPUTE THROUGH THE COURTS

After considering the alternatives and their costs, management may decide that it is in the company's interest to bring (or defend against) a lawsuit. With regard to the basic trial procedures, lawsuits involving a business will not differ significantly from lawsuits involving nonbusiness parties. With rare exception, all parties must follow the procedural rules of the court system where the dispute is to be resolved.

Although there are no basic procedural differences between business and nonbusiness trials, there are other important differences. Those differences are important because they may affect both the decision to become involved in a lawsuit and the tactics and strategies the attorney for the business may employ in that lawsuit. The following are several of the more important differences between business and nonbusiness cases:

(1) The typical business case is more complex.

(2) It generally involves a greater need for documents and exhibits as evidence.

(3) It relies more heavily on expert testimony.

(4) It takes more time to complete.

(5) The damage award will be larger if the business loses.

■ THE COMPLEXITY IN RESOLVING A BUSINESS DISPUTE

The legal issues in a business dispute are typically more complex than in a nonbusiness dispute. Business activities that supposedly violate federal regulatory law can involve complicated fact situations that can take several months to unwind. In a recent antitrust case, for example, the presiding judge required both sides to write out in detail what they intended to prove. Even after the judge ordered several refinements, the response was nearly 5,000 pages long. Given that degree of complexity, it is not uncommon for several teams of attorneys to be involved in preparing and presenting the case.

TABLE 4–1
CIVIL LAW CASES IN FIVE STATES (1989)

Case Type	Connecticut	Florida	Kansas	Minnesota	North Dakota
Tort	8%	11%	3%	5%	2%
Contract	13	9	41	4	22
Real property	9	20	11	14	5
Estate	23	8	9	7	11
Small claims	30	23	13	46	20
Other	17	29	23	24	40
Cases filed per 1,000 people	65	69	59	48	50
Maximum small claims $	$1,000	$2,500	$1,000	$2,000	$2,000

Statute Differences Among States.   Most suits involving businesses are filed in state courts. As discussed in the previous chapter, the law differs in each state, and management must take into account the different rules that may exist as its business expands into another state. Table 4–1 shows that some states have more lawsuits per person than other states and that the type of lawsuit varies from state to state. That is, what may be called a property case in one state may be called a contract case in another state.

Documents and Exhibits Used as Evidence.   In resolving a complex business dispute, thousands of documents and exhibits could be presented at the trial. More importantly, the documents involved may be part of a series of related documents, thereby adding to the complexity of the case. The documents, for example, may be part of a series of related papers, correspondence, internal memos, an exchange of letters that make up a contract, or annual reports. The judge and the jury will have a difficult task in such a case just to simply understand the documents and exhibits.

Reliance on Expert Testimony.   The testimony of the expert witnesses often is an important part of the successful business lawsuit. Even a relatively simple business dispute can require expert testimony at the trial on basic economic and finance issues. In environmental pollution cases, for example, the presentation of the issues may require testimony from a variety of experts, including scientists, medical doctors, engineers, and economists. In more complex cases and where there is more at stake, the expert testimony can involve complicated statistical models presented by experts in the field. The cost of such testimony can represent a large portion of the total costs of the lawsuit. Attorneys involved in the Hunt silver case (the Hunts were accused of attempting to monopolize the silver market), for example, estimated that the bill for expert testimony alone exceeded $2 million.

Longer Trials.   Because of the complexity of the issues involved, the average business lawsuit is considerably longer than a nonbusiness lawsuit. While a simple business lawsuit trial may last three or fewer days, a more complex case may take a year or more. Each party could call many witnesses and present thousands of documents and exhibits. In addition, it is not uncommon for several years to pass before the dispute even reaches the trial stage. The AT&T antitrust case, for example, was filed in 1974 but did not reach the courts until the 1980s. Legal fees in that case exceeded $100 million.

■ THE GROWING SIGNIFICANCE OF BUSINESS LITIGATION

Over the past thirty years, the United States has experienced an explosion in business litigation. Since 1960, the number of disputes brought to the court system has increased by more than 300 percent. As Table 4–2 shows, more than 120,000 business lawsuits—about 500 suits every working day—were litigated in federal district courts alone in 1988.

■ SIZE OF JUDGMENTS AGAINST BUSINESSES

Not only has the number of lawsuits increased, but the size of the judgments has also increased. According to Jury Verdict Research, average jury awards in product liability cases nearly tripled between the 1970s and the 1980s. Through the 1980s, the average verdict exceeded $1 million, and there is every expectation that the size of awards will continue to increase through the 1990s.

Among noteworthy cases, $100 million was awarded to the family of a chemical worker who died of leukemia as a result of workplace exposure to the chemical benzene. A Texas jury returned a 10.3-billion-dollar verdict against Texaco, finding that Texaco had interfered with Pennzoil's attempted merger with Getty Oil Company. Texaco responded by filing for bankruptcy. With $35 billion in assets, Texaco became the largest company in U.S. history to file for bankruptcy. The companies eventually settled the case for $3 billion.

TABLE 4–2
BUSINESS LITIGATION, U.S. DISTRICT COURTS 1988

Nature of Dispute	Number of Cases
Contracts	44,135
Real property	12,209
Product liability	16,166
Asbestos	10,715
Bankruptcy	5,558
Environmental matters	889
Commerce (ICC)	1,694
Patent, copyright, trademark	6,059
Labor laws	12,688
Employment discrimination	8,563
Securities and commodities	2,638
Total business cases	**121,314**

SOURCE: *1989 Annual Report of the Director*, Administration Office of the U.S. Courts.

Texaco was not the only blue-chip company to be adversely affected by legal proceedings in the 1980s. The A. H. Robbins Company filed for bankruptcy to stall the some 6,000 legal liabilities associated with its manufacture of the Dalkon Shield, a contraceptive device. The company, which had nearly $500 million in assets when it filed, was required to establish a fund of over $2 billion to compensate victims.

Larger Damage Awards Imposed on Businesses.   In litigation where the remedy being sought is monetary damages, businesses—and particularly large businesses—are often viewed as "deep pockets." That is, the jury will often award a larger damage award to a party injured by a business than to a party injured in the same way by another individual. The business is viewed by the jury as having more than enough resources—either in the form of insurance or profits—to compensate injured victims. An important jury study found that injured plaintiffs who sue businesses receive awards that are four times larger, on the average, than awards to plaintiffs with similar injuries who sue individuals.

It is clear that the costs associated with both resolving and preventing disputes have become a significant cost of doing business. It is also clear that these costs will likely continue to increase. While some businesses have always carefully monitored their legal environments, it was not until recently that the importance of such monitoring became apparent.

BASIC TRIAL PROCEDURES

As discussed at the beginning of the chapter, the American legal system follows the adversary system of justice. That is, the responsibility for bringing a lawsuit, shaping its issues, and presenting convincing evidence rests upon the parties to the dispute and no one else. This section discusses the major procedural rules governing the civil litigation process. A summary of a typical lawsuit is presented in Figure 4–1.

PLEADINGS STAGE

For the litigatory process to begin, the plaintiff must first determine in which court to bring the action. The plaintiff will select a court that has both subject-matter jurisdiction and jurisdiction over the parties to the dispute. The plaintiff will then give notice to the defendant by *service of process,* typically consisting of a summons (refer to Exhibit 3–1 for an example).

With the summons, the plaintiff will serve the defendant with the first of the pleadings, called the *complaint* (see Exhibit 4–1). The complaint is a written statement that sets forth the plaintiff's claim against the defendant. The complaint will contain the following:

(1) A statement setting forth the facts necessary for the court to take jurisdiction.

(2) A short statement of the facts necessary to show that the plaintiff is entitled to a remedy.

(3) A statement of the remedy the plaintiff is seeking.

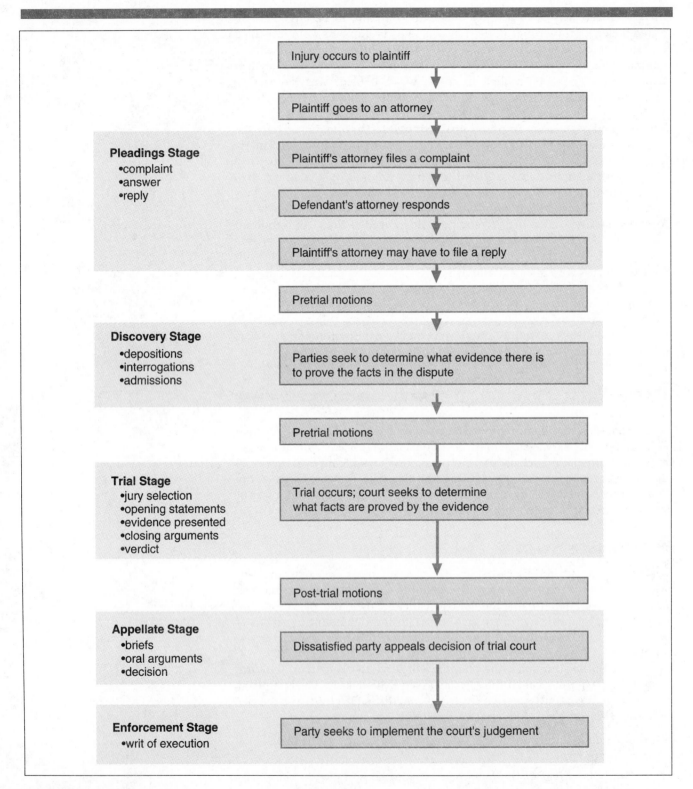

FIGURE 4–1

Example of a Typical Lawsuit

EXHIBIT 4–1 ▆▆▆▆▆▆▆▆▆▆▆▆▆▆▆▆▆▆▆▆▆▆▆▆▆▆

Example of a Typical Complaint

UNITED STATES DISTRICT COURT
FOR THE
SOUTHERN DISTRICT OF NEW YORK

Civil No. 2–80151

Franco Gori
Plaintiff

vs.   COMPLAINT

Tom Eyestone Company,
Defendant

Comes now the plaintiff and for his cause of action against the defendant alleges and states as follows:

1. The plaintiff is a citizen of the state of New York and defendant is a corporation incorporated under the laws of the state of Delaware having its principal place of business in the state of Massachusetts. There is diversity of citizenship between parties.

2. The amount in controversy, exclusive of interest and costs, exceeds the sum of ten thousand dollars.

3. On January 10, 1993, in a public highway called Pleasant Street in Newburyport, Massachusetts, defendant's agent, John Kluttz, negligently drove a motor vehicle against plaintiff who was then crossing said highway.

4. As a result, plaintiff was thrown down and had his leg broken and was otherwise injured, was prevented from transacting his business, suffered great pain of body and mind, and incurred expenses for medical attention and hospitalization.

5. The costs plaintiff incurred included: $20,000 in medical care and $5,000 in lost business.

WHEREFORE plaintiff demands judgment against defendant in the sum of $25,000 and costs.

by
Ronald Johnson
Attorney for Plaintiff
5450 Trump Tower
New York, New York

Dated: 5/15/93

Responses to the Complaint and Summons.   Following the service of the plaintiff's complaint, the defendant must file a pleading to respond. Depending on the circumstances, the defendant may file (1) a motion to dismiss or (2) an answer with or without an affirmative defense, or (3) a counterclaim.

Motion to Dismiss.   The defendant may first respond by challenging the plaintiff's complaint by filing a *motion to dismiss*. This motion may ask the court to dismiss the action because it does not have jurisdiction over either the subject matter of the dispute or the defendant's person. This motion may also challenge the venue (location) or the sufficiency of the service of process.

The defendant may also file a *motion to dismiss for failure to state a claim or cause of action,* which is a statement on the part of the defendant that even if the facts presented in the complaint are true, the injury claimed by the plaintiff is not an injury for which the law furnishes a remedy. In addition, the defendant may file this motion if he or she believes that the plaintiff has failed to include in the pleadings an important part of the case.

Answer.   The defendant must file an *answer* with the court if the defendant's motion to dismiss is denied by the judge or if the defendant does not make that motion. In this pleading, the defendant must admit or deny the allegations made by the plaintiff in the complaint. If the defendant admits all the allegations or fails to deny the claims, the plaintiff wins the lawsuit. If the defendant denies the allegations, the dispute will be set for trial.

Affirmative Defenses.   In answering the complaint, the defendant may admit to the plaintiff's allegations but may assert additional facts that will result in the action's being dismissed. These additional facts are called an *affirmative defense.* The defendant admits that he or she has injured the plaintiff but that the additional facts he or she has provided the court form a defense (a legal excuse) to the plaintiff's complaint. The defendant could admit to being negligent in a car accident involving him or her and the plaintiff, for example, but could also tell the court that the claim is now prohibited by the statute of limitations.

Counterclaim.   The defendant can deny the allegations and assert his or her own claim against the plaintiff. This claim by the defendant is called a *counterclaim* or *cross-complaint*. The counterclaim is in essence a complaint by the defendant. The plaintiff will have to respond to it just as the defendant had to respond to the original complaint.

Reply.   In the majority of state court systems, the pleadings stage ends after the answer. Any new matters raised by the defendant in his or her answer are automatically taken as denied by the plaintiff. In situations when the defendant does file a counterclaim, the plaintiff may answer it with an additional pleading called a *reply,* which is in essence an answer to the counterclaim.

The complaint, answer, and, if present, the counterclaim and reply form the *pleadings*. The purpose of the pleadings is to notify each of the parties of the claims, defenses, and counterclaims of the other party. The pleadings focus the issues, thereby removing the element of surprise from the resolution of the dispute.

■ DISCOVERY STAGE: OBTAINING INFORMATION BEFORE TRIAL

After the pleadings, the litigation enters the discovery stage. During this stage, the parties are allowed to use a variety of legal tools to obtain information and gather evidence about the dispute. The attorneys will be particularly interested in gathering information from the opposing parties. The process of obtaining information is known as *discovery*. The Federal Rules of Civil Procedure and the corresponding state procedural codes set down the basic rules for discovery.

The discovery rules offer several methods of obtaining information from an opposing party or witness. Discovery rules allow an attorney to gain access to the testimony of the parties, relevant documents and records, and virtually any other type of evidence relevant to the resolution of the dispute. The specific tools of discovery include depositions, written interrogatories, orders for production of documents, requests for admissions, and orders for a mental or physical examination. The rules of civil procedure generally require that the party seeking information select a discovery tool that is not "unduly burdensome" to the other party.

Depositions and Interrogatories.   The principal discovery tool is the *deposition*—the sworn testimony of a witness recorded by a court official. In this procedure, the person whose deposition is to be taken is questioned by attorneys from both sides. The questions and the answers are taken down, sworn to, and signed. Some states also allow the use of videotaped depositions.

The deposition is useful in finding information that is important to the resolution of the dispute, including finding important leads to other witnesses or documents. It is also useful during the trial. Occasionally, a witness will attempt to change his or her story at the trial. An attorney will use prior statements from the deposition to show that the witness has no credibility. Finally, the deposition of a witness who is unavailable at the time of the trial may, in some circumstances, be used in place of live testimony.

A discovery tool particularly useful in determining the content of an opponent's case is *written interrogatories*—written questions submitted by the opposing party. The party receiving the interrogatories must prepare written answers with the aid of an attorney and then sign them under oath. The interrogatories will require the party to provide information from his or her records and files—the kind of information that one does not carry in one's head.

Orders for the Production of Documents.   An order for the production of documents allows a party to gain access to information in the sole possession of the other party. Such information might include medical bills, business records, letters, and repair bills. The party seeking the information usually has the right to gain access for the purposes of inspection, examination, and reproduction. If a trade secret is involved, a company can get a *protective order* to ensure the confidentiality of that secret.

Requests for Admissions.   Either party can serve the other party with a written request for an admission of the truth in matters relating to the dispute. Requests for admissions are to be used to force admissions of facts about which there are no real disputes between the parties. In a contract dispute over product price, for example, one party may ask the other party to admit to the fact that deliveries were made and accepted according to the terms of the contract. After a party has admitted the truthfulness of a fact related to the dispute, the parties are relieved of the burden of proving the fact, and trial time is reduced.

Mental and Physical Examinations.   In disputes where the physical or mental condition of a party is an issue, the court may be asked to order that party to submit to an examination. Because of concerns for the other party's right to privacy, the party requesting the order must show a greater need for the information than in requests for other forms of discovery. Generally, the party requesting the order specifies the exact type of mental or physical examination desired, the time, the place, and the specialists who are to do the examination.

Sanctions for Failing to Respond to a Discovery Request.   Under the Federal Rules of Civil Procedure and the procedural codes of most states, the court has broad powers to impose sanctions against a party who fails to comply with discovery requirements. If a party fails to comply with the requirements of a deposition, written interrogatories, or a request, the court may issue an order directing the party to comply. If the party does not comply with the order, the court may find the party in *contempt of court* (resulting in imprisonment or fines).

■ DISCOVERY: IMPACTS ON BUSINESS

Despite its value to the litigation process, discovery can impose significant costs on businesses, managers, and executives. Businesses can be forced to endure the expense and disruption of their administrative and executive staff while the various officers and employees answer questions and produce documents. In one regulatory dispute between Ford Motor Company and the Federal Trade Commission, it cost Ford nearly $4 million just to copy and produce required documents.

Of all discovery tools, depositions are often the major source of expense for a business involved in litigation. The burdens imposed by depositions are particularly heavy when administrative and executive personnel have to take time to provide a deposition. In disputes involving technical matters, the deposition of the manager with the responsibility for the project may take two weeks or more.

Further, in many disputes, it is not uncommon for the chief executive officer of the corporation to be issued a subpoena requesting that he or she appear to make a deposition. In the majority of cases, the knowledge or information being sought is in the hands of subordinates, not the chief executive officer. The court will generally attempt to protect executives if the purpose in seeking the deposition is largely to harass them. In some cases, the courts will examine the circumstances and recommend an alternative discovery tool. Plaintiffs seeking damages for injuries from an alleged defective design in a Dodge van, for example, sought the deposition of Lee Iacocca, chairman of the board of Chrysler Corporation. The court held that although "[Iacocca's] prestigious position is an unimpressive paper barrier shielding him from the judicial process, . . . he is a singularly unique and important individual who can be easily subjected to harassment and abuse. . . . Therefore, . . . an orderly discovery process will be best served by resorting to interrogatories at this time. . . ." In the following case, the court is confronted with a similar request for a deposition of executives.

TRAVELERS RENTAL COMPANY v. FORD MOTOR COMPANY

United States District Court, District of Massachusetts
116 F.R.D. 140 (1987)

Case Background
Travelers (the plaintiff), doing business as Dollar Rent a Car, alleged in its complaint that Ford (the defendant) had violated antitrust laws in a program it had developed with Hertz and Avis. Under the program, Ford had agreed to give Hertz and Avis—but not Dollar—a guaranteed resale price after using the Ford cars in their rental businesses. To establish its claim, Travelers sought to take the depositions of several high-level executives at Ford, including the president and executive vice president. Ford refused to produce the executives. Ford stated that Travelers was demanding the depositions "solely for the purpose of harassment and oppression, and not because the additional depositions are reasonably calculated to lead to the discovery of admissable evidence." Travelers asserted that there was an important connection between the executives and the issues in the case.

Case Decision
The district court held that Travelers was entitled to take the depositions of the Ford executives. The court ruled that

Travelers was trying to explore Ford's motives in implementing and administering the guaranteed resale plan. When the motives behind corporate actions are at issue, an opposing party usually has to depose those officers and employees who approved and administered the particular action. Here, the executives had exchanged memorandums regarding the program, had the authority to implement it, requested relevant reports, and provided written approval of it.

Managerial Considerations
While discovery serves several important functions in dispute resolution, it has become an abusive tool in the hands of certain attorneys. Executives, particularly chief executive officers of major corporations, are unique and important individuals who can easily be subjected to harassment and abuse. The company should make efforts to protect its executives from potential abuse by determining which lower level managerial personnel have better information on the action being questioned. Further, the company's attorneys should try to encourage the use of written interrogatories in questioning company executives.

■ PRETRIAL STAGE

Either party or the court may request a pretrial conference. Usually the conference involves the attorneys and the judge, but it may also involve the parties themselves. The pretrial conference is intended to be a forum for planning the course of the trial. To ensure a meaningful trial, the judge may find it necessary to request that the parties seek additional admissions of facts or limit the number of witnesses. In some state court systems, the pretrial conference is viewed as a forum for obtaining settlements.

If through discovery it is determined that there are no disagreements about the facts to a dispute, either party may move for *summary judgment*. Because there are no facts in dispute, the judge will be asked simply to apply the law to those facts and resolve the dispute. In reaching a decision, the judge will be free to consider evidence not contained in the pleadings. Motions for summary judgment may be made before or during the trial. They will be granted only if there are no disagreements about the facts.

■ TRIAL STAGE

After the completion of discovery, and if it has not been resolved by dismissal, summary judgment, or settlement, the dispute must be set for *trial*. In many court systems, the trial calendar is quite long. It is not uncommon for there to be delays of up to three years before a dispute is finally called to trial.

The Jury. The Seventh Amendment to the U.S. Constitution and most state constitutions provide for the right to a *jury trial*. In the federal court system, the right is guaranteed if the amount in controversy exceeds $20. Most state court systems have similar guarantees, although the minimum amount in controversy may be higher. Iowa, for example, requires that the amount in controversy equal or exceed $1,000. In disputes where the plaintiff requests that the court direct or prohibit a specified action by the defendant—an equitable remedy—and not a judgment for monetary damages, there is no right to a jury trial.

The right to a jury trial, however, does not have to be exercised. If a jury has not been requested, the judge will both determine the true facts in the dispute and apply the law to resolve it.

The jury selection process formally begins when the clerk of the court sends a notice requesting individuals to appear for jury duty. The screening process used in selecting the actual jury members from this group of individuals is called *voir dire*. The purpose of this process is to determine whether any of the prospective jurors are likely to be so biased or prejudiced that they could not reach an objective decision from the *evidence* to be presented. A jury is typically a panel of twelve persons. Increasingly, however, panels of fewer than twelve—frequently six—are being used.

The Trial. Although the judge has some freedom to change the order of the trial, he or she will usually require that the order not differ much from the order as summarized in Table 4–3. Although jury and nonjury trials are generally handled in much the same way, they can have a number of important procedural differences. For example, the judge in nonjury trials will often eliminate the attorney's opening statements and closing arguments. The following discussion details the various steps involved in a typical jury trial.

Opening Statements. After the jurors have been sworn in, both attorneys are allowed to make *opening statements*. In these statements, the attorneys tell the jury the crucial facts to the dispute and how they will prove that those facts support their positions. These statements are generally limited to twenty minutes. The plaintiff's attorney normally presents the first statement.

TABLE 4–3
SUMMARIES OF TYPICAL JURY AND NONJURY TRIALS

Jury Trial	Nonjury Trial
1. The selection of a jury.	1. Plaintiff's presentation of direct evidence.
2. Plaintiff's opening statement.	2. Defendant's presentation of direct evidence.
3. Defendant's opening statement.	3. Plaintiff's presentation of rebuttal evidence.
4. Plaintiff's presentation of direct evidence.	4. Defendant's presentation of rebuttal evidence.
5. Defendant's presentation of direct evidence.	5. Judge's deliberation and verdict.
6. Plaintiff's presentation of rebuttal evidence.	
7. Defendant's presentation of rebuttal evidence.	
8. Opening final argument by the plaintiff.	
9. Defendant's final argument.	
10. Closing final argument by the plaintiff.	
11. Instructions to the jury.	
12. Jury deliberation and verdict.	

Presentation of Direct Testimony.   Following the opening statements, the plaintiff's attorney calls witnesses. The plaintiff goes first and has the burden of proving that his or her claims are correct. Each of the plaintiff's witnesses is first questioned by the plaintiff's attorney. This is called *direct examination.* The defendant's attorney then questions the witness. This is called *cross-examination.* There are rules that dictate the types of questions attorneys may ask and the kinds of testimony a witness may provide.

After having called and examined all witnesses, the plaintiff *rests.* The defendant's attorney may then ask for a *directed verdict* on the grounds that the plaintiff has not presented sufficient evidence to support the claims. As the following case illustrates, the plaintiff must present the evidence to demonstrate that the defendant's actions caused the injuries.

MAY v. HALL COUNTY LIVESTOCK IMPROVEMENT ASSOCIATION

Supreme Court of Nebraska
216 Neb. 476, 344 N.W.2d 629 (1984)

Case Background
May (the plaintiff) slipped and fell at a racetrack owned by Hall County (the defendant). She had started to climb the steps from the area where she had been seated. Her left foot slipped, and she was unable to break her fall. After she regained consciousness, she noted that the bottom of her right pant leg was wet. The food concession manager, who arrived at the site shortly after the accident, noted that there were no spills, debris, or liquids where the plaintiff had fallen.

The plaintiff brought an action against the defendant for the injuries she incurred in the fall. At the close of the plain-tiff's case, the trial court sustained the defendant's motion for a directed verdict. The court asserted that although the plaintiff's evidence had established her injuries, it did not provide a basis for finding the defendant responsible. The plaintiff appealed. The issue before the Supreme Court of Nebraska was whether the facts presented were sufficient to sustain the plaintiff's action.

Case Decision
The Supreme Court of Nebraska affirmed the lower court's decision to dismiss the case. The Supreme Court said that the plaintiff failed to produce evidence establishing that the condition of the defendant's place of business was the

(*continued*)

cause of the plaintiff's injuries. According to the general rule, when no supporting evidence has been presented by the plaintiff, it is the duty of the court to dismiss the case rather than submit the issue to a jury.

Managerial Considerations

From a managerial perspective, this case illustrates the importance of being prepared in the event that a customer or supplier is injured by an employee or a product or on the property of the company. In this case, the concession manager attended to the injured plaintiff immediately. In addition, the manager noted the circumstances surrounding the accident to determine whether the racetrack could be responsible for the injury.

Managers should advise their employees and agents on how to handle similar situations to avoid or reduce liability. The management of Delta Airlines, for example, developed a procedure to be followed in the event of an air crash. It is estimated that Delta saved millions of dollars in liability claims by requiring employees to make special efforts to tend to the needs of the victims' families shortly after a recent crash. Later, Delta was able to work out settlements with those families. Largely because of the personal relationships Delta had developed, the terms of those settlements were more favorable for the company. Had Delta taken a distant, uninterested, and adversarial posture and allowed the terms to be dictated by a jury in a court of law, it most likely would have had to pay much much more than it did.

If the motion for a directed verdict is denied by the court (which is usually the case), the defendant will present his or her own case. Like the plaintiff, the defendant will call witnesses to present his or her side of the dispute. With the defendant's attorney now going first, the defendant's witnesses will be subject to the same process of direct and cross-examination as the plaintiff's witnesses.

Closing Arguments.   Before the case goes to the jury, each attorney presents a *closing argument.* The attorneys try to organize the evidence for the jury in a manner most favorable to their case. Normally, the plaintiff may present closing arguments both before and after the defendant. As in the opening statement, the judge will limit the time available to the attorneys for their closing arguments. It is improper for an attorney to discuss a matter that was excluded from the trial by the judge or that was not discussed at the trial.

Instructions to the Jury.   Before the jury retires to decide the verdict, the judge gives the jury *instructions* (or *charges*). In the instructions, the judge tells the jury about the applicable law, summarizes the facts and issues of the dispute, and states which of the parties has the *burden of persuasion.*

The jurors then consider carefully among themselves to reach an agreement and find either for the plaintiff or for the defendant. Ordinarily in a civil trial, the burden of persuasion requires that the responsible party prove its contentions by a *preponderance of the evidence.* That is, if jurors are unable to resolve an issue in their mind, they should find against the party who has the burden of persuasion for that issue. In some cases, however, juries are unable to reach a unanimous decision. If such is the case, the jury is said to be *hung,* and a new trial before a different jury is necessary. The jury is then discharged and a *mistrial* declared.

Motions After the Verdict.   After the verdict has been presented, the parties may challenge it with certain *post-trial motions.* The challenging party may move for a *judgment notwithstanding the verdict,* or *judgment n.o.v.* This motion raises the same question as the motion for a directed verdict.

The party asking for the judgment n.o.v. is stating that a reasonable jury would not have found for the other party. That is, the jury's verdict is not supportable by the evidence presented at the trial. If the judge agrees, the jury's verdict is reversed.

The losing party can also move for a new trial. There are several important bases for this motion. Most commonly, an attorney will argue that the judge erred in admitting certain evidence; the judge's instructions to the jury were inappropriate; there was misconduct on the part of the attorneys, parties, or the jurors; or the monetary damages awarded were either too much or inadequate. In any case, the party making the motion is asking the court to set aside the current verdict and hold a new trial. A new trial may also be granted if new and important evidence, a clerical mistake, or fraud is discovered after the trial. However, the granting of a new trial under these circumstances is very rare. The following case considers the important issue of jury misconduct.

CATERPILLAR TRACTOR COMPANY v. HULVEY

Supreme Court of Virginia
233 Va. 77, 353 S.E.2d 747 (1987)

Case Background
Hulvey was a forklift operator. He brought a product liability action against Caterpillar, the forklift manufacturer, for injuries sustained while operating the forklift. Three trials were held. The first trial resulted in a hung jury. In the second trial, although the jury found for the defendant, the verdict was set aside for jury misconduct, and a new trial was ordered. In the third trial, the jury found for the plaintiff and awarded him $250,000.

The jury misconduct in the second trial centered around one of the jurors, named Olmstead, who was a corporate attorney. One juror testified that because Olmstead was a lawyer, he had "an advantage" and swayed other jurors. Members of the jury testified that Olmstead read to them from an insurance newsletter (discussing the rapid increase in injury lawsuits) and made insulting comments about people who sued for injuries. Olmstead also commented on the plaintiff's ability to sit in a chair for long periods of time despite supposedly being in pain from the injuries alleged.

Caterpillar appealed the second verdict that had been set aside for jury misconduct. The issue before the Supreme Court of Virginia was whether there had been jury misconduct in the second trial.

Case Decision
The Supreme Court of Virginia held that Olmstead's actions did not constitute jury misconduct. Therefore, the third ver-

dict in favor of Hulvey was reversed, and the verdict of the second trial in favor of Caterpillar was reinstated.

As a general rule, a court should set aside a verdict if misconduct outside the jury room adversely affects the jury's deliberation. The court felt, however, that most of the alleged misconduct in this case occurred within the jury room. The court stated that it would not be beneficial to restrict discussions in the jury room. Since Olmstead's conduct occurred for the most part in the jury room and swayed only two jurors, the court felt there was no reason to set aside the second verdict.

Management Considerations
Being involved in litigation can be expensive for a company. Here, Caterpillar had to defend itself three times because of difficulties associated with the jury. These and other difficulties encourage companies to settle (often prematurely) or adopt alternative dispute resolution processes such as arbitration or mediation (as GM did in the Manager's Legal Challenge feature).

In electing to present its case before a judge or jury, managers with their lawyers will consider the judge's temperament, the complexity of the evidence, and the degree to which the emotions of the jury will likely affect the judgment. Management may be concerned that the resolution of disputes with its consumers or suppliers may be affected by the emotions of a jury. In such cases, it may want to implement an alternative dispute resolution process to eliminate the potential for a substantial judgment being awarded by a jury.

■ APPELLATE STAGE

The case may enter the appellate stage if one of the parties believes that an *error of law* was made during the trial. The parties cannot, however, appeal the factual determinations made at the trial. Common bases for appeal include errors made by the trial court judge in admitting evidence that should have been excluded, refusals to admit evidence that should have been heard, improper instructions given to the jury, and the granting or denying of motions to dismiss the case. A principal function served by the appellate courts is to ensure the fairness of a trial, that is, to make sure that the trial court judge correctly applied the law.

The parties present their arguments to the appellate court through written *briefs* and *oral arguments.* These arguments are restricted to discussions of law, not the facts in the case. There will always be more than one judge hearing the appeal, with three judges being the most common number for the first appeal. In reviewing the trial court's decision, the appellate court has the authority to review any ruling of law made by the trial judge. It has the power to *affirm, reverse,* or *modify* the judgment of the trial court.

The appellate court decision will be accompanied by a written *opinion* that presents the views of the majority of the court. *Concurring opinions*—opinions by judges who agree with the decision of the majority but for different reasons—and *dissenting opinions*—opinions written by judges who disagree with the decision of the majority—may also be filed. Those written opinions are intended to set forth the rationale for the judges' decisions. They also furnish guidance for the resolution of similar future disputes to attorneys, judges, and the public.

■ ENFORCEMENT STAGE

After a dispute has been tried at the trial level, and if no appeal is taken or if no further appeal is available, the *judgment* becomes final. The same dispute cannot be considered again in this or any other forum. It is *res judicata*—literally, a thing decided.

The judgment may be in the form of a monetary award to the plaintiff, a declaration of the rights between the parties, or an order requiring or prohibiting some activity on the part of the defendant. In cases where the defendant wins, the judgment generally will not involve an award of money. However, it will state that the defendant is not responsible for the plaintiff's injuries. In some instances, the court may require that the plaintiff pay the defendant's legal expenses.

In the case where the plaintiff recovers a monetary damage award, it is the plaintiff's responsibility to collect from the defendant. In the event the defendant does not pay, the plaintiff can seek a *writ of execution.* The writ will command an official such as a sheriff to seize the property of the defendant and, if necessary, to sell the property to satisfy the judgment.

BASIC TRIAL PROCEDURES | INTERNATIONAL ASPECTS

The rules governing trial procedures can differ dramatically from country to country. The Italian rules of procedure, for example, combine the pleading, discovery, and pretrial conference stages of U.S. civil procedure into the initial "pleadings" stage. In contrast to civil cases in the United States, juries are not used in France, Germany, Italy, and most other civil law countries, or in the common law countries of England and Canada.

In several civil law countries, witnesses do not appear in open court. Rather, their testimonies are given to an investigation judge, who then presents their testimony in summary form to the judges charged with resolving the dispute. In contrast to the United States, where the emphasis is on monetary damages, the primary objective in the Italian system is to rehabilitate the person and return him or her to a productive life as quickly as possible. Thus, while our courts are clogged with automobile cases, a very small percentage of such cases end up in Italian court.

DISPUTE RESOLUTION ALTERNATIVES TO THE COURT SYSTEM

The business litigation explosion in the United States, combined with the high costs and delay associated with the court system, has brought about an increased use of *alternative dispute resolution* (ADR) processes. A growing dissatisfaction with juries in business litigation has led to dramatic changes in the business community's feelings toward these processes. This frustration with the court system was well stated by former Supreme Court Chief Justice Warren Burger:

> We, as lawyers, know that litigation is not only stressful and frustrating but expensive and frequently unrewarding for litigants. . . . Commercial litigation takes business executives and their staffs away from the creative paths of the development and production [of goods and services] and often inflicts more wear and tear on them than the most difficult business problems.

Alternatives to the court system are used because they provide a neutral, low-cost, rapid method for resolving disputes. If these alternatives were not available, many more disputes would be resolved in the court system. Because of the strongly competitive nature of the court system, however, the underlying business relationship is usually damaged beyond repair. As a rule, the choice of an alternative to the court system in resolving disputes must be agreed upon by the parties before a dispute occurs. Often parties will include a clause in the contract calling for the parties to submit disputes to a particular alternative method of dispute resolution. The most common ADR processes include arbitration, minitrials, and negotiation. Figure 4–2 shows that negotiation provides the parties with the

FIGURE 4–2

Relative Comparison of Disputant Control Under Various ADR Processes
SOURCE: Adapted from Larry Ray, "Emerging Options in Dispute Resolution," *ABA Journal,* June 1989, pp. 66–68.

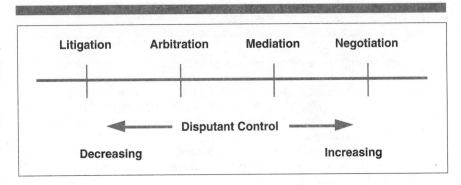

most control over the process and outcome. However, it is important to note that all ADR processes provide the parties with more control than using the court system.

■ ARBITRATION

Arbitration is the most widely recognized and accepted ADR process. It is a legal process in which two or more persons agree to allow an impartial person (or panel) to resolve their disputes. The impartial person, called the *arbiter,* is often an expert in the field who understands the technical nuances of the dispute. Business litigants frequently find the opinion of such a third party invaluable in deciding how best to settle complicated disputes. The decision of the arbiter may be legally binding and can be appealed to the courts only under specific and limited circumstances. As Figure 4–3 illustrates, there has been a steady increase in the number of business cases going to arbitration.

Court-Annexed Arbitration.   A few court systems require arbitration before a trial. Called *court-annexed arbitration,* these programs have been limited to disputes in which the amount in controversy is relatively small. Eligible cases are referred to mandatory pretrial arbitration. The proceeding is typically conducted by a practicing attorney, a retired judge, or, in some court systems, a panel of three attorneys. The procedure used usually consists of a hearing that is similar to a regular trial.

Either party may reject the arbitration decision and insist on a trial before a judge or a jury. Relatively few cases submitted to the process, however, have later proceeded to trial. Courts using this process have experienced significant reductions in both case backlogs and case processing time. In Pittsburgh, for example, this ADR process ends nearly three-quarters of all disputes referred to it. The average delay before an arbitration hearing is only three months, in contrast to the eighteen-month delay before a trial. Surveys of both attorneys and the parties whose disputes have been submitted to this ADR process have also reported a high level of satisfaction.

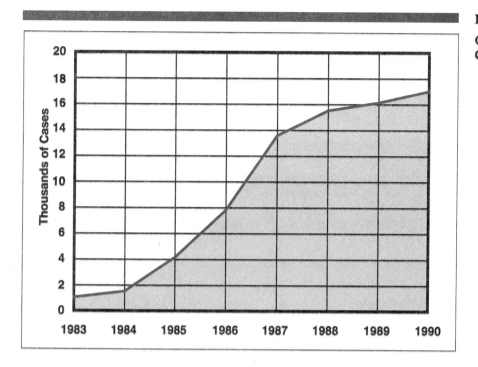

FIGURE 4-3

Growth in Commercial Cases Going to Arbitration

MINITRIALS

As the name implies, *minitrials* are shortened, nonbinding hearings on disputed matters. The hearings take place before an expert selected by the parties. The expert will provide a confidential opinion on the strengths and weaknesses of each party's case. That opinion is then used to assist in settlement negotiations. The procedures to be used in the hearing are decided upon by the parties. This ADR process has been successful in dealing with a variety of intellectual property, product liability, and breach of contract disputes.

NEGOTIATION

In the ADR process of *negotiation*, the parties choose to work out their differences among themselves rather than through either arbitration or litigation. The process of negotiation can take on many different forms and approaches.

The best-known and most widely used negotiation technique is *mediation*, which involves the use of a neutral outsider who helps the parties reach a permanent resolution to their dispute. Collective bargaining in labor-management relations has been a big user of mediation techniques.

Mediators essentially manage the negotiation process, arranging the scheduling, setting the agenda, and maintaining the records of the dispute. They also assist communications outside the meetings by holding confidential talks with the individual parties and suggesting areas where a party may be unreasonable, such as asking for many times more than actual losses. In some circumstances, the mediator may offer creative suggestions, remind the parties of the costs if they fail to reach an agreement (and decide to go to court), and recommend the terms of an agreement.

■ ADVANTAGES OF ADR PROCESSES TO BUSINESSES

The use of ADR processes by the business community has increased dramatically in the past fifteen years. Businesses have used these processes to resolve both large and small disputes between themselves, with their consumers, and with the government. (See, for example, this chapter's Manager's Legal Challenge feature.)

Several important factors contribute to this increase. Some of the more important factors include the following:

1. The avoidance of high-cost litigation.
2. The fear that litigation will result in an outcome far worse than reasonably anticipated.
3. The need to return employees involved in the litigation to more productive activities.
4. The desire to maintain the business relationship.

SUMMARY: A GUIDE FOR MANAGERS

- The adversary system of justice requires people to decide whether they wish to file a lawsuit to have a court determine whether they have a legitimate case that may be resolved. Before filing a suit, one must consider the costs involved, the impact on one's reputation, the likelihood of success, and the odds of collecting a judgment, even if a case is won. Expert counsel is usually required to make these determinations; business litigation can be complex and expensive.

- Litigation begins with pleadings. The plaintiff must notify the defendant by service of process that a complaint has been filed with a court. The defendant must answer the complaint with a motion to dismiss, a defense, or a counterclaim, or the plaintiff wins automatically. The plaintiff may respond with a reply.

- Before trial, the discovery process allows both parties to gather legal evidence. Depositions or interrogatories may be taken from witnesses. The discovery process allows both parties to know what the trial is to be about so few surprises arise. Gathering evidence may cause the parties to change their claims or settle the case as the likely outcome becomes clear.

- At most trials, the defendant has the right to ask for a jury trial; attorneys discuss with clients the advisability of a jury trial or a trial where the judge hears and determines the whole matter. Different courts have different rules about how juries are selected. When a jury is used, it is the finder of fact. After both parties have presented their evidence and arguments, the judge instructs the jury on the law and how to apply it to the facts; the jury decides the outcome.

- The judge can set aside the verdict of a jury, but this is rare. In most cases, a party unhappy with the result must bear the costs of an appeal to the court of appeals, which reviews the application of the law to the facts that were determined at the trial and makes sure there was no error of law that requires a reversal or modification of the trial court decision.

- Because of the expense of litigation and the long time it takes for most civil litigation, many parties volunteer for arbitration or negotiation of a dispute. Alternative dispute resolution (ADR) is popular and settles more business disputes than does regular litigation. Many business contracts require use of ADR and the courts uphold such contracts. Once ADR is chosen, it is rare to then be able to seek court litigation instead.

MANAGER'S ETHICAL DILEMMA

Heading Off Legal Troubles

Shearson Lehman Brothers is the second largest securities firm in the United States. Like all securities firms, its stockbrokers have control over funds invested by clients. Some brokers make trades (buying and selling stocks and bonds) without client approval and lose money. Other brokers have authority to make trades, but when they lose money, their clients get angry. In other cases, the brokers simply make more trades than make sense because they get a commission on every trade.

Most disputes between clients and brokerage firms are handled by arbitration, which is called for in the agreement signed by investors when they start doing business with the brokerage firm. In 1990, an average of 250 arbitrations a month took place involving Wall Street brokerage firms. About twenty-five cases a month involved Shearson. Shearson lost 60 percent of the cases, paying an average of $85,000 per case.

Since it is not possible for Shearson's management to know whether every broker makes every trade properly, management may not learn about a problem until it has become serious. Since Shearson is liable for illegal use of clients' funds by its brokers—even if the brokers are breaking company rules—the company has legal incentives to treat clients right.

To try to reduce the number of cases, in 1992, Shearson assigned about three dozen lawyers to go work with branch managers to work on ways to reduce the number of investor disputes and subsequent arbitration and litigation.

Some branch managers feel they are caught in a trap: the lawyers want things run more carefully; and the branch managers say that the lawyers' demands for more controls reduce the effectiveness of the brokers, which means the best ones will leave for other firms.

Questions

Suppose that if a lawyer reviewed every trade made by brokers, no illegal trades or even dubious trades would be made. This would be very expensive. Is such high-quality legal and ethical guidance desirable? Brokers already know that they can be fired, fined, and sued for illegal trades or trades in violation of clients' orders. What else can Shearson and other firms do to give brokers an incentive to make fewer mistakes? What if they paid brokers salaries rather than commissions?

REVIEW AND DISCUSSION QUESTIONS

1. Define the following terms:

   complaint   voire dire
   motion to dismiss   evidence
   affirmative defense   arbitration
   summary judgment

2. Compare and contrast the following concepts:
   a. Motion to dismiss and a motion for directed verdict.
   b. Deposition and written interrogatories.
   c. Burden of persuasion and preponderance of the evidence.
   d. Procedures at the trial court versus the appellate court.

3. Describe the decision-making process a business goes through in determining whether to undertake a lawsuit.

4. How do lawsuits involving a business differ from lawsuits involving individuals?

5. What advantages do alternative dispute resolution processes provide to a business?

■ CASE QUESTIONS

6. Larry Folsom, an independent truck driver, was unloading potatoes at A & P's warehouse. During the unloading process, he was injured. Folsom brought an action against A & P, alleging that A & P's negligence brought about his injuries. At the close of a two-and-one-half-day trial, the jury deliberated just thirty-five minutes and found for A & P. Folsom alleges jury misconduct and moves for a new trial. What will be the result? [*Folsom* v. *Great Atlantic & Pacific Tea Company,* 521 A.2d 678 (Me.1987)]

7. A union employee was covered by an employment agreement that requires the use of arbitration to resolve any grievance that arises on the job. He was fired after he was arrested for possession and use of marijuana on company property during working hours. His job entailed working with dangerous machinery that had been involved in some serious injuries. He had been reprimanded twice recently for poor job performance. The arbitrator required the employer to rehire the worker. The company took the case to court. The district court reversed the arbitration award. The court of appeals affirmed the decision of the district court, ruling that reinstatement would violate public policy "against the operation of dangerous machinery by persons under the influence of drugs." That decision was appealed to the U.S. Supreme Court. What will be its decision? [*United Paperworkers International Union* v. *Misco Inc.,* 484 U.S. 29, 108 S.Ct. 364 (1987)]

8. A franchise agreement (contract) between the parent company franchisor and the franchisees who operated 7-Eleven stores said that any dispute between the franchisor and franchisees would be settled by arbitration. A franchisee sued the franchisor in state court, claiming that some actions of the franchisor were in violation of state law concerning franchises. The state supreme court ruled that the issues covered by the state law could be tried in state court and did not have to be submitted to arbitration. What did the U.S. Supreme Court hold about the choice between arbitration and litigation? [*Southland Corp.* v. *Keating,* 465 U.S. 1, 104 S.Ct. 852 (1984)]

■ BUSINESS POLICY QUESTIONS

9. A party who deliberately disobeys a court order requiring cooperation with a discovery request can be held in contempt of court. He or she can be fined or imprisoned *except* in those cases where the party has refused to submit to a physical examination. Why?

10. A person may legally be his or her own attorney in almost any legal matter. In what circumstances and for what reasons would it be unwise for a person to act as his or her own attorney?

11. In the 1980s, the Audi 5000 was alleged to suffer from a problem called "sudden acceleration." Without warning, the automobile allegedly would suddenly accelerate, causing damage and injury to anything in its path. The company developed a very timid strategic plan in fighting these allegations. New-car sales declined by more than 50 percent, Audi 5000 used-car values nose-dived, and Audi was forced to discard its 5000 series and develop a new series for the U.S. market.

   Suzuki had a similar problem with its four-wheel drive vehicle, the Samurai. *Consumer Reports,* finding that the vehicle supposedly tipped over easily in hard cornering, advised its readers not to buy the car. In contrast to Audi, Suzuki adopted a very aggressive strategic plan to reduce liability and protect its public image. It attacked the *Consumer Reports* findings in newspaper advertisements and on television talk shows. As a consequence, Suzuki's sales declined only about 5 percent. Compare and contrast the two companies' strategic plans.

■ ETHICS QUESTIONS

12. As the text discussed, businesses are considered by juries to be "deep pockets." Suppose a business found itself in the following circumstances:

   A large energy company comprises an exploration division, a development division, a transportation division, and a marketing division. The transportation division purchased natural gas from the company's own development division, but the majority of the company's purchases were from smaller producers. The contracts called for the transportation division to take and pay for gas, regardless of whether it had sold it. Energy prices dropped dramatically, and the transportation division found that for every ten units of natural gas it was forced to take and pay for, it could sell only one unit. At some point, the transportation division will not be able to continue this uneconomic practice caused by its contracts. The producers will sue the company, which has sufficient assets to pay the judgments. Or, the company could protect its assets by selling the transportation division. The new owner could then threaten to put the transportation company—which has far fewer assets than the whole company—into bankruptcy if the producers do not renegotiate the contracts.

   What do you suggest?

13. In giving instructions to the jury, should judges be allowed to comment on the evidence presented at the trial? Consider the following charge provided to the jury:

   . . . I am going to tell you what I think of the defendant's testimony. You may have noticed, Mr. Foreman and ladies and gentlemen, that the defendant wiped his hands during his testimony. It is rather a curious thing, but that is almost always an indication of lying. Why it should be so, we don't know, but that is a fact. I think that every single word that man said was a lie.

BUSINESS AND THE CONSTITUTION

CHAPTER 5

MANAGER'S LEGAL CHALLENGE

Newspapers are for-profit businesses. Their main source of revenue is advertising. How much a newspaper can charge for advertisements depends on the newspaper's circulation. The number of subscriptions to a paper depend on the publication's quality: news coverage, comics, sports, advertisements, and special features that are of interest to purchasers of the paper.

News editors always pride themselves on good, original reporting of news. A reporter or editor makes a reputation in the news profession by noteworthy, tough, insightful reporting. In many cities, such reporting will include critical stories about businesses or entire professions. While the readers of the newspaper find such stories interesting and such stories help make the reputation of an editor or a reporter, the subjects of critical stories in local papers are not likely to be happy.

To protest critical news coverage, a business can stop advertising in the newspaper. If the business does a lot of advertising in the paper, the income consequences can be significant. For example, the *Daily Spectrum* of St. George, Utah, told readers how to haggle over price when shopping for a car. The auto dealers protested the story, and all quit advertising in the newspaper, which was then forced to apologize for the story. The publisher admits the paper now stays away from offering advice that might anger advertisers. The *News-Tribune* of Duluth, Minnesota, suffered a similar reaction by real estate advertisers, who were angry about a story telling people how to sell their homes without the help of a realtor. The newspaper publicly apologized for the story, and the writer resigned.

In these two instances, no particular business was attacked; the advertisers simply did not like the informative content of the articles. In other cases, after a paper has published a critical story about one business, the business threatens to cut off advertising or actually does so. The advertising manager is told that it is not right for the newspaper to attack a business that supports the newspaper with its advertising business.

Freedom of the press is one of the best-known constitutional rights. Managers of newspapers must decide whether to tell the newspeople not to be concerned about advertising revenues when they do stories, or they must consider the financial position of the newspaper and tell news editors to look for stories that will not upset advertisers—or at least tone down critical stories.

Managers of businesses subject to critical news stories must decide if they will take their lumps or fight back by cutting newspaper advertising. Most managers favor freedom of the press, but when their business is attacked, they believe that the reporter got the facts wrong and are more critical than they otherwise would be. If the paper will not set the record straight, it is legitimate to let the management of the paper know that such reporting will not be tolerated. Managers have to balance the interests of business against the interest of constitutional rights of the free press.

While issues of constitutional law usually do not arise daily for most businesses, managers do have occasion to deal with parts of the Constitution. The Constitution provides safeguards against overzealous law enforcement agencies, especially through the Bill of Rights. These rights are commonly known in their application to individuals accused of crimes, but many of the same issues are at stake in the business world.

BACKGROUND ON THE CONSTITUTION

George Washington presided over a convention in Philadelphia from May to September 1787 at which the Constitution of the United States was drafted. Having been ratified by nine of the thirteen original states, the Constitution became effective in March 1789. It is composed of the preamble and seven articles. The preamble reads:

> We the people of the United States, in order to form a more perfect Union, establish justice, insure domestic tranquility, provide for the common defense, promote the general welfare, and secure the blessings of liberty to ourselves and our posterity, do ordain and establish this Constitution for the United States of America.

The Articles, which are divided into sections, provide for the following:

 I. Composition and powers of Congress
 II. Selection and powers of the president
 III. Creation and powers of the federal judiciary
 IV. Role of the states in the federal system
 V. Methods of amending the Constitution
 VI. Declaring the Constitution to be supreme law of the land
 VII. Method for ratifying the Constitution

The process of amending the Constitution began almost immediately. In 1791, the first ten amendments (*the Bill of Rights*) were ratified by the states after having been approved by the first session of Congress. The Twenty-sixth Amendment, lowering the voting age to eighteen, was ratified in 1971. Numerous other amendments have been proposed, but many, such as the Equal Rights Amendment, have failed. A proposed amendment must pass three-fourths of the state legislatures within a time period specified by Congress, which must pass amendments by a two-thirds vote in the Senate and House. The Constitution is reprinted in Appendix B of this book.

Except for a few rights that are clearly expressed, most of the Constitution is written in general terms or in terms that can be interpreted in different ways. Justice Joseph Story noted this in 1816 in *Martin v. Hunter's Lessee:*

> The constitution unavoidably deals in general language. It did not suit the purposes of the people, in framing this great charter of our liberties, to provide for minute specifications of its powers, or to declare the means by which those powers should be carried into execution. It was foreseen that this would be a perilous and difficult, if not an impracticable, task. The instrument was not intended to provide merely for the exigencies of a few years, but was to endure through a long lapse of ages, the events of which were locked up in the inscrutable purposes of Providence. It could not be foreseen what new changes and modifications of power might be indispensable to effectuate the general objects of the charter; and restrictions and specifications which, at the present, might seem salutary, might, in the end, prove the overthrow of the system itself. Hence its powers are expressed in general terms, leaving to the legislature, from time to time, to adopt its own means to effectuate legitimate objects, and to mold and model the exercise of its powers, as its own wisdom and the public interest should require.

CONSTITUTIONAL BASIS OF REGULATION

The Constitution has a significant effect on the operations of business. While the Constitution applies to everyone in the United States, certain provisions have a much bigger impact on the business community than other parts have. The Supreme Court has reversed itself on major constitutional issues over the years, reading the same words in an opposite manner. While some say this means that the Court is political, others believe that it reflects the Court's response to changes in technology, social values, economic conditions, and political realities.

■ THE COMMERCE CLAUSE

"The Congress shall have Power . . . To regulate Commerce with foreign Nations, and among the several States, and with the Indian Tribes," states Article I, Section 8, of the Constitution. Known as the *commerce clause*, these few words have been interpreted to give Congress the power to enact most of the federal regulation of business discussed in this text. Many other important parts of the Constitution affect business, but the commerce clause is without a doubt the single most important provision.

Defining Commerce among the Several States.   Although most federal regulation of business evolved in the twentieth century, Congress has had broad regulatory powers since the early days of the Republic. In 1824, Chief Justice John Marshall established some of the basic guidelines of the commerce clause in *Gibbons* v. *Ogden.* He held that commerce among the states means *interstate commerce,* that is, "commerce which concerns more States than one." Further, Justice Marshall held, "What is this power? It is the power to regulate; that is, to prescribe the rule by which commerce is to be governed. This power, like all others vested in Congress, is complete in itself, may be exercised to its utmost extent, and acknowledges no limitations other than are prescribed in the Constitution." Congress has exclusive power over regulation of foreign trade.

Interstate Commerce Broadly Defined.   As the Supreme Court has ruled, Congress has broad power to regulate interstate commerce. However, much commerce may be mostly intrastate. That is, most of the activity of a business may be located within a single state, but some part of the business activity may be in other states. The Court has held that such a business may be termed *interstate* for purposes of congressional control. The part of the business that is intrastate is not necessarily exempt from regulation. If part of a business is interstate, all of the intrastate business is considered interstate for regulatory purposes, unless Congress specifies otherwise.

▨ THE NECESSARY AND PROPER CLAUSE

The Constitution specifies a long list of congressional powers, such as collecting taxes, regulating interstate commerce, and providing for national defense. At the end of the list, clause 18 of Article I, Section 8, gives Congress power "to make all Laws which shall be necessary and proper for carrying into Execution the foregoing Powers, and all other Powers vested by this Constitution in the Government of the United States, or in any Department or Officer thereof." This provision is known as the *necessary and proper clause.*

The necessary and proper clause, along with the commerce clause, has been held to provide justification for broad congressional control of commerce. Often the distinction between these two clauses is difficult to find. Essentially, the necessary and proper clause gives Congress power to deal with matters beyond the list of specified federal concerns as long as control of those matters will help Congress be more effective in executing control over specified concerns. For example, the Supreme Court has held that a federal statute limiting tort liabilities arising out of nuclear accidents was necessary and proper to achieving a congressional objective of encouraging the development of privately operated nuclear power plants.

▨ LIMITS ON CONGRESSIONAL POWERS TO REGULATE COMMERCE

Some limits are placed on congressional power to regulate commerce. Intrastate commerce may be subject to federal regulation only to assist in the regulation of interstate commerce. Congressional power is left flexible. Thus, in the 1937 Supreme Court decision *NLRB* v. *Jones & Laughlin Steel Corp.,* the Court said that it is not possible to have a mechanical definition of when a federal law may affect intrastate commerce. Rather, congressional control applies when the intrastate activities being regulated "have such a close and substantial relation to interstate commerce that their control is essential or appropriate to protect that commerce from burdens and obstructions."

Small Business Generally Not Exempt.   Just because the effect of a business on interstate commerce is small does not mean that the business will be exempt from federal regulation. For example, in the 1942 Supreme Court decision *Wickard* v. *Filburn,* federal controls on the production of wheat were held to apply to a small farm in Ohio that produced only 239 bushels of wheat for consumption on the farm. The Court reasoned that Congress intended to regulate the wheat industry. To control wheat prices effectively, there could not be an exemption for small intrastate producers. The Court reasoned that although one farmer would not make a difference, all the small farmers added together would have a substantial impact on the wheat market.

In another decision, *Perez* v. *United States* (1971), the Supreme Court upheld federal regulation of local loan-sharking activities. The Court held that even though the activity may be local, the funds behind local loan sharks are often interstate in origin, since they may come from organized crime, which is a national concern.

In the *Katzenbach* v. *McClung* decision, the Court used the commerce clause to extend nondiscrimination requirements of the 1964 Civil Rights Act to essentially local operations.

KATZENBACH v. McCLUNG

United States Supreme Court
379 U.S. 294, 85 S.Ct. 377 (1964)

Case Background
Ollie's Barbecue was a family-owned restaurant in Birmingham, Alabama. It provided 220 seats for white customers. Although two-thirds of the employees were black, black customers were only allowed to buy food at the take-out window. The government sued the restaurant for violating Title II of the 1964 Civil Rights Act, which prohibits segregation on grounds of race in places of public accommodation. These places include restaurants that offer "to serve interstate travelers or [if] a substantial portion of the food which it serves ... has moved in interstate commerce." Ollie's contended that its customers were local, not interstate travelers. The government noted that about half the food that Ollie's bought had moved in interstate commerce. The district court agreed with the government, and Ollie's appealed to the Supreme Court.

Case Decision
The Court held that the Civil Rights Act was constitutional as applied to public accommodations under the necessary and proper clause. The Court stated that although the amount of food that Ollie's alone bought was small, when all restaurants that discriminated on the basis of race were considered, the illegal direct effect on commerce could be substantial. Further, there was an illegal indirect effect on commerce: because few restaurants would serve blacks, it limited blacks' ability to travel without obstruction, thereby injuring interstate commerce.

Managerial Considerations
The Court rarely limits the constitutional right of Congress to regulate commerce. All business decisions, although they may be individually small, directly or indirectly affect interstate commerce. Management's efforts to escape regulation by being small or operating in a small area are likely to be ineffective. Even if Ollie's had shown that it only bought food grown in Alabama and only served Alabama residents, the Court still could find an indirect effect on commerce. The business of one restaurant affects the business of other restaurants; if Ollie's went out of business, its competitors' businesses would benefit.

■ FEDERAL/STATE REGULATORY RELATIONS

Sometimes states regulate the same business as does Congress. When this occurs, federal regulation takes precedence over state regulation that directly contradicts or reduces the standards imposed by federal law. In addition, states may not enact laws that create an unreasonable burden on interstate commerce. In some areas, such as postal authority, Congress is said to have preempted the power of the states to regulate at all. States may not pass laws in these areas, even if the laws do not contradict federal laws.

State Law May Further Federal Law.   The limits on state regulatory activities have given the Supreme Court problems for years. As federal regulation of business became more common in this century, the Court had to give more weight to congressional action or make it ineffective because of conflicting state rules.

It is clear that if Congress passes a regulation that is constitutional, the states may not pass regulations that would impede the effect of the federal rule. In most cases, the states may add their own rules that strengthen the impact of the federal rules, so long as the rules do not conflict with the intent of the federal law or the desire for unimpeded interstate commerce. However, Congress can prohibit the states from imposing any regulations that differ from the federal standards.

When State Law Impedes Interstate Commerce.   In 1945, the Supreme Court, in *Southern Pacific Co.* v. *Arizona*, had to consider Arizona regulations that for "safety considerations" required trains to be shorter in that state than in other states. Although the Arizona law was not intended to conflict with the federal rules about train length, its effect was to impede interstate commerce. At the Arizona border, trains had to be shortened.

The Supreme Court struck down the Arizona law. Chief Justice Harlan Fiske Stone said, "The decisive question is whether in the circumstances the total effect of the law as a safety measure in reducing accidents and casualties is so slight or problematical as not to outweigh the national interest in keeping interstate commerce free from interferences which seriously impede it. . . ." He noted further, "The matters for ultimate determination here are the nature and extent of the burden which the state regulation of interstate trains, adopted as a safety measure, imposes on interstate commerce, and whether the relative weights of the state and national interests involved are such as to make inapplicable the rule, generally observed, that the free flow of interstate commerce . . . [is] safeguarded by the commerce clause from state interference."

Since there are numerous Supreme Court decisions concerning state and federal regulatory conflicts, the exact boundaries of the constitutional rules are constantly being probed. For example, in 1988, there were three Supreme Court decisions on point:

■ In *Schneidewind* v. *ANR Pipeline Co.*, the Court held that the federal Natural Gas Act prevented the state of Michigan from regulating the issuance of new securities by natural gas companies in interstate commerce. Since state control over the securities could affect the financing of the gas companies, it could influence the companies' ability to do interstate business, which means that the Michigan statute could conflict with the commerce clause.

- In *New York City* v. *Federal Communications Commission*, the right of the Federal Communications Commission (FCC) to preempt existing state and local regulations of cable television was upheld. Since Congress gave the FCC broad regulatory powers, the commission's action was reasonable, since Congress did not prevent it from replacing existing state regulations, and because it acted to prevent conflicting state standards.

- In *Mississippi Power & Light Co.* v. *Mississippi,* the Federal Energy Regulatory Commission (FERC) assigned costs to various utilities of a nuclear power plant that utilities in several states were sharing. The Court held that the costs set by the FERC preempted those that state utility regulators attempted to fix.

The Supreme Court addressed this issue in several cases in 1992:

- In *Chemical Waste Management Inc.* v. *Hunt* the Court held that it was a violation of the Commerce Clause for Alabama to impose a higher fee for hazardous waste generated outside the state than was charged for hazardous waste generated within the state when both were disposed at commercial disposal facilities in Alabama.

- *Fort Gratiot Santitary Landfill Inc.* v. *Michigan Department of Natural Resources* challenged a Michigan law prohibiting private landfill operators from accepting solid waste from another county, state, or country unless given permission by the county in which the landfill was located. The Court struck down this law as a violation of the Commerce Clause.

- In *Morales* v. *Trans World Airlines Inc.* the Court held that the Airline Deregulation Act of 1978 prohibits the states from regulating airline rates, routes, or services. Therefore, state attorneys general may not sue the airlines under state consumer protection statutes even though they contend that airline fare advertising is injuring consumers.

▉ THE CONTRACT CLAUSE

Article I, Section 10, clause 1, of the Constitution appears to be quite simple: "No State shall . . . pass any . . . Law impairing the Obligation of Contracts. . . ." Generally, in applying the *contract clause,* the Court has attempted to accommodate both the legitimate interests of the contracting parties and the need of the state to pass rules in the public interest.

One important decision is *United States Trust Co. of New York* v. *New Jersey* (1977). The Port Authority of New York and New Jersey was established in 1921 to improve transportation facilities connected with the port of New York. Bonds were sold to private investors to finance construction. To enhance the marketability of its bonds, the Port Authority in 1962 placed a ceiling on the amount of mass transit deficits it could finance at any time. This decision was backed by statutes passed by New York and New Jersey.

In 1974, the mass transit system was in financial trouble. To provide the increase in funding needed to keep the system in operation and to expand it, the states repealed the 1962 debt limits. Because of the increased uncertainty of the financial viability of the system, the value of bonds sold before 1974 dropped. The bondholders sued the states, claiming that the repeal of the 1962 bond agreement was a violation of the contract clause of the Constitution. The Supreme Court agreed with the bondholders. The repeal in 1974 of the 1962 statute broke a contractual obligation.

The Court noted that in some cases, contractual obligations could be impaired by the states. "The Contract Clause does not require a State to adhere to a contract that surrenders an essential attribute of its sovereignty." That is, a state legislature cannot bargain away state police powers and other essential powers. A contract may be broken by the states if it is reasonable and necessary to serve an important public purpose. In this case, since the states knew of the impending mass transit problems, they had time to act responsibly without impairing the rights of existing bondholders.

■ THE TAXING POWER

Congress is given the power to "lay and collect Taxes, Duties, Imposts and Excises" by Article I, Section 8, clause 1, of the Constitution. Although this text does not investigate federal taxation (since that is a complex topic requiring specialized courses), it should be remembered that taxation can be a potent tool of regulation. Taxes can be used for more than simply raising revenue. They can be used to deter and to punish certain behavior. For example, a tax may be tied to a requirement to keep detailed records about sales subject to the tax. In this manner, goods such as explosives, firearms, drugs, and liquors may be kept under federal supervision.

Federal Taxation Schemes.   The Supreme Court rarely questions federal taxing schemes. In 1937, the Court noted in *Sonzinsky* v. *United States,* "Inquiry into the hidden motives which may move Congress to exercise a power constitutionally conferred upon it is beyond the competency of courts. . . . We are not free to speculate as to the motives which moved Congress to impose it, or as to the extent to which it may operate to restrict the activities taxed. As it is not attended by offensive regulation, and since it operates as a tax, it is within the taxing power."

The Court has upheld taxes on illegal gambling, narcotics, and marijuana. This makes it easier for the government to prosecute those involved in illegal activities. If income from illegal activities is reported, such as by reporting income from cocaine sales, the government has evidence of illegal drug dealing. If the income from cocaine deals or other illegal activities is not reported and the money is found, the tax laws have been violated. It is not uncommon for big-time criminals to be convicted for tax fraud—they are not caught doing illegal deals but are caught failing to report the income from their deals. In *United States* v. *Kahriger* (1953), the Court held, "It is axiomatic that the power of Congress to tax is extensive and sometimes falls with crushing effect on businesses deemed unessential or inimical to the public welfare, or where, as in dealings with narcotics, the collection of the tax also is difficult."

State Taxes May Not Impede International Commerce.   Since the Constitution gives Congress the power to regulate international trade, the states may not interfere with international commerce. The Supreme Court emphasized this restriction in the 1979 decision *Japan Line, Ltd.* v. *County of*

Los Angeles. Several California cities and counties imposed a property tax on cargo shipping containers owned by Japanese companies. The containers were used only in international commerce on Japanese ships. The taxes in California were levied on the presence of the containers in the state during loading and unloading. The Supreme Court held the tax to be unconstitutional. The commerce clause reserves to Congress the power over foreign commerce. Even in the absence of congressional action, the states may not tax foreign trade. Only the federal government may speak on foreign trade and tax matters.

State Taxes May Not Impede Interstate Commerce.   Since most commerce is interstate, what can the states tax? The intent of the Constitution is to protect interstate commerce from impediments established by state taxes. As the Court noted in the 1959 decision *Northwestern States Portland Cement Co.* v. *Minnesota:* ''. . . a State 'cannot impose taxes upon persons passing through the state or coming into it merely for a temporary purpose'. . . . Moreover, it is beyond dispute that a State may not lay a tax on the 'privilege' of engaging in interstate commerce. . . . Nor may a State impose a tax which discriminates against interstate commerce either by providing a direct commercial advantage to local business . . . or by subjecting interstate commerce to the burden of 'multiple taxation.' . . . Such impositions have been stricken because the States, under the Commerce Clause, are not allowed 'one single tax-dollar worth of direct interference with the free flow of commerce.' ''

Consider the following cases in which the Supreme Court reviewed state taxing schemes to decide whether they interfered with interstate commerce:

- The state of Hawaii imposed a tax on all alcoholic beverages except for a local product. The Court struck this down in 1984, holding that the tax imposed on alcoholic products had to be the same regardless of origin.

- Pennsylvania imposed an annual tax on out-of-state trucks that carried goods through the state. The tax was not imposed on trucks registered in Pennsylvania, because those trucks paid an annual registration fee. The Court struck this down in 1987 as a violation of the commerce clause because it imposed a heavier tax burden on out-of-state businesses engaged in interstate commerce in Pennsylvania than it did on Pennsylvania businesses engaged in interstate commerce.

- Illinois imposes a 5 percent tax on all long-distance calls to or from the state. If a taxpayer can show that another state has billed the call, the Illinois tax will be refunded. This tax was held by the Supreme Court not to violate the commerce clause in *Goldberg* v. *Sweet* (1989) because it satisfies a four-part test:

1. The tax applies to an activity having a substantial nexus within the state.

2. The tax is fairly apportioned.

3. The tax does not discriminate against interstate commerce, compared to intrastate commerce.

4. The tax is fairly related to services that the state provides to the benefit of taxpayers.

■ Oklahoma required coal-burning power plants in the state to burn at least 10 percent Oklahoma-mined coal. Wyoming challenged the regulation, because it meant less Wyoming coal was sold to Oklahoma. The Court held, in *Wyoming* v. *Oklahoma* (1992), that the Oklahoma law was discriminatory on its face and interfered with interstate commerce.

Apportioning State Tax Burden. The Court in *Northwestern States* went on to note that the income of businesses may be taxed by the states—so long as the proceeds are fairly apportioned among the states—using formulas that account for the intrastate share of interstate commerce. A tax on income "from interstate commerce, as distinguished from a tax on the privilege of engaging in interstate commerce, does not conflict with the Commerce Clause. . . ." For example, in 1981, the Supreme Court struck down a tax imposed by the state of Louisiana on natural gas that passed through the state for sale in other states. The tax was held to be an illegal restraint on interstate commerce, not a tax on the share of business that occurred in the state.

Apportionment generates substantial litigation because there are many difficult issues. Firms often have manufacturing and distribution systems that involve activities in numerous states. It is nearly impossible to know how to assign the various costs to the different portions of an operation—different accounting techniques will produce different legitimate results. A state may tax the portion of a business that occurs within its borders. The federal courts are concerned not with the level of taxation but with whether the intent or effect of a tax is to impose greater burdens on transactions that cross state lines than on those that occur entirely within a state.

BUSINESS AND FREE SPEECH ■■■■■■■

The First Amendment restricts congressional encroachment on freedom of speech: "Congress shall make no law . . . abridging the freedom of speech. . . ." Since this right is not absolute—it will not protect someone who falsely shouts "fire" in a theatre and causes panic—the Supreme Court has to define what speech may be regulated.

People have debated whether commercial speech, advertisements, and political statements by corporations, such as statements about public issues, deserve the same freedoms as political speech by private citizens. Political speech is generally provided First Amendment protection. While it is clear that citizens have very broad rights of free speech, some people contend that commercial speech, since it is for profit, does not deserve the same protections as political speech. Others say it does deserve the same freedoms.

The Constitution did not distinguish between the two kinds of speech. In both cases, the parties—private or public—are usually trying to convince some group of people about something—to buy soap, to support a political program, or to vote for a politician. In recent years, the Supreme Court has helped resolve the issue in several important cases that have tended to extend First Amendment protection to commercial speech.

■ POLITICAL SPEECH BY CORPORATIONS

First National Bank of Boston v. *Bellotti* (1978) provided the Supreme Court the opportunity to address the issue of *political speech* by corporations and

First Amendment freedoms. A Massachusetts criminal statute prohibited corporations from making contributions or expenditures "for the purpose of . . . influencing or affecting the vote on any question submitted to the voters, other than one materially affecting any of the property, business or assets of the corporation." The First National Bank of Boston wished to make contributions to help defeat a referendum proposition to amend the Massachusetts Constitution.

The U.S. Supreme Court struck down the statute: "The speech proposed by appellants is at the heart of the First Amendment's protection. The freedom of speech . . . guaranteed by the Constitution embraces at the least the liberty to discuss publicly and truthfully all matters of public concern without previous restraint or fear of subsequent punishment. . . ." The Court could "find no support in the First or Fourteenth Amendments . . . for the proposition that speech that otherwise would be within the protection of the First Amendment loses that protection simply because its source is a corporation that cannot prove, to the satisfaction of a court, a material effect on its business or property. . . . it amounts to an impermissible legislative prohibition of speech based on the identity of the interests that spokesmen may represent in public debate over controversial issues. . . ."

The Court reemphasized the right of free speech regarding political issues on the part of business in the *Consolidated Edison Co.* v. *Public Service Commission* decision.

CONSOLIDATED EDISON CO. v. PUBLIC SERVICE COMMISSION OF NEW YORK

United States Supreme Court
447 U.S. 530, 100 S.Ct. 2326 (1980)

Case Background
Consolidated Edison inserted with the monthly utilities bill sent to its customers a flyer in support of nuclear power. The Public Service Commission, which regulates utilities in New York, ruled that utilities could not mail controversial or political material to customers because they are a captive audience. The Supreme Court was asked to determine whether the First Amendment of the Constitution is violated by this kind of restriction.

Case Decision
The Court held that the regulation suppressing the mailing of inserts with bills to customers directly infringes on the First Amendment. The Court stated that such regulations must be "(1) a reasonable time, place, or manner restriction, (2) a permissible subject-matter regulation, or (3) a narrowly tailored means of serving a compelling state interest." The regulation here fails the tests—it is a broad restriction on public discussion of a major topic. If customers do not want to read the insert, they can throw it away.

Managerial Considerations
Regulated or not, businesses—and their managers—have wide latitude to engage in political debates. The management of companies that are regulated must think of the strategic implications—can their public pronouncements irritate the regulators in some way that could worsen their political position? Similarly, the management of unregulated companies must consider the impact of being affiliated with controversial views.

If management takes a position on an issue that customers think is wrong, customers may boycott the company. The managers must decide whether the right to speak out as a commercial establishment outweighs the possible loss of profits. Customers who are unconcerned with the issue involved may wonder whether the company management is paying too little attention to business and too much attention to political issues. Because of such problems, some companies have decided that neither the company nor senior managers may take positions on controversial issues.

In the 1987 decision *Board of Airport Commissioners of Los Angeles* v. *Jews for Jesus* the Supreme Court held that complete prohibitions on speech in commercial establishments will not be allowed by the First Amendment. The Court held that the airport authority could not impose an outright ban on all political and other controversial speech in the Los Angeles International Airport. However, the Court indicated, as in *Consolidated Edison,* that some restrictions may be allowed but will be reviewed for their reasonableness.

An example of a reasonable restriction allowed to stand comes from the 1990 decision *Austin* v. *Michigan Chamber of Commerce.* The Supreme Court upheld a Michigan statute (and similar ones in twenty other states) that prohibits the use of general corporate money for supporting political candidates. Rather, political expenditures must come from corporate monies that have been set aside for specific political purposes. The compelling government interest that allows this regulation is the desire to eliminate distortions in the political process caused by unregulated expenditures out of unrestricted corporate treasuries.

■ COMMERCIAL SPEECH

Drawing the line between *commercial speech,* such as advertising a product for sale, and *political speech* by a corporation is difficult. In many cases, the intent is the same: to increase profits. In one case, it is done by trying to convince people to buy a product. In another case, it is done by trying to influence governmental policy in a way that will favor the business or to reduce the prospects of passage of a law that would hurt the business. The Supreme Court holds that both commercial speech and political speech by business are protected.

In 1980, in *Central Hudson Gas & Electric Corp.* v. *Public Service Commission of New York,* the Court addressed the issue of controls on commercial speech and discussed a four-part test that must be met to justify restrictions on commercial speech.

■ CENTRAL HUDSON GAS & ELECTRIC CORP. v. PUBLIC SERVICE COMMISSION OF NEW YORK

United States Supreme Court
447 U.S. 557, 100 S.Ct. 2343 (1980)

Case Background
Because of the energy crisis of the 1970s, the Public Service Commission of New York ordered all utilities to cease all advertising that promoted the use of electricity. The Commission declared that such advertising was contrary to the national policy of conserving energy. The Commission ruled that it would review any proposed advertising that would encourage energy conservation. Central Hudson

Gas and Electric appealed this regulatory scheme to the Supreme Court.

Case Decision
The Court struck down this restriction on commercial speech as a violation of the First Amendment rights of utility companies to distribute information and of consumers to receive such information. The speech here concerns a lawful activity and does not mislead. It is irrelevant that the utility company is in a noncompetitive market; even monop-

(continued)

olists have constitutional guarantees regarding commercial speech. While energy conservation may be vital to the public interest, it does not justify this violation of the First Amendment. When such regulations are challenged, the state bears the burden of justifying the restriction on speech.

Managerial Considerations
The regulatory agency reached too far in this case. Had the agency not claimed the right to censor ads before their publication but had attempted only to limit ads that encouraged more electricity use while there was a national energy crisis, the decision would have been much closer. If the public interest is found to overwhelm the right of free commercial speech, then limited restrictions may be imposed on companies and their managers. There is little doubt that regulated industries, especially monopolies like utilities, can face more restrictions on commercial speech than can firms in highly competitive industries.

Speech and Competition.   Part of the push for fewer restrictions on commercial speech came with the enforcement of the antitrust laws. In some cases, restrictions were put on commercial speech to limit competition. Such restrictions have not been viewed favorably in recent years.

In 1975, in *Bigelow* v. *Virginia*, the Supreme Court reversed a conviction of a Virginia newspaper editor who published ads about the availability of low-cost abortions in New York City. A Virginia law prohibited publications from encouraging abortions. The Court held that speech that is related to the marketplace of products or services is not valueless in the marketplace of ideas.

The following year, in *Virginia State Board of Pharmacy* v. *Virginia Citizens Consumer Council,* the Court struck down a Virginia law prohibiting the advertising of prices of prescription drugs. Justice Blackmun held, "It is clear . . . that speech does not lose its First Amendment protection because money is spent . . . as in a paid advertisement. . . ." The Board of Pharmacy argued that the restrictions on advertising were needed to protect the public from their ignorance about drugs. The Court responded, "There is, of course, an alternative to this highly paternalistic approach (of prohibiting advertising of drug prices). That alternative is to assume that this information is not in itself harmful, that people will perceive their own best interests if only they are well enough informed, and that the best means to that end is to open the channels of communication rather than to close them."

The Supreme Court has ruled in several cases that First Amendment rights may be violated by restrictions on advertising of professional services, such as those offered by lawyers. Most recently, in *Shapero* v. *Kentucky Bar Association* (1989), the Court held that the Kentucky Bar Association violated the First Amendment by prohibiting lawyers from soliciting business by sending truthful and nondeceptive letters to potential clients known to face particular legal problems. If an attorney engages in misleading or deceptive solicitation practices, the attorney may be punished by the bar for doing so, but the bar may not act as a censor for commercial speech.

Freedom To Criticize.   Freedom of speech can mean that a business will find itself criticized in a commercial setting. The Supreme Court upheld this right in the 1984 decision *Bose Corp.* v. *Consumers Union.* Consumers Union published a report in *Consumer Reports* that was critical of the quality of a Bose stereo speaker. Bose sued, claiming product disparagement.

The Supreme Court held that there must be actual malice for a public figure, such as a corporation selling products, to recover damages for a defamatory falsehood. Since actual malice was not shown in this case, the suit was dismissed. Speaking for the majority, Justice Stevens said: "The First Amendment presupposes that the freedom to speak one's mind is not only an aspect of individual liberty—and thus a good unto itself—but also is essential to the common quest for truth and the vitality of society as a whole. Under our Constitution 'there is no such thing as a false idea. However pernicious an opinion may seem, we depend for its correction not on the conscience of judges and juries but on the competition of other ideas.' " Nevertheless, libelous speech is limited by the First Amendment, but the standard is strong in the case of most commercial speech.

The First Amendment right to criticize is not the right to make false statements that injure others. As the Supreme Court noted in the 1990 decision *Milkovich* v. *Lorain Journal Co.*, a business such as a newspaper is not protected by the First Amendment when it makes false statements that defame someone. If a reasonable person can conclude that there is injury to reputation, it does not matter whether the false information is stated as an opinion or as fact. The Court also held in *Cohen* v. *Cowles Media Co.* (1991) that the First Amendment does not shield a newspaper from liability for publishing the identity of a news source in breach of a promise of confidentiality. Although in this case the information printed was true, revealing the source injured the reputation of the person who gave the story in confidence to the newspaper.

UNREASONABLE SEARCH AND SEIZURE

The Fourth Amendment reads: "The right of the people to be secure in their persons, houses, papers, and effects, against unreasonable searches and seizures, shall not be violated, and no Warrants shall issue, but upon probable cause. . . ." Most cases arising under this amendment are criminal and concern the proper method of search and seizure of suspected criminals and evidence. However, there have been a number of cases brought under the Fourth Amendment in response to the methods used by regulatory agencies executing their functions.

In Fourth Amendment cases asking whether proper search and seizure procedures were used, the Supreme Court consistently refers to the 1968 decision *Katz* v. *United States*, which said that in such cases the premier issue is whether a person has a constitutionally protected reasonable expectation of privacy. Essentially, closed places, such as homes and businesses, are not subject to random police searches.

■ LIMITATIONS ON BUSINESS SEARCHES AND INSPECTIONS

If a government inspector shows up at a business and asks to inspect the premises or search company records for some purpose related to the laws being enforced by the inspector's agency, does the business have to allow admission? Not without a warrant, the Supreme Court held in *Marshall* v.

Barlow's, Inc. (1978). In that decision, an inspector for the Occupational Safety and Health Administration (OSHA) had arrived at Barlow's plant in Pocatello, Idaho, and asked to search the work areas. Barlow asked the inspector whether he had a warrant. Since the inspector did not, Barlow refused him admission to the plant.

OSHA asked the Court to require businesses to admit inspectors to conduct warrantless searches. The Court refused, saying that warrantless searches are generally unreasonable and that this rule applies to commercial premises as well as homes. The government argued that if inspectors had to obtain warrants, businesses would have time to hide safety and health defects on work sites. The Court responded: "We are unconvinced . . . that requiring warrants to inspect will impose serious burdens on the inspection system or the courts, will prevent inspections necessary to enforce the statute, or will make them less effective. In the first place the great majority of businessmen can be expected in normal course to consent to inspection without warrant; the Secretary (of Labor) has not brought to this Court's attention any widespread pattern of refusal . . . ." As the Court predicted, in fact, most businesses do allow warrantless searches; the requirement to obtain a warrant when demanded has not become burdensome or retarded law enforcement.

■ RESTRICTIONS ON THE USE OF EVIDENCE COLLECTED

When evidence is collected by an inspector, with or without a warrant, the evidence is to be used for the purposes intended. The government cannot abuse the evidence by passing it around to various federal agencies for their inspection or releasing it to the public. Hence, protections of the constitutional rights of businesses have remained similar to those of individuals in this regard.

Evidence gathered by enforcement officials in a manner that violates Fourth Amendment rights regarding search and seizure may not be used in prosecution under the exclusionary rule. That is, illegally obtained evidence is excluded from use in legal proceedings.

CONSTITUTIONAL LAW IN FOREIGN JURISDICTIONS | INTERNATIONAL ASPECTS

The United Kingdom, unlike the United States and most other nations, does not have a written constitution, yet it has a body of constitutional law. The courts there recognize three kinds of rules: statutory law, case law, and custom or constitutional convention. Statutory law, which comes from Parliament, is potentially unlimited in scope.

The courts may not strike down statutes because of constitutional restrictions, as may U.S. courts. There is no official separation of powers; the courts in the U.K. cannot use constitutional custom to overrule parliamentary law. By custom, the current monarch (Queen Elizabeth) cannot veto laws, but prior monarchs did have such authority.

The United Kingdom is clearly a democratic nation with a high regard for civil liberties. While that nation works well without a formal constitution, it was that

(continued)

lack of fixed constitutional standards that convinced the founders of the United States that a written constitution was desirable. In the United Kingdom, constitutional customs change over time, just as the U.S. Supreme Court infers different standards at different times from the Constitution, often reflecting changes in social values and economic realities.

It should be remembered that U.S. constitutional rights do not protect American citizens if they are subject to legal action in another nation. Similarly, U.S. constitutional rights do not always extend to noncitizens not in the United States. The Supreme Court, in *U.S.* v. *Verdugo-Urquidez* (1990), held that the Fourth Amendment does not apply to a warrantless search and seizure by U.S. agents of property located outside the United States that is owned by a non-U.S. citizen. The Amendment protects people in the United States against arbitrary action by the government; it does not restrain the federal government's actions against aliens outside American territory.

SELF-INCRIMINATION

The Fifth Amendment protects individuals against self-incrimination: "No person shall be . . . compelled in any criminal case to be a witness against himself." This constitutional protection applies to persons, not to corporations. Although corporate executives cannot be made to testify against themselves, business records that might incriminate the corporation (and executives) must be produced, since such records are not protected by the Fifth Amendment.

A number of businesses have contested fines imposed by an agency resulting from this mandatory self-reporting of information. They argue that the reporting of self-incriminating evidence violates the Fifth Amendment. Self-incrimination in criminal cases cannot be required, but many regulatory statutes impose civil penalties, which do not receive the same level of constitutional protection.

The Supreme Court discussed an interesting twist on self-incrimination in the 1988 decision *John Doe* v. *U.S.*, where Doe was the target of a federal investigation into suspected illegal manipulation of oil cargo and failure to report income from the deal. Doe refused to answer questions about the existence or location of foreign bank accounts he owned. The Court held that Doe could be required to sign a form authorizing the foreign bank to release his records to the U.S. government, even though the records could be incriminating. Doe has the right to refuse to testify about the records but cannot refuse to cooperate in producing testimony.

JUST COMPENSATION

The Fifth Amendment states, ". . . nor shall private property be taken for public use, without just compensation." Termed the *just compensation* or *takings clause,* its traditional primary use was to require governments to pay for property the government required someone to sell because public officials determined that the property should be used for some specific purpose, such as a highway or a military base.

The Supreme Court appears to have broadened the application of the just compensation clause by two 1987 decisions. Before these decisions, the clause had not changed much in interpretation for many years. Local governments, where most land use requirements are determined, had broad powers to change zoning and land use requirements without paying compensation, even though the value of the land may be affected by the change. This power has been restricted by the *First English* decision.

FIRST ENGLISH EVANGELICAL LUTHERAN CHURCH OF GLENDALE v. LOS ANGELES COUNTY

United States Supreme Court
482 U.S. 304, 107 S.Ct. 2378 (1987)

Case Background
The church owned a retreat center and recreational area for disabled children on twenty-one acres in a rural canyon. In 1977, when the center was twenty years old, a forest fire upstream from the camp destroyed a watershed. Consequently, rains caused a flood that destroyed the camp buildings in 1978. To protect public health and safety, the county then passed a temporary ordinance prohibiting any building in the area. Six years later, the church had made no progress in attempting to force the county to let them rebuild, buy the property from them, or take some other concrete action. The California Supreme Court upheld the right of the county to let the matter drag on unresolved for years, leaving the future of the property in question. The church appealed to the U.S. Supreme Court.

Case Decision
The U.S. Supreme Court reversed the California court's decision, holding that it is unreasonable for a governmental body to deprive property owners of the use or value of their property for an unreasonably long time. The just compensation clause of the Fifth Amendment requires that the government pay the landowner for the value of the use of the land during such a time, because a taking of property has occurred. The government had two reasonable options: it could have used eminent domain and forced the church to sell the property to the government or to some other owner for a particular use, or it could have passed new ordinances in a timely fashion regarding building standards to allow the property owner to rebuild.

Managerial Considerations
This decision and the companion decision discussed below are possible landmarks in the theory of taking. Many challenges are now in the courts to see how these decisions will be applied and to see whether the Supreme Court will elaborate on what constitutes a taking that requires just compensation.

Businesses frequently are required to stop production or construction because of a new regulation. While governments have broad regulatory powers, the Supreme Court is making governments and agencies more conscious of the time value of property. Unreasonable delays or forced changes in plans may allow managers to sue for damages, a remedy that, before these cases, was not very promising. Clear records of dealings with government agencies over time may be important evidence in showing that a business suffered an unreasonable burden because of governmental foot dragging.

The 1987 Supreme Court decision *Nollan* v. *California Coastal Commission* also addressed compensation in land use rules. The Nollans wished to tear down their house and build a larger one on their beach property in Ventura, California. The California Coastal Commission told the Nollans that their permit would be granted only if they agreed to allow the public an easement (access) to pass across their beach. The historic high tide line determines the lot's oceanside boundary. The Coastal Commission wanted the public to have the right to walk across what had been the Nollans's backyard—above the high tide line—along the beach. This was a common requirement that had been imposed for several years whenever private property owners requested a building permit.

The Supreme Court reversed the decision of the California Court of Appeals by holding that the takings clause of the Fifth Amendment had been violated. The state could not tie a rebuilding permit to an easement that it would have to pay for if it simply imposed the easement. "California is free to advance its 'comprehensive program,' if it wishes [of increased beach access] by using its power of eminent domain for this 'public purpose,' but if it wants an easement across the Nollans' property, it must pay for it."

RIGHT TO TRIAL

The Sixth Amendment addresses the right of persons to trial by jury in criminal cases. The Seventh Amendment provides for the right to jury trial in common law cases. Although the law is well established about the constitutional right to jury trial in criminal and common law cases, what about cases in which a business is charged with a violation of a statute that regulates it? If the charge is criminal, the right to request a jury trial remains.

What if the charge is only civil? The Supreme Court addressed that question in 1987 in *Tull* v. *United States*. Tull, a real estate developer, was charged by the federal government with violating the Clean Water Act. The Act authorizes injunctive relief against violators (such as a court order to stop work on the land) and subjects violators to a civil penalty not to exceed $10,000 per day. The government sued Tull, charging violations of the Clean Water Act with respect to damage to wetlands. The government sought an injunction to force Tull to stop work and asked for $23 million in civil penalties. Tull requested a jury trial, which was denied by the federal district court. At the bench trial, Tull did not deny he lacked the required permits or dumped fill dirt where the government claimed. He did claim, however, that because the land in question was not wetland covered by the statute, he was not liable. The district court held that the lands were wetlands and ordered Tull to restore the lands to their original condition and to pay several hundred thousand dollars in civil penalties.

On appeal, the Supreme Court ruled that Tull was due a jury trial under the Seventh Amendment with respect to the issue of whether he was liable because the lands were wetlands. If the only question was that of imposing civil penalties, no right to jury trial existed. Since civil penalties are imposed by statute, there is no constitutional right to trial on such matters. There is a right to jury trial on the question of liability of the defendant only when there is the "substance of the common-law right of trial by jury." That is, when the legal issue involved is close to that of a common law right, jury trial rights exist. If the legal issue is one of statutory law that may impose only civil penalties, there is no right to jury trial to determine liability.

EXCESSIVE FINES

The Eighth Amendment is most famous for its restriction on *cruel and unusual punishments*, but it also holds that *no excessive fines* may be imposed. Since large jury awards have become more common in the past two decades, as we will see in the chapters on torts and products liability, defendants have looked to see whether the Eighth Amendment offers protection against huge awards.

A jury awarded the plaintiff in a tort suit $51,146 in compensatory damages and $6 million in punitive damages. The defendant appealed to the Supreme Court, claiming the punitive damages violated the Eighth Amendment. In 1989, in *Browning-Ferris Industries* v. *Kelco Disposal*, the Court held that the excessive fines clause does not apply to punitive damage awards in cases between private parties. Reaching back as far as the Magna Carta, the Court found that the purpose of the Eighth Amendment was to restrict the potential for governmental abuse of prosecutorial power by the imposition of excessive fines. The issue of high punitive damages, which is of great concern to many businesses, was next attacked as a violation of the Fourteenth Amendment, as we see below.

DUE PROCESS

The Fourteenth Amendment holds, in part, "No state shall . . . deprive any person of life, liberty, or property, without due process of law; nor deny to any person within its jurisdiction the equal protection of the laws." This amendment, called the *due process clause*, has been a powerful device for extending federal constitutional guarantees to the states and preventing states from passing laws that diminish any federal constitutional protections.

Does the Fourteenth Amendment's due process clause act as a check on unlimited jury discretion to award punitive damages in the absence of any express statutory limit? The Supreme Court considered this issue in the 1991 decision *Pacific Mutual Life Insurance* v. *Haslip*.

PACIFIC MUTUAL LIFE INSURANCE CO. v. HASLIP

United States Supreme Court,
499 U.S. _____ , 111 S.Ct. 1032 (1991)

Case Background
An employer attempted to buy life and health insurance for its employees from an agent, Ruffin, who sold insurance for a number of companies, including Pacific Mutual. Although Pacific Mutual does not sell health insurance, Ruffin falsely told the employer that it did through Union Fidelity, which he claimed was a subsidiary of Pacific Mutual. The agent

"sold" health insurance to the employer but never told either insurance company of the alleged sale, and he pocketed the insurance premiums. When Clara Haslip and other employees filed claims, they were told by the insurance company that there was no policy and they had to pay for the medical care themselves. The employees sued Pacific Mutual and Ruffin for fraud. Haslip was awarded $1.04 million dollars in compensatory and punitive damages—a sum four times what she requested and 200 times her medical
(continued)

expenses. Pacific Mutual appealed, noting that the law in Alabama, where the case occurred, placed no restrictions on what juries could award when they decide to make the defendant pay punitive damages. Pacific Mutual claimed this was unbridled jury discretion and thus violated due process.

Case Decision
The Court concluded that Pacific Mutual's due process rights had not been violated either by the discretion of the jury in imposing punitive damages or by the size of the award. The Court made the following points:

1. We have carefully reviewed the instructions to the jury. By these instructions, the trial court expressly described for the jury the purpose of punitive damages, namely, "not to compensate the plaintiff for any injury "but" to punish the defendant". . . .
2. Before the trial in this case took place, the Supreme Court of Alabama had established post-trial procedures for scrutinizing punitive damages. . . .
3. By its review of punitive awards, the Alabama Supreme Court provides an additional check on the jury's or trial court's discretion. . . .

Pacific Mutual thus had the benefit of the full panoply of Alabama's procedural protections. . . . While the monetary comparisons [between the actual damages and the sum awarded] are wide and, indeed, may be close to the line,

the award here did not lack objective criteria. We conclude, after careful consideration, that in this case it does not cross the line into the area of constitutional impropriety.

Managerial Considerations
Pacific Mutual argued that it was not aware that Ruffin sold the nonexistent health policy or that he was stealing premiums until this all came to light. While Ruffin was an agent for Pacific Mutual, his actions violated his contract with them. Pacific Mutual's claim that it should be dismissed from the suit was rejected by all courts because Ruffin had authority to enter into contracts on Pacific Mutual's behalf. The employer and employees who bought the bogus health insurance policies had no reason to know that Ruffin was lying, since Ruffin was an agent for Pacific Mutual.

Since companies know that some agents and employees may try to cheat them, a company must take steps to protect itself and its customers against such instances. The likelihood of this event might have been reduced had Pacific required all premium payments to be sent to the parent company directly so that agents did not collect checks. Perhaps policies could state on them in a conspicuous place that they are not effective without direct home office approval. In other words, managers must think of how to arrange affairs so as to minimize the likelihood of destructive lawsuits such as this one.

While it was previously noted that foreigners cannot ask for U.S. constitutional protection for events that happen outside the United States, when foreign parties are made subject to litigation in the United States, they are protected. This point is made in the *Asahi Metal* decision, which concerns a foreign business's being sued in California.

ASAHI METAL INDUSTRY CO. v. SUPERIOR COURT OF CALIFORNIA

United States Supreme Court
480 U.S. 102, 107 S.Ct. 1026 (1987)

Case Background
Asahi, a Japanese company, did business worldwide but only a trivial amount in California. It sold component parts to a Taiwanese manufacturer, who sold its finished products in California. The Taiwanese company (Cheng Shin) was sued in California in a product liability suit. It settled the case but sued Asahi in California for indemnity. Asahi argued that California courts could not exercise jurisdiction over Asahi and force it to appear in court in this matter. The California Supreme Court held that the fact that some of

Asahi's parts ended up in a product in commerce in California made Asahi subject to jurisdiction under California's long-arm statute. Asahi appealed to the U.S. Supreme Court.

Case Decision
The Supreme Court reversed the California high court and ordered the case by the Taiwanese company against Asahi dismissed. The due process clause of the Fourteenth Amendment prohibits state courts from exercising jurisdiction under circumstances that would violate "traditional notions of fair play and substantial justice." Because the

(continued)

state had little interest in the matter and because the case placed high costs on the defendant, the case could not be forced to proceed.

Managerial Considerations

This case does not indicate that American companies that sell foreign products may be able to escape responsibility for any problems caused by their products. The American seller, even if only a retailer, may well be held responsible to the consumer for damages if the producer cannot be reached. Hence, given the difficulties of getting a foreign company into court in the United States, management should consider whether the foreign company has sufficient assets and business ties to the United States to give it an incentive to defend itself and the resources to pay possible damages. A U.S. distributor that deals with a foreign company that has no assets in the United States and places low value on future business in the United States may be stuck with the full bill in case of a product defect or some other problem. Suing foreign producers in their home courts for damages incurred in the United States is generally very difficult. In addition, note that many U.S. retailers and distributors now require proof of insurance before they will accept foreign manufactured products.

Due process, on one hand, concerns the fairness of law enforcement procedures, as in the *Asahi* decision. The substance of due process, however, concerns the content of legislation. All laws must be constitutional so as not to violate the due process clause. If a law restricts a fundamental constitutional right, there must be a compelling interest for it. As we have seen already, when it comes to the regulation of business, most regulations will meet constitutionality tests.

The fact that due process rights are not as strong in business matters as in the personal sphere can be seen in the 1988 Supreme Court decision *Federal Deposit Insurance Corp.* v. *Mallen*. Under a federal statute, the Federal Deposit Insurance Corp. (FDIC) suspended Mallen from his job as president of a bank when he was indicted for conspiracy to commit mail fraud. The law allowed such suspensions to protect public confidence in banks. Mallen claimed that his due process rights meant that he should have been allowed a hearing by the FDIC before his suspension, that he should have been allowed a hearing immediately after the suspension, and that he should have been allowed to give oral testimony at a hearing.

The Court held that he had no such rights. The Court stated that the FDIC, acting under the statute, behaved properly and did not have to allow a hearing before the suspension, did not have to accept any oral testimony if written testimony was sufficient, and only had to have a hearing within the ninety days set by the statute. Clearly, fewer substantive guarantees exist under the Constitution for businesses than for individuals.

EQUAL PROTECTION

The Fourteenth Amendment, as noted above, says that "No state shall . . . deny . . . the equal protection of the laws." This *equal protection clause*, often is closely tied to the due process clause. The equal protection clause arose in two cases involving business and state governments.

In 1988, in *Pennell* v. *City of San Jose*, the Supreme Court upheld the San Jose rent control ordinance. That ordinance limited rent increases to a maximum of 8 percent per year, unless the tenant objected, in which case there was a hearing to determine whether a rent increase was justified. The Court held that this did not violate the taking clause or the due process clause. The rent controls also did not violate the equal protection clause, because they met the test of being "rationally related to a legitimate state interest." The controls exist to protect the interests of tenants, which is a legitimate concern of the state, so they may stand.

In the 1989 decision *Allegheny Pittsburgh Coal Co.* v. *County Commission of Webster County,* the Supreme Court struck down certain features of the West Virginia property tax system as violating the equal protection clause. West Virginia counties would assess real property taxes on the basis of recent purchase price but would make only minor modifications to assessments of properties not recently transferred. The result was that there arose over time a great disparity in assessed values of comparable properties. For taxpayers to be treated so differently was held to violate the equal protection clause of the Fourteenth Amendment.

SUMMARY: A GUIDE FOR MANAGERS

- The commerce clause and the necessary and proper clause give Congress nearly unlimited discretion to regulate and tax business. Unless a statute specifies that certain businesses are exempt, regulations apply to all, since even local (intrastate) business has been held to affect interstate business.

- States may impose regulations that do not conflict with federal regulations or may impose regulations in areas in which Congress gives them specific regulatory authority, but states may not impose burdens on interstate commerce. Numerous state regulatory and taxing schemes have been limited because they violate the commerce clause of the Constitution.

- Commercial speech is afforded a high level of First Amendment protection. Businesses have the right to participate in political discussion whether or not it concerns an issue that directly affects business.

- Restrictions on commercial speech are subject to constitutional guidelines concerning strong public necessity. Truthful speech about lawful activities may be regulated only if the regulation would advance a substantial governmental interest and the regulation is no more extensive than is necessary.

- Since companies have Fourth Amendment guarantees against unreasonable searches and seizures, law enforcement authorities can be required to obtain warrants for most inspections. The business sensibility of requiring an inspector to obtain a warrant for a routine inspection is dubious.

- Companies may not withhold documents or testimony requested by prosecutors on the grounds that the evidence will incriminate the company; only individuals may invoke that Fifth Amendment right. Efforts to evade the requirement to testify by holding corporate evidence out of the country will not necessarily work.

- When government agencies prevent property from being used in a legitimate manner due to long, unjustified procedural delays or if agencies impose rules that substantially change the property value, compensation under the just compensation clause of the Fifth Amendment may be sought.

- The Supreme Court has held that large damage awards by juries against businesses, including punitive damages, do not violate the Eighth Amendment protection against excessive fines, nor do they violate Fourteenth Amendment due process clause protections of fair play and substantial justice.

MANAGER'S ETHICAL DILEMMA

VALUES, RIGHTS, OR PROFITS?

Sexually explicit magazines, within limits, are generally legal. Southland Corporation, which owns 7-Eleven stores, bowed to pressure from Christian advocacy groups, such as the American Family Association, and took *Penthouse* and similar magazines off the shelf. Just as some women's rights groups oppose the "sexploitation" of women in such magazines and call for the boycott of the magazines and those who sell them or advertise in them, the Christian groups have the right to suggest that economic pressure be brought to bear on those who sell products they find offensive.

PepsiCo took a multimillion-dollar loss when it scrapped a contract with rock star Madonna because of opposition by Christian groups over the "profane" implications of the ads she produced for Pepsi. PepsiCo managers were concerned that a public dispute over values unrelated to their product could hurt sales and profits.

Similarly, television producers face criticism and possible loss of sponsors' advertising dollars for shows that some regard as counter to Christian values, the dignity of minorities or women, or the values they want children to learn. Tipper Gore, wife of Senator Al Gore, has led a public attack on music producers and radio stations that produce and play music that she contends causes young people to lose basic values and engage in self-destructive behavior.

Rarely is the right of the producers and sellers of any of the products in question challenged. While some would like constitutional restrictions on "dirty" books, music, and television shows, such limits are unlikely. Some civil rights advocates claim that while we may not like the values implied by some products, in a free society we should not look for legal restrictions but simply should ignore the products. If there is no demand for the products, they will not be sold.

QUESTIONS

Should the producers of television shows, music, magazines, and so forth attempt to satisfy groups that may be offended by their products? As long as production is legal, should profit maximization be the only concern of managers in those companies producing products that have social implications? Should managers attempt to instill social values in their company's products, such as television shows? If so, whose values? Should managers stop selling a product (such as *Penthouse* in 7-Eleven stores) or cancel an ad campaign (such as Madonna for Pepsi) because of pressure or fear of controversy, or does yielding to such pressure essentially forfeit the constitutional rights of the company and of consumers who are not offended?

REVIEW AND DISCUSSION QUESTIONS

1. Define the following terms:

commerce clause	political speech
interstate commerce	just compensation (takings) clause
necessary and proper clause	due process clause
contract clause	equal protection clause
commercial speech	

2. Taken together, do the commerce clause and necessary and proper clause, as read by the Supreme Court, restrict to a significant degree the ability of Congress to regulate business?

3. Suppose Congress imposes a water pollution restriction. Can a state set limits on water pollution that are higher or lower than the federal limits?

4. Goods are produced in New Mexico. Some are shipped to Louisiana by truck for further processing. Can the state of Texas place a tax on those goods as they are shipped across the state that is the same as the tax it imposes on such goods that are produced in Texas for shipment within and outside Texas?

5. Congress requires that you report to the Internal Revenue Service any income from illegal activities, such as drug dealing. If you report the income, you reveal your illegal activities. If you do not report the income and the dealing is discovered, you can be charged with income tax evasion. Does this violate the Fifth Amendment? If not, why not?

■ CASE QUESTIONS

6. An employee hears a news report that terrorists were suspected of trying to set off a bomb to kill the President. The employee says to other employees, "I hope they kill that no-good jerk." The employer fires the employee for the statement. Is the statement protected by the First Amendment? What if the employee made the statement in public, such as by a letter to the editor of the newspaper?

7. Hospitals are regulated by state statute. The state sends inspectors to hospitals to check on such conditions as sanitation and proper procedure and to assure that only qualified personnel are performing certain functions. A state inspector enters a hospital without being recognized or volunteering the purpose of the visit. While looking around, the inspector discovers some prescription medicines on a nurse's desk without any evidence that there is a prescription. He asks the nurse if the pills belong to her; she says yes. The inspector then identifies himself and asks the nurse to produce a prescription, which she cannot do. The inspector files charges against the nurse, who will say only that a doctor gave her the pills but not which doctor. Is the evidence gathered in this case good evidence, or will it be tossed out?

8. Randy Braswell operated his business in Mississippi as a corporation of which he was sole shareholder. A grand jury ordered Braswell to produce the books and records of his corporation. Braswell refused. He argued that although normally a business cannot refuse to produce its records under the collective entity rule, since he was the sole owner of the corporation, forcing production of corporate records would be the same as forcing him to testify against himself in violation of his Fifth Amendment rights. Does Braswell have to produce the records? [*Braswell* v. *United States*, 487 U.S. 99, 108 S.Ct. 2284 (1988)]

9. Taylor sold live minnows as fishing bait in Maine. He imported some minnows from another state in violation of Maine law. He was then indicted under a federal law that makes it illegal to move fish in interstate commerce in violation of state law. Taylor claimed that the indictment should be dismissed because the Maine statute unconstitutionally burdened interstate commerce. Maine argued that it needed the statute to protect the state's fisheries from diseases and undesired varieties of fish. The U.S. Court of Appeals sided with Taylor, and the state of Maine appealed to the Supreme Court. Do the indictment and the statute stand? [*Maine* v. *Taylor*, 477 U.S. 131, 106 S.Ct. 2440 (1986)]

10. The city of San Diego passed an ordinance regulating outdoor advertising. Signs were allowed on the property where the advertised goods and services were located, but off-property fixed-structure signs (billboards) for commercial and noncommercial advertisements were prohibited, except for temporary political campaign signs. The Supreme Court of California held that the ordinance did not violate the First Amendment and was a proper use of the city's police power. The sign companies took the case to the U.S. Supreme Court. What was the result? [*Metromedia, Inc.* v. *City of San Diego,* 453 U.S. 490, 101 S.Ct. 2882 (1981)]

11. California law requires employers to provide leave for employees who are disabled by pregnancy, then to reinstate them to their job afterwards. Federal law prohibits discrimination on the basis of pregnancy, but does not state that leave must be given or that employees must be reinstated afterwards. A woman who worked for California Federal Savings and Loan took pregnancy disability leave. When she was ready to return to work she was told that her job had been filled and no similar position was available. She filed a complaint with the State of California, which charged her employer with a violation of state law. The employer filed suit in federal court, claiming that the state law was inconsistent with federal law concerning pregnancy discrimination, so the state law should be stricken. What did the Supreme Court say about the differences between the two sets of laws? [*California Federal Savings and Loan* v. *Guerra,* 479 U.S. 272, 107 S.C. 683 (1987)]

 BUSINESS POLICY QUESTIONS

12. Some intrastate business is not regulated by Congress. Would it be more desirable to have all regulations apply equally to all businesses? That is, is it desirable that some firms be subject to certain regulations that are not imposed on small intrastate firms? Is there any restriction on Congress specifying that various regulations will, in fact, be imposed on all firms in commerce?

13. Would a constitutional restriction on political speech that is sponsored by commercial interests produce a less biased, more fair system of political decision making?

ETHICS QUESTIONS

14. Since it is now legal for physicians and other professionals to engage in a certain amount of commercial advertising, a physician puts an ad in the newspaper telling people that the flu season could be bad this year and that the flu kills hundreds of people every year (which is true). She urges people to come to her office to get a flu shot to protect themselves. Is this ethical? The medical associations used to hold such ads unethical.

15. A firm subject to OSHA inspections requires an OSHA inspector who shows up unexpectedly one day to get a warrant before engaging in the search. The firm owner knows that the inspector is a genuine inspector and that there is no question that the warrant to search will be issued. However, requiring the inspector to get the warrant takes half a day of the inspector's time (which is paid for by taxpayers). Is this ethical?

GOVERNMENT AGENCIES AND THE ADMINISTRATIVE PROCESS

CHAPTER 6

MANAGER'S LEGAL CHALLENGE

The Beech Nut Nutrition Company is a Fortune 500 company. It is the second largest manufacturer of baby food and, among other things, sells fruit juices, including apple juice, in interstate commerce.

In 1977, the Universal Juice Company became Beech Nut's sole supplier of apple juice concentrate. Beech Nut processed and bottled the concentrate for distribution and sale under its own label. It advertised and labeled the bottled product as pure fruit juice with no sugar added. Shortly after it began to purchase concentrate from Universal, Beech Nut received information that the concentrate being supplied by Universal was being made from syrups and edible substances other than apples. Employees within Beech Nut confirmed the evidence, establishing that Universal's apple concentrate was not apple juice. The information, however, was not made public.

The management of Beech Nut faced several difficult decisions. The apple juice concentrate being purchased from Universal cost the company from fifty cents to one dollar less per gallon than would concentrate purchased from other suppliers. Because the company could purchase concentrate at that price, the "apple juice" market was very profitable to it. Further, recall of the fake apple juice would cause a serious financial loss and injure consumer goodwill and the reputation of the company. Realizing that the federal Food and Drug Administration (FDA) had no subpoena power, management elected to delay withdrawal of the product and avoid FDA inquiries.

Several government agencies soon became suspicious of Beech Nut's practices. To avoid seizure of the product by government agencies, management moved the product out of the state of New York at night. Records of the shipment were withheld from the FDA. Finally, the FDA notified Beech Nut that it was going to seize all of its apple juice made from Universal's concentrate. Management negotiated with the FDA for a limited recall, further delaying the removal of the product from the marketplace. By the time a nationwide recall was implemented, more than

97 percent of the fake juice had been sold to consumers who thought they were buying real apple juice.

The FDA pressed on, eventually obtaining a 470-count indictment against Beech Nut and its management, including one count of conspiracy, 20 counts of mail fraud, and 449 Food and Drug Act violations. The company eventually pleaded guilty and was fined $2 million plus $140,000 for the FDA's investigation costs. Several managers were sentenced to prison for their participation in and approval of the company's activities.

As the Beech Nut case illustrates, government agencies play an important role in implementing, policing, and enforcing the law. Since the first administrative agency was established in 1887, agencies have had a significant impact on the legal environment of business. More than fifty federal agencies share responsibility of regulating virtually all aspects of business. Those agencies regulate business activity from the transportation of raw materials to the quality of final products.

The chapter begins with a discussion of the nature of administrative agencies and the administrative process. It also examines the history of administrative agencies and the impact of social and economic conditions on their creation and development. Next, it considers the powers delegated to the administrative agencies by Congress, including their legislative, investigative, adjudicatory, and enforcement powers. The discussion then turns to the concept of judicial review—the power of the judicial branch of government to review an agency's actions or decisions. The chapter closes with a discussion of the limits placed on the power and authorities of administrative agencies by Congress.

ADMINISTRATIVE AGENCIES AND ADMINISTRATIVE LAW

Administrative agencies have become a fundamental part of modern U.S. government. In a relatively short time, they have become the primary tool used by the government to perform regulatory functions. In the words of the Supreme Court in *FTC* v. *Ruberoid Company* (1952):

> The rise of administration bodies probably has been the most significant legal trend of the last century and perhaps more values today are affected by their decisions than by those of all the courts. . . . They have become a veritable fourth branch of the government. . . .

■ CREATING AN ADMINISTRATIVE AGENCY

An *administrative agency* is an authority of the government—other than a legislature or a court—created to carry out a particular law. An agency will generally be provided with the authority to perform at least some functions of the three constitutional branches of government: legislative, judicial, and executive. The agency's authority will generally be provided by Congress in the legislation that creates the agency.

In creating an administrative agency, Congress gives the agency power and authority through a *legislative delegation*. Among the powers generally delegated to the agency is the authorization to perform its specific regulatory purpose, formulate appropriate public policy, and perform certain fundamental activities in implementing that policy. A statute delegating those powers to the agency is called an *enabling statute*.

The Purpose of Agencies.   Administrative agencies are generally created by Congress when solving a problem is viewed as requiring expertise, flexibility, and continuous supervision. In the late 1960s, for example, Congress and the general public became very concerned about air pollution. Congress could have enacted a law requiring that air pollution from factories be reduced or eliminated. However, Congress has neither the time nor the expertise to determine how such a law might be applied to the thousands of factories emitting air pollution. Instead, Congress enacted the Clean Air Act and delegated the responsibility for the Act's implementation to the Environmental Protection Agency. The Clean Air Act provided the agency with legislative, investigative, adjudicatory, and enforcement powers to accomplish the task.

Administrative agencies offer several advantages over Congress and the courts in the management of complex and technical regulatory problems. Because agencies are specialized bodies, they can consider technical details more effectively than can Congress. In comparison to the judicial system, agencies have the ability to monitor a regulated industry continuously. In contrast, the courts generally monitor business behavior only after a dispute or a violation has a risen.

ADMINISTRATIVE LAW

Administrative law consists of those legal rules that define the authority and structure of administrative agencies. The primary sources of administrative law include the following:

1. The enabling statutes of the administrative agencies.
2. The Administrative Procedures Act.
3. Decisions of the courts that review the validity of agency actions or decisions.

In addition, Congress has enacted several statutes that have had a significant impact on administrative agencies, including the Freedom of Information Act and the Government in the Sunshine Act. Those acts created new opportunities for public participation.

The most fundamental administrative law is the Administrative Procedures Act (APA). Enacted by Congress in 1946, the APA was intended to provide the basic procedural rules and formalities for all federal agencies. An agency is required to follow APA requirements unless Congress has passed a law specifically imposing different or additional requirements on that agency. The major provisions of the APA are summarized in Table 6–1.

TABLE 6-1
SUMMARY OF THE MAJOR PROVISIONS OF THE ADMINISTRATIVE PROCEDURES ACT

Section	United States Code	Summary of Provision
2	5 U.S.C. § 551	Provides definitions of the Act's terms and coverage.
3	5 U.S.C. § 552	Sets forth requirements for the publication of certain rules and regulations in the Federal Register; requires agencies to make other documents available to the public upon request.
4-8	5 U.S.C. §§ 553-558	Establishes the basic rules applicable to agency actions, including the procedures in rulemaking and adjudication.
10	5 U.S.C. §§ 701-706	Establishes judicial review of agency decisions.

DEVELOPMENT OF REGULATORY AGENCIES

The development of administrative agencies began with the regulation of private economic activity in the late 1800s. State governments first developed agencies to regulate railroads, grain elevators, and other natural monopolies. The state regulatory requirements on railroads helped bring about the creation of the first federal regulatory agency—the Interstate Commerce Commission (ICC). In 1887, Congress established the ICC to regulate railroad prices and routes "in the public interest," a function it still performs.

Numerous federal administrative agencies were developed in the years following the creation of the ICC. For example, the Food and Drug Administration, responsible for monitoring food and drug safety, was created in 1907. The Federal Trade Commission, which protects the free enterprise system from monopoly and corruption by unfair or deceptive trade practices, was established in 1914. However, the first big expansion in administrative agencies came during the New Deal era of the 1930s.

■ NEW DEAL AGENCIES

The New Deal era changed the face of government and stimulated the development of modern administrative law. During that era, regulation was imposed on business in response to concerns generated by the Great Depression. The Depression was viewed as demonstrating that the unregulated market could not be trusted to serve the welfare of the nation. In response, Congress created several administrative agencies.

Most significant of the New Deal agencies are the Securities and Exchange Commission (SEC), the Civil Aeronautics Board (CAB), and the Federal Communications Commission (FCC). Other agencies formed by

Congress during the New Deal era regulate banking, labor relations, energy, and agriculture. The Airline Deregulation Act of 1978 phased out many of the federal regulations imposed on the airline industry by the CAB, which ceased to exist in 1985.

◼ SOCIAL REFORM AND THE AGENCIES OF THE 1960S AND 1970S

Agencies created in the 1960s and 1970s are generally not oriented toward a specific industry as were earlier agencies. During those earlier years, the regulatory focus shifted from direct control of industry to social reform. This period saw the creation of such agencies as the Environmental Protection Agency (EPA), whose function is "to assure protection of the environment"; the Occupational Safety and Health Administration (OSHA), whose function is to "enforce . . . occupational health and safety standards"; the Equal Employment Opportunity Commission (EEOC), whose function is to "end discrimination based on race, color, religion, sex, or national origin in hiring, promoting, firing, wages, testing, training, apprenticeship, and all other conditions of employment"; and the Consumer Product Safety Commission (CPSC), whose function is "to reduce the risk of injury to consumers from consumer products."

Since the creation of the ICC over 100 years ago, administrative agencies have grown to become a dominant part of the federal government. Today there are over fifty independent agencies and government corporations, along with fourteen cabinet-level departments—all with significant regulatory responsibilities. Those agencies issue more than 50,000 pages of rules per year. Table 6–2 is a selected list of administrative agencies that perform a broad range of regulatory tasks.

REGULATORY POWERS OF ADMINISTRATIVE AGENCIES ▬▬▬▬▬

Congress gives an agency significant regulatory powers to enact rules and regulations. An agency also has the power to investigate violations of its rules and regulations and to prosecute violators. Although these specific powers differ from agency to agency, it is possible to generalize to a typical administrative agency.

◼ LEGISLATIVE OR RULEMAKING POWER

Most agencies have the authority to engage in *rulemaking*. Through its rulemaking procedures, an agency seeks to develop administrative rules and to state its regulatory policy. Agency rulemaking has been called "the most distinctive administrative process" and "one of the greatest inventions of modern government."

A precise definition of an administrative rule resulting from agency rulemaking is somewhat difficult. Compounding the difficulty of defining such a rule is the fact that agencies maintain their own distinctive terminologies. The Department of the Treasury, for example, calls its rules

TABLE 6–2
SELECTED FEDERAL ADMINISTRATIVE AGENCIES

Direct and Indirect Regulators of Business

Commission on Civil Rights (1957)
Consumer Product Safety Commission (1972)
Council of Environmental Quality (1970)
Council of Consumer Affairs (1971)
Department of Agriculture (1862)
Department of Commerce (1913)
Department of Energy (1977)
Department of Health and Human Services (1980)
Department of Housing and Urban Development (1965)
Department of the Interior (1849)
Department of Labor (1913)
Department of Transportation (1966)
Department of the Treasury (1789)
Environmental Protection Agency (1970)
Equal Employment Opportunity Commission (1965)
Federal Communications Commission (1934)
Federal Deposit Insurance Corporation (1933)
Federal Energy Regulatory Commission (1977)
Federal Maritime Commission (1961)
Federal Reserve System (1913)
Federal Trade Commission (1914)
Food and Drug Administration (1907)
Interstate Commerce Commission (1887)
National Labor Relations Board (1935)
National Railroad Passenger Corporation (Amtrak) (1970)
Nuclear Regulatory Commission (1975)
Occupational Safety and Health Review Commission (1970)
Office of Federal Contract Compliance Programs (1965)
Regulatory Analysis Review Group (1978)
Regulatory Council (1978)
Securities and Exchange Commission (1934)
Small Business Administration (1953)
Tennessee Valley Authority (1933)
United States Postal Service (1971)
United States Tariff Commission (1916)

"decisions"; other agencies refer to their rules as standards, guidelines, or opinions. The APA defines a rule as follows:

> The whole or part of an agency statement of general or particular applicability and future effect designed to implement, interpret, or prescribe law or policy describing the organization, procedure, or practice requirements of an agency.

As an aid to a more precise definition, administrative rules are classified as substantive (legislative), interpretative, or procedural.

Substantive or Legislative Rules.   Substantive rules are, in effect, administrative statutes with the same force of law as statutes enacted by Congress. Before issuing such a rule, the agency is generally required by the APA to provide public notice and the opportunity for interested parties to comment. In some circumstances, a legislative rule may be required to be on the record. The agency is then required to conduct a formal trial-like hearing to allow interested parties to present evidence for or against the proposed rule.

Interpretative Rules. Interpretative rules are statements issued by an agency to provide both its staff and the public with guidance regarding the interpretation of a statute or regulation. That is, interpretative rules are statements as to what an agency thinks a statute or regulation means. Interpretative rules range from informal *general policy statements* to authoritative rulings that are binding on the agency.

In contrast to legislative rules, interpretative rules are exempt from the notice and comment requirements of the APA. As a consequence, an agency is able to issue interpretative rules without inviting input from interested parties. However, interested parties frequently challenge an agency's interpretative rule by arguing that it is really a legislative rule. If the challenge is successful, the agency is required to provide public notice. Interested parties then have the opportunity to comment. Thus, the ability of an agency to distinguish between the two types of rules is important. The following case discusses the distinction between legislative and interpretative rules in that regard.

UNITED TECHNOLOGIES CORPORATION v. U.S. ENVIRONMENTAL PROTECTION AGENCY

United States Court of Appeals, District of Columbia Circuit
821 F.2d 714 (1987)

Case Background
The EPA enacted a final rule intended to make its existing hazardous waste regulations conform with new statutory provisions enacted by Congress. United Technologies Corporation argued that the final rule was a legislative rule enacted without notice and comment as required by the APA. Therefore, it contended, the rule must be invalidated. The EPA, on the other hand, maintained that the final rule was an interpretative rule and therefore did not require notice and comment.

Case Decision
The court agreed with the EPA. The APA specifically states that interpretative rules need not follow notice and comment procedures. An interpretative rule is intended to set forth what the agency thinks the statute means. A legislative rule is intended to create new legal rights and duties separate from that statute. The final rule here was an attempt by the EPA to analyze specific statutory provisions imposed upon it and therefore must be considered as an interpretative rule.

Managerial Considerations
The notice and comment requirements of the APA are intended to provide businesses and their managers with an opportunity to directly influence regulatory policy. Businesses' right to be proactive, however, is limited to legislative rather than interpretative rules. In either case, management will want to be informed of both changes and proposed changes in the legal and regulatory environments. By failing to monitor the regulatory environment effectively, many businesses are surprised and hurt by new rules. Waiting to respond to new rules after they are enacted has proven to be expensive and relatively unsuccessful for most businesses.

Businesses that respond to the regulatory environment by monitoring and challenging proposed rules are better able to influence regulatory policy. Businesses find that involvement in policymaking generally produces a legal environment much more compatible with their operations.

Monitoring is frequently performed by an industry's trade association, providing small- and medium-sized companies with this important but expensive service. Without a trade association or similar organization, those companies would likely not be able to afford to participate in policymaking.

Procedural Rules.   Procedural rules define an agency's organization, describe its method of operation, and detail its internal practices. The power to enact such rules is generally provided by the agency's enabling statute. The agency is bound by its procedural rules. A challenge to an agency decision will usually be upheld if the challenging party can demonstrate that the agency did not comply with its own procedural rules in reaching its decision.

■ INVESTIGATIVE POWERS

Without information, administrative agencies could not perform their responsibilities. Whatever the administrative action, its effectiveness is determined by the information the agency has or can obtain. The agency's authority to investigate possible violations of its rules is one of the functions that makes agencies different from courts.

Most information is obtained through staff analysis and the agency's records. In some cases, information is obtained from private sources willing to tell what they know. When these sources prove inadequate, however, an agency may rely on its statutory authority to seek further information. Because the need for information varies widely among agencies, Congress has traditionally given broad and expansive investigative power to agencies. Those powers are limited by the Constitution, particularly the Fourth Amendment. Despite these constitutional limitations, if an agency is persistent and careful, very little information in the possession of a business is beyond its reach.

Agencies usually obtain information in one of three ways:

1. The regulated business is required to do self-reporting on a regular basis.
2. Direct observation is made through inspections to determine whether a particular business is meeting the requirements of the law.
3. Agency subpoena power is used, requiring the business to produce documents from its files.

Requiring Businesses to Monitor and Self-Report.   Agencies increasingly have required businesses to monitor their own behavior. Generally an agency will require a business to report certain information to it either at preset time intervals or when an event (often a violation) deemed important by the agency occurs.

Businesses have incentives to comply with self-reporting requirements. The failure to report or the reporting of false information can lead to fines and other more severe agency sanctions. On the other hand, the *accurate* reporting of information can also lead to fines and sanctions. If, for example, the information indicates that the business has acted in violation of agency rules, the agency may use the information and impose a fine. Businesses have contested fines resulting from the mandatory self-reporting of data, arguing that the reporting of self-incriminating evidence violates the Fifth Amendment. The Supreme Court has ruled, however, that the self-incrimination privilege of the Fifth Amendment applies only to individuals and does not protect corporations and other legal entities.

Direct Observation by Agency. Agencies also acquire information through direct observation of the business and its activities. Techniques frequently employed include, for example, work site safety inspections conducted by OSHA or the detection by the EPA of excessive air pollution emissions from a smokestack.

In some situations, however, agency inspections may violate the constitutional rights of the owner of the business. In the past, agency inspectors were not required to have a search warrant. In recent years, however, the Supreme Court has limited warrantless investigations by administrative agencies. Beginning with its decision in *Marshall v. Barlow's, Inc.* (1978), the Supreme Court has held that agencies are required to obtain warrants for routine inspections.

There are several exceptions to the warrant requirement. The Court in *Barlow's* recognized that businesses are free to consent to routine agency inspections, in which case no warrant would be required. In addition, no warrant is required if an agency's evidence is obtained from an "open field" observation. That is, a warrant is not required if the evidence is gathered by the inspector from his or her observations in areas where the public has access. In the following case, the Court considers whether the taking of photographs from an airplane flying over a factory falls within the open field exception.

DOW CHEMICAL COMPANY v. UNITED STATES

United States Supreme Court
476 U.S. 227, 106 S.Ct. 1819 (1986)

Case Background
Dow Chemical Company brought an action to stop the EPA from taking photographs of its industrial complex. The EPA had requested an onsite inspection of the plant, but Dow Chemical had denied the request. Instead of obtaining an administrative search warrant for an onsite inspection, the EPA employed a commercial aerial photographer, who took photographs of the facility using a precision mapping camera. The photographs were taken from various altitudes, all within the lawful airspace.

Dow Chemical brought suit in federal district court, alleging that the EPA's action violated the Constitution's Fourth Amendment protections against unlawful searches and seizures. The district court granted summary judgment for Dow Chemical, but the court of appeals reversed. Dow Chemical then appealed to the U.S. Supreme Court.

Case Decision
The U.S. Supreme Court affirmed the decision of the court of appeals, holding that the Fourth Amendment was not violated by the EPA's aerial surveillance. In this case, a manufacturing facility was observed through the use of photographs of the sort commonly used in mapmaking. Any person with an airplane and an aerial camera could take such photographs. Those areas observable by the general public are considered observable by a government inspector without a warrant. Had the surveillance involved the use of electronic devices for the purpose of penetrating walls to hear and record confidential information concerning trade secrets or chemical formulas, it would have raised constitutional concerns. However, the complex was open to observation by persons in aircraft lawfully in the public airspace and within camera range. As a result, there was no constitutional violation.

Managerial Considerations
The investigatory authority of administrative agencies is far-reaching. Unlike private dwellings, commercial properties are subject to warrantless searches under certain circumstances. The Dow Chemical case outlines one instance where an area open to plain view by the general public is subject to observation by an agency without a search warrant. Management should be concerned as well about competitors making similar observations. As competition becomes more intense, the loss of a production secret or other competitive advantage to an observant competitor could affect profits more substantially than an agency observation.

Agency Subpoena Power.   An agency may also attempt to obtain information by issuing a subpoena if the power to do so has been provided by Congress. A *subpoena* is a legal instrument that directs the person receiving it to appear at a specified time and place either to testify or to produce documents. The Clean Air Act provides a typical example of a congressional authorization of the power to issue subpoenas and the normal procedure used to enforce them:

> [F]or purposes of obtaining information . . . the Administrator may issue subpoenas for the attendance and testimony of witnesses and the production of relevant papers, books, and documents, and he may administer oaths. . . . In case of . . . refusal to obey a subpoena served upon any person . . . , the district court for any district in which such person is found or resides or transacts business . . . shall have jurisdiction to issue an order requiring such person to appear and give testimony before the Administrator . . . and any failure to obey such an order may be punished by such court as a contempt thereof.

Unless the request for information by the agency is vague, or if the burden imposed on the business clearly outweighs the possible benefits to the agency, the business is required to comply with the subpoena. Even trade secrets and other confidential information cannot necessarily be kept from the agency. If a business asserts that the information requested by the subpoena deserves confidential treatment, the agency will allow the information to be presented secretly to it by the business.

ADJUDICATORY POWER

Administrative agencies have the power not only to investigate but also to adjudicate parties who violate their rules. In this sense, the agency is empowered to act much like a court of law. The administrative agency equivalent to a trial in a court of law is called an *adjudication*. As in a judicial trial, witnesses may be cross-examined.

ENFORCEMENT POWER

Congress generally provides an agency with a broad selection of enforcement tools. Those tools are intended to be used to encourage voluntary compliance with the regulatory law, agency rules, and an agency's adjudicatory outcomes. The EPA, for example, can assure compliance with air pollution control requirements by seeking civil and criminal penalties and injunctions. In the Clean Air Act, for example, Congress provided that

> The Administrator shall commence a civil action for a permanent or temporary injunction, or to assess and recover a civil penalty of not more than $25,000 per day of violation, or both, whenever [the owner or operator of a major stationary source of pollution] . . . violates or fails to comply with any order. . . .

In addition to having the authority to sue in federal court to impose civil and criminal penalties, agencies are generally given authority to impose several other types of sanctions. To illustrate the various sanctions available to an agency, consider the examples offered by the APA in its definition of the term *sanction*:

1. Prohibition, requirement, limitation, or other condition affecting the freedom of a person.
2. Withholding of relief.
3. Imposition of a penalty or fine.
4. Destruction, taking, seizing, or withholding of property.
5. Assessment of damages, reimbursement, restitution, compensation, costs, charges, or fees.
6. Requirement, revocation, or suspension of a license.
7. Taking other compulsory or restrictive action.

The actual techniques of enforcement vary from agency to agency. Some agencies, for example, have found that threatening a company with public exposure of a violation is often sufficient to bring about compliance.

ADMINISTRATIVE PROCESS AND PROCEDURES

Administrative law concerns itself primarily with the procedural requirements imposed upon agencies by the APA. The APA, however, imposes procedural requirements only when the agency is engaged in (1) formal procedures, such as rulemaking, or (2) determining the application of its rules to a particular situation through an adjudication. For the vast majority of an agency's informal decisions, the APA provides little procedural guidance. This section discusses the basic agency formal and informal procedures.

■ INFORMAL AGENCY PROCEDURES

As agency regulatory activities have expanded, agencies have relied more heavily on informal procedures. Because of their nature, informal procedures lie outside the procedural controls provided by the APA. Since informal procedures generally require less time and are less costly than formal procedures in bringing about industry compliance—primarily because few procedural controls are applied—agencies prefer to employ them whenever possible.

Nature of an Informal Procedure.   Informal agency procedures include tests and inspections, day-to-day supervision, the processing of applications and permits, settlements and negotiations, and the exchange of interpretative advice in the form of advisory opinions. Publicity or the threat of it is often considered as an additional (and very potent) informal procedure through which an agency can encourage industry compliance with its rules and regulations.

In many cases, the agency's decision is based on an inspector's on-the-spot analysis. For example, an OSHA inspector, upon finding that a manufacturing process places a worker's health in peril, may order immediate changes. In other situations, the mere existence of the agency in its supervisory and enforcement role may "encourage" the desired industry behavior. When the FDA finds botulism in canned foods, for example, the manufacturer will "voluntarily" withdraw the product from the shelves and destroy it in response to an implied threat of prosecution by the FDA.

Review of an Agency Decision in an Informal Procedure.   A business dissatisfied with an agency decision from an informal procedure may appeal through the same process available for appeals from formal procedures. The decision is reviewed by the agency. If dissatisfied with the agency's final decision, parties may seek review by the appropriate federal court. In reviewing agency informal procedures, the courts are generally most concerned with whether the particular agency procedure was fair and the decision was consistent with the expectations of Congress.

■ FORMAL AGENCY PROCEDURES

The two basic *formal procedures* used by most federal regulatory agencies are adjudicatory and investigatory hearings. The manner in which such hearings are generally defined and conducted is dictated by the APA. In some instances, however, an agency's enabling statute may require procedures that are different somewhat from those provided by the APA.

Adjudicatory Hearings.   Under the APA, an *adjudicatory hearing* is a formal process involving the agency and an individual or a small group of individuals. The procedures required by the APA for an adjudicatory hearing are similar to those followed in a court trial. In contrast to the industry-wide coverage of a rule enacted by an agency, the decision reached at the close of an adjudicatory hearing is applicable only to the party involved in the hearing.

As Figure 6–1 shows, an adjudicatory hearing is typically initiated by the agency (or a citizen, the U.S. Attorney General, or an injured party) filing a complaint against a business whose behavior is in question. The business is then required to respond to the complaint. In some cases, the agency will do research, collect information relevant to the charges, and reach a decision as to whether a hearing is appropriate. If it is determined that a hearing is appropriate, an administrative law judge (ALJ) from the agency will be selected to preside over the hearing. The ALJ differs from a judge in a trial court in that the ALJ is a civil service employee of the agency. The agency is represented by its counsel, who presents the agency's evidence in support of the complaint; the business then presents its evidence. Witnesses may be cross-examined just as in a trial court.

The adjudicatory hearing must conform to the procedural due process guarantees provided by the Constitution. However, the litigants in an agency adjudicatory hearing are not entitled to a jury trial. In the following case, the Supreme Court discusses the applicability of the Seventh Amendment's guarantee of the right to a jury trial to an agency adjudicatory hearing.

ATLAS ROOFING COMPANY, INC. v. OCCUPATIONAL SAFETY AND HEALTH REVIEW COMMISSION

United States Supreme Court
430 U.S. 442, 97 S.Ct. 1261 (1977)

Case Background
In response to growing workplace safety concerns, Congress enacted the Occupational Safety and Health Act in 1970. Two new remedies provided by the Act permitted the federal government to (1) obtain abatement orders requiring employers to correct unsafe working conditions and (2) impose civil penalties on any employer maintaining any unsafe working conditions.

If an employer wishes to contest the penalty or the abatement order, a hearing is held before an ALJ within the Occupational Safety and Health Review Commission. The judge has the authority to affirm, modify, or vacate the abatement order or penalty. The judge's decision is subject to review by the full commission. If review is granted, the full commission's subsequent order requiring abatement and the payment of any penalty becomes final unless the employer petitions the appropriate court of appeals for judicial review. If review by the court of appeals is granted, the Act specifies that "the findings of the Full Commission with respect to questions of fact, if supported by substantial evidence, shall be conclusive." If the employer fails to pay the penalty, the secretary of the commission may begin a collection action in a federal district court. In that proceeding, neither the facts of the violation nor the penalty may be reexamined.

Atlas Roofing was issued an abatement order and penalty for safety violations and appealed the case through the review procedures outlined above. It then challenged the constitutionality of the proceedings, arguing that the Commission failed to provide for a jury trial, a violation of the Seventh Amendment. The court of appeals affirmed the commission's findings and stated that jury trials are not required in agency hearings. The Supreme Court granted certiorari to consider whether the Seventh Amendment's right to a jury trial applies to an agency adjudication.

Case Decision
The Supreme Court affirmed the decision of the court of appeals. The Court found that agency adjudicatory hearings are not unconstitutional because jury trials are not provided. The Court stated that the Seventh Amendment provides a right to a jury for "suits at common law" when the value in controversy exceeds twenty dollars. The Court emphasized that *statutory* proceedings initiated by Congress are not "common law," nor are they of the nature of usual common law cases. Further, administration agency hearings and reviews are not compatible with a jury. Thus, the Seventh Amendment's guarantee of a right to a jury trial does not prohibit the enforcement of statutory rights outside the regular courts of law.

Managerial Considerations
Public laws created by Congress and regulated and enforced by the administrative agencies significantly affect management's day-to-day decision making. Generally, management will work to comply voluntarily with an agency's rules and regulations. When an agency becomes dissatisfied with a company's performance and an enforcement action is initiated, management should be aware of the company's rights in that proceeding. Although the company is not entitled to a jury trial, it is entitled to a fair hearing.

The administrative agency adjudicatory process can be complicated and time-consuming. Thus, management should make every effort to avoid becoming involved in the process. By monitoring the legal environment and periodically conducting legal audits, management can reduce the probability of an enforcement action. However, if violations do occur, management should fully assess the costs of an agency proceeding. Often the threat of publicity alone is a sufficient inducement for management to give in to an agency's demands.

Shortly after the hearing ends, the ALJ gives a decision, usually in the form of a written opinion. If the business does not object to the decision, the agency normally adopts the decision. If the business is dissatisfied with the ALJ's decision, the commissioners or agency administrator will review the decision in the same manner as an appellate court. If the business is dissatisfied after this final agency review, it may then proceed to the federal court system for further review.

Investigatory Hearings: Rulemaking Under the APA.   An agency's legislative or rulemaking function under the APA takes place in investigatory

FIGURE 6–1

Formal Agency Procedures: Adjudicatory Hearing

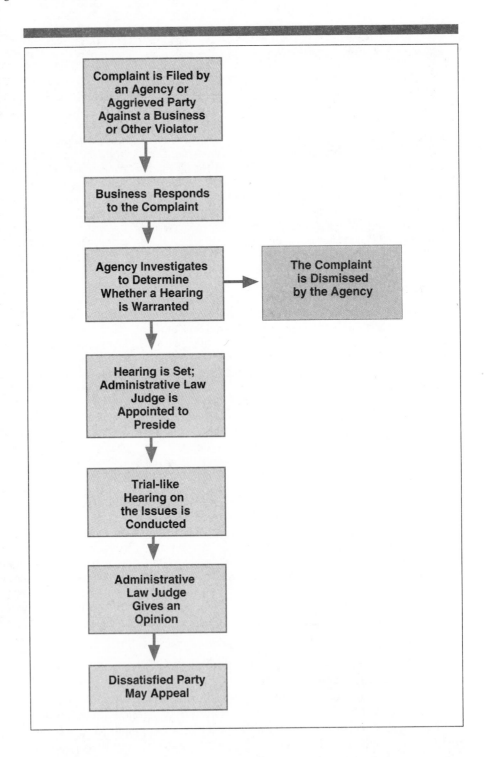

hearings. Under the APA, an investigatory hearing deals with the formulation of a regulatory policy. The agency will apply that policy in the future to all parties engaged in the regulated activity. The agency's principal goal in an investigatory hearing is to gather information about the feasibility and desirability of a regulatory policy.

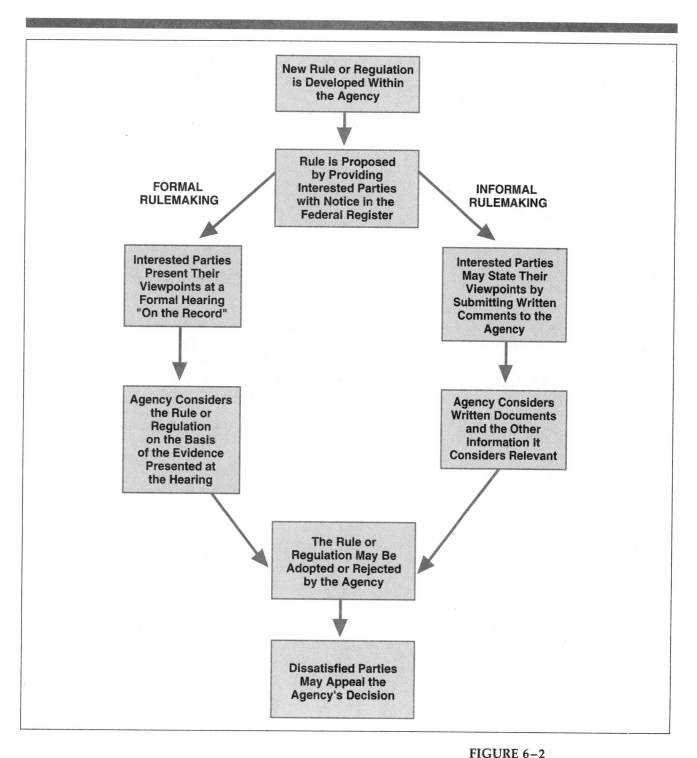

FIGURE 6–2

Formal Agency Procedures:
Formal vs. Informal Rulemaking

   The APA provides for both formal and informal rulemaking procedures. Figure 6–2 compares the two types of procedures. Regardless of which procedure is used, the agency begins by proposing a specific rule or regulation. The APA requires official notice of that proposed rule in the *Federal Register*. The notice will generally appear as a Notice of Proposed

Rulemaking by the agency. It will contain information on the nature (formal or informal) of the rulemaking and the time frame in which interested parties must respond. If a formal hearing is to be held, the notice will provide information about the time and place of the hearing. The notice will also contain a discussion of the proposed rule or regulation.

Informal Rulemaking.   If the rulemaking is informal, the APA provides that interested parties may submit written comments to the agency stating their position on the proposed rule. Oral testimony and cross-examination of witnesses, however, are generally not permitted in an informal rulemaking. In addition, in deciding whether the rule or regulation should be enacted, the agency is free to consider sources of information other than the written comments submitted by interested parties.

Formal Rulemaking.   Under some statutes, rules must be made "on the record" after the opportunity for an agency hearing. In such situations, the agency is required to undertake a formal, trial-like investigatory hearing. Interested parties may introduce exhibits and call witnesses, who are then subject to examination and cross-examination.

Only a small number of federal statutes provide for rulemaking proceedings on the record. There is reason to believe that formal rulemaking may provide interested parties with a greater opportunity to be heard. However, the costs—particularly with regard to the time required to formulate and implement policy—can be considerably greater than under informal rulemaking.

As with other agency decisions, dissatisfied parties may seek review of rules promulgated through either formal or informal rulemaking. First, appeal must be made to the agency. Then, after agency procedures have been exhausted, review with the appropriate federal court may be sought.

INTERNATIONAL ASPECTS | ADMINISTRATIVE AGENCIES IN JAPAN

Along with differences in the law and legal structures among the developed countries, there are important differences in administrative agencies and administrative law. These differences can significantly impact the legal environment of business for firms interested in operating in other countries. For example, one of the most interesting and worrisome areas of Japanese law and legal culture for an American company is the formal body of administrative "law" known as "administrative guidance" (*gyosei shido*). This term generally includes all the different things the ministries and agencies of the Japanese government can do to exert formal and informal regulatory authority over businesses in Japan. An administrative agency, for example, may issue guidance by direction (*shiji*), request (*yobo*), warning (*keikoku*), encouragement (*kansho*), or suggestion (*kankoku*).

The power basis of administrative guidance in Japan is found in the government's power over foreign trade, foreign exchange, or loanable funds. However, the subject of such guidance might extend far beyond these fields. In theory, businesses are not forced to comply with such administrative guidance. A busi-

(continued)

ness that ignores a foreign government's suggestion, however, might find that its quota of imported raw materials has been reduced, that it cannot get the necessary legal permission for foreign currencies needed in its business, that it is being denied long-term government financing for future expansion, or that some other governmental sanction is imposed unrelated to that area in which the original guidance was given. The Foreign Exchange Control and Foreign Investment Acts, for example, require that any agreement or contract involving expenditures abroad must be approved by the Foreign Investment Council. A business that has not complied with an agency's request that a pollution control device be installed might find that a contract requiring expenditures abroad has not been approved.

This type of government influence assumes business cooperation on a voluntary basis. However, it clearly draws its authority from the ability of agencies to punish noncompliance by a business in a variety of ways. The Japanese judiciary has taken a hands-off policy toward administrative guidance. As long as the agency action is within its discretion, the action will not be reviewed unfavorably even if it is abusive. This gives Japanese administrative agencies considerably more power than U.S. agencies.

JUDICIAL REVIEW: CONSTRAINT ON AGENCY POWERS

The APA sets forth procedural requirements for a party seeking a court review of an agency decision. If those requirements are met, the party may challenge the decision with an appeal to the appropriate federal court of appeals. That appeal is referred to as *judicial review,* a powerful and effective external check on administrative agency power. Its existence ensures that agencies are careful to follow required procedures, prepared to justify their actions, and respectful of the constitutional and legal rights of individuals.

■ PROCEDURAL REQUIREMENTS: THE RIGHT TO JUDICIAL REVIEW

Several threshold *procedural requirements* must be overcome by a party challenging an agency decision through judicial review, the most prominent are jurisdiction, reviewability, standing, ripeness, and exhaustion. If a party challenging an agency decision is unable to meet the requirement, it will be denied judicial review. These procedural requirements are summarized in Table 6–3.

Jurisdiction. Most regulatory statutes provide for judicial review of agency actions. Most commonly, statutory provisions provide that a party can petition a particular court of appeals for review. The Clean Air Act, for example, provides that

> A petition for review of an action of the [EPA] Administrator in promulgating any national ambient air quality standard . . . or any other nationally applicable regulation . . . may be filed only in the United States Court of Appeals for the District of Columbia. A petition for review of the

TABLE 6–3	
JUDICIAL REVIEW OF AGENCY ACTIONS: SUMMARY OF PROCEDURAL REQUIREMENTS	

Procedural Requirement	Definition
1. Jurisdiction	The injured party may seek judicial review only in courts that have the power to hear the case. Most statutes specify which courts have jurisdiction to hear an appeal from an agency action implementing the statute.
2. Reviewability	The appellate court has power to examine an agency decision to determine whether a correction or modification is needed.
3. Standing	A party seeking judicial review must demonstrate that it has incurred an injury or is threatened with injury as a consequence of the agency's decision.
4. Ripeness	There may be no judicial review until the agency's action is final so that the court will have the *final* issues before it and not a hypothetical question.
5. Exhaustion	This is a "gatekeeping" device, requiring that a party seeking judicial review has sought relief through agency appeal processes *before* seeking relief from the courts.

Administrator's actions in approving or promulgating any . . . regulation . . . or any other final action . . . which is locally or regionally applicable may be filed only in the United States Court of Appeals for the appropriate circuit. . . . Any petition for review . . . shall be filed within sixty days from the date of notice of such promulgation . . . or action.

Reviewability.   Statutes giving jurisdiction to courts to review agency actions are often broadly drafted. As a consequence, most decisions made by an agency within its delegated authority are subject to judicial review.

An exception from judicial review is for agency actions that have a compelling need for speed, flexibility, or secrecy that is inconsistent with the open processes of judicial review. If a court finds that a compelling reason exists for denying review, it may decide that the agency's action is not reviewable.

In addition, in some statutes delegating authority to an agency, Congress has elected to provide specific exceptions to the general availability of judicial review. The Secretary of Veteran Affairs, for example, has the final authority over the determination of benefits due veterans. As long as precluding judicial review is constitutional, the courts must follow those congressional directives. As a rule, however, there is a strong presumption of reviewability. However, those who seek review have a specified time period in which to file for review—usually thirty days.

Standing.   A party seeking a court challenge to an agency decision or action must have *standing* to seek judicial review. American administrative law has traditionally restricted the right of judicial review to those who can show an injury recognized by law as entitled to protection. A party who is unable to demonstrate such an injury is prohibited from obtaining judicial review and is said to lack standing.

The Supreme Court addressed this issue in *Lujan* v. *Defenders of Wildlife* (1992). In that case, environmental groups claimed that United States government actions were causing species in other countries to be endangered. For example, foreign aid to Egypt helps to build dams on the Nile River. Those dams are endangering the Nile crocodile. Plaintiffs claimed that the agency providing the foreign aid should comply with the Endangered Species Act. The Court said there was no "injury in fact" to the plaintiffs, therefore they did not have standing to bring the case. Having a grievance about government policy is not the same as showing concrete injury from a policy.

The standing requirement is rooted in Section 2 of Article III of the U.S. Constitution, which limits the judicial power to *actual cases or controversies*. Federal courts cannot hear complaints from parties who have no stake in a real dispute or who raise only hypothetical questions. The test for standing is whether the agency decision challenged has caused the party seeking review *injury in fact*, economic or otherwise, and whether the interest sought to be protected falls within the *zone of interests* governed by the statute in question.

Ripeness and Exhaustion.   Procedural requirements control the appropriate time in which a party can obtain judicial review of an agency decision. Two significant requirements are the doctrines of ripeness and exhaustion. The *ripeness doctrine* is concerned with whether the agency decision is final enough to warrant judicial review. According to the Supreme Court in *Lujan* v. *National Wildlife Federation* (1990), the judiciary cannot review agency decisions until agency action and appeals are complete—when the legal issue is "ripe."

The *exhaustion doctrine* requires a party to complete agency appeals procedures before turning to a court for review. That is, parties may not resort to the courts for assistance until they have exhausted all internal agency review procedures. Until an action is considered final by the agency, the possibility remains open that the agency will change its mind. Given that possibility, courts are reluctant to assert their jurisdiction.

■ Scope of Judicial Review

After all procedural requirements have been met, the court of appeals can review the agency's decision. The court's *scope of review* determines how far the court can go in examining the decision. Generally, that will depend on whether the issue before the court involves a question of procedure, statutory interpretation, or substantive law. Each imposes different requirements on the reviewing court.

Review of Agency's Substantive Determinations.   The court's review of an agency's substantive determinations is generally provided the lowest scope of judicial review. As a rule, the courts are willing to yield to the agency's judgment in technical matters. The courts will generally not find that an agency's actions or decisions are *arbitrary, capricious,* or *an abuse of discretion* if the following are true:

1. The agency has sufficiently explained the facts and its policy concerns.
2. Those facts have some basis in the agency's record.
3. On the basis of those facts and legislative concerns, a reasonable person could reach the same judgments the agency has reached.

Review of Agency's Statutory Interpretation.   The court's review of an agency's statutory interpretation is generally afforded a middle intensity scope of review. In contrast to the technical judgments required of the agency in implementing a statute, the courts have primary responsibility for the interpretation of the reach and meaning of statutes enacted by Congress. Although the courts give great weight to the interpretation of a statute by the agency responsible for its implementation, they will reject that interpretation if it does not comply with interpretations dictated by established principles of statutory construction.

Review of Agency's Procedural Requirements.   The court's review of the agency's procedural requirements is provided the most intense scope of review. The court is responsible for ensuring that the agency has not acted unfairly or in disregard of statutorily prescribed procedures. The courts have been regarded historically as the authority in procedural fair play. According to the Court in *Weyerhaeuser* v. *Costle* (1978):

> [W]e are willing to entrust the agency with wide ranging regulatory discretion, and even, to a lesser extent, with an interpretive discretion vis-à-vis its statutory mandate, so long as we are assured that its promulgation process as a whole and in each of its major aspects provides a degree of public awareness, understanding, and participation commensurate with the complexity and intrusiveness of the resulting regulations.

CONGRESSIONAL RESTRICTIONS ON AGENCY POWER

Congress can check agency powers in several ways. Just as it is able to delegate powers to an agency, Congress may also revoke those powers. In most instances, however, the interests of Congress and the general public may be better served by checks on agency behavior and performance. This section discusses measures that Congress has used or considered in providing those checks.

■ DIRECT CONGRESSIONAL CHECKS ON AGENCY POWER

Public awareness and concern about the costs and effectiveness of regulation have prompted various responses from Congress. With its responses, Congress has intended to improve its control over agency activities. The most immediate control mechanism enjoyed by Congress is the ability to influence agency activity through the budget process. In addition, members of Congress have proposed bills calling for, among other things, *sunset provisions, legislative vetoes,* and a mandatory *cost-benefit analysis.*

Agency Appropriations. Administrative agencies depend on public funding to support their programs. Each year they are required to submit their budget requests for review first by the President and then by Congress. The President or Congress can cut the agency's budget if either is opposed to its activities. Budget cuts reduce the overall effectiveness of an agency. Furthermore, Congress can require in the budget that an agency address a specific issue. Thus, control of an agency's budget gives both Congress and the President control to influence agency regulatory policy.

Statutory Reporting Requirements. In more recent enactments, Congress has required agencies to report their progress on certain programs or activities on a regular basis. The reporting requirements vary from annual reports on specific programs to more frequent reports on other agency activities. Consider, for example, the reporting requirements imposed by Congress on the EPA in the Clean Air Act:

> [N]ot later than January 10 of each calendar year . . . , the Administrator shall report to the Congress on measures taken toward implementing the purpose and intent of this [Act] including, but not limited to, (1) the progress and problems associated with control of automotive exhaust emissions and the research efforts related thereto; (2) the development of air quality criteria and recommended emission control requirements; [and] (3) the status of enforcement actions taken pursuant to this [Act]. . . .

Sunset Laws. To increase its control over administrative agencies, Congress has considered including mandatory sunset provisions in all federal regulatory laws. A sunset provision would require Congress to review an agency's regulations, programs, or general usefulness on a regular basis. If it is determined that the agency is no longer needed, it is abolished; that is, the sun is allowed to set upon it. Sunset provisions would require Congress to be more involved in evaluating agency activities and agencies to be more responsive to Congress. While not common at the federal level, some states have routine sunset review of all agencies.

Legislative Veto. By including a legislative veto provision in a regulatory state, Congress gives itself veto power over any individual regulation enacted by an agency. The legislative veto is intended to increase congressional control over the regulatory process. The legislative veto has two variants: the two-house veto, under which both houses of Congress must veto a regulation for the veto to be effective; and the one-house veto, under which only one house need veto the regulation. The Supreme Court, however, found the one-house legislative veto unconstitutional in *Chadha* v. *Immigration and Naturalization Service* (1980). Congress is considering alternatives that could meet the test for legislative vetoes established by the Court in that decision.

Mandatory Cost-Benefit Analysis.   A mandatory agency cost-benefit analysis requires an administrative agency to weigh the costs and benefits of all regulations it proposes. When the costs exceed the benefits derived from a regulation, the regulation is eliminated or scaled down. The aim of mandatory cost-benefit analysis is to make the government's decision-making process more cost effective. According to the Supreme Court in *American Textile Manufacturers Institute* v. *Donovan* (1981), a cost-benefit requirement must be expressly provided in the enabling statute. In the absence of an explicit requirement in the enabling statute, an agency is not required to undertake a cost-benefit analysis of the regulations it issues.

▓ INDIRECT CONGRESSIONAL CHECKS ON AGENCY POWER

In recent years, Congress has passed several acts that have had the effect of indirectly controlling the power and authority of administrative agencies. Through those acts, which include the Freedom of Information Act, the Privacy Act, and the Government in the Sunshine Act, Congress made it easier for parties outside the agency to obtain information in the possession of the agency.

Freedom of Information Act.   The Freedom of Information Act (FOIA) was enacted in 1966 and amended in 1974. The FOIA makes most documents submitted to or held by federal agencies available to the general public. Unless the document falls within one of the specifically exempted categories, it must be released upon a request for a copy by a citizen. Exempted categories include trade secrets and documents that would, if disclosed, constitute an unwarranted invasion of personal privacy. Agencies are required to respond to a request for information within ten days after receipt of the request.

Privacy Act.   The Privacy Act, enacted in 1974, is intended to give citizens more control over what information is collected about them and how that information is used. It requires that unless an exception applies, notice and prior consent are needed before an agency can disclose information that concerns and identifies an individual. Individuals are given rights of access to agency records and rights to request amendments to correct inaccuracies. The Act provides that individuals can enforce their rights under it in the federal district courts.

Government in the Sunshine Act.   In 1976, Congress enacted the Federal Sunshine Act. In combination with the Federal Advisory Committee Act of 1972, the Sunshine Act limits secret meetings by agencies. Its purpose is to improve citizen access to government operations.

Under the Sunshine Act, the public is entitled to at least one week's notice of the time, place, and subject matter of any agency meeting. In addition, the agency must specify whether the meeting is open or closed to the public. It must also provide the name and phone number of the official designated by the agency to respond to requests for information about the meeting.

The Sunshine Act lists numerous situations in which a meeting may be properly closed. An open meeting is not required, for example, when the meeting is likely to concern disclosure of matters to be kept secret in the interest of national defense or disclosure of certain trade secrets and commercial or financial information. Agency day-to-day activities are not subject to the Act's requirements.

Federal courts are given authority to enforce the provisions of the Sunshine Act. They may not, however, invalidate an agency action taken at a meeting in violation of the Sunshine Act merely because of such violation; some other basis for overturning an agency action must be established. The court may grant an injunction against future violations of the Sunshine Act.

SUMMARY: A GUIDE FOR MANAGERS

- Administrative agencies have become an important part of modern U.S. government. They are created by Congress and granted legislative, investigative, adjudicatory, and enforcement powers. Congress has created an administrative agency when confronted with problems requiring expertise, flexibility, and supervision.

- Administrative agencies were first used by state governments to regulate private economic activities in the late 1800s. The first federal agency was the Interstate Commerce Commission, established by Congress in 1887. The most significant growth periods in the history of administrative agencies took place during the New Deal era of the 1930s and the social reform era of the 1960s and 1970s.

- Administrative law consists of legal rules defining the authority and structure of administrative agencies, specifying procedural requirements, and defining the roles of government bodies (particularly the courts) in their relationship with agencies. The most fundamental administrative law is the Administrative Procedures Act (APA).

- Agencies perform regulatory responsibilities by the use of informal and formal procedures. Informal procedures, which consist of tests and inspections, are not subject to the procedural requirements of the APA. Formal procedures, which include adjudicatory and investigative hearings, must meet the APA's procedural requirements.

- Except in emergencies, agencies must allow interested parties, such as businesses that will be subject to a regulation, to comment publicly about proposed regulations. Agencies must show that they based regulations on substantial evidence and took into account the comments provided by interested parties.

- Judicial review of an agency decision must be based on a complaint brought

> by an identifiable plaintiff whose zone of interest;
> has been injured or is threatened with injury;
> by a specific agency action;
> that is a final action found in violation of the intent of Congress.

■ Since agencies are authorized by Congress, they are subject to constant oversight by congressional committees. Agencies' budgets can be cut, and agencies can be ordered to stop certain actions and to do certain things. Hence, special interest pleading with Congress can result in agencies' being forced to stop investigations or change regulations.

MANAGER'S ETHICAL DILEMMA

MY FRIEND, THE POLITICIAN

Tough competition, while publicly praised by most business leaders, is rarely favored by those in an industry subject to it. Companies thus seek special privileges from Congress, often to be administered by administrative agencies. Many federal laws have been written specifically to provide relief for certain companies from certain regulations. For example, a provision in one law exempted Massachusetts firms with a value of between $72 million and $73 million. That is, one company persuaded a friend in Congress to put a provision in a general law that applied only to itself. Of course, since it would not look good to name the one company getting special treatment, the company's name is hidden by language that refers to a dollar value that applies to only one company. Other laws force competitors to comply with costly regulations that existing firms can avoid.

Deregulation of airlines in 1978 forced the restructuring of the airlines industry. A number of airlines went broke. Some had become sloppy in their managerial practices. Since they had monopoly routes, new competitors were not allowed, and fares were fixed by the government, genius was not required for staying in the industry. The arrival of competition meant survival by the most efficient and best managed.

While the most successful airlines—such as American, Delta, and United—have stood behind deregulation, others, who continue to suffer from the rigors of competition, yearn for a return to regulation, or at least for the regulations that would benefit them in particular.

Northwest Airlines has had a tough time dealing with deregulation. Once considered one of the best airlines, industry analysts now wonder whether it can survive. The head of Northwest was one of presidential candidate Bill Clinton's biggest financial supporters in 1992. It may be because he believed that Clinton would be a great president; but some suggested it may be because the Clinton administration might promote regulations that would help the airline and thereby make it more profitable at the expense of its competitors and the public.

Corporate and union support for candidates is common. Northwest Airlines executives are no different from most other business and union leaders who know that political leaders can provide assistance with the regulatory process. That is a major reason why Political Action Committees (PACs), which are mostly special interest groups, provided over $116 million in campaign contributions to incumbent members of Congress running for reelection in 1990, while giving their challengers less than $16 million.

QUESTIONS

Should companies and unions be involved in contributing to political campaigns? Is it ethical to lobby members of Congress for special privileges for particular companies, such as exemptions from regulations?

REVIEW AND DISCUSSION QUESTIONS

1. Define the following terms and concepts:
   enabling statute
   New Deal agency
   rulemaking

2. Compare and contrast the following concepts:
   a. Investigatory hearing and adjudicatory hearing.
   b. Agency order and agency regulation.
   c. Informal and formal agency procedures.

3. What are the advantages of informal agency procedures over formal procedures?

4. What advantages does an agency have over the judicial system in monitoring business behavior?

5. Many of the regulatory agencies established before the 1960s were oriented to regulating a specific industry—air travel, trucking, railroads, securities, communications, and shipping. Many of the regulatory agencies established in the 1960s and 1970s apply to business in general—the environment, employee relations, worker safety, and product quality. Why would there be such a shift in emphasis from single-industry orientation to general business? What factors might have caused such a change?

6. Congress often gives the regulatory agencies it creates very broad requirements. It may say something to the effect of "go regulate the environment in the public interest." The agencies then devise regulations to execute the intent of Congress. Should Congress be more specific when it creates agencies?

■ CASE QUESTIONS

7. Dewey owned a mine in Wisconsin. He refused to allow agents of the Department of Labor to inspect the mine without a search warrant. The Department of Labor wanted to determine whether twenty-five violations discovered in a previous search had been corrected. The Federal Mine Safety and Health Act authorizes a specific number of warrantless inspections, but it does not dictate the procedures that inspectors must follow. Will the warrantless search violate Dewey's Fourth Amendment rights?

8. Suppose the Federal Trade Commission has decided to act to eliminate vacation scams—telephone calls by high-pressure salespeople who are selling worthless vacations. Discuss how the FTC could attack this problem through a rulemaking strategy. Conversely, discuss how it could attack the problem by adopting an adjudicatory strategy. Are there any major differences in the two strategies?

9. In 1977, the U.S. Department of Transportation (DOT) adopted a regulation that would require new cars to have either air bags or automatic seat belts (the kind that strap you to the seat when you get in the car). The carmakers protested that this would be too expensive and would not work. In 1981, DOT, under new leadership, repealed the regulation, saying that since it had evidence that people would unhook the seat belts, the regulation was not effective. Car insurance companies sued DOT, claiming that the agency could not repeal the regulation. The court of appeals held that since the repeal was not

based on sufficient evidence, the regulation must be reimposed. What did the Supreme Court have to say? [*Motor Vehicle Manufacturers Assn.* v. *State Farm,* 463 U.S. 29, 103 S.Ct. 2856 (1983)]

10. The EPA proposed expensive new pollution control regulations for coal-burning electricity plants. After receiving comments in the public review period and informal feedback from members of Congress, the EPA published its final regulations, which were not as strict as originally proposed. Some environmental groups sued, claiming that the EPA had been influenced by informal comments and that such comments to agency heads are illegal or should be in the public record. Did the regulation stand? [*Sierra Club* v. *Costle,* 657 F.2d 298 (D.C. Cir. 1981)]

■ BUSINESS POLICY QUESTIONS

11. Are the regulatory reform measures—cost-benefit analysis, sunset laws, and legislative vetoes—good ideas, or are they likely to cause more problems than they will solve? Do they allow private interests to have more say in the continued existence of regulations?

12. The Fudor Paper Company makes specialty paper products at a number of plants throughout the southeastern United States. The company has been in operation for more than 100 years. Over the past several years, the impacts on it of the regulatory and legal environments have been severe. Workplace, employment, transportation, product, and other regulations have significantly increased costs and reduced profitability.

    The regulations that have most affected the company, however, are environmental. The imposition of pollution controls will make several plants noncompetitive with international companies importing into this country. As the general manager of Fudor, you face a difficult decision. The regulations imposed by the EPA were designed for a slightly different technology than what is being used in Fudor's plants. Businesses opposing regulations because of such technical differences, however, often have been viewed as simply trying to avoid governmental regulation.

    Management is considering adopting a strategy that would involve its work force and the state and local governments. Although Fudor has asked these groups to help it in the past, the response has generally been noncommital. Under the proposed strategy, management intends to announce the closing of the plant as a result of the environmental regulations. Fudor anticipates that because it is the principal employer in the towns where its plants are located, the work force and local governments will seek a modification of the pollution control requirements from state and federal officials. It further anticipates that the workers and the local government officials will find the EPA much more willing to listen to them than to the company management. If the pollution control requirement is not relaxed, the company will then decide whether the plants will continue to operate. Assess the company's strategy. Should the work force have any say in the extent of pollution control to be applied? Should agencies take potential unemployment into account in forcing a company to comply with their regulations?

■ ETHICS QUESTIONS

13. The vast majority of regulatory matters are settled informally. Only a very small number of disputes result in litigation. When a company is engaged in a dispute with a federal agency, it knows that if it does not reach a settlement, there

can be costly litigation. From the perspective of the government agency, the litigation is costless—the taxpayers foot the bill. The government representatives know that the threat of costly litigation enhances their chance of extracting a settlement from the company. Should the government use this leverage to extract more in a settlement than it knows it would be likely to get in a court-resolved dispute?

14. Suppose you are working for an agency that has you collecting information about a business to determine whether the business has violated the agency's rules or regulations. In the process, you discover how the company develops and markets it products. If you were to use that information, you are convinced you could make a lot of money. Should agency employees use such information for personal gain?

15. The EPA requires your company to self-report pollution discharges on a day-to-day basis. Your job is to make those reports. You and your superior know that the reports could be easily fudged in the event the company exceeded its designated limits. Suppose that any such excessive discharge would cost the company $25,000 for each day its limit is exceeded. One morning, your superior negligently failed to start the pollution control device, and the designated amount of pollution was exceeded. Your superior has strongly implied that if you do not fudge the figures, you may not be employed at the end of the day because of the costs that will be imposed on the business by the EPA. Should you report the correct figures to the EPA? Would your answer be different if you knew whether the excessive pollution caused serious damage or no damage at all?

BUSINESS AND THE COMMON LAW

The common law is the basis of private legal relationships and has a strong influence on how regulatory law functions. The common law has a long history of evolving to deal with the impact of changes in technology and society. It explain to us how we deal with one another in voluntary business arrangements and what happens when injury is inflicted on someone. The key parts are reviewed in these chapters:

- *Chapter 7 — Business and the Law of Torts* develops the major areas of tort law—legal wrongs for which remedies may be sought. The law of torts is concerned with what happens when a business inflicts an injury on someone.

- *Chapter 8 — Products Liability and Intellectual Property* looks at two of the most important areas of law that have evolved from torts: the modern products liability suits that involve billions of dollars each year and the protection of intellectual property by patents, copyright, trademarks, and trade secrets.

- *Chapter 9 — Business and the Law of Contracts* reviews the key element of business dealings—how we obligate ourselves to exchanges.

- *Chapter 10 — Sales and the UCC* explains the key parts of contract law as applied to business sales and the main parts of the law of sales that has been written down in the Uniform Commercial Code.

- *Chapter 11 — Business Organizations and the Law of Agency* provides an overview of the major ways in which business can be organized; agency law is the study of how we delegate authority in business organizations.

BUSINESS AND THE LAW OF TORTS

CHAPTER 7

MANAGER'S
LEGAL CHALLENGE

Tort liabaility has become a major financial conern for the business community. Rising judgments in tort cases and the rapidly increasing costs of liability insurance have prompted the managements of many companies to assess more fully their potential sources of liability.

Activities that were once considered to be outside of business are being brought into the business environment. For example, in 1991, a jury in Tampa, Florida, imposed an 800,000-dollar punitive damages verdict on Carroll Air Systems, Inc., because one of its salesmen got drunk while entertaining clients and later killed two people in an automobile accident.

The jury concluded that Carroll Air was responsible for the actions of James Mills, one of its salesmen, who rammed another car, killing its two occupants. Mr. Mills was found to be legally drunk. He had just left a convention in a Fort Lauderdale hotel, where he had entertained guests with the company president, who paid for the drinks.

Mr. Mills was, of course, liable for the damages, but the employer was held jointly and separately liable, which meant that as the deep pocket, it would pay most of the damages.

This case is one in a new line of cases in which corporate liability is extended to employees' off-business-property actions. In other cases, companies have been found liable for accidents that result after drunken company-sponsored events, such as Christmas parties and picnics. At least ten states, including New York, New Jersey, and Texas, have adopted a rule that social hosts, including businesses, may be liable for car accidents that result after parties at which the hosts served or paid for liquor.

Managers in states in which there has been no such ruling cannot presume that the rule would not apply to them if such a situation happened involving their company. Juries and judges are free to change the law and adopt the social host liability rule when a case appears in their state.

Since the consumption of alcohol is legal and a common part of social gatherings, and since consumption in moderation is fine for many people, what steps can managers take to reduce the chance of liability? Some companies have adopted no-alcohol rules across the board—none on company property, at company functions, or on company expense accounts. Others mandate two-drink rules at social events, so consumption is allowed, but not enough to produce legal intoxication for most people. Of course, monitoring consumption is a problem. If an employee appears intoxicated, there may be an unpleasant confrontation when the employee is told not to drive home. As in other areas, when social and legal rules change, managers must implement policy changes or risk damaging legal results.

This chapter reviews the tort law and how it affects the business community. It begins with a general discussion that defines the term *tort*, describes the various avenues through which a business may find itself involved in a tort action, and considers the costs of tort litigation. Torts classified as intentional torts are discussed, including wrongs generally designated as either intentional interference with personal rights or intentional interference with property rights. The discussion is followed by an examination of the tort of negligence, including the elements to a negligence action and the defenses available in such an action. Strict liability in tort—often defined as liability without fault—is then discussed. The final section of the chapter considers those torts called business torts, such as interference with contractual relations and interference with business relations.

THE SCOPE OF TORT LAW

Although there are many definitions of the word *tort*, a completely satisfactory definition is hard to give. The word is derived from the Latin *tortus* (twisted) and means "wrong" in French. Although the word faded from common use in the nineteenth century, it remained in the law and has acquired a technical meaning. Today, *tort* is broadly defined as a civil wrong, other than a breach of contract, for which the law provides a remedy.

■ PURPOSES OF TORT LAW

Many accidents and injuries occur each year that result in personal injury and property damage. To constitute a legal action in tort, however, the injury an individual or a business has sustained must be the *consequence* of the wrongdoing of another. In a tort action, the injured individual or business sues the party allegedly responsible for the injury.

Unlike the purpose of the criminal law, the purpose of the law of torts is not to punish the wrongdoer. Rather, the main purposes of tort law are to provide compensation for wrongful injuries and to place the burden of compensation on the wrongdoer who, in justice, ought to bear it. In addition, it is hoped that payment or fear of payment of compensation for tortious conduct will deter future dangerous or injurious behavior by individuals and businesses.

■ BUSINESS AND THE LAW OF TORTS

Broadly speaking, a business can become involved in a tort action in one of three ways: (1) a person is harmed or injured by the actions of a business or its employees, (2) a person is harmed or injured by a product manufactured or distributed by a business, or (3) a business is harmed or injured by the wrongful actions of another business or person.

Injuries suffered by employees while at work are generally covered by state workers' compensation laws and are rarely the subject of tort actions. State workers' compensation laws are specifically designed to compensate workers and their families for work-related injury, disease, or death. Tort actions for injuries caused by the products manufactured or distributed by the business involve the law of products liability, discussed in detail in Chapter 8, which also discusses the application of tort law to intellectual property. The law applicable to the other ways in which a business may become involved in a tort action—where the actions of employees injure another individual or when the business harms or injures another business—is the principal subject of this chapter.

Torts are traditionally classified on the basis of how the harm or injury was inflicted: intentionally, negligently, or without fault (strict liability). In the study of the legal environment of business, however, emphasis is placed on those laws most affecting business. Thus, a fourth classification may be included, called *business torts*, which emphasize the harms or injuries a business may inflict on other businesses.

■ COSTS OF TORT LITIGATION

In 1992, more than one-half million lawsuits involving a tort claim were initiated in our nation's court systems, most in state courts. As Figure 7–1 illustrates, injured party compensation—the principal purpose of tort law—accounted for less than half the total cost of such lawsuits. The rising costs associated with tort litigation have prompted concern about the ability of our court system to effectively and efficiently compensate injured parties.

The cost of the tort system is difficult to calculate. A conservative estimate of the direct costs in 1992 is at least $40 billion. The President's Council on Competitiveness claims that the indirect costs are about three times the direct costs, meaning the total costs of the tort system in 1992 will run closer to $150 billion. Since a large fraction of the cost, whatever it is, falls on business, it is an important part of the legal environment.

INTENTIONAL TORTS

In the law, there is a tendency to attach greater blame to intentional misconduct than to lesser degrees of fault. In such circumstances, the law imposes a greater degree of responsibility upon a defendant. The rules are

FIGURE 7–1

The Distribution of Tort Litigation Costs
SOURCE: Institute for Civil Justice, Rand Corporation

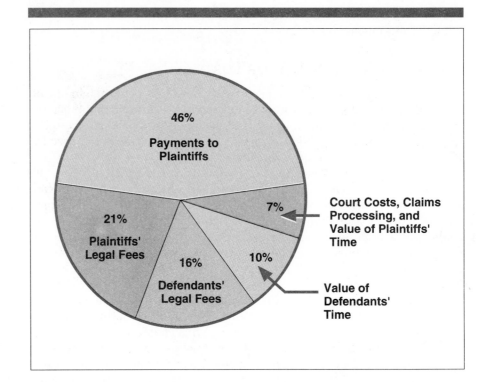

much more liberally applied, imposing liability on a broader range of the defendant's activities, requiring less certainty in the proof presented by the plaintiff as a basis upon which to find the defendant liable, and allowing compensation for wider range of injuries and damages. The defendant's interests are given less weight than are the plaintiff's claim to protection where an *intentional tort* is found.

Intentional torts are based on *willful misconduct* or an intentional wrong. To establish *liability* for an intentional tort, the injured party needs to prove that the wrongdoer intentionally invaded a protected interest. The requirement of *intent* for tort liability is not concerned with malicious intent to do serious harm to another. Rather, there must be an intent to invade the rights or interests of another in a way that the law does not permit. Even in cases where the wrongdoer meant to help someone but the person is injured in the process, the required intent may be present for purposes of tort liability.

■ INTERFERENCE WITH PERSONAL RIGHTS

A business will ordinarily find itself involved in a lawsuit for an intentional tort involving *interference with personal rights* through the wrongful actions of an employee. As discussed in Chapter 11, and as the case in this chapter's Manager's Legal Challenge illustrated, a business is liable under the *law of agency* for the torts of its workers if the tort results from an activity carried out within the scope of the worker's employment. Intentional torts involving interference with personal rights include assault, battery, false imprisonment, defamation, emotional distress, and invasion of privacy.

Assault and Battery. *Assault* is intentional conduct directed at a person that places the person in fear of immediate bodily harm or offensive contact. Contact with the body is not necessary. For example, pointing a gun or swinging a club at another can be an assault. The requirement of fear is satisfied if a reasonable person under similar circumstances would have fear of bodily harm or offensive contact. An essential element of this tort is that the individual in danger of harm must know of the danger and be fearful of its immediate threat. If an individual points a gun at another while the other person is sleeping, for example, there is no assault.

Battery is an unlawful touching—an intentional physical contact without consent. The contact may be direct or may be made with anything that is attached to or identified with the wrongdoer. For example, contact by use of a stick or a gun may cause the unlawful touching. Even if the touching does not cause actual physical harm, it is unlawful if it would offend a reasonable person's sense of dignity.

Although assault and battery often go together, the offenses are separate. The basic requirements of fear of an offensive physical contact for an assault and of actual physical contact for a battery is the principal distinction between the two torts. The two torts are separable. A person may strike another who is asleep, for example, thus committing battery but not assault. On the other hand, a person may shoot at another and miss, thereby creating an assault but no battery. The following is a classic case involving an employee of Western Union Telegraph who was accused of assaulting a customer.

WESTERN UNION TELEGRAPH COMPANY v. HILL

Supreme Court of Alabama
25 Ala.App. 540, 150 So. 709 (1933)

Case Background
Sapp was the agent and manager of a telegraph office belonging to Western Union Telegraph Company. Hill owned an electric clock, the repair of which was under contract with Western Union. If the clock needed repair, Hill was to report that fact to Sapp. One evening, Hill's wife went to the Western Union office to report that the clock needed repair. She found Sapp behind the counter, "still slightly feeling the effects of whiskey." Mrs. Hill told Sapp that she needed the clock repaired. While reaching toward her across the counter, Sapp stated, "If you will come back here and let me love and pet you, I will fix your clock."

Mr. Hill filed damages against the Western Union Telegraph Company for the assault on his wife. The evidence presented at the trial established that Sapp did not touch Mrs. Hill. In fact, even if Sapp had wanted to, he could not have reached Mrs. Hill, because the counter was too high. The trial court found for Mr. Hill and awarded damages. The defendant appealed.

Case Decision
The appellate court found that there was no error by the trial judge in his application of the law to the alleged assault. There was sufficient evidence suggesting Mrs. Hill feared an assault to allow a jury to find that an assault had occurred. The court noted that an assault does not require a battery. Assault is usually an attempt to commit a battery that is not completed. What is required is "a well-founded fear of an imminent battery."

(continued)

Managerial Considerations

This case brings to the manager's attention an important concern in tort law. Notice that although the assault was committed by Sapp, the defendant was Western Union—Sapp's employer. Under the general principles of agency law, if an employee is acting within the scope of employment, the principal (the employer) will be liable for the agent's tortious conduct. Even though Western Union would never have condoned Sapp's actions, it was still liable for the assault.

Managers should be concerned, therefore, with employee conduct during working hours. As society has become less tolerant of sexual harassment, a number of assault suits have been filed against employers for assaults at the workplace. Even though there may be no touching, the fear of harmful or offensive contact constitutes the assault. Similarly, many battery suits now involve offensive contact—such as a man touching a woman—that does not injure the person but is nonetheless offensive. As discussed in the chapter on employment discrimination, employers must have clear policies to put employees on notice that the company will not tolerate harassment and must offer to assist employees who believe they are victims of assaults.

The law recognizes that persons alleged to have committed the torts of assault and battery may have a *defense*—a legally recognized justification for their actions—that relieves them of liability. Two of the most common defenses to assault and battery—and most other intentional torts—are consent and privilege.

Consent occurs when the injured party gives permission to the wrongdoer to interfere with a personal right. The consent may be either expressed or implied by words or conduct. An example of consent in a battery case includes the voluntary participation in a contact sport, such as boxing or football.

A *privilege* involves a right to an immunity from liability. An individual may, for example, have a privilege to use force or the threat of force for self-defense or to evict another lawfully from his or her property. The force used must be reasonable under the circumstances. For example, it is not reasonable to shoot someone to prevent the person from stealing the hubcaps from your car.

False Imprisonment.   The tort of *false imprisonment* (or false arrest) is the intentional holding or detaining of a person within boundaries if the person knows about the detention or is harmed by it. The required detention need not be physical; verbal restraints, such as threats, may be the basis of an action for false imprisonment. As with assault and battery, if the accused is able to prove the consent of the injured party or privileged action, there may be no liability.

Until recently, businesses commonly faced false imprisonment suits from the detention of suspected shoplifters. If the suspected shoplifters were found innocent, it was not uncommon for them to sue the business for false imprisonment. Despite the fact that shoplifters cost stores billions of dollars each year, such suits deterred stores in their attempts to catch shoplifters. As a consequence, most states passed anti-shoplifting statutes, which provide businesses with a defense to a charge of false imprisonment for detaining a shoplifter. The merchant must, however, have a reasonable basis for the detention. Such a statute is the subject of the following case.

JACQUES v. SEARS, ROEBUCK AND COMPANY

Court of Appeals of New York
30 N.Y.2d 466, 334 N.Y.S.2d 632,
285 N.E.2d 871 (1972)

Case Background
Section 218 of the General Business Law of New York gives retail merchants a defense in an action for false arrest and imprisonment for the detention of a suspected shoplifter. The statute provides that if the suspected shoplifter is detained for a reasonable time and if there are reasonable grounds for detaining the suspect, the merchant has a complete defense to a charge of false imprisonment.

Jacques entered a store owned by Sears. He picked up nineteen reflector letters and numbers worth ten cents apiece and put them in his pocket. He selected a mailbox and had two extra keys made. He paid for the mailbox and keys but left the store without paying for the letters. A Sears security guard observed Jacques putting the letters in his pocket and leave the store without paying. The guard stopped him, told him he was under arrest, and took him back to the security office. Sears' security officers called the police, who arrived a few minutes later. With the security officers, the police took Jacques to police headquarters, booked him for petty larceny, and released him on bail. Later, the larceny charge was dismissed because of a lack of proof of intent.

Jacques then brought an action for false imprisonment against Sears. The trial court ruled for Sears, finding that

Jacques had been detained for a reasonable time at Sears and that there were reasonable grounds to detain him. Jacques appealed.

Case Decision
The appellate court affirmed the decision of the trial court, holding that since the detention was reasonable, Sears could not be charged with false imprisonment under Section 218. The court stated that it was the intent of the legislature to protect merchants from false arrest suits even when there was no criminal conviction but where there were reasonable grounds for the arrest.

Managerial Considerations
Each year, billions of dollars are lost as a result of shoplifting and employee theft. Before the enactment of shoplifting statutes, managers were leery about detaining a possible shoplifter for fear of a false imprisonment suit if the alleged shoplifter was not convicted. That reluctance had the effect of further encouraging shoplifting. Thus, merchants and consumers were forced to bear the costs of shoplifting. Shoplifting statutes and improved electronic theft-prevention and surveillance equipment have discouraged shoplifting and reduced losses. However, managers must still take care in the instruction and supervision of employees involved in surveillance to ensure that any detention meets the standards set by legislatures and the courts.

Defamation. The tort of *defamation* is an intentional false communication that injures a person's reputation or good name. If the defamatory communication is spoken, *slander* is the tort. If the communication is printed, written, a picture, or a radio or television broadcast, the tort is *libel.* The elements of both torts involve the following:

1. Making a false or defamatory statement about another individual.
2. Publishing or communicating the statement to a third person.
3. Causing harm to the individual about whom the statement was made.

Some statements are considered *defamation per se.* That is, they are presumed by law to be harmful to the individual to whom they were directed and therefore require no proof of harm or injury. Statements that an individual has committed a serious crime, has a sexually communicable disease, or has improperly carried out business activities can be defamatory per se.

Defenses. Truth and privilege are defenses to an action for defamation. If the statement that caused harm to a person's reputation is the truth, some states hold that that is a complete defense regardless of the purpose or intent in publishing the statement. The defense of *truth* is a common defense to a defamation suit.

Depending on the circumstances, there are three privileges—absolute, conditional, and constitutional—that may be defenses to a defamation action. *Absolute privilege* is an immunity applied in situations where public policy favors complete freedom of speech. For example, state legislators in legislative sessions and participants in judicial proceedings have absolute immunity from liability that could result from their statements. A *conditional privilege* exempts a potential wrongdoer from liability when the defamatory statement was published in good faith and with proper motives. An individual has a conditional privilege, for example, to publish defamatory matter to protect his or her own legitimate interests or to reasonably defend his or her reputation against the defamation of another.

As discussed in Chapter 5, the First Amendment to the Constitution guarantees freedom of speech and freedom of press. This *constitutional privilege* protects members of the press who publish otherwise defamatory material about public officials or public figures. However, this privilege is lost if the statement was made with *actual malice*—knowledge that it was false or with reckless disregard for the truth. In addition, members of Congress are protected from tort liability for defamatory statements by the speech or debate clause of the Constitution (Article I, Section 6). The constitutional privilege for members of Congress does not extend beyond the legislative forum.

INTERNATIONAL ASPECTS | LIBEL IN FOREIGN COURTS

Unlike the United States, many foreign countries do not provide constitutional freedom of speech and press guarantees to the news media. The news media in the United States can communicate defamatory material about public officials and figures or individuals of legitimate public interest as long as the material is provided without actual malice. In the United Kingdom, the news media are not provided with this extensive privilege. Plaintiffs need show only that the alleged defamatory statement was communicated in the United Kingdom and that their reputation as previously held by the people of the country was damaged. To avoid liability, a defendant in the United Kingdom must then demonstrate either that the statements made were, in fact, true or that they had been made in either a court of law or Parliament.

As a consequence of this important difference in the law of defamation, a growing number of U.S. communications and publishing companies are finding themselves in foreign courts defending against defamation suits. Although the broadcasts and publications in question may have originated in the United States and may even have been rebroadcast or distributed in the foreign country without the consent of the U.S. company, the responsible company will not be relieved of liability on that basis alone. In addition, the fact that the U.S. government may have printed a document containing the alleged defamatory material will not relieve the company of liability.

(continued)

The need to defend against libel actions in foreign jurisdictions, however, is not the aspect of this problem that has U.S. companies concerned. Rather these companies' primary concern is with the growing number of libel suits being filed by individuals who are admittedly filing them outside the United States to take advantage of the more favorable laws. The majority of such cases would not likely prevail in U.S. courts. *Time* magazine, NBC, and Dow Jones have faced serious libel actions in foreign jurisdictions. In each case, the plaintiff has selected the foreign court knowing that they would not prevail in the U.S. courts.

Emotional Distress.   One of the newer torts at common law is *emotional distress*. The tort of emotional distress involves intentional conduct so reckless or outrageous that it creates severe mental or emotional distress. This cause of action will compensate a person for conduct that goes beyond the bounds of decency but not from mere bad manners or rough language. Some courts were reluctant to find this tort without accompanying physical injury. Most courts, however, have moved away from that requirement as our understanding about psychological harm has increased.

Businesspeople most often involved in emotional distress suits are bill collectors, landlords, and insurance adjusters. Debt collection is a particularly common area if the debt collector is "overenthusiastic" in collections efforts. Badgering, late-night phone calls, profanity, threats, and name calling lay the groundwork for a potential emotional distress suit.

Invasion of Privacy.   The tort of *invasion of privacy* is a fairly recent development in tort law and is not fully defined by the courts. The concept behind the tort is an individual's right to solitude and to be free from unwarranted public exposure. The tort of invasion of privacy has been committed in the following ways:

1. The use of a person's name or picture without permission (a practice in which advertisers and marketing companies have found themselves liable).

2. Intrusion into a person's solitude (illegal wiretapping, illegal searches of one's residence, and harassment through unwanted and continual telephoning).

3. Placing a person in a false light (for example, the publication of a story claiming that an individual has certain ideas and beliefs when, in fact, he or she does not).

4. Public exposure of facts that are private (such as the public disclosure of one's nonpayment of debts).

In addition to the common law developments, some states have passed statutes to recognize a right to privacy. In either case, the right to privacy is largely waived when a person becomes a public figure, such as an entertainer, a politician, or a sports personality. In addition, the publication of information about an individual taken from public files does not constitute an invasion of privacy.

■ INTERFERENCE WITH PROPERTY RIGHTS

Some wrongs do not harm people but harm their property rights or property interests. Property refers to both *real property*—land and things attached to it—and *personal property*—a person's possessions other than an interest in land. While a business most often finds itself involved in tort actions for the intentional interference with personal rights through its employees, both the business and its employees become involved in tort actions for interference with property rights. The tort actions that may be initiated for violations of the property rights of another include trespass to land, nuisance, trespass to personal property, and conversion.

Trespass to Land.   The tort of *trespass to land* is an unauthorized intrusion by a person or a thing on land belonging to another. If the intruder intended to be on another's property, it is irrelevant whether the intruder incorrectly believed he or she owned the land or had permission to enter it. In addition, it is not necessary for the property owner to demonstrate actual injury to the property. For example, shooting a gun across another's property may create an action for the tort of trespass to land even though there is no damage to the property. Further, the intruder may be liable for trespass even if the entry resulted in an improvement to another's land. If, however, an individual enters another's property to protect the property from damage or to help someone on the property who is in danger, that is a defense against the tort of trespass to land.

The original idea of possession of land included control over a space "from the center of the earth to the heavens." A trespass could be committed on, beneath, or above the surface of the land. That rule is much more relaxed today. An airplane flying over a property owner's airspace does not create an action in trespass so long as it is flying at a reasonable altitude.

Nuisance (Private and Public).   The common law of torts recognizes two kinds of nuisance: a private nuisance and a public nuisance. A *private nuisance* is an activity that substantially and unreasonably interferes with the use and enjoyment of land. The interference may be physical, such as vibration, the destruction of crops, or the throwing of objects upon the land. The interference may cause discomfort or poor health from water pollution, odors, smoke, excessive noise, dust, or noxious fumes. A nuisance may include offensive conditions on adjoining land that impair the occupants' mental tranquility through the fear that those conditions impart or simply through their offensive nature. A person may find, for example, that the use of the house next door for drug deals is upsetting to mental tranquility.

Common law nuisance actions have been useful for challenging environmental damage. In fact, nuisance actions have challenged virtually every major industrial activity that causes some form of pollution. The chapter on environmental law discusses the importance of common law nuisance.

A *public nuisance* is an unreasonable interference with a right held in common by the general public. Generally, a public nuisance involves interference with the public health and welfare. For example, illegal liquor and gambling establishments, bad odors and smells, and the obstruction of a highway would be grounds for a public nuisance action.

Whether an activity creates a private or a public nuisance depends on who is affected by it. The pollution of a river is a private nuisance if it interferes only with one or two landowners living next to the polluter. The suit will be brought privately by those landowners against the polluters. If the pollution adversely affects the public water supply, however, it is also a public nuisance. In such circumstances, the legal representative of the community will bring the action for the people against the polluters.

In addition to the common law, every state has a number of statutes that define a wide variety of activities as being public nuisances. For example, certain manufacturing plants, buildings where drugs are sold, and unhealthy dwellings have been declared by statute to be public nuisances. In the *City of Virginia Beach* decision, the court is asked to consider the constitutionality of such a statute. In its analysis, the court is required to distinguish between a public and a private nuisance.

CITY OF VIRGINIA BEACH v. MURPHY

Supreme Court of Virginia
239 Va. 353, 389 S.E.2d 462 (1990)

Case Background
Maureen Murphy (the defendant) was prosecuted for violating a Virginia Beach City noise ordinance because she permitted loud music to emanate from her restaurant located in the City of Virginia Beach (the plaintiff). The noise ordinance provided:

(a) It shall be unlawful for any person to create, or allow to be created any unreasonably loud, disturbing and unnecessary noise in the city or any noise of such character, intensity and duration as to be detrimental to the life or health of any person or persons or to unreasonably disturb or annoy the quiet, comfort or repose of any person or persons. The following acts, among others, are declared to be loud, disturbing and unnecessary noise in violation of this section, but such enumeration shall not be deemed to be exclusive:

(1) The playing of any television set, radio, tape player, phonograph or any musical instrument in such a manner or with such volume as to annoy or disturb the quiet, comfort or repose of any person or persons.

At the conclusion of the city's case in a non-jury trial, the trial court found the noise ordinance to be unconstitutional because the city "may not under its general police power undertake to make conduct which affects only one person a public nuisance." The city appealed to the state supreme court.

Case Decision
The Supreme Court reversed the trial court, holding the city's noise ordinance to be a legitimate use of its powers to protect citizens from public nuisances. The right not to be subject to "unreasonably loud, disturbing and unnecessary noise," as provided by the city ordinance, combats a nuisance that could bother many people. At any particular time, only one person may be bothered by the noise, but the noise could invade the rights of many people who do not wish to suffer from it. In contrast, "a private nuisance is one which . . . interferes with a right or interest that is unique to an individual, such as an interest in land. . . ."

Managerial Considerations
What is a nuisance is different to different people and in different places. Some activities that are acceptable in large cities would be prohibited in small towns. Businesses attempting to open new operations may be attacked as producing a public nuisance because of the pollution or congestion they cause. As the case here shows, local governments can clarify what is a nuisance and enforce the law so as to protect certain interests. For example, a retirement community may want strict prohibitions on noise to protect the character of the community. Businesses located in such places often help press for such rules not only because the rules are desired by most residents but also because the businesses rely on the stability of the community.

Trespass to Personal Property.   The intentional and wrongful interference with the possession of personal property of another without consent is a *trespass to personal property*. An important element in this tort is that an individual has interfered with the right of the owner to exclusive possession and enjoyment of personal property. Liability usually occurs where the trespasser damages the property or deprives the owner of the use of the property for a time. However, if interference with the personal property is warranted, there is a defense to the trespass. Many states have statutes that allow innkeepers to hold the personal property of guests who have not paid their lodging bills.

Conversion.   The tort of *conversion* is an intentional and unlawful control or appropriation of the personal property of another. In contrast to trespass to personal property, conversion requires that the interference with the owner's right of control be serious enough to justify payment for the property. Several factors are considered in determining whether the interference is serious enough to warrant a finding of conversion: the extent of dominion or control, the length of the interference, the damage to the property, and the inconvenience and expense to the owner.

As with trespass to land, mistake does not constitute a defense to conversion. Generally, one who wrongfully acquires possession of another's personal property—as by theft, duress, or fraud—is said to have committed the tort of conversion. Even a good-faith purchaser who buys converted (stolen) goods, believing the seller had a right to sell the goods, is liable for conversion. However, there is no liability if the property was purchased from one who acquired it through duress or fraud. Suppose, for example, that Mobley buys a cement mixer from RMC, Inc., a masonry contractor. If Mobley believes that RMC is the owner of the mixer and has the right to sell it, Mobley is a good-faith purchaser. Later, if it is held that RMC has committed the tort of conversion, having stolen the cement mixer from Baumer Distributing Company, Mobley has also committed conversion. If RMC had wrongly obtained possession of the cement mixer from Baumer through fraud or duress, however, RMC would be liable in conversion, but Mobley, the good-faith purchaser, would not.

INTERNATIONAL ASPECTS | **IS JAPAN REALLY DIFFERENT?**

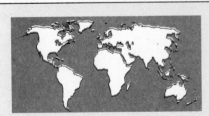

Some politicians want legislation to restrict tort litigation. They often cite Japan as an example of where there is less litigation and fewer lawyers. This is supposed to make the Japanese more competitive than the United States, where tort cases are claimed to be out of control.

The United States has twenty-five times more lawyers per person than Japan because the government of Japan allows only between 300 and 500 new attorneys each year. However, Japanese universities produce 50 percent *more* legal specialists per person than do American universities. These Japanese "nonlawyers" do all legal work except represent clients in court for a fee. Although the nonlawyers are not called lawyers, they are paid to do what Americans call legal work.

(continued)

A study of fatal traffic accidents in Japan by UCLA law professor Mark Ramseyer and Hitotsubashi University law professor Minoru Nakazato found that the American and Japanese tort systems do not look all that different. The systems are organized differently because of the small number of people in Japan called lawyers, but the results are surprising for those who think that Americans are the only people in the world who file lawsuits and that American juries are too sympathetic to plaintiffs. The authors found that Japanese plaintiffs win a higher percentage of tort liability suits than do American plaintiffs. They also found the payments to Japanese plaintiffs to be very close to those given to American plaintiffs in similar tort suits.

Many of the rules in Japan are different from those in the United States, but a close examination makes the actual operation of the two tort systems look more alike than one would suspect.

NEGLIGENCE

Unlike intentional torts, torts based on *negligence* protect individuals from harm from others' unintentional but careless conduct. As a general rule, all individuals are under a duty to conduct themselves in all their activities so as to not create an unreasonable risk of harm or injury to others. People who do not exercise due care in their conduct will be liable for negligence if the following elements can be shown by the injured party:

1. The wrongdoer owed a duty to the injured party (often known as the duty of ordinary care).

2. The duty of care owed to the injured party was breached through some act or omission on the part of the wrongdoer (often this breach itself is termed negligence).

3. There is a causal connection between the wrongdoer's negligent conduct and the resulting harm to the injured party.

4. The injured party suffered actual harm or damage recognized as actionable by law as a result of the negligent conduct.

Broadly defined, then, negligence is conduct—an act or omission—by an individual that results in harm to another to whom the individual owes a duty of care. In contrast to an intentional tort, the harmful results of an individual's conduct are not based on an intended invasion of another person's rights. If the individual's conduct creates an *unreasonable risk of harm* to others, such conduct may be termed negligent even though there was no intent to cause harm. Thus, if a person intentionally runs over another while driving, he or she has committed the intentional tort of battery. However, a person who unintentionally runs over another while driving carelessly has committed a tort based on negligence.

THE REASONABLE PERSON STANDARD

In determining whether a person's conduct is negligent, the law applies a standard of reasonableness. The standard is usually stated as *ordinary care* or *due care,* as measured against the conduct of a hypothetical person—the *reasonable* person.

The reasonable person represents a standard of how typical persons in the community *ought* to behave. If the person is a skilled professional, such as a doctor, an attorney, or an accountant, the standard is that of a reasonably skilled and competent person who is a qualified member of the profession. In determining whether a person's conduct was negligent, the question is, What would a reasonable person have done under the same or similar circumstances? If the conduct was not that of a reasonable person in the eyes of the jury or the judge, the person has failed the reasonableness test and has acted in a negligent manner.

The reasonableness standard or the reasonable person standard is a theoretical concept created in law. It describes a person who acts in a reasonable manner under the circumstances. The standard is not always easy to live up to. Although the law does not require perfection, errors in judgment must be reasonable or excusable under the circumstances, or negligence will be found. Note that juries in different parts of the country may have slightly different standards, since local customs play a role in common law cases.

■ CAUSATION

A basic element of the tort of negligence is *causation* between the act or omission of an individual and another's injury. For a person to have caused an injury to another and be held negligent, the acts must have been the cause in fact and the proximate cause of the other's injury.

Cause in Fact.   *Cause in fact* is established by evidence showing that a person's conduct is the cause of an event because the event would not have occurred without it. Courts express this as a rule commonly referred to as the *but for* or *sine qua non* rule. That is, the individual's injury would not have occurred "but for" the conduct of the wrongdoer. A hotel's failure to install a proper fire escape, for example, is not the cause in fact for the death of an individual who suffocated in bed from smoke. The individual would have died regardless of whether the hotel had properly installed a fire escape.

Proximate Cause.   An injured party must prove that the defendant's act or omission was not only the cause in fact of the injury but also the proximate cause of the injury. *Proximate cause* is a judicially imposed limit on liability for the consequences of negligence. Liability is limited to consequences that bear a reasonable relationship to the negligent conduct. Consequences that are too remote or too far removed from negligent conduct will not result in liability.

A person's act may set off a chain of events and injuries that were not *foreseeable*. For example, the principal cause in fact of the Great Chicago Fire may have been Mrs. O'Leary's negligent conduct of leaving a lamp for her cow to kick, but no court would hold Mrs. O'Leary liable for the full consequences of her initial act. The chain of events was not foreseeable, as the court explains in *Palsgraf*.

PALSGRAF v. LONG ISLAND RAILROAD COMPANY

Court of Appeals of New York
248 N.Y. 339, 162 N.E. 99 (1928)

Case Background
The plaintiff, Helen Palsgraf, was waiting on a platform to catch a train to Rockaway Beach. As she stood there, another train stopped at the station. As the other train began leaving the station, two men ran to catch it. One man was able to get aboard without a problem, but the other man, who was carrying a package wrapped in newspaper, jumped on the car but appeared to fall from the train. One of the guards on the train was holding the door open for the man. He reached forward to help the falling man, while another guard, who was standing on the platform, pushed the teetering man from behind. As the man regained his balance, the package he was holding fell onto the rails. The package contained fireworks, and when the package fell, the fireworks exploded. The shock from the explosion caused some scales that were located on the other end of the platform to fall, striking the plaintiff and injuring her seriously.

The plaintiff sued the railroad company for the negligence of its employees during this event. The jury found in favor of the plaintiff, and the appellate division affirmed the jury's decision. The defendant appealed to the Court of Appeals of New York.

Case Decision
The high court of New York reversed the lower courts and ruled for the defendant. In one of the most cited opinions in

legal history, Judge Cardozo explained why. "Negligence is not actionable unless it involves the invasion of a legally protected interest, the violation of a right." Unfortunately for Helen Palsgraf, no action was directed at her that violated any right. She was not involved in the situation that resulted in the explosion. The people involved in the incident were not aware of her presence. "Here . . . there was nothing in the situation to suggest to the most cautious mind that the parcel wrapped in newspaper would spread wreckage through the station." The possibility of danger from the situation was not foreseeable as to Palsgraf.

Managerial Considerations
The person who was negligent in this case was the passenger who got on the train, leaving injury behind. It is not uncommon for businesses to become responsible for a situation caused by the carelessness of a customer or a stranger. In a store or restaurant, for example, a customer may spill liquid on the floor, on which another person falls and is injured. The culprit is usually gone when the injury occurs and, even if not, is not the deep pockets worth suing for the injury. Since managers know that spills will occur, they must instruct the staff to watch for such things and clean them up or rope the area off. Knowing the kinds of careless things that happen on company property, managers must take steps to protect those on their property.

The majority of courts stand by *Palsgraf* today. Several Supreme courts in 1990 cases restated the proposition. The Missouri court held that the duty owed by the plaintiff to the defendant "is generally measured by whether or not a reasonably prudent person would have anticipated danger and provided against it. . . ." The New Mexico court explained: "A duty to the individual is closely intertwined with the foreseeability of injury to *that individual* resulting from an activity conducted with less than reasonable care. . . ." And the Texas court stated that "before liability will be imposed, there must be sufficient evidence indicating that the defendant knew of or should have known that harm would eventually befall a victim."

However, a few state supreme courts reject the *Palsgraf* doctrine. In *Mitchell* v. *Gonzales* (1991), the California Supreme Court rejected proximate cause in favor of a *substantial factor* test. The court said that juries were confused by the instructions they were given about proximte cause. Juries were told they could not find a negligent defendant liable for injury to a plaintiff unless the injury would not have occurred "but for" the negligence of the defendant. This caused juries to let negligent defendants off the hook because there may have been other factors involved or because the defendant was not on the scene at the moment of the injury. The substantial factor test allows a jury to hold a defendant liable even if there is more than one cause of harm and if the jury finds that a defendant's conduct was a substantial factor in bringing about the injury.

Intervening Conduct.   One problem with determining proximate cause is the possibility of *intervening conduct*. The breaking of the causal connection between a person's act and the resulting harm to another by an intervening act or event, is called a *superseding cause*. If the causal relationship between the defendant's act and resulting harm is *broken* by the intervening act, which was unforeseeable under the circumstances, the defendant will likely not be liable in negligence. Suppose, for example, that LMN, Inc., negligently leaves uncovered a ditch that its workers dug to lay a pipe and the ditch crosses a public sidewalk. If Washburn intentionally shoves Daft into the ditch, LMN is not liable to Daft for its negligence. Washburn's conduct is a superseding cause that relieves LMN of liability. Suppose, however, that Daft had accidentally fallen into the ditch that had negligently been left uncovered and was drowning because the ditch was filled with rainwater. Frierson dives into the ditch to save Daft and drowns. LMN will be responsible to both parties. Because *danger invites rescue*, the common law policy is that the negligent party will be responsible for the losses suffered by those who attempt to save people in danger because of the negligence of others.

■ DEFENSES TO A NEGLIGENCE ACTION

Even if an injured party establishes the required elements of negligence, the party may be denied compensation if the alleged wrongdoer establishes a *valid defense*. As a general rule, any defense to an intentional tort is also available in a negligence action. In addition, several other defenses are available to defendants in negligence actions, including assumption of risk, contributory negligence, comparative negligence, and the last clear chance.

Assumption of Risk.   An injured party who had voluntarily assumed the risk of harm that arose from the negligent conduct of another person will generally not recover compensation for his or her losses. Such a decision by the injured party is called *assumption of risk* and creates a defense for the wrongdoer. This defense requires that the injured party knew or *should* have known of the risk and that the risk was voluntarily assumed. Thus, athletes, such as football players, are said to assume the risk of some injuries on the field. Similarly, spectators at sporting events such as baseball games assume the risk for injuries that result from the usual playing of the game and the reaction of the crowd.

Assumption of risk is an affirmative defense. It must be specifically raised by the defendant in order to take advantage of it. When established, assumption of risk may bar the plaintiff from any recovery—even if the defendant was negligent—or limit the amount that may be recovered.

Contributory Negligence.   We have established that a person who does not use reasonable care in the exercise of a duty to another may be liable for the injuries that result. In some situations, however, both parties will have acted in an unreasonable manner. If the defendant in a negligence action can prove that the plaintiff failed to exercise due care, in some courts the negligence of the injured party creates a *complete defense,* called *contributory negligence.* Under this defense, the injured party's conduct is found to fall below a standard reasonable for his or her own protection, and as a consequence, the injured party has legally contributed to the wrongdoer's negligence in bringing about the harmed caused. In effect, the injured party's own negligence has become the superseding cause of the injury. For example, in a negligence suit in which the injured party is claiming damages for injuries resulting from an automobile accident, if it can be demonstrated that the injured party contributed to the cause of the accident—he or she had been drinking—the wrongdoer has a complete defense to the negligence suit.

Comparative Negligence.   Because of the harshness of the contributory negligence doctrine in creating a complete bar to recovery, a majority of the states (44 at last count) are substituting the doctrine of *comparative negligence.* Under comparative negligence, damages are reduced by the percentage of the injuries caused by the plaintiff's own negligence. Suppose, for example, that Eyestone runs over Glenn with his automobile. As a consequence, Glenn sustains $10,000 in injuries and sues Eyestone. If the court determines that Eyestone's negligence contributed 80 percent to Glenn's injuries and that Glenn's negligence contributed 20 percent, the court would award Glenn $8,000. Note, however, that many courts allow no recovery under comparative negligence when the injured party's degree of negligence is equal to or greater than that of the wrongdoer, that is, 50 percent or more. The *Brooks* decision looks at the distribution of fault in a case in which both parties were negligent.

BROOKS v. CITY OF BATON ROUGE

Court of Appeals of Louisiana, First Circuit
558 So.2d 1177 (1990)

Case Background
Brooks (the plaintiff) was driving her car on O'Neal Lane in Baton Rouge. For some reason, she allowed the right wheels of her car to drift off the paved road and onto loose shoulder gravel. Trying to get the car back on the pavement, she jerked the steering wheel, oversteered, crossed the center line, and was hit by a car coming from the other direction. She died as a result of the accident.

O'Neal Lane had recently been repaved, and new lines painted. City workers who did the shoulder work used size

No. 57 limestone aggregate. Experts agreed that size No. 610 would have been better for shoulder surfacing because of its compaction ability. On that basis, the Brooks estate sued the City of Baton Rouge for negligence in the construction of the highway shoulder.

Applying the comparative negligence doctrine, the trial court found Mrs. Brooks 15 percent at fault and the defendant 85 percent at fault for the accident. The defendant appealed, claiming that Brooks's negligence accounted for more than 15 percent of the cause of the accident.

(continued)

Case Decision

[The state's] Supreme Court has indicated which factors should be considered in order to apportion fault under a system of comparative fault:

In determining the percentages of fault, the trier of fact shall consider both the nature of the conduct of each party at fault and the extent of the causal relation between the conduct and the damages claimed. In assessing the nature of the conduct of the parties various factors may influence the degree of fault assigned, including: (1) whether the conduct resulted from inadvertence of involved an awareness of the danger, (2) how great a risk was created by the conduct, (3) the significance of what was sought by the conduct, (4) the capacities of the extenuating circumstances which might require the actor to proceed in haste without proper thought. And of course, as evidenced by concepts such as last clear chance, the relationship between the fault/negligent conduct and the harm to the plaintiff are considerations in determining the relative fault of the parties.

Mrs. Brooks committed two acts of negligence: her inattention which caused her to leave the roadway, and her improper attempt to regain the paved portion of the highway before reducing speed.

Since the road was straight and the weather clear, the court noted that the only factor that lessened Mrs. Brooks's percent of fault was that her reaction to the situation was instinctive. On the other hand, the City should have known better than to use the wrong material on the shoulder of the road, which caused the plaintiff's car to drop down when it left the pavement. That would not have happened if the City had used the correct limestone aggregate. The appeals court concluded that the trial court should have allocated 50 percent of the responsibility to Brooks.

Managerial Considerations

Anyone who provides a good or a service, such as paving a road, is held to know what experts in that particular field know to be safe and proper. It is not a defense for the people responsible for paving to say that they thought the limestone aggregate they used was good enough; they had a duty to know what should have been used. People will be negligent in their use of goods and services, but that does not mean that all liability will be avoided. If negligence contributes to injury, legal responsibility is likely to be found.

Last Clear Chance. The most commonly accepted modification of the strict rule of contributory negligence is the *last clear chance doctrine*, which allows an injured party to recover from a wrongdoer, despite the injured party's contributory negligence, if the wrongdoer was the last actor under the circumstances able to avoid the injury. Suppose, for example, that a worker for DEF, Inc., was digging a ditch across a public sidewalk but had negligently failed to post warning signs. Katz, who was driving her moped along the sidewalk, saw the ditch in sufficient time to stop. However, Katz negligently pulled on the accelerator rather than the brake and ran into the ditch, injuring the worker. Because Katz had the last clear chance to stop her moped before going into the ditch, the worker's contributory negligence is excused.

INTERNATIONAL ASPECTS | TORT LIABILITY IN FRANCE

In France, a wrongdoer's liability is established in the Civil Code. In general, the Civil Code makes a wrongdoer liable for all damages that result from his or her negligence. In particular, the Civil Code specifically permits recovery for economic loss arising from negligent conduct (*quasi-delit*). The only limitations on damages are that they must be the immediate and direct consequence of the tort.

The wrongdoer's liability, however, is conditioned on finding the specific elements of the tort. First, the harm, either physical or economic, must be specific and certain. Second, there must be a finding of fault on the part of the negligent party. The U.S. doctrine of strict liability in tort is not present to any significant extent in the French system. Third, there must be a finding of causality, and the courts use the notion of proximate cause. Finally, the extent of the harm and the recoverable loss is determined by a judge and not by a jury.

STRICT LIABILITY IN TORT ▬▬▬▬▬▬▬▬▬

Strict liability can be defined as liability without fault. That is, unlike intentional tort, there is no need to prove intent. In contrast to negligence, liability under the doctrine of *strict liability in tort* will be established if the following elements can be shown by the injured party:

1. A causal connection exists between the wrongdoer's conduct and the resulting harm to the injured party.

2. The injured party suffered harm, recognized as actionable by law, as a result of the wrongdoer's conduct.

▨ ABNORMALLY DANGEROUS ACTIVITIES

Although the use of strict liability has been expanded recently, the concept is not a new one. In an early English case, *Rylands* v. *Fletcher* (1868), the defendants were found liable for damages when water from an abandoned coal mine on their property broke through and flooded the plaintiff's active mine. At the time, the case did not fit into any of the conventional tort liability theories, since the defendant was free of negligence and did not know of the abandoned coal shaft, so there could be no intentional tort. The court introduced the concept of strict liability, emphasizing the abnormal character of the activity that caused the harm.

Today courts impose strict liability for harms resulting from the undertaking of exceptionally dangerous or inappropriate activities. Such activities as blasting with dynamite, storing or using dangerous substances, or keeping dangerous animals have all been held to be sufficiently dangerous to justify strict liability. Thus, if Randy's Construction Company is using dynamite to blast a path for a new roadway and a bystander that Randy's was unaware of is injured, Randy's is strictly liable for the bystander's injuries.

The tort of strict liability for dangerous activities has been applied in *toxic tort* cases involving people injured by exposure to toxic or hazardous substances. In the following case, the state government is using strict liability to impose responsibility upon several companies to clean up a toxic dump site.

STATE DEPARTMENT OF ENVIRONMENTAL PROTECTION v. VENTRON CORPORATION

Supreme Court of New Jersey
94 N.J. 473, 468 A.2d 150 (1983)

Case Background
The case involves the responsibility of Ventron for the cleanup of pollution seeping from its land into Berry's Creek, a tidal estuary of the Hackensack River that flows through the Meadowlands. Beneath its surface, the land is saturated by hundreds of tons of toxic waste, primarily mercury. For several thousand feet, the concentration of mercury is among the highest found in fresh water in the world. The contamination results from mercury processing operations at the site for almost fifty years.

The New Jersey Department of Environmental Protection filed a complaint against Ventron, charging it with, among other things, creating and maintaining a nuisance. The trial court found Ventron strictly liable for the cleanup of the mercury. The appellate court affirmed the judgment. The Supreme Court of New Jersey granted an appeal to
(*continued*)

consider the application of strict liability for the removal of the mercury in Berry's Creek.

Case Decision
The high court affirmed the decision of the lower courts, holding that the company is liable for the damages caused under the doctrine of strict liability for abnormally dangerous activities. The court stated that the company was "unleashing a dangerous substance during nonnatural use of the land." In imposing strict liability, it said that "an ultrahazardous activity which introduces an unusual danger into the community should pay its own way in the event it actually causes damage to others."

Managerial Considerations
In recent years, courts have been less tolerant about polluting industries. Increasingly, the courts are looking to strict liability as a theory under which those affected by industrial pollution can find relief. Managers in industries that have a history of land pollution should consider environmental audits and, if necessary, the development of detailed cleanup plans. It is likely to be cheaper to initiate such an action than to have it imposed either by the courts or by a regulatory agency.

In addition, managers should be careful when purchasing real estate. Efforts should be made to ensure that the land does not contain hidden environmental problems. If management has not been diligent in determining the existence of such a problem, it could be burdened with the unexpected responsibility of cleaning up the pollution. A simple cleanup involving digging up the site and disposing of the waste and any contaminated soils could cost several million dollars.

■ PRODUCTS LIABILITY

A manufacturer is strictly liable for harm caused by its defective products. Although the manufacturer may not have been negligent or intended to cause harm, the law will impose strict liability upon the manufacturer for production of a product that was unreasonably dangerous to the consumer and resulted in harm. Under this doctrine, the injured party must show the following:

1. The product was defective.
2. The defect created an unreasonably dangerous product.
3. The defect was the proximate cause of injury.

The rationale given for strict liability for manufacturers of defective products is that negligence is often difficult to prove, strict liability provides manufacturers with needed safety incentives, and the manufacturer is in a better position to bear accident costs. Because of the great importance of products liability to business, it is discussed in detail in the next chapter.

BUSINESS TORTS

Our economy is based on general principles of competition and free enterprise. Its strength lies in the ability of individuals to maximize the value of their assets in the market by being able to compete in the most efficient manner. The policy of the common law has always been in favor of this notion of free competition.

Some overzealous competitors may act to the detriment of society and the market system. The concept of fair competition under the law restrains businesspeople from intentionally or carelessly injuring others involved in business. This area of the law is concerned with business torts—those torts unique to business forums. A *business tort* is defined as the wrongful interference with the business rights of another. The business tort theories discussed below include disparagement, intentional interference with contractual relations of another, and interference with a business relationship.

■ DISPARAGEMENT

Disparagement is a false communication that injures other people in their business. Unlike defamation, the false and damaging statement applies to business, not to personal reputation. Sometimes called trade disparagement, this tort arises when an untrue statement is published regarding a business or a person's business dealings, and the statement convinces others not to deal with that business.

The disparaging statement can take many forms, including statements about a business's goods, credit, honesty, or efficiency. The disparaging statement, for example, may falsely claim that a firm's liquor is watered down, its food is contaminated, or its gasoline is low quality. It may also refer to the principal asset of the business, such as a disparaging statement about a hotel or a restaurant.

In most circumstances, the business must prove it has suffered a monetary loss. That loss may be from a single transaction or from a general decline in customers. Like defamation, this tort is subject to the defenses of truth and privilege.

Business Communications and Defamation.   Letters or other communications between businesses regarding the work performance of past employees have become a major source of defamation suits. Accounting for nearly one-third of defamation suits, the typical case involves a person who has been fired by a company and is seeking employment with another. The letter describing the work performance of the person becomes the focus for why the person failed to get hired. The person then brings an action against the former employer alleging defamation. As the *Buck* decision illustrates, the jury awards can be substantial. However, even if the court agrees with the defendant, the costs of defending against a defamation suit are substantial. As a consequence, several major companies have made it company policy not to provide information—good or bad—on past or current employees.

FRANK B. HALL & COMPANY, INC. v. BUCK

Court of Appeals of Texas,
Fourteenth District
678 S.W.2d 612 (1984)

Case Background
Buck, the plaintiff, was a successful insurance salesman when he was hired by Frank B. Hall & Company, the defendant, in 1976. During the next several months, Buck generated substantial commission income for Hall and suc-

ceeded in bringing several major accounts to the firm. At a meeting in 1977, Lester Eckert, Hall & Company's office manager, abruptly fired Buck. Buck sought employment at several other insurance firms, but his efforts were fruitless. Buck hired an investigator, Lloyd Barber, in an attempt to discover why Hall had fired him. On the basis of statements made by Eckert, Buck sued Hall for defamation of character. The jury found for Buck and awarded $1.9 million in

(continued)

damages, plus interest, attorney's fees, and court costs. Hall & Company appealed.

Case Decision

Eckert, Hall & Company's office manager, had told Barber that Buck was horrible in a business sense, irrational, ruthless, and disliked by office personnel. He described Buck as a "classical sociopath," who would verbally abuse and embarrass Hall employees. Eckert said Buck had stolen files and records from [his previous company]. He called Buck "a zero," "a Jekyll and Hyde person" who was "lacking . . . in scruples." . . . Charles Burton, then president of another large insurance brokerage firm . . . testified that Buck had contacted him in the summer of 1977 to discuss employment possibilities with [his company]. When asked why he was no longer with Hall & Company, Buck told Burton that he "really (didn't) know." Because he was seriously interested in hiring Buck, Burton telephoned Eckert to find out the circumstances surrounding Buck's termination. Eckert told Burton, "Larry didn't reach his production goals." Burton, who was very familiar with Buck's exceptional record as a good producer in the insurance business, was surprised at Eckert's response. When pressed for more information, Eckert declined to comment, stating, "I can't go into it." Burton then asked if Eckert would rehire Buck, to which Eckert answered, "No."

Burton testified that Eckert made the statements and that because of Eckert's comments, he was not willing to extend an offer of employment to Buck. He stated, "When I talked to Mr. Eckert at Frank B. Hall agency, he led me to believe that there was something that he was unable to discuss with me" and "(t)here was something that he was unwilling to tell me about that I had to know."

The jury found (1) Eckert made a statement calculated to convey that Buck had been terminated because of serious misconduct; (2) the statement was slanderous or libelous; (3) the statement was made with malice; (4) the statement was published; and (5) damage directly resulted from the statement. The jury also found the statements were not substantially true and determined that the statements, which were capable of a defamatory meaning, were understood as such by Burton. The judgment of the trial court was affirmed.

Managerial Considerations

Buck had good, strong evidence to present in this case. In other cases, a straightforward letter of recommendation to a potential employer was attacked for not being glowing enough in its contents. One must thus be very careful, especially when in a managerial position, about what is said about another's work ability. What may seem perfectly obvious at the time can look very different to a jury removed from the work situation when negative comments are repeated. Further, the comments that are made to someone who is a friend can come back to haunt if the friend ends up on the other side at a later time. Even when it hurts to keep opinions private, unless there is clear evidence of lack of performance, discretion is advised.

■ INTERFERENCE WITH CONTRACTUAL RELATIONS

One of the more common business torts is *intentional interference with contractual relations of another*. The basis of the claim is that the injured business's contractual relations were wrongfully interfered with by another business. The elements of this tort are

1. The existence of a valid contract between the injured business and another party.
2. The contract was known to the wrongdoer.
3. The wrongdoer intentionally interfered with the contract.

When a wrongdoer intentionally causes another party to break a good contract, it does not matter what the motive is. The point is that the breach of contract is induced to benefit the wrongdoer. This causes injury to the party who suffers the breach of contract. The party who suffers the breach may sue both the party who breached the contract for breach and the wrongdoer for the tort of interference with the contract.

The most spectacular case in history involved the purchase of Getty Oil by Texaco. It was known that Pennzoil was in the process of buying Getty Oil. Texaco stepped in and offered a higher price for Getty, which accepted the offer. Pennzoil sued. The court found that Getty intended to contract with Pennzoil and that Texaco knew of the impending contract but induced the deal not to be completed. Texaco was ordered to pay Pennzoil over $10 billion in damages, which bankrupted Texaco. The case was settled for $3 billion. More common, and less spectacular, are cases in which an employee is induced to breach a contract with an employer, as we see in the *Kemper* case.

JAMES S. KEMPER & COMPANY v. COX & ASSOCIATES

Supreme Court of Alabama
434 So.2d 1380 (1983)

Case Background
Kemper was an insurance brokerage company with one office in Alabama. It employed Earl Tillery beginning in 1963. Tillery's employment contract included a covenant not to compete. Tillery was Kemper's only salesman in Alabama until his resignation in 1981. He then went to work for Cox & Associates. Although Tillery had informed Cox of the covenant, Cox authorized and paid for a trip by Tillery through Alabama to call on Kemper clients to solicit business for Cox. Cox encouraged Tillery to exploit his longstanding relations with Kemper's customers to secure their business.

Kemper brought an action against Tillery and Cox, seeking injunctive relief and damages for interference with contractual relations. The trial court granted partial injunctive relief but denied damages. Cox appealed.

Case Decision
The supreme court held that there was interference with contractual relations and reversed the trial court's decision with instructions to grant damages to Kemper. The court stated that in employer-employee relationships, interference with a contract is not legal if it is "intentional, knowing, malicious, unjustified or unlawful." In this case, Cox knew of Tillery's covenant not to compete but financed the trip to visit Kemper's customers anyway. The damages were the loss of Kemper's customers to Cox.

Managerial Considerations
In hiring new employees, managers should be aware of their past employment and take care that they do not breach duties explicit in past contracts or implied at law. Not the least of these are covenants not to compete and interfere with contractual relationships. Knowledge of a relationship between the new employee and a competitor should make the manager particularly cautious. Although competitive practices are encouraged by the court, predatory behavior is not. While most states uphold no-compete clauses in employment contracts, as long as they are reasonable as to place and length of time, a few states, like California, do not like such clauses.

◼ INTERFERENCE WITH A BUSINESS RELATIONSHIP

Similar to the tort of interference with contractual rights is the tort of *interference with a business relationship*. While businesses devise countless schemes to attract customers, it is a tort when a business attempts to improve its place in the market by interfering with another's business in an unreasonable and improper manner. An employee of Ira's Liquors, for example, cannot be positioned at the entrance of JJ's Liquors for the purpose of diverting customers to Ira's. Most courts define such conduct as *predatory behavior*. If this type of business activity were permitted, Ira's could reap the benefits of JJ's advertising. If the behavior of the defendant is merely competitive and not predatory in nature—for example, the defendant is so effective in advertising and marketing that customers are drawn from the other business—the courts will not find the defendant liable. Such activity is, in the spirit of free competition, considered privileged. We see an example of this in the *Miller* decision.

MILLER CHEMICAL COMPANY v. TAMS

Supreme Court of Nebraska
211 Neb. 837, 320 N.W.2d 759 (1982)

Case Background
Miller, the plaintiff, distributed agricultural chemicals and animal feed additives for livestock and crops. In February 1979, Miller feared it would lose sales in southeastern Iowa, so it sent a letter to its customers in that area offering 5 percent discounts for large orders. A week after the letter was sent out, Miller learned that some of its customers outside the area had also received copies of the letter. Several of those customers inquired about the discount. As a consequence of having to extend the discounts, Miller lost nearly $9,000. It later learned that Robert Tams, a former Miller employee now in competition with Miller, had received the letter, made copies of it, and distributed it to customers of Miller outside the southeastern Iowa area. Miller brought an action for interference with a business relationship against Tams. The trial court found no interference. The plaintiff appealed.

Case Decision

The essential elements of tortious interference with business relationships are: (1) The existence of a valid business relationship or expectancy; (2) Knowledge by the interferer of the relationship or expectancy; (3) An intentional act of interference on the part of the interferer; (4) Proof that the interference caused the harm sustained; and (5) Damage to the party whose relationship or expectancy was disrupted. . . .

The Restatement of Torts recognizes the privilege of a competitor and provides: "(1) One is privileged purposely to cause a third person not to enter into or continue a business relation with a competitor of the actor if (a) the relation concerns a matter involved in the competition between the actor and the competitor, and (b) the actor does not employ improper means, and (c) the actor does not intend thereby to create or continue an illegal restraint of competition, and (d) the actor's purpose is at least in part to advance his interest in his competition with the other.

The judgment of the trial court was affirmed. The court said that the action was competitive in nature. No contracts between Miller and Miller's customers had been breached. Even if Tams acted out of hate or revenge, that "is insufficient to make interference improper if the conduct is directed at least in part to advancement of his own competitive interest."

Managerial Considerations
Fair competition is beneficial to the market as a whole but not to individual competitors. As A Manager's Ethical Dilemma at the end of the chapter illustrates, managers can become so convinced of the evil of their competitors and of the correctness of their position that they go beyond what is acceptable in competitive actions. Counsel by persons not wrapped up in the day-to-day affairs of the business can help provide a broader perspective on the advisability of going after competitors.

SUMMARY:
A GUIDE FOR MANAGERS

- Managers should periodically assess the potential sources of tort liability within their company. Efforts should be made to reduce the likelihood of an incident capable of generating liability. Managers must be aware that the company is generally responsible for the torts of its employees. A policy that deals with alcohol and other drugs should be considered. This can improve worker quality and reduce a major source of potential liability.

- Intentional torts are based on willful misconduct that invades a right of another and causes injury. The rights that are intentionally violated can be the rights of persons to be safe and secure in their person or in their property. Wrongdoers will be expected to pay damages to compensate for injuries inflicted.

- Intentional interference with personal rights includes assault—when a person is placed in fear of bodily harm or offensive contact; battery—unlawful physical contact without consent; false imprisonment—detaining someone within boundaries against their will; defamation—false communication that injures a person's reputation; emotional distress—caused by outrageous conduct; and invasion of privacy—a violation of a person's right to be free from unwanted exposure.

- Intentional interference with property rights includes trespass to land—an intrusion on land belonging to another; nuisance—interference with the use and enjoyment of private land or interference with a right held in common by the public; trespass to personal property—interference with a person's right to use his or her personal property; and conversion—unlawful control over another person's personal property.

- Tort liability for negligence arises when the duty of ordinary care—the care expected of a reasonable person under the circumstances—to another person is breached, usually by an act, which is the proximate cause of harm to the other person. Liability may be avoided if the other person can be shown to have assumed the risk or to have been negligent.

- Strict liability in tort, or liability without fault, has long been imposed on those who handle unusually dangerous substances, such as toxic chemicals, or substances involved in dangerous activities, such as blasting. In such cases, if there is a causal connection between the handling of the substance or the activity and an injury that is suffered, liability is imposed.

- While businesses may be sued in tort for any of the classes of torts mentioned above, businesses are particularly subject to cases involving disparagement—a false communication that injures others in their business; interference with contractual relations—in which a person induces another party to breach a valid contract that he or she knew existed; and interference with a business relationship—where a business attempts to improve its position by improper interference with another's lawful business.

- To avoid illegally interfering with the business or the contracts of other companies, the personnel manager should check the employment history of new employees. Covenants not to compete in past employment contracts can be a source of potential tort liability.

MANAGER'S ETHICAL DILEMMA

HOW DO YOU MAKE THINGS RIGHT WHEN YOU WERE WRONG?

American Express (AE) bought a Swiss bank from Edmond Safra for $550 million in 1983 to give AE entry into the highest levels of Swiss banking in hopes of securing the banking business of the rich and famous. Safra was made chairman of the new AE banking operation. It was soon obvious that he did not want to do business the way AE wanted it done, so he resigned in 1984, promising not to start a new bank in Switzerland in competition with AE before 1988.

Safra intended to start a new bank in 1988 and began to assemble a team to run it. Fearing that the rich and famous clients would defect from AE's bank to Safra's new bank, AE began an investigation to see whether Safra was engaged in any bad deeds that potential banking clients would want to know about. AE filed criminal charges against Safra in Switzerland and tried to block his application to begin a new bank in 1988. Its complaints were brushed aside by the Swiss, who gave Safra a new banking license.

Having hired private investigators, high-level AE personnel, who were in contact with James Robinson, the chairman and CEO of AE, began a smear campaign against Safra, hoping to discourage bank customers from switching to his new bank. Articles appeared in papers around the world claiming that Safra laundered money for major drug dealers in South America and was involved in many other illegal activities. This false information was taken to congressional staff and the major news media in hopes of generating more bad publicity for Safra.

Safra, shocked by the stories that were destroying his reputation and knowing they would damage his new bank, hired attorneys and investigators to track down the source of the smear. In March 1989, Safra personally confronted Robinson, who denied any involvement by AE. When Safra's lawyers moved to file suit, AE settled, paying $4 million to Safra and $4 million to the charities of his choice, and Robinson issued a public apology.

One executive who was involved retired but is on generous contract with AE; the executive who did much of the dirty work was promoted to senior vice president; Robinson is still chairman and CEO of AE. Safra is still combating false stories that show up about him in various places.

QUESTIONS

AE says it has tightened its internal controls to stop such a thing from happening again. Is that sufficient? What other steps could the company take? Should Robinson and all other senior executives involved have been fired by the board, or was the public apology sufficient penance?

REVIEW AND DISCUSSION QUESTIONS

1. Define the following terms and expressions:

tort	conversion
false imprisonment	trespass
defamation	nuisance
slander	proximate cause
libel	

2. Compare and contrast the following concepts:
   a. intentional tort and negligence
   b. negligence and strict liability in tort
   c. assault and battery
   d. public nuisance and private nuisance

3. Are most accidents and injuries covered by tort law?

■ CASE QUESTIONS

4. While Rouse was looking at new cars at a dealership, he gave his car keys to a sales rep so that his car could be examined for its tradein value. When Rouse decided to leave without buying, the keys were hidden from him—supposedly lost—for about a half hour. The sales rep thought this was a joke; Rouse sued and was awarded $5,000 in punitive damages. What was the tort claimed, and would the damages be allowed on appeal? [*Russell-Vaughn Ford* v. *Rouse*, 281 Ala. 567, 206 So.2d 371 (1968)]

5. Florida land developer Lehigh would show prospective buyers Lehigh Acres and have the buyers stay at its motel. Competitor Azar would watch for the buyers, contact them at the motel, tell them that under federal law they had three days to cancel any contract with Lehigh, and then show them less expensive property that he was selling. Lehigh wanted a court order to keep Azar away from its customers because Azar was interfering with business relationships. Will the court tell Azar to stay away? [*Azar* v. *Lehigh Corp.,* 364 So.2d 860 (Fla. App. 1978)]

6. McKenzie lived next to a gas station run by Yommer. Unknown to Yommer, a gas storage tank developed a leak, polluting McKenzie's well water, making the water unfit for drinking or bathing. Yommer replaced the storage tank, but the problem with McKenzie's water persisted, and McKenzie sued. What tort was claimed? What, if any, is the basis for liability? [*Yommer* v. *McKenzie,* 255 Md. 220, 257 A.2d 138 (1969)]

7. Dun & Bradstreet, a company that reports on the credit history of businesses, incorrectly stated that Greenmoss Builders had once gone bankrupt when in fact it had not. Greenmoss claimed that it lost business because of the incorrect report, which was sent to prospective customers. Greenmoss sued for damages for defamation and won. Dun & Bradstreet said that since there was no "actual malice" in what was said, it could not be held liable. What did the U.S. Supreme Court say? [*Dun & Bradstreet* v. *Greenmoss Builders,* 472 U.S. 749, 105 S.Ct. 2939 (1985)]

8. Fran Gabas owns a condo at Winding Lake II. Shortly after moving in, she began to experience difficulties with cold, dampness, and mildew on various interior walls. The builder's efforts to remedy the situation proved fruitless. Gabas and other occupants then stationed themselves in front of the sales office to the condo complex and proceeded to walk about carrying signs and speaking to passersby. One sign read: "Open House, See Mildew, Feel Dampness, No Extra Charge." Several prospective buyers departed from the project without visiting the sales office. No new units were sold during the time in which the occupants walked about. The company has brought an action against Gabas and the other occupants who participated. What will be the action alleged, and what will be the result? [*Zimmerman* v. *D.C.A. at Welleby, Inc.* 505 So.2d 1371 (Fla. 1987)]

9. Jerry Katz was a politician who stated he would not raise taxes if elected. The local newspaper supported Katz, who won the election. At his first board meeting, Katz moved to raise taxes. His actions prompted an editorial that began "Jerry Katz is a liar. He has lied to us in the past, and he will lie to us in the future." Katz brought an action against the newspaper. What will that action be, and what will be the likely result? [*Costello* v. *Capital Cities Communications,* 153 Ill. App. 3d 956, 106 Ill. Dec. 154, 505 N.E.2d 701 (1987)]

■ BUSINESS POLICY QUESTIONS

10. Because of the defamation lawsuits that have been filed by former employees who claim that letters of recommendation from former employers prevented them from getting a job they wanted, some companies have policies—no comments about any former employees, good or bad. This reduced flow of information hurts employers and employees, since most of the information was accurate. What should business do to solve this legal problem? Lobby Congress for a statutory exemption from defamation suits by former employees unless malice can be shown? Have a major business group, like the U.S. Chamber of Commerce, establish a code that all businesses agree to follow in recommendations?

■ ETHICS QUESTION

11. An employee at the supermarket you manage mopped one of the aisles in the store and placed signs at the ends of the aisles to warn people not to use the aisle until the floor dried. One customer walked around the sign, slipped, fell, and suffered serious injuries. Her lawyer comes to you with the following story. He says that he is going to sue the store for negligence that led to her injuries. However, he says that he doubts that he can win, since case law in the state makes it clear that the sign is considered a reasonable warning so that contributory negligence by the customer would eliminate liability of the store. This means that the customer will get nothing, but one can never be completely sure. The worst part is that the customer has no insurance, has incurred large hospital bills, cannot work for several months, and has no source of support. The lawyer makes the following deal. He will forgo any fee for the case and will sue only for an amount equal to the medical costs incurred and the wages lost if you will agree to testify that there was no sign in place to warn that the floor was wet. The payment will be made by the insurance company. This will not affect your position with the insurance company, and you will save attorney's fees. Should you make such a deal? What if you knew that the law in most states would provide an award because their law held that warning signs were not sufficient and a complete physical barrier had to be in place?

PRODUCTS LIABILITY AND INTELLECTUAL PROPERTY

CHAPTER 8

MANAGER'S LEGAL CHALLENGE

Heart valves control the flow of blood into and out of the heart. When they weaken, a person often has constant fatigue, seizures, and other medical problems that lead to early death. Mechanical heart valves that are implanted to replace failing natural valves have saved and improved hundreds of thousands of lives in the past couple of decades.

Pfizer Inc. sold 86,000 valves for about $2,000 each that were implanted beginning in 1979. The valve was ordered off the market in 1986 because of production flaws that caused an unacceptably high failure rate. By 1990, over 250 people who had this valve had died because of the valve's failure. The worst valve produced by any other company was believed to have killed fewer than ten people.

What did Pfizer do other than pull the valve off the market, as forced to by the Food and Drug Administration? Very little. Three years later, Pfizer sent 5,000 heart specialists a letter telling them about the problem so that the specialists could advise their patients. In some cases, the valve can be replaced, but because of the difficulty of the operation, often a replacement is tried only if the valve actually fails. This requires fast action at a hospital that can do open-heart surgery, which many patients were not aware of. Facing increasing criticism in 1990, Pfizer sent 275,000 letters to doctors and emergency medical workers.

Many patients learned about the Pfizer valve problem from the media, who had learned of it from former employees and who began reporting the problems in 1987. The former employees had openly spoken about what they thought was shoddy work. Pfizer said little in public and not much more to patients who asked about the problem.

Why did Pfizer not notify patients so that they could talk to their doctors about the problem? The company had not kept good records of who had the valves. Some lives might have been saved had the patients been told what steps to take in case of valve failure.

Now Pfizer is facing many lawsuits, most of which are settled. The California Supreme Court is allowing patients who have a Pfizer valve to sue for emotional distress. Some patients say they worry all the time about possible failure and have changed their lifestyle to avoid strains that they think could cause their heart to pump harder and break the valve.

The losses Pfizer will incur from lawsuits far outweigh the income from the sale of the valves. The problem started with poor quality control in production and was compounded first by poor record keeping about patients and then by claims of a cover-up of the problem, which kept patients in the dark about the problem. Obviously the company regrets the problem. It did not have a strategy in place to deal with such a product problem when it arose. It simply floundered along, dealing with the lawsuits as they arose. As one of Pfizer's top experts on the valve said, "The heart-valve problem was paralyzing the company."

As the situation involving the Pfizer heart valve shows, products liability—and the readiness of management to deal with the problems of defective products—plays an important role in the modern legal environment of business. This chapter reviews how the modern law evolved and the heavy responsibility it places on product manufacturers. The Pfizer heart valve was, like many products, protected by the law of intellectual property—specifically, patent law. Intellectual property is a major part of most companies' business and is subject to tort law and various statutes. This chapter reviews some of the key features of this form of property.

The chapter begins with a discussion of early common law liability rules as applied to unsafe products. Initially, in an effort to stimulate the industrialization of the U.S. economy, the courts favored the manufacturer by placing the burden for product-related injuries on consumers. As society evolved to an industrialized mass production economy with a strong consumer orientation, the courts gradually relaxed those rigid early products liability rules. The chapter traces the evolution in liability rules, discussing both the procedures and rationale for the court's application of negligence standards in the early twentieth century and then the application of strict liability doctrines in recent years.

CONSUMER PRODUCTS AND NEGLIGENCE

In the nineteenth century, the courts adopted the rule that a manufacturer was liable for injuries caused by defects in its products to parties with whom the manufacturer had a contractual relationship regarding the product. The term *privity of contract* refers to the relationship that exists between two contracting parties. It is essential to a legal action involving a contract that privity exist between the plaintiff and the defendant. Since consumers rarely purchased products directly from manufacturers, there was no privity, so producers were effectively isolated from liability for most product-related injuries.

■ RULE OF CAVEAT EMPTOR

Parties who were injured by a defective product and did not have privity of contract with the manufacturer were forced to operate under the rule of *caveat emptor,* which means "let the buyer beware." According to the Supreme Court, the rule of *caveat emptor* "requires that the buyer examine, judge, and test [the product] for himself." Thus, a consumer without privity took the risk that a product was of adequate quality. In the event the product did not meet the consumer's safety expectations and an injury resulted, the financial burdens caused by that injury were the responsibility of the consumer.

In a product related injury case, the injured party would contend that the manufacturer was under a duty to provide reasonably safe products. However, if no privity was found to exist, the courts held that no legal duty existed between the manufacturer and the consumer. Thus, the manufacturer could not be found negligent in the construction or design of its product in cases brought by an injured consumer who lacked privity. The law of tort did not apply.

■ RISE OF NEGLIGENCE IN TORT

In justifying the privity rule, the courts reasoned that the rule would place too heavy a burden on manufacturers to hold them responsible to consumers located all over and whose identity they did not know. The rule raised concerns, however, because it often left injured consumers without redress. In response to the harsh result the rule would frequently impose, the courts began to recognize several exceptions. Finally in 1916, in the famous case of *MacPherson* v. *Buick Motor Company,* New York struck down the privity rule and held a manufacturer liable in tort for negligence for a product-related injury.

MACPHERSON v. BUICK MOTOR COMPANY

New York Court of Appeals
217 N.Y. 382, 111 N.E. 1050 (1916)

Case Background
Buick Motor Company produced cars and sold them to retail dealers. MacPherson bought a new Buick from a dealer in New York. The wheels on MacPherson's Buick were made by another company for Buick. Not long after MacPherson bought the car, one of the wheels suddenly collapsed, causing an accident that injured MacPherson, who sued Buick. MacPherson's suit against Buick traditionally would have been barred because of lack of privity. Buick sold the car to the dealer, who in turn sold it to MacPherson. The dealer had privity with MacPherson but

was not responsible for the defect. The trial court and the appellate division ruled for MacPherson, finding Buick liable in tort for injuries caused by the defect. Buick appealed to the highest court in New York.

Case Decision
The distinguished Justice Benjamin Cardozo, later a member of the U.S. Supreme Court, delivered the opinion of the court. The old rule of privity in contract being needed to have a claim against the producer of a defective product was rejected in favor of a new rule of liability in tort for negligence. Since a manufacturer has primary control over product design and safety, it makes sense to hold the pro-

(continued)

ducer responsible for what it makes and what it purchases as components of the product it sells.

Managerial Considerations
This case reflects the common law tradition of courts disposing of rules that seem not to make sense any longer, given changes in technology or society. Cases are brought that go against the traditional rule because there is a chance that the courts will overturn precedent. This case also established the rule that the primary producer of a product is responsible for the entire product. That is, Buick could not escape liability because a component part—

wheels—were supplied by another company. It is not a defense that the problem was caused by a defective part that was supplied by another company. The two companies can deal with that matter in another lawsuit. An injured party, whether the purchaser of the defective product or a user, has the right to sue the primary producer if there seems to have been a defect in the product that caused the harm. In this case, Buick also argued that since only one out of 60,000 wheels sold had collapsed, it should not be held negligent. The court said no. Since Buick failed to test a product that could cause serious injury or death if defective, it is responsible.

With the elimination of the requirement of a contractual relationship between the manufacturer and the consumer, manufacturers were held to assume a responsibility for product safety to consumers. Manufacturers must, therefore, produce products using proper care to eliminate foreseeable harm, or they risk being found negligent if a consumer is injured by a defective product. The rule originating with *MacPherson,* and eventually adopted by the courts in every state, provided that

> The manufacturer of a product is liable in the production and sale of a product for negligence, if the product may reasonably be expected to inflict harm on the user if the product is defective.

■ THE NEGLIGENCE STANDARD

As we saw in the previous chapter, when liability is based on negligence, a manufacturer is required to exercise *reasonable care* under the circumstances in the production of its product. The circumstances include the probability of a defect, magnitude of the possible harm, cost of effective inspection, and customs of the business. Liability may be imposed on the manufacturer for negligence in the preparation of the product—for failing to inspect or test the materials, workmanship, or finished product—or for failing to discover possible defects. Defects and dangers must be revealed, even if the manufacturer becomes aware of them after the sale of the product to the consumer. Reasonable care must also be taken by the manufacturer in presenting the product to the public—through advertisements or other promotions—to avoid misrepresentation. If a causal connection can be established between the failure of the manufacturer to exercise reasonable care in any of these areas and an injury suffered by a consumer, liability for damages will be imposed on the manufacturer.

■ CURRENT APPLICATIONS OF NEGLIGENCE

For fifty years after *MacPherson,* negligence was the universal law of products liability. Beginning in the early 1960s, however, the courts began to apply strict liability to manufactured products, and that has become the common method for holding manufacturers liable for product-related injuries. Despite the predominance of strict liability, there are still several product-related injuries that are brought under a theory of negligence.

One important area in which the theory of negligence is applied by the courts is in cases where the crashworthiness of automobiles is called into question. To avoid being held negligent in the design and construction of their products, automobile manufacturers must design automobiles to prevent *foreseeable dangers* to occupants in the event of a crash. *Mickle v. Blackmon* concerns the application of negligence in cases involving injuries to the occupants of an automobile involved in a crash.

MICKLE v. BLACKMON

Supreme Court of South Carolina
252 S.C. 202, 166 S.E.2d 173 (1969)

Case Background
In 1962, seventeen-year-old Janet Mickle was a passenger in a 1949 Ford that was in a collision with a car driven by Larry Blackmon. Mickle was thrown against the gearshift lever on the steering column. The knob on the lever shattered, and Mickle was impaled on the lever, suffered spinal damage, and was left paralyzed. Mickle sued Blackmon for causing the accident and Ford for producing a defective gearshift knob that would shatter in such an accident. The jury awarded her $312,000. The state appellate court upheld the award, but only against Blackmon. The verdict against Ford was set aside. Since Blackmon could not pay the judgment, Mickle appealed the verdict with respect to Ford.

Case Decision
The high court reversed the decision of the trial judge and held Ford liable for Mickle's injuries. The court ruled that the jury could find Ford's production of the gearshift knob to be negligent. Producers have a duty to minimize the likelihood of death or injury by designing cars to take into account the fact that accidents do occur.

Ford should have foreseen that many thousands of the one million vehicles produced by it in 1949 would, in the course of time, be operated millions of miles with gearshift lever balls which, while yet serving adequately as handholds, would furnish no protection to an occupant who might be thrown against the gearshift lever. The jury could reasonably conclude that Ford's conduct, in manufacturing a needed safety device of a material which could not tolerate a frequently encountered aspect of the environment in which it would be employed, exposed many users of its product to unreasonably great risk of harm.

Managerial considerations
It is not a good defense to say that cars are not intended to be in accidents. Since everyone knows that cars are in accidents, the interior of cars must be designed to account for what will happen to occupants in an accident. Producers must think of what is likely to happen to their product while it is used. Many products are used for purposes other than those for which they were originally intended and producers must anticipate such uses and change product design as soon as they become aware of potential problems.

West Virginia was one of the last states to adopt the crashworthiness doctrine. In *Blankenship* v. *General Motors* (1991), the high court of West Virginia stated that in such cases, the issue is not a defect in the automobile but that the vehicle could have reasonably been built safer: "... the plaintiff must offer proof of an alternative, safer design, practicable under the circumstances. ..." The alternative design must be shown to have been likely to reduce the injury suffered by the plaintiff.

In recent years, thousands of crashworthiness suits have been filed for injuries in accidents that were made worse to backseat occupants who had only lap seat belts rather than lap and shoulder seat belts. Lap belts were standard equipment in many cars before the government made lap and shoulder belts mandatory in late 1989. Plaintiffs argue that since the automakers had known before then of the safety value of the three-point belts, which are not expensive, they should have installed them. Verdicts up to $6 million per accident have been awarded.

STRICT LIABILITY

Consumers became increasingly frustrated with how negligence was applied in product-related injury cases, in particular, with the difficulties in establishing that the manufacturer had not exercised reasonable care in the production of its product. The *strict liability* doctrine requires manufacturers to pay compensation to consumers injured by defective products even though the manufacturer exercised all reasonable care. Thus, the injured party is not required to attack the conduct of the manufacturer but rather is required to attack the product. To be successful, an injured party must show the following:

1. The product was defective.
2. The defect created an unreasonably dangerous product.
3. The defect was the proximate cause of his or her injury.

Strict liability was first applied to product-related injuries through a warranty theory under contract law. After strict liability under contract law proved to be too restrictive, the courts began to apply a rule of strict liability in tort. Later, the adoption of strict liability in tort by the American Law Institute brought about a modification of the authoritative *Second Restatement of Torts* and helped spur the adoption of strict liability in tort in product-related injury cases throughout the country.

■ STRICT LIABILITY UNDER CONTRACT LAW

Strict liability under contract law is based on the relationship between the injured party and the manufacturer by the existence of a warranty. The concept of *warranty* is based upon the manufacturer's promise to the consumer that the product will meet certain quality and performance standards.

A warranty may be either express or implied. An *implied warranty* is one that the law derives by an implication or inference from the nature of the transaction between the parties. A manufacturer can create an *express warranty* by making either oral or written representations about the quality, condition, description, or performance of the product. Strict liability under contract as applied to product-related injuries can be based on either an express or an implied warranty.

Strict Liability Based on Implied Warranty.   The first major application to consumer products of the doctrine of strict liability was in the area of food and drink. In a 1913 case from the state of Washington, *Mazetti* v. *Armour,* a court disregarded the privity of contract requirement and held that a manufacturer of food *implies* the food's safety for human consumption simply by selling it to the public. There is an *implied warranty of safety* governing the quality of food and drink products. A consumer injury caused by a defective food or drink product constitutes a breach of that warranty, and the manufacturer is strictly liable for the injury. By the mid-1950s, the majority of courts in defective food and drink cases were imposing strict liability based on an implied warranty of safety as originally established by *Mazetti*.

In 1960, the Supreme Court of New Jersey extended an implied warranty of safety to a vast array of consumer products. In the leading case *Henningsen* v. *Bloomfield Motors, Inc.*, the New Jersey court held both the manufacturer of an automobile and the dealer who sold the car to the purchaser's wife (who was driving the automobile when the accident occurred) strictly liable for the woman's injuries and damages on the basis of an implied warranty of safety. It was the first major decision to expand the implied warranty theory beyond its application in food and drink cases.

The *Henningsen* decision had a dramatic impact on the liability rules to be applied to product-related injury cases. According to Professor Keeton:

> What followed [the *Henningsen* case] was the most rapid and altogether spectacular overturn of an established rule in the entire history of the law of torts. There was a deluge of cases in other jurisdictions following the lead of New Jersey, and finding an implied warranty of safety as to a wide assortment of products [e.g., tires, airplane, power golf cart, water heater, and an insecticide]. It [was] clear that the "citadel of privity" [had] fallen.

In addition to the implied warranties of safety under the common law, the *Uniform Commercial Code* (UCC) creates two statutory implied warranties governing product quality and performance that has been adopted in all states. Under Section 2-314, the UCC provides that if the seller of a product is a merchant under the Code—defined as an individual who deals in the kinds of products sold to the consumer—the products are statutorily warranted as *merchantable*. A product is considered merchantable if it is fit for the purpose for which it is being sold. In addition, Section 2-315 of the UCC provides that where the seller knows how the buyer intends to use the product and the buyer relies on the seller's expertise to supply a suitable product, there is an implied warranty that the goods will be fit for that particular purpose.

Strict Liability Based on Express Warranty.   Strict liability under contract law was also applied where a manufacturer made an express claim about its product to consumers. A manufacturer, for example, could have advertisements that made certain quality or performance claims about its product. To the extent such claims became part of the bargain between the manufacturer and consumers, the manufacturer was held to have a duty of performance as to the claims.

As the court's decision in *Baxter* v. *Ford Motor* illustrates, the courts often disregarded privity of contract as necessary to recovery where the consumer had purchased the product from someone other than the manufacturer. Injured consumers were not required to prove fault, because the courts held the manufacturer was obligated to guarantee the truthfulness of its claims. Hence, strict liability was imposed.

BAXTER v. FORD MOTOR COMPANY

Supreme Court of Washington
168 Wash. 456, 12 P.2d 409 (1932)

Case Background
Baxter purchased a new Model A Ford from a Ford dealer in Washington state in May 1930. Printed material from Ford, distributed by the dealer, stated that the windshield of the car was "Triple Shatter-Proof Glass." This innovation was advertised by Ford as a safety feature. The windshield "will not fly or shatter under the hardest impact . . . it eliminates the dangers of flying glass." Several months later, when Baxter was driving his car, a rock flipped up by a passing car hit the windshield, causing a small piece of glass to fly into Baxter's left eye, leaving the eye sightless. Ford asserted that since the purchase document said nothing about the shatterproof glass, Baxter should not have a warranty claim against the manufacturer. The trial court did not allow Ford's advertisement about the windshield to be admitted in evidence and ruled for Ford.

Case Decision
The Supreme Court of Washington reversed in favor of Baxter. The court stated that the printed sales materials distributed by Ford should have been admitted in evidence. The materials make clear the producer's claims to the public about safety features. Even though there was no privity of contract between Baxter and Ford, Baxter had the right to rely on representations made by Ford creating a warranty that accompanied the product. Since the product was defective and caused injury to Baxter, the express warranty was violated, and strict liability could be imposed.

Managerial Considerations
When companies make specific claims about the virtues of their products, consumers should be able to rely on those claims. Under warranty law, claims become a part of the purchase package of the product. Consumers thus have stronger cases against a manufacturer when a product fails to meet a specific claim made by the manufacturer. Hence, management should not make statements about its products unless it intends to live up to those claims. Most cases involving injuries from defective products fall under tort law. However, when there is found to be a contractual promise of safety created by claims about a product, an injured consumer may have a case that would not exist under tort law.

The UCC also creates express warranties. Section 2-313 provides that if the seller makes promises or statements about the product that become part of the basis of the bargain for sale between the seller and buyer, an express warranty is created by those promises or statements. Importantly, as under the common law, the UCC provides that the seller need not use the word *warranty* or *guarantee* for an express warranty to be created.

■ STRICT LIABILITY IN TORT

When imposing strict liability under contract law, the courts were often faced with determining what constituted a warranty. In addition, the courts were frequently confounded by the express limits on liability that manufacturers put in their warranties. In response to such difficulties, the courts supplemented strict liability under contract law with a simple rule of *strict liability in tort*. The Supreme Court of California was the first court to adopt strict liability in tort in product-related injury cases with its 1963 decision *Greenman* v. *Yuba Power Products.*

GREENMAN v. YUBA POWER PRODUCTS, INC.

Supreme Court of California
59 Cal.2d 57, 27 Cal.Rptr. 697, 377 P.2d 897 (1963)

Case Background
Greenman's wife bought Greenman a Shopsmith—a power tool that could be used as a saw, drill, and wood lathe—for Christmas in 1955. Greenman had studied material about the product and had requested that his wife buy it for him. Two years later, when he was using the machine as a lathe, a piece of wood suddenly flew out of the machine and struck him on the head, inflicting serious injuries. Greenman sued the producer, Shopsmith, and the retailer, Yuba Power, claiming breaches of warranties and negligence. The lower court found for Greenman, and Yuba appealed.

Case Decision
The California high court upheld the verdict for Greenman and established the rule of strict liability in tort for manufacturers of products sold to consumers.

> A manufacturer is strictly liable in tort when an article he places on the market, knowing that it is to be used without inspection for defects, proves to have a defect that causes injury to a human being. . . . The remedies of injured consumers ought not to be made to depend upon the intricacies of the law of sales. To establish the manufacturer's liability it was sufficient that Greenman proved that he was injured while using the Shopsmith in a way it was intended to be used as a result of a defect in design and manufacture of which Greenman was not aware that made the Shopsmith unsafe for its intended use.

Managerial Considerations
By the mid-1970s, every state supreme court had adopted this rule. Strict liability in tort cannot be waived by attaching a paper to consumer products that disclaims liability except for whatever is admitted to by the producer. Management can best limit potential liability created by its products by inspecting the products carefully for defects, developing design features that are likely to be associated with the least injuries, explaining clearly how to use the product properly, and warning of dangers in use.

The principal author of the *Second Restatement of Torts*, the American Law Institute (ALI), adopted a strict liability in tort rule in product-related injury cases similar to that imposed in *Greenman*. This helped to bring about nationwide acceptance of the strict liability in tort rule. The *Restatement's* strict liability in tort rule is found in Section 402A:

> Sec. 402A (1) One who sells any product in a defective condition unreasonably dangerous to the user or consumer or to his property is subject to liability for physical harm thereby caused to the ultimate user or consumer, or to his property, if
>
> (a) the seller is engaged in the business of selling such a product, and
>
> (b) it is expected to and does reach the user or consumer without substantial change in the condition in which it is sold.
>
> (2) The rule stated in Subsection (1) applies although
>
> (a) the seller has exercised all possible care in the preparation and sale of his product, and
>
> (b) the user or consumer has not bought the product from or entered into any contractual relation with the seller.

■ EXTENSIONS OF STRICT LIABILITY

The *Greenman* decision illustrates the application of the strict liability in tort doctrine to a case in which a defective product has caused an injury to a consumer. This application of the doctrine is relatively simple and uncontroversial. Since the *Greenman* decision, however, the application of the doctrine has been extended to more controversial product injury cases. Those extensions include cases in which (1) the manufacturer has failed to warn the consumer of known hazards in certain uses of the product, (2) the product is poorly designed (as opposed to simply being defectively manufactured), and (3) the product produces latent injuries (injuries that occur years after the consumer has used the product).

Failure to Warn.   Even before the widespread adoption of strict liability, the manufacturer's *failure to warn* consumers of dangers involved in the use of a product or to instruct consumers about proper procedures in using a product was actionable under the rule of negligence. Manufacturers have to think of possible dangers in the use, storage, and handling of their products. For example, although household cleansers are dangerous and not intended for consumption, manufacturers know that parents often leave such products in places where children might get at them. Thus, it may be a product defect not to warn people of such dangers and to take steps to reduce possible tragedies, such as by using containers that are not attractive to children, using hard-to-remove caps, and putting danger labels or symbols on the containers.

How far does the failure-to-warn application of strict liability in tort extend? While the limits of the application are still being defined by the courts, several recent decisions provide insights:

- A Pennsylvania court found that a gun manufacturer that had failed to warn users of possible damage to their hearing from long-term exposure to gunfire was strictly liable for such injuries.

- A Texas court found a liquor manufacturer liable for failing to warn consumers about the adverse health effects associated with drinking its products. In the case, an eighteen-year-old first-year college student had died after consuming a large quantity of tequila.

- The Supreme Court of Alaska upheld a verdict against a diet-food producer who failed to provide adequate warnings about using the adult diet food as baby food. Because the food was safe for dieting adults but not for infants, the company should have stated so on its product rather than assume that adults would have enough sense not to use the product as baby food.

- The highest court of New York held the producer of a commercial pizza dough roller machine liable for injuries suffered by a worker who stuck his hands into the machine while it was on as he tried to clean it. Although the machine had a safety switch that was supposed to be used in such cases, the worker had turned off the safety switch so that he could stick his hands into the machine. The manufacturer failed to warn when it did not clearly explain the dangers of turning off the safety switch.

- The Eleventh Circuit Court of Appeals held that the warnings printed on a bottle of Campho-Phenique, an external medicine, stating "Keep out of reach of children," "For external use," and "in case of ingestion—seek medical help and call poison center'' were not strong enough to explain the dangers. A four-year-old child drank the medicine and suffered severe injuries. The suit proceeded on the basis of failure to warn.

Design Defects.   Unlike defective product cases, *design defect* cases are not concerned with a particular unit of a product that has been poorly manufactured and sold to a consumer and then has caused injury. A design defect case, for example, would not involve a determination of whether the manufacturer was liable for injuries caused by a defectively manufactured toaster. Rather, a design defect case focuses on the determination of whether a particular injury to users could have been prevented by a differently designed product. The inquiry is relevant even if the product itself is not defectively manufactured. In that regard, consider the following design defect cases:

- In a Washington State case a worker received a 750,000-dollar judgment for the loss of a leg from an accident that occurred at work. Coworkers had removed a metal plate from the top of the machine. When they finished repairing the machine, the workers failed to put the metal plate back on and covered the machine with cardboard. The plaintiff later walked on what he thought was the metal plate, as was customary, and fell into the machine. The court held that it was a design defect to allow the machine to be able to run when the metal plate was removed.

- A restaurant employee was seriously burned when he tried to retrieve something that fell out of his shirt pocket and into a commercial French fryer machine. The D.C. Circuit Court of Appeals held that since a jury could find that a safer alternative design of the machine was possible, it could impose liability.

- A child pushed the emergency stop button on an escalator, causing a person to fall and be injured. The Seventh Circuit Court of Appeals ruled that it was a design defect to both make the button red (because the color is attractive to children) and place the button so that it was accessible to children.

- In an Eleventh Circuit Court of Appeals case, the plaintiff was injured when he took his riding mower up a hill that was too steep, the mower rolled over, and he was cut by the whirring blades. The court held that there was technology in existence at the time the mower was built that would have caused the mower to automatically shut off when it was lifted off the ground or when the rider let go of the controls. Because such technology was not included in the product's design, the manufacturer was strictly liable for the plaintiff's injuries.

Unknown Hazards.   The largest dollar volume and number of products liability cases are now based on *unknown hazards*—dangers that were not known or not fully appreciated at the time the product was manufactured. Since the hazard associated with the product may not be learned for years, neither the producer nor the consumer may be able to do anything to prevent injury.

Billions of dollars have been awarded in thousands of suits involving the health effects of asbestos, injuries caused by IUDs, and damage caused by the side effects of drugs that did not appear for years. For example, A. H. Robins marketed the Dalkon Shield contraceptive device in the early 1970s. The device caused injuries ranging from spontaneous abortion to sterility in tens of thousands of women. The result was bankruptcy in 1985 and a 2.35-billion-dollar settlement fund that began operation in 1990. Over 100,000 small claims were settled in 1991, but tens of thousands of larger claims are bogged down, unhappy with the settlements offered by the court-appointed administrators of the fund.

The most notable area of activity has involved asbestos, which has resulted in billions of dollars being awarded by all asbestos makers to tens of thousands of plaintiffs. By 1991, over two-thirds of all products liability suits filed in federal court were asbestos related. In an attempt to get the cases organized a panel of judges ordered the 27,000 asbestos suits in federal court transferred to one court. Another 60,000 asbestos suits remain in state courts, with the numbers expected to grow.

Claims far outweigh the assets of the defendants. Manville, the largest supplier of asbestos, filed for bankruptcy when it faced $2 billion in claims but had only $1 billion of net worth. In such cases, the companies have continued to operate under bankruptcy supervision, with most claims being pooled and then paid out of a fund generated by company earnings. The *Borel* decision was one of the most important in opening the way for the asbestos litigation.

BOREL v. FIBREBOARD PAPER PRODUCTS CORPORATION

United States Court of Appeals, Fifth Circuit
493 F.2d 1076 (1973)

Case Background
Clarence Borel, an industrial insulation worker, was exposed to asbestos from 1936 through 1969 as he worked at various jobs in Texas. In 1964, an X ray showed his lungs to be cloudy, and his doctor advised him to avoid asbestos dust as much as possible. In 1969, a lung biopsy revealed pulmonary asbestosis. Within a year, Borel had a lung removed because of lung cancer, and he died shortly thereafter. His heirs continued the litigation he had initiated against eleven makers of asbestos insulation materials he had used over the years. Four of the makers settled out of court, and one was dismissed at trial. The jury found the six remaining producers, including Fibreboard, liable under strict liability.

Case Decision
The federal court of appeals upheld the jury verdict against the asbestos makers. The court noted that the producers had known about the hazards of asbestos since the 1930s. Despite their knowledge, or knowledge they should have had, there was no evidence that they ever warned contrac-

tors or installers of the dangers of inhaling asbestos dust. Strict liability is imposed on manufacturers when a defect makes the product unreasonably dangerous. The lack of warnings was the defect.

Managerial Considerations
Managers are held to have expert knowledge about the product they produce. It is not a defense to claim that one was not aware of a problem—managers are legally responsible for knowing the latest information about their products and for acting on the information as it becomes available. Managers must communicate company knowledge to likely users of the company's products to warn them of newly discovered dangers. All products have some dangers associated with them. Managers must balance the utility of their products—including their risks—against the likelihood of losses caused by injuries.

There was evidence in this case that the levels of asbestos Borel was exposed to were within "safe" levels established by federal government studies. The studies were wrong, as we now know. Considerable debate occurs over whether managers should be allowed to rely on such studies as evidence that they met acceptable safety standards and so be relieved of liability.

The *Collins* v. *Eli Lilly* case is another example of liability being imposed for injuries from an unknown hazard. In this case, the defect was impossible to know until the product had been used for twenty years, because the injury occurred to the adult daughters of the mothers who took a prescription drug. Manufacturers argue against such liability, saying that they should not be responsible for damages that at the time the product was made and sold they could not have known were going to occur. In many states, the courts have ruled that strict liability does apply. Real injuries have occurred, and it makes more sense to impose the costs on the manufacturers than on society as a whole or on the consumers who suffered the injuries.

COLLINS v. ELI LILLY COMPANY

Wisconsin Supreme Court
116 Wis.2d 166, 342 N.W.2d 37 (1984)

Case Background
Therese Collins was born in 1958. Her mother had taken the prescription drug DES (diethylstilbestrol) during pregnancy to reduce the risk of miscarriage. DES was banned in 1971 when its cancer risks to the reproductive organs of adult women whose mothers had taken the drug became known. Collins had radical cancer surgery in 1975. Like over 1,000 other such cancer victims, she attributed the cancer to the DES taken by her mother and sued a dozen producers of DES. Tort law requires a plaintiff to specify a responsible defendant. That was not possible in this case, because the specific producer of the DES pills taken by her mother was not known. The Supreme Court of Wisconsin had to decide how to handle this matter.

Case Holding
The court ruled that Collins could sue any or all of the drug manufacturers in question, even though she did not know which one made the pills that directly caused the injury.

Each defendant contributed to the *risk* of injury to the public and, consequently, the risk of injury to individual plaintiffs such as Therese Collins. Thus each defendant shares, in some measure, a degree of culpability in producing or marketing what the FDA, many scientists, and medical researchers ultimately concluded was a drug with possibly harmful side effects. . . . We conclude that it is better to have drug companies or consumers share the cost of the injury than to place the burden solely on the innocent plaintiff.

Managerial Consideration
The Wisconsin court, like other courts, fashioned a remedy to allow injured plaintiffs to bring suit against any or all manufacturers of a defective product. If only one or a few manufacturers are sued, they have the right to sue all other manufacturers of the product, so that all are likely to share in the cost of the verdict. The case means that manufacturers of generic products or those that are not brand names will not be able to escape liability because of lack of consumer identification.

■ MARKET SHARE LIABILITY

An intriguing development in products liability arose in a 1980 California decision, *Sindell* v. *Abbott Laboratories*. The decision pioneered the notion of *market liability*, or *market share liability*. This application of strict liability arose in response to a number of suits filed involving the adult daughters of women who had taken DES (diethylstilbestrol) during pregnancy as in the *Collins* case. Because DES (a synthetic estrogen) was produced by numerous companies and was consumed twenty or more years ago, plaintiffs could not identify the manufacturer of the drug taken by their mothers. The California court allowed plaintiffs to sue all drug manufacturers who marketed DES and said that those manufacturers would proportion the liability according to their share of the market for the drug.

The Wisconsin Supreme Court addressed the same question in *Collins* v. *Eli Lilly.* It rejected the market share liability approach but held that plaintiff(s) could sue any or all manufacturers and that the manufacturers could bring in other manufacturers as defendants so they would all share the liability. This is the more traditional *joint and several liability* rule that allows any defendant to be responsible for all damages.

Rules similar to the rule adopted in the *Sindell* decision have appeared elsewhere. In a 1984 decision, *Abel* v. *Eli Lilly,* the Supreme Court of Michigan adopted a "DES-modified alternative liability" that allows plaintiffs to sue any or all manufacturers of the drug in question at the time it was taken by plaintiffs' mothers.

■ DEFENSES

The application of strict liability holds manufacturers to a high standard of product safety. Manufacturers can escape liability in some instances if the consumer has undertaken some activity that increases the risk of injury. Most courts recognize product abuse, assumption of risk, and contributory negligence as defenses in product-related injury cases. Defenses to tort actions were discussed more generally in Chapter 7.

Product Abuse.   If it can be shown that the product was abused, was combined with another product to make it dangerous, was used in some unforeseen and unusual manner, or was mishandled, the negligence of the consumer may preclude recovery for damages. If proper warnings and instructions concerning the use of the product (especially in a situation whereby the consumer could be expected to heed the warnings) are ignored by the consumer and lead to injury, it is possible that liability will not be imposed on the manufacturer.

In one case, the court barred recovery by plaintiffs who were injured when the blowout of a fairly new tire was shown to be caused by improper air pressure inserted by plaintiff in the tires. The court noted, "To hold otherwise would be to convert a strict liability cause of action into one of absolute liability."

Assumption of Risk.   Two primary types of products are of concern here: (1) medicinal drugs that have unavoidable, known side effects that physicians and consumers have been warned about and (2) goods, such as cigarettes and alcohol, that inflict undesirable side effects. If a person smokes cigarettes for forty years and develops lung cancer, should the cigarette manufacturer be held liable? If one drinks large quantities of alcohol for years and develops cirrhosis of the liver, should the liquor industry be liable? In general, the courts have said no; the persons using the cigarettes and alcohol know of the risks involved and will bear the costs.

It is not hard to imagine what the impact would be on the liquor and cigarette industries if they were held liable for health problems believed associated with the use of their products. Society seems willing to let this set of products inflict their costs where they may because of the common use of the products and the general knowledge of the risks involved in using them.

Contributory Negligence.   Some states allow the defense of *contributory negligence*. If the manufacturer can prove that the injured party failed to exercise due care for his or her own protection in the use, handling, or storage of the product, that failure will create a complete defense. Generally, this must involve the user of the product having voluntarily proceeded (assumed the risk) to use a product known to be defective or to use the product in a situation involving unreasonable danger. Remember that in most jurisdictions, *comparative negligence* will determine whether the fault is to be shared or to fall all on one party.

PRODUCTS LIABILITY IN EUROPE | INTERNATIONAL ASPECTS

Products liability law is more developed in the United States than in other Western countries. While many Western countries are undertaking efforts to evaluate and change their products liability law, most currently apply some form of negligence standard. The differences between the United States and other Western countries in the application of traditional negligence law in product-related injury cases is best illustrated by litigation in Britain involving the severely deformed children of women who took the drug thalidomide. That litigation spanned two decades and resulted in relatively modest recoveries for plaintiffs with very severe deformities. In this country, the theory of recovery would have been strict liability in tort, and the recovery would very likely have been substantial.

Several countries, however, are moving toward legal standards that make it easier for plaintiffs to recover in product-related injury cases. West Germany, for example, statutorily imposes strict liability on drug manufacturers. In addition, it has made recovery easier under its negligent standard for other product-related injuries by requiring the manufacturer to disprove a presumption of fault once the plaintiff has demonstrated a defect. France has developed a theory of products liability not based on fault, but the theory is being applied only in certain courts.

These countries also have several procedural rules that inhibit a plaintiff's ability to recover. For example, plaintiffs face prohibitions on discovery, punitive damages, and the use of juries. The biggest difference between these countries and the United States, however, may be that contingency fees (refer to Chapter 4) are generally not available in other countries. Injured parties must be prepared to manage the full financial burden of bringing the lawsuit, including the defense costs, if they lose. These procedural restrictions greatly reduce the number of products-liability suits in Europe and the United Kingdom.

■ DOES PRODUCTS LIABILITY NEED REFORM?

Manufacturers are pushing for statutes that would limit strict liability for producers. They claim there is a liability crisis that is making America less competitive in world markets. The annual cost to the economy is claimed to be in the hundreds of billions of dollars, consuming 2.5 percent of GNP, compared to about 0.5 percent of GNP in most other developed nations. The threat of liability forces good products off the market in the United States and results in less research for new products. Compounding the problem are punitive damage awards that are often much greater than the actual damage award. As a result, liability insurance in the United States often costs many times more than what it costs for similar businesses in Canada, Japan, or Europe because, in the United States, liability awards are so much higher and liability suits are easier to bring.

Organized opposition to the proposed legislation mostly comes from trial lawyers associations, which assert that liability is a reflection of our society's belief that if you injure people, you should pay for the costs of their injuries. In any event, the cost estimates are overstated. If mass torts cases such as asbestos are subtracted, there was little change in the number of products liability suits filed annually in the 1980s. While there are some large punitive damage awards, they are relatively rare and do serve to punish companies that have not been responsible.

A study issued by the Roscoe Pound Foundation found that from 1965 to 1990, there was an average of fourteen punitive damage verdicts per year in all state and federal courts, one quarter of which involved asbestos. About half of the punitive damage verdicts were tossed out on appeal, making huge payouts relatively rare events.

A Middle Ground?   Trial lawyers argue for no changes in the products liability system. Business groups want to limit damages, limit the bases for liability, and return some product cases to the rule of negligence instead of strict liability. Many states have passed laws to restrict liability and to put caps on damages. Some of these laws have been struck down as unconstitutional, but caps on damages for "pain and suffering" have been upheld in California, Florida, Illinois, Indiana, Maryland, and several other states.

Perhaps a middle ground is provided by the prestigious American Law Institute, which in 1991 produced a report by leading legal scholars recommending liability reform. Among the recommendations:

- Awards for pain and suffering would be for severely injured plaintiffs only.
- Juries would be given a scale setting dollar amounts for specific injuries to determine damages.
- Payment received by a plaintiff from private insurance would offset jury awards to prevent double collection.
- Compliance with government standards would be a strong defense in a lawsuit and provide a bar against punitive damages.
- Defendants would pay the legal fees of successful plaintiffs.

INTELLECTUAL PROPERTY

Physical property, like houses, land, and cars, is obvious because it is visible or tangible. We can see it, stand on it, or sit in it. *Intellectual property* is another form of property, sometimes called *intangible property* because it is not as easy to see and is harder to value. The term *intellectual property* is used because such property is produced mostly by thinking, not by physical labor.

Major forms of intellectual property include trademarks, trade names, copyrights, patents, and trade secrets. The common law has a long tradition of providing protection for such property. The Constitution expresses its importance: Article I, Section 8, authorizes Congress "To promote the Progress of Science and useful Arts, by securing for limited Times to Authors and Inventors the exclusive Right to their respective Writings and Discoveries." Today, the Commissioner of Patents and Trademarks annually issues over 100,000 patents—half to Americans and half to foreigners—and over 60,000 trademarks, and over 600,000 copyrights are registered annually.

As discussed in the previous chapter, the law of torts helps people protect their right not to have others trespass or interfere with their real or personal property. The common law also provides protection for intellectual property by allowing property owners to sue in case of *infringement*. Wrongful, unauthorized use of intellectual property in violation of the owner's rights is the basis for a tort action for damages. This protection has been enhanced by various statutes. How important is protection of intellectual property? The U.S. government estimates that counterfeit and fraudulent use of intellectual property costs business over $60 billion a year.

■ TRADEMARKS

A *trademark* is a design, logo, distinctive mark, or word that a manufacturer prints on its goods so the goods can be readily identified in the marketplace. Producers cannot impersonate or counterfeit genuine trademarks. Since companies spend huge sums so that consumers will come to recognize their products and trust their quality, the common law has long recognized the right to protect this property. Federal trademark law allows trademarks to be registered if they are distinctive and unique. As long as the owner continues to use and protect the trademark, the trademark's exclusive use can be perpetual.

Most colleges have trademarks for their name, or a distinctive use of letters in their name, and for their sports team name and mascot. Collegiate Licensing is a licensing agent for many universities and the manufacturers that make clothing and various items with university logos. This allows colleges to collect royalties from and control the use of their trademarks so the trademarks are not used in ways the colleges do not approve.

Counterfeiting of trademarks owned by universities, Major League Baseball, and well-known companies such as Nike, Disney, and Levi Strauss means that the owners must work to protect their property. Levi's seized 1.3 million pairs of counterfeit pants in 1991 alone. Not only are profits lost to counterfeiters, but since counterfeit goods are usually low quality, consumers might think that the trademarks do not represent quality, and the reputation of the owner can suffer. The *Hard Rock Cafe* case provides an example.

HARD ROCK CAFE LICENSING CORP. v. CONCESSION SERVICES, INC.

United States Court of Appeals, Seventh Circuit
955 F.2d 1143 (1992)

Case Background
Hard Rock Cafe Licensing Corp. owns various Hard Rock trademarks and licenses use of its trademarks to the limited partnerships that own and operate various Hard Rock Cafe restaurants. Hard Rock Cafe t-shirts may only be sold at the restaurants. Since 1986 the Chicago Hard Rock Cafe restaurant had sold over 500,000 t-shirts at a profit of over $10 per shirt. Learning that counterfeit Hard Rock Cafe t-shirts were being sold, the Chicago restaurant hired private investigators to track them down. They found counterfeit shirts sold at independently run booths at "Swap-O-Rama" flea markets managed by Concession Services, Inc. (CSI).

(continued)

One of the booth operators paid $30,000 to settle the case out-of-court. The trial court issued a permanent injunction against further sales at flea markets operated by CSI. Both parties appealed.

Case Decision

The Court remanded the case to the district court, holding that if the court found that CSI knew or had reason to know that counterfeit shirts were being sold at its flea markets, then CSI was contributorily liable for the trademark violation. CSI was required "to understand what a reasonably prudent person would understand," but it did not have "any duty to seek out and prevent violations" to make sure that counterfeit goods were not being sold at the flea markets. That is, it did not have a positive duty to watch out for Hard Rock's commercial interests. The Court held that CSI was not vicariously liable to Hard Rock for the actions of the shirt sellers, since CSI and the shirt sellers had not acted together to violate the trademark. The injunction against further sales of counterfeit shirts at CSI flea-markets was upheld.

Managerial Considerations

Hard Rock and many other trademark owners take action against vendors selling imitations of their goods. The loss of sales from any one vendor is trivial, but if the companies do not invest in trademark protection, the counterfeiting will become widespread, sales will be lost, and customers will not know the difference between the real thing and the counterfeit. Eventually, the right to protect the trademark would be lost. If you take no steps to protect your property when it is taken, at some point you are presumed to have abandoned it. In its discussion, the Court made it clear that it was likely that CSI knew that some vendors at its flea-markets were selling counterfeits. Being "willfully blind as to the counterfeit nature of the t-shirts" would not get them off the hook; that is, you cannot proclaim ignorance about law violations within the scope of your control when everyone knows what is really going on.

Note that even if people are told that the counterfeit goods are counterfeit—so that no one is being fooled—the trademark has still been counterfeited. For example, Ferrari makes very expensive cars with distinctive body designs. Ferrari sued companies that made fiberglass imitations of its car bodies that could be placed on car frames. Even though everyone knew the bodies were not Ferrari and there was a name other than Ferrari on the bodies, the distinctive design of Ferrari was held to be a trademark that could be protected against imitations.

The Supreme Court extended trademark protection to what is known as *trade dress* in the 1992 case, *Two Pesos Inc.* v. *Taco Cabana Inc.* One Mexican-style restaurant could not copy the decor of its competitor, which included distinctive exterior decorations and interior design. To qualify for trade dress protection, a company need only show that its appearance is "inherently distinctive."

■ TRADE NAMES

A *trade name* identifies the services and products of various businesses. Just as others cannot use your name and pretend to be you, the trade name of a business cannot be used by impostors. Unlike trademarks, trade names must be earned by actual use over time. The bigger the market and the better known the name, the broader the protection offered the owner of the trade name.

Companies that fail to protect their names from use by others will find them lost to common usage. The words *elevator* and *zipper* were trade names that became generic. Recently, Rollerblade Inc. has been fighting to protect the name "Rollerblade" from becoming generic. Some words that are very valuable are *Coke* and *Coca-Cola*. Because these words are well-known worldwide, they have broad protection that applies to products other than soft drinks. No one may open the Coca-Cola Motel without permission of the Coca-Cola Company—even though the company is not in the motel business—because of the value the word imports to any business and because Coca-Cola could license its trade name to motel operators. The Coca-Cola Company works constantly to protect its name from infringement, as the *Koke* case shows.

COCA-COLA COMPANY v. KOKE COMPANY OF AMERICA

United States Supreme Court
254 U.S. 143, 41 S.Ct. 113 (1920)

Case Background
Koke Company was imitating the soft drink Coca-Cola under the name of "Koke." The Coca-Cola Company sought to prevent Koke Company from infringing on its trade name, Coca-Cola. According to the arguments of the Koke Company, prior to 1900 the Coca-Cola Company has used small amounts of cocaine in its drink to induce consumers to drink it. However, with the enactment of the Food and Drug Act in the early 1900s, Coca-Cola stopped putting the drug in its beverage. While coca leaves were still used in making the drink, their treatment in the manufacturing process left only a small amount of caffeine. Koke claimed the Coca-Cola Company used the cola nut and coca leaves in its advertising with the intent to allude to the past use of cocaine in the drink, which is a fraudulent misrepresentation. Thus, since the Coca-Cola trade name was a fraudulent representation, the company was not entitled to any relief from the courts. The federal district court issued a decree for Coca-Cola Company, but the court of appeals reversed. Coca-Cola Company appealed to the U.S. Supreme Court.

Case Decision
The Supreme Court reversed the appellate court's decision. The Court held that the Coca-Cola Company had not defrauded the public through the use of the coca name and therefore should be allowed trademark protection by the courts. The Court stated that the Coca-Cola Company does not use any drug in its beverage, nor does it advertise the beverage as medicinal. Rather, the product is a soft drink to be sold at soda fountains. The name "Coca-Cola" represents to most people the name of a particular beverage and no more. The Court further stated that "it would be going too far to deny the plaintiff relief . . . because here and there an ignorant person might call for the drink with the hope for incipient cocaine intoxication."

Managerial Considerations
The protection offered by trade name and trademark law is substantial and valuable. However, protection is afforded only to parties who have "clean hands." A manager must be cautious that any representation by the company does not induce fraud or misrepresent the product's performance capabilities. Although the use of overstatement, humor, puns, and hyperbole—puffing—in advertising is common, such techniques must be clearly construed as such. In other words, puffing must be easily understood by the public as just that and not a representation of the truth. Any consistent advertising and marketing communication that leads to misrepresentation could have the adverse result that the defendant sought in this case. That is, the courts will not protect trade names that have misled or defrauded the public. The marketing manager should closely scrutinize all marketing and advertised strategies to ensure that this does not occur.

■ COPYRIGHTS

A *copyright* provides the copyright holder with the exclusive right to print, reprint, publish, copy, and sell books, periodicals, newspapers, dramatic and musical compositions, letters, works of art, photographs, pictorial illustrations, and motion pictures for the period of the author's life plus fifty years. The Copyright Act governs the rights of copyright owners. Federal protection begins automatically with the author's creation of a work and will run for the author's lifetime plus fifty years.

Copyright law requires that the work be original. You cannot copyright a 200-year-old song, because you did not create an original work. The

Supreme Court made this point in the 1991 decision *Feist Publications* v. *Rural Telephone Service Co.*, where one company copied the white page telephone listings of another company. The Court said there is nothing original in listing telephone users names, addresses, and phone numbers alphabetically—a "garden variety white pages directory, devoid of even the slightest trace of creativity." Public facts not presented in an original manner deserve no copyright protection. Of course, public facts are used in many publications, but there must be some original element in the work for copyright protection.

The law provides for the limited use of the copyrighted material for purposes of research, comment, news reporting, and teaching without permission if the use is reasonable and not harmful to the copyright owner (referred to as "fair use"). The *Sony* decision considers whether videotaping television programs for home use violates the copyright laws.

SONY CORPORATION OF AMERICA v. UNIVERSAL CITY STUDIOS, INC.

United States Supreme Court
464 U.S. 417, 104 S.Ct. 774 (1984)

Case Background
Universal City Studios, the plaintiff, owns the copyrights on several television programs that are aired on television. Sony, the defendant, makes videotape recorders (VCRs) that allow its customers to record Universal's programs at home. Universal has asserted that such recordings are an infringement of its copyright and that Sony is liable because it sold the machines. The federal district court denied relief, finding that home use for noncommercial purposes was not a copyright infringement. The court of appeals reversed the decision. The defendant appealed to the Supreme Court.

Case Decision
The Supreme Court reversed the court of appeals decision, finding that since Universal had suffered no harm to its copyrighted materials or to the creative processes necessary for the further creation of such materials, the recording of televised programs for home viewing was a fair use. The

Court stated that not all uses of copyrighted materials constitute an infringement. Under the fair use doctrine, for example, copyrighted material may be used for the purposes of research, news reporting, and teaching without permission. One of the overriding concerns of the fair use doctrine is whether the use is commercial or noncommercial in its purposes. The use of VCRs for home use is a noncommercial, nonprofit activity that does not adversely affect the potential market for the copyrighted work. The time shifting of videotaped programs for home viewing, therefore, falls within the fair use doctrine.

Managerial Considerations
This case could have long-run implications for managers well beyond it, holding that noncommercial taping for home use is fair use and does not create copyright infringement. The important consideration for managers is that Sony, the *producer* of the VCR, would have been liable if its product had been found to be a tool used by others to infringement on copyrights. To what extent a company is liable for creating products that will be used by other parties in violation of the law remains unclear.

Copyright protection exists at common law, but the Copyright Act provides for specific steps to be taken to get statutory protection. A short form is filled out and filed with the Registrar of Copyrights in Washington, along with a copy of the material being copyrighted. This filing makes clear the date and coverage of the material copyrighted. It is best to put a copyright symbol, ©, on copyrighted material, but that is not required by the law, as one can presume that most materials are copyrighted.

Infringement of copyrighted material covers more than exact duplication; it can be copying a part of a work or a substantial part of the expression. That has been the key point in copyright cases involving songs—even though some of the words were different, the general expression of the song was the same as the original. Infringement suits usually ask for the profits earned by the copier to be given over to the copyright owner, or the court can award up to $100,000 in damages.

■ PATENTS

A *patent* is a grant from the government conveying and securing for an inventor the exclusive right to make, use, and sell an invention for seventeen years. To be patentable, the invention, design, or process must be genuine, useful, novel, and not obvious in light of presently known technology. The owner of the patent may also profit by licensing others to use the invention on a royalty basis.

A major advantage of patents is the strong protection provided. For example, Polaroid won a billion-dollar judgment against Kodak for infringement on its instant camera and film patents. However, there are drawbacks to the patent process. The application process is technical, expensive, and very time consuming. Usually it takes about two years to find out whether a patent application will be approved. Further, once a patent is approved, the patent application, which contains all the details, is made public. That means that competitors can gain a lot of valuable information. As a result, many companies prefer to use trade secrets for some innovations. A hundred years ago, the Coca-Cola company decided to keep the formula for Coke a secret. Had it gotten a patent instead, the formula could have been used by anyone after about 1907. Some firms use a combination of trade secrecy and patents to protect their innovations.

JAPANESE AND AMERICAN PATENTS	INTERNATIONAL ASPECTS

The World Intellectual Property Organization is working to make patent laws consistent around the world. U.S. patents tend to be broad compared to the patents issued in Japan, which tend to be very specific in coverage. Hence, a U.S. patent may cover an entire invention, whereas in Japan, there would be numerous patent applications to cover each little part of the same invention. Small changes will be patented in Japan; in the United States, they may be rejected as too trivial or even seen as an infringement.

The result is frequent litigation between American and Japanese companies in the same market over patent infringement. For example, in 1992, Honeywell won a 96-million-dollar judgment against Minolta for infringement on Honeywell's autofocus patents on cameras. The decision made the camera industry nervous because the jury seemed to give Honeywell broader ownership over autofocus than most firms thought Honeywell really owned.

Having to review over 10,000 patent applications per month, the U.S. Patent Office is swamped. It relies on old-fashioned research by its examiners, who determine whether a patent application covers inventions that already exist. Mistakes are made, and patents are granted that were already covered, which leads to litigation. Facing the same problem, the Japanese government is spending over $1 billion on an advanced computer system for its patent office to speed research and improve accuracy.

Few complaints are made about the fairness of treatment of foreigners in the American or Japanese patent offices. The problems are created by differences in the patent laws.

■ TRADE SECRETS

Coca-Cola has kept a valuable secret for over 100 years—the formula for Coke. Businesses have a lot of information that are *trade secrets.* The information could be patented, like the Coke formula, or copyrighted, like a list of customers, but the firm prefers to keep it secret. Other information may not be eligible for patent or copyright protection but is still a valuable secret. Tort law protects such information. The *Restatement of Torts* defines such secret information as follows: ''A trade secret may consist of any formula, pattern, device, or compilation of information which is used in one's business, and which gives him an opportunity to obtain an advantage over competitors who do not know or use it.''

The word *secret* means both that such information is not known by the competition and that if the competition were to obtain it, the business would lose its advantage. If the trade secret is stolen by another business either by the abuse of confidence of an employee or by means such as trespass, electronic surveillance, or bribery, the courts will provide relief to the injured business by way of injunction and damages.

Generally, businesses with trade secrets protect themselves by having employees agree in their employment contracts never to divulge those secrets. Still, the classic example of a theft of a trade secret involves an employee who steals a secret and then uses it in direct competition with the former employer or sells it to a competitor for personal gain. The general requirement, however, is that the stolen information be confidential. As the following case illustrates, if the employee draws on general knowledge gained in the course of employment, the courts will not find liability under this tort if the employee later uses that general knowledge for personal gain.

TEMPLETON v. CREATIVE LOAFING TAMPA, INC.

District Court of Appeal of Florida, Second District
552 So.2d 288 (1989)

Case Background
For eight years, Templeton was an employee of Steppin' Out-Suncoast Edition, Inc. (Steppin' Out), the owner of a publication known as *Music*, which was distributed to local restaurants and music stores in the Tampa Bay area. The magazine was free at the establishments that carried it, and the company derived its revenues solely from its advertisers, most of whom were local merchants. Templeton worked in both the editorial and the advertising departments of *Music* and was the principal contact for the magazine's advertising clients. During his employment, Templeton developed a list of potential advertisers, including actual advertisers in *Music* and a larger number of merchants who fit into the class likely to advertise in the publication but who had not chosen to do so. The list contained the names, addresses, and contact persons of the various merchants.

Templeton also kept a distribution list, which contained information regarding the order of delivery and the number of magazines to be dropped off at each location.

Steppin' Out was purchased by Creative Loafing, which began to publish a magazine in the Tampa Bay area. Approximately two weeks after the sale, Templeton resigned and started a competing magazine called *Music Pulse*. Most of the 80 to 100 advertisers in *Music Pulse* were the same merchants who had advertised in *Music*, and *Music Pulse* was distributed to many of the same establishments to which *Music* had been distributed.

Creative Loafing sued Templeton, seeking damages and injunctive relief against Templeton for the use of Creative Loafing's trade secrets, consisting of the allegedly confidential information contained in the advertiser and distribution lists. After evidentiary hearings, the trial court granted Creative Loafing's motion for temporary injunction, finding that Creative Loafing had suffered irreparable harm as a

(continued)

result of Templeton's use of its trade secrets. The trial court enjoined Templeton from using the lists and from soliciting or contacting any advertisers on the advertiser list or delivering to anyone on the distribution list. Templeton appealed.

Case Decision

In our view, the lists in question do not qualify as trade secrets entitled to injunctive protection. There is no evidence that they are the product of any great expense or effort, that they are distillations of larger lists, or that they include information not available from public sources.

In fact, the information on the lists is easy to obtain merely by looking at the advertisements in past issues of *Music*, in addition to many other sources, such as the weekend sections of local newspapers and the yellow pages.

The appeals court reversed the trial court. The only secret information Templeton had was the names of persons on the advertiser list, whom he all knew personally anyway. He was free to use such business expertise.

Managerial Considerations

While Templeton worked for Creative Loafing he was a loyal employee. The main problem was that there was no convenant not to compete signed by Templeton while at Creative Loafing. That would have deterred Templeton from going into direct competition. Such contracts must be limited as to time, place, and scope, and the law varies from state to state. Making sure employees know that what information they possess is a trade secret is important for reducing the likelihood of theft and for winning a lawsuit later if that comes about.

SUMMARY: A GUIDE FOR MANAGERS

- The rule of negligence in tort dominated products liability the first half of this century. Still good law, it requires producers to take the care of a reasonable person when making products to prevent foreseeable injury. The reasonable person is held to the skill of an expert in the industry. This rule applies in most states to the crashworthiness of automobiles— that they be constructed to help minimize the injuries suffered by those in accidents.

- In recent decades, the rule of strict liability in tort has applied to most consumer products. If there is a defect in a product that causes an injury to a consumer, the producer is liable for damages. The defect may be due to a failure to warn consumers of dangers or a defect in product design.

- Many strict liability suits have concerned unknown hazards, such as those associated with asbestos, where the danger did not become known until many years later. When claims of thousands of persons exceed all funds of defendants, the claims may be joined together for settlement. When many companies have made the same product, they may be held joint and severally liable, requiring all to pay equal compensation, or the damages may be apportioned among the producers based on market share.

- Defenses in strict liability cases include product abuse and negligence, which may lead to a split of liability between producer and consumer. For products known to be dangerous, such as alcohol and tobacco, the consumer is presumed to have assumed the risk.

- Intellectual property is a major form of wealth. It is protected by a combination of tort law and statutes. Like real and personal property, others may not infringe on one's right to enjoy the use of property that is mostly created by one's mental work.

- Trademarks are designs, logos, or distinctive marks put on products. Huge sums have been invested in trademarks so that consumers come to know and trust the quality of products associated with those marks. Use of trademarks without permission—regardless of intent and product quality—is counterfeiting.

- Trade names are earned by use over time as consumers come to recognize the name of companies. Companies must protect their names by suing those who use their name or a similar version of it. If such use is not challenged, the word becomes generic and may be used by anyone.

- Copyrights are long-term legal rights to exclusive control over original written works, musical compositions, art, and photography. One cannot copyright common knowledge, and one cannot prevent others from fair use of copyrighted material, such as for personal use, news reporting, or teaching.

- Patents are exclusive grants for seventeen years granted by the government to protect an invention, design, or process that is genuine, useful, novel, and not obvious.

- Trade secrets—formulas, patterns, devices, or compilations of information used in business that have been kept secret—are protected by the law of tort from use by others for profit. Employers can require employees to sign contracts not to reveal trade secrets and not to use them later in competition.

MANAGER'S ETHICAL DILEMMA

SHOULD LOCAL FOLKS PAY THEIR OWN TORT BILLS?

A New Yorker rented a car from Avis. He lent the car, in violation of the rental agreement, to a friend who hit several people. Avis paid out $3.6 million in claims.

Four British sailors rented a car from Alamo in Florida. The driver lost control, killing himself and two of the other sailors. No problem with the car was found, but Alamo was ordered to pay $7.8 million to the estates of the deceased.

In both cases, car rental companies were held liable for the negligence of the drivers of their cars. New York and Florida, along with six other states (and two others to a lesser extent), have the doctrine of *vicarious liability*, which allows blame to be assigned to the owner or producer of a product, regardless of fault, for the costs that arise from tort claims. Traditionally, this doctrine applied only to employers held responsible for the acts of their employees or to business partners held responsible for the acts of their partners that were associated with the business.

Advocates of vicarious liability say the rule is good. When car rental companies enter commerce, they should pay anyone injured. The head of the Florida Trial Lawyers says the rule "puts the burden where it should be, on the company that makes money on renting cars." Car companies that want to cut their risks should not rent to people with bad driving records.

Opponents of vicarious liability say it is difficult and expensive to check driving records of car renters. Such checking is not a perfect predictor of future accidents anyway, and it is impossible to stop a renter from giving the car to someone else in violation of the rental contract.

From 1988 to 1990, Hertz paid $45 million in vicarious liability claims in New York City. Avis paid out $25 million in similar claims. These are claims that would not have been paid in most of the country, because most states reject this application of the rule of vicarious liability.

In 1992, Hertz announced it would impose surcharges as high as $56 a day on car rentals in high-risk, lawsuit-likely parts of New York City. These surcharges will cover the cost of expected payouts from the rule of vicarious liability. Avis said it would not impose such a sur- charge, because it would cause customer resentment. New York officials claimed that this was unfair discrimination.

QUESTIONS

The common law produces different rules in different states, such as vicarious liability, which imposes cost differences. Hertz is going to have the costs covered where they arise. Avis is going to have the costs covered by customers from all over the country. Which approach makes more sense? Is there anything unethical about having renters in New York, Florida, or other vicarious liability states charged more for rental costs than the laws of their states impose? Is it fair for residents of Illinois and other states with no vicarious liability to have to pay for the bills incurred in New York because of New York's law?

REVIEW AND DISCUSSION QUESTIONS

1. Define the following terms:

    caveat emptor   intellectual property
    strict liability   trademark
    design defect   trade name
    failure to warn   copyright
    unknown hazard   patent
    market share liability   trade secret

2. Compare the standards of care a producer must take under the rule of negligence compared to under the rule of strict liability. Can you think of a stricter standard of care to hold producers to?

3. Distinguish the logic between *express* and *implied* in the cases of express warranty and implied warranty.

4. Refer to Section 402A of the *Second Restatement of Torts:* What does "the seller is engaged in the business of selling such a product" mean? Who is excluded by this? What does "it is expected to and does reach the user or consumer without substantial change in the condition in which it is sold" mean? What situations does this cover? What is the difference between the idea that the rule applies although "the seller has exercised all possible care in the preparation and sale of his product" and the rule of negligence? What is covered by the provision "the user or consumer has not bought the product from or entered into any contractual relation with the seller"?

5. Except for patents, how much of intellectual property protection depends on statutes compared to common law?

■ CASE QUESTIONS

6. Many crimes involve the use of cheap handguns. Producers and sellers of such handguns know that some percentage of these guns will be used in crimes by the purchaser of the gun or by a criminal who steals the gun. Could the producers and retailers of such handguns be held liable for the injuries suffered by persons shot by such handguns used during the commission of a crime? That is, should such a producer be held strictly liable or negligent for selling a product that is "defective" in that one of its known end uses is crime? [See *Patterson v. Rohm Gesellschaft,* 608 F.Supp. 1206 (N.D. Tex 1985).]

7. A company sells pesticides nationwide that are usually used for agricultural purposes. All bags of the pesticides are clearly labeled with respect to ingredients, proper usage, and dangers. Some farm workers speak only Spanish, and some cannot read at all. Does the producer have a legal responsibility for such users of the product? If so, how can the matter be handled?

8. Defendant flew his plane over a chemical plant being built by duPont and took numerous photos of the construction. Although the plant was guarded on the ground from outsiders, it was not guarded from aerial inspection. The photographs reveal a lot about secret processes. Defendant said that if duPont cared, it would have covered the construction site. Does duPont have a legitimate trade secret action against the photographer? [*E.I. duPont De Nemours & Co.v. Christopher*, 431 F.2d 1012 (5th Cir. 1970)]

9. A rainstorm blew water into a grocery store every time the door was opened by a customer going in or out, and customers tracked water into the store. The manager had an employee frequently mop up the water around the door. Nevertheless, a women entering the store slipped in the water on the floor inside the door, fell, and was injured. No sign had been posted to warn customers of the water. Was the store liable for her injuries? [*H.E. Butt Grocery Company* v. *Hawkins*, 594 S.W.2d 187 (Tex. Cir. App. 1980)]

■ BUSINESS POLICY QUESTIONS

10. In recent years, drug companies have been held liable for side effects of drugs that are widely distributed for public health reasons. That is, our population is inoculated against polio, whooping cough, and other diseases that used to kill thousands of people each year. However, some people who receive the shots will die from them or suffer permanent injuries. The shots they receive are not defective, and it is not possible to predict who will suffer such horrible consequences. Should drug companies and doctors be required to tell all potential recipients of these inoculations—including parents of children who get the shots—about the risk involved and let them decide if they want the shots or not? If everyone else gets the shots, the person who does not is probably safe from the disease because no one else will carry it. Some people know this, so they avoid the shots and let everyone else provide the public health benefit by getting the shots. Should public policy considerations take precedence over personal wishes? That is, should we all be forced to get the shots, or do we let everyone choose, even though it increases the risk of disease for many more people? Given that some people will be injured or killed by the shots, what should the policy be—nothing (tough luck), the producer of the shots pays the victims, or the government has a special fund to compensate the victims?

■ ETHICS QUESTIONS

11. You are an executive with a drug company that has recently been selling a highly effective, FDA-approved prescription drug that greatly reduces the pain of migraine headaches. This patented drug is earning a high rate of return for your company and is expected to do so for several years. One of the research scientists comes to you and reports that she thinks that the drug may have long-term effects that lead to brain tumors. She says that tests on rats and mice are not conclusive and probably will not be. There will have to be long, expensive tests run on other animals to determine whether this is the case, but she believes that the results are likely to be bad. She claims that a small percentage of the users will develop tumors after about twenty years. Since no one else is

likely to run the tests needed to determine whether this is true, if you do nothing there may be no consequences for twenty years. Since it may not be true, there may never be any consequences. You know that twenty years from now, you will no longer be where you are and, in any event, cannot be held liable for what happens. You can do nothing, order more rat and mice tests, or order expensive testing of other animals. You know that if word gets out about this, sales may drop and your job security may be threatened. Suppose you think tests should be started, but your superiors say no. What should you do?

12. Many copyrighted books are published each year that list a famous person, such as a president or would-be president, as the author. In fact, the famous person did not write the book but merely talked to a good writer, who wrote the book and split the payment for the book with the famous person. Should book publishers always inform us that ghost authors actually wrote the book? Some book serials are published with the name of a well-liked author who has died or no longer writes. Obviously the "author" who is listed did not participate in writing the book at all. Are these practices unethical?

13. An unhappy employee from a competitor offers to sell your company secret information from the other company. Having the information will save you a lot of money and, at the least, keep you more competitive with the other company—which could mean lower prices for consumers because of the added competition. While it is illegal, is it unethical to buy the information if it leads to lower prices? What if the employee offers to *give* you the information?

BUSINESS AND THE LAW OF CONTRACTS

CHAPTER 9

MANAGER'S LEGAL CHALLENGE

Contracts are a fundamental aspect of doing business in the United States. Contracting and contract law are more developed in this country than in any other Western industrial country. For example, in Japan, the emphasis has traditionally been placed on business relationships rather than on business contracts. Businesses in this country place a high value on the terms and conditions in their contracts. The courts have supported businesses when the other party to a contract has failed to fulfill its commitments.

In 1983, the management of Pennzoil made the strategic decision to expand its oil and gas reserve holdings. To be competitive and to grow in the oil industry of the 1980s and 1990s, Pennzoil had to acquire a stable and reasonably priced supply of crude oil and natural gas. To that end, management decided to acquire Getty Oil Company. In December 1983, Pennzoil undertook efforts to buy 20 percent of Getty's stock.

The companies negotiated through December. On January 3, 1984, the parties reached an agreement in principle to merge Getty Oil Company with a new corporation co-owned by Gordon P. Getty and Pennzoil. The agreement was subject to the execution of a definitive merger agreement, including approval by Getty Oil shareholders. According to the understanding between the parties, Pennzoil would acquire 43 percent of Getty Oil's shares for approximately $110 each. Getty, who previously owned 40.2 percent of Getty Oil, would control a 57 percent interest in the new company.

Before Pennzoil had time to celebrate, however, Texaco entered negotiations with Getty Oil. On January 5, 1984, Texaco offered $125 per share for Getty Oil stock. Getty agreed to recommend that Getty Oil's board of directors approve a proposal allowing Texaco to purchase the Getty Oil shares at that price. Despite protests from Pennzoil management, Texaco announced the signing of a formal agreement with Getty Oil on January 8, 1989.

The management of Pennzoil was shocked at the turn of events. It made the decision to challenge Texaco's actions in court. The suit was filed against Texaco in Texas state court. The company argued that Texaco had wrongfully interfered with Pennzoil's contractual and business relationship with Getty Oil.

The result of the jury trial was shocking. The Texas jury awarded Pennzoil $7.53 billion in actual damages, $3 billion in punitive damages, and $470 million in interest. The appellate court upheld the decision but decided to reduce the punitive damages from $3 billion to $2 billion. The Texas Supreme Court refused to hear the case. On December 19, 1987, the parties reached a settlement under which Texaco agreed to pay Pennzoil $3 billion.

Several theories have been offered by businesspeople and scholars to explain this incident. Some place blame on the jury system. They argue that if the jurors as consumers had fully understood the impact of the decision, they would have decided the case differently. Others place the blame on the management of Texaco for two reasons. First, management clearly underestimated the force of contract law and contract principles. If it did not ignore those principles, the moral justification of their activities between January 3 and January 5 is questionable. Second, Texaco's management apparently underestimated the ability of Pennzoil to defend itself in a court of law. Several commentators were skeptical that Pennzoil could win, given that it did not have a signed agreement with Getty. They have speculated that perhaps Texaco management felt the same way. Thus, perhaps Texaco management did not make the effort to meet the legal challenge as effectively as Pennzoil management did.

Business transactions and the law of contracts are examined in this chapter, which begins by considering the fundamental concept of freedom of contract and some of the limitations and restrictions contract law places on that freedom. A further discussion is provided on the principal sources of contract law, including common law judicial opinions, the *Restatement of Contracts* (2d), and the Uniform Commercial Code. Next, the chapter examines the definition of contract and the various classifications of contracts.

The chapter then develops the basic elements of a contract, including the agreement, consideration, legal capacity, lawful subject matter, and genuine consent. It lastly discusses the various ways in which a contract can be discharged and the remedies available to the parties in the event of a breach.

THE NOTION OF FREEDOM OF CONTRACT

The *law of contracts* enters into practically every aspect of domestic and international business. It establishes the legal rules governing agreements between businesses and their employees, customers, and suppliers. In day-to-day commercial activity, businesses enter into a multitude of contractual relationships. From selling a Coke to creating a purchase contract for a large quantity of goods, a business day is filled with contracts and contracting.

Basic to the law of contracts is the underlying principle that every business has the freedom to enter into nearly any contract it desires. Businesses can bind suppliers to exacting specifications on product or service requirements, customers to specific purchase agreements and payment terms, and employees to designated salaries and responsibilities, all with the intent to facilitate commerce.

Business and economic historians have called *freedom of contract* the fundamental and indispensable requisite of progress. This freedom is not, however, without restrictions and limitations imposed by contract law. Prohibitions, for example, are placed on contracts for criminal purposes, contracts among businesses designed to restrain trade, and contracts that do not comply with regulatory restrictions. Contracts for these purposes will not be judged valid or enforceable by the courts. For example, business's freedom to enter into employment contracts is highly restricted by a wide range of federal and state laws concerning wages, hours, working conditions, and required social insurance programs. These and many other restrictions on a business's freedom of contract are imposed by the government and the courts to achieve public policy goals and objectives.

■ SOURCES OF CONTRACT LAW

Contract law is primarily state common law. It has developed through centuries of judicial opinions that have resolved virtually every kind of contract dispute. The *Restatement of Contracts*, now in its second edition, is an authoritative document that provides a summary of the common law of contract.

Common law principles of contract are significantly influenced by many legislative enactments. Of particular importance are Articles 2 and 9 of the *Uniform Commercial Code* (UCC). The UCC is a statute adopted in similar form in all the states. Article 2 of the UCC applies to sales of goods (discussed in Chapter 10), while Article 9 deals in part with the assignment (transfer) of some contractual rights. The UCC was designed to promote uniformity of the laws relating to commercial transactions among the states. It does not apply, however, to employment contracts, service contracts, insurance contracts, contracts involving real property (land and anything attached to it), and contracts for the sale of intangibles, such as patents and copyrights, all of which are governed by general contract law.

DEFINITION AND CLASSIFICATIONS OF CONTRACTS

Before discussing contracts, we will define a contract and discuss the important classifications of contracts. A contract is one of the most basic tools used by a business. Its fundamental purpose is to allow voluntary exchanges and to allocate risk among contracting parties in transactions where time is an important factor. Contract law serves a valuable social function by providing a legal environment that promotes such transactions.

■ DEFINITIONS OF A CONTRACT

Sir William Blackstone, a famous English jurist, defined a *contract* simply as "an agreement, upon sufficient consideration, to do or not to do a particular thing." Modern definitions center on a *promise*—the element common to all contracts. Section I of the *Restatement of Contracts* (2d), for example, defines a contract as "a promise or a set of promises for the breach of which the law gives a remedy, or the performance of which the law in some way recognizes as a duty." The *Restatement* (2d) then defines a promise as "a manifestation of the intention [of a party] to act or refrain from acting in a specified manner."

A contract, then, is the legal relationship that consists of the rights and duties of the contracting parties growing out of promises. Contract law governs the enforceability of that legal relationship.

Not all promises, however, are enforceable contracts. A promise may be either binding (contractual) or nonbinding (noncontractual). For a promise to be binding, and thus enforceable, it must meet all of the basic requirements of a contract. If a party fails to perform a nonbinding promise—that is, if he or she is in breach of the promise—contract law will not provide a remedy. This concept is important because it emphasizes the necessity of meeting the requirements of a contract when the parties want their exchange of promises to be binding.

■ CLASSIFICATIONS OF CONTRACTS

Contracts can be classified in a variety of ways, ranging from their method of formation to their legal effect. The standard classifications are express and implied contracts; bilateral and unilateral contracts; executory and executed contracts; valid, void, voidable, and unenforceable contracts; and quasi-contracts. Note that a particular contract could actually fall into several classifications. A bilateral contract, for example, can also be an express, executory, and valid contract.

Express and Implied Contracts. An *express contract* is a contract created by a direct statement by the parties of a promise or promises to each other. Nothing is left to implication. The statement may be either oral or in writing. If Ms. A offers to sell her car for $400 to Mr. B, who then states to her that he will buy it for that price, an express contract has been created orally for buying and selling the automobile for $400. If Ms. A makes the same offer in a letter and Mr. B accepts by letter, an express contract has been created in writing.

In an *implied contract*, the parties do not state directly the promise or promises to one another. Rather, the promises are inferred from the behavior of the parties or the circumstances in which they find themselves. Words, conduct, gestures, and the like will reasonably imply the existence of certain kinds of contracts. Suppose a woman enters a service station and tells the operators that she wants her car's engine oil changed but says nothing about the price. After the oil has been changed, the woman refuses to pay because the price is too high. A court will infer from the conduct of the parties that the parties have bargained for the oil change and that the woman promised to pay the standard fee for the service.

Bilateral and Unilateral Contracts. Every contract has an offeror and an offeree. The individual making the offer is called the *offeror*. The individual to whom the offer is made is called the *offeree*. A contract is formed only when the offer is accepted by the offeree. The offeree may accept the offer either by a promise to perform in the future or by immediate performance. If the offeree accepts the offer through an exchange of a mutual promise, a *bilateral contract* is formed. If the offeree accepts the offer through the exchange of performance for the offeror's promise, a *unilateral contract* is formed. Figure 9–1 compares unilateral and bilateral contracts.

Most contracts are bilateral in nature. However, there are situations where unilateral contracts are a standard business practice. In contracts for the sale of real estate, for example, the seller of property often promises to pay a real estate agent a commission upon the sale of the property. The contract is unilateral because the real estate agent accepts the seller's promise to pay a commission only by selling the property. The sale of the property is the performance required in this unilateral contract. There is no obligation to pay if the property is not sold.

Executory and Executed Contracts. Some contracts are classified on the basis of when they are performed. *Executory contracts* are contracts that have not been fully performed by either party. *Executed contracts* are those that have been fully performed by both parties. Contracts fully performed by one party but not by the other are partially executed, or partially performed. The difference is important because it affects the remedies available to the parties. The remedies available depend on whether the party has performed fully or partially.

Valid, Void, Voidable, and Unenforceable Contracts. A *valid contract* is one in which all the elements of a contract are present. Such contracts are enforceable at law. A *void contract* is one that does not exist at law. Examples of a void contract would include a contract whose subject matter is illegal and a contract made by an individual without capacity to make a contract.

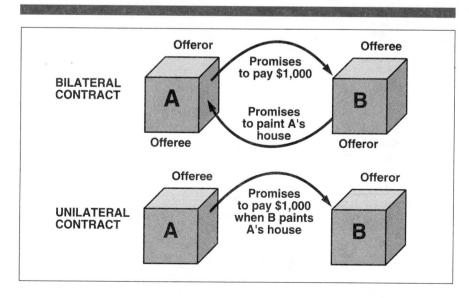

FIGURE 9–1

Comparing Bilateral and Unilateral Contracts

A *voidable contract* is a valid contract. However, one of the parties to the contract has the right to avoid his or her legal obligation without incurring liability. For this reason, the contract is not void but rather is voidable, or capable of becoming void at one party's option. A contract entered into by an individual of less than the legal age (a minor), for example, is a voidable contract. The contract is valid but may become void at the minor's request.

Unenforceable contracts are contracts that once were valid but because of a subsequent illegality will not be enforced by the courts. The passing of a statute that makes previously valid contracts illegal creates an unenforceable contract.

Quasi-Contracts.   A *quasi-contract* is not a true contract. This term is used by the courts to impose obligations on one party to a dispute when to do otherwise would create an injustice to the other party. Suppose that Glaze's son, without Glaze's permission, asks Pokorny Construction Company to build an addition onto a warehouse owned by Glaze. Pokorny builds the addition over a period of several days. Glaze watches the warehouse being built and knows that Pokorny will expect to be paid. When the warehouse is built, Glaze refuses to pay, saying there was not a contract between him and Pokorny. The court would require Glaze to pay under quasi-contract. Glaze was unjustly enriched by the construction of the addition to the warehouse.

INTERNATIONAL ASPECTS	**DEVELOPING CONTRACT RIGHTS IN CENTRAL AND EASTERN EUROPE**

Contract rights play a fundamental role in business. In most Western countries, the right to contract and contract law are often taken for granted. However, for contracts to be effective as a means of exchange within a society, three things must be present in some form:

contract law

private property rights

freedom to acquire and protect knowledge and information

Under the communism imposed by the former Soviet Union, there were no private property rights in Central and Eastern Europe. All property was owned by the government. All production decisions, and thus all decisions regarding the allocation of resources, were made by the government. The countries' business and legal systems had little need for contracts or contract law.

Recently, Central and Eastern Europe have experienced dramatic political changes. With the fall of communism, those countries are now making efforts to implement a democratic form of government. To attract foreign investors and businesspeople, they are working to create open market systems. Eventually, most production decisions will be made by private citizens and not by the government.

To implement the changes, the new governments are moving to develop contract law principles. Any long-term investment will require some form of con-

(continued)

tract, which will set forth the obligations of the parties. One party—probably the foreign partner—will contribute money, and the other party will agree to pay it back over time. Investors will not be willing to invest unless they are confident that contracts will be enforced. Most countries have invited Western legal scholars and practitioners to teach contract law to local lawyers. Slowly, Western investors are gaining more and more confidence in the ability of the European legal systems to enforce contracts.

Another serious roadblock is the lack of private property. It is difficult to enter into a lease or other sales contract if the party contracting does not have clear legal rights to the property. Each of the countries is now developing a process to place property back into the hands of private citizens. This process is called privatization. Most countries are finding the process difficult to implement. Should each family be given the house it is living in? What if that house had been taken away from one family and given to another during a war or other conflict? Does the previous family have any rights to the house? Should each worker be given equal shares in the business where he or she has been working? Should managers receive more than other workers? What if the government had taken business property away from the original business owners during a war? Should the original owners have any rights to the business now? Clearly it will be some time before many of these roadblocks to the freedom to contract are resolved.

ELEMENTS OF A CONTRACT

A contract provides businesses with reasonable confidence that its bargained-for exchanges will be enforceable. This section develops and discusses the basic elements necessary for a bargain between two or more parties to be a valid contract. While most business contracts today consist of standardized forms, the basic elements of a contract remain unchanged. Those elements include agreement, consideration, legal capacity of the parties to contract, lawful subject matter, and genuine consent to the contract. In addition, compliance may be necessary with the Statute of Frauds. To be a valid contract, an agreement must comply with the principles these basic elements represent.

■ THE AGREEMENT

In contract law, an *agreement* means that there is a mutual understanding between the parties as to the substance of the contract. This agreement between the parties is reached through a process of *offer* and *acceptance*. Table 9–1 provides a summary of offer and acceptance communications and their legal effect.

The Offer.   An *offer* is a promise to do or refrain from doing some specified thing. The party making an offer to another party is called the *offeror*. The *offeree* is the party to whom the offer is made. To be an effective offer, three requirements must be met: clear manifestation of intent, definite terms and conditions, and communication of the offer.

Manifestation of Intent.   In making an offer to enter into a contract, the offeror must have the intent to be bound to the contract, and that

TABLE 9-1
SUMMARY OF LEGAL EFFECT OF OFFER AND ACCEPTANCE COMMUNICATIONS

Communications	Time Effective	Legal Effect
By offeror		
1. Offer	When received by offeree.	Creates in offeree the power to form a contract.
2. Revocation	When received by offeree.	Terminates offeree's power to form a contract.
By offeree		
1. Rejection	When received by offeror.	Terminates the offer.
2. Counteroffer	When received by offeror.	Terminates the offer.
3. Acceptance	When sent by offeree.	Forms a contract.*

*Contract will also require consideration, legal capacity, lawful subject matter, genuine consent, and, in some cases, compliance with the Statute of Frauds.

intent must be clearly manifested. *Preliminary negotiations* are not viewed as an offer. Rather, they are invitations to negotiate or to make an offer. Many advertisements, an auctioneer's invitation for a bid at an auction, and dickering with a car salesperson about price are examples of preliminary negotiations. There is *intent* to negotiate but not to create a firm offer.

Definite Terms and Conditions. Not every detail of the offer needs to be present or completely clear. The terms of the offer must be sufficiently detailed so that each party's promises are reasonably certain. An offer whose terms are *ambiguous* or *missing* cannot serve as the basis for a contract. Sometimes the court will supply the missing terms if they are minor so that the offer (and subsequently the contract) will not fail for *indefiniteness.*

In a business transaction, the terms of trade generally used by the industry may supply the missing terms. Under the UCC, an offer or a contract for the sale of goods does not fail for indefiniteness of terms even though one or more terms are left open. UCC Section 2-305, for example, provides that if no price is stated or if the price is left open to be agreed upon later, the price is reasonable at the time of delivery.

Communication of the Offer. An appropriate acceptance requires prior *knowledge of the offer* by the offeree. The case of an individual who captures a fugitive and then learns of a reward is a good example of an offer failing for lack of communication. Because the communication of the offer occurred after the act of acceptance (the capturing of the fugitive), a proper acceptance did not take place. It is impossible to form a contract by accepting an unknown offer.

Terminating the Offer. *Termination* of the offer can occur either through the action of the parties or by the operation of law. The parties can *terminate* the offer by withdrawing it (by the offeror) or rejecting it (by the offere) or through lapse of time (by the inaction of the offeree). Termination of the offer by operation of law may occur through intervening illegality, destruction of the subject matter of the offer, or death or insanity of the offeror or the offeree.

Termination by the Parties.   The offeror can terminate the offer by withdrawing it anytime before it has been accepted by the offeree. The withdrawal of the offer by the offeror is termed a *revocation.* To be effective, the revocation must be communicated to the offeree. Generally, the offeror may revoke the offer anytime before acceptance. An offer can also state that it must be accepted within a designated time period. The expiration of that time period terminates the offer.

After the offer has been made by the offeror, the offeree has the power to create a contract by accepting the offer or to terminate the offer by rejecting it. One important form of rejection is a *counteroffer*—a proposal by the offeree to change the terms of the original offer. By indicating an unwillingness to agree to the original terms of the offer, the counteroffer operates as a rejection. For example, if Mr. Smith (the *offeror*) offers to buy Mr. White's (the *offeree*) automobile for $500 and Mr. White says that he will sell the automobile for $600, a counteroffer has been made. The original offer made by Mr. Smith is terminated by the counteroffer. The offeree now has to wait for the offeror's acceptance or a rejection of the counteroffer to determine whether a contract is formed.

Finally, the offer may terminate through *lapse of time.* If the offer does not state a specific time period for acceptance, the passage of a reasonable length of time after the offer has been made will work to terminate it. What is considered reasonable will depend upon the circumstances. An offer to buy stock in a company at a set price will terminate through lapse of time much more quickly than, for example, an offer to sell a building.

Termination by the Operation of Law.   Termination of the offer by operation of law through *intervening illegality* occurs when a court decision or legislative enactment makes an offer illegal after it has been made. Suppose that Horace Grant starts a business in South Carolina that offers to sell Florida lottery tickets to people in South Carolina. The state of South Carolina does not have its own lottery. Suppose the state decides that it is opposed to lotteries and enacts a law forbidding the sale of any lottery tickets within its boundaries. Grant's offer to sell Florida lottery tickets in the state of South Carolina is terminated by an intervening illegality.

An offer will also terminate by law if the subject matter of the offer is destroyed. The subject matter, however, must be destroyed before the offer is accepted. Suppose that Alisa Cook offers to sell Joanne Washburn an automobile. Before Washburn accepts Cook's offer, an accident destroys the automobile. The courts will hold that the offer terminated when the accident occurred.

The *death or insanity of the offeror or the offeree* will terminate an offer by operation of law. Upon the death or insanity of the offeror, the offer is terminated because the offeror no longer has capacity to enter into a contract. The death of the offeree terminates the offer because an offer can be accepted only by the person to whom it is made. Upon insanity, the offeree no longer has legal capacity to enter into a contract and thus cannot accept an offer.

The Acceptance.   In contract law, the term *acceptance* is defined as the offeree's expression of agreement to the exact terms of the offer. To be effective, an acceptance must be unconditional, unequivocal, and legally communicated. An acceptance that lacks one or more of these elements will generally not bring about a binding contract between the parties.

Must Be Unconditional.   The offeree must accept the offer as presented by the offeror. In effect, the acceptance must be the *mirror image* of the offer. The common law rule is that an acceptance that adds conditions to the original offer operates as a counteroffer. By changing the terms of the offer, the offeree rejects the offer.

Must Be Unequivocal.   The acceptance must be unequivocal or definite. Suppose that an offeree receives an offer to buy some merchandise for $10,000. If the offeree responds to the offer with "I see" or "What a good idea," the expressions will fail the unequivocal test. There will be no acceptance.

The words "I accept" would be a clear indication of an offeree's acceptance. However, any words or conduct expressing the offeree's intent to accept the offer is an effective acceptance. The standard is whether a reasonable person would consider the words as an acceptance of the offer.

Must Be Legally Communicated.   The final requirement of an effective acceptance is that it must be legally communicated to the offeror. Three factors are important in meeting this requirement: the method of acceptance, the timeliness of acceptance, and, in the case of unilateral contracts, performance as acceptance.

The general rule in communicating an acceptance is that any reasonable method or medium will be adequate. Problems arise when the offeror authorizes one method of communicating the acceptance but the offeree uses another. If, for example, the offeror requires that acceptance be made by telegram, a response by letter will not create an acceptance. If no method of acceptance is specified, the offeree may use any reasonable means to communicate his or her acceptance. The safest approach is to use the method used by the offeror in communicating the offer.

The timeliness of the acceptance is important, especially when the distance between the parties creates the potential for long passages of time between the offer and the acceptance. To deal with this time problem, the courts created the following rule: if the method of acceptance is reasonable under the circumstances, the acceptance is effective when it is sent.

In those circumstances where the offeror attempted to revoke the offer before the offeree's acceptance, the courts developed the *mailbox rule,* which states that acceptance is effective when it is sent by the offeror and revocation is effective when it is received by the offeree. For example, the offeror sends the offer July 1, and the offer is received by the offeree on July 3. The offeror then sends a revocation of the offer on July 2. The revocation is received by the offeree on July 4. If the offeree had sent an acceptance to the offeror on July 3 and the acceptance had reached the offeror on July 5, would there be a valid acceptance?

Applying the mailbox rule, the answer is yes, since the acceptance is effective upon being sent or dispatched by the offeree (July 3). The revocation is effective upon receipt (July 4). Thus, the acceptance is created by the offeree before the revocation by the offeror. A valid contract is formed. The following case provides an interesting example of the application of the mailbox rule.

CUSHING v. THOMSON

Court of Appeals of New Hampshire
118 N.H. 292, 386 A.2d 805 (1978)

Case Background
On March 30, 1978, the office of the adjutant general for the state of New Hampshire received an application from Portsmouth Clamshell Alliance to use the state armory for a dance to be held April 29, 1978. The Portsmouth Clamshell Alliance was an antinuclear protest group. The adjutant general mailed the signed contract on March 31, agreeing to rent the armory to the group. For the agreement to be binding, it was to be signed by the renter and returned to the adjutant general's office within five days after its receipt. On April 3, Cushing received the contract, signed it on behalf of the Portsmouth Clamshell Alliance, and placed it in the out box for mailing. At 6:30 P.M. on April 4, the adjutant general called Cushing, stating that Governor Meldrim Thomson, Jr., had ordered the offer to be withdrawn. Cushing stated that the contract was already in the mail. On April 5, the adjutant general sent Cushing a confirmation of the withdrawal. On April 6, the adjutant general received the agreement. It was signed and dated April 3 and postmarked April 5. The adjutant general, however, refused to recognize the existence of a contract.

Cushing and other members of the protest group brought this suit against Governor Thomson and the adjutant general. The Alliance sought specific performance of the contract. Thomson argued that there was no contract by virtue of the timely revocation by the adjutant general on April 4, along with the fact that the plaintiff's acceptance was postmarked April 5. The trial court ruled that a binding contract existed, and the defendant appealed.

Case Decision
The court of appeals affirmed the trial court's decision that a binding contract existed. The court held that since Cushing had placed the acceptance in the out box for mailing, the acceptance was effectively "sent" on April 3, prior to the defendant's revocation.

Managerial Considerations
The timing of acceptance and revocation are critical in contracting. Although the mailbox rule is relatively straightforward, confusion can result as to when acceptance and revocation take place if managers are not knowledgeable about it. Many courts today are struggling with the use of the mailbox rule when offers and acceptances are sent by telegram, FAX, or computer communication. The hour, or even the second, a communication is sent through these media may be critical in deciding whether a valid contract exists—especially when there are overlapping communications. Depending on the nature of the transaction, managers will want to make sure that they fully understand the possible consequences of their actions.

Special considerations govern the acceptance of unilateral contracts. As discussed earlier, a unilateral contract is a contract in which a promise is made in exchange for a performance. Thus, a unilateral contract offer is accepted by *performance*. Could the offeror revoke the offer just before the offeree was to complete the performance? Courts usually require that the performance be completed for the acceptance to take place. Some courts, however, take the view that if performance has begun, the offeror loses the right to revoke the offer.

■ CONSIDERATION

Consideration is defined as something of value or something bargained for in exchange for a promise. It is the element of a contract that keeps it from being gratuitous. If consideration is absent, neither party can enforce the promise or agreement. The traditional rule is that an exchange will be consideration if it creates a legal detriment to the promisee (the party to whom a promise is made) *or* a legal benefit to the promisor (the party making a promise). A *legal detriment* is defined as an act, a promise to act, or the refraining from acting in a way that one is not legally obligated to do. A *legal benefit* to the promisor exists when the promisor acquires some legal right through the promisee's act, promise to act, or refraining to do some act.

The definition of consideration requires either a legal detriment to the promisee or a legal benefit to the promisor. In actuality, both concepts often occur at the same time. Suppose that Sarah Leasure buys a watch from Art Glasgow for $100. Leasure suffers a legal detriment (gives up the right to keep the $100) in exchange for a benefit (the watch). Glasgow also suffers a legal detriment (gives up the watch) in exchange for a benefit (the $100). As the following case illustrates, many courts use this *detriment-benefit test* to determine whether there is consideration for a contract.

HAMER v. SIDWAY

Court of Appeals of New York, Second Division
124 N.Y. 538, 27 N.E. 256 (1891)

Case Background
William E. Story, Sr., was the uncle of William E. Story, II. During a celebration with several family members and guests present, William E. Story, Sr. promised his nephew that he would pay him $5,000 if he would refrain from "drinking, using tobacco, swearing, and playing cards or billiards for money" until he was twenty-one years old. In January 1875, the nephew wrote to the uncle informing him that he had performed his part of the agreement and wished to be awarded the $5,000. The uncle wrote a letter to the nephew stating, "Your letter . . . came to my hand all right, saying that you had lived up to the promise made to me several years ago. I have no doubt but you have, [and] you shall have five thousand dollars as I promised you." The uncle then stated the terms and conditions under which the money was to be given to the nephew. The nephew consented to those stated conditions and terms.

Two years later, the uncle died without having paid the nephew the $5,000. During that time, the nephew had assigned his interest in the $5,000 to Hamer. Sidway, the executor of the estate, refused to pay the $5,000. Sidway stated that there had been no consideration on the part of the nephew for the money. He asserted that there was no consideration because the promisee-nephew incurred a benefit rather than a detriment by refraining from using tobacco, drinking, swearing, and gambling. Hamer then brought this action. The trial court held that there was no consideration, and Hamer appealed.

Case Decision.
The court of appeals reversed the trial court's decision. The court stated that the nephew had a legal right to use tobacco and drink. He incurred a detriment by abandoning those legal rights based on the uncle's promise. By refraining from drinking, using tobacco, swearing, and playing cards or billiards for money, the nephew had provided sufficient consideration to establish a contract with his uncle. Hamer, having been assigned the rights to the contract by the nephew, was entitled to collect the $5,000.

Managerial Considerations
Managers often remember the definition of consideration as either a legal detriment to the promisee or a legal benefit to the promisor, or both. As indicated by *Hamer* v. *Sidway*, the courts have defined detriment and benefit to include more than money, time, or product. Managers should therefore be cautious when making promises that induce or constrain an action by other parties.

Adequacy of Consideration. For the most part, courts do not like to inquire into the *adequacy of consideration* given in a contract. In a business transaction, this places the bargaining responsibility on the parties to the contract. Even if one party bargains poorly and the values of the items to be exchanged are unequal, the courts will generally not interfere. In fact, a majority of the courts will support contracts that are bargained for, even if the consideration is one dollar or some other trivial amount.

Preexisting Obligations and Past Consideration. Consideration is a present detriment to the promisee or a present benefit to the promisor.

Obligations that existed before the present agreement will not constitute consideration for the present agreement. The reasoning behind this requirement is that the promisee has not incurred a detriment if there already is a prior obligation to perform it; without a detriment, there can be no consideration. Promises based on past considerations are thus unenforceable because of their failure to provide new or added consideration. For example, suppose that Oklahoma Natural Gas Company promised to deliver natural gas to Mississippi River Pipeline Company, and Mississippi River promised to pay $3.00 per unit for the gas. Thereafter, Oklahoma decided the price was not sufficient and increased the price to $3.50. Mississippi agreed to pay the higher price. After delivering the gas, Mississippi River paid $3.00 per unit, claiming that the promise to pay the additional fifty cents was unsupported by new consideration. Under these circumstances, Mississippi River would ordinarily win. Only if the parties had changed the existing contract—say by increasing the quantity of gas being bought and sold—would there be new consideration.

As a second example, consider the professional baseball player who becomes unhappy with his contract because other athletes are now making more money than he is making. Suppose the club is interested in making the player happy. In many cases, the club's management will give the athlete a salary increase. However, an agreement to provide the salary increase alone under the existing contract would not be supported by consideration on the part of the athlete. Only the club would be incurring a detriment. The athlete had already agreed to perform for the club at the original contract amount (past consideration). To provide the needed present consideration, the club's management usually requires the athlete to agree to a contract extension. The club's detriment is the additional salary, and the athlete's detriment is the additional years he agrees to play for the club at the new, higher salary.

Settlement of Business Debts.   Sometimes in business relationships debts become due that the debtor cannot or will not pay. In such situations, it is often the best solution for the debtor and the creditor to enter into a *settlement agreement*. Under such an agreement, the creditor releases the debtor from the full obligation of the debt in return for some partial payment. At law, such a settlement agreement is called an *accord and satisfaction*.

The *accord* occurs when one of the parties agrees to perform by making the partial payment. The *satisfaction* occurs when the accord has been fully executed. If the creditor wishes later to claim the remainder of the amount owed by the debtor, the ability to do so is dependent on whether the debt is defined as a liquidated debt or an unliquidated debt.

Liquidated Debt.   A *liquidated debt* exists when there is no dispute about the amount owed. Agreements to pay an amount less than the original debt usually do not stop later claims by the creditor for the remainder owed. The rationale is that the debtor promised to pay a particular amount when the original contract with the creditor was created. Therefore, the new settlement agreement is likely to fail for lack of new consideration.

Unliquidated Debt.   An *unliquidated debt* exists when there is a genuine dispute between the parties as to the amount owed by the debtor.

The general rule is that settlement agreements for unliquidated debts are binding. The creditor may not later claim the remainder of the original amount owed. The rationale is that the debtor and creditor have given new consideration in the creation of the settlement agreement—the debtor has promised to pay an amount that he or she otherwise did not feel he or she had the responsibility to pay (thereby giving up a legal right). The creditor has promised not to sue the debtor for the amount believed to be owed (giving up the legal right to enforce the claim in court).

Enforceable Promises Without Consideration.   There are circumstances where consideration for a promise is not required by the courts for the promise to be enforceable. Suppose a business makes a promise to a customer who needs a particular product for a proposed office renovation project. The customer has been unable to find the product and is reluctant to start the project. The business then promises to find the product and deliver it to the customer at a fair price. Like any other reasonable person, on that basis the customer begins the work. The courts will find that the business is bound by its promise if it later refuses to deliver the product to the customer. The doctrine used by the courts to bind such a promisor is called *promissory estoppel* (or *detrimental reliance*). The rationale to the doctrine is that it will avoid an injustice due to the promisee's reliance on the promisor's promise. As in the *Red Owl* decision, the doctrine is being applied in a growing number of business situations.

HOFFMAN v. RED OWL STORES, INC.

Supreme Court of Wisconsin
26 Wis.2d 683, 133 N.W.2d 267 (1965)

Case Background
Hoffman owned a bakery. He wanted to expand his business operations through the ownership of a grocery store. In 1959, he contacted Red Owl, which owns and operates a chain of supermarkets and provides franchises to selected individuals. Several conversations between Hoffman and Red Owl took place. It was eventually decided that a Red Owl franchise store should be established in Wautoma, Wisconsin. It was discussed that Hoffman would need $18,000 in capital to invest in the business. Since Hoffman felt that he needed more experience in the grocery business, he leased a building, bought inventory and fixtures, and began operating a small grocery store in Wautoma.

After three months, Red Owl advised Hoffman to sell the store, despite the fact that it was making a profit. Red Owl assured Hoffman that it would find a larger store for him. Hoffman sold the fixtures and inventory in June 1961. Before Hoffman sold the store, he told Red Owl that he had $18,000 for the start-up costs of the Red Owl franchise.

Red Owl selected a site, and at Red Owl's suggestion, Hoffman obtained an option on the site with a payment of $1,000. Upon the assurances of Red Owl that the business was ready to begin, Hoffman sold the bakery for $10,000, incurring a loss of $2,000.

In November, Red Owl and Hoffman met to discuss Hoffman's financial standing. A document entitled "Proposed Financing for an Agency Store" stated that Hoffman was to contribute $24,100 instead of the original $18,000. Through a series of loans, Hoffman came up with the new amount. A week or two later, Hoffman was told that if he could get another $2,000 together, the deal would be made for $26,000.

Hoffman objected to the further demands by Red Owl. Negotiations between the two parties were terminated. Hoffman sued Red Owl under breach of contract. Red Owl defended that no contract had been completed because of a lack of consideration. There was no franchise agreement, and no formal financing plan had been agreed upon by the parties. Hoffman, however, contended that Red Owl was liable under the theory of promissory estoppel. The trial court held for Hoffman, stating that an injustice would result if Hoffman was not granted relief. Red Owl appealed.

(continued)

Case Decision
The trial court's decision was affirmed. The appellate court adopted the theory of promissory estoppel. The high court stated injustice would result if Hoffman was not granted some relief. Red Owl had failed to keep promises that had induced Hoffman to act to his detriment.

Managerial Considerations
In dealing with parties who have less business experience, managers should be careful not to make statements that may induce the other parties to act to their detriment. Hoffman was most anxious to please Red Owl and to follow any advice it provided, even to his detriment. Red Owl's management was either to busy to notice Hoffman's dilemma or simply insensitive to it. When this behavior is viewed later by the courts, the appearance is often that the business has taken advantage of the less experienced party.

■ CAPACITY TO CONTRACT

One of the essential elements of a contract is the *contractual capacity,* or *legal capacity,* to create a contract. The term *capacity* refers to a party's ability to perform legally valid acts, acquire legal rights, and incur legal liabilities. Generally, minors, intoxicated persons, and the insane lack capacity to contract. A party claiming incapacity has the burden of proving it.

Most individuals have complete capacity to contract. If an individual, such as an insane person, has no capacity to contract, the contract entered into is void. If an individual, such as a minor or an intoxicated person, has *partial capacity,* the contract is enforceable unless the individual exercises his or her right to disaffirm the contract. Contracts created by those with partial capacity are said to be voidable. A summary of the legal effects on contracts resulting from less than complete capacity is presented in Table 9–2.

Minors.   A *minor* is a person under the legal age of majority. The common law age of majority is twenty-one for men and women. At common law, the general rule is that a minor may enter into contracts. However, those contracts are voidable at the option of the minor. This *right to disaffirm* contracts stems from the traditions of the English courts wishing to protect the young from the results "of their own folly." As the following case shows, a minor's contract is voidable at his or her option almost without exception.

TABLE 9–2
A SUMMARY OF CONTRACTUAL CAPACITY

Incapacity	Degree of Incapacity	Legal Effect on Contract
Minor	Partial capacity	Voidable
Intoxicated person	Partial capacity	Voidable
Mentally insane		
Adjudicated	No capacity	Void
Insane in fact	Partial capacity	Voidable

ROBERTSON v. KING

Supreme Court of Arkansas
225 Ark. 276, 280 S.W.2d 402 (1955)

Case Background
Robertson entered into a sales agreement with King and Julian, doing business as Julian Pontiac Company, for the purchase of a pickup truck. Robertson was seventeen years old on the day of the purchase. The purchase price of the truck was $1,743.85. Robertson was given $723.85 in trade for his old car.

Robertson had considerable trouble with the truck's wiring and returned the truck several times for repairs. About two months after Robertson purchased it, the truck caught fire and was destroyed. The automobile dealer's insurance company refused to pay when it found out Robertson was only seventeen years of age. Robertson sought to disaffirm the contract on the basis that he was a minor. He also sought to recover $776.51 from the automobile dealer ($723.85 for the trade-in plus one monthly payment of $52.66). The trial court ruled in favor of the automobile dealer. Robertson appealed.

Case Decision
The supreme court reversed the lower court's decision. The court stated that a minor can rescind a purchase contract when the property is not a necessary (a necessity to life). The defendant did not meet the burden of proving that the article purchased was a necessary. The damages awarded as a result of the rescission are "the reasonable value of the property at the time of the purchase, rather than the value fixed in the purchase agreement." In this case, the minor traded in his car for $723.85.

Managerial Considerations
Managers should take care when entering into contracts with minors. The right of the minor to rescind a contract is a one-sided right in favor of the minor, with the adult bearing the risk of loss. This does not mean, however, that managers should never enter into contracts with minors. A co-signature by an adult would allow the minor to enter into the contract and still protect the manager. Furthermore, some items are known to be necessities, and minors cannot rescind such contracts. In addition, a manager may want to include a clause in the contract stating that all parties are of lawful age to enter into the contract. The presence of such a clause may establish bad faith on the part of the minor if the minor signs the contract. Such a fraud by a minor will offer some protection by the courts in the event the minor tries later to rescind the contract.

There are some contracts, however, that minors may not disaffirm. Enlistment contracts and marriage contracts are classic examples of *non-voidable contracts*. Further, some states do not allow minors to disaffirm contracts for insurance, educational loans, medical care loans, bank account agreements, and transfers of stock.

After a minor reaches the age of majority, most states provide that the individual may *ratify* contracts made while a minor. The minor must generally show an intent to be bound. This intent may be either expressed through words or a writing or implied by the individual's conduct.

Insane and Intoxicated Persons. If an individual is *intoxicated* at the time a contract is made, most courts hold that the contract is voidable. The test is whether the individual was so intoxicated that he or she did not understand the nature of the agreement. When the intoxicated person becomes sober, he or she may then disaffirm the contract.

Contract law classifies insane persons as either adjudicated insane or insane in fact. An individual is *adjudicated insane* if a court rules that the individual is not competent to carry on contractual activities. A contract entered into by an individual who is adjudicated insane is void.

An insane individual not adjudicated insane but who nonetheless lacks the capacity to enter into a contract is *insane in fact*. An individual who is insane in fact has the right to disaffirm a contract. The right either to disaffirm or to ratify a contract arises after an insane individual is restored to competency or after a guardian is appointed to act in his or her behalf. A guardian may disaffirm or ratify an existing contract and may enter into a new contract on behalf of the insane individual. A few states do not allow disaffirmance of a contract made by an insane person if the contract is just and reasonable.

■ LEGALITY

For a contract to be valid, its subject matter must be *lawful*. The contract will be illegal and unenforceable if its subject matter violates a state or federal statutory law or the common law or is contrary to public policy. Commentators often insist on using the term *illegal bargain* or *illegal agreement* rather than illegal contract. The word *contract* by definition refers to a legal and enforceable agreement.

Contracts Contrary to Public Policy.   Some contracts are unenforceable because their subject matter is *contrary to public policy*. In some situations, a contract will not violate any particular statute or law. However, its effect is said to have a negative impact on public welfare. Some of the types of contracts that courts have frequently found to be contrary to public policy are exculpatory agreements, unconscionable contracts, contracts with public servants, and contracts in restraint of trade.

   Exculpatory Agreements.   An *exculpatory agreement* releases one party from the consequences brought about by his or her wrongful acts or negligence. An example of an exculpatory agreement is an employment contract with a clause stating that the employee will not hold the employer liable for any harm to him or her caused by the employer while on the job. Such exculpatory clauses are frequently objected to on the grounds that they tend to induce a lack of care on the part of the employer. The employer is less careful because he or she is no longer concerned about being sued for negligent acts. Such clauses are generally held to be contrary to public policy and not enforceable.

   Unconscionable Contracts.   Usually the courts will not concern themselves with the fairness of a bargain struck by contracting parties. If a contract, however, is grossly unfair to an innocent party, the courts, in equity, will not enforce it. Such contracts are called *unconscionable contracts* and occur when one of the parties, being in a strong bargaining position, takes advantage of the other party. The stronger party convinces the other party to enter into a contract contrary to his or her well-being. Such agreements are generally held to violate public policy and are not enforceable.

   Contracts with Public Servants.   A contract to influence a public servant to violate the duty the public servant owes to the general public is contrary to public policy and illegal. For example, if a lobbyist contracts to pay a legislator if a bill is passed or not passed, the contract would be unenforceable. However, note that a lobbying contract under which a person is hired to influence a legislator's vote or decision is not illegal unless it also includes direct payments to legislators for their votes on certain issues.

Contracts in Restraint of Trade.   Contracts that restrain trade or unreasonably restrict competition are considered contrary to public policy and are not enforced by the courts. Part of the common law on this subject became the basis for the federal antitrust laws, especially the Sherman and Clayton Acts. Antitrust laws are discussed in Chapter 16.

Effect of Illegal Agreements.   Generally, the courts will not enforce *illegal agreements.* They will leave parties as they found them and will not allow the parties to recover damages for breach or for services already rendered. Under some circumstances, however, the courts will enforce obligations even though the agreement is basically illegal. When one of the parties is innocent of wrongdoing, for example, the courts will ordinarily grant relief to the innocent party and refuse any relief to the guilty party. Or, if the contract can be separated into an illegal portion and a legal portion, some courts will enforce the promises in the legal portion.

■ REALITY AND GENUINENESS OF CONSENT

The concept of freedom of contract is based on the right of individuals to enter into the bargains of their choice. The courts will assume that if an individual has entered into a contract, the individual had a desire to do so. Under some circumstances, however, an individual (or both individuals) may enter into an agreement without full knowledge of the consequences. Without full knowledge, there is no *reality of consent* or *genuineness of assent* by the parties, and the contract is void or voidable depending upon the circumstances. It is often said that there must be a meeting of the minds for there to be consent to the contract. If the parties enter into a contract by *mutual mistake,* the contract may be voidable. If an individual consents to a contract due to *fraud, deceit, duress,* or *undue influence,* that individual has the right to disaffirm the contract.

In some circumstances, reality or genuineness of consent is governed by statute. Typical statutes deal with high-pressure selling techniques by door-to-door salespeople. These "home solicitation" statutes allow contracts to be voided if the innocent party entered into the contract under undue influence or duress. Under federal law, the Federal Trade Commission's cooling-off rule allows purchasers of door-to-door sales with a value over twenty-five dollars to void the contract in writing within three business days.

■ CONTRACTS IN WRITING AND THE STATUTE OF FRAUDS

In contract law, the general rule is that an express or implied contract, written or oral, is enforceable. Some contracts, however, must be in writing and signed to be enforceable. Such contracts are subject to the requirements of the *Statute of Frauds.*

The Statute of Frauds evolved from a 1677 English statute called "An Act for the Prevention of Frauds and Perjuries." The purpose of the act was to prevent individuals from committing fraud by claiming that a contract existed when in fact it did not. To prevent this fraud, the statute required that for certain contractual transactions to be enforceable, they must be in writing and be signed.

Virtually every state has a statute similar to the English act. Most states have six types of contracts that are covered by the Statute of Frauds and that must therefore be in writing: contracts for the sale of land and real property, contracts that cannot be performed within one year, promises to pay the debt of another, promises by an administrator to personally pay the debts of the estate, promises made in consideration of marriage, and contracts for the sale of goods under the UCC.

Sufficiency of the Writing. For a writing to be *sufficient* under the Statute of Frauds, it must set out all the material terms in writing and must be signed. Courts usually require it to contain the names of the parties and outline of the consideration tendered by the parties, the subject matter of the contract, and other terms material to the agreement. However, confirmations, invoices, telegrams, sales orders, and even checks may sometimes satisfy the sufficiency of the writing requirement.

Parol Evidence Rule. In most cases, the parties will negotiate the terms of their contract before actually entering into the contract. The parties may exchange letters, memorandums, and other similar communications before signing the actual contract. Occasionally, the parties will omit from the final contract items they agreed on in negotiations. In a later lawsuit over the contract, if the parties disagree about those items, oral evidence about the items will not be admitted into evidence by the court. It will be excluded on the basis of the parol evidence rule.

The *parol evidence rule* prohibits the introduction of oral evidence into a lawsuit where the evidence to be presented is contrary to the terms of a written contract. Oral evidence cannot contradict, change, or add terms to a written contract. Oral or parol evidence may, however, be introduced when the written contract is incomplete or ambiguous, when it will prove fraud, mistake, or misrepresentation, or when the parol evidence will explain the written instrument through previous trade usage or course of dealing.

CONTRACTING WITH THE JAPANESE	INTERNATIONAL ASPECTS

The attitude of Japanese businesses toward contracts is very different from that of U.S. businesses. The typical U.S. view is that a contract defines the rights and responsibilities of the parties and seeks to cover all possible contingencies. The traditional Japanese view, however, is that a contract is secondary in a business transaction; the basis upon which two parties should do business is an ongoing, harmonious relationship, with both parties committed to the pursuit of similar objectives. Consequently, relationships, not contracts, are negotiated in Japan.

The specific details of a Japanese contract are seldom negotiated with much intensity. Legal documents are usually kept as brief and flexible as possible. Brevity and flexibility are believed to be important to accommodate the evolving relationship between the parties. Contracts are often viewed lightheartedly, as tentative agreements that may be redefined as the circumstances between the
(continued)

parties change. Long legal agreements drafted by one side, especially a foreign firm, are often viewed with suspicion by the Japanese and almost immediately portray the other side as an adversary. The Japanese believe that the relationship should take precedence over formal rights and obligations and that all practical problems can be resolved through mutual compromise and accommodation. Reflecting this belief, the Japanese not uncommonly include a good-faith clause in contracts with Westerners. The clause will state that disputes are to be resolved through good-faith discussions among the parties. This desire to establish and maintain mutual trust as a basis for a business relationship may account for the longer time it takes to negotiate an agreement with the Japanese.

Japanese contract-negotiating teams are generally larger than American teams. Depending upon the nature of the transaction, there may be ten or more people on the Japanese side. It is common for there to be just two or three people on the U.S. side. Often members of the Japanese group will excuse themselves during a session by saying that they must caucus. In discussing an issue among themselves in this manner, the Japanese work to obtain a consensus both within the team and within the company. As a rule, the negotiations proceed at a slow pace. Japanese businesspeople do not appear to operate with the urgency typical of American businesspeople. The Japanese take as much time as they need until they are absolutely sure of a decision and have reached consensus among themselves.

DISCHARGE OF CONTRACTS

Eventually contracts must come to an end. When the obligations of a contract are satisfied, the contract is terminated or *discharged*. Just as there are laws to govern the creation of contracts, so are there laws to govern the discharge of contracts. The various ways in which a contract can be discharged and the legal effects of a discharge on the parties are summarized in Figure 9–2.

■ DISCHARGE BY PERFORMANCE

Most contracts are terminated by the *complete performance* of the parties' obligations under the contract. A promisor is obligated to perform as promised. Sometimes, however, parties do not perform their obligations. The nonperformance of the obligations promised in a contract is called a *breach of contract*.

If the performance provided by a party is clearly inferior to the requirements of the contract, there is a *material breach*. The party wronged by the breach has a cause of action against the breaching party for any damages and is discharged from his or her performance promised under the contract. If, however, the breaching party has deviated from the contract only slightly and not in bad faith, there has been *substantial performance* of the contract. The courts will usually provide the breaching party with payment for services performed, less any damages resulting from the incomplete performance expected under the contract.

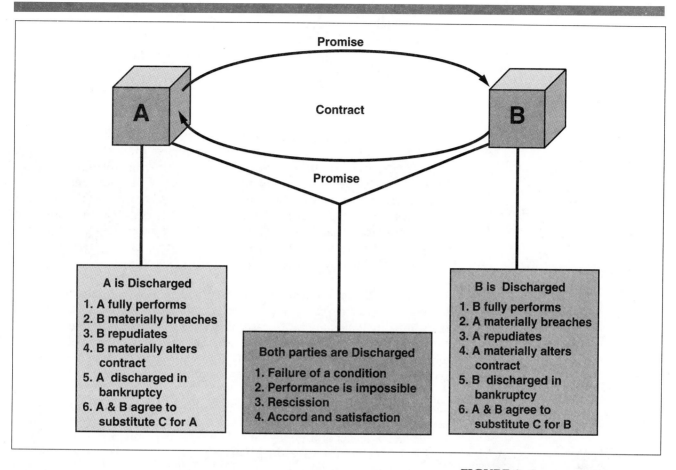

FIGURE 9–2

Summary of Discharge of a Contract and Its Effect on the Parties

■ ANTICIPATORY BREACH

Before the performance of the contract is to take place, an *anticipatory breach,* or *repudiation,* occurs if one party expresses an inability or lack of desire to perform the contract. The doctrine of anticipatory breach discharges the duties of the nonbreaching party under the contract and allows the nonbreaching party to sue for damages incurred from the repudiation. However, until the nonbreaching party treats the expression not to perform as a repudiation, the breaching party may retract the repudiation, and the duties of the contract will be reinstated.

■ DISCHARGE BY FAILURE OF CONDITION PRECEDENT AND BY OCCURRENCE OF EXPRESS CONDITION SUBSEQUENT

A party's duty to perform under a contract is not always certain. Sometimes the duty of the party is *conditioned* on the occurrence or nonoccurrence of some event. The condition is often stated expressly in the contract. The contract might state, for example, that the party will perform as promised if the price of a product "rises above three dollars" or "as soon as a warehouse is built." Contract law defines three kinds of conditions: *conditions precedent*, where some stated event must take place before the promises of the parties become operative; *conditions subsequent*, where the occurrence of an event will terminate the duties of the parties to the contract; and *conditions concurrent*, where performance of the promises of the parties to the contract must occur at the same time.

Failure of a Condition Precedent.   Contracts may be discharged by the *failure of a condition precedent*. For example, suppose the businesses along a street agree that "If the city paves the street in front of our shops by March 19, 1993, we agree to plant trees between the sidewalk and the street in front of our shops by May 1, 1993." The businesses have created a contract based on a condition precedent. The city must pave the street by March 19 before the businesses must begin performance—planting the trees. If the city does not pave the street, the contract among the businesses will be discharged by failure of the condition precedent.

Express Condition Subsequent.   Contracts may also be discharged by an *express condition subsequent*. For example, contracts between U.S. and German firms in 1939 stated: "In case of declared war between our nations, this contract will become null and void." The outbreak of war between the United States and Germany in 1941 (the express condition subsequent) terminated the obligations of the parties under such contracts.

Condition Concurrent.   Duties under a contract that occur simultaneously are termed *concurrent conditions*. A sales contract for a house between a buyer and a seller is a good example of the performance of concurrent conditions. If either party does not perform, the other party's duty to perform does not arise.

■ DISCHARGE BY IMPOSSIBILITY

The doctrine of *discharge by legal impossibility* is used to discharge the obligations of the parties to a contract when some event occurs that makes performance impossible by one or both of the parties. In determining whether the parties to a contract are discharged from their duties, the courts distinguish between objective impossibility (or true impossibility) and subjective impossibility.

Objective impossibility occurs when a party to a contract dies or is incapacitated, a law is passed making performance of the contract illegal, there is complete destruction of the subject matter of the contract, or the performance contemplated by the contract turns out to be massively more expensive or difficult than anticipated. Objective impossibility discharges the obligations of the parties to the contract.

Subjective impossibility does not, however, discharge the obligations of the parties. Such events as shortages in supplies, strikes by workers, or mere loss of profits anticipated from a contract will rarely, if ever, be termed by the courts as objective impossibilities. The rationale behind this rule is that the business assumes the risk of certain occurrences. The following case applies the concept of subjective impossibility.

F. J. BUSSE, INC. v. DEPARTMENT OF GENERAL SERVICES

Commonwealth Court of Pennsylvania
47 Pa.Cmwlth. 539, 408 A.2d 578 (1979)

Case Background
Busse and the General State Authority (GSA) entered into a contract on May 25, 1972, for the construction of a fountain at Point State Park in Pittsburgh, Pennsylvania. The construction site was at the point where the Allegheny and Monongahela rivers join to form the Ohio River. Flooding had frequently occurred in that area.

Busse began construction. Just as the grading and excavation work were almost completed, Hurricane Agnes struck. The hurricane deposited six to eight inches of silt and dirt on the site. Busse had to remove the dirt and silt to complete construction under the contract.

Busse delivered an additional claim under the contract to the GSA for over $85,000, the cost of the additional work to remove the silt and mud. The GSA did not accept the claim. It alleged that the risk of loss from the damage caused by Hurricane Agnes was on Busse. Busse completed construction and then filed a complaint against the GSA with the Board of Arbitration of Claims. The board denied Busse's claim for the costs to remove the silt and mud. Busse appealed to the Pennsylvania court system.

Case Decision
The decision of the Board of Arbitration of Claims to deny Busse's claim was affirmed. Under the language of the contract, Busse was to bear the risk of loss. The court stated that if the work cannot be performed because of an act of God, performance of the contract would be impossible. In this case, Hurricane Agnes was an act of God. However, although the flooding it caused made the job more expensive, it did not make it impossible.

Managerial Considerations
Since the courts do not like to use the impossibility rule except in extreme cases, the message to management should be clear. The court will not provide assistance when the losses occur as a "normal" course of business. Thus, managers must have a complete understanding of the business and those outside influences that could adversely affect performance of a contract. The court will not help managers who do not anticipate possible risks that the industry expects them to be prepared to bear. Since most losses due to acts of God or vandalism are beyond the control of managers, it is wise to insure against such losses. Insurance is a good tool for managing the risk of loss.

■ DISCHARGE BY OPERATION OF LAW

The occurrence of certain legal events will sometimes terminate the obligations of the parties to a contract. This termination is called *discharge by operation of law.* The material alteration of the contract by one of the parties, for example, will discharge the innocent party's duties to perform under the contract. When a contract has been breached, the running of the statute of limitations will discharge the obligations of the parties if the injured party does not bring a suit within a specified time period. Also, a bankruptcy proceeding will often result in the discharge of contractual obligations of the bankrupt party.

■ DISCHARGE BY AGREEMENT OF THE PARTIES

Just as parties have the freedom to contract, they also have the freedom to agree to modify or to terminate their obligations under the contracts. Discharge by agreement between the parties may take various forms. Among the most important ones are rescission, novation, and accord and satisfaction.

Rescission.   A *rescission* occurs when both parties agree that their contractual relationship should be terminated without performance. A rescission discharges completely the obligations of both parties under the contract.

Suppose that Ordan Trading Company enters into a contract with Alimenta Food Machinery Company. Ordan agrees to buy 10 million pounds of pasta from a pasta plant that Alimenta promises to build to meet Ordan's needs. Although the parties both negotiated the contract in good faith, other events cause the parties to push the plant farther and farther into the future. Finally, the parties simply agree that they will not be able to complete the project because of other commitments. Thus, the parties agree to rescind—cancel—the contract. That rescission discharges the obligations of both parties.

Novation.   In a *novation* the parties agree to discharge one party from the contract and create a new contract with another party who is to become responsible for the discharged party's performance. Suppose, for example, that A and B have a contract. Later, A, B, and C all agree that C will perform B's obligations under that contract. This new agreement will be called a novation. The effect of the new agreement is to release B from the original contract and replace B with C.

Accord and Satisfaction.   Another way parties may agree to discharge their duties to one another under a contract is through *accord and satisfaction*. An *accord* is an agreement by the parties to give and accept some performance different from that originally bargained for. *Satisfaction* is the actual performance of substituted obligation. The original obligation is discharged when the substituted obligation is performed.

REMEDIES

In the large majority of the contracts written every day, the parties perform as required. Interestingly, of those contracts where one of the parties does not perform, relatively few are then resolved in a court of law. Professor Friedman found an explanation for this in a study by Macaulay:

> Macaulay explored the behavior of businessmen in Wisconsin. He found that many of them tended to avoid formal contract law and contract doctrine. They especially shied away from suing each other, even when they had a "good case" according to law. The reason was not at all mysterious. Businessmen depended upon each other; they lived and worked in networks of continuing relationships. A manufacturer might buy paper clips, pens, and office supplies from the same dealer, year in and year out. Suing at the drop of a hat, or arguing excessively, or sticking up for abstract "rights," was disruptive; it tended to rip apart these valuable relationships. Also, there were norms, practices, and conceptions of honor and fairness that businessmen customarily followed. These were more subtle, more complicated, than the formal norms of the lawyers. (Friedman, *American Law*, pg. 143)

Still, thousands of contract disputes are resolved through the court system every year. In the resolution of such disputes, there is a basic premise in contract law. After a breach, innocent parties should be placed in the same economic position they would have been in had the contract been fully performed. Under normal business circumstances, a monetary judgment for damages will place the injured party in such a position. If,

TABLE 9–3
CONTRACT REMEDIES

Monetary Damages	Equitable Remedies
Compensatory damages	Specific performance
Expectancy damages	Injunction
Liquidated damages	
Nominal damages	
Punitive damages	
Special damages	

however, the circumstances are such that the legal remedy of monetary damages is inadequate, the court may grant the injured party an appropriate equitable remedy. The types of remedies available to the parties are presented in Table 9–3.

■ MONETARY DAMAGES

The legal remedy usually granted for breach of contract is monetary damages. The court will rule that the wrongdoer must pay a sum of money to the injured party. The injured party will seek a monetary judgment for the thing contracted for, for lost profit, and for any other special damages incurred. A variety of monetary damage awards are available to the courts, including compensatory, expectancy, liquidated, nominal, punitive, and special damages.

Compensatory Damages.   The rationale behind *compensatory damages* is to provide the injured party with the sum of money necessary to restore him or her to the financial position he or she was in before entering into the contract. Suppose, for example, that an individual contracts to buy lumber from a lumber company for $1,000. Based on that contract, suppose the individual creates another contract to sell the lumber for $1,200. If the lumber company breaches the contract (fails to deliver the lumber) and the individual must pay $1,300 for the lumber elsewhere, the individual has a net loss of $100 after selling the lumber for $1,200 as required by the sales contract. In such a case, the individual could sue for compensatory damages of $100. The right to recover compensatory damages for breach of contract is always available to the injured party.

Expectancy Damages.   Many courts provide an expectancy damage award to the injured party to allow him or her to recover the expectation interest in the contract. *Expectancy damages* may be given instead of compensatory damages when the loss from the breach can be estimated with a fair degree of certainty. In the example just given, the individual expected to pay $1,000 but had to pay $1,300 for the lumber. The expectancy damages are $300. Expectancy damages are intended to place the individual in the same economic position she would have been in had the contract been performed as promised.

Liquidated Damages. *Liquidated damages* are damages specified in the contract to be paid in the event of breach by either party. They serve to discourage both parties from taking actions that will result in a breach of contract. Liquidated damages will not be allowed if the court finds they are so excessive that they actually impose a penalty. The court will then provide the innocent party with an amount more in line with the costs actually incurred because of the other party's failure to perform.

Nominal Damages.   When a plaintiff has suffered a technical injury in contract law but has not suffered an actual loss, the courts will sometimes award *nominal damages*. The amount of recovery to the injured party will often be as little as a dollar plus the court costs. Such awards are important because courts are able to establish a precedent that effectively states that even technical wrongs will be recognized at law. Such cases confirm the importance of contractual obligations.

Punitive Damages.   *Punitive* or *exemplary damages* are usually awarded when the wrongdoer's conduct has been intentional or malicious. They punish the wrongdoer by allowing the plaintiff to receive relief beyond compensatory or expectancy damages. Punitive damages are intended to discourage the wrongdoer and others from similar conduct in the future. As a rule, however, punitive damages are not traditionally awarded in contract cases.

Special Damages.   *Special damages* are damages not considered by the parties at the time the contract was made. If there are factors that may cause damages and those factors were foreseeable to the parties at the time the contract was entered into, the court will grant special damages. Suppose, for example, that a wholesale seller of food states that a product it is selling is wholesome when in fact it is not. If a restaurant buys the product and serves it and its customers become ill, the seller will be liable for the medical and hospital expenses of the restaurant's customers. The restaurant will recover payments for the product as compensatory damages. The medical and hospital expenses are special damages. Those special damages may be far in excess of the price of the product.

■ MITIGATION OF DAMAGES

When a breach of contract does occur, the injured party is required to undertake reasonable efforts to *mitigate* or lessen the losses that may be incurred. The injured party may not recover for losses that could have easily been avoided. If a buyer does not receive goods he or she has ordered under contract, for example, the buyer is required to make reasonable efforts to secure substitutes. Suppose George Eyestone is a manufacturer of a product that requires a plastic resin. If his supplier does not deliver, Eyestone is required to mitigate the damages by attempting to secure a substitute resin from another supplier. The damages are then the difference in price between the substitute and the resin of the supplier under contract. In the *Copenhaver* case, the plaintiff avoided the loss but attempted to recover the full value of the contract.

COPENHAVER v. BERRYMAN

Texas Court of Civil Appeals
602 S.W.2d 540 (1980)

Case Background
Copenhaver, the plaintiff, was the owner of a laundry business. Berryman, the defendant, owned a large apartment complex. Copenhaver and Berryman had signed a five-year contract. According to the contract, Berryman agreed to let Copenhaver own and operate a laundry service in the apartment complex. The laundry service was to be used by the occupants of the complex. With forty-seven months remaining on the contract, Berryman terminated it. Within six months after the termination of the contract, Copenhaver had moved the equipment to other locations.

Copenhaver sued Berryman for the termination. He argued that he was entitled to operate the laundry for the full term of the contract. Because of the early termination, Copenhaver argued that he had suffered $13,886.58 in lost profits. The trial court awarded Copenhaver $3,525.84. Copenhaver was not satisfied with the award and appealed the decision.

Case Decision
The appellate court agreed with the lower court's decision. The court found that Copenhaver was entitled to be compensated for the losses caused by Berryman's breach. However, Copenhaver had the responsibility to make a reasonable effort to minimize his losses from the breach. After the breach by Berryman, Copenhaver was able to move the equipment to other locations. From the time the machines began operating in those new locations, Copenhaver was not able to prove to the satisfaction of the court that there were any additional damages caused by breach.

Managerial Considerations
Copenhaver responded properly to the breach by working to minimize losses. The equipment was moved to other locations to generate income for the company. However, Copenhaver was fortunate to be operating in a growing market. It was relatively easy to move the equipment from the Berryman complex to a new (and profitable) location. The breach by Berryman never threatened the survival of the company. On the other hand, if the market had not been good, it would have been more difficult to move the equipment. The company could have incurred lost profits for the entire length of the contract. Under such conditions, the size of the damage award to Copenhaver would have been larger. Unfortunately, for many small businesses such awards may come too late to assist the company.

Businesses must examine such risks carefully. Strategic planning forces management to consider the positive and the negative consequences of their actions and activities. Managers must ask the following questions: What is the probability that one of our suppliers or buyers will go out of business? (Since even large companies go bankrupt, size alone is no guarantee that a company is solid financially.) If a supplier or buyer goes out of business, how will that affect contractual relationships? Will we be able to move our machinery, equipment, and workers to other jobs and locations? If not, what are our strategic alternatives? What can management do in advance to protect the company in the event of such an occurrence?

By considering such problems, the legal requirements to minimize losses will coincide with the financial incentives of the company. Companies that do not undertake this approach will find themselves penalized both by the courts and by the market for not working to minimize losses.

◼ EQUITABLE REMEDIES

If money damages are inadequate to compensate for the injury caused by the breach of contract, *equitable remedies,* such as specific performance or an injunction, are available. These remedies are available to injured parties only at the discretion of the courts. They will generally not be granted where an adequate monetary damage remedy exists or where enforcement would be a great burden to the defendant.

Specific Performance. In some circumstances, a plaintiff in a contract action may be entitled to specific performance. *Specific performance* is an order by the court requiring the party who created the wrong to perform the obligations he or she had promised in the contract to perform. The remedy is frequently granted for breach of a contract in those circumstances where the payment of money damages is inadequate. Contracts for the sale of a particular piece of property or for the performance of a personal service are the type of contract where specific performance may be granted by the courts.

Injunction.   As with the remedy of specific performance, the remedy of injunction is allowed by the courts in circumstances where the payment of damages does not offer a satisfactory substitute for the performance promised. An *injunction* is an order by the court that requires one of the parties to do or to refrain from doing certain acts. For example, suppose an individual is a partner in a business and the partnership agreement has a clause stating that if a partner quits, he or she may not compete against the partnership for three years. The individual quits the partnership to start a competing firm. If the business partner sues to enforce the partnership agreement, the payment of damages may be an inadequate remedy for the partnership. The court, through the granting of an injunction, may order the individual to stop operating the new business.

SUMMARY:
A GUIDE FOR MANAGERS

- The law of contracts enters into virtually every aspect of domestic and international business. It is one of the most important laws making up the legal environment of business. It affects managers at all levels of the business.
- Basic to the law of contracts is freedom of contract. This underlying notion is not without its restrictions. Because of important public policy goals, state and federal laws place some restrictions on the kinds of contracts business can enter into.
- Contract law is basically common or judge-made law. The *Restatement of Contracts* is an authoritative document providing a summary of the common law of contract. Additional contract law is provided by the Uniform Commercial Code.
- A contract is a promise or set of promises that creates an agreement between parties. It creates legal rights and duties enforceable under the law.
- Contracts may be classified as express or implied; bilateral or unilateral; executory or executed; valid, void, voidable, or unenforceable contracts; and quasi-contracts. A contract may fall into several categories; for example, a contract may be express, bilateral, executed, and valid.
- Under the common law, enforceable contracts have several elements in common:
    1. There must be an agreement (offer and acceptance).
    2. The parties to a contract must provide consideration.
    3. The parties must have the legal capacity to contract.
    4. The subject matter of the contract must be legal.
    5. The consent of the parties must be genuine.

- Some contracts must be in writing to fulfill requirements of the Statute of Frauds. They include contracts for the sale of land and real property, contracts that cannot be completed within one year, promises to pay the debt of another, and contracts for goods under the UCC.

- Contracts may be discharged—or terminated—in several ways: by performance, through a breach by one or both of the parties to the contract, by the failure of a condition precedent or the occurrence of an express condition subsequent, by the impossibility of performance, by operation of law, or by mutual agreement of the parties.

- In the event of a breach of contract, the injured party may ask the court for relief. To the extent possible, the injured party has the responsibility to minimize losses from the breach. For the remaining losses, the courts can award monetary damages or provide equitable relief.

MANAGER'S ETHICAL DILEMMA

IS IT CHEATING OR IS IT BUSINESS?

During the fall of 1987 and the spring of 1988, the United States and Europe suffered from a shortage of tomato paste. The cost of paste increased from about twenty-seven cents to more than a dollar per pound in less than three months. The price increase affected many consumer products made from tomato paste, including catsups, soups, spaghetti sauces, pizza sauces, and Mexican salsas. Both large and small food companies found themselves unable to find supplies of tomato paste at prices that would allow them to meet their contractual obligations. They had one of two basic choices: (1) not deliver under their contracts (and thus cause damage to long-term and important contract relationships) or (2) deliver at a loss (because the price they were paying for the tomato paste would cause them to lose money on the finished products they were making from the tomato paste). Most companies chose to preserve their contractual relationships and to deliver if at all possible.

Throughout the world there were many small tomato producers. Many of those producers had never sold their product in world markets. With plentiful supplies available in the United States (primarily from California), there was little need for U.S. food companies to look to foreign suppliers. Thus, many foreign suppliers were generally not connected with any major U.S. food company. With the shortage, the major food companies began to look for ways to gain access to those foreign suppliers. One important way was through the use of food brokers—small companies that specialize in finding food products (particularly raw

materials) for the major food companies. These brokers generally work on a commission basis. That is, they receive a percentage of the sale (often between one percent and three percent of the total contract value) as their compensation. Their primary product is information—knowing where a processing company can readily obtain the raw food product it needs.

Columbia Soup Company needed tomato paste to meet its contractual obligations. It entered into discussions with Ordan Trading Company in March of 1988. Ordan had not done business with Columbia in the past. The fact that Columbia was a world-recognized company gave Ordan confidence. The fact that Ordan at least claimed to have paste gave Columbia good reason to talk with Ordan. The parties exchanged information about the product and began to negotiate about such matters as price and delivery conditions.

During this time, there had been many false sales of tomato paste. Brokers who claimed they had the product for sale often did not. Because it had not done business with Ordan in the past, Columbia was very suspicious about Ordan's activities. Would Ordan be able to deliver the paste? Thus, Columbia was unwilling to enter into a formal contract with Ordan for the purchase of the paste until it was sure that Ordan could deliver.

Near the final stages of the negotiations, Ordan's salesman became confident in his relationship with Columbia. Perhaps by accident, he told the Columbia representative the name and general location of the tomato paste producer. The parties continued to nego-tiate, including discussions about specific shipping dates and vessels.

On the day the product was to be shipped, the management of Columbia found itself in an interesting dilemma. With the information the Ordan salesman had revealed, Columbia personnel had located the producer. The producer had been talked into selling the product directly to Columbia by a company representative. Ordan had agreed to purchase the paste from the producer for 53 cents a pound. Ordan had been asking Columbia to pay 93 cents a pound. Because 93 cents was well below the $1.08 market price, Columbia management was willing to pay Ordan that price. If the deal is made, Ordan would make a profit of $640,000 on this single sale.

QUESTIONS

Under the agreement between the producer and Columbia, the price would be 73 cents. The producer would make more money ($320,000), and Columbia would save money ($320,0000). Ordan, of course, would be the loser. Management had to decide what strategy it should take. Did it have a contract with Ordan? If not, should the company simply agree to the terms set forth in negotiations with Ordan? Could it be sued by Ordan if it went directly to the producer? If so, could Ordan afford to sue Columbia? Or would Ordan fear that a lawsuit would damage its reputation with its other clients? Would the very size of Columbia alone frighten Ordan away? Is the manager asking the right questions to resolve its dilemma?

REVIEW AND DISCUSSION QUESTIONS

1. Define the following terms and expressions:

    | offer | discharge |
    | acceptance | breach of contract |
    | consideration | impossibility |
    | promissory estoppel | damages |
    | legal capacity | mitigation of damages |
    | parol evidence rule | |

2. Compare and contrast the following concepts:
    a. binding and nonbinding promises
    b. bilateral and unilateral contracts
    c. contracts and quasi-contracts
    d. offer and acceptance and offer and counteroffer
    e. monetary damages and equitable relief

3. What is the concept of freedom to contract? How does it affect the law of contracts?

4. Suskind walks into a grocery store, puts fifty cents down on the counter, and says, "A Coke please." Under contract law, what has just occurred? If the grocery store owner hands him a Coke and takes the fifty cents, what type of contract has been agreed upon?

5. What are the differences between valid, void, voidable, and unenforceable contracts?

6. What is the purpose of the Statute of Frauds in modern contract law?

■ CASE QUESTIONS

7. Burt executed a pledge for $50,000 in 1968. The pledge was delivered to St. Joseph's Hospital. It provided that "In consideration of and to induce the subscription of others, I promise to pay to St. Joseph's Hospital the sum of $50,000 in five installments." Burt made two installment payments of $10,000

each before his death. The hospital filed a claim for the unpaid balance against his estate. Is this a contract for which the estate is now liable? [*Mount Sinai Hospital* v. *Jordan,* 290 So.2d 484 (Fla.1974)]

8. Rose, a minor, purchased a new car from Sheehan Buick for $5,000. Rose later elected to disaffirm the purchase and notified Sheehan of her decision. She also requested a full refund of the purchase price. Sheehan refused, and Rose brought an action to invalidate the contract and to seek a refund of the purchase price. What will be the likely result? [*Rose* v. *Sheehan Buick, Inc.,* 204 So.2d 903 (Fla.App.1967)]

9. Monica wishes to rent a hall for her class reunion dance. She writes to the owner of the hall asking for the rental price. The owner replies, "Agreed that you may have the hall for the class reunion dance May 29. Price is $100." Monica sends a reply, "Look forward to the 29th. $100 is acceptable price." Upon inquiring, the owner learns that other halls are renting for $150. He writes to Monica, "Original price is off. Will rent hall for $200." His note reaches Monica the day after her last letter was sent. Was there an offer, acceptance, revocation, or counteroffer?

10. Louise and Mary are partaking of too much wine when Louise says to Mary, "You have been such a dear friend this year. Please accept my car in payment for your friendship." Coming to her senses the next day, Louise decides not to turn over her car to Mary. Have Louise and Mary entered into a contractual relationship?

11. BZB Corporation agreed to sell property to C & S Corporation for a new development project. Five days before the actual sale date, BZB backed out of the contract. As a result, C & S lost $170,000 in related building contracts. Is there a breach? If it is a breach, what remedies are available to C & S?

12. XYZ Corporation contracted with Smith Company to build a twenty-story building within a twelve-month period. Because of labor strikes, heavy weather, and increased costs of building materials, XYZ is unable to perform within the specified period of time. Are XYZ's duties discharged under the impossibility doctrine? Why or why not?

■ BUSINESS POLICY QUESTIONS

13. How does contract law encourage mutually beneficial exchange, and why is that important? Are there alternative systems of exchange?

14. What function does contract law play in the allocation of risk between the parties to a contract?

■ ETHICS QUESTIONS

15. Michele works long and hard to develop the perfect recipe for chocolate-covered ants. After perfecting the method, she has it patented but fails to sell much of her product. Web buys the patent rights from Michele for $100. The next year there is a craze for chocolate-covered ants. Web makes a fortune; Michele gets nothing. The contract between the two was legal in every respect. Should Web give Michele some portion of the profits? Suppose, instead, that Michele had promised to supply Web all the boxes of chocolate-covered ants that he wanted for one dollar a box for five years. Because of the subsequent craze for chocolate-covered ants, Web can sell the boxes for ten dollars each. Should he share the unexpected profits with Michele? Suppose the price of chocolate and ants rose so that Michele lost one cent on each box supplied to Web but Web continued to make high profits. Should Web be forced to rewrite the terms of the deal? Should he, as an ethical businessman, voluntarily do so?

16. Three armed men robbed the First State Bank of Kentucky of over $30,000. The Kentucky Bankers Association provided and advertised a reward of $500 for the arrest and conviction of the bank robbers. The robbers were later captured and convicted. The arresting officers and the employees of the bank who provided important information leading to the arrest have all claimed the reward. Is there a contract between these parties and the Bankers Association? [*Denney* v. *Reppert*, 432 S.W.2d 647 (Ky.1968)]

SALES AND THE UCC

CHAPTER 10

MANAGER'S LEGAL CHALLENGE

The Lamon Brothers Plastic Fabricators started as a two-person partnership in 1958. The company provided special, made-to-order plastic and light-metal products for a few larger customers. By 1965, Lamon Brothers employed ten people, all in the production area of the business. The brothers still maintained responsibility for all sales and marketing.

Primarily because of the nature of their business, the brothers relied on a sales contract they had developed over time. The contract was rigid, with a large number of contingencies covered explicitly. Because of their familiarity with the contract, the brothers were able to adapt it to the various circumstances they encountered.

Beginning in the early 1970s, the company began to experience significant growth. In one year alone, sales increased by more than 230 percent. The increase in growth eventually caused the brothers to incorporate the business under the name of TechniPlastica. The first order of business was to increase the size of the sales and clerical staffs.

As the company continued to grow, the brothers found themselves unable to monitor every sale. With the sales staff relatively inexperienced, the company standard contract very quickly became a burden. The sales staff found it to be time-consuming. Not infrequently, customers balked at some of its lengthy (and often inapplicable) clauses. In an effort to close a deal, sales staff members often found themselves trying to modify the contract to better fit the needs of the customer. In a few unfortunate instances, a salesperson overcommitted the company in the contract, and lawsuits followed. Somewhat surprisingly, the company contract had become an obstacle to company growth.

In the late 1970s, the company made a concerted effort to streamline its contract and sales processes. The managerial challenge was to make the process more flexible, free the sales staff from paperwork burdens, and still make sure that the company was protected. Using contracting practices made legal by the Uniform Commercial Code, the company developed contracting processes that moved the company away from the demands of the original contract. The UCC allowed the company to write contracts with the price, delivery time, and quantities left open to be determined at a later date by the parties. The first result was that the cost of taking orders declined markedly. The sales staff, freed from paperwork burdens, was able to increase the amount of time spent on actually selling the product. Those sales that were done on a continuous reorder basis did not require a new contract each time. In addition, the amount of time that elapsed between sales and production was also reduced substantially. Eventually, the company was able to implement an electronic ordering process that further decreased costs and increased profits.

As the management of TechniPlastica discovered, the *Uniform Commercial Code* (UCC) has had a significant impact on business and its legal environment. Specifically, *Article 2* of the UCC governs the law of sales. The concept of a *sale* is fundamental to business. Final sales to consumers within the U.S. economy exceeded $1.8 trillion in 1991. For every final sale, however, there may be several important preliminary sales—sales, for example, between a retailer and a wholesaler, a wholesaler and a manufacturer, and a manufacturer and its several suppliers. With buying and selling goods the primary activity of most commercial enterprises, it is not surprising that the law of sales is an important part of the legal environment of business.

This chapter provides a general overview of the law of sales as set forth in Article 2 of the UCC. The chapter begins with a discussion of the UCC, its origins, structure, purpose, and relationship with the common law of contracts. It then considers the nature of sales contracts under the UCC and the special requirements the UCC places upon merchants. After considering the concept of title under Article 2, the chapter discusses the basic performance obligations of a seller and buyer engaged in a contract for the sale of goods. It next examines the warranty rights and obligations of the parties to a sales contract. The chapter closes with the discussion of the remedies available to buyers and sellers in the event the other party breaches the sales contract.

THE ORIGIN OF THE UNIFORM COMMERCIAL CODE

As discussed in Chapter 9, contract law is primarily state common, or judge-made, law. Before the turn of the century, the management of a company had to be concerned with the common law of contracts in each of the states in which the company did business. To the extent the common law rules were the same in each state, the legal challenges confronting managers were workable. However, by the turn of the century, serious differences in contract law rules had developed among the states. A particular clause that was acceptable in one state might produce an entirely different (and perhaps unacceptable) result in another state.

Managers attempted to control the legal difficulties these inconsistent rules created by writing different contracts for different states. The managerial challenges created by this legal environment significantly increased the costs of doing business across state lines. As those costs increased, managers viewed the legal environment as a serious deterrent to economic growth.

■ THE MOVEMENT TOWARD UNIFICATION

In response to pressures from the business community, the legal and political communities moved to make sales law more uniform among the states. Unfortunately, the first laws developed did little to improve the situation. By the early 1940s, it was well recognized that a serious revision was needed. After several years and several revisions, the Uniform Commercial Code was developed. In one form or another, the UCC has now been adopted by every state.

As Table 10–1 shows, the UCC contains nine articles. It is intended to deal with all aspects of a business transaction. Of particular interest for this chapter is Article 2, which specifically governs contracts for the sale of goods. The following are the stated purposes of Article 2:

1. To simplify, clarify, and modernize the law governing sales.
2. To permit the continued development of business practices through custom, usage, and agreement of the parties.
3. To make the laws uniform among the various state jurisdictions.

■ RELATIONSHIP BETWEEN ARTICLE 2 AND THE COMMON LAW

Article 2 of the UCC governs contracts for the sale of goods, or *sales contracts*. Under Article 2, a sales contract is governed by the same basic principles that are applied under the common law of contracts: offer, acceptance, consideration, capacity, genuineness of consent, and legality. However, Article 2 makes several important changes in these traditional contract principles. Where Article 2 so states, those changes override the corresponding common law rule. On the other hand, where Article 2 of the

---

TABLE 10–1
THE PRINCIPAL ARTICLES OF THE UNIFORM COMMERCIAL CODE

Article	Coverage
1	General Provisions
2	Sale of Goods
3	Commercial Paper
4	Bank Deposits and Collections
5	Letters of Credit
6	Bulk Transfers
7	Warehouse Receipts, Bills of Lading, and Other Documents of Titles
8	Investment Securities
9	Secured Transactions

UCC neither restates nor modifies the common law, the UCC supplements the common law of contracts. That is, the common law of contracts continues to govern unless it is specifically overridden by Article 2 (or other parts of the UCC). Thus, Article 2 is actually a specialized part of the common law of contracts.

Contracts Outside the Coverage of the UCC.   General contract law continues to govern all contractual transactions that fall outside the area of coverage or scope of the UCC. Transactions excluded from the application of the UCC specifically include insurance contracts, employment contracts, service contracts, contracts involving real property (real estate), and contracts involving intangible property (such as stocks and bonds, bank accounts, patents, and copyrights).

The UCC and Mixed Transactions.   As just stated, service contracts are not within the coverage of the UCC. Service contracts—such as a contract to do maintenance work not involving any replacement parts or other sales of goods—would be governed by the common law of contracts. However, a problem can arise when a contract involves both a service and a sale of goods—a *mixed transaction*. For example, suppose a company enters into a contract to buy a photocopier for its office. Included in the contract is a maintenance agreement. Is the contract a service contract governed by the common law or a sales of goods governed by the UCC?

The courts will generally look to see whether the more dominant feature of the contract as a whole is a sale of goods or a sale of services. If the sale of goods—here, a photocopier—is the more dominant feature, the contract is a contract for the sale of goods governed by the UCC. If the service component is the more dominant, the common law of contracts will govern the relationship between the parties.

SALES CONTRACTS UNDER THE UCC: SCOPE OF COVERAGE ▪▪▪▪▪▪

Before the UCC can be applied, it must first be determined whether the sales contract falls within the scope of the UCC. As a general rule, any transaction involving a *sale of goods* will fall under the UCC. In addition, the UCC sometimes—but not always—requires that the parties to the contract to *merchants* before some parts of Article 2 will apply to the sale.

▪ SALE UNDER THE UCC

Under Article 2, a *sale* occurs when there is a "passing of title from the seller to the buyer for a price." Thus, to be a sale for purposes of the UCC, the transaction must involve a "passing of title," and a price must be paid for the goods. Under this definition, there are a number of important transactions that are *not* sales of goods. Many of these transactions do affect goods significantly.

For example, a *gift* is not a sale, because no price is included in the transaction; that is, it involves a transaction without consideration. *Bailments* are excluded because there is no passing of title in such transactions.

Rather, possession of the goods is transferred for only a specified prede-termined period of time.

Suppose you place your goods in another company's warehouse for storage. Under the law, you are a bailee and the warehouse owner is a bailor. The contract for storage—the bailment contract—does not give the bailee-/warehouse owner title to your goods. The owner will keep your goods in its warehouse only for the length of time stated in the bailment contract. Thus, the contract is not a sale of goods subject to Article 2 of the UCC.

■ GOODS UNDER THE UCC

The UCC defines *goods* as "all things which are movable at the time of iden-tification to the contract for sale." In other words, the subject matter of a sales contract is not considered a good under Article 2 unless it is both tangible and movable. A good is considered *movable* if it can be carried from one location to another. Thus, real estate and fixtures attached permanently to that real estate are excluded from Article 2's coverage because they are not movable.

A good is considered *tangible* when it has a physical existence; that is, it can be seen and touched. Thus, services and intangible interests in property—such as stocks, bonds, bank accounts, patents, and copyrights, all of which are said to have a conceptual but not a physical existence—are not goods under Article 2. A contract to buy these items would be gov-erned by the common law of contracts and not by the UCC.

■ SALES BY AND BETWEEN MERCHANTS

Article 2 holds all parties who enter into a sales contract that falls within its scope of coverage to a standard of *good faith,* or honest, dealing. Good faith dealing is defined by the UCC as "honesty in fact in the conduct or trans-action incurred." In addition, Article 2 places additional burdens of hon-esty on merchants, who are treated differently from other parties because they possess more business expertise. A seller or buyer is considered to be a merchant when he or she does any of the following:

1. Regularly deals in goods of the kind involved in the transaction.
2. By occupation presents him or herself as having knowledge or skill specialized to the transaction.
3. Employs an agent or broker who holds him or herself out as having the requisite knowledge or skill.

THE FORMATION OF A SALES CONTRACT

As previously stated, sales contracts are governed by the common law of contracts unless the UCC specifically changes or modifies the rule. In most instances, the changes imposed by the UCC modernize general contract law to promote greater fairness and efficiency. This section considers the effect of the UCC's Article 2 on general contract law principles. As you read this section, consider the basic differences between the UCC and the com-mon law as presented in Figure 10–1.

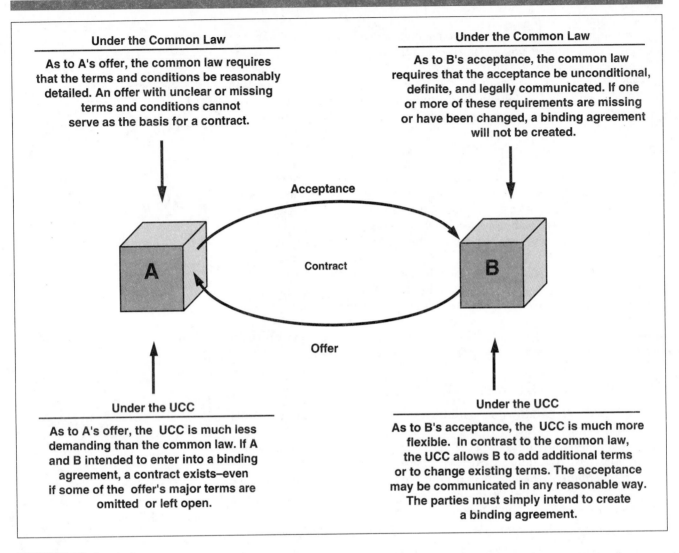

Under the Common Law

As to A's offer, the common law requires that the terms and conditions be reasonably detailed. An offer with unclear or missing terms and conditions cannot serve as the basis for a contract.

Under the Common Law

As to B's acceptance, the common law requires that the acceptance be unconditional, definite, and legally communicated. If one or more of these requirements are missing or have been changed, a binding agreement will not be created.

Acceptance

Contract

A

B

Offer

Under the UCC

As to A's offer, the UCC is much less demanding than the common law. If A and B intended to enter into a binding agreement, a contract exists—even if some of the offer's major terms are omitted or left open.

Under the UCC

As to B's acceptance, the UCC is much more flexible. In contrast to the common law, the UCC allows B to add additional terms or to change existing terms. The acceptance may be communicated in any reasonable way. The parties must simply intend to create a binding agreement.

FIGURE 10–1

Offer and Acceptance:
Comparing the UCC and the
Common Law of Contracts

■ INTENT TO CONTRACT

Under the common law, a contract is not formed until there is no question that the offer has been accepted. This offer-acceptance rule is normally rigidly applied. Article 2 relaxes this rule; it provides that a contract can be formed in any manner that shows an agreement between the parties. For example, suppose a buyer and a seller have been doing business together for several months. On Tuesdays, the seller delivers restaurant supplies to the buyer's restaurant. On Thursdays, the buyer pays the invoice by mail. Under the UCC, a contract has been formed by the conduct of the parties. In that regard, it does not matter that the exact moment of contract formation is unknown.

Under Article 2, the intent of the parties to reach an agreement determines whether the parties have formed a contract. No special rituals or formalities are necessary. Suppose the buyer in the preceding example for some reason becomes dissatisfied. Article 2 would not allow the buyer to claim that she does not have to pay for the supplies because no formal contract ever existed between the parties.

■ AN INDEFINITE OFFER

The common law requires that an offer specify all of the relevant terms. Article 2 is much less demanding. If the parties intended to enter into a binding agreement on the basis of the offer, a contract exists. This is the case even though some of the offer's major terms were omitted or were simply just left open for determination later. When terms are left open by the parties, Article 2 provides rules for determining those terms.

Open Price Term.   There are occasions when buyers and sellers are unable to specify a contract price in advance. The price may be left open to be determined later when the goods are custom-made, when market conditions are changing rapidly, or when deliveries are postponed to some future date and the seller cannot accurately estimate his or her production costs that far in advance. Article 2 allows the parties to enter into a binding agreement even though the contract price is to be determined at a later date. The contract price in such cases is to be a "reasonable price at the time of delivery." In addition, the price must be determined in good faith.

Open Quantity Terms.   As a general rule, the buyer and seller must agree on the quantities of the goods to be exchanged, or the agreement will be too indefinite to constitute a contract. Important exceptions to this rule can arise in two instances: (1) when the buyer has agreed to purchase the total output of the seller (called an *output contract*) and (2) when the seller has agreed to supply the full requirements of the buyer (called a *requirements contract*). In either of these instances, a contract for the sale of goods need not specify a definite quantity. Relying on the good faith of the parties, Article 2 fixes the contract quantity at the actual output of the seller or the actual requirements of the buyer. These rules encourage managers to enter into contracts that provide some degree of flexibility. *O&R* v. *Amerada Hess* considers an open quantity term in a requirements contract.

ORANGE AND ROCKLAND UTILITIES, INC. v. AMERADA HESS CORPORATION

Appellate Division of the New York Supreme Court
59 A.D.2d 110, 397 N.Y.S.2d 814 (1977)

Case Background
In December 1969, the Amerada Hess Corporation (Hess) agreed to supply Orange and Rockland Utilities, Inc. (O&R) with "all of the fuel oil required for its Lovett Generating Plant until September 30, 1974." The written contract included estimates of O&R's annual fuel oil requirements.

The contract price was fixed at $2.14 per barrel. Several months later, the market price of fuel oil began increasing rapidly. By May 1970, it had reached $3.00 per barrel. During the same period, O&R continually notified Hess of increases in its fuel oil requirements. Additional supplies were needed because O&R was substituting oil for costly natural gas as a boiler fuel and then selling large amounts of electricity at attractive prices to neighboring utilities.

(continued)

At the end of June 1970, O&R's projected demand was more than 63 percent over the original estimate. Hess refused to meet the revised requirements but did increase supplies about 10 percent above the contract estimates. O&R responded by purchasing additional fuel oil from other suppliers at considerably higher prices. By 1971, its annual purchases of fuel oil were more than double the estimates presented in the Hess contract.

In 1972, O&R sued Hess for the difference between its actual costs of fuel oil and what those costs would have been if Hess had supplied its total requirements at the $2.14 per barrel contract price. The trial court denied recovery, finding a lack of good faith by O&R. Hess appealed.

Case Decision
The appellate court affirmed the decision of the trial court. The court found ample evidence to justify a finding of lack of good faith on O&R's part. Nonfirm sales from O&R's Lovett plant to the New York Power Pool had increased from 67,867 megawatt hours in 1969 to 390,017 megawatt hours

in 1970. Those sales did not enter into the estimates that formed the basis of the contract. Such an increase was not foreseeable. The conclusion is inescapable that this dramatic increase came about as a result of the requirements contract between the parties. The contract insured O&R a steady flow of cheap oil despite swiftly rising prices. O&R's use of the contract to suddenly and dramatically become one of the largest sellers of power to other utilities is evidence of a lack of good faith dealing.

Managerial Considerations
In such circumstances, management would be well advised to consider carefully the potential contingencies that might arise and cause a change in the value of the contract. For example, Hess possibly could have included a clause in the original contract that limited the amount of oil that O&R could purchase. Hess could also have stipulated that the price would be increased if its costs increased by a specified amount. O&R, of course, would have resisted those additions but likely could have been persuaded to accept them.

Open Delivery Term.   Article 2 sets forth several rules for use in determining open delivery terms. It provides that goods must be delivered to the buyer at the seller's place of business or at the seller's residence if the seller has no place of business.

If the goods are in another location known to the parties when the contract was made, that location is the place of delivery. Suppose, for example, that the parties agree to the sale of office equipment over the telephone. At the time of the sale, both parties are aware that the seller does not have the item requested in stock. The item is available only at an outlet in another part of the city. Unless the parties have otherwise agreed, the place of delivery is the other outlet where the item is in stock. If the contract has left open the delivery time, Article 2 provides that deliveries must be made within a reasonable time and at a reasonable hour.

Open Payment Term.   In the event the parties do not specify the terms of payment, Article 2 provides that payment is due in full at the time and place where the buyer is to receive the goods. If unspecified, payment can be made in any manner used in the ordinary course of business, including by check or credit card. If at the time of delivery the seller demands cash, the buyer must be given a reasonable time to secure it.

■ Merchant's Firm Offer

Article 2 also modifies the contract rules governing when an offer may be revoked. Under the common law of contract law, an offer can be revoked at any time before acceptance. The principal common law exception is the *option contract,* under which the offeree pays consideration for the offeror's promise to keep the offer open for a stated time period. Article 2 provides another exception. Under Article 2 if a merchant-offeror gives assurances in a signed writing that the offer will remain open for a given period, the merchant's firm offer is irrevocable. Importantly, the merchant's firm offer is irrevocable without the need for consideration. If the period is not stated in the offer, the offer will stay open for a reasonable time not to exceed three months.

■ ACCEPTANCE

Article 2 modifies the common law rules of contract for acceptances in several important ways. With the intent to bring the common law rules of acceptance more in line with business practices, the UCC provides greater flexibility in the way an acceptance can be communicated. If the offeror does not clearly demand a particular method of acceptance, a contract is formed when the offer is accepted in any reasonable manner under the circumstances. Further, a contract exists under the UCC even if the acceptance is received late by the offeror—as long as the acceptance was sent before the expiration of the specified deadline. The UCC's flexibility allows the legal rules governing acceptance to keep pace with new and emerging modes of communication.

Unlike the common law, the UCC also provides that an acceptance may be valid even if the offeree has either included additional terms or changed existing terms in an offer. Under the common law of contracts, an acceptance cannot deviate from the terms of the offer without being considered either a rejection or a counteroffer. Article 2 makes an acceptance valid when the parties intend to form a contract—even though the offeree's acceptance contains different terms from those in the offer.

■ CONTRACT MODIFICATION AND CONSIDERATION REQUIREMENTS

Under the common law, contract modifications must be supported by new consideration to be binding on the parties. The UCC makes a significant change in the common law rule by providing that the parties need not exchange new consideration to modify an existing sales contract. Such a modification to a sales contract, however, must meet the UCC's test of *good faith dealing.* For example, a buyer who has taken delivery of an order could threaten to withhold payment unfairly until the seller has agreed to lower the contract price. Later, if sued for full payment, the buyer could claim that the lower price was a modification of the sales contract. The UCC makes such extorted modifications unenforceable because of bad faith dealing. The UCC's requirement of good faith dealing largely prevents such misconduct by demanding a legitimate business reason for any contract modification.

The UCC's relaxed consideration requirements for contract modifications is very similar to international standards. Consider these and other differences in the general discussion of international sales contracts in the *International Aspects* feature.

INTERNATIONAL ASPECTS | INTERNATIONAL SALES OF GOODS

When American businesses become involved in international business for the first time, they are often most surprised by contract law issues. Some countries that have been under communist rule have little if any form of modern contract law principles. Several of those countries have requested assistance in developing contract law from leading American legal organizations.

Other well-developed, civil law countries (like Italy, France, Germany, and Japan) have contract rules that are very different from American rules. These differences in contract rules and principles can be managed to some extent by including the *United Nations Convention on the International Sale of Goods* into international contracts for the sales of goods. The Sales Convention represents the consequences of lengthy negotiations among sixty-two countries.

Since civil law countries are in the majority among world legal systems, it is not surprising that the Convention follows civil law concepts more closely than American common law concepts. Thus, the Convention can be a trap for unwary American businesses. For example, the Convention does not include a statute of frauds. Thus, it allows for the enforcement of both oral and written contracts for the sale of goods.

Perhaps more interesting to American lawyers and businesspeople is the fact that the Convention does not require consideration for the creation of a contract. Clearly, American businesses will want to be very careful in drafting international business contracts to avoid confusion and potentially serious legal consequences.

TITLE TO GOODS

Before the enactment of the UCC, the common law of sales placed the risk of loss or damage in a sales transaction upon the party who had *title*, or the legal right of ownership, to the goods. If goods subject to a sales transaction were lost or damaged, the common law imposed the financial responsibility for the loss upon the party with title. In contrast, Article 2 of the UCC makes the determination of the responsibility for loss or damage to goods less dependent on title to the goods and more dependent on possession and control.

◼ IDENTIFICATION

Before title to the goods can pass from the seller to the buyer, two requirements must be met under Article 2:

1. The goods must be *in existence*.
2. They must be *identified* to the contract.

Goods that fail to meet the first requirement are considered *future goods.* For example, a contract that calls for delivery of oranges to be grown and harvested two years from now would be a contract for future goods. Under the UCC, since the oranges are not considered to be currently in existence, title cannot pass.

To meet the second requirement, the goods subject to the sales contract must be identified in such a way that they are distinguishable from all other similar goods. *Identification* is the process of specifying the actual goods that are covered by a contract. Normally, the seller begins to take steps to identify the goods after the formation of the contract—by ordering, manufacturing, or in some other way preparing the goods necessary to fulfill contractual obligations. In the simplest of cases, identification may require little more than listing on the sales contract the serial numbers of the goods purchased.

■ PASSAGE OF TITLE

The UCC allows the parties to determine how title to the goods will pass between them. However, if the buyer and the seller have not stated how title will pass, Article 2 provides rules for determining it. The determination of when title passes is most influenced by whether or not the goods must be moved to be delivered.

Delivery By Moving the Goods. In those instances where the goods are to be shipped to be delivered, title will pass to the buyer once the seller has completed "physical delivery" of the goods. If the buyer has purchased on the basis of a *shipment contract*, which requires the goods to be shipped to the buyer, title passes at the time of shipment. The seller's sole obligation is to deliver the goods to the carrier—the truck, rail, or air transport company. Upon delivery to the carrier, title passes to the buyer.

The buyer could also purchase from the seller on the basis of a *destination contract*, which requires the seller to deliver the goods to the buyer at a particular place. Title passes when the goods are given to the buyer at that destination. Title to the goods passes to the buyer at the designated place regardless of whether the seller ships the goods personally or ships them by an independent carrier.

Delivery Without Moving the Goods. In those instances where the goods are to be delivered without being moved—the buyer, for example, has agreed to pick up the goods or have them stored either in the seller's or some other party's warehouse—the passage of title will depend upon whether the seller is required to deliver a document of title to the buyer. If the seller is required to deliver such a document, title will pass when that document is delivered. If no document of title is required, title will pass to the buyer at the time and place the sales contract was made—but only if the goods are then identified to the contract. In the event the goods are not identified, title will not pass until identification takes place. Consider, for example, the identification problem and its impact on the passage of title in *Reeves* v. *Pillsbury.*

REEVES v. PILLSBURY COMPANY

Supreme Court of Kansas
229 Kan. 423, 625 P.2d 440 (1981)

Case Background
Reeves contracted to sell 5,000 bushels of wheat to the Brownville Grain Company on October 30, 1975. As was customary, the contract did not specify a time, manner, or place of delivery. Instead, farmers under contract to Brownville usually transported their wheat to local elevators and received scale tickets in the names of both the farmer and Brownsville showing the quantity delivered. These tickets were negotiable instruments entitling the holder to ownership of the wheat. After a ten-day waiting period, a farmer could present the tickets to Brownville for payment and complete a sale.

Shortly after delivering the wheat to Brownsville, Reeves heard that Brownville was having financial difficulties. Reeves became concerned that he would not be paid for the wheat he had placed in the Brownville elevator. He shipped the 5,000 bushels of wheat to an elevator owned by the Pillsbury Company and received scale tickets in his name alone. Thus, if Brownville solved its financial problems, Reeves could fulfill his contract by giving his scale tickets to Brownville for payment. On the other hand, if Brownville went bankrupt, Reeves could sell his wheat to Pillsbury or to another grain company.

Unfortunately, a Pillsbury employee heard about the delivery and paid Brownville for the wheat Reeves had stored in the Pillsbury elevator. Brownville then went bankrupt without paying Reeves. Unable to collect from Brownville, Reeves sued Pillsbury for conversion—the tort of improperly exercising dominion and control over someone else's property. Pillsbury defended itself by arguing that payment was proper because the wheat stored in its elevator was committed to Brownville by the October 30 "contract."

The trial and appellate courts found that the wheat was never identified to the contract. Therefore, Reeves retained title to the wheat, and Pillsbury converted it. Pillsbury appealed to the state supreme court.

Case Decision
The state supreme court agreed with the decisions of the lower courts. It reasoned that the wheat delivered by Reeves to Brownville was not sufficiently identified to contract between Reeves and Pillsbury to allow title to pass to Brownville. The usual conduct of the area farmers was to identify grain by either (1) notifying Brownville of the delivery or (2) presenting the scale ticket to Brownville for payment. There was no evidence that Reeves did either. Thus, title to the wheat remained with Reeves. It had not passed to Brownville under a contract between Reeves and Brownville at the time that Pillsbury made payment to Brownsville. Since Pillsbury wrongfully paid Brownville for the wheat and refused to pay Reeves, Pillsbury was liable for conversion of the wheat.

Managerial Considerations
Managers should take special precautions in dealing with property and other assets in their possession when that property belongs to another. They should be particularly careful when there is some ambiguity about ownership and the property is of such a type that it could easily become confused with the company's properties. In situations like that presented in this case, a manager in the position of Pillsbury should make sure that property is not released improperly.

■ SPECIAL PROBLEMS REGARDING TITLE

In the overwhelming majority of transactions, title passes between seller and buyer with no difficulty. The title transferred to the buyer will constitute a full legal ownership, and the courts will protect that ownership from all other claimants. There are, however, several instances where special problems regarding title can arise. For example, the strength of the buyer's claim to title may be affected by the fact that the buyer has bought stolen goods. Or, the buyer may have bought goods from a seller who is making the sale to avoid or defraud creditors.

Under such circumstances, the UCC provides special rules to resolve disputes regarding ownership rights and responsibilities. Particular attention is placed on the rights of a *good faith purchaser*—a purchaser who has given value for the goods and did not know about the seller's lack of title. A good faith purchaser always believes that the seller of goods is the true owner or has the authority to sell on behalf of the true owner.

Sale of Goods By Nonowners.   If the seller is selling stolen goods, the true owner has the right to reclaim the goods from the buyer. This is the rule under Article 2 even if the buyer is a good faith purchaser. Of course, a good faith purchaser of stolen goods who subsequently loses the goods to the true owner can recover the amount paid by suing the seller—if the seller is still available.

If the seller has obtained the goods through fraud, has paid with a bad check, or has purchased the goods on credit while insolvent, the true owner cannot recover the goods from a good faith purchaser. Under these circumstances, the seller can transfer goods title to a good faith purchaser despite the fact he or she does not have perfect title to the goods. Suppose, for example, that Oak & Brass Furniture purchased a shipment of oak tables from A&B Wholesale Furniture and paid with a company check. If the check is no good, A&B can recover the goods if they are still in the possession of Oak & Brass. However, suppose Oak & Brass has sold the tables to Larry Catlin, who paid for the tables without knowledge that the check from Oak & Brass to A&B had bounced (Catlin is a good faith purchaser). A&B cannot recover the goods from Catlin. Catlin has a title in the goods superior to that of A&B.

Rights of Creditors to Goods.   There may be instances where the seller's creditors will try to recover goods from a buyer in an effort to gain repayment for the seller's debts. In most cases, Article 2 places the buyer's rights above the rights of the seller's creditors. Thus, a good faith purchaser is protected from the seller's creditors should they attempt to collect on the seller's debt by recovering goods.

There are, however, exceptions to this general rule when the seller transfers goods to a buyer but does so fraudulently. For example, it is common for banks and other creditors to loan money to businesses and use goods in inventory as collateral (a pledge or security for repayment). However, there can be situations where a dishonest seller has already sold some of those goods in inventory to a buyer. Thus, in reality, the collateral does not exist. A creditor who is defrauded in this manner may treat the sale as being canceled and retrieve the goods from the buyer.

The more important exception concerns efforts by an insolvent seller to deliberately defraud a creditor by transferring goods to a "buyer." In a *fraudulent transfer,* goods are sold to a friend or relative of the insolvent seller at less than fair market value. The friend or relative in effect is "storing" the goods for the seller until the creditor has been avoided. The seller may later repurchase the products and sell them to another buyer at market value. In a *voidable preference,* the seller transfers goods to a favored creditor to satisfy a preexisting debt. The transfer gives that creditor preference over other creditors. In either case, the creditors may recover the goods from the buyer.

STATUTE OF FRAUDS

Article 2 also provides a *statute of frauds* provision. Under Article 2's statute of frauds, the basic rule is that a contract for the sale of goods priced at $500 or more is not enforceable unless it is in writing and signed by the party against whom enforcement is sought. In comparison to the common law, Article 2 relaxes the requirements for the sufficiency of a writing to satisfy the statute of frauds. Under Article 2, the writing need not specify every material term in the contract. The key element is that there is some basis for believing that the parties made a contract for the sale of goods.

Any writing such as a written contract, memorandum, or confirmation is enough to show an agreement between the parties. In addition, the writing must be signed by the party against whom enforcement is sought, and it must specify a quantity (except in a dispute that involves an output or requirements contract).

If a dispute arises, a specified quantity will enable a court to fashion an appropriate remedy for the injured party. For example, suppose a buyer writes a letter to a seller indicating an intent to enter into a contract for the purchase of shipping cartons. Later, because the market price of shipping cartons is falling and other sellers are offering lower prices, the buyer wants to get out of the contract. If the buyer indicated an intent to enter into an agreement by writing and signing the letter, the writing is "sufficient" under Article 2 to be binding. The letter must be signed by the buyer, since the seller is seeking enforcement against the buyer.

PERFORMANCE AND OBLIGATIONS

Once a buyer and a seller have formed a contract for the sale of goods, each party must perform his or her obligations under that contract or risk being found in breach. The general duties and obligations assumed by each party to a contract for the sale of goods include those duties and obligations specified by the contract, imposed by the UCC, and, where necessary, provided by trade custom. Under Article 2 of the UCC, the buyer is obligated to accept and pay for the goods in accordance with the contract, and the seller is obligated to transfer and deliver the goods to the buyer.

In performing or enforcing the duties and obligations created by contractual relationship, the UCC requires the parties to act in good faith. This requirement applies whether the parties are merchants or nonmerchants. In the event of a breach of the contract, the UCC's good faith requirement extends even to the nonbreaching party. In their contracts, the parties cannot disclaim these good faith requirements.

SELLER'S OBLIGATIONS

The seller's basic obligation under the UCC is to transfer and deliver conforming goods to the buyer. In meeting those obligations, the seller must be concerned about the appropriate manner and timeliness of delivery, the place of tender, and the quality of tender. The proper tender of such goods to and their acceptance by the buyer entitles the seller to be paid according to the contract.

Under the common law, the *perfect tender rule* doctrine developed. Under this doctrine, the seller's tender of delivery was required to conform in every detail to the terms of the agreement between the parties. In the absence of perfect tender, the buyer either rejected the entire delivery or accepted it. The UCC essentially restates the perfect tender rule to provide the following:

> [I]f the goods or the tender of delivery fail in any respect to conform to the contract, the buyer may:
>
> **(a)** reject the whole;
>
> **(b)** accept the whole; or,
>
> **(c)** accept any commercial unit or units and reject the rest.

The last of these options does modify the common law doctrine by allowing the buyer to accept less than the entire shipment. Like its common law counterpart, the UCC's perfect tender rule can be very harsh on unwary sellers. The rule allows buyers to reject goods that do not conform fully to the contract, no matter how small the discrepancy. The rationale for the rule is that buyers are entitled to receive those goods they have bargained and paid for—and not something less.

On the other hand, allowing the buyer to simply reject the shipment when the nonconformities are slight may enable the buyer to escape payment obligations. This is particularly a problem when the market price of the goods is falling. The buyer can simply find some small nonconformity, cancel the contract, and purchase the goods at a lower price from another seller. Under Article 2's general policy of enforcing contracts whenever possible, such unfair behavior is discouraged. The UCC provides three modifications to the buyer's right to reject the seller's goods for failure to comply with the perfect tender rule:

1. In an agreement of the parties.
2. Through cure by the seller.
3. Under an installment contract.

Agreement of the Parties.   In their contract for the sale of goods, the parties may agree to limit the operation of the perfect tender rule. The parties, for example, may agree that the "seller shall have the right to repair or to replace defective goods or parts thereof."

Cure by the Seller.   The UCC provides limited opportunities for a seller to *cure* an improper tender of goods that has been rejected by the buyer. After the buyer has rightfully rejected a shipment as not conforming to the contract, the seller may cure the defective tender or delivery if

1. The time for the seller's performance under the contract has not yet passed.
2. The seller notifies the buyer in a timely manner of an intent to cure the defect.
3. The seller properly repairs or replaces the defective goods within the time allowed for his or her performance.

In *Ramirez* v. *Autosport*, the buyer rejected nonconforming goods and provided the seller with an extended period in which to cure the improper tender.

RAMIREZ v. AUTOSPORT

New Jersey Supreme Court
88 N.J. 277, 440 A.2d 1345 (1982)

Case Background
On July 20, 1978, Mr. & Mrs. Ernest Ramirez contracted to purchase a camper van from Autosport. The van cost $14,100, and Autosport gave the Ramirezes $4,700 for their old van as a trade-in. The Ramirezes agreed to turn in their old van immediately and to take delivery of the new van on August 3.

On August 3, the Ramirezes tendered payment. However, the new van was not ready. The new van had several paint scratches, missing electric and sewer hookups, and damaged hubcaps. Autosport agreed to fix all the problems. After repeated phone calls, Autosport promised delivery on August 14.

On August 14, the van was still not ready. This time, the repainted surfaces were not dry, and the seat cushions were soaking wet because the windows had been left open during a rainstorm. A third delivery date was set for September 1, but the new van was again not ready for delivery.

Finally, in October, the Ramirezes returned with their attorney and canceled the contract. They also demanded the return of their old van. Unfortunately, Autosport had sold it to another customer.

The Ramirezes filed suit against Autosport for rescission of the contract and recovery of the value of their old van. Autosport counterclaimed for breach of contract. The trial court found for the Ramirezes. Autosport appealed to the New Jersey Supreme Court.

Case Decision
The New Jersey Supreme Court affirmed the trial court's decision. The court found that the Ramirezes had properly rejected the new van notwithstanding Autosport's efforts to fix the van's admittedly minor defects. The court noted that the UCC permits a buyer who rightfully rejects goods to cancel a sales contract. The court then reasoned that because a buyer may reject goods with insubstantial defects, he or she may also cancel the contract if those defects remain uncured. Otherwise, a seller's failure to cure minor defects would compel a buyer to accept imperfect goods.

Managerial Considerations
The key managerial issue here is the extent to which people are willing to act on faith rather than on performance. The Ramirezes acted on faith by turning over their old van without completing the remainder of the agreement. An alternative approach might have been to retain possession of their old van—and their payment—until the new van was acceptable to them. It might have pressured Autosport into being more energetic.

On the other hand, the management of Autosport was very careless in its approach to solving this problem. Simple scheduling and attention to detail could have solved the problem easily. Perhaps the company had a only a small profit in the sale to the Ramirezes. Still, solving the problem in a timely fashion would have been less expensive than the outlays for the lawsuit and the repairs to Autosport's public image.

As the case suggests, the seller can be provided with additional time to cure beyond the time for performance with the buyer's consent. In addition, the seller may have a right to cure after the time allowed for performance. To establish this right, Article 2 requires that a seller must have had reasonable grounds to believe that the nonconforming goods sent would be acceptable to the buyer. Frequently, the seller will provide the buyer with a price discount for nonconforming goods. The discount will serve as the "reasonable grounds to believe" the buyer would accept the nonconforming goods. The seller would then have the right to cure after the time for performance had passed. In other situations, the buyer's past acceptance of nonconforming goods could serve as the seller's reasonable basis. In either situation, the seller would then have additional time to cure the nonconformity.

Installment Contracts.   An *installment contract* is a single contract that provides for delivery in two or more separate lots. Each lot is to be accepted and paid for separately. In an installment contract, a buyer can reject an installment, but "only if the nonconformity substantially impairs the value" of the installment and cannot be cured. The entire installment contract is breached only when one or more nonconforming installments "substantially" impair the value of the "whole contract." If the buyer subsequently accepts a nonconforming installment and fails to notify the seller of cancellation, the contract is reinstated.

■ BUYER'S OBLIGATIONS

In general, the buyer's obligations begin when the seller tenders delivery of goods that conform to the sales contract. The buyer is required to accept conforming goods and to pay for them according to the contract. The decision by the buyer to accept or reject the goods will dictate how the seller will continue to perform. If the buyer accepts the goods, the seller will await payment. If the buyer rejects the goods as nonconforming, the seller may need to remedy the problem. One solution may be to start a lawsuit for breach of contract against the buyer.

Buyer's Right of Inspection.   Unless the parties have agreed otherwise, the buyer has a right to inspect the goods before accepting or paying for them. This inspection allows the buyer to verify that the goods received are those the seller had agreed to deliver. The buyer must pay for any expenses associated with an inspection. However, those expenses can be recovered from the seller as damages if the goods do not conform to the contract.

Buyer's Right of Rejection.   Under the perfect tender rule, a buyer who receives goods that are nonconforming may reject them and withhold payment. The buyer may also cancel the contract and recover from the seller any prepayments made. The buyer must notify the seller of a rejection in a timely manner to allow the seller to either cure the nonconformity or reclaim the goods.

Buyer's Duty of Acceptance.   When the seller has properly tendered conforming goods, the buyer has the duty to accept them. That is, the buyer has the duty to express a willingness to become the owner of the goods tendered by the seller. The buyer may notify the seller, pay for the goods, use the goods, or simply put the goods into inventory.

Accepting goods from the seller imposes several obligations on the buyer. Most obviously, an acceptance of the goods obligates the buyer to pay the seller at the contract rate. By accepting the goods, the buyer is precluded from rejecting them. However, the buyer may revoke an acceptance later if a nonconformity is discovered. The nonconformity must have been difficult to discover upon inspection and must *substantially impair* the value of the goods to the buyer. A determination of substantial impairment will depend on the circumstances of the transaction. If done properly, such a revocation of acceptance provides the buyer with virtually the same rights and obligations as if the goods had been rejected.

Obligation of Payment.   Unless otherwise agreed, payment is due at the time and place at which the buyer receives the goods. Even in those circumstance where the contract calls for the seller to deliver the goods to a transportation company for further shipment to the buyer, the buyer's payment for the goods is not due until the buyer receives them. Payment upon receipt gives the buyer a chance to inspect the goods before paying for them.

SALES WARRANTIES

Broadly speaking, a *warranty* is a statement or other representation made by a seller that the goods being sold conform to the specified standards of quality, safety, performance, and title. If the goods do not conform to the standards created by the warranty, the seller can be held liable in damages for breach of warranty. Article 2 of the UCC provides five types of warranties that can arise in a sales contract:

1. Warranty of Title.
2. Express Warranty.
3. Implied Warranty of Merchantability.
4. Implied Warranty of Fitness for a Particular Purpose.
5. Implied Warranty Arising from the Course of Dealing or Trade.

These warranties are summarized in Table 10–2.

■ WARRANTIES OF TITLE

A *warranty of title* is the seller's promise or guarantee that the seller is the rightful owner of the goods being sold. Under the common law, an implied

---

TABLE 10–2
SUMMARY OF WARRANTIES UNDER THE UCC

Warranty of Title	Seller is the rightful owner of the goods, the goods are free of any liens, and there are no infringements.
Express Warranty	Seller's promise as to quality, safety, performance, or title. May be created by the seller's statements, description, or models.
Implied Warranties	
Merchantability	Imposed on the seller by the UCC; requires that the goods being sold are reasonably fit for the purposes they are being sold for; also applies to packaging and labeling; generally means goods of fair, average, or medium quality.
Fitness for a Particular Purpose	Imposed on the seller by the UCC: If the buyer relies on the seller's skill or judgment in selecting goods for a particular purpose, the goods must be able to perform that purpose.
Trade Usage	Imposed on the seller by the UCC; the seller must provide the goods to the buyer in the manner customary in the trade.

warranty of title is assumed when an innocent buyer purchases goods from a seller. Article 2 of the UCC overrides the common law's implied warranty and imposes an obligation of a warranty of title on the seller. However, Article 2 does not designate it as either an express or an implied warranty.

Specifically, the warranties of title under Article 2 require good title and rightful transfer, the absence of any liens or other interests, and the absence of any infringements (for example, on the trademarks, trade-names, or copyrights of others). In most sales contracts, these warranties of title arise automatically. With these warranties, the buyer should expect that he or she will not have to defend title in a subsequent lawsuit. If after purchasing a good from a seller, the buyer is forced into litigation over title, the seller is obligated to pay the costs of the lawsuit.

As a general rule, litigation arises when a third party asserts ownership over the goods. As *Jefferson* v. *Jones* illustrates, the buyer must show that the third party made a credible claim of ownership. The buyer will then be able to show that the seller has breached a warranty of title.

JEFFERSON v. JONES

Maryland Court of Appeals
286 Md. 544, 408 A.2d 1036 (1979)

Case Background
In July 1975, Thomas Jefferson purchased a motorcycle from Lawrence Jones. Jones gave the motorcycle to Jefferson and signed over his certificate of title. Shortly thereafter, the state Motor Vehicle Administration reissued the title in Jefferson's name. Two years later, the police who believed the vehicle had been stolen, asked Jefferson to prove he owned the motorcycle. When Jefferson showed the police his title certificate, the vehicle identification number on the certificate did not match the number on the motorcycle. The police seized the motorcycle. Jefferson sued the police to get the motorcycle back and won because no other person could be found with a superior title.

Jefferson then demanded that Jones reimburse him for his legal expenses. When Jones refused, Jefferson sued him for breach of warranty of title under the UCC. The trial court found that no breach occurred, because Jefferson had failed to prove that someone else had a superior title. Jefferson appealed to the Maryland Court of Appeals. He argued that just the disruption in the use and enjoyment of the motorcycle by a seemingly genuine claim of superior title was sufficient to breach the warranty of title.

Case Decision
The Maryland Court of Appeals reversed the trial court's decision. It found that the warranty of title provided by the UCC does not require proof of a superior title in a third party to establish a breach of its provisions. Rather, it required only a claim that is not fictitious. The court reasoned that an unconditional aspect of possessing good title is that a purchaser be "enabled . . . to hold the property in peace and, if he wishes to sell it, to be reasonably certain that [nothing] will appear to disturb its market value. Whenever the title to personal property is evidenced by a document which is an aid to proving ownership, as in the case of motor vehicles, any substantial defect in that document necessarily creates a reasonable doubt as to that ownership."

Managerial Consideration
Buyers and sellers should take appropriate precautions to ensure that merchandise and titles agree. Suppose that a business orders five new IBM personal computers. Each computer will have a serial number. When the manager takes delivery of the machines, he or she should compare the serial numbers on the units with the numbers on the invoice. Similarly, if the company sells the machines to another business two years later, both the seller and the buyer should agree that the serial numbers match all relevant documentation regarding the sale.

■ EXPRESS WARRANTIES OF QUALITY

An *express warranty* is created by a seller's promise or guarantee as to the quality, safety, performance, or title to the goods being sold. In the course of negotiations, the seller often induces the buyer to purchase goods by making statements or by taking other actions. When those statements or actions relate to the quality, description, condition, or performance of the goods, the seller may create an express warranty. Article 2 provides three circumstances where an express warranty may be created.

1. Seller's confirmation or promise of fact made to the buyer regarding the goods.
2. Seller's description of the goods provided to the buyer.
3. Seller's sample or model of the goods.

The seller's intentions are irrelevant in determining whether the statements or actions create an express warranty of quality. It is unnecessary that the seller have specific intent to create warranty. It is also unnecessary that the seller use words like *warrant* or *guarantee* in a presentation to the buyer to create a warranty. Article 2 will also assume that the buyer relied on the seller's representations. However, it is unnecessary that the buyer actually relied upon the representations for a warranty to be created.

■ IMPLIED WARRANTIES OF QUALITY

An *implied warranty* is a minimum quality standard imposed automatically by operation of law. In a contract for the sale of goods, implied warranties are created and imposed by Article 2 of the UCC. When imposed by Article 2, an implied warranty will exist regardless of whether it is written into the sales contract. Article 2 of the UCC provides two implied warranties of quality:

1. An implied warranty of merchantability.
2. An implied warranty of fitness for a particular purpose.

Implied Warranty of Merchantability.   Article 2 provides that unless the parties expressly agree otherwise, an implied warranty of merchantability accompanies every sale by a merchant. The goods sold must be the kind of goods that a merchant/seller regularly deals in. Article 2 imposes an obligation on the merchant/seller that the goods being sold are reasonably fit for the purposes they are being sold for. It also requires that the goods be of fair, average, merchantable quality. Article 2 provides minimum requirements that goods must satisfy to be considered *merchantable*, as follows:

1. *Conform to Contract Description.* The goods received must conform to the trade meaning of the goods described in the contract. This requirement has been interpreted over time to mean fair, average, or medium quality. That is, the seller is not obligated to supply the highest quality of the goods described in the contract and the buyer is not obligated to accept the lowest quality.
2. *In the Case of Fungible Goods.* If the goods are bulk agricultural (such as wheat or corn) or other similar fungible commodities, they must be of "fair average quality" within the contract description. Goods are considered *fungible* if one unit is at least roughly identical to any other unit.
3. *Fit for Ordinary Uses.* To be considered merchantable, the goods must be fit for the ordinary purposes that they are to be used for. That is, the goods being sold must be capable of performing the functions ordinarily required of similar goods.

4. *Even Kind, Quality, and Quantity.* The goods must have an evenness of kind, quality, and quantity in each unit and among the units. This requirement is intended to protect a buyer who expects that goods sold in large lots will be interchangeable. Not uncommonly, the buyer and seller will agree to limited variations between the units to the extent trade usage allows. They may also agree that the seller will replace units exceeding specified tolerances.

5. *Adequacy of Packaging and Labeling.* In the event the goods are to be packaged and/or labeled, the packaging and labeling must be as adequate as the agreement between the parties may require.

6. *Conform to Label Description.* If the goods come delivered in a container or with a label, they must conform to any statements or promises on that label. The UCC requires that any labeling be accurate, even if it is not required by the terms of the contract. This requirement reflects the common expectation of buyers that goods will not be delivered with false representations on the package or label.

In *Reid* v. *Eckerds Drugs,* the court is asked to judge the adequacy of the labeling on a consumer product. By examining the label, the court will determine whether the seller has breached an implied warranty of merchantability.

REID v. ECKERDS DRUGS, INC.

North Carolina Court of Appeals
40 N.C.App. 476, 253 S.E.2d 344 (1979)

Case Background
Reid purchased an aerosol can of deodorant from Eckerds Drugs. The label on the can included the following statement:

> WARNING: Use only as directed. Do not apply to broken, irritated or sensitive skin. If rash or irritation develops discontinue use. Never spray towards face or flame. Do not puncture or incinerate can. Do not expose or store at temperature above 120°F. Intentional misuse by deliberately concentrating and inhaling the contents can be harmful or fatal. Keep out of reach of children.

One morning, Reid liberally sprayed his underarms and neck with the deodorant. He then put the can down, walked across the room, and lit a cigarette. He immediately burst into flames and was severely burned on his upper torso where the deodorant had been applied. He sued the seller, Eckerds Drugs, and the manufacturer, the J.P. Williams Company, alleging breach of the implied warranty of merchantability.

At trial, the defendants proved that the deodorant could not be ignited unless an open flame was within ¼ inch of the surface coated with it. They also showed that large quantities of the deodorant had been sold without injuring other consumers. The trial court granted the defendants' motion for summary judgment without allowing a jury to determine liability. Reid appealed to the North Carolina Court of Appeals.

Case Decision
The Court of Appeals reversed and remanded the trial court's decision. The court found that a failure to warn consumers of all dangerous tendencies of a product may breach the implied warranty of merchantability provided in the UCC. The jury had the right to determine whether the defendants had provided adequate warning. If the jury found that the defendants had provided adequate warning, there was no breach of the implied warranty.

Managerial Considerations
Given the ambiguities and uncertainties associated with warranties, product misuse, and so forth, management must be very careful in its warranty statements. Consumer testing and continual review of relevant judicial decisions through a legal audit should be undertaken to keep as current as possible about potential liabilities. Relevant information from such review should then be incorporated into written warranties and disclaimers to the maximum extent possible.

Implied Warranty of Fitness for a Particular Purpose.   In some situations, a buyer will purchase goods with a definite use in mind. Article 2 is more demanding about a seller who had reason to know the buyer's particular purpose for purchasing the goods. The seller can be either a merchant or a nonmerchant. If the buyer actually relies on the seller's skill or judgment to select the goods for the particular purpose, an implied warranty that the goods are suited for that purpose is created. The goods must be intended for something more specific than the general purpose for which they were made.

The buyer is required to demonstrate "actual reliance" the seller's expertise. The buyer must also show that the seller had "reason to know"—not necessarily actual knowledge—of the buyer's purpose. Suppose, for example, that Flodden needs to paint some rain gutters on his house. He enters a paint store and tells the salesperson what he needs. He also informs the salesperson that he is very concerned about chipping and peeling and asks for a recommendation. The salesperson recommends Pittura Exterior. If Flodden buys Pittura based on the salesperson's recommendation and the paint chips and peels, there is a breach of implied warranty of fitness for a particular purpose.

Implied Warranties Arising Under Trade Usage.   Implied warranties can also arise from course of dealing, course of performance, or trade usage. In some sales relationships, the sellers will be very knowledgeable about the goods, the practices used in selling the goods to their customers, and the uses those customers will put the goods to. In such cases, the courts will infer that the buyer and seller intended for those customs to apply to their contract.

The parties may, of course, specifically state that they do not intend for the custom to apply. For example, it is customary for new car dealers to thoroughly check new cars prior to delivery to their customers. Suppose that the new car manager at Clay Smith Mazda failed to check a car with a simple problem in its onboard computer system. If the manager had checked the car, he would have discovered the problem. Instead, the problem caused the engine's exhaust system to be diverted into the passenger compartment. While driving the car, the buyer was overcome by carbon monoxide and ran into a tree. The dealer may be held liable to the buyer for the damages under a breach of an implied warranty arising from trade usage. If the dealership had performed according to trade custom, the problem would have been discovered and repaired before the buyer drove the car.

■ CONFLICTING WARRANTIES

On occasion, a single sales contract between a buyer and a seller will involve several warranties. An electronics manufacturer, for example, may provide an express warranty in the sales contract stating that the components are warranted against defects for one year. In addition to this express warranty, there is also an implied warranty that the components will be fit for the use to which they are going to be placed. While such warranties are generally compatible, there are occasions when they are inconsistent or even in conflict with one another. In such cases, the UCC provides that the warranties will be construed as consistent and cumulative whenever possible.

◼ WARRANTY DISCLAIMERS

To avoid warranty liability obligations, sellers often rely on *warranty disclaimers*—contractual limitations or exclusions on implied and express warranties put in the sales contract by the seller. Under Article 2, a seller can exclude any express or implied warranty, limit the time period in which a warranty is to be effective, or limit the buyer's remedies for breach of warranty. However, the manner in which a warranty can be limited or excluded is defined specifically by Article 2.

Disclaiming Express Warranties.   The policy of the UCC is to protect buyers from sellers who either make express warranties during negotiations between the parties and then disclaim them later in a form contract or put language in a written agreement that both creates and disclaims a warranty. Suppose, for example, that a sales contract contained the following language: "The digital components supplied by the seller are warranted against defective workmanship for a period of one year." Another clause in the sales contract reads: "Seller hereby excludes all warranties, express and implied." Article 2 directs that wherever possible, words or conduct excluding or limiting an express warranty shall be interpreted as consistent with any other words or conduct that created the warranty. If is not possible to make the warranties consistent, however, the intended disclaimer is ineffective. Thus, the express warranty exclusion in this sales contract is inoperative under the UCC because it is not possible to make it consistent with other warranties. These rules give the courts wide latitude in striking down a seller's disclaimers.

Disclaiming Warranties of Title.   A seller can exclude or limit the warranty of title, but only in one of two ways:

1. By specific language in the contract.
2. By circumstances informing the buyer that the seller either does not claim full title or is selling only whatever title he or she may have.

These latter circumstances include, for example, the purchase of goods at a sheriff's sale. In such instances, buyers know or should know that the goods have been seized to satisfy unpaid debts and thus are not the property of the party selling them.

Disclaiming Implied Warranties.   If the seller wants to disclaim the implied warranty of merchantability or the implied warranty of fitness for a particular purpose, the UCC provides explicit methods for doing so. The implied warranty of merchantability can be excluded or limited by a "conspicuous writing" that includes the word *merchantability*. General statements may suffice as a proper disclaimer. For example, including the phrase "SELLER MAKES NO WARRANTY OF MERCHANTABILITY WITH RESPECT TO GOODS SOLD UNDER THIS AGREEMENT" will work if the seller brings it to the attention of the buyer. Language like "as is" and "with all faults" is equally effective to alert the buyer that there are no implied warranties of any kind.

An implied warranty of fitness for a particular purpose can also be excluded by a conspicuous writing. The UCC provides model language sufficient to disclaim any implied warranty of fitness: "THERE ARE NO WARRANTIES THAT EXTEND BEYOND THE DESCRIPTION ON THE FACE HEREOF." Other language can also operate as a disclaimer if it specifically excludes or limits an implied warranty.

THIRD-PARTY BENEFICIARIES OF WARRANTIES

The UCC extends any express warranty made by the seller to the buyer to designated third parties. It also extends the implied warranty of merchantability. All warranty disclaimers made to the buyer by the seller also apply equally to third parties. However, the seller is barred from giving a warranty to the buyer but excluding or limiting its application to third parties. This rule gives some, but not all, third parties the benefit of the same warranties the buyer received in the contract for sale.

Which third parties were to be covered by the rule generated considerable disagreement among the states. To minimize those concerns, three alternative versions for the imposition of liability under Article 2 were drafted. States may choose to limit third parties to the buyer's family and house guests; to any natural person; or to any person, which would also include businesses. Each state is allowed to choose that alternative that best suits its existing case law.

RIGHTS AND REMEDIES

When a buyer or seller breaches a contract for the sale of goods, the UCC provides the nonbreaching party with a number of remedies. Those remedies are designed to place the nonbreaching party in the same position as if the contract had been performed according to its terms. In applying its remedies, the UCC directs the courts to liberally interpret those remedies.

SELLER'S RIGHTS AND REMEDIES

The buyer may default on his or her contractual obligations by rejecting a tender of goods that conforms to the contract, wrongfully revoking an acceptance, repudiating the contract, failing to make a payment, or failing to complete some other performance required by the contract. In each of these situations, the UCC provides the seller with remedies. The seller is not restricted to any one remedy in particular. Rather, the seller may use several remedies at the same time. The seller's remedies under the UCC include the following:

1. Withholding delivery of the goods.
2. Stopping delivery by a carrier or bailee.
3. Identifying the goods to the contract and salvaging them if necessary.

4. Reselling the goods and recovering any deficiency as damages.

5. Recovering damages for wrongful acceptance or, in limited situations, recovering the purchase price.

6. Canceling the contract.

The remedies available to the seller depend on whether the buyer breached before or after receiving the goods (see Table 10–3). When the buyer breaches before receiving the goods, the seller may elect to cancel the contract, resell or salvage (recycle) the goods, or withhold or stop delivery. If the buyer breaches after receiving the goods, the remedies available to the seller will depend upon whether the seller reclaims the goods. If the seller is not able to reclaim the goods, the seller may sue the buyer to recover the purchase price and any resulting incidental damages. If the goods are reclaimed by the seller, the seller may use any of the same remedies available had the buyer's breach occurred before receiving the goods.

Withholding or Stopping Deliveries.   In the event the buyer wrongfully rejects the goods or revokes an acceptance, fails to make a payment due on or before delivery, or repudiates the contract, the UCC protects the seller

TABLE 10–3 SUMMARY OF SELLER'S RIGHTS AND REMEDIES	
Status of the Goods	**Seller's Rights and Remedies**
Buyer breaches before receiving the goods	**The seller may** 1. Cancel the contract. 2. Identify the goods; minimize losses if necessary by completing manufacture of the goods or by stopping the manufacturing process and salvaging the goods. 3. Withhold delivery or, if the circumstances warrant, stop delivery. 4. Resell the goods in a commercially reasonable manner. 5. Sue the buyer to recover the purchase price and any resulting incidental damages. 6. Stop the goods in transit.

Buyer breaches after receiving the goods	1. If the buyer does not pay, the seller may sue to recover the purchase price and resulting incidental damages.
	 2. If the buyer wrongfully rejects the goods or revokes an acceptance, the remedies depend on whether the seller reclaims the goods:
	   a. If the seller reclaims the goods, the rights and remedies are the same as if the buyer breached before receiving the goods.
	   b. If the seller does not reclaim the goods, the seller can sue to recover the purchase price and any resulting incidental damages.

from further loss by allowing delivery to be withheld. If the goods have already been shipped but have not been received by the buyer when the buyer breaches, the seller may be able to stop delivery of the goods by the carrier. A seller who rightfully stops delivery to a nonperforming buyer regains all original rights to the goods.

Identifying Goods to the Contract for Resale or Salvage.   If the buyer breaches while the goods are still in the possession of the seller, the seller is authorized to identify goods conforming to the contract if they had not been identified previously. Recall that the identification process basically involves specifying those goods that are the subject of the sales contract. After identifying the goods, the seller has one of two options:

1. Finish manufacturing the goods, if necessary, and then resell them to another buyer.
2. Sell unfinished goods for their scrap or salvage value.

The seller's decision between these options must express a reasonable commercial judgment to minimize losses.

Reselling Goods.   After a buyer has breached the contract, the seller can often minimize losses by reselling the goods (or the remaining balance of the goods) to another buyer. In reselling the goods, the seller may use either a public or a private sale as long as the manner, time, place, and terms of the resale are *commercially reasonable*. After the sale, the seller may also look to the original buyer to make up any difference between the contract price and the resale price. However, the seller does not have to give the original buyer any profit obtained from the resale.

▇ SELLER'S INCIDENTAL DAMAGES

When reclaiming and reselling the goods does not fully compensate the seller for the buyer's breach of contract, damages are the proper remedy. All of the UCC's damage measures are designed to put the seller in as good a position as if the buyer had fully performed his or her contractual obligations. Furthermore, the seller is allowed to seek incidental damages for recovery of those costs resulting from the breach. Those costs may include expenses associated with stopping delivery, transporting and taking care of the goods after the breach, returning or reselling the goods, and taking any other necessary action. Attorney's fees, however, are not allowed as incidental damages.

▇ BUYER'S RIGHTS AND REMEDIES

A seller usually breaches a sales contract in one of the following ways:

1. The seller repudiates the contract before tendering the goods.
2. The seller fails to make a scheduled delivery on time.
3. The seller delivers nonconforming goods.

The buyer's remedies will vary somewhat depending on the type of breach by the seller. In any case, the buyer may respond by canceling the contract,

TABLE 10–4	
SUMMARY OF BUYER'S RIGHTS AND REMEDIES	

Status of the Goods	Buyer's Rights and Remedies
Seller repudiates the contract before delivery	**The buyer may** 1. Cancel the contract. 2. Obtain or arrange to obtain goods from another supplier (cover). 3. Sue the seller for incidental and consequential damages and to recover advance payments.
Seller fails to deliver on time	**The buyer may** 1. Cancel the contract. 2. Obtain or arrange to obtain goods from another supplier (cover). 3. Sue the seller for incidental and consequential damages.
Seller delivers nonconforming goods, buyer rejects	**The buyer may** 1. Cancel the contract. 2. Obtain or arrange to obtain goods from another supplier (cover) if goods are rejected. 3. Sue the seller for incidental and consequential damages. 4. Sell rejected goods to recover advance payments. 5. If no advance payment, store or reship goods.
Seller delivers nonconforming goods, buyer accepts	**The buyer may** 1. Deduct damages from price of goods. 2. Sue the seller for damages. 3. Sue for breach of warranty.

arranging to obtain the goods from another supplier, and suing the nonperforming seller for damages. Buyer's rights and remedies are summarized in Table 10–4.

Buyer's Disposition of Rejected Goods.   After rightfully rejecting a tender of goods or revoking a prior acceptance, a buyer may become concerned about getting the seller to refund advance payments. Generally, sellers will refund advance payments to dissatisfied buyers. However, if the seller does not refund, the payments are recoverable under the UCC whenever the seller breaches the contract by repudiating it, failing to make a timely delivery, or tendering nonconforming goods. To use the UCC's provisions, the circumstances of the breach must give the buyer temporary possession of any goods identified to the contract.

Resale of Rejected Goods.   Under the UCC, the buyer may elect to resell the contract goods in his or her possession to recover all advance payments. (The buyer may still bring a lawsuit to recover damages for the seller's breach.) The buyer must resell the goods according to the same rules the UCC imposes on sellers; that is, the buyer may use either a public or a private sale as long as the manner, time, place, and terms of the resale are commercially reasonable. But unlike sellers, a buyer who resells contract goods after breach may keep only those proceeds that equal payments and expenses. Any excess must be remitted to the seller.

Other Disposition of Rejected Goods.   The UCC does not compel the buyer to resell goods that remain in his or her possession following the seller's breach. The buyer is obligated only to use reasonable care in holding rejected goods so that the seller can reclaim them. Normally, the buyer will surrender the goods to the seller in exchange for a refund of all holding costs and advance payments. When the seller has been given timely notice of the buyer's rejection or revocation of acceptance but provides the buyer with no instructions for disposing of the goods, the buyer has the option of storing or reshipping the goods. If the goods are perishable or threaten to decline rapidly in value, a merchant buyer must make a reasonable effort to resell them on the seller's behalf.

The Buyer's Right to Cover.   When a seller has breached the contract, the buyer will usually want to protect him or herself by obtaining similar goods from another supplier as soon as possible. Obtaining such goods enables a manufacturer/buyer to keep production processes operating, a retailer/buyer to maintain an adequate inventory for resale, and a consumer/buyer to continue using the goods as planned. The UCC uses the term *cover* to describe the buyer's purchase or arrangements to purchase substitute goods following a breach of contract by the seller.

The buyer may recover damages from the nonperforming seller equal to the difference between the contract price and the cover price, plus incidental and consequential damages. In principle, this remedy—cover plus additional costs as damages—puts the buyer in the same economic position as if the original seller had fully performed the contract. As the following case illustrates, as long as the buyer acts reasonably and in good faith, cover will be viewed as proper. This will be the case even if hindsight reveals that the arrangement made was not the best possible under the circumstances.

HUNTINGTON BEACH UNION HIGH SCHOOL DISTRICT v. CONTINENTAL INFORMATION SYSTEMS CORPORATION

United States Court of Appeals, Ninth Circuit
621 F.2d 353 (1980)

Case Background
The Huntington Beach Union High School District had requested bids for a computer system. The computer system was to be installed at the end of July 1977. Bids could be received by the school district on or before July 11. The bids were to be opened and the contract awarded on July 12.

On July 12, the winning bidder was Continental Information Systems, with a bid of $332,939. Continental was a computer broker who purchased systems from other companies for resale. However, on July 12, Continental had not yet acquired a system for the school district from another computer company. On the other hand, the second best bidder ($379,960.60) was prepared to deliver the computer system to the school district. The school district nevertheless decided to accept Continental's bid and let the other bids expire. By July 31, Continental still had not been able to obtain the computer system. The school district covered by rebidding the contract.

The new bidding process caused the installation of the computer system to be delayed by three months. In addi-

(continued)

tion, the new winning bid was for $392,363.66, or $59,424.66 higher than Continental's original bid. To recover this loss, the school district sued Continental for breach of contract and won. However, the trial court awarded damages for cover of only $12,403.06. The court reasoned that the school district would have been "more reasonable" to have accepted the second best bid. The school district knew that on July 12 Continental did not have the system and that the second best bidder did. Thus, the court calculated damages as the difference between the new bid and the second best bid from the original bid letting. The school district appealed to Ninth Circuit Court of Appeals.

Case Decision

The appellate court found that the trial court had erred in its calculations of damages. It found that cover damages in this case should be calculated at $59,424.66, the difference between the new bid and the Continental bid. The court reasoned that the test of proper cover is whether the buyer had acted in good faith and in a reasonable manner. It is

immaterial that hindsight may later prove that the method of cover used was not the most effective. The school district had acted reasonably in accepting the Continental bid, even though in retrospect it would have been more reasonable to have rejected Continental's bid and taken the second best bid.

Managerial Considerations

The case shows managerial failings on both sides. The management of the school district should have stayed in closer contact with contractors to monitor potential problems. For example, by monitoring the situation more closely, the school district would have had some warning about Continental's inability to meet the requirements of the contract. The management of Continental should have been more careful about entering into an agreement where it was doubtful that the company would be able to meet its obligations. If the damages imposed by the court did not put the company out of business, the damage to its reputation just might have.

Damages When the Buyer Elects Not to Cover.   It is not always desirable for the buyer to cover a seller's nondelivery or repudiation of a sales contract. For example, with perishable goods, the breach may occur so late in the season that the buyer cannot purchase the goods from another supplier. Also, the breach may motivate the buyer/manager to change the company's business plans and strategies so that the goods or substitutes are no longer needed. Still, the buyer has been injured—changing company strategies can produce expenses that should be compensated by the nonperforming seller. When the buyer elects not to cover, damages are calculated as the difference between the market price of the goods at the time the buyer learned of the breach and the price established in the original contract.

BUYER'S INCIDENTAL AND CONSEQUENTIAL DAMAGES

Like the seller's damage provisions, the buyer's damage provisions under the UCC are designed to put the buyer in as good a position as if the seller had performed according to the contract. Like the seller's provisions, the buyer is allowed to seek incidental damages for recovery of those costs resulting from the breach. In addition, the buyer is allowed to recover consequential damages.

Incidental Damages.   When the buyer rejects a delivery rightfully, his or her incidental damages include the reasonable costs of inspecting, receiving, transporting, and taking care of the goods while they remain in his or her possession. If there was no delivery at all or if delivery is late, the buyer's incidental damages will include all reasonable costs associated with the delay in receiving the goods.

Consequential Damages.   Consequential damages are the foreseeable, although not necessarily foreseen, damages that result from the seller's breach. They differ from incidental damages in that they result from the buyer's relations with parties other than the seller. For example, the breach may cause the buyer to lose other sales (and profits).

Consequential damages may also include injuries to people or property that are (proximately) caused by the seller's breach of any warranty. Suppose, for example, that a California winery shipped its vintner's reserve Cabernet to J.J.'s Fine Wines. The wine was improperly filtered and began to ferment in the bottle for a second time. The second fermentation caused the wine to blow its corks and spew wine all over J.J.'s fine white carpeting and onto several customers. The value of the carpet and any other damages to the building, the building's contents, and J.J.'s customers are consequential damages. However, if J.J. knew of the defect in the wine or reasonably should have known of it, J.J.'s could not recover consequential damages.

SUMMARY: A MANAGER'S GUIDE

- A fundamental aspect of business and its legal environment is the concept of a sale and the sales contract. In an effort to unify state contract law, the Uniform Commercial Code, or UCC, was developed. The UCC governs contracts for the sale of goods under Article 2.
- Under the UCC, a good is defined as all tangible things that are movable at the time of the identification of the contract. By definition, real estate, fixtures attached permanently to real estate, services, stocks, bonds, bank accounts, patents, and copyrights are not goods under the UCC. A sales transaction involving those things will be governed by the common law of contracts.
- Although the UCC governs all contracts for the sale of goods, merchants involved in such contracts are often treated differently from nonmerchants. An individual is considered to be a merchant if he or she deals, holds him or herself out as having special knowledge, or employs an agent, broker, or other intermediary who holds him or herself out as having special knowledge in the goods involved in the transaction. Merchants are required not only to conduct their activities in good faith like nonmerchants but also to adhere to all business practices common in the trade.
- The UCC's law of sales is a subset of the common law of contracts. The common law of contracts governs a transaction unless the UCC specifically modifies or changes the effect of the common law. Generally speaking, where the UCC modifies or changes the common law, the effect is usually to be less demanding than the common law. An acceptance under the UCC, for example, does not have to be unequivocal to form a contract. An indefinite offer can form the basis of a contract (even with open price, quantity, delivery, and payment terms) under the UCC but not under the common law.
- The basic obligation of the seller is to transfer and deliver the goods. The buyer is obligated to accept and pay for them.

- In performing their obligations under the contract—in its performance and its enforcement—the parties are required by the UCC to act in good faith.

- In delivering conforming goods to the buyer, the seller is concerned with the appropriate manner and timeliness of delivery, place of tender, and the quality of tender.

- The common law's perfect tender rule requires that the seller's tender of delivery conform in every detail to the terms of the contract. Since this rule can have harsh consequences, the UCC modifies the buyer's common law right to reject the goods by providing the seller with the right to cure defects.

- The UCC's warranty provisions provide buyers with significant protection with regard to product safety, performance, and title. The UCC provides five types of warranties: warranty of titles, express warranty of quality, implied warranty of merchantability, implied warranty of fitness for a particular purpose, and implied warranty arising from the course of dealing or trade usage.

- The UCC obligates the seller to warrant title to the goods being sold to the buyer. In warranting title, the seller warrants good title, the absence of any interests or other liens on the goods, and that the goods are free of any patent, copyright, or trademark infringements.

- A seller may create an express warranty under the UCC by making a statement to the buyer regarding the goods, providing the buyer with a description of the goods, or providing the buyer with a sample or model of the goods.

- The UCC provides two implied warranties of quality: an implied warranty of merchantability and an implied warranty of fitness for a particular purpose. To be merchantable, the goods must conform to the contract description, be fit for the purposes for which it is intended, be of even kind, quality, and quantity, be adequately labeled, and conform to label descriptions. If a seller knows that a buyer has a particular purpose for purchasing a good and the buyer relies on the seller's skill or judgment in selecting a good, an implied warranty of fitness for a particular purpose may be created.

- It is not uncommon for a sales transaction to be affected by several warranties. Although warranties are generally compatible, there are occasions when they can be in conflict. The UCC provides that warranties in such situations will be construed as consistent and cumulative whenever possible.

- The UCC extends to designated third parties any express warranty made by the seller to a buyer. To allow the UCC to be consistent with other third-party beneficiary rules within a state, the UCC provides three alternative third-party beneficiary rules.

- When a buyer or seller breaches a contract for the sale of goods, the UCC provides the nonbreaching party with a number of remedies. Those remedies are designed to place the nonbreaching party in the same position as if the contract had been performed according to its terms. The seller and the buyer are allowed to seek incidental damages for recovery of those costs resulting from the breach. In addition, the buyer is allowed to recover consequential damages.

MANAGER'S ETHICAL DILEMMA

MEETING THE REQUIRED SPECIFICATIONS

Regis Tool and Machinery has been a respected producer of machine tools for more than fifty years. The company has manufactured a variety of equipment for major electrical and transportation companies worldwide. As part of its successful business strategy, the company employs only 150 workers, relying heavily on local subcontractors to do much of the detail work.

In March 1992, the company entered into a large, multiyear contract with a Japanese electrical supply company called Samsuo. The contract called for Regis to build several large, diesel-powered electrical generators and sell them to Samsuo. This was new work for Regis. To gain access to a supply of components, Regis encouraged a local entrepreneur to start a new business, called Modolo Electronics. Within five weeks, Modolo employed more than fifty people. Within eight weeks, it was to deliver its first components to Regis.

At about the same time Regis had encouraged the development of Modolo, the management of Samsuo had encouraged the development of a similar supplier. Unknown to the management of Regis, it was Samsuo's intention to begin by supplying these critical components. Then, if business was good, it would either begin to make the generator itself in the United States or attempt to buy out Regis.

In October 1992, Modolo delivered the first of the required components. Despite varying from the contract specifications in seemingly minor ways, the components were acceptable to the management of Regis. Regis, however, did inform Modolo that the quality had to improve to meet the required specifications.

After three months of deliveries, Samsuo began to complain about the Modolo components. It offered the components of "another" supplier (the fact that it was Samsuo's supplier was not known to Regis). Samsuo was able to demonstrate that the components more closely fit the required contract specifications.

Regis found itself in a difficult position. It had encouraged Modolo to develop but now was being forced to abandon the company. Modolo's attorneys informed management that technically Regis could cancel the contract because Modolo was supplying nonconforming goods. However, management knew that the nonconformity really did not impact the overall quality of the product. The customer, on the other hand, had stated that the Modolo nonconformity did affect the quality from its perspective. Samsuo had also made it clear that if Modolo was not replaced, it would cancel the overall contract.

QUESTIONS

What do you recommend that Regis management do? Is Modolo unethically exploiting a legal technicality for purposes entirely unrelated?

REVIEW AND DISCUSSION QUESTIONS

1. Define the following terms:

sales contracts	title
merchant	identification
warranty of title	perfect tender
merchantability	

2. Compare and contrast the following terms and concepts:
   a. output contract and requirements contract
   b. consequential damages and incidental damages
   c. implied warranty of merchantability and implied warranty of fitness for a particular purpose
   d. good faith and honesty in fact
   e. right of inspection and right of rejection
   f. cure and cover

■ CASE QUESTIONS

3. A seller of used steel pipe negotiated the sale of 30,000 feet of pipe at a fixed price with a buyer. In August, the seller mailed a written offer to the buyer. The buyer accepted the offer by mail. However, the buyer changed the final delivery date for the shipment of pipe from October 15 to December 15. Included with the acceptance was a check for $20,000 in partial payment. The seller deposited the check in its bank account. The seller then promptly sent the buyer a written confirmation of the agreement that contained the original delivery date of October 15 with a note that read, "We will work it out." The buyer received 22,937 feet of pipe in September and October. The seller then refused to ship any more pipe. The buyer sued the seller for breach of contract on the 7,063 feet of pipe not delivered by December 15. The seller argued that a contract existed only for the pipe actually received and not for the 30,000 feet because the buyer's acceptance did not conform to the delivery date in the offer. What result?

4. Roth went to the haristylist to have her hair bleached. She had been going to this stylist for more than seven years. The stylist proposed using a new product developed by Roux Laboratories. In the past, the stylist had used other Roux products with good results. However, the use of this new product severely damaged Roth's hair. The damage caused Roth embarrassment and distress until Roth's hair finally grew back several months later. The product's label stated that use of the product would not cause damage to hair. Roth sued both the stylist and Roux Laboratories, alleging negligence and breach of implied and express warranties. Did the product's performance breach a warranty? [*Roth* v. *Ray-Stel's Hair Stylists,* 18 Mass.App. Ct. 975, 470 N.E.2d 137 (1984)]

5. Community Television Services (CTS) contracted with Dresser Industries to design, construct, and install a 2,000-foot antenna tower in South Dakota. The price was $385,000. The contract contained technical specifications warranting that the tower would withstand winds of 120 mph on bare, flat surfaces. During the preliminary negotiations, Dresser had given to CTS a sales brochures that contained the following statements:

> Wind force creates the most critical loads to which a tower is normally subjected. When ice forms on the tower members, thereby increasing the surface area resisting the passage of wind, the load is increased. Properly designed towers will safely withstand the maximum wind velocities and ice loads to which they are likely to be subjected. Dresser . . . can make wind and ice load recommendations to you for your area based on U.S. Weather Bureau data. In the winter, loaded with ice and hammered repeatedly with gale force winds, these towers absorb some of the roughest punishment that towers take anywhere in the country . . . yet continue to give dependable, uninterrupted service.

The parties entered into a contract. The tower was built according to the contract's technical specifications. Later, the tower collapsed. The evidence indicated that it collapsed partly because of accumulated ice from a winter storm that produced winds of 80 mph. Is Dresser liable for breach of an express warranty?

6. In 1975, Nederlandse Draadindustrie (NDI) contracted to manufacture 1,180 metric tons of ½-inch steel strand for the Grand Pre-Stressed Corporation at a price of about $675 per ton. The strand is used to reinforce concrete. NDI was to deliver the strand over a seven-month period, and Grand agreed to pay for each shipment. Thereafter, Grand accepted deliveries of 221.113 tons and still

owed $57,960.03 for them when it repudiated the contract in May 1976. Of the 958.887 tons of strand that remained for delivery under the contract, NDI had already produced 317.891 tons and later sold them privately to other customers at prices averaging $608.47 per ton. At all times during 1975 and 1976, NDI had sufficient capacity to produce 12,500 tons of strand annually at an average cost of $394.57 per ton. NDI sued Grand for breach of contract and won. Can you calculate the damages under the UCC? Are there any damages? [*Nederlandse Draadindustrie Ndi B.V.* v. *Grand Pre-Stressed Corporation,* 466 F.Supp. 846, (E.D.N.Y. 1979)]

 7. ServBest Foods entered into a sales contract with Emessee. The contract called for Emessee to purchase 200,000 pounds of beef trimmings from ServBest at 52.5 cents per pound. ServBest delivered the warehouse receipts and the invoice for the beef trimmings to Emessee. The market price of beef trimmings then fell significantly, providing Emessee with the opportunity to buy the trimmings from another seller at a lower price. Emessee returned the warehouse receipts and invoice to ServBest and canceled the contract. ServBest sold the trimmings for 20.25 cents per pound and sued Emessee for damages for breach of contract plus incidental damages. Should Emessee be required to pay damages in this case? [*ServBest Foods, Inc.* v. *Emessee Industries, Inc.,* 37 Ill. Dec. 945, 403 N.E.2d 1 (1980)]

 8. In January 1974, T.W. Oil Company purchased fuel oil that was still at sea on the tanker *Khamsin.* After the purchase, T.W. Oil then entered into a contract for the sale of the oil to Consolidated Edison (ConEd). The contract called for a delivery date between January 24 and January 30 and for the oil to have a sulfur content of 0.5 percent. During its negotiations with ConEd, T.W. Oil learned that ConEd was authorized to use oils with sulfur contents up to 1.0 percent. ConEd also had the capability to mix oils containing more than 1.0 percent with oils containing less to maintain an average of 1.0 percent.

The *Khamsin* arrived on time. However, the oil tested at 0.92 percent sulfur content, 0.42 percent higher than specified in the contract. On February 14, ConEd rejected the shipment. T.W. Oil then offered ConEd a reduced price. On February 20, ConEd rejected the lower price offer. On February 21, T.W. Oil offered to cure by providing a substitute due to arrive on February 28. ConEd also rejected T.W. Oil's offer to cure. Was T.W. Oil's offer to cure properly rejected by ConEd? Was ConEd required to accept the substitute shipment tendered by T.W. Oil? [*T.W. Oil, Inc.* v. *Consolidated Edison Company,* 57 N.Y.2d 574, 457 N.Y. S.2d 458, 443 N.E.2d 932 (1982)]

■ BUSINESS POLICY QUESTIONS

9. Why would the UCC allow the true owner to reclaim his or her stolen goods from a good faith purchaser and then not allow a creditor of the seller to reclaim goods from the same purchaser?

10. Consider the following statements:

> This car has 10,000 miles on it, and we just mounted new radial tires on all four wheels.

> This is the best car for the money.

If made by a seller, does either statement create a warranty? Is there a difference?

ETHICS QUESTIONS

11. Joseph Steiner conducted extensive negotiations with representatives of the Mobil Oil Corporation to operate a service station. During these negotiations, Steiner made it very clear that he would not operate the service station unless Mobil gave him a 1.4-cent-per-gallon discount from the tank wagon price for a period of ten years. However, Mobil's standard dealer contract provided that Mobil could revoke or modify the discount at any time. A Mobil representative sent Steiner a letter guaranteeing him a 1.4-cent discount for ten years. Shortly thereafter, Mobil gave Steiner a package of forms that described their agreement. But unknown to Steiner, one of the forms reduced the discount to 0.5 cent per gallon. Without looking at the agreement, Steiner signed the contract modification. What result?

BUSINESS ORGANIZATIONS AND THE LAW OF AGENCY

CHAPTER 11

MANAGER'S LEGAL CHALLENGE

The Columbia Organic Chemical Company (COCC) leased four acres of land outside Columbia, South Carolina, in 1972. The landowners were told that COCC would store chemicals there used in its production processes. Three people affiliated with COCC formed South Carolina Recycling and Disposal Incorporated (SCRDI), which ran a hazardous waste operation on the land. Companies that needed to dispose of toxic wastes shipped their chemicals to SCRDI.

Thousands of drums of highly toxic materials were dumped on the land. No records were kept. The chemicals spilled on the ground and mixed together, causing fires and toxic fumes. Because of the dangers, the EPA and the South Carolina Department of Health and Environmental Control shut down the operation in 1978. Under the federal Superfund program, a cleanup of the land was ordered. Federal law requires the responsible parties to be sued by the EPA to recover the costs of the cleanup. The responsible parties were held to be the owners of the land; COCC, which leased the land; SCRDI, which leased the land from COCC; and the companies that sent their toxic waste to the facility. With millions to be paid, the parties blamed each other or claimed that they were not legally responsible because they were not parties to the activities.

In *U.S.* v. *SCRDI* (653 F.Supp. 984 (1985)) the court found each party legally responsible for the costs of cleaning up the mess. Environmental responsibility of each party arose from the party's agency or business organization relationship to the situation.

COCC claimed it was not responsible. SCRDI, which was set up by some COCC people, was responsible. The court found COCC liable because its agents (employees), including the vice president for the chemicals division, set up SCRDI to take care of chemical disposal activities. While there was no paperwork to show the linkage between COCC and SCRDI, COCC employees had the apparent authority as agents of COCC to engage in activities at SCRDI for the benefit of COCC. Since improper handling of hazardous chemicals is a tort, COCC was liable for the actions of its agents under the rule of respondeat superior.

Even though there was no written contract that formed a partnership or other formal venture between COCC and SCRDI, at law a joint venture existed. It was clear that agents of COCC, acting under apparent authority, did business with SCRDI for the benefit of COCC. Parties to joint ventures are mutually liable for harms caused by the venture. Therefore, COCC is responsible for the mess left by SCRDI.

Under federal law, companies that shipped chemicals to the improper disposal site are liable for cleanup costs. After EPA had closed the dump site, a company never involved in the dumping bought one of the companies that had been involved in sending chemical waste to the SCRDI site. The new corporation was sued for the cleanup costs. It claimed that when it bought the other company, the contract to buy it excluded any environmental liability, and the seller of the company swore that it had not operated in violation of any environmental law. The court held that regardless of the terms of the sale of the old company, the new corporation assumed the liabilities of the old corporation.

Here, the principles of agency and business organization tied parties to a very costly environmental action. This shows the importance of managers' being aware of the key responsibilities imposed by the law of agency and business organization so that they do not blunder into unexpected legal obligations.

This chapter discusses the common law of agency and the various forms of business organization. Since most business transactions or contracts can be performed by an agent, it is common practice for businesses to make extensive use of agency relationships. The agency relationship is a basic arrangement for much commercial activity around the world.

The chapter begins with a discussion of the nature of the agency relationship, how it is created, and the legal constraints imposed on its formation and functions. Next, the chapter discusses the agent's authority to act for the principal and how it affects the principal's liability for the contracts and torts of the agent. The chapter then discusses the ways an agency relationship can be terminated.

While the corporation is often considered to be synonymous with the term *business*, there are many other forms of business organization. After considering several factors, a business organizer may select the form of organization that provides the least costly way of conducting affairs. The type of organization selected can significantly influence a business's legal environment.

The chapter provides a general discussion of the dominant forms of business organization, including sole proprietorships, partnerships, limited partnerships, and corporations. It then considers alternative forms that may have important applications in special circumstances, including joint ventures, joint stock companies, syndicates, and cooperatives. Finally, the chapter considers several factors that may influence the choice of business organization.

THE AGENCY RELATIONSHIP

According to *Black's Law Dictionary,* an *agency relationship* involves the following:

> An employment [of an agent] for the purpose of representation in establishing legal relations between a principal and third parties.

An agency relationship is created whenever a person or company—the *agent*—agrees to act on behalf of, and for, and to be subject to the control of another person or company—the *principal.* Through the agency relationship, the agent becomes a business representative of the principal. The agent may negotiate the terms of and legally bind the principal to contracts with third parties as long as he or she is acting within the scope of the authority granted by the principal. In dealing with third parties—normally the customers or suppliers of the principal—the agent is granted authority to act for and in the name of and in place of the principal. The typical agency relationship is compared with the typical two-party business contract in Figure 11–1.

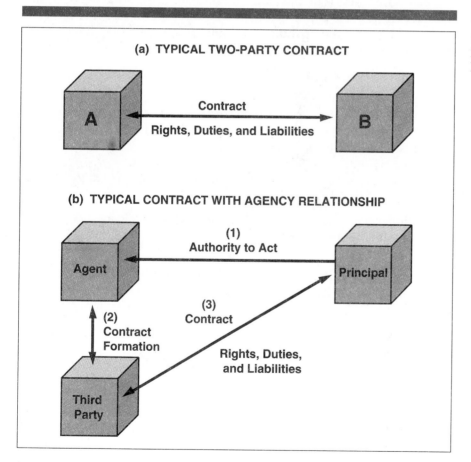

FIGURE 11–1

Comparison of an Agency Relationship to a Contract Relationship

■ CREATING AN AGENCY

An agency is usually formed by the voluntary consent and agreement of the parties. The principal and agent may establish the agency by an oral or written contract, but a contract is not generally required. However, in several instances, a written contract is required by law. For example, where the agency is to be longer than one year or is for the sale of land, many states require that the agency be in writing. However, most agencies are established by consensual agreements that are not contracts. The basis of the relationship is that the agent acts for the benefit of the principal and is subject to the principal's control.

Generally, whatever business activity a person may do legally may also be conducted through an agent. However, an agency may be void or voidable if the principal lacks contractual capacity or the purpose of the agency relationship is illegal or unlawful.

■ PRINCIPAL'S DUTIES TO AN AGENT

The law of agency places primary emphasis on the duties the agent owes to the principal. This is understandable, since the acts central to the agency relationship are to be performed by the agent. Nevertheless, the principal does owe the agent certain duties. Basically, unless the parties have agreed otherwise, the principal is required to do the following:

1. Cooperate with the agent so that the purpose of the agency can be fulfilled.
2. Pay the agent for services rendered—either the amount agreed or an amount that is customary for such services.
3. Reimburse the agent for reasonable expenses incurred in the course of performing duties.
4. Provide safe working conditions and meet any legal obligations, such as provide insurance, if required by law.
5. Indemnify (pay back) the agent for legal liabilities incurred while performing the duties of the agency.

■ AGENT'S DUTIES TO THE PRINCIPAL

The agent's duties to the principal arise from the fact that the agent is a *fiduciary* of the principal. That is, the agent occupies a position of trust, honesty, and confidence with respect to the principal. In addition to whatever specific responsibilities the principal and agent agree on in establishing the agency, the law imposes fiduciary duties upon an agent: loyalty, obedience, reasonable care and performance, accounting, and notification.

Duty of Loyalty.   An agent is required to meet a higher standard of conduct than that ordinarily imposed upon parties to business dealings. This *duty of loyalty* requires the agent to place the principal's interests before the agent's personal interests or those of any third party. Thus, it would be a violation of this duty if the agent also represented another person whose interests were in conflict with those of the principal. Suppose that a sales agent represents an electronics manufacturer and the agent's primary responsibility in the agency is to locate potential customers for the manufacturer's products and to attempt to arrange sales. If the agent also represents a competing manufacturer, there would be a violation of the duty of loyalty to the first manufacturer. Of course, the agent could legally represent both manufacturers with their consent.

Duty of Obedience.   An agent is under a duty to perform all instructions provided by the principal as closely as possible. The agent violates this *duty of obedience* and is liable to the principal by ignoring the principal's instructions. Of course, in an emergency, the agent has the right to use good sense to do what is necessary. An agent has no obligation to engage in illegal activity on behalf of a principal that would lead to personal liability. Nor is it a breach of this duty if the agent refuses to engage in behavior that would be considered unethical. A sales clerk in a sporting goods store who refuses to inform customers falsely (as instructed by the principal) that sleeping bags are filled with goose down, when in fact they are filled with a less expensive mixture, would not be in violation of this duty.

Duty of Reasonable Care and Performance.   An agent is required to exercise *reasonable care* and skill in the *performance* of duties. Unless the agent has claimed to be an expert in the particular subject matter of the agency relationship or to possess a special skill as in the case of an attorney or a broker, the duty is to perform responsibilities with the degree of care that a reasonable person would exercise under the circumstances. An accountant employed as an agent to prepare an income tax return who failed to take advantage of a legal tax deduction would violate this duty of reasonable care.

Duty to Account.   An agent acquires a *duty to account* for the funds and property of the principal that have been entrusted to or come into possession of the agent. This does not mean that an agent must be a bookkeeper or an accountant, but that the agent must keep a record of all money or property received in the course of the agency. The agent must be able to show where money and property come from and go to. An agent must also avoid mixing personal funds with funds of the principal. If funds are mixed without the principal's permission, a violation of the duty to account has occurred whether or not the principal is harmed in any way.

Duty To Notify.   Finally, the agent is under a duty to *notify* the principal of all facts and events relevant to the agency. Suppose that Clayton employs Pokorny as his agent to sell 500 acres of farmland at a given price per acre. Suppose that Pokorny finds that in the next several months, the farmland will likely increase in value because of a major new highway planned to be constructed nearby. Pokorny is under a duty to notify Clayton of this information so that Clayton can decide whether he still wants Pokorny to proceed according to the original instructions.

AGENT'S AUTHORITY TO ACT FOR THE PRINCIPAL

An agent's ability to transact business on behalf of a principal depends in large part upon the scope of authority given to the agent by the principal. The scope of an agent's authority is determined from the oral or written expressions of the principal, the principal's conduct, or the customs of the business in which the agent is employed. An agent can possess two general classifications of authority: actual authority and apparent authority. Although each arises in a different fashion, both may be present at the same time.

◼ ACTUAL AUTHORITY

Actual authority is sometimes referred to as real authority because it is authority given by the principal to the agent. Actual authority can be divided into express and implied authority. If, for example, the owner of an automobile franchise told the sales personnel to give a 10 percent discount on all compact car sales, the sales personnel would have *express authority* to do so. If a landowner authorizes a real estate agent to find a buyer for some property, the landowner need not tell the agent each step that could be taken to try to locate a buyer. Thus, even though the parties never explicitly discussed the matter, the agent would have the *implied authority* to post a "For Sale" sign on the property, advertise the offer for sale in a newspaper, and take prospective purchasers onto the property to inspect it unless instructed by the principal to the contrary. In either case, actual authority confers upon an agent the power and the right to change the principal's legal status.

◼ APPARENT AUTHORITY

On occasion, principals can be bound by unauthorized actions of agents if the agent appears to have authority to act. Unlike actual authority, which is given by the principal to the agent, *apparent authority* results from a third party's reasonable perceptions from the principal's behavior. That is, apparent authority arises when the principal creates an appearance of authority in an agent that leads a third party to conclude reasonably that the agent has actual authority to perform certain acts for the principal. We see an example of this in the situation described in the Manager's Legal Challenge feature that opened this chapter. Note, however, that apparent authority cannot be created by the agent. It can exist only when the principal acts in such a way as to lead a reasonably prudent third person to believe that the agent has authority to act for the principal.

LIABILITY FOR CONTRACTS AND TORTS

The fundamental purpose of an agency is to provide the principal with a legal means to expand business opportunities and activities. That purpose is accomplished by authorizing agents to enter into contracts on behalf of the principal. The principal is thus able to do business in several places simultaneously.

CONTRACT LIABILITY OF DISCLOSED AND PARTIALLY DISCLOSED PRINCIPALS

As illustrated in Figure 11–2(a), a principal is liable to a third party for a contract made by the agent if the agent has actual authority to so act on behalf of the principal. The agent under such circumstances will have no contractual liability if either the principal or the third party does not perform. Suppose, that Cook instructs Chan, her agent, to purchase a vehicle for her use. Suppose further that Chan enters into a contract for such a vehicle with a third party who knows that Chan is acting as an agent. Cook is bound by the contract and must honor it. The third-party seller of the vehicle is entitled to sue Cook if she fails to perform according to the agreement made on her behalf by Chan.

In the event the principal's liability is based on the apparent authority of the agent, the agent has violated the duty of obedience to the principal. As a consequence, and as illustrated in Figure 11–2(b), the agent is liable to the principal for any losses incurred due to the agent's exceeding his or her authority. To illustrate, suppose in the preceding example that Cook did not provide Chan with express authority to purchase a vehicle. Suppose further that Cook's conduct in the past has led third parties to believe that Chan has such authority. If Chan enters into a contract for a vehicle, Cook is bound by it, but Chan must indemnify Cook for losses incurred as a consequence.

LIABILITY FOR TORTS OF THE AGENT

In addition to creating contractual liability on behalf of a principal, an agent can create tort liability. The principal can be liable for the torts of an agent if the agent's tort was authorized by the principal or was unauthorized but occurred within the scope of the agent's employment. In general, if an agent commits a tort outside the scope of employment, the agent is liable to the third party for damages incurred.

Principal's Liability.   It is obvious that a principal is liable for torts committed by an agent that are ordered by the principal. If Mike the building contractor tells Marty the bricklayer to skimp on concrete and use low-quality bricks, and that later causes a building to collapse, Mike the contractor is liable in tort for any injuries that are suffered as a result of the shoddy work done by his agent Marty.

Under the rule of *vicarious liability,* a principal can also be liable for the unauthorized torts of an agent. A principal is likely to be liable for the unauthorized intentional or negligent torts of an agent if the agent was acting within the scope of employment. The rule of law imposing vicarious liability upon an innocent principal for the torts of an agent acting within the scope of employment is known as *respondeat superior.* This doctrine has been justified on the grounds that the principal is in a better position to

FIGURE 11–2

Contract Liabilities If Principal
Is Disclosed or Partially
Disclosed

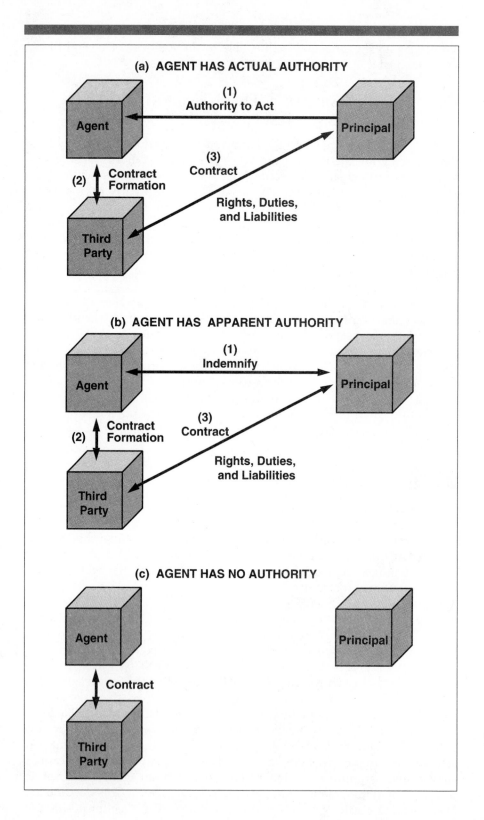

both protect the public from such torts (through careful selection of agents) and compensate those injured (through its ability to acquire insurance).

The Agent's Liability.   An agent may be required to indemnify the principal for damages the principal has to pay to the wronged party as a consequence of the agent's unauthorized torts. This issue is discussed in the *Biggs* case. In most cases, however, the agent is unable to reimburse the principal, who must then bear the brunt of the liability.

BIGGS v. SURREY BROADCASTING CO.

Court of Appeals of Oklahoma, Division 2
811 P.2d 111 (1991)

Case Background
Susan Kelly worked for Greg Biggs, sales manager for Surrey Broadcasting at radio station KATT-FM in Oklahoma City. Biggs fired Kelly in 1985. Kelly then sued Surrey for wrongful discharge in retaliation for her resisting Biggs' sexual harassment. Biggs was then fired by Surrey. Biggs admitted that he appeared naked in front of Kelly at a hotel when they were at a business meeting together and that there were other incidents. Surrey paid Kelly $65,000 to settle her lawsuit. Biggs then sued Surrey demanding that he be paid severance pay and be paid for the value of his lost sick leave and vacation time. Surrey rejected Biggs's demands and countersued Biggs for indemnification for the costs it incurred as a result of the Kelly lawsuit.

Case Decision
The appeals court upheld the decision of the trial court that Biggs would get no severance pay or pay for lost sick leave because he was terminated from employment for gross misconduct. However, since company policy promised payment of lost vacation days, Surrey did have to pay Biggs for the value of that time. The appeals court reversed the trial court on the issue of indemnification, ruling that Surrey could sue Biggs to recover its costs. Assuming the payment from Surrey to Kelly was reasonable, Biggs, an agent of Surrey the principal, was responsible for indemnification to Surrey due to his tort, which imposed vicarious liability on his principal.

Managerial Considerations
The issue of sexual harassment is covered in Chapter 13. The point here is that while companies cannot always prevent their employees from committing illegal acts for which the employer may be held responsible, they can reduce the likelihood of such instances by making sure that all employees (agents) have the consequences of such actions made clear. For example, one of the most costly tort actions for many companies result from accidents of drivers. Managers have found they can reduce the number of accidents and, therefore, their vicarious liability for torts by investing in driver education, monitoring driving practices, making it clear that bad drivers will be fired, and not giving employees incentives to drive fast.

As a rule, the principal is not liable for the torts of an agent when the tort is both unauthorized and outside the scope of employment. In such cases, the agent alone is liable to the wronged party. More difficult to decide, however, are those cases where the agent was not clearly doing his or her job at the time of the tort but may have been engaged in an authorized action, such as carelessly driving a company car when going to lunch.

TERMINATION OF AN AGENCY

The agency relationship is largely consensual. Thus, when the principal withdraws or when consent otherwise ends, the agency is *terminated*. Once an agency is terminated, the agent's actual authority to act for the principal ceases. It may be necessary, however, to give notice of the termination to some and constructive notice to other third parties to end the agent's apparent authority.

While many different events can terminate agencies, they are most commonly ended by mutual agreement of the parties, by one of the parties, through lapse of time, or by the fulfillment of the agency's purpose. An agency relationship is terminated *by operation of law* without any required action by the principal or the agent if either the principal or the agent dies, the subject matter of the agreement is destroyed, or the principal or the agent declares bankruptcy.

MAJOR FORMS OF BUSINESS ORGANIZATION

The forms of business organization used most frequently are the sole proprietorship, partnership, limited partnership, and corporation. Less frequently employed forms include joint ventures, joint stock companies, cooperatives, and syndicates. Every state has laws concerning some aspects of corporation and partnership formation, operation, and dissolution, but business organizations are primarily created by actions and contracts. The statutory rules are not onerous. Depending upon the business, each of the forms has distinct advantages and disadvantages when compared to another.

■ A STATISTICAL OVERVIEW

As Table 11–1 shows, there are more than 18 million businesses in the United States. Sole proprietorships account for more than 70 percent of U.S. businesses. Despite their greater numbers, however, sole proprietor-

TABLE 11–1
BUSINESSES BY MAJOR FORMS OF ORGANIZATION, 1970–1987

Item	Unit	1970	1975	1980	1985	1987
Total number	1,000	8,371	10,318	13,023	16,920	18,351
Business receipts	$billion	1,997	3,540	6,869	8,939	10,207
Net income	$billion	106	191	302	310	428
Proprietorships, number (nonfarm)	1,000	5,770	7,221	8,932	11,929	13,091
Business receipts	$billion	199	274	411	540	611
Net income	$billion	30	40	55	79	105
Partnership, number	1,000	936	1,073	1,380	1,714	1,648
Business receipts	$billion	92	146	286	349	411
Net income	$billion	10	8	8	−9	−5
Corporations, number	1,000	1,665	2,024	2,711	3,277	3,612
Business receipts	$billion	1,706	3,120	6,172	8,050	9,185
Net income	$billion	66	143	239	240	328

SOURCE: U.S. Statistical Abstract (1991), based on tax returns.

ships account for only about 6 percent of all business receipts. Sole proprietorships are principally made up of small businesses, such as hardware stores, beauty shops, dry cleaners, and restaurants. In contrast, corporations are far fewer in number (less than 20 percent of the total) but account for over 90 percent of all business receipts. Clearly, most large businesses in the United States are corporations. Finally, partnerships provide about 4 percent of all business receipts while making up a little less than 10 percent of all U.S. businesses.

■ SOLE PROPRIETORSHIPS

A person conducting business for himself or herself is termed a *sole proprietor;* the business organization is termed a *sole proprietorship.* The sole proprietorship is the oldest and simplest form of business organization. As a sole proprietor, a person may simply begin to do business without formality in those enterprises that do not require a government license or permit. The proprietor owns all or most of the business property and has sole responsibility for the control, liabilities, and management of the business.

In a sole proprietorship, legally and practically *the owner is the business,* and any capital must come from the owner's own resources or from borrowed resources. The availability of limited alternatives for raising capital is perhaps the greatest disadvantage for most sole proprietorships. Because the profits of the business are taxed to the owner personally, no formal tax return in the business's name is required. The operational and recordkeeping formalities of the business are at the owner's discretion as long as the various taxing authorities are satisfied.

■ GENERAL PARTNERSHIPS

A *general partnership* is a business made up of two or more persons (called *partners* or *general partners*) who have entered into an agreement, either express or implied, to carry on a business venture for a profit. The partners are the co-owners of the business and share control over the business's operations and profits. Many attorneys, doctors and dentists, and small retail stores are organized as general partnerships.

At common law, a partnership was generally not treated as an independent legal entity. As a consequence, a legal action could not be brought by or against the business. Rather, the partners making up the partnership had to sue or be sued individually. A number of states, however, now provide that for certain purposes, a partnership may be treated as an independent entity (e.g., ownership in property). Thus, a partnership may sue or be sued and collect judgments in its own name. In addition, the federal courts provide that in a variety of circumstances, a partnership will be treated as a legal entity.

Partnership law has its origins in the common law. It is now codified in the *Uniform Partnership Act* (UPA), which has been adopted in forty-eight states, and governs partnerships and partnership relations. The UPA dictates the operation of partnerships where the partnership agreement is silent or where there is no formal agreement among the partners.

Formation of a Partnership.   A partnership can begin with a simple oral agreement between two or more people to do business as partners or with a tacit agreement that may be inferred from the conduct of the partners as they do business together. Typically, however, the parties formalize their relationship by a written partnership agreement expressly providing how the partnership business will be conducted and profits will be shared. Any person having legal capacity to enter a contract may also enter a partnership agreement and become a partner in a business venture.

The written partnership agreement will usually specify such matters as the business name, relative ownership interests of the partners, the partners' responsibilities within the partnership, method of accounting, duration of the partnership, and procedures for the partnership's dissolution. Exhibit 11–1 is an example of a partnership agreement. In the absence of specific agreement, the UPA will specify and govern the relationship of the parties.

Relationship of the Parties.   A partnership is a relationship based on extraordinary trust and loyalty. As a consequence, the law specifies that the partners owe a *fiduciary duty* to one another. That fiduciary relationship requires that each partner act in good faith for the benefit of the partnership. As in the fiduciary relationship between a principal and agents, the partners must place their individual interests below those of the partnership. Partners, as Justice Cardozo once said, "owe to one another . . . the duty of finest loyalty."

Unless otherwise specified by contract, the basic rule in a partnership is that each partner has an equal voice in the management and conduct of partnership affairs. Regardless of the size of the interest in the partnership, each partner has one vote in managerial decisions. Except in the case of major managerial decisions that require unanimous consent of the partners—such as decisions to change the nature of the partnership's business, to admit new partners, or to sell the business—a majority vote is controlling. In most large partnerships, however, the partners usually agree to delegate day-to-day management responsibilities to one person or group, often referred to as the managing partner or partners.

Termination of the Partnership.   A change in the relationship of the partners showing an unwillingness or an inability to continue with the business of the partnership will bring about termination of the partnership. A complete termination comes about only after the partnership has been dissolved and its affairs have been wound up. The *dissolution* of the partnership occurs when an event takes place that precludes the partners from engaging in any new business. The *winding up* of partnership affairs involves completing any unfinished business of the partnership and then collecting and distributing the partnership's assets.

The dissolution of the partnership can be brought about in several ways. Any change in the composition of the partners will result in a new partnership and the dissolution of the old one. Thus, the withdrawal or death of a partner will cause the partnership to be dissolved. Similarly, the partnership will be dissolved if a partner is found to be bankrupt. In winding up the partnership's affairs, the partners have a duty to each other to disclose fully all financial aspects of the partnership.

EXHIBIT 11–1

Example of a Basic Partnership Agreement

[Name]
PARTNERSHIP AGREEMENT

This agreement, made and entered into as of the [Date], by and among [Names] (hereinafter collectively sometimes referred to as ''Partners'').

WITNESSETH:

Whereas, the Parties hereto desire to form a General Partnership (hereinafter referred to as the ''Partnership'') for the term and upon the conditions hereinafter set forth;

Now, therefore, in consideration of the mutual covenants hereinafter contained, it is agreed by and among the Parties hereto as follows:

Article I: BASIC STRUCTURE

1.1 Form. The Parties hereby form a General Partnership pursuant to the Laws of [Name of State].

1.2 Name. The business of the Partnership shall be conducted under the name of [Name].

1.3 Place of Business. The principal office and place of business of the Partnership shall be located at [Describe], or such other place as the Partners may from time to time designate.

1.4 Term. The Partnership shall commence on [Date], and shall continue for [Number] years, unless earlier terminated in the following manner:

(a) By the completion of the purpose intended, or

(b) Pursuant to this Agreement, or

(c) By applicable [State] law, or

(d) By death, insanity, bankruptcy, retirement, withdrawal, resignation, expulsion, or disability of all of the then Partners.

1.5 Purpose—General. The purpose for which the Partnership is organized is _____ .

Article II: FINANCIAL ARRANGEMENTS

2.1 Initial Contributions of Partners. Each Partner has contributed to the initial capital of the Partnership property in the amount and form indicated on Schedule A attached hereto and made a part hereof. Capital contributions to the Partnership shall not earn interest. An individual capital account shall be maintained for each Partner.

2.2 Additional Capital Contributions. If at any time during the existence of the Partnership it shall become necessary to increase the capital with which the said Partnership is doing business, then (upon the vote of the Managing Partner(s)) each party to this Agreement shall contribute to the capital of this Partnership within _____ days notice of such need in an amount according to his then Percentage Share of Capital as called for by the Managing Partner(s).

2.3 Percentage Share of Profits and Capital. (a) The Percentage Share of Profits and Capital of each Partner shall be (unless otherwise modified by the terms of this Agreement) as follows:

Names	Initial Percentage Share of Profits and Capital
_____	_____
_____	_____

2.4 Interest. No interest shall be paid on any contribution to the capital of the Partnership.

2.5 Return of Capital Contributions. No Partner shall have the right to demand the return of his capital contributions except as herein provided.

(continued)

EXHIBIT 11–1

Example of a Basic Partnership Agreement   *(continued)*

2.6 Rights of Priority. Except as herein provided, the individual Partners shall have no right to any priority over each other as to the return of capital contributions except as herein provided.

2.7 Distributions. Distributions to the Partners of net operating profits of the Partnership, as hereinafter defined, shall be made at (least monthly/at such times as the Managing Partner(s) shall reasonably agree.) Such distributions shall be made to the Partners simultaneously.

2.8 Compensation. No Partner shall be entitled to receive any compensation from the Partnership, nor shall any Partner receive any drawing account from the Partnership.

Article III: MANAGEMENT

3.1 Managing Partners. The Managing Partner(s) shall be [Names or "all partners"].

3.2 Voting. All Managing Partner(s) shall have the right to vote as to the management and conduct of the business of the Partnership according to their then Percentage Share of [Capital/Income]. Except as otherwise herein set forth, a majority of such [Capital/Income] shall control.

Article IV: DISSOLUTION

4.1 Dissolutions. In the event that the Partnership shall hereafter be dissolved for any reason whatsoever, a full and general account of its assets, liabilities and transactions shall at once be taken. Such assets may be sold and turned into cash as soon as possible and all debts and other amounts due the Partnership collected. The proceeds thereof shall thereupon be applied as follows:

(a) To discharge the debts and liabilities of the Partnership and the expenses of liquidation.

(b) To pay each Partner or his legal representative any unpaid salary, drawing account, interest or profits to which he shall then be entitled and, in addition, to repay to any Partner his capital contributions in excess of his original capital contribution.

(c) To divide the surplus, if any, among the Partners or their representatives as follows:

   (1) First (to the extent of each Partner's then capital account) in proportion to their then capital accounts.

   (2) Then according to each Partner's then Percentage Share of Capital/Income.

4.2 Right To Demand Property. No Partner shall have the right to demand and receive property in kind for his distribution.

Article V: MISCELLANEOUS

5.1 Accounting Year, Books, Statements. The Partnership's fiscal year shall commence on January 1 of each year and shall end on December 31 of each year. Full and accurate books of account shall be kept at such place as the Managing Partner(s) may from time to time designate, showing the condition of the business and finances of the Partnership; and each Partner shall have access to such books of account and shall be entitled to examine them at any time during ordinary business hours.

5.2 Arbitration. Any controversy or claim arising out of or relating to this Agreement shall only be settled by arbitration in accordance with the rules of the American Arbitration Association, one Arbitrator, and shall be enforceable in any court having competent jurisdiction.

Witnesses   **Partners**

_____   _____

_____   _____

Dated: _____

■ LIMITED PARTNERSHIP

A limited partnership is a special form of partnership. Like a general partnership, a *limited partnership* is a business made up of two or more persons (called *partners*) who have entered into an agreement to carry on a business venture for a profit. Unlike a general partnership, however, not all the partners involved in a limited partnership have unlimited personal liability for the debts of the business venture.

Formation of a Limited Partnership.   Every state provides by statute for the formation of limited partnerships. All but two states use some form of the *Uniform Limited Partnership Act.* Partners are required to execute a written agreement—called a *certificate of limited partnership*—and file it with the appropriate state official, often the secretary of state. The Uniform Limited Partnership Act requires that the certificate contain the following information:

1. Name of the business.
2. Type or character of the business.
3. Address of an agent who is designated to receive legal process.
4. Names and addresses of each general and limited partner.
5. Contributions (cash and property) each partner has made and any additional contributions they will make.
6. Duration of the limited partnership.
7. The rights for any personnel changes in the partnership and the continuance of the partnership upon those changes.
8. The proportion of the partnership's profits or other compensation that each partner is entitled to receive.

In addition, the parties to the limited partnership agreement may agree to bind themselves in ways not required by the certificate. Exhibit 11–2 is an example of a limited partnership certificate.

Relationship of the Parties.   A limited partnership consists of at least one *general partner* and one or more *limited partners.* The general partners are treated by the law in the same manner as general partners in a general partnership. They have sole responsibility for managing the business and are personally liable to the partnership's creditors.

The limited partners are investors who do not (and may not) participate in the management of the business. Although they have the same rights as the general partners to see the partnership books and participate in the dissolution of the business, limited partners are not liable for the debts or torts of the limited partnership beyond their capital contributions. Limited partners lose their limited liability, and become general partners, by taking an active role in the management of the business. Hence, limited partners must not take control of the firm, contribute services to the business, or allow their names to appear in the name of the business.

Just as in general partnerships, all partners, limited or general, in a limited partnership have a fiduciary obligation to one another. This

EXHIBIT 11–2 ▰▰▰▰▰▰▰▰▰▰▰▰▰▰▰

Example of a Certificate of Limited Partnership

CERTIFICATE OF FORMATION OF LIMITED PARTNERSHIP

The undersigned, being desirous of forming a Limited Partnership under the Act of _____ , entitled "The Uniform Limited Partnership Act," hereby make and sign the following certificate for that purpose:

  1. **Name.** The name under which the Partnership is to be conducted is _____ .
  2. **Purpose.** The purpose of the Partnership shall be to [describe].
  3. **Location.** The location of the Partnership's principal place of business is _____ .
  4. **Partners.** The names and places of residence of the General and Limited Partners are:

_____	**General Partner**	**(Address)**
_____	**General Partner**	**(Address)**
_____	**Limited Partner**	**(Address)**
_____	**Limited Partner**	**(Address)**

  5. **Term.** The Partnership shall continue for an indefinite term.

  6. **Initial Contributions.** The Limited Partners have contributed the following cash to the Partnership:

_____   _____

_____   _____

  7. **Additional Contributions.** Each Limited Partner may make any additional contributions to the capital of the Partnership as may from time to time be agreed upon by the General Partners.
  8. **Withdrawals.** Each Limited Partner may make those withdrawals from his capital account as may from time to time be agreed upon by the General Partners.
  9. **Profits.** By reason of their contributions the Limited Partners shall receive the following percentages of the net profits of the Partnership:

_____   _____

_____   _____

  10. **Dissolution.** In the event of the retirement, death, or insanity of a General Partner, the remaining Partners shall have the right to continue the business of the Partnership under the same name by themselves or in conjunction with any other person or persons they may select.

  In witness whereof, we have hereunto set our hands and seals this _____ day of _____ , 19__ .

_____	_____
Limited Partner	**General Partner**
_____	_____
Limited Partner	**General Partner**

Witnesses:

_____

_____

STATE OF _____   County of _____

_____ and _____ , being duly sworn according to law, depose and certify that they are the General Partners named in the foregoing certificate and that the facts set forth therein are true and correct.

_____

_____

means all partners must be open and honest in all business dealings relevant to the partnership. Since limited partners are required to be passive investors, problems can arise where the general partner takes advantage of their lack of knowledge of the details of the operation, as the following case illustrates.

REMENCHIK v. WHITTINGTON

Court of Appeals of Texas, 14th District
757 S.W.2d 836 (1988)

Case Background
Remenchik and others were limited partners in Corpus Project I, Ltd., a limited partnership formed to build a six-story atrium office building in Corpus Christi, Texas. The limited partners contributed the capital to build the building in exchange for 48 percent of the profits generated. Whittington, the general partner of Corpus Project I and president of Whitco Development Corporation, was given 52 percent of the profits from the building project in exchange for the contribution of his services to get the building built and then leased or sold. The building, which cost $2,518,817, was built by Evans, a friend of Whittington. After seven years of almost no profits, the limited partners audited the books of Corpus Project I and discovered that Whittington had overpaid Evans by $275,000. Investigation revealed that Evans had paid $150,000 of that back to Whittington and Whitco. The limited partners sued Evans, the contractor, for fraud and Whittington, the general partner, for fraud and for breach of fiduciary duty. Evans argued that he was not liable because he was an agent of Whittington, his principal, and hence, he had acted within the scope of his agency.

Case Decision
The court held Evans and Whittington jointly and severally liable for the $275,000. Whittington violated his fiduciary duty to the limited partners and was personally liable to them for the damages. The fact that he did this through his corporation, Whitco, is irrelevant. Evans was liable because he was an agent of the limited partnership, not just of Whittington, and he had conspired with Whittington to defraud the principal. Since Whittington had violated his fiduciary duty to the limited partners, he could not claim to have been acting on their behalf in his dealing with Evans.

Managerial Considerations
Fraud and breaches of fiduciary duty are not protected by a web of complicated business organizations that are used to try to shield the guilty parties. However, this case shows how difficult it can be for partners to know whether their partners, on whom they must rely, are being honest. This fraud could easily have gone unnoticed. It is often embarrassing for partners to call in auditors to look at the books to try to uncover the self-dealing of other partners. If the general partner had known up front that the books would be reviewed by an expert, this situation might never have arisen.

Termination of a Limited Partnership.   A limited partnership is terminated in much the same way as a general partnership. Events that affect a general partner and would bring about the dissolution of a general partnership will also dissolve a limited partnership. Thus, the bankruptcy of a general partner would dissolve a limited partnership, although the bankruptcy of a limited partner usually would not.

As in the dissolution of a general partnership, the business continues to operate while it is winding up. The business may not enter into any new commitments but must complete all existing commitments before the partnership's dissolution. In the final dispersal of limited partnership assets, creditors come before partners. The limited partners receive their share of the profits and their capital contributions before general partners receive anything, unless the partnership agreement holds otherwise.

◼ CORPORATIONS

When most people think of a business, they think of the *corporation*. Most large, well-known businesses—such as Exxon, Coca-Cola, IBM, and Ford

Motor Company—are corporations. Although businesses have produced and traded goods for thousands of years, the modern corporation is a more recent development.

The modern corporation was developed in the United States during the late 1700s. State governments drew on their English heritage and issued *corporate charters* to selected businesses. Because the charter usually contained some special privilege, there was intense competition in the state legislature to decide who received charters. A charter might, for example, give a business the exclusive privilege of operating a toll bridge over a river or having the only bank in a town. Hence, monopoly power was associated with early corporate charters.

It was not until the late 1800s that the first "liberal" *general incorporation statute* was enacted. That act established a simple procedure for incorporating a business. Incorporation was thereby made available to virtually all businesses regardless of their field of operation or size.

The Corporation as a Legal Entity.   Unlike sole proprietorships and, in most instances, partnerships, the corporation is a *legal entity*. It is recognized under both federal and state law as a "person" and enjoys many of the rights and privileges accorded U.S. citizens. Corporations are thus entitled to most constitutional protections, including free speech, equal protection under the law, and protections against unreasonable searches and seizures. As a person, a corporation has the right of access to the courts as an entity that may sue and be sued. However, although the officers and employees of a corporation enjoy the privilege against self-incrimination under the Fifth Amendment, the corporation itself does not.

Method of Creation.   Every state has a general incorporation statute that sets forth a procedure for the incorporation of a business. Although the procedures for incorporation vary among the states, the basic requirements are similar. In general, the corporation's *articles of incorporation* along with an application must be filed with the appropriate officer of the state. (Exhibit 11–3 is an example of articles of incorporation.) The articles of incorporation must generally provide the following:

1. Name of the corporation.
2. Address of the corporation and name of its registered agent.
3. Purpose of the business.
4. The class(es) of stock to be issued and their par value.
5. Names and mailing addresses of the incorporators.

After reviewing the corporation's application for completeness, the state issues a *certificate of incorporation*. As a rule, the incorporators of the business will wait until the state has issued the certificate before holding their first organizational meeting. At that meeting, the incorporators will elect a board of directors, enact the corporation's bylaws (the rules that regulate and govern the internal operations of the corporation), and issue the corporation's stock. The shareholders, directors, and officers of the corporation are required to abide by the *bylaws* in conducting corporate business

EXHIBIT 11–3 ▉▉▉

Example of Articles of Incorporation

CERTIFICATE OF INCORPORATION

OF

_____ **CORPORATION**

1. **Name.** The name of the Corporation is _____ Corporation.

2. **Registered Office and Registered Agent.** The address of the Corporation's registered office in Delaware is _____ Street in the City of _____ and County of _____ , and the name of its registered agent at such address _____ .

3. **Purposes.** The purpose of the Corporation is to engage in any lawful act or activity for which Corporations may be now or hereafter organized under the General Corporation Law of Delaware.

4. **Capital Stock (Providing for Two Classes of Stock, One Voting and One Nonvoting).** The total number of shares of all classes of stock which the Corporation shall have authority to issue is _____ , all of which are to be without par value. _____ of such shares shall be Class A voting shares and _____ of such shares shall be Class B nonvoting shares. The Class A shares and the Class B shares shall have identical rights except that the Class B shares shall not entitle the holder thereof to vote on any matter unless specifically required by law.

5. **Incorporators.** The names and mailing addresses of the incorporators are:

Name	Mailing Address
_____	_____
_____	_____
_____	_____

6. **Regulatory Provisions.** [The Corporations may insert additional provisions for the management of the business and for the conduct of the affairs of the Corporation, and creating, defining, limiting, and regulating the powers of the Corporation, the Directors and the shareholders, or any class of shareholders.]

7. **Personal Liability.** The shareholders shall be liable for the debts of the Corporation in the proportion that their stock bears to the total outstanding stock of the Corporation.

8. **Amendment.** The Corporation reserves the right to amend, alter, change or repeal any provision contained in the Certificate of INCORPORATION, in the manner now or hereafter prescribed by statute, and all rights conferred upon shareholders herein are granted subject to this reservation.

We, the undersigned, being all of the incorporations above named, for the purpose of forming a Corporation pursuant to the General Corporation Law of Delaware, sign and acknowledge this Certificate of Incorporation this _____ day of _____ , 19 __ .

Acknowledgement

STATE OF_____
County of_____

On this _____ day of _____ , 19 __, before me personally came _____ , one of the persons who signed the foregoing certificate of incorporation, known to me personally to be such, and acknowledged that the said certificate is his act and deed and that the facts stated therein are true.

_____

Notary Public

[seal]

activities. Of course, the bylaws must not conflict with the corporation's articles of incorporation.

Relationship of the Parties.   A corporation consists of three distinct groups of individuals: the shareholders, the board of directors, and the officers. Each shares specific duties and responsibilities to the other groups, to the corporation, and to third parties.

   Shareholders.   The *shareholders* are the owners of the corporation. Ownership shares may be shown on a *stock certificate*, but as a practical matter, these are not used much. The shareholder has first right over other purchasers to buy any new stock issued by the corporation. Shareholders also enjoy a limited right to inspect the corporation's books and records. As a rule, inspections are provided to shareholders if it is for a proper purpose and a request is made in advance. Finally, unless stated to the contrary on the stock certificate, shareholders are not restricted from selling or giving their stock to someone else.

   The shareholders do not have responsibility for the management of the corporation. That is the legal responsibility of the board of directors, which generally delegates that responsibility to hired managers. Shareholders are generally required to elect the board of directors and to vote on matters that may effect a change in the corporation's structure or existence (such as a merger or an amendment to the corporation's articles of incorporation).

   Elections take place at the shareholder meetings, which generally must be held annually. Notice of the shareholder meetings must be provided in advance, and a quorum—usually more than 50 percent of the total shares held—must be represented at the meeting. Most shareholders give third parties their *proxy*—a written authorization to cast their vote at the meeting. The proxy is often solicited by the corporation's management.

   At the meeting, corporate business is presented to the shareholders in the form of *resolutions.* After considering a resolution, shareholders then vote to approve or disapprove it. As a rule, resolutions are passed if a majority of the votes cast are in favor of it. However, the articles of incorporation usually require more than a simple majority for a resolution for actions not within the ordinary course of business. Such actions might include amendments to the articles of incorporation and the bylaws, the extraordinary sale of corporate assets, or the dissolution or merger of the corporation.

   Shareholders have no legal relationship with creditors of the corporation. A shareholder's obligation to those creditors is usually limited to the capital contribution. The shareholder may, however, also be a creditor of the corporation (for example, by supplying some of the corporation's raw material needs or by working for the business) and enjoy the same rights of recovery against the corporation as any other creditor.

   Board of Directors.   The initial *board of directors* is either specified in the articles of incorporation or designated by the incorporators at the first corporate meeting. Thereafter, the selection and retention of directors is exclusively a shareholder responsibility. Once elected, directors are allowed to serve full terms, although the shareholders can remove a director from office *for cause* (generally for a *breach of duty* or *misconduct*.)

The functions of the board of directors include making basic corporate policy, such as the sale of corporate assets, entrance into new product lines, major financing decisions, appointment and compensation of corporate officers, and oversight of labor-management agreements. The directors, however, must act as a body and not as individuals to exert management power. Directors are under a *duty of care* to conduct themselves in the same manner as a reasonably prudent person in the conduct of personal business affairs. Honest mistakes in judgment not resulting from negligence will usually not result in personal liability to the directors. In most cases, courts give both directors and managers the benefit of the doubt and do not impose liability by applying the *business judgment rule,* which protects directors and managers who have made honest mistakes in judgment.

Directors are subject to a *fiduciary duty of loyalty,* which requires that directors place the interests of the corporation before their own interests. Directors can be held answerable to the corporation and its shareholders for a breach of their duties of care or loyalty. As the following case illustrates, the duties owed to shareholders by the board of directors are often affected by the circumstances in which the business finds itself. As a rule, the board has the duty to undertake those courses of action intended to preserve the corporate entity. That duty may be different, however, in the event the business becomes the target of a takeover attempt by another business. Note that decisions on corporate law by Delaware courts are especially important, since over one-half of the Fortune 500 firms are incorporated there.

REVLON, INC. v. MacANDREWS & FORBES HOLDINGS, INC.

Supreme Court of Delaware
506 A.2d 173 (1985)

Case Background
This case considers the duties a board of directors owes to a company's shareholders. The court was concerned that in their efforts to stop a takeover attempt by Pantry Pride (owned by MacAndrews), the directors of Revlon breached their duties to Revlon's shareholders. To avoid the takeover, the directors of Revlon had undertaken several defensive measures:

> **1.** Revlon entered into an agreement with Forstmann Little & Company that called for Revlon to sell assets to Forstmann if another company managed to purchase 40 percent of Revlon shares (called a "lock-up agreement," it effectively barred another company from gaining control of Revlon).
> **2.** Revlon agreed to deal exclusively with Forstmann in the event of a takeover attempt (called a "no-shop provision").
> **3.** Revlon agreed to pay Forstmann $25 million if the deal was aborted (called a cancellation fee provision).

Forstmann offered $57.25 per share for Revlon's stock and agreed to protect Revlon's creditors. The evidence showed that the directors' efforts to avoid the takeover were motivated in large part by the dislike of Revlon's chairman of the board for MacAndrews, chairman of Pantry Pride.

Pantry Pride challenged the lock-up, no-shop, and cancellation fee provisions and offered $58 per share for Revlon. The Court of Chancery enjoined the provisions and concluded that the Revlon directors had breached their duty of loyalty by making concessions to Forstmann rather than maximizing the sales price of the company for the shareholders' benefit. Revlon appealed to the Delaware Supreme Court.

Case Decision
The decision of the Court of Chancery was affirmed. Revlon's directors breached their duty of care to the Revlon shareholders. When the sale of a corporation is inevitable, the directors' fiduciary duty to the shareholders changes from a duty to preserve the corporate entity to a duty to maximize the corporation's value. During such times, the board must act "in good faith, and in the honest belief that the action taken (is) in the best interests of the company." If there is evidence that a board attempts to stop a takeover,

(continued)

the board must prove that it acted in good faith and reasonably investigated the reasons for the takeover and alternatives to it.

Regarding the lock-up provision, the court stated that such provisions are not necessarily illegal. In some cases, such provisions allow a "white knight," such as Forstmann, to play a beneficial role in the interests of the shareholders. However, care must be taken so that the lock-up provisions do not preclude other bidders and therefore create a detriment to the shareholders. In this case, the lock-up provision in Revlon's agreement with Forstmann did not help the bidding process but destroyed it.

Likewise, the no-shop provision is not necessarily illegal. However, the use of the no-shop provision was to end the bidding, which injured the shareholders. Complete favoritism to the white knight is not permissible when it hurts the shareholders' interests. "Market forces must be allowed to operate freely to bring . . . shareholders the best price available for their equity."

Managerial Considerations
Care must be taken during takeovers or the sale of corporate assets. It appears that Revlon's chairman's dislike for the chairman of Pantry Pride interfered with his decisions and with the duties owed to the Revlon shareholders. Managers must beware of personal feelings that may interfere with good business judgment. Had the Revlon board been able to justify economically the measures it took to stop Pantry Pride's takeover, the court would have allowed such measures as within the boundaries of the law. However, the courts will not support measures that harm shareholders, especially when the motives appear to be personal.

Management of the Corporation.   The corporation's board of directors is usually empowered to hire *managers* to operate the business on a day-to-day basis. The extent of managerial control and the compensation package for hired managers are matters of contract and agency between the board of directors and the managers. Once hired, managers have the same duties of care and loyalty as the directors. The use of hired management is a significant advantage of the corporate form of business where management by the owners of the business is impractical.

Termination of the Corporation.   The termination of a corporation, like the termination of a partnership, is essentially conducted in two phases: the dissolution phase and the winding-up phase. *Dissolution* of a corporation may be either voluntary or involuntary and effectively marks the end of the corporation. Upon its dissolution, the corporation is prevented from taking on any new business. A *voluntary dissolution* would normally involve the approval of the shareholders and the board of directors. The *involuntary dissolution* of a corporation usually happens because of bankruptcy but could also happen because of fraud in the establishment of the corporation.

When a corporation is dissolved through voluntary action, the board of directors (acting as trustee) is responsible for *winding up* the affairs of the corporation. If the board refuses to act as trustee or if shareholders or creditors object, the court will appoint a trustee (just as it would if the dissolution were involuntary). After the corporation's affairs have been completed, the assets are liquidated. The proceeds of the liquidation are first used to satisfy creditors, with any remainder going to the shareholders.

FACTORS IN THE CHOICE OF BUSINESS ORGANIZATION

Business organizers may, on more than one occasion, be faced with a choice of forms of business organization. For example, a business might begin as a sole proprietorship or a partnership and later, as it becomes more successful, find it advantageous to incorporate. The business also might consider an international business venture independently of its existing business, as a part of its existing business, or in a partnership with a foreign company.

Several important factors will influence the choice of business organization, including the potential liabilities imposed on the owners, the transferability of ownership rights, the ability of the business organization to continue in the event of the death or withdrawal of one or more of the owners, the capital requirements of the business, and the tax rate applicable to the business organization selected. Table 11–2 summarizes the differences between proprietorships, partnerships, and corporations on the basis of these factors.

TABLE 11–2
CHARACTERISTICS OF MAJOR FORMS OF BUSINESS ORGANIZATION

	Proprietorship	Partnership	Corporation
Method of Creation	Owner begins business operations.	Created by agreement of parties.	Charter issued by state—created by statutory authority.
Entity Status	Not separate from owner.	Separate from owners for some purposes.	Legal entity distinct from owners.
Liability of Owners	Owner personally liable for all debts.	Unlimited liability except for limited partner in a limited partnership.	Shareholders liable only to the extent of paid-in capital.
Duration	Same as owner.	Terminated by agreement of partners, by the death or withdrawal of a partner, or by bankruptcy.	May have perpetual existence.
Transferability of Interest	May be sold at any time; new proprietorship formed.	Generally, sale of partnership interest creates a new partnership.	Shares of stock can usually be readily transferred.
Control	By owner.	General partners have equal management control unless agreed to otherwise by partnership agreement; limited partners have no management rights.	Shareholders elect board of directors that sets policy and appoints officers to manage.
Capital	Limited to what owner can raise.	Limited to what partners can raise.	Sale of more ownership shares increases capital; may also borrow.
Taxation	Profits taxed to owner as individual.	Profits taxed proportionately to each owner as agreed in contract, or all share equally whether or not distributed.	Double taxation: profits of corporation are taxed to corporation, and shareholders pay income tax on their share of profits.

■ LIABILITY

One factor influencing the choice of business organization is the extent of liability protection provided to owners. *Limited liability* allows people to invest without placing all of their personal wealth at risk. Limited liability requires investors to be passive toward the internal management of the business.

Unlimited Liability.   Sole proprietors and general partners have unlimited personal liability for the debts of the business, including its torts. Some states require that judgment creditors exhaust the business partnership property before moving against the personal property of the partners. After those assets are exhausted, however, the creditor may require any of the partners to pay the entire remaining debt. Partners forced to pay more than their proportionate share of a debt may be entitled to reimbursement from the other partners unless the original agreement provides otherwise.

Limited Liability.   The liability of a limited partner is limited to the capital the partner has contributed to the partnership. Like the limited partner, shareholders of corporations risk only their capital investment if the corporation fails. They are not personally liable for the business debts or torts of the corporation unless they contract to make themselves personally liable.

In certain circumstances, the court will "pierce the corporate veil" and hold shareholders personally liable. That is, the court will disregard the corporate entity by finding that the corporation is a sham and that the owners are actually intending to operate the business as a proprietorship or partnership. Although a rare occurrence, the court will impose liability on shareholders in instances of fraud, undercapitalization, or failure to follow corporate formalities. As the following case illustrates, the corporate form of business organization may not be used merely to avoid business obligations.

TIGRETT v. POINTER

Court of Civil Appeals of Texas
580 S.W.2d 375 (1978)

Case Background
In April 1974, Tigrett sued Heritage Building Company. A judgment was rendered against Heritage Building Company in August 1976 for $49 per week for 401 weeks. However, Heritage's president and sole shareholder, Pointer, testified that the company was insolvent. In May 1974, Pointer transferred all of Heritage's assets to himself to repay a loan he had made to the company. On the same day, Pointer transferred those same assets to Heritage Corporation (a new corporation) as a loan.

Based on the previous judgment, Tigrett brought this suit in the form of an application for a writ of garnishment against Pointer and Heritage Corporation. She alleged that Pointer and Heritage Corporation were indebted to Heritage Building Company as a result of a fraudulent transfer of its assets. She further alleged that Heritage Building Company and the Heritage Corporation were merely the alter egos of Pointer and as a consequence were all jointly and severally liable for the previous judgment. The trial court found for Pointer, and Tigrett appealed.

Case Decision
The appellate court ruled that the trial court erred in failing to hold Pointer personally liable for the debts of Heritage Building Company. When a corporation transfers virtually all of its assets to its controlling shareholder to repay cash

(continued)

advances without providing for other creditors, the court may consider whether the manipulation of the corporate form to serve personal interests justifies the imposition of personal liability.

The domination of the corporation by a sole shareholder will not by itself create a piercing of the corporate veil and impose personal liability. However, if some "unfair device" has been used to deprive a creditor of corporate assets, the shareholder will be liable. One device considered unfair is grossly inadequate capitalization. The Heritage Building Company had $1,000 in capital, and yet it carried a $484,218 loan to Pointer. To carry a debt/assets ratio of 500 to 1 is considered by most courts as gross undercapitalization.

Managerial Considerations

The problems outlined in this case tend to affect small corporations, which are more likely to have a limited number of shareholders. Generally created for tax or liability purposes, the small corporation is susceptible to treatment as a mere shell under which the shareholders do as they please. Care should be taken that the identities of the shareholders and the corporation are not confused. If they are, the corporate veil may be pierced and personal liability may fall on the shareholders. If shareholders are careful to follow the rules of behavior imposed on corporate entities, personal liability is rarely imposed.

■ TRANSFERABILITY OF OWNERSHIP INTERESTS

The *transferability* of ownership rights refers to the ability of owners in business ventures to sell or otherwise pass their interests to others. In particular, it refers to the impact such a transfer will have on the existing business venture and the ease of making such transfers. The ability of owners to transfer ownership interests differs significantly among the various forms of business organizations.

Difficult Transfers. The proprietor of sole proprietorship is, in essence, the business. A decision to transfer the business to another clearly brings about the termination of the existing proprietorship and the creation of a new one. Selling proprietorships and partnerships can be expensive because the businesses are hard to price. Often a specialist is hired to help determine the market value of the business.

The sale of partnership shares is almost always covered by the partnership agreement, which spells out what is to happen if one partner wants out or dies. Otherwise, a costly legal battle can occur that forces the partnership to dissolve and a new one to be formed. Most partnership agreements allow sale of shares in such a way that the partnership keeps going despite the sale. Since existing partners usually have first right to buy the shares of other partners, they can control who becomes partners. The method used to determine the value of the partnership at time of sale is normally also spelled out in the agreement. The sale and control of shares in a small corporation, called a *close corporation*, is essentially the same as that in partnerships. Because of the small number of people involved, methods of handling sale of shares should be specified in advance.

Simple Transfers. The stock of corporations that is traded on a stock exchange, like the New York Stock Exchange, is very simple and done at very low cost. Hence, the transfer of ownership shares in complex corporations like IBM is easier than the transfer of ownership rights in proprietorships, partnerships, or close corporations. Since the price of shares is determined by the many buyers and sellers of the stock, no specialists needed be hired to help evaluate the corporation, and the exchange itself is handled by a stockbroker for a modest commission.

■ DURATION

A business's *duration* refers to its ability to continue to operate in the event of the death, retirement, or incapacity of an owner of the business. The ability of a business to continue under such circumstances can depend on the form of organization.

Noncorporate Entities.   A sole proprietorship terminates with the death or incapacity of the proprietor. Similarly, at common law a partnership is dissolved by the death, retirement, or incapacity of a partner but is not necessarily terminated. After the partnership has been dissolved, it may be terminated by liquidation, but the remaining partners probably do not want that to happen. To avoid liquidation, partners may assure that the partnership will continue, despite the departure of a partner, by having a continuation agreement. The agreement usually allows the remaining partners to continue to operate the business until a settlement is reached with the retired partner or with the deceased partner's legal representative.

Corporations.   Unless its articles of incorporation provide for a specified period of duration, a corporation has *perpetual existence.* A corporation is a legal entity that is normally dissolved only by intentional acts of the board of directors. Because of perpetual existence, the death, retirement, or incapacity of a shareholder does not bring about the termination of the corporation. In most large corporations, the death of a shareholder has no impact on the operations of the business. In a close corporation, death of a key shareholder can be of practical importance, since control of the shares may mean control of the business.

■ CAPITAL REQUIREMENTS

The forms of business organization differ in the alternatives they provide to the owners for raising financial capital. Depending upon the financial needs of a business, the business's legal form can be an important factor in the business's long-run viability.

Noncorporate Entities.   Sole proprietorships are the most limited form of business organization in terms of the alternatives available to the business for raising capital. The principal source of capital is the proprietor's personal wealth and any capital the proprietor may be able to borrow from other people or from financial institutions. Creditors of businesses can insist on some managerial control to help protect the funds they have invested, so even a sole proprietor may not end up in complete control of the business.

Partnerships allow a number of persons to pool their capital and to share the borrowing power they have, which is mostly a function of their personal wealth to back up the debt. The more partners, the less control any one partner will have.

Through the investment of limited partners, limited partnerships provide additional alternatives for raising capital. Recall that limited partners are essentially passive investors who have no control in the day-to-day operation of the business. Limited partners are often seeking investment opportunities with the hope of reaping large returns from a successful venture.

Corporations.   A major factor influencing the selection of the corporation as a form of business organization is the corporation's ability to raise capital. Corporations can raise capital from two sources: through the issuance of stock and from the selling of bonds. The issuance of stock is termed *equity financing* because the buyers of the stock purchase an ownership, or equitable, interest in the corporation. When the corporation sells bonds, it raises capital through *debt financing*. The bond represents a promise on the part of the corporation to repay the purchase price of the bond plus interest after a specified number of years. The proceeds of the sale of stocks and bonds are then used to finance the expansion of the business.

■ TAXATION CONSIDERATIONS

The federal tax system has large effects on behavior by affecting incentives for business activity. The tax treatment differs among forms of business organizations. Tax considerations are particularly important to small businesses and may dominate the selection decision.

Noncorporate Entities.   The income from a sole proprietorship or a partnership is taxed as personal income of the sole proprietor or partner. The business itself does not pay taxes on its profits. Partnerships, however, must file an informational return with the Internal Revenue Service.

Corporations.   Unlike the profits of proprietorships and partnerships, the profits of a corporation are taxed directly. Further, shareholders must pay income tax on the dividends or capital gains they receive from the corporation. Thus, corporate income is subject to double taxation, first on the corporate net income at corporate rates and then at a shareholder's personal income tax rate. Shareholders are taxed on the capital gains upon the sale of their stock and on any dividend income they receive for the stock they own.

For a business owner who finds incorporation an advantage but double taxation a drawback, an *S corporation* under Subchapter S of the Internal Revenue Code may be beneficial. An S corporation is created, operated, and dissolved in the same manner as regular corporations. If the corporation meets certain requirements, it may notify the IRS of its election to be taxed as a partnership. The entire profits of the corporation may then be taxed as personal income whether the income is distributed or not.

OTHER FORMS OF BUSINESS ORGANIZATION ▬▬▬▬▬▬

A number of other forms of business organization are available, including joint ventures, joint stock companies, syndicates, and cooperatives. These alternative forms are generally used as vehicles to manage a specific project or business concept.

◼ JOINT VENTURES

The Supreme Court has defined a *joint venture* as a general partnership for a limited time and purpose. Generally, a joint venture has several of the same characteristics of a general partnership, including same rights of control, risks of loss, and the manner in which profits are taxed. It usually involves two or more persons who agree to combine in a specific project and to share in the subsequent losses or profits. The joint venture exists as a business entity until the project is completed or the joint venture is terminated.

A joint venture is not usually considered a legal entity and therefore may not sue or be sued in its own name. In addition, the members of a joint venture usually have limited authority to bind each other to matters not directly related to the project. Joint ventures vary in size and are most popular as an international business organization. As the situation in the Manager's Legal Challenge feature shows, a joint venture may be held to exist at law, even though the parties to the venture never intended to form one.

◼ JOINT STOCK COMPANIES

A *joint stock company* is a business organization involving a unique mixture of partnership and corporation characteristics. Despite the mixture of characteristics, however, joint stock companies are generally treated like partnerships. Although not widely used, a modern example is the American Express Company, which was a joint stock company until 1965.

The joint stock company resembles the corporate form of business organization in that ownership is represented by shares of stock. In addition, joint stock companies are usually managed by directors and officers in a way very similar to that employed in most corporations. Like a corporation, a joint stock company can also have perpetual life.

In resembling a partnership, the joint stock company is usually created by an agreement and not according to state statute. In addition, company property is held in the names of the shareholder/members who have personal liability for all company actions. The company is generally not considered a legal entity and therefore may not sue or be sued in its own name.

◼ COOPERATIVES

A *cooperative* is a business (that may or may not be incorporated) organized to provide an economic service to its members. Cooperatives are usually formed by people who want to pool their purchasing power to gain some advantage in the marketplace. Generally, they get lower product prices for their members by the purchase of products in large quantities at a discount.

Cooperatives that are not incorporated are usually treated as partnerships; the members are jointly liable for the acts of the cooperative. If the cooperative is to be formed as a corporation, it must meet state laws governing nonprofit cooperations. In contrast to typical corporate dividends, however, cooperative dividends are provided on the basis of the volume of a member's (shareholder's) purchases from the cooperative rather than on the basis of capital contributed.

■ SYNDICATES

A *syndicate* is the name given to a group of persons who join together to finance a specific project. A common example of a syndicate is a large real estate development, such as a shopping center or professional office building. Although the specific structure such organizations take varies considerably, syndicates may exist as general partnerships, limited partnerships, or corporations. It is not uncommon for the members of a syndicate to simply own property together with no other formal business organization.

SUMMARY: A GUIDE FOR MANAGERS

- The common law of agency allows principals and agents to form legal relationships for limited business purposes. The agent is subject to control by the principal and may not exceed the authority granted by the principal or authority consistent with what can be presumed to be given an agent under the circumstances of a given agency.

- Principals must cooperate with agents, compensate them for services rendered, reimburse them for reasonable expenses, provide safe working conditions, and indemnify them for legal liabilities they incur in the course of the agency.

- Agents have a fiduciary duty to their principals. This requires the highest level of loyalty and obedience within the agency. Agents must perform with reasonable care and skill under the circumstances and must account honestly to principals about finances and notify them of events that are important to the purpose of the agency. Agents must indemnify principals for unauthorized torts they commit or contracts they enter into for which the principal is held financially responsible.

- Agency relationships arise when actual expressed or implied authority is granted to an agent. Principals are also responsible for the acts of agents when it appears to reasonable people that the agents have apparent authority to act as agents.

- Sole proprietorships automatically come into existence whenever people begin to do business for themselves. Legally a sole proprietor is the business, responsible for its debts and torts, liable for its taxes, and in control of the business and its transfer.

- Partnerships may be structured in almost any manner desired by partners forming a business. When a partnership agreement does not specify what happens in some instance, such as death of a partner, the law of partnership, codified in the Uniform Partnership Act, determines the result. In general, partners are fully liable for all acts of the partnership.

They share in the managerial control, debts, tort liability, and profits of the business. They are taxed personally on the gains from the partnership.

- Limited partnerships are governed by state law. They require that such partnerships have at least one general partner. The limited partners are primarily investors. They may not share in managerial control of the business. Their liability is limited to the amount they invest unless they try to exercise managerial control and, therefore, become general partners.

- Corporations are recognized as legal entities. They have their own legal life, which is potentially perpetual. They are responsible for their own debts and tort liabilities; shareholders are liable only to the amount they invest in the corporation.

- Shareholders are investors in corporations. They are passive except that they vote to elect the board of directors and must vote on major issues such as selling the corporation. The board of directors is the principal of a corporation. It has legal responsibility for determining how the company is to be operated and, in that capacity, to hire and instruct the management. Hired managers are agents of the board and respond to the instructions provided by the board.

MANAGER'S ETHICAL DILEMMA

Are We Our Employees' Keepers?

Suppose you manage a small business. You hire a local accountant to do your accounting. One day, while working on your books at his office, your accountant sexually assaults his secretary. Are you responsible for the assault? No, it happened at another place of business. The accountant was your agent for the purpose of doing the books; the assault was not related to that. The accountant was an independent contractor, not an employee. But if you had employed the accountant as an employee at your office and the assault had occurred there, then you, the employer, may very well be responsible under the rule of vicarious liability for the injury suffered by the employee who was assaulted. This illustrates one of the advantages of hiring independent contractors rather than employees.

While it is clear that your company should not be responsible in this case, what about the following situation? Your company delivers supplies all over town. You have full-time drivers who use their own car to do this. These drivers can be employees on salary and compensated for the use of their cars, or they can be independent contractors, paid to use their cars full-time to deliver your supplies. One of the drivers is at fault in an accident. If the driver is an employee, you are liable. If the driver is an independent contractor, you *might* escape liability.

Further consider that if you hire a driver as an employee, you will have to pay workers' compensation, Social Security, and Medicare and comply with other laws, which may include a requirement to provide health insurance. But if you hire the same driver as an independent contractor, you have no such concerns—you can just pay the driver a flat monthly agreed-upon fee, and the driver can worry about taxes and health insurance.

Many working-age people who do not have medical insurance do not have it because they work as independent contractors rather than as employees. They do not buy insurance for themselves, thinking that they do not need it, or, as independent contractors not part of a group of employees, they find it very difficult to obtain insurance.

Many states are changing common law rules regarding independent contractor status, looking to the reality of the employment arrangement, not the form. Some states are requiring the purchase of health insurance for all employees—independent contractors or not—if they are full-time employees, so that the state does not have to provide medical care for so many people who have failed to purchase insurance but then cannot afford private medical care.

QUESTIONS

Is it ethical to hire independent contractors in hopes of reducing tort liability, even though the work performed will be the same whether the person is an employee or an independent contractor?

Is it ethical for an employer to hire persons as independent contractors if the real purpose is to avoid paying tax or insurance or complying with other regulatory requirements?

REVIEW AND DISCUSSION QUESTIONS

1. Define the following terms:

   agency relationship   general partner
   agent   limited partnership
   principal   limited liability
   sole proprietor   corporation

2. Compare and contrast the following:
   a. apparent authority and actual authority
   b. express authority and implied authority
   c. partnership and joint venture
   d. dissolution of a partnership and the winding up of a partnership
   e. general partner and limited partner
   f. shareholder and limited partner
   g. piercing the corporate veil and limited liability for shareholders
   h. articles of incorporation and bylaws

3. Under what circumstances would a principal be liable for the following:
   a. the negligence of an agent
   b. the intentional tort of an agent
   c. the contracts of an agent

4. What is the definition of a partnership? Are four doctors who jointly own a summer cottage and use it solely for their personal enjoyment a partnership?

5. Mrs. Ehsani owns one share in Exxon. She is convinced that because her interest is so small, she has no rights with regard to the company's affairs. She is particularly concerned about whether she can attend the shareholders' meeting and what her rights and responsibilities are during that meeting. She would also like to inspect the company's books. What are her rights?

6. Which factors might most influence the selection of a form of business organization in the following businesses? Which form would be most appropriate?
   a. operation of a hazardous waste disposal facility
   b. a research and development facility that has just begun to develop its own products
   c. a company with the patent to a unique but inexpensive product that is expected to generate large profits
   d. a coin-operated laundry near a college campus
   e. a business intending to undertake labor-intensive manufacturing in Korea

■ CASE QUESTIONS

7. Mary Kidd sued Thomas A. Edison, Inc. (Edison), alleging that a Mr. Fuller, acting for Edison, contracted with her to sing at a series of recitals for record dealers. At the recitals, Kidd was to sing so the dealers could compare her recorded voice with her actual voice. Kidd was not paid and brought suit against Edison. According to Edison, Fuller never agreed that Edison would pay Kidd, because Fuller's only authority was to hire Kidd for those recitals for which he could persuade record dealers to pay. Is Edison liable to Kidd? Why or why not? [*Kidd* v. *Thomas A. Edison, Inc.*, 239 Fed. 405 (S.D.N.Y. 1917)]

8. Witlin was a partner in a partnership. When he died, per the partnership agreement, the other partners bought Witlin's share, paying the proceeds to Witlin's estate. The partners sold the entire partnership for more than three times the share price they had paid the estate. The estate sued the partners, claiming that since the partners had violated their fiduciary duty to tell the estate's heirs of the pending sale, the heirs should be paid the higher price. Was their claim correct? [*Estate of Witlin*, 83 Cal.App.3d 167, 147 Cal.Rptr. 723 (1978)]

9. A limited partnership had a general partner and eighteen limited partners. It could not pay a bill due a contractor. The contractor sued, claiming the limited partners should have to pay the bill, since the general partner and the partnership itself could not. Did the limited partners have to pay? [*Northampton Valley Contractors, Inc.* v. *Horne-Lang Associates*, 310 Pa.Super. 559, 456 A.2d 1077 (1983)]

10. Cloney was president of the Boston Athletic Association (BAA), a nonprofit corporation that sponsored the Boston Marathon. The board of directors authorized Cloney to negotiate the best deal he could get for the sponsorship of the marathon. Cloney signed a contract with a company that turned the marathon over to it in exchange for a certain payment, and this deal would last forever if the new company wanted it to. Hence, BAA no longer had control over the marathon. The board sued Cloney and the other company, claiming that the president of the BAA had exceeded his authority. Any such long-term, binding deal would have to have been approved by the board of directors. Was the board right? [*BAA* v. *International Marathons, Inc.*, 362 Mass. 356, 467 N.E.2d 58 (1984)].

11. Nockels and Everett formed a limited partnership. Nockels, who contributed office space, is the general partner, and Everett, who contributed $20,000 to the partnership, is the limited partner. About six months after the partnership began its operations, Nockels became very ill, and Everett took over the management of the operations of the business. During this time period, Everett negotiated and entered into a large contract with James Knott. After several weeks, it became apparent that the partnership was not going to be able to fulfill its contractual obligations and Knott was going to suffer a significant loss. Knott has filed suit against both Everett and Nockels, asserting they are personally liable for the losses despite the appearance of a limited partnership. Can Everett support his claim that he is a limited partner and therefore avoid personal liability beyond the amount of his contribution to the partnership?

12. Charles Gabus was appointed to the board of directors for Ironhorse Automotive, Inc., a corporation that owned several new car dealerships. In the next eighteen months, the business deteriorated rapidly, in part because of poor managerial decisions. Gabus neither attended board meetings nor examined the business records or books during the period. Could he be personally liable to the shareholders for the losses of the corporation?

■ BUSINESS POLICY QUESTIONS

13. What advantages and disadvantages are there in having a nationally accepted statute for the regulation of partnerships in various states?

14. In selecting a state in which to incorporate, businesses often look for one that offers the most advantageous tax or incorporation provisions in its incorporation statutes. Historically, Delaware has had the least restrictive incorporation statutes. Should states be able to compete on the basis of incorporation statutes? Are there advantages to consumers in allowing states to compete? Are there disadvantages?

■ ETHICS QUESTIONS

15. Jensen and Cross entered into a partnership agreement to sell insulation to residential and commercial contractors. The business was very successful, and the two became quite wealthy. As the business grew, the partners discussed seriously the need to incorporate the business to take advantage of the corporate form of business organization. Since their partnership agreement had served them well, they did not undertake the change to a corporation until 1983. In that year, the partners first realized that some of the workers for the contractors to whom they sold their insulation were developing serious illnesses that appeared to be caused by long-term exposure to the insulation. By incorporating, Jensen and Cross hoped to avoid personal liability for the injuries to those workers. Was the move to incorporate good business practice?

16. Cook and Smith entered into a limited partnership called Trinity Development to develop a shopping center. Adjacent to the shopping center property was a ten-acre tract of undeveloped land that came up for sale after the limited partnership had begun its operations. Cook, the general partner, purchased the property from McCade, but only after McCade had refused to sell the property to Trinity. His stated purpose was that he did not want to do business with Smith. Cook then sold the property to another developer for a $60,000 profit. If Cook had sold the property to Trinity, Trinity could have avoided the need to build an access road. Trinity has objected to the sale and purchase by Cook. What alternatives did Cook have? With regard to his employment with Trinity, what was the ethical choice? How was Trinity damaged? With regard to his relationship with McCade, what were his alternatives?

BUSINESS AND THE REGULATORY ENVIRONMENT

Regulation of business has increased consistently during the twentieth century. It began with restraints on monopolistic practices early in the century, moved to control of specific industries during the depression of the 1930s, and has focused on broader social regulation since the 1960s. These chapters focus on the areas of key importance:

- *Chapter 12 — Labor Relations Law* begins with a look at traditional labor union law and then moves to labor law of more recent importance, such as employment-at-will and how businesses deal with substance abuse.

- *Chapter 13 — Employment Discrimination* studies the law that has developed concerning discrimination in employment, especially when based on race, sex, religion, age, or disability.

- *Chapter 14 — Environmental Regulation* reviews the key areas of environmental law that have developed in the past twenty years that control business use of air, water, land, and species — all aspects of our physical world.

- *Chapter 15 — Consumer Protection* focuses on the regulations that have the largest impact on business-consumer relations: food and drug regulation, consumer credit, and consumer fraud.

- *Chapter 16 — Antitrust Law* explains the major parts of laws that restrict business activities defined as anticompetitive or monopolistic.

- *Chapter 17 — Securities Regulation* looks at the key parts of federal controls on the sale and trading of stocks, bonds, and other securities and reviews the regulation of the sale of a rapidly growing business form — franchises.

- *Chapter 18 — International Legal Environment of Business* reviews some legal controls on international business relations, the forefront of business developments today.

329

LABOR RELATIONS LAW

CHAPTER 12

MANAGER'S LEGAL CHALLENGE

The largest provider of drug testing services in the country, SmithKline Beecham, reported that 9.3 percent of the workers and job applicants it tested were positive for illegal drugs in 1991, down from 11 percent in 1990. Substance abuse, which used to be mostly ignored in the workplace, is now a major managerial issue that has many legal implications.

Companies have many economic reasons for caring whether or not employees are substance abusers. Drug users, on the average, are worse employees than nondrug users. A study reported in *Journal of the American Medical Association* found that those who tested positive in preemployment drug tests were 50 percent more likely to be fired, injured, disciplined, or absent than those who tested drug free. Alcohol and other drug abusers have substantially more medical problems, driving up the cost of health insurance for employers. Further, substance abusers are more likely to be involved in accidents, for which the employer may be legally responsible.

This chapter considers the legal aspects of substance abuse policy. Besides knowing what can be done legally, are companies aware of the kind of alcohol and other drug abuse programs that seem to work? Some companies only post notices about abuse policies and still largely ignore the problem. Other companies, large and small, are taking the problem head on.

A paving company, Chamberlain Contractors, in Laurel, Maryland, adopted a comprehensive program of preemployment drug tests, random tests twice a year, mandatory tests after accidents, quarterly sessions for all employees, and an employee assistance program that offers counseling on substance abuse and other major problems, since personal problems are often mixed with alcohol and other drug problems.

The rules apply to all sixty-five employees, starting with the president. So far, the program has cost only about $7,000 a year. Drug users have not been hired, and several were fired. The payoff has been substantial. Workers' compensation insurance premiums fell $50,000 per year because of a sharp reduction in accidents.

Motorola, which has 60,000 employees, spends over $1 million a year on drug testing and substance abuse programs, not counting rehabilitation costs. The company estimates it will save about $200 million per year, primarily from increased productivity. Not only do substance abusers miss work more often and become ill more often, but the quality of their work is frequently lower—especially at a company such as Motorola that makes sensitive electronic equipment.

Management at Motorola discovered that most of the workers agreed there should be a tough policy—so long as it was universal, starting with the president. All employees are subject to the same testing rules. A worker who has an alcohol problem or who tests positive for other drugs has the right to go through company-sponsored rehabilitation. Those who refuse or who again test positive are fired. The company president says that the get-tough approach is required if the company is to be an international competitor with high-quality products coming from a high-quality labor force.

Laws affecting the labor-management relationship are the subject of this chapter, which first examines federal labor legislation, including the Norris-LaGuardia Act, the Wagner Act, the Taft-Hartley Act, and the Landrum-Griffin Act, and then turns to the processes and procedures of the National Labor Relations Board. Unions, collective bargaining, and unlawful labor activities such as secondary boycotts are considered next. The chapter also discusses other laws affecting the labor relationship, including employment-at-will; laws concerning worker safety, health, and retirement rights; workers' compensation; and occupational regulation.

Before 1890, attempts to organize labor were greatly restricted. The primary barrier was the common law rule that infliction of economic harm is a tort. Hence, when workers banded together and refused to work—and thus boycotted a business—they could be held guilty of conspiring to commit a tort. Although not all courts accepted this rule, there was little legal support for organized labor activities.

After 1890, with the enactment of the Sherman Act, restraints of trade were restricted by statute. Since organized boycotts by labor are clearly restraints of trade, union activities were restricted. The Clayton Act of 1914 liberalized the rules regarding union activities, but it was not until the Great Depression that public and political attitudes toward unions changed sufficiently to provide affirmative support for organized labor activities. Thus, although various craft and trade unions existed during the 1800s, labor law is a twentieth-century phenomenon.

Union membership and representation has declined significantly since the 1950s. From 1975 to 1990, the percentage of the labor force belonging to unions fell from about 29 percent to about 16 percent. Table 12–1 shows who belongs to unions by labor force category as of 1990.

FEDERAL LABOR LEGISLATION

Several federal statutes regulate labor-management relations. However, the federal labor code, generally referred to as the *National Labor Relations*

TABLE 12–1
THE WORK FORCE AND UNIONS IN 1991

Characteristic	Number of Workers*	% Union Members	% Union Represented
Total	102,786	16.1	18.2
By Sex			
Men	53,931	19.3	21.3
Women	48,856	12.6	14.8
By Race			
African American	11,318	21.4	24.4
Hispanic	8,193	15.6	17.7
White	87,981	15.4	17.4
By Employer			
Private	84,811	11.7	12.9
Government	17,975	36.9	43.3
By Occupation			
Managerial and Professional	26,018	14.6	17.7
Technical, Sales & Administrative	32,649	10.4	12.4
Service Occupations	14,649	13.9	15.4
Precision Production	11,189	25.9	27.8
Machine Operators, Transport & Laborers	16,492	26.3	28.0

*In thousands.

Note: Only employed workers are counted. "Union Represented" includes union members and workers who are not union members but are represented by a union at their workplace.

SOURCE: U.S. Bureau of Labor Statistics, *Employment and Earnings.*

Act, was enacted in three major phases: the Wagner Act in 1935, the Taft-Hartley Act in 1947, and the Landrum-Griffin Act in 1959. The public policy of the United States with regard to unions was first developed in the Norris-La Guardia Act of 1932. We will briefly review the major acts and then discuss in more detail some of the major aspects of labor law.

■ NORRIS-LA GUARDIA ACT

Federal courts played an active role in labor-management relations before passage of the *Norris-La Guardia Act* in 1932. The courts, however, showed little consistency in their decisions. Some courts held union activities to be criminal conspiracies, while others upheld the same activities as legal. In 1908, in the *Danbury Hatters* case, the Supreme Court held a union responsible for treble damages under the Sherman Act for organizing a boycott of retail stores. Those retail stores were selling hats produced by a manufacturer that was being struck by the union. The Clayton Act reduced the antitrust liabilities of unions, but the courts continued to thwart union activities.

The most common tactic of employers was to plead for a court injunction to stop union strikes, boycotts, and other activities. The Norris-La Guardia Act ended this widespread practice. The intent of the statute was to make the federal government neutral with respect to labor policy. This was a substantial benefit to union activity. The Norris-La Guardia Act declared the public policy of the United States to be that the individual worker should "have full freedom of association, self-organization, and designation of representatives of his own choosing, to negotiate terms and conditions of his employment."

Injunctions Prohibited in Nonviolent Labor Disputes.   The Norris-La Guardia Act prohibits federal courts from issuing injunctions in nonviolent *labor disputes,* thereby increasing the freedom of the unions to use economic force to compel employers to bargain over employment terms and conditions with unions. The specific actions that the Act says are not subject to federal court injunctions include *striking* or quitting work, belonging to a labor organization, paying strike or unemployment benefits to labor dispute participants, publicizing the existence of a labor dispute, picketing, peacefully assembling to promote interests in a labor dispute, and advising others to do any of these acts without violence or fraud.

The 1982 Supreme Court case *Jacksonville Bulk Terminals* indicates how far-reaching the Norris-LaGuardia Act is in keeping courts out of labor disputes. In that case, to protest the Russian invasion of Afghanistan, the union at the port of Jacksonville (Florida) told the workers to refuse to load goods onto ships that were bound for the Soviet Union, which meant that the goods sat on the dock. The shippers said the issue was a political dispute concerning Russian foreign policy, not a labor dispute, and wanted a court order to force the workers to go back to work. The Supreme Court said that since the Act prohibits court involvement in "any labor dispute," the courts could not intervene in this dispute even though the motive was political.

Besides limiting the ability of employers to seek injunctions to stop union activities, the Act also prohibits employers from requiring employees to sign *yellow-dog contracts*. Under such a contract, the employee agrees not to join a union, with the understanding that joining a union is a contract violation that means dismissal.

■ WAGNER ACT OF 1935

The basic goal of the *Wagner Act* of 1935 (the National Labor Relations Act, or NLRA) is to provide employees with the right to "self-organization, to form, join, or assist labor organizations, to bargain collectively through representatives of their own choosing, and to engage in other concerted activities for the purpose of collective bargaining or other mutual aid or protection. . . ." To achieve this goal, the legislation created the *National Labor Relations Board* (NLRB) to monitor unfair labor practices and assure that union representation elections were held in a fair manner. The NLRB, however, does not regulate the substance of bargaining—the actual terms and conditions of employment—between employers and employees.

In general, *unfair labor practices* by employers are actions that would impair the goal of the Wagner Act. Such practices include employer interference with employee rights guaranteed by the Act; employer-formed or dominated "company unions"; discrimination by employers on account of union activity in hiring, firing, or other matters of employment; discrimination by employers against employees who testify or file charges before the NLRB; and failure by employers to bargain collectively with the employees' union.

THE TAFT-HARTLEY ACT OF 1947

The *Taft-Hartley Act* of 1947 (the Labor-Management Relations Act), which amended the NLRA, marked a change in federal policy from one of actively encouraging labor union formation to one of a favorable attitude toward unionization coupled with regulation. The Taft-Hartley Act prohibits unions from the following activities:

1. Coercing employees with respect to their collective bargaining rights.
2. Refusing to bargain in good faith with employers about wages and working conditions.
3. Carrying out certain kinds of strikes, such as secondary boycotts, charging "excessive" union initiation fees or dues, or engaging in *featherbedding* (i.e., employers having to pay for work not performed).

THE LANDRUM-GRIFFIN ACT OF 1959

The *Landrum-Griffin Act* of 1959 (Labor-Management Reporting and Disclosure Act), which amended the NLRA, increased regulation of internal union affairs. Senate investigations revealed the improper use of union funds and other problems. Congress took action to help protect union members from improper actions by union leaders.

Monitoring Union Leadership.   The financial status of unions is subject to federal review, and a report must be available to union members so that they know how their dues are used. Penalties were established to punish union officials who betrayed the trust of office. Penalties were also established to reduce incidences of employer wrongdoing, such as bribing union officials or attempting to hold off union activities by other illegal means. Employers must report annually to the Secretary of Labor about company expenditures to attempt to influence collective bargaining activities.

Union Member Bill of Rights.   A bill of rights for union members was included in the Landrum-Griffin Act that requires a more democratic procedure in the operation of unions than was previously used. It provides for rights in nomination of candidates for union offices, fair election procedures, and participation in union business, subject to "reasonable" union rules. Union dues and fees are to be set by a majority vote of the members. If a union member is to be disciplined by the union, procedural safeguards must be followed to protect the rights of the member, and no punishment may be inflicted on members who challenge union leadership or its actions. Further, members must be given copies of all collective bargaining agreements and be made aware of their rights under the Landrum-Griffin Act.

In the 1989 decision *Sheet Metal Workers* v. *Lynn,* the Supreme Court held it a violation of the Landrum-Griffin Act for a union leader to fire another union official who had spoken out at a union meeting in opposition to a proposal favored by the union leader. Union members have the right of freedom of speech that should not be chilled by such retaliation.

THE NATIONAL LABOR RELATIONS BOARD

It is the NLRB's responsibility to administer the National Labor Relations Act. The NLRB has five board members, a General Counsel, regional directors, and administrative law judges. The board members are appointed by the President, with the consent of the Senate, to five-year terms, with the term of one member expiring each year. The board acts as a quasi-judicial body in deciding cases upon formal records, generally upon review from decisions of regional directors or administrative law judges. The General Counsel is responsible for overseeing the investigation and prosecution of unfair labor practice charges and for representing the NLRB in court. Headquartered in Washington, D.C., the NLRB has thirty-three regional offices and sixteen smaller field offices around the country.

JURISDICTION OF THE NLRB

The NLRB has jurisdiction over all employers engaged in interstate commerce and all employees in businesses where a labor dispute would affect interstate commerce. The NLRB has refused to assert jurisdiction over small employers whose businesses are local. Also, certain classes of employees—federal, state, and municipal employees (the public sector); supervisors; managers; independent contractors; employees of railroads and airlines (covered by the Railway Labor Act of 1926); domestic servants; and agricultural laborers—are not covered by the National Labor Relations Act and thus are outside NLRB jurisdiction.

NLRB COMPLAINT PROCEDURE

Over 50,000 cases a year are filed with the NLRB, the majority of which— about 40,000—involve charges of *unfair labor practice.* Over the years, charges filed against employers have outnumbered those filed against unions by almost two to one. Each NLRB case, whether it involves an unfair labor practice or a matter of representation, must be initiated by a private party, such as an individual worker, a union, or an employer.

Most unfair labor practice casework is done in the field through the regional offices and involves the following process. Charges of unfair labor practice are filed at field offices, where they are then investigated. If the investigation shows that a case is meritorious, the regional director will file a complaint.

About two-thirds of the charges filed do not lead to a complaint being filed, as they are either dismissed by the regional director or withdrawn by the complaining party when informed of their probable lack of success. Of the charges that do lead to a complaint, over 80 percent are settled before a hearing takes place.

An administrative law judge presides over complaints that are not settled. After taking evidence and receiving briefs, the judge issues a decision and order. The order either sets out the appropriate remedy or suggests that the complaint be dismissed. Unless one of the parties involved files an exception, the judge's decision becomes final.

If an exception to the decision is filed, the case is reviewed in Washington by a panel of three board members if the case is routine or by the entire board if the case is considered particularly important. The board members hear no evidence and see no witnesses; in that sense the board is similar to an appellate court. The board issues decisions in about 1,600 cases a year.

If one of the parties refuses to accept the board's decision, the case is referred to the U.S. Court of Appeals for enforcement or review of the order. Most decisions of the board referred to the court of appeals are upheld. In rare instances, the case may be taken for final review by the U.S. Supreme Court.

UNIONIZATION

A major responsibility of the NLRB is to determine whether employees want to be represented by a union. The NLRA focuses on the right of employees to "self-organization, to form, join, or assist labor organizations." To ensure that the employees' right of self-organization can be exercised in a manner consistent with employer rights to the proper functioning of business, the NLRB has rules governing employer and union conduct.

MOVEMENT TO UNIONIZATION

If the employees of a company are not represented by a union, a movement toward unionization might be brought about by some interested employees who contact a union for assistance or by a union agent who contacts the company's employees to determine whether interest exists. The union then undertakes an organizing drive. A committee of employees is formed and, with the help of a union organizer, holds informational meetings and distributes information.

Representation Elections.   If the union collects *authorization cards* from 30 percent or more of the employees asking the union to be their agent in collective bargaining (the cards are kept secret from the employer), it turns the cards over to the NLRB and requests a *representation election*. The election will determine whether a majority of the employees want a union as their agent. Some employees sign authorization cards but do not vote to have the union as their bargaining agent. During the past decade, unions won slightly less than half of the representation elections. As employers have become more sophisticated in responding to union challenges, the trend over time has been against unions.

Before the NLRB-run election, there is a campaign in which the union tells the workers of the benefits of unionization and management tells the workers the benefits the company provides without a union. The company is prohibited from threatening those who favor unionization, nor may it promise, say, a 10 percent pay raise if the workers defeat the union. Rather, the company must argue in more general terms, with discussions limited to possible problems with unionization.

Union Certification.   NLRB agents supervise the election, which is often held at the workplace. Shortly after the election is held, the NLRB certifies the results. If more than 50 percent of the employees vote for the union, it will be *certified* by the NLRB as the exclusive *bargaining agent* for all employees at the workplace and must be recognized as such by the company. Dissenting employees are bound by the recognition of the union as their bargaining agent.

On the other side of the coin, employers or workers can call for elections to attempt to *decertify* unions—get a majority of employees to vote to remove the union as bargaining agent. The number of such elections has increased in recent years.

■ AGENCY SHOPS

When a union is selected to be the collective bargaining agent for the workers at a work site, the workers who join the union must pay union dues. What about the workers who do not want to be union members?

The NLRA prohibits *closed shops*, where an employee must be a union member before going to work at a unionized work site. It also prohibits *union shops*—work sites where being a member of the union is a condition of employment. *Agency shops*—places of employment where a majority of employees have voted to be represented by a union in a collective bargaining agreement—are legal. In an agency shop, employees who belong to the union pay union dues, while nonunion employees pay agency fees. That is, nonunion employees have fees deducted from their paychecks that are given to the union to cover the costs of union services. Agency fees are lower than union dues.

The use of the fees paid by nonunion employees in agency shops has raised concerns regarding the constitutional rights of those employees. Of particular concern is the use of fees paid by nonunion employers to support union political activities unrelated to the union's duties as an exclusive bargaining representative. There have been a number of Supreme Court cases on this issue in recent years. In a 1986 case, *Chicago Teachers Union*, the Court listed four requirements on agency fees paid by nonunion workers to unions at unionized workplaces:

1. An adequate explanation of the basis for the fee.

2. A reasonably prompt explanation of the basis for the fee.

3. A reasonably prompt opportunity to challenge the amount of the fee before an impartial decision maker.

4. An escrow for the amounts reasonably in dispute while such challenges are pending.

The Court revisited the issue in the *Ferris Faculty* case.

LEHNERT v. FERRIS FACULTY ASSOCIATION

United States Supreme Court
____ U.S. ____ , 111 S.Ct. 1950 (1991)

Case Background
Since 1975, Ferris State College has entered into collective bargaining agreements with agency shop provisions with the Ferris Faculty Association (FFA), an affiliate of the Michigan Education Association (MEA) and the National Education Association (NEA). Lehnert and some other faculty members at Ferris State objected that they were required to pay agency fees equal to the dues paid by faculty who were union (FFA) members. Most of the fees (and union dues) went to the MEA and the NEA and, according to Lehnert, were used mostly for political purposes, such as lobbying, not related to collective bargaining costs at Ferris State. The Supreme Court had to consider the constitutional issues of union activities supported by agency fees.

Case Decision
The Court held that nonunion members may be charged fees that cover (1) pro rata share of costs of collective bargaining activities of state (MEA) and national (NEA) affiliates that are not directly related to the bargaining unit (FFA); (2) NEA program expenditures for other states and expenses of the MEA's publications that are related to collective bargaining; (3) MEA publications that concern teaching and education, professional development, and other nonpolitical informational matters; (4) participation of delegates at affiliated union conventions; and (5) expenses related to preparation for strikes. They may not be charged for (1) expenses of lobbying or other political activities unrelated to contract ratification, (2) union programs designed to secure funds for public education, (3) litigation unrelated to the bargaining unit, and (4) union public relations efforts.

Managerial Considerations
By encouraging nonunion workers to exercise their rights to limit agency fees to the legally allowed areas, managers can make clear to all workers that unions spend an average of 75 percent of dues on political activities, which may reduce interest in unionization.

President Bush issued an Executive Order in 1992 that requires most employers to inform workers of their rights in this regard. The notices must state that: workers may not be compelled to join or maintain membership in a union; employees may not be forced to contribute to union activities other than collective bargaining and other direct costs involved in union representation; and that objecting employees may be entitled to refunds or future reduction in fees spent for political activity and other union actions not related to worker representation.

Right-to-Work.   One of the most hotly contested features of the Taft-Hartley Act is the provision that allows states to pass *right-to-work laws* that prohibit agency shops. Even if a majority of the employees vote for union representation and pay union initiation fees and dues, no employees can be required to pay agency fees, even though their wages and working conditions are determined by the collective bargaining agreement signed by the union on behalf of all employees. Since some employees receive the benefits of the union without paying dues, unions claim they are free riders. Right-to-work laws, in effect in twenty-one Southern and Western states, clearly retard the effectiveness of unions in such states.

■ EMPLOYER RESPONSES TO UNION ORGANIZING

When Congress enacted the Wagner Act in 1935, it used broad language to declare it illegal for an employer to interfere with, restrain, or coerce employees in the exercise of the rights to organize and bargain collectively. However, employer conduct may be lawful if it advances a substantial and legitimate employer interest in plant safety, efficiency, or discipline. Thus, courts and the NLRB must strike a balance between these employer interests and the interests of the employees concerning union participation and activities.

Union Solicitation on Company Property.   The NLRB and the courts accommodate the employee's right to access union communications and the employer's interest in managing the business. As a general rule, the NLRB and the courts will not permit access to company property by outside organizers. The Supreme Court reviewed this issue again in the *Lechmere* case.

LECHMERE INC. v. NATIONAL LABOR RELATIONS BOARD

United States Supreme Court
____ U.S. ____ , 112 S.Ct. 841 (1992)

Case Background
The AFL-CIO wanted to organize the 200 employees of Lechmere's retail store in Newington, Connecticut. Union organizers entered Lechmere's property and put handbills on the windshields of cars parked in the store's employee parking lot. The store manager told the organizers that Lechmere prohibited any solicitations or handbill distribution on its property and told them to leave. Lechmere personnel removed the handbills from the windshields. This event was repeated two more times. The organizers then stood at a public entrance to the parking lot and passed out handbills to cars entering and leaving the parking lot at peak times for employee traffic and picketed the store for months. They copied the license plate numbers of cars parked in the employee lot, obtained names and addresses from the Department of Motor Vehicles, and sent four mailings to these employees. The result of this activity was one signed union authorization card.

The union filed an unfair labor practice charge with the NLRB, which ruled for the union, holding that members could go into the parking lot to distribute handbills in their effort to make contact with employees. The Court of Appeals upheld this order against Lechmere, which appealed to the Supreme Court.

Case Decision
The Court reversed in favor of Lechmere, holding that the store had not commited an unfair labor practice. The NLRA's guarantee to employees of the right to organize does not mean that employers cannot exclude nonemployee union organizers from its property, except in rare cases, such as if the employees live on company property. Since the employees were well aware of the union efforts, including the picketing and the mailings, they were accessible to the union. "*Access* to employees, not *success* in winning them over, is the critical issue. . . ."

Managerial Considerations
Although it is trespass for union organizers or other non-employees to enter company property without permission, company employees who would like to be in a union can obviously be on company property. While they may not use work time to campaign for the union, they may talk to other employees about unionization during breaks and before and after working hours. Most companies have learned to be less combative with labor, in part because open communication helps to head off likely unionization efforts.

Employer Communications.   One of the most controversial aspects of union organizing involves what employers may say during union election campaigns. The NLRA provides:

> The expressing of any views, argument, or opinion or the dissemination thereof, whether in written, printed, graphic, or visual form, shall not constitute or be evidence of an unfair labor practice under any of the provisions of this Act, if such expression contains no threat of reprisal or force or promise of benefit.

However, as the following leading case illustrates, interpreting the precise limits of the law has not been a simple matter.

NATIONAL LABOR RELATIONS BOARD v. GOLUB CORPORATION

United States Court of Appeals, Second Circuit
388 F.2d 921 (1967)

Case Background
During a union representation campaign, the employer made speeches and sent letters to the employees that said that the union might make excessive demands on the company. The employer said that companies forced to meet excessive demands sometimes go out of business or have to cut the number of employees. The NLRB ruled these statements to be "threats of reprisal" that were unfair labor practices. The company appealed.

Case Decision
The U.S. Court of Appeals rejected the decision of the NLRB, ruling that an employer's prediction of adverse consequences from unionization is not sufficient to constitute an illegal threat of reprisal.

Managerial Considerations
"The error of the Board in finding violations of the Act in the two passages . . . predicting loss of work, harder work, or even a close-down as a result of unionization is apparent. Nothing in these communications could reasonably be interpreted as a threat to make the employees' lot harder in retaliation for their voting for the union . . . . The only fair reading is that the employer would take these steps solely from economic necessity and with regret. . . ."

A manager may make statements about the possible negative effects of unionization on the company's future and on the future prospects for employment so long as there is a credible basis for such statements. In fact, some companies have closed operations or cut labor forces after being unionized. Such communications must be straightforward and not viewed as a threat. Managers who wish to fight a unionization effort often hire consultants who know how to carry on such battles within the limits of the law.

COLLECTIVE BARGAINING

Once employees choose a bargaining representative, that representative— the union—is now their legal representative. The employer must bargain with the union. The term *collective bargaining* refers to the process by which the employer and the union negotiate a contract, setting forth the terms and conditions of employment for a given period of time. Collective bargaining is more than the initial contract negotiation; it is the entire process of contract administration resulting in a continuous relationship between the employer and the employee representative.

GOOD FAITH BARGAINING

The duty to bargain in good faith is defined in the National Labor Relations Act as follows:

> [T]o bargain collectively is the performance of the mutual obligation of the employer and the representative of the employees to meet at reasonable times and confer in *good faith* with respect to wages, hours, and other terms and conditions of employment, or the negotiation of an agreement, or any question arising thereunder, and the execution of a written contract incorporating any agreement reached if requested by either party, but such obligation does not compel either party to agree to a proposal or require the making of a concession . . . [emphasis added].

The principal difficulty lies in defining what constitutes good faith, since it can involve trying to interpret another's state of mind. Essentially, *good faith* means an obligation to meet and be willing to present proposals and explain reasons, to listen to and consider the proposals of the other party, and to search for some common ground that can serve as the basis for an agreement—but with no requirement of an agreement.

So long as no unfair labor practices are used by the employer or the union, even if it appears that bitterness exists on one or both sides, the use of legal labor practices will not be seen as a failure to bargain in good faith. In general, the Supreme Court has indicated that it is best that the NLRB and the courts not become too involved in the details of labor practices as they relate to the bargaining process, since Congress did not intend for direct intervention in the substance of labor bargains. Rather, Congress took the position that the parties should be free to reach an agreement of their own making.

Actions Not in Good Faith.   Certain actions are recognized as a failure to bargain in good faith. For example, in *NLRB* v. *Katz* in 1962, the Supreme Court said that an employer cannot unilaterally change the terms of an existing agreement with a union. To increase or decrease employment terms—wages or benefits—without consulting the union may be held to be a bad faith attempt to convince the workers that they do not need the union or to create confusion in bargaining. In remedying bad faith bargaining, the NLRB is limited to issuing a cease and desist order; it cannot insert a clause into a collective bargaining agreement.

■ MANDATORY SUBJECTS OF BARGAINING

The NLRA states that bargaining in good faith must occur with respect to "wages, hours, and other terms and conditions of employment." These are *mandatory subjects,* about which employers and unions must bargain in good faith but about which either party may insist on its position and back that insistence with a strike or a lockout.

Employers and unions are free to bargain over any topics they agree to discuss. The following are among the topics that may be placed on the bargaining table because they have been determined by the NLRB or the courts to be subject to mandatory bargaining:

- Pay rate
- Insurance plans
- Holidays
- Overtime pay
- Vacations
- Retirement plans
- Work hours
- Individual merit raises
- Breaks and lunch periods
- Safety practices
- Seniority rights
- Discipline procedures
- Termination procedures
- Layoff procedures

- Recall rights
- Union dues collection
- Grievance procedures
- Arbitration procedures
- No-strike clauses
- Drug testing
- Christmas bonuses

There is no requirement that every such issue be covered in a collective bargaining contract, only that the employer must consider demands about such issues raised by the union. In the event of a stalemate between the employer and the union, a private arbitrator may be called in to help get the talks going, or either party may request the assistance of the Federal Mediation and Conciliation Service. These negotiators have no authority to impose a settlement but often help the parties reach a settlement.

COLLECTIVE BARGAINING AND ARBITRATION

Section 301 of the Taft-Hartley Act—which made *collective bargaining agreements* directly enforceable in federal court—has played a role in the growth of *grievance arbitration* clauses and the establishment of arbitration mechanisms in collective bargaining agreements. Under such clauses, a dispute regarding a collective bargaining agreement between the employer and the union is to be resolved by an internal grievance procedure. If the result of these discussions is not satisfactory, the dispute is heard by an outside labor arbitrator. If the arbitration decision is violated or is believed unjust by one of the parties, the parties may then go to federal court for relief.

Currently, over 90 percent of existing collective bargaining agreements contain such dispute resolution clauses. The federal courts encourage the use of the grievance arbitration process. This has helped prevent the federal court system from being clogged with thousands of disputes.

CONCERTED ACTIVITIES

For productive collective bargaining, both the employer and the union must be able to back up their positions. Both parties can insist on a position and then back it up with a strike, lockout, or some other action that brings economic pressure on the other party. Essentially, these are economic weapons to pressure the opposing party to meet demands. To promote productive collective bargaining, Congress provided that certain activities would be protected so that the parties could effectively support their bargaining demands.

Definition of Concerted Activities.   The NLRA protects the rights of employees, individually or in groups, to engage in *concerted activities* for mutual aid or protection. Usually protected concerted activity involves union organizing efforts. However, concerted activity also involves any joint actions by employees, union or not, such as a refusal to work because of hazards beyond what the employees believe safe or because of other poor working conditions that endanger health or safety.

That concerted activity by employees is protected whether or not a union is involved was made clear by the Supreme Court in *NLRB* v. *Washington Aluminum Co.* (1962). In that case, seven employees who did not belong to a union left work without permission because the furnace at their plant was broken; it was eleven degrees outside and very cold in the plant. The company fired the workers, claiming they had to make specific demands to which the company could respond rather than just walk out. The Court held that activities by employees for the purpose of protecting themselves from intolerable working conditions is a concerted activity protected by the NLRA. Since the decision to walk out was reasonable given the conditions, the workers could not be fired.

Unprotected Activities.   Workers who engage in threats or acts of violence will not be protected by the law, and the employer may discipline or fire them. The Supreme Court has held that employers may fire employees for insubordination, disobedience, or disloyalty unless the reason for such activity involves protected concerted activity. That is, the worker may not be fired for engaging in a union-organizing activity the employer feels to be disloyal. However, a worker who simply attacks the company in public without tying the attack to a union issue may be disciplined or fired.

■ EMPLOYER ECONOMIC RESPONSES

Although employers are not permitted to retaliate against employees for engaging in protected concerted activities, they have the right to use economic weapons and take actions to promote their interests. In a labor dispute, an employer may decide to use a lockout against the employees. A *lockout* occurs when an employer refuses to permit employees to work until a dispute with the union is settled.

Lockouts are legal so long as evidence of bad intent is not shown, such as trying to break the union or punish the workers. However, the employer cannot then allow new workers or strikebreakers to work in place of those workers locked out. That is an unfair labor practice. Rather, the lockout must be *defensive*. It is done in response to a strike, to prevent a sitdown strike in the plant, or to prevent some other activity that would be destructive to the plant or its materials. So long as the lockout is seen as promoting the settlement of the collective bargaining process, it should be upheld as legal.

A tactic successfully used by companies in recent years is the hiring of nonunion workers to replace striking workers. Once a collective bargaining agreement expires, if the union and the employer have not agreed to a new contract and the union calls for a strike, the employer is free to hire new (nonunion) workers and to keep using existing workers who will cross the picket line (crossovers). In some cases, a strike went on so long and there were enough new hires and crossovers that the union simply disappeared or lost substantial strength by the time a new agreement was signed. This was particularly true in the airline industry, as illustrated by the *TWA* case, where deregulation forced firms to be much more cost conscious than they had been in earlier years.

TRANS WORLD AIRLINES, INC. v. INDEPENDENT FEDERATION OF FLIGHT ATTENDANTS

United States Supreme Court
489 U.S. 425, 109 S.Ct. 1225 (1989)

Case Background
TWA and the flight attendants union began bargaining in March 1984 on a new collective bargaining agreement to replace the contract that expired in July 1984. By March 1986 attendants were still working under the old contract and a strike was called. TWA announced that it intended to keep in operation and would hire permanent replacements for striking attendants but that it welcomed attendants who would continue working. One-quarter of the 5,000 attendants continued to work, and TWA hired 2,350 new attendants. When the strike was settled after seventy-two days with a new contract, TWA recalled only 197 of the striking attendants. By May 1988, only 1,100 strikers had been recalled—all with full seniority.

The union sued, claiming (1) that it was an unfair labor practice to hire new attendants and (2) even if hiring the new attendants was legal, the striking attendants had to be hired back because they had more seniority than the newly hired attendants.

Case Decision
The Court ruled in favor of TWA. An employer is not required to lay off junior crossover employees or newly hired employees in order to bring back more senior employees who were on strike.

[T]he decision to guarantee to crossovers the same protections lawfully applied to new hires was a simple decision to apply the preexisting seniority terms of the collective bargaining agreement uniformly to all working employees. That this decision had the effect of encouraging prestrike workers to remain on the job during the strike or to abandon the strike and return to work before all vacancies were filled was an effect of the exercise of TWA's peaceful economic power, a power that the company was legally free to deploy once the parties had exhausted the private dispute resolution mechanisms.

Managerial Considerations
Hiring permanent replacement workers has become a very effective tool for companies to use to encourage unions to settle without a strike. Some companies have agreed to collective bargaining agreements that guarantee seniority even in the event of a strike that occurs after the collective bargaining agreement has ended. This means the company has given up a tool it may wish it had in the future. Note that the Supreme Court has said that an employer may not ask new employees what they think about unionization. It is possible that the new employees will want to vote to bring back the union, but that does not happen in most cases.

UNLAWFUL LABOR ACTIVITIES

Various strikes and forms of picketing by employees are unlawful under the NLRA. If picketing involves violence or threats of violence and the union is held responsible for the actions, it is an unfair labor practice. There are also state laws against such violent acts. However, the fact that union members are involved does not necessarily mean that the union is at fault. Such acts must be based on union policy or occur at the behest of union leaders. Also, a strike can be an unfair labor practice if it violates an NLRB rule or the union's collective bargaining agreement.

■ SECONDARY BOYCOTTS

The most important restrictions on strikes are limitations on *secondary boycotts*. No clear definition of secondary boycott exists. A *primary boycott*—the strike or other concerted action by a union against the employer whose collective bargaining agreement is in question—is clearly legal. In general, a secondary boycott occurs when a union tries to force others to stop doing business with an employer not directly involved in the primary labor dispute. The following forms of secondary activities are illegal:

1. A strike against or refusing to handle goods or perform services for an employer other than the one involved in the primary labor dispute.
2. Threatening, coercing, or restraining any person engaged in commerce—usually an employee—in an effort to spread the dispute beyond the primary employer.

In a strike against a plant owned by the food manufacturer Hormel, the union picketed seven banks, only three of which did business directly with Hormel. The NLRB ruled that the union could not picket any of the banks, since none were involved in the distribution of Hormel products. The picketing was an illegal secondary boycott.

In another line of cases, the Supreme Court held it illegal for a state or local government to intrude in labor disputes that are under the NLRA. In the 1986 decision *Golden State Transit Corp. v. City of Los Angeles,* a taxi company licensed by the city of Los Angeles was struck by its drivers. The city, attempting to support the drivers' strike, told the taxi company that it would not renew its license to operate unless it settled with the union. The Court said that for states to impose additional restrictions on either party in a labor dispute is in conflict with congressional intent regarding labor law. The City of Los Angeles was required to pay $11 million for meddling in the labor dispute.

Legal Activities.   An exception to the rule against secondary boycotts against firms that do business with the primary employer occurs when the *ally doctrine* may be invoked. Because of a strike, an employer may be able to complete only part of the production process. An agreement is then reached with another firm to take the partly completed product and finish it for marketing. A picket around the firm that agrees to finish the product would be legal, even though it is secondary, because the firm has become an ally of the primary employer only because of the strike. The union may picket and ask the employees of the ally of the primary employer to go on strike in support of the primary strike. When another employer is neutral, its employees should not be encouraged to join in the strike.

One way to make a strike more effective is to get cooperation from the customers of the employer. A union may make a peaceful request to other firms or the public not to buy certain products. That is a right of free speech, just as is the right to picket a store peacefully to give customers information about certain products sold at the store that the union would like to see the public stop buying. For example, in the 1988 Supreme Court decision *Edward J. DeBartolo Corp. v. Florida Gulf Coast Building & Construction Trades Council,* it was held legal for the union to pass out leaflets at a shopping mall urging customers not to shop there because of a labor dispute between the union and a construction company building a store at the mall.

LABOR RELATIONS IN JAPAN

INTERNATIONAL ASPECTS

Many American managers believe that if their firms can be organized more like Japanese firms, they might have more success in international competition. The following are some of the most-cited significant features of Japanese labor relations:

1. Since long-term employment is more prevalent and dismissals and layoffs are rare, workers have enough job security to identify with the company and accept changes in it over time.

2. Wages are tied more to seniority in Japan, and workers receive a substantial share of their pay in bonuses twice a year, which may be tied to profitability.

3. Japanese labor contracts with unions are brief and general, giving more emphasis to decision making on the job, which often involves worker input. American labor contracts are lengthy and rigid.

4. Quality circles are used more often and more effectively in Japan.

5. Decisions in Japanese firms are based on consensus building, including substantial consultation with labor. Such procedures are said to increase communication and harmony and make labor feel that it plays a more important role in the organization.

Some of these factors may represent cultural differences that cannot be easily adapted to American firms; others would require a change in the legal labor relationships. While not easily emulated, firms that enhance labor satisfaction usually increase both productivity and profits.

EMPLOYMENT-AT-WILL

The traditional common law rule is that employees serve their employer at will. That is, employers are free to discharge employees for any reason at any time, and employees are free to quit their jobs for any reason at any time. The *employment-at-will* doctrine is, of course, limited by collective bargaining agreements or any other contract that specifies length, terms, and conditions of employment.

Many employees, especially those in managerial and supervisory positions, are clearly at will in employment. Although there is little evidence that this produces abuse on a large scale, cases do arise in which an employee's dismissal seems unjust. For example, in a 1974 Pennsylvania Supreme Court case, United States Steel was sued by Geary, a former employee who was fired by his boss for going over his head to report a serious product problem. Higher management agreed with Geary that the product defect was serious and withdrew the product from the market. Higher management also failed to protect Geary when he was fired by his boss, who had ignored Geary's comments about the defective product and had told him to ignore it. The court noted that although Geary had been a loyal employee—and in this case may have saved his company millions of dollars—under employment-at-will, Geary had no legal complaint.

■ PUBLIC POLICY EXCEPTIONS

The supreme courts of many states have chipped away at the strength of the employment-at-will doctrine. There are *public policy exceptions* to at-will discharges for acts that public policy encourages or for refusal to do an act that public policy condemns. In most states, it is clear that employees may not be terminated at will for the following:

1. Refusing to commit an illegal act (such as falsifying reports required by a government agency).

2. Performing an important public duty (such as reporting for jury duty when called).

3. Exercising a public right (such as filing a claim for workers' compensation benefits).

The Arizona Supreme Court and some others allow a fourth exception on grounds of public policy, called the *whistle blower* exception. This occurs when an employee who is aware of an illegal act of the employer brings the act to the attention of the proper authorities, even though the employee was not legally responsible for the act in question. More cases can be expected to test the limits of this rule. The general test is that the whistle blowing is primarily for the public good—to enhance law enforcement and to expose unsafe conditions—rather than primarily for private gain.

EMPLOYEE HANDBOOKS

Many employers issue handbooks to employees to explain company policy, benefits, and procedures. As the Supreme Court of Illinois noted in a 1987 case, most courts now hold *employee handbooks* to create binding contractual obligations—if one can show the elements of offer, acceptance, and consideration in the employment process. That is, if the employer makes it clear that rules in the handbook are to be followed and if the handbook discusses proper termination procedure, employees have a right to have that procedure followed.

If the handbook says that employees can be dismissed only for "good cause," most courts now hold that that dismissal is no longer at will. If a firm experiences a downturn in business and fires one-third of its employees—is that "good cause"? Yes, because it is a valid business reason, not like dismissal on the whim of a supervisor. Since the courts may turn to the handbooks as conditions of employment, the handbooks should be written with some precision so as not to open the door to needless litigation, where employees can sue for compensatory damages for wrongful dismissal.

Punitive Damages.   Of even greater concern to employers are such decisions as the 1986 Montana Supreme Court case that upheld a 1.3-million-dollar punitive damage verdict against a bank that fired an employee of twenty-eight years. The court said that because the employee was given no clue that her job performance was unsatisfactory, her expectation of continued employment had been violated. The possibility of such cases in other states means that employers should consider specifying terms and conditions of employment, even if employment is simply to be at will.

The California Supreme Court joined a number of other courts by holding that punitive damages for wrongful dismissal should be rare. In a 1988 case, the California high court upheld the rights of employees to sue employers for breach of an employment contract, whether the contract is written, verbal, or implied. However, the court concluded that because "the employment relationship is fundamentally contractual . . . , contractual remedies should remain the sole available relief for breaches of . . . good faith and fair dealing in the employment context." Therefore, when an employee has a valid claim of a breach of an employment contract, the damages will be compensatory (primarily lost wages).

SUBSTANCE ABUSE

Some abused substances, such as cocaine, are illegal; others, like Valium, are legal but are dispensed illegally. Because of the illegality, the full extent of the problem is unknown. The most common abused substance is alcohol. The National Institute of Mental Health reports the 13.6 percent of all adults have experienced alcohol addiction or abuse in their lives. About 8 percent of the working population are alcoholics, that is, abusers of a legal drug that is legally dispensed. Add to this the estimated 5 percent to 10 percent of the adult population who abuse or are addicted to illegal and improperly dispensed drugs, and it means that about one in six working-age people have a substance abuse problem.

PRACTICAL PROBLEMS FOR BUSINESS

Tragic stories about lives ruined by substance abuse are common. Substance abuse directly affects employers primarily because it means reduced productivity and higher medical insurance costs, which cost employers well over $100 billion per year. The National Institute on Alcoholism and Alcohol Abuse estimates that the average health care (insurance) costs for families with an alcoholic are double the costs incurred by families with no alcoholics. The huge cost of substance abuse obscures the costs imposed by another widely used, highly addictive legal drug—nicotine—which also reduces productivity and increases medical expenses.

Expensive Consequences.   The oil spill caused by the wreck of the Exxon *Valdez* off the Alaska coast in 1989 raised issues beyond environmental liability, because it appears to have been a problem directly related to substance abuse. The captain of the ship had a history of alcohol abuse and was found guilty of operating the ship under the influence of alcohol. While he suffered a small legal penalty for his action, Exxon suffered over a billion dollars in costs. The company subsequently announced that all known alcohol and other drug abusers, even after treatment, would not be allowed to return to critical duties such as piloting a ship or operating a refinery. Such workers would be given less sensitive—and less productive—assignments. Obviously, had Exxon understood all the factors that could produce that environmental catastrophe, it would have taken steps to avoid it.

The problem is not unique to that incident. The U.S. Chamber of Commerce reports that workers under the influence of alcohol or other drugs are 3.6 times more likely to suffer an injury or cause one to someone else. The Federal Railroad Administration found that between 1975 and 1984, forty-eight railroad accidents that killed thirty-seven people and caused millions of dollars in damages were caused by alcohol- or other drug-impaired workers. The National Transportation Safety Board found alcohol or other drugs in one-third of the accidents involving truck drivers killed in highway accidents.

Testing and Treatment.   While some drugs are new to the market, substance abuse is not new; it is a problem that only recently been brought into the open. In 1983, only three percent of the *Fortune 500* firms had drug testing programs of any sort. Five years later, over 50 percent had testing programs.

Most companies provide employee assistance programs to help deal with alcohol and other drug problems. Treatment is expensive. For example, in 1990, Motorola spent $4,000 to $10,000 for each of 100 to 125 employees a month who volunteered for detoxification treatment. Even if employers do not offer assistance with such expensive programs as a part of employees' health benefits, the costs of dealing with substance abuse show up in various ways. Companies must balance the costs of treatment against the costs of lower productivity and the prospect of liability from accidents caused by employee substance abuse.

■ LEGAL ISSUES IN DRUG TESTING

Companies that are unionized cannot impose a drug testing program for their workers. Since a testing program is a condition affecting work, the NLRA requires that the employer negotiate with the union for a program that is spelled out in the collective bargaining agreement. Hence, the discussion here largely concerns nonunionized places of employment. Further, a substance abuser may have certain rights under the Rehabilitation Act of 1973 and the Disabilities Act of 1990, an issue that is discussed in the next chapter.

Drug-Free Workplace Act.   The *Drug-Free Workplace Act* of 1988 requires all companies of any size with more than $25,000 worth of business with the federal government to certify that they will provide a "drug-free" workplace. The primary requirements are that the employer

1. Publish a policy statement that substance abuse in the workplace will not be tolerated.

2. Establish a drug awareness program to inform employees of the dangers of drug abuse.

3. Make known to employees the availability of programs to help those with substance abuse problems.

Employers failing to comply may lose their business with the federal government. This statute is simple to deal with and is not regarded as significant in fighting substance abuse.

State Statutory Standards.   State legislatures have enacted a variety of statutes concerning drug testing, and one must be aware of local requirements. Iowa allows employees to be tested if

1. The employer has "probable cause" to believe that the employee's job performance is impaired by drug use.

2. The employee poses a safety danger to persons or property.

3. The drug test is sent to a state-approved laboratory.

There may be no disciplinary action for a first drug offense if the employee completes the treatment that is recommended upon evaluation.

Minnesota allows testing of job applicants if a job offer is extended, if all applicants in the same job classes are required to be tested, and if those who fail the test are notified. Like Connecticut, Minnesota allows random drug testing of current employees only for those in safety-sensitive positions. Those two states, as well as Vermont, Montana, and Rhode Island, allow testing of employees only if there is "reasonable suspicion" or "probable cause" to believe that alcohol or other drug use is impairing job performance.

Maryland and Nebraska do not restrict the conditions under which drug tests may be required but do provide quality and procedural safeguards for the tests to ensure that records are kept properly and that there is a chance for independent verification of test results.

Utah holds employers immune from liability for action taken by employees dismissed for drug usage or by applicants rejected because they failed a drug test, so long as the employer has a written policy, informs employees of positive tests, and maintains proper documentation of tests.

Court Rulings.   As the different statutory standards indicate, the law in this area is emerging and not settled. Since the law of contract and agency is the basis of most of the employment relationship, employers are presumed to have wide latitude to adopt drug policies. However, there have been a variety of conflicting court cases as cases arise based on tort and contract law and on claims brought under Fourth Amendment protection against "unreasonable searches and seizures." The law cannot be summarized because it is so uncertain, but the Supreme Court has started to give some guidance, as seen in the *Skinner* case. While this case concerns workers in an industry subject to direct federal regulation, the opinion provides broader guidance.

SKINNER v. RAILWAY LABOR EXECUTIVES' ASSOCIATION

United States Supreme Court
489 U.S. 1, 109 S.Ct. 1402 (1989)

Case Background
Based on evidence that alcohol and other drug abuse by railroad employees caused or contributed to a number of fatal train accidents, the Federal Railroad Administration (FRA) issued regulations as a part of its safety standards, requiring railroads to conduct blood and urine tests of employees involved in train accidents. The FRA also encouraged railroads to adopt breath and urine test programs to administer when employees were involved in other safety violations. The Supreme Court was asked whether such tests violate the Fourth Amendment.

Case Decision
The Supreme Court upheld federal regulations that imposed alcohol and other drug tests on workers involved in railroad accidents. The Court also upheld the right of railroad companies to adopt their own alcohol and other drug tests in situations involving other safety violations.

> The possession of unlawful drugs is a criminal offense that the Government may punish, but it is a separate and far more dangerous wrong to perform certain sensitive tasks while under the influence of those substances. Performing those tasks while impaired by alcohol is, of course, equally dangerous, though consumption of alcohol is legal in most other contexts. The Government may take all necessary and reasonable regulatory steps to prevent or deter that hazardous conduct, and since the gravamen of the evil is performing certain functions while concealing the substance in the body, it may be necessary, as in the case before us, to examine the body or its fluids to accomplish the regulatory purpose. The necessity to perform that regulatory function with respect to railroad employees engaged in safety-sensitive tasks, and the reasonableness of the system for doing so, have been established in this case.

Managerial Considerations
Intrusive alcohol or other drug tests—especially taking blood—are harder to justify than less intrusive tests like breath or urine samples. Nevertheless, employers may not randomly impose such tests, which must be given as part of the company's substance abuse policy. If certain employees are to be singled out for tests on demand (rather than a policy of all employee testing at random), there needs to be a safety rationale for testing rather than testing done merely at the whim of a supervisor. The most successful drug policies are often developed with the input of employees, who have insights as to substance abuse on the job; and employee participation in planning increases likelihood of acceptance.

In a companion case to *Skinner,* the Court considered the legality of drug testing of U.S. Customs Service employees who sought a transfer or promotion to positions involving drug interception, enforcement of related laws, carrying of firearms, or handling of classified material. The Court concluded in *Treasury Employees* v. *Von Raab* that the program was legal and that warrants to impose the test were not required. The circumstances in which the testing was mandated were specified and covered all employees equally; that is, agency officials would have no discretion to determine who would or would not have to take a test. Given the safety and sensitivity issues involved, the benefits of the suspicionless searches outweigh the privacy interests of the employees.

■ EMPLOYER SUBSTANCE ABUSE POLICY

Like any matter involving employee rights, a *substance abuse policy* should not be adopted without careful consideration of the legal issues. In general, an employer should have a clear policy statement that demonstrates that testing is not discriminatory or haphazard. The policy should state why the tests are being done, what is being tested for, what will be done with the results, and what will be the consequences of the test results. Rather than test only employees that supervisors think may be drug users, companies should test all employees in certain categories or when a specific safety or security issue is involved.

The Exxon *Valdez* story provides another lesson about improper substance abuse policy. After the Alaska oil spill, Exxon banned employees with histories of alcoholism from key positions on oil tankers. The chief engineer on a tanker was removed from his position because of his history of alcohol abuse and was given a job at the same pay on land. He sued Exxon, claiming discrimination; and in 1992, a federal district court jury awarded him $750,000 in damages. Companies cannot always change job conditions for current employees without giving employees the opportunity to comply with new substance abuse policies.

Helping Abusers.   Companies should have a plan of action for those who test positive. In general, companies that try to help people with a drug problem rather than dismiss them will have fewer problems. Since drug tests have a certain rate of incorrect results, employees who test positive should be given a second test rather than rely on a possible false reading. The credibility of the testing laboratory should be high. Because the legal developments in this area will generate substantial interest in the public and contain legally explosive issues for employers, they should be followed with care.

Nicotine.   Another addictive substance drawing the increasing attention of employers is nicotine. Some companies and governmental units no longer hire smokers and have banned smoking among certain categories of employees. Some employers ban smoking on all company property. Smoking bans are defended because of the lower health insurance premiums for nonsmokers and the fewer days lost to illness, on the average, by nonsmokers.

The National Center for Health Promotion estimated in 1990 that smokers added an average of $350 per year per employee in costs borne by employers. This translates into tens of billions of dollars per year higher labor costs due to lost workdays and higher medical services due to smoking—not including the lowered productivity. The tobacco industry attacks such bans as a violation of individual rights and is lobbying for statutes, such as the one passed in Virginia, that prohibit discrimination against smokers.

PROTECTION OF WORKER SAFETY AND HEALTH

Concern about worker safety dates to the mid-1800s and the early state regulation of coal-mine safety. In the late 1800s, federal regulations on job safety in coal mines were first enacted. This early legislative effort concentrated on issues of job safety—accidents, injuries, and deaths—not occupational health. Between 1890 and 1920, most states enacted a job safety law, although many were merely cosmetic and most were poorly enforced.

▉ OCCUPATIONAL SAFETY AND HEALTH ACT

In 1970, the National Safety Council reported that 14,000 workers died and two million workers suffered disabling injuries on the job every year. Other studies estimated that hundreds of thousands of cases of occupational illnesses caused many additional deaths each year. Congress enacted the Occupational Safety and Health Act of 1970 (OSHAct), which created the Occupational Safety and Health Administration (OSHA). The Act requires employers to comply with OSHA's standards, including keeping records of work-related injuries, illnesses, and deaths, and to provide a workplace "free from recognized hazards that are causing or are likely to cause death or serious physical hardship to employees."

Establishing Safety and Health Standards.   The general procedure used to establish a new *permanent standard* requires several steps. First, standards are recommended by the National Institute of Occupational Safety and Health (NIOSH), a government agency that conducts research related to occupational safety and health. An advisory committee established by OSHA then reviews and, if necessary, amends the proposed standards. This committee is composed of representatives from industry, labor (usually a labor union representative), and the public.

The proposed standards are then published in the *Federal Register*, and interested parties can comment. After considering the comments, the Secretary of Labor issues the standards, giving them the force of law. The process can be time consuming. For example, in 1971, the steel industry asked OSHA for coke-oven emissions standards. NIOSH issued its recommendations in the spring of 1973. The advisory committee issued its report in the spring of 1974. The proposed standards were issued by OSHA in the summer of 1975. The final standards were finally issued in October of 1976 — more than five years after the process began.

OSHA Workplace Inspections.   Although the OSHAct provided OSHA with the authority to conduct surprise workplace inspections, the Supreme Court in *Marshall* v. *Barlow's, Inc.* (1978) held that the Fourth Amendment of the Constitution prohibits warrantless searches by OSHA. However, the Court required OSHA to obtain only administrative warrants, thereby exempting the agency from showing probable cause and other conditions ordinarily required to secure a criminal warrant.

The typical workplace inspection includes an examination of appropriate health and safety records, interviews with employees, and a walk-around inspection of the plant. Representatives of both the company and the employees have the right to accompany the inspector. Since 1977, OSHA has attempted to concentrate its inspection efforts in those industries where health and safety problems are perceived to be the worst — industries such as construction, petrochemicals, and heavy manufacturing.

Employee Rights.   It is unlawful for an employer to punish an employee for participating in an OSHA workplace inspection or exercising any right guaranteed by the OSHAct. In particular, employees have the right to refuse work assignments they believe may pose a serious threat to their safety or health.

The Supreme Court reviewed such an incident in *Whirlpool Corp. v. Marshall* (1980). Two employees at a manufacturing plant refused to perform maintenance duties that required them to work on a screen twenty feet above the plant floor. The safety of the screen was at issue, since one employee had fallen through it and had been killed and there had been several other close calls. When the employees refused to work on the screen, they were sent home, lost six hours of pay each, and had a reprimand placed in their file. OSHA, through the Secretary of Labor, sued the employer on behalf of the workers, asking that their records be cleared and they be paid the lost wages. The Supreme Court supported the workers, holding that the OSHA rule that allows employees to refuse to obey orders that pose a risk of death or serious injury was within the intent of Congress when the law was passed.

Duty of Employees.   OSHA does not place the entire safety burden on employers. The Act provides that employees "shall comply with occupational safety and health standards and all rules, regulations, and orders." OSHA does not penalize employees who ignore rules of which they are aware, but it may relieve the employer of liability. However, an employer cannot always use the defense that the employees ignored safety procedures. It is the company's duty to work to enforce safety standards, even if the workers dislike them.

OSHA Penalties.   Based on inspections by OSHA compliance officers, citations may be issued for rule violations, and monetary penalties may be imposed. Section 17 of OSHAct provides for the following penalties:

- For a willful or repeated violation—up to $10,000.
- For a serious violation (chance of death or serious injury)—up to $1,000.
- For a nonserious violation—up to $1,000.
- For failure to correct a violation—up to $1,000 per day.
- For a willful violation resulting in the death of an employee, first conviction—up to $10,000 and six months in jail; subsequent convictions—up to $20,000 and one year in jail.

OSHA fines can be large, such as the $4 million Phillips Petroleum paid in 1991 for willful safety violations in connection with explosions in 1989 that killed twenty-three workers at a chemical plant near Houston. But in total, fines are small, especially compared to the liability in tort or in workers' compensation payments.

■ WORKERS AND TOXIC SUBSTANCES

Most OSHA standards concern safety. Thousands of specifications concern physical safety—such as machine design and placement, stairway design, and the height of fire extinguishers. A small number of health standards have been issued: for asbestos, vinyl chloride, coke-oven emissions, and other industrial carcinogens.

Toxic Substance Standards.   With regard to health standards for worker exposure to toxic substances, OSHA must issue standards that "most adequately assure, to the extent feasible, . . . that no employee will suffer material impairment of health or functional capacity even if such employee has regular exposure to the hazard . . . for the period of his working life." Every health standard that OSHA has issued or proposed has been attacked by both industry and labor. Two important Supreme Court decisions that have resulted from those attacks now influence OSHA's health-standard-setting process. The cases involved health standards for benzene and cotton dust.

Significant Health Risk Requirement.   A study of benzene, a substance known to be dangerous to humans at certain levels, resulted in a NIOSH report that benzene be considered carcinogenic in humans. OSHA established standards for benzene in 1977. The American Petroleum Institute and others attacked the regulations as too extreme and unjustified. In its review in *Industrial Union* v. *American Petroleum Institute* (1980) (the "benzene case"), the Supreme Court found that the agency did not have adequate information regarding the actual effects of benzene. The Court held that before OSHA requires that worker exposure to a carcinogen be reduced to its lowest feasible level, the agency must first find that the existing exposure to the substance "poses a significant health risk in the workplace."

Cost Benefit Analysis Not Required.   The Court noted in the "benzene case" that the cost of implementing the standard was expected to be hundreds of millions of dollars. Should OSHA's health standards reflect a reasonable relationship between their costs and benefits? That question was answered in the "cotton dust case," *American Textile Manufacturers Institute* v. *Donovan* (1981). The Supreme Court held that cost benefit analysis is not required as a justification for an OSHA standard. The statute says that standards must be feasible. Congress "chose to place pre-eminent value on assuring employees a safe and healthful working environment, limited only by the feasibility of achieving such an environment." Thus, the costs of complying with a health or safety standard may outweigh the economic benefits.

Hazard Communication Standard.   A major step was taken in 1988 to ensure that chemical hazards in the workplace are evaluated. The *hazard communication standard* (HCS) covers all employees exposed to hazardous chemicals in the normal course of operations. Chemical producers and importers must conduct a "hazard determination" of each chemical they produce or sell in which they identify and consider scientific evidence about the hazards of each chemical. Information about chemical hazards must be updated as new evidence becomes available. Where hazardous chemicals are used, employers must have

1. A written hazard communication program that lists all hazardous chemicals in the workplace.
2. Labels for all chemical containers with hazard warnings and the name and address of the producer.

3. Material safety data sheets, which must accompany every chemical contained, with details of the chemical such as its physical and health hazards, precautions, and emergency procedures.

4. Employee training programs about hazardous chemicals and information about precautions and procedures.

Environmentalism in the workplace is now a major issue for employers, who work with OSHA and the Environmental Protection Agency on issues that are now expanding to cover concerns such as the ill effects of tobacco smoke on nonsmokers in the workplace.

WORKERS' COMPENSATION

Beginning in 1910, the states enacted *workers' compensation laws* that require employers to pay employees a benefit set by a compensation schedule. The benefits are paid regardless of the cause of a work-related injury (no-fault insurance). Workers' compensation acts as a system of mandatory insurance. Benefits are set by a state agency, and premiums are paid by employers. In exchange for paying the premiums, the employer becomes immune from employee damage suits (tort) arising from on-the-job accidents.

The following objectives underlie workers' compensation laws:

1. Provide sure, prompt, and reasonable income and medical benefits to work-related accident victims or income benefits to their dependents, regardless of fault.

2. Provide a certain remedy and reduce court costs and time delays associated with personal injury litigation.

3. Prevent public and private charities from incurring the financial strains that would accompany uncompensated accidents.

4. Reduce or eliminate payment of fees to lawyers and expert witnesses.

5. Encourage employer interest in safety and rehabilitation of workers through an insurance scheme that bases rates on the experience rating of the employer.

6. Promote open discussion of the causes of accidents rather than encourage concealment of fault, thereby helping to reduce future accidents and health hazards.

■ COMPENSATION PROVIDED

Workers' compensation generally has five benefit categories: death, total disability, permanent partial disability, temporary partial disability, and medical expenses. Most states do not restrict the amount or duration of medical benefits. While some injuries require only medical assistance, others take the worker out of the workplace for some recovery period, sometimes forever. Workers usually receive about two-thirds of their gross wages as disability income up to a state-imposed weekly maximum, as low as $200 in some states to as high as $700 in others. In some states, the benefits run for over ten years for temporary disability. For permanent disability, the benefits last a lifetime but may be offset by Social Security Disability payments.

■ INCENTIVES FOR SAFETY

Generally, workers' compensation provides employers with financial incentives to invest in safety on the work site. Insurance premiums are based on safety and injury claims records. Hence, firms with the lowest number of injuries, and therefore the fewest claims, have the lowest premiums. (See Table 12–2.)

Further incentives to participate in the system exist. If an employer chooses not to comply (which is allowed in some cases) or if an employer fails to comply, an injured employee can sue the employer in tort for negligence and collect the full cost of the accident. In such a case, there is no statutory limit to the amount of damages recoverable by an injured worker or his or her family.

■ BASIS FOR A CLAIM

About 90 percent of all workers are covered by workers' compensation laws. Many of those who are not covered are protected by other laws, such as the Federal Employer's Liability Act. For an employee to have a claim, it must generally be shown that the worker received a personal injury as a result of an accident that arose out of and in the course of employment. The negligence or fault of the employer in causing the injury is not an issue. The application of the law is broad. Compensable injuries can include mental and nervous disorders and heart attacks that occur on the job.

Most courts are strict in interpreting state statutes that clearly state that the liability coverage of workers' compensation "shall be exclusive in place of any and all other liability to such employees . . . entitled to damages in any action at law or otherwise on account of any injury or

---

TABLE 12–2
WORKERS' COMPENSATION PREMIUMS, NORTH CAROLINA, 1992

Occupation	Base Rate*
Lawyers and employees	$00.23
Physicians and assistants	.29
Upholsterers	1.37
AVERAGE FOR EMPLOYER IN NORTH CAROLINA	1.95
Taxidermists	2.87
Street pavers	6.17
Welders	12.09
Traveling carnival employees	17.80
Athletes on contract	38.67
High metal structure painters	52.24

*Base insurance premium rates, per $100 paid to employees.

SOURCE: North Carolina Rate Bureau.

death . . . ." The actions of the employer, employee, or third person become relevant only if there was intentional infliction of harm, that is, an intentional tort. The employee may then file a civil action for damages outside the workers' compensation system. Attempts to evade the worker's compensation system by claims of mental distress imposed by supervisory harassment are not allowed except in cases of intentional harm. As noted previously, employers are forbidden by statute or by public policy from firing employees who seek compensation by filing claims.

■ A FLAWED SYSTEM?

Employers complain that workers' compensation insurance is too expensive. Workers' compensation now costs over $60 billion a year—triple what it was ten years ago—and amounts to $500 per employee annually. One reason for the expense appears to be that there are too many awards for permanent partial disability, which results in lifetime payment awards, when the worker is in fact not permanently disabled.

On the other side, consider the amounts paid for losses suffered in injuries, which are usually fixed by a schedule. Suppose a worker loses a foot but is able to return to work. Medical expenses and lost work time aside, how much is a foot worth? As of 1989, on the lower end, the state of Georgia said it was worth $23,625. On the higher end, the state of North Carolina said $54,144. It is likely that if a jury was allowed to determine the worth of the loss of a foot for a lifetime, if an employer was negligent, the award would be much larger. So it is unlikely that employers would prefer to operate under the tort system rather than under this system of awards determined by statute.

GENERAL REGULATION OF LABOR MARKETS

Besides the law we have already covered, restrictions are placed on the labor market by a variety of controls. Federal immigration laws restrict who is allowed to work in the country. The minimum wage law sets a lower limit on what employees may be paid. Many states restrict entry into occupations by a series of licensing requirements. And employee pensions are subject to federal regulation.

■ RESTRICTIONS ON IMMIGRATION

The United States is a nation of immigrants and is the most popular destination for peoples from many countries where there are fewer opportunities. Millions of illegal immigrants work in the country, most of whom are concentrated in California, Arizona, New Mexico, Texas, and Florida. The *Immigration Reform and Control Act* of 1986 sets strict standards for employees and employers. To be hired legally in the United States, a person must be able to present certain documents to show his or her identity and authorization to work. Such documentary proof may be required even if the person is a U.S. citizen.

Since violations of the law can mean criminal penalties, employers must be sure to meet the basic requirements. Employers must collect evidence of citizenship or of legal work status for all new employees. Any of the following documents is legal proof of employment eligibility:

- U.S. passport
- Certificate of U.S. citizenship
- Certificate of naturalization
- Foreign passport with employment authorization
- Alien registration card with photograph

Combinations of other documents, such as driver's license, school ID card, original Social Security card, or birth certificate, may be put together to provide legal proof to satisfy Immigration and Naturalization Service requirements.

■ FEDERAL MINIMUM WAGE REQUIREMENTS

Federal minimum wage requirements were initiated in 1938 as a part of the Fair Labor Standards Act. Over the years, the minimum wage has increased so that it is now equal to about 50 percent of the average manufacturing wage. In 1991, the minimum wage became $4.25 an hour. Employers must also pay Social Security tax (7.65 percent), workers' compensation insurance, and unemployment insurance taxes. The law has also been amended to expand the sectors of the labor force that are covered. Initially, less than half of all nonsupervisory employees in the private, nonagricultural sector were covered; now over 90 percent are covered. This expansion, combined with legislation in most states that complements the federal law, means that most jobs are covered by the minimum wage requirement.

Supporters of the minimum wage contend that the law requires employers to pay a fair wage to employees and, although the wage is relatively low, will not allow workers to be paid so little that they have trouble buying even the necessities of life. On the other side are those who argue that the law results in lower demand for workers in the minimum wage category—usually young persons, often minorities, with little education or job experience. The result is relatively high unemployment among persons in those groups who never get the opportunity to work to develop labor skills that will command higher wages.

The overall impact of the minimum wage is difficult to assess. The minimum wage makes some people better off—those who obtain jobs at higher wages than they would have in the absence of the law. It also makes some people worse off—those who cannot obtain jobs because of the reduction in demand for low-skill, poorly educated workers.

■ OCCUPATIONAL LICENSURE AND REGULATION

Entry into many occupations is controlled by various regulations or *licensing requirements*. In such occupations, an individual cannot simply set up and begin to operate a business. Rather, permission from the regulating agency is required that usually involves some demonstration of competency or payment of a high entry fee. The expressed purpose of these labor restrictions is to protect the consumer by guaranteeing that businesses will provide service of a certain quality and that fewer unscrupulous people will operate in certain professions.

Regulation Set by State Law.   Although a few occupations have entry restrictions set at the federal level, most restrictions are set at the state level. In most states, an individual must receive a license or certificate from the state to practice as a lawyer, doctor, dentist, nurse, veterinarian, optometrist, optician, barber, cosmetologist, or architect. In various states, an individual must be licensed to be a dog groomer, beekeeper, industrial psychologist, building contractor, electrician, plumber, or massage parlor operator. Usually, a state commission is established to determine what the entry criteria will be for one to be licensed to practice. In most cases, there is a formal education requirement; and in some cases, an apprenticeship period is required, or a standardized test of knowledge about the profession must be passed.

Impact on Consumers.   Some aspects of such occupational licensing have been criticized for practices that may be detrimental to consumers. The Supreme Court has prohibited price fixing by lawyers through state bar associations. Similarly, restrictions on advertising, especially restrictions on price advertising, have been attacked and removed in recent years. Regardless of the impact of licensing on the quality and price of service to consumers, such procedures raise the cost of entering many professions, making it more difficult for new entrants to get into the profession and to compete with existing professionals. In addition, some critics have charged that occupational licensing particularly discriminates against minorities and women, many of whom are just now being given the education and opportunities to enter professions that were previously very difficult to enter.

◼ THE REGULATION OF PRIVATE EMPLOYEE RETIREMENT PLANS

The most important legislation regulating private employee retirement plans is the *Employee Retirement Income Security Act* of 1974 (ERISA). The main objective of ERISA is to guarantee the expectations of retirement plan participants and to promote the growth of private pension plans. ERISA was prompted by horror stories about employees who made years of contributions to retirement funds only to receive nothing. For example, the closing of Studebaker in 1963 left more than 8,500 employees without retirement benefits.

ERISA is directed at most employee benefit plans, including medical, surgical, or hospital benefits; sickness, accident, or disability benefits; death benefits; unemployment benefits; vacation benefits; apprenticeship or training benefits; day-care centers; scholarship funds; prepaid legal services; retirement income programs; and deferred income programs.

Vesting Requirements.   The law establishes *vesting* requirements; that is, it guarantees that plan participants will receive some retirement benefits after a reasonable length of employment. All plans must be adequately funded to meet their expected liabilities. A termination insurance program is to be provided in case of the failure of a plan. The law provides standards of conduct for trustees and fiduciaries of employee benefit plans.

The major problem covered by ERISA is that of the loss of all benefits by employees who had many years of service with a company and then either quit or were fired. The law makes all full-time employees over the age of twenty-five with one year of service eligible for participation in employee benefit plans. In 1992 the Supreme Court held that who is an "employee" covered by ERISA is determined by traditional agency law criteria for establishing employer-employee relationships. Employers cannot call employees something else if they are employees under agency law principles.

Mandatory *vesting* (when the employee becomes the owner of the retirement proceeds) was established by ERISA. It provides the employer with three options: (1) to have 100 percent vesting after ten years of employment; (2) to have 25 percent vesting after five years, then 5 percent vesting a year for five years, then 10 percent vesting a year for five years, to achieve 100 percent vesting in fifteen years; and (3) vesting under the rule-of-forty-five vesting. Under the rule of forty-five, if the age and years of service of an employee total forty-five or if an employee has ten years' service, there must be at least 50 percent vesting. Each added year of employment provides 10 percent more vesting so that an employee will be fully vested within fifteen years.

Funding Shortages?   Concern is developing that despite the standards set by ERISA, many pension funds may not be properly funded. The Pension Benefit Guaranty Corporation is the federal agency that insures the solvency of pension funds. As of 1990, it estimated that the fifty corporations with the largest amounts of unfunded pension liabilities were $14 billion in the red. Like the savings and loan industry, the taxpayers may end up with a major bailout on their hands if better solvency rules are not put into effect.

SUMMARY: A GUIDE FOR MANAGERS

- Under the Norris-La Guardia Act, federal courts may not issue injunctions against unions in labor disputes. Employers must bargain with unions according to the terms of the collective bargaining agreement rather than seek relief in federal court.

- The National Labor Relations Act (NLRA), which originated with the Wagner Act in 1935, gives employees the right to organize unions and to bargain collectively through representatives of their choosing. The Act made it illegal for an employer to interfere with employees in the exercise of those rights, and employee actions could not interfere with the employer's interest in plant safety, efficiency, and discipline. The Act also created the National Labor Relations Board (NLRB), which is responsible for resolving unfair labor practice disputes and supervising matters of union representation.

- The Landrum-Griffin Act, a part of the NLRA, provides federal regulation of internal union affairs. The law is to make union procedures and elections democratic. It covers the election of union leadership, protects the right of union members to speak out about union matters, and assures union members the right to see the books of the union, which are audited by the Department of Labor.

- If more than 30 percent of the workers at a workplace petition for a union representation election, the NLRB holds an election to determine whether a majority of the workers want union representation. Workers can also vote to terminate union representation. Both the employer and the union have the right to argue about the pros and cons of union representation.

- When a majority of the workers at a workplace vote for union representation, all workers are covered by the collective bargaining agreement settled by management and the union, and all workers must follow the procedures established for handling complaints. Workers who are not union members must follow the rules set by the collective bargaining contract.

- Workers who work at a unionized workplace must either join the union and pay dues or, if they do not want to join the union, pay agency fees to the union. Agency fees cannot include money used for union political purposes; they are to cover the cost of union representation. In the twenty-one right-to-work states, workers at unionized workplaces cannot be forced to pay agency fees, making unions less effective in such states.

- Most workers are governed by the law of employment-at-will, which is a part of the law of agency and of contract. There are public policy and statutory exceptions to the rule of employment-at-will, but most aspects of job conditions and rights are determined by written, verbal, or implied contracts, which can include the terms established in a firm's employee handbook. Companies must be sensitive to establishing contracts that can leave them open to charges of unjust dismissal if they do not follow promised procedures.

- While the law is not settled, companies have the right to have policies regarding testing for substance abuse and steps that must be taken by the employee if abuse is detected. Generally, companies are free to require drug tests of job applicants. Companies may wish to control substance abuse to reduce medical expenses, improve worker productivity, and reduce accidents.

- OSHA has primary responsibility for determining work safety and health regulations and for enforcing those regulations. If a company fails to meet minimal safety standards, workers have the right to walk off the job to protect their health. Such regulations must be justified by documented need, but there is no requirement they be cost effective. Recently, OSHA has turned more attention to health issues, such as worker protection from hazardous chemicals.

- Most employers must pay for workers' compensation insurance to ensure that injured employees, regardless of fault, will have medical expenses covered and receive partial compensation for lost wages. Regulations of labor markets require that employers collect evidence to show that all new employees are U.S. citizens or are noncitizens with a legal work status. Employers must also comply with federal minimum wage requirements. Entry into many occupations is controlled by state regulations, which often require certain levels of education and passage of competency examinations. Finally, the Employee Retirement Income Security Act is designed to give employees the right to their pension benefits after a certain time of service and to provide federal inspection and guarantee of the solvency of pension funds.

MANAGER'S ETHICAL DILEMMA

SHOULD EMPLOYERS DICTATE EMPLOYEE LIFESTYLE?

Most skilled workers—blue-collar and white-collar—receive thousands of dollars each year in health and life insurance benefits. As medical technology continues to improve and diseases that used to be hopeless can be treated—but at high cost—the cost of health insurance can be expected to continue to rise.

To help contain medical benefits costs, managers have adopted numerous strategies. Some have installed fitness centers, where employees can exercise and get advice on proper diet. There is clear statistical evidence that on the average, workers who stay in shape will miss fewer workdays and will not need as much medical care. Company productivity is thereby increased and insurance costs reduced.

As noted in the chapter, some companies have adopted a policy of not hiring smokers or people who fail drug tests. The problems of drug abuse are well-known; at the same time, smokers on the average have more health problems and miss more days of work than nonsmokers.

QUESTIONS

How far should managers be allowed to go in discriminating among employees with various lifestyles? While drug abuse is illegal, alcohol abuse and smoking are not. Further, there is good evidence that obese people have more health costs than nonobese people. Can a manager implement a policy not to hire obese people? Since certain diets are more likely to lead to heart disease than other diets, can managers screen employees diets? Can managers forbid employees from riding motorcycles, since they are more dangerous than riding in cars?

On one side, some claim that managers should pay no attention to any personal attributes of employees other than their ability to do the job. On the other side, if employees who have "unhealthful" habits irritate other employees and incur higher medical costs, why should the "healthy" employees subsidize the costs of the habits of the "unhealthy" employees? This argument can apply to drugs, sexual practices, alcohol, smoking, diet, and many other elements of life. There are many issues here that will be litigated and will also have a direct impact on company profitability and employee satisfaction. How do you distinguish between the interests of the manager in the company and the interests of the employees?

REVIEW AND DISCUSSION QUESTIONS

1. Define the following terms and phrases:

Yellow-dog contract	Concerted activity
Agency shop	Secondary boycott
Agency fees	Lockout
Right-to-work law	Employment-at-will
Authorization card	Employee handbooks
Union certification	Workers' compensation
Collective bargaining	Vesting
Mandatory subjects of bargaining	

2. Give some examples of secondary boycotts or actions that may be generally classified as secondary boycotts. Why should there be prohibitions against such activities? If these are voluntary actions by the workers involved, should the workers not have the right to bring pressure on whomever they choose?

3. Do employers have the right to test all job applicants and to refuse to hire applicants who test positive for drugs, even if there are no safety issues?

■ CASE QUESTIONS

4. An employee knows that a company manager is engaged in serious personal income tax fraud and reports this to the IRS. The IRS investigates and wins litigation involving the manager. The manager discovers who blew the whistle with the IRS and has the employee fired. Will the courts protect the employee whose job is at will? What if the fraud was committed by corporate managers with the taxes owed by the corporation?

5. RMC Company had long provided its employees with an in-house cafeteria. The cafeteria was managed by Ira's Deli, but RMC reserved the right to review and approve the quality and prices of the food served. When RMC notified the union representing its employees that it was going to increase prices, the union requested bargaining over the prices and service. RMC refused to bargain. Are the cafeteria's prices and services "other terms and conditions of employment" and therefore subject to bargaining?

6. The employees of Bierman's High Fashion Apparel Incorporated wanted to distribute a union newsletter. The newsletter was to be distributed in the non-working areas of Bierman's plant on the employees' time. The newsletter contained two articles to which the management of Bierman's objected. One article criticized President Bush's veto of a minimum wage increase, and the other encouraged employees to write their state representative to oppose the incorporation of the state's right-to-work statute into a revised state constitution. Is the distribution of the newsletter the kind of concerted activity that is protected from employer interference by the National Labor Relations Act?

7. Monte was president of a company where Helen Chizmar had been office manager for many years. Among the employees Chizmar supervised were her sister, daughter, and daughter-in-law. Those three relatives and other clerical staff selected a union as their bargaining agent. When Monte found out about the unionization, he blew up and fired Chizmar. Even though Chizmar was not involved in the unionization, it was made clear to employees that she was fired because her relatives supported the union. Monte threatened to fire all of the family members, who filed an unfair labor practice complaint with the NLRB. Could Chizmar make a complaint under this law even though she was not involved in the union effort? (*Kenrich Petrochemicals, Inc.* v. *NLRB,* 907 F.2d 400 (3d Cir. 1990))

8. During a campaign for a company's production facility to become unionized, the management showed a movie to employees that dramatized some supposed risks of unionization. The union complained that this was an unfair labor practice, and the NLRB agreed. The company claimed this was protected by freedom of speech and was not an unfair labor practice. What was the result when the case was appealed to federal court of appeals? [*Luxuray of New York* v. *NLRB,* 447 F.2d 112 (2d Cir. 1971)]

9. An engineer worked for a company for ten years with no written employment contract. The company's personnel policy manual said that employees could be fired only for good cause. Soon after the engineer wrote a memo about a structural problem with one of the company's buildings, he was fired. He sued, claiming that he was fired without good cause and that an implied contract

existed because of the policy manual. The lower courts ruled that he did not have a claim. What was the result of the appeal to the state supreme court? [*Woolley* v. *Hoffmann-La Roche,* 99 N.J. 284, 491 A.2d 1257 (1985)]

◼ BUSINESS POLICY QUESTIONS

10. Does it not seem like a restriction on freedom of speech to prohibit many forms of secondary boycotts? That is, if the Hormel workers wanted to have a picket at a bank telling the public that the bank should be boycotted unless it supported the union against Hormel, should that not be protected political speech so long as access to the bank was not blocked?

11. Should OSHA concentrate more efforts on worker health issues than on safety issues, as critics have asserted it should? Why do the critics make this argument? What is the difference in employers' incentives with respect to safety and health issues? Should a cost/benefit test be used in determining whether to allow a particular health measure, such as limiting worker exposure to cotton dust? Although the costs of cotton dust control are fairly easy to measure, how does one measure the benefits? What is involved?

◼ ETHICS QUESTIONS

12. Employees of Glasgow's Nouvelle Shoes wanted to form a union. Mr. Glasgow said that he did not want the employees unionized and would liquidate the business if a union was voted in. After the union won the representative election, Mr. Glasgow closed the shoe factory and sold all its assets. What he did was legal, but was it ethical? Instead of selling the assets, could Mr. Glasgow open the business up again after the employees denounced the union?

13. Contemplating the opening of a factory, you discover that it appears to be a toss-up between building a plant that uses cheaper machinery and two hundred workers who will earn an average of $6 an hour and building a plant that uses more expensive, sophisticated machinery and seventy workers likely to earn about $15 an hour. Is it more responsible to build one kind of factory than another? What if you know that the first factory will probably never be unionized but the second factory is most likely going to be unionized?

14. The employees' handbook for your company is rather poorly written and says things to the effect that "so long as your work record is good, you have no reason to expect to be fired." You realize that although never used, this could be used as evidence of a contractual standard in a court case by a terminated employee. You are pretty sure that if you revise the manual so that it conforms to the employment-at-will standard, employees will probably not realize they may have lost some valuable employment rights. What do you do?

EMPLOYMENT DISCRIMINATION

CHAPTER 13

MANAGER'S LEGAL CHALLENGE

Corning Glass Works is a large manufacturer with headquarters in a small town in New York. The company has a reputation as a high-quality employer that provides many benefits—such as child care and flextime schedules—that most companies do not offer. Yet, the company has had a difficult time keeping female and African American professionals, who quit the company for other opportunities at about double the rate of white male professionals.

The Corning situation illustrates a modern managerial problem. At well-managed firms that moved to follow the requirements of the Equal Opportunity Employment Act, the overt forms of discrimination against women and minorities have been eliminated. Those companies are not faced with the employment discrimination problems that they had ten or twenty years ago.

The chairman of Corning has set goals for his company to retain more female and African American professionals, to increase their representation at the highest level of management, and to take steps to ensure that subtle forms of discrimination are not a part of the problem. The chairman stated that the promotions of white male executives would depend in part on how well they helped women and minorities "reach their fullest potential."

Consultants to the company find that at Corning, as at most companies, there are subtle forms of discrimination that are not illegal but discourage the full integration of women and African Americans. For example, white male managers exclude women and African Americans of similar rank from participation in informal get-togethers, which are an important part of learning how the company team works. Women and minorities also claim that they are ignored at meetings, where all the discussion occurs among the white males.

After attending a series of workshops on racism and sexism in the workplace, some of the male attendees said they became aware for the first time of some forms of discrimination. Conscious efforts are made to deal with subtle forms of discrimination, and more white males are now aware of them. On the other side is the concern that all promotions will go to women or minorities, even if they are less qualified than white males. That, of course, can cause workers to be discouraged and defect to other companies.

Since 85 percent of new workers are women, minorities, and immigrants, managers must learn how to integrate men and women of all races into the work force better than in the past. Not only does that affect the ability of companies to attract and retain talented workers, but it is likely that more subtle forms of discrimination will be the basis for legal action in the future. Previously, managers met the duties imposed by the law by eliminating the obvious features of discrimination. Now they must begin to do more to be competitive in a work force in which white males have become a minority.

The laws providing for equal opportunity in employment are reviewed in this chapter. The chapter begins with a discussion of the historical background of the federal law of employment discrimination, including the Equal Pay Act of 1963, the first federal law governing employment discrimination on the basis of sex.

The chapter then discusses Title VII of the Civil Rights Act of 1964, the most important federal law intended to correct and deter discriminatory employment practices. The law prohibits employers, unions, and employment agencies from discriminating on the basis of race, color, sex, religion, and national origin. In practice, most cases have concerned race and sex discrimination. To remedy race or sex discrimination, affirmative action programs may be implemented voluntarily or may be imposed on an employer. In recent years, the Civil Rights Acts of 1866 and 1871, which had been unused for years, were revived and can be used to bring suit for injury due to racial discrimination.

The chapter also reviews the Age Discrimination in Employment Act, which added age to the list of personal characteristics on which discrimination suits may be based. The chapter concludes with a discussion of the Rehabilitation Act and the Americans with Disabilities Act of 1990 — the primary basis of federal employment rights for mentally and physically disabled persons.

BACKGROUND TO DISCRIMINATION LAW

Problems of discrimination in employment due to sex, color, race, religion, or national origin are not unique to the American culture. Most countries consciously or unconsciously practice some form of employment discrimination. For example, in Japan, female executives are much more uncommon than in the United States.

As in other countries, there are large statistical differences between races and ethnic groups in the United States. For example, the unemployment rate for African Americans is regularly twice the unemployment rate for whites. The percentage of African American and Hispanic families living below the poverty line is much greater than that of white families. Of those working, about one in four African Americans secures a white-collar job, whereas one in two working whites secures such employment. White male wage workers earn an average of 20 percent more than African American male wage workers. Males predominate in the higher paying professions, such as in medicine, law, and management, while females have traditionally been concentrated in the lower paying professions such as nursing, paralegal, and clerical. White male wage workers earn an average of 40 percent more than female wage workers.

Much of the difference between men and women and between races and ethnic groups may be unconscious and attributable to employment patterns. Much of the "wage gap" is attributed to differences in education, training, family demands, and years of experience in the work force. Still, possibly some of the disparity is due to stereotyped assumptions and expectations about productivity and to worker preferences to associate in the workplace with "one's own kind." It is this kind of employment discrimination that has produced a legal response.

■ THE CIVIL RIGHTS MOVEMENT

Historically, the common law permitted employers to hire and fire—within contractual limits—at will. The employer was relatively unconstrained to establish the terms and conditions of employment. Employers could discriminate or not discriminate as they wished. Similarly, labor unions could impose discriminatory membership policies. Although some states enacted statutes limiting discriminatory practices, employers and unions were largely free to conduct their affairs without judicial or administrative interference under the common law.

By the early 1960s, the National Labor Relations Board had interpreted the National Labor Relations Act as prohibiting most blatant forms of discrimination by unions. Executive Orders in the 1940s and 1950s had placed some restraints on racial discrimination by government employers and employers under government contract. The drive for civil rights in employment and in other aspects of life that arose in the South in the 1950s became a national movement in the early 1960s. Thus, there was an emerging but incomplete patchwork of remedies for employment discrimination coupled with a rapidly rising public concern. In partial response, Congress enacted the first federal employment discrimination statute in 1963—the Equal Pay Act—followed by the Civil Rights Act of 1964, the cornerstone of federal employment discrimination law.

■ EQUAL PAY ACT OF 1963

The *Equal Pay Act of 1963* was the first federal law that specifically addressed equal employment. The law prohibits discrimination in pay on the basis of sex. The law does not apply to any other discriminatory practice. The Act is interpreted and enforced by the Equal Employment Opportunity Commission (EEOC).

Scope and Coverage of the Act.   The Act holds that it is illegal to pay a wage to female employees that is different from that paid to male employees where the jobs require equal skill, effort, and responsibility and the same working conditions. Job titles are not relevant; it is the content of the jobs that is scrutinized. However, the Equal Pay Act does allow differences in wages if such differences are due to ''(i) a seniority system; (ii) a merit system; (iii) a system which measures earnings by quantity or quality of production; or (iv) a differential based on any factor other than sex. . . .'' Pay differentials on the basis of sex are eliminated by raising the pay of the female employees, not by lowering the pay of the male employees. The only exceptions permitted by the Act are some small retail and agricultural employers.

Enforcement Provisions.   To permit enforcement of the Act, employers are required to keep records of each employee's hours, wages, and other relevant information. Government investigators may enter a business to examine the records, which must be kept for several years. If a firm is found to be in violation, the most likely result will be an order to pay employees who have been discriminated against an amount equal to the wages they should have been receiving. The employees may also receive an additional amount to serve as a penalty to the employer. If the employees have to hire an attorney to settle the suit and they win, they may be awarded reasonable attorney's fees and court costs.

TITLE VII OF THE 1964 CIVIL RIGHTS ACT

The single most important source of antidiscrimination in employment law is *Title VII of the Civil Rights Act of 1964*. The Act was amended by the *Equal Employment Opportunity Act* in 1972 to give the *Equal Employment Opportunity Commission (EEOC)* the power to enforce the Act, and by the *Pregnancy Discrimination Act* in 1978. The Civil Rights Act makes it an unlawful employment practice for an employer

> (1) to fail or refuse to hire or to discharge any individual, or otherwise to discriminate against any individual with respect to his compensation, terms, conditions, or privileges of employment; or
>
> (2) to limit, segregate, or classify his employees or applicants for employment in any way which would deprive or tend to deprive any individual of employment opportunities or otherwise adversely affect his status as an employee because of such individual's race, color, religion, sex, or national origin.

■ COVERAGE AND ENFORCEMENT

Title VII applies to employers, employment agencies, and labor unions in the private and public sectors. In general, it forbids *discrimination* in all aspects of employment on the basis of *race, color, religion, sex, or national origin*. Employers with fifteen or more employees and unions with fifteen or more members are covered by the Act, as are educational institutions and state and local governments, regardless of size. The Supreme Court has stated that law firms and other partnership organizations are also covered by the law.

Administrative Procedure.   A person who believes that he or she has been the victim of a discriminatory act must, to seek relief under Title VII, file a charge with his or her state or local Equal Employment Opportunity agency. Such agencies exist in almost all states under state statutes similar to Title VII. Many complaints are handled at the state level, much like the EEOC procedure described in the following subsection. But if the charge is dismissed at the state level or the relief is not satisfactory, the employee may then take the complaint to the EEOC, which will investigate.

The EEOC will notify the employer to come to the EEOC office for a conference to discuss the allegations. An EEOC agent will have the employer and employee present their views and will suggest a settlement. Many complaints are settled at this point. If there is no settlement, the EEOC completes an investigation to determine whether there is reasonable cause to believe that discrimination has occurred. Results of the investigation are given to both parties. If reasonable cause is found, the employee is given a right-to-sue letter.

Litigation.   The right-to-sue letter gives the employee the right to sue the employer in federal court. The EEOC may sue the employer but rarely does so—the burden is on the employee to carry the case forward. The Supreme Court established a four-part test in *McDonnell-Douglas Corp.* v. *Green* (1983) that a plaintiff must meet to provide a *prima facie* case of discrimination:

1. The person belongs to a protected class.
2. The person applied for a job and met the qualifications for a job that was open.
3. The person was rejected.
4. The employer continued to seek applications from persons with similar qualifications.

While the court applied the test to applications for employment, the same test holds for all aspects of employment—promotion, compensation, discipline, and termination.

Once the employee has presented a *rebuttable presumption of discrimination*, the defendant-employer must provide "legitimate, nondiscriminatory reasons" for what happened. The charge of discrimination must be answered directly, or the plaintiff wins. Assuming that the defendant responds, the plaintiff answers by showing that the defendant's explanation is only a pretext to disguise discrimination. The Supreme Court addressed the standard of proof in the *Price Waterhouse* case.

PRICE WATERHOUSE v. HOPKINS

United States Supreme Court
490 U.S. 228, 109 S. Ct. 1775 (1989)

Case Background
Ann Hopkins worked at Price Waterhouse, a nationwide accounting partnership, as a senior manager. She was the only woman proposed for partnership in 1982 (along with eighty-seven male candidates). Her evaluations indicated her performance was "outstanding." The main issue appeared to be personality. The trial judge (Gesell) found that both supporters and opponents indicated that she could be "overly aggressive, unduly harsh, difficult to work with and impatient with staff." One partner said she was "macho"; another said she should take "a course at charm school"; and one said that she should "walk more femininely, talk more femininely, dress more femininely, wear more make-up, have her hair styled, and wear jewelry." Her candidacy for partnership was put on hold for a year, at which time she was not renominated for partnership. She sued under Title VII, charging that her employer had discriminated against her on the basis of sex. She won at District Court (Judge Gesell) and Court of Appeals; the issue is what standard of evidence must be met.

Case Decision
[O]ur assumption always has been that if an employer allows gender to affect its decisionmaking process, then it must carry the burden of justifying its ultimate decision. We have not in the past required women whose gender has proved relevant to an employment decision to establish the negative proposition that they would not have been subject to that decision had they been men, and we do not do so today.

In saying that gender played a motivating part in an employment decision, we mean that, if we asked the employer at the moment of the decision what its reasons were and if we received a truthful response, one of those reasons would be that the applicant or employee was a woman. In the specific context of sex stereotyping, an employer who acts on the basis of a belief that a woman cannot be aggressive, or that she must not be, has acted on the basis of gender. . . .

Remarks at work that are based on sex stereotypes do not inevitably prove that gender played a part in a particular employment decision. The plaintiff must show that the employer actually relied on her gender in making its decision. In making this showing, stereotyped remarks can certainly be *evidence* that gender played a part. In any event, the stereotyping in this case did not simply consist of stray remarks. On the contrary, Hopkins proved that Price Waterhouse invited partners to submit comments; that some of the comments stemmed from sex stereotypes; that an important part of the Policy Board's decision on Hopkins was an assessment of the submitted comments; and that Price Waterhouse in no way disclaimed reliance on the sex-linked evaluations. This is not, as Price Waterhouse suggests, "discrimination in the air"; rather, it is, as Hopkins puts it, "discrimination brought to ground and visited upon" an employee.

The Supreme Court affirmed the verdict in favor of Hopkins, holding that if an employee establishes that a discriminatory element was involved in an employment decision, the employer will be liable under Title VII unless it proves, by a preponderance of the evidence, that it would have made the same decision even if it had not taken that element into account. On remand to the District Court, Hopkins was granted partnership retroactive to 1982 and $371,000 in back pay.

Managerial Considerations
Insensitivity to discrimination caused this expensive result—and loss of reputation—to Price Waterhouse. Professional training of those in decision-making positions about sexism and racism might reduce the number of such incidents. It is difficult for people to get rid of personal feelings, but they can learn to separate their feelings from what is permissible at work.

■ PROTECTED CLASSES UNDER TITLE VII

Title VII provides for *equal employment opportunity* without regard for race, color, religion, sex, or national origin. Congress sought to protect certain classes of people who historically had been discriminated against in employment relationships. These classes are referred to as the *protected classes* for the purposes of Title VII coverage.

Race and Color.   Relative to the other protected classes, the courts have had little difficulty in determining the protected racial class. Congress expressly acknowledged that its primary legislative purpose in enacting Title VII was "to open employment opportunities for Negroes in occupations which have been traditionally closed to them." In addition to African Americans, there are four other major racial groupings: white, Native American, Hispanic, and Asian. Since whites form the majority, the other groups are considered protected classes under Title VII.

Congress's emphasis on eliminating racial discrimination does not mean that whites are not protected under Title VII. That was rejected by the Court in *McDonald* v. *Sante Fe Trail Transportation Company* (1976). In *McDonald*, an African American employee and a white employee had misappropriated the property of their employer. The African American employee was reprimanded but allowed to keep his job, while the white employee was discharged. In declaring that Title VII protected whites against racial discrimination, the Court stated:

> Title VII prohibits racial discrimination against the white petitioners upon the same standards as would be applicable were they Negroes. . . . While Santa Fe may decide that participation in a theft of cargo may render an employee unqualified for employment, this criteria must be applied alike to members of all races. . . . [W]hatever factors the mechanisms of compromise may take into account in mitigating discipline of some employees, under Title VII race may not be among them.

While *reverse discrimination*—giving preferential treatment to minorities—is illegal, where minorities or women are underrepresented in a particular job classification, it is legal for an employer to take steps voluntarily to see that more minorities or women are hired to increase their share of the jobs. *Affirmative action programs* (discussed later), designed to remedy past or present discrimination against minorities or women, may be adopted and not violate the rule against reverse discrimination.

Religion.   Title VII does not define the term *religion* but states that "religion includes all aspects of religious observances and practice." The courts have defined the term broadly to resolve constitutional issues. According to the Court in *United States* v. *Seeger* (1965):

> [All that is required is a] sincere and meaningful belief occupying in the life of its possessor a place parallel to that filled by the God of those [religions generally recognized].

The employer is required to reasonably accommodate an employee's or a prospective employee's religious observance or practice. The employer may discriminate, however, if the accommodation will impose an *undue hardship* on the conduct of the business. The Court has stated that undue hardship is created by accommodations that would cost an employer more than a minimal amount. A religious institution, like a seminary, may discriminate in hiring on the basis of religion.

Sex.   The prohibition against sex discrimination was added with little legislative insight into how Congress intended to define the scope of the term sex discrimination under Title VII. Thus, the courts have taken an active role in defining the limits on sex as a protected class under Title VII.

The courts have taken the position that the term *sex* should be given the meaning it has in ordinary communications. Thus, early decisions interpreted Title VII as prohibiting sex discrimination simply on the basis of whether a person was male or female. In that light, the courts have uniformly held that discrimination on the basis of sexual preference is not protected by Title VII. Nor has Title VII been held to prohibit discrimination on the basis of marital status—as long as the employer applies the rule uniformly to employees of both sexes.

Pregnancy and Sex Discrimination.   Title VII was amended in 1978 by the *Pregnancy Discrimination Act*, which states that prohibitions on sex discrimination include pregnancy, childbirth, and related medical conditions. Women affected by these conditions "shall be treated the same for all employment-related purposes, including receipt of benefits under fringe benefit programs."

Examples of pregnancy discrimination include the following:

- Denying a woman a job, assignment, or promotion only because she is pregnant.
- Requiring a pregnant woman to go on leave when she is able to do her job.
- Treating maternity leave from work different from other leaves for temporary disabilities.
- Discriminating with regard to fringe benefits such as health insurance with the intent of discouraging women of childbearing age from working.

Sexual Harassment and Sex Discrimination.   The courts have held that a hostile sexual environment constitutes sex discrimination within the meaning of Title VII. The U.S. Department of Health and Human Services has defined *sexual harassment* as follows:

1. Explicit or implicit promise of career advancement (e.g., promotion, training, awards, details, lax timekeeping, and lower standards of performance) in return for sexual favors.
2. Explicit or implicit threats that the employee's career will be adversely affected (e.g., nonpromotion, poor performance appraisal, reassignment to a less desirable position or location) if the sexual demands are rejected.
3. Deliberate, repeated, unsolicited verbal comments, gestures, or physical actions of a sexual nature (e.g., touching, pinching, or patting the employee).

Many employers have established policies regarding sexual harassment and train supervisors to be sensitive to such matters because the employer may be liable for harassment, even when it is committed by lower level employees. Although the exact boundaries of sexual harassment under Title VII are still to be determined, the Supreme Court did offer some guidance in its 1986 decision in *Meritor Savings Bank* v. *Vinson*.

MERITOR SAVINGS BANK v. VINSON

United States Supreme Court
477 U.S. 57, 106 S.Ct. 2399 (1986)

Case Background

Mechelle Vinson was hired in 1974 by Sidney Taylor, vice president of Meritor Savings. She worked for the bank until 1978, when she was fired by Taylor for taking too much sick leave. Taylor had consistently given Vinson high work evaluations and three promotions before she was fired. Vinson sued Taylor and the bank for damages, claiming that she had been subject to constant sexual harassment by Taylor in violation of Title VII. Vinson testified that soon after she began work at the bank, Taylor took her to dinner and then suggested they go to a motel. She said she agreed for fear of losing her job. She said that over the next several years, Taylor made repeated sexual demands of her, they had intercourse forty to fifty times, and there were several forcible rapes. In addition, as witnesses agreed, Taylor was seen fondling Vinson in front of other employees. These activities ceased in 1978 when Vinson started going with a steady boyfriend, and Vinson was soon dismissed. Vinson never reported Taylor's harassment to his supervisors and never made use of the bank's complaint procedure, because she was afraid of Taylor. Taylor denied all of Vinson's claims, and the bank denied responsibility because it was never notified of the alleged activities, which, if true, were in violation of bank policy. The district court ruled against Vinson because the relations appeared to be voluntary and had nothing to do with her employment at the bank. Further, the bank had no notice of any possible problem. The federal court of appeals reversed in favor of Vinson, holding that Vinson had established a case of sexual harassment.

Case Decision

The gravamen of any sexual harassment claim is that the alleged sexual advances were "unwelcome." . . . The correct inquiry is whether respondent by her conduct indicated that the alleged sexual advances were unwelcome, not whether her actual participation in sexual intercourse was voluntary. . . . While "voluntariness" in the sense of consent is not a defense to such a claim, it does not follow that a complainant's sexually provocative speech or dress is irrelevant as a matter of law in determining whether he or she found particular sexual advances unwelcome. To the contrary, such evidence is obviously relevant. The EEOC guidelines emphasize that the trier of fact must determine the existence of sexual-harassment in light of "the record as a whole" and "the totality of circumstances, such as the nature of the sexual advances and the context in which the alleged incidents occurred." . . .

[W]e reject petitioner's view that the mere existence of a grievance procedure and a policy against discrimination, coupled with respondent's failure to invoke that procedure, must insulate petitioner from liability. While those facts are plainly relevant, the situation before us demonstrates why they are not necessarily dispositive. Petitioner's general nondiscrimination policy did not address sexual harassment in particular, and thus did not alert employees to their employer's interest in correcting that form of discrimination. Moreover, the bank's grievance procedure apparently required an employee to complain first to her supervisor, in this case Taylor. Since Taylor was the alleged perpetrator, it is not altogether surprising that respondent failed to invoke the procedure and report her grievance to him. Petitioner's contention that respondent's failure should insulate it from liability might be substantially stronger if its procedures were better calculated to encourage victims of harassment to come forward.

All nine justices agreed on several points: sexual harassment in a hostile environment is in violation of Title VII; in such cases there need be no "economic" consequence to the employee from the hostile environment; if an employee was subject to unwelcome sexual advances, later participation in sexual activity, even if "voluntary," does not prevent a charge of sexual harassment; evidence of the employee's sexually provocative dress or speech may be considered to determine whether sexual language or advances were unwelcome; and for sexual harassment to be actionable, it must be sufficiently severe to alter the conditions of employment and create an abusive working environment. The judgment for Vinson was upheld.

Managerial Considerations

Four justices, in a concurring opinion, said that they would hold the company liable in all instances, regardless of its knowledge about what was going on. It is clear that there is a heavy burden of responsibility on managers to try to prevent sexual harassment on the job. Company management must have clear policies opposing sexual harassment and make sure that all employees have been clearly informed of the policy and made aware that they can be fired for violating the policy. Further, there must be a system in place that allows complaints of harassment to be given in confidence for investigation without fear of retaliation.

National Origin.   According to the Supreme Court in *Espinoza* v. *Farah Manufacturing* (1973), the term *national origin* is to be given the meaning it has in ordinary communications:

> [The term national origin] refers to the country where a person is born or . . . the country from which his or her ancestors came.

Employment discrimination can take place when an employer allows ethnic slurs to occur and does not take steps to prevent such actions. Discrimination has been held to exist because a person has a physical, cultural, or speech characteristic of a national origin group. It is also discrimination to require that English be spoken at all times in the workplace. However, if business necessity requires that English be spoken, speaking English may be a legitimate job requirement. Such discrimination is further restricted by the Immigration Reform and Control Act that outlaws national origin discrimination by employers with four or more employees.

■ THEORIES OF DISCRIMINATION UNDER TITLE VII

To select among applicants for employment or among employees for promotion, the employer must differentiate between those individuals to make a decision. Although Title VII does not restrict the process, it restricts the grounds upon which the employer can make that decision. If an employer differentiates between applicants or employees on the basis of race, color, religion, sex, or national origin, there may be a violation of Title VII's prohibitions against discriminatory employment practices.

To find discrimination, it is not necessary that the employer intended to discriminate. To determine whether an employer's decision is unlawful discrimination, the courts have used three basic approaches or "theories":

1. Individual instances of disparate treatment or direct discrimination.
2. Neutral rules that perpetuate past intentional discrimination.
3. Neutral rules that have an adverse or disparate impact that are not justified by a business necessity.

Disparate Treatment.   An employee may bring a suit charging an employer with violating Title VII based on *disparate treatment*. If race, color, religion, sex, or national origin plays a significant role in an employer's decision to hire, promote, or fire—unless the employer can show that other factors were in fact the basis of the employment-related decision—there probably is a violation of the Act. In most disparate treatment cases, although the employer does not have a written policy against hiring or promoting individuals from a certain group, qualified individuals from that group are simply not being hired or promoted in the employer's business.

Perpetuating Past Patterns of Intentional Discrimination.   A violation of Title VII can be established by a "neutral" employment rule that *perpetuates a past pattern of intentional discrimination*. That is, although the employer does not actively engage in discrimination on the basis of race, color, religion, sex, or national origin, the effect of being neutral on such basis is to perpetuate past actions that did involve intentional discrimination.

For example, before the enactment of Title VII, some labor unions restricted membership to whites only. After the Act, the unions imposed a membership requirement that new members had to be related to or recommended by current members. The court found that although the union's membership rule was neutral on its face, it perpetuated the past purposeful exclusion.

Disparate Impact.   A third theory under which a violation of Title VII can be established involves a neutral employment rule that has a *disparate impact* on a certain group. Employment procedure often requires that applicants have a high school diploma, achieve a minimum score on a specified test, or meet some other specified selection device. If it is asserted that the employer's hiring or promotion practices have a discriminatory impact on an applicant, the employer must show that the applicant was rejected not because of race, color, religion, sex, or national origin but because the qualification requirements of the job were not met. The impact of employment rules, such as having a high school diploma, must be neutral—that is, not have a disparate impact on a protected class. Congress reemphasized this point in the 1991 Civil Rights Act.

The relationship between the use of such rules and Title VII was established in *Griggs* v. *Duke Power Company,* which determined that neutral employment criteria will be judged by their impact, not by the good or bad faith involved in their implementation.

GRIGGS v. DUKE POWER COMPANY

United States Supreme Court
401 U.S. 424, 91 S.Ct. 849 (1971)

Case Background
Duke Power was a segregated company before the passage of the 1964 Civil Rights Act. African Americans were hired to work only in certain low-level jobs; all higher level jobs were held by whites. When Title VII took effect, Duke Power allowed all persons to compete for all jobs. Except for certain manual labor jobs that were already held by African Americans, all jobs required a high school diploma and certain scores on two aptitude tests. These requirements, while neutral on their face, were claimed to discriminate against African American applicants. At that time, 34 percent of the white men in North Carolina had high school diplomas, compared to only 12 percent of African American men. In addition, 58 percent of the whites passed the aptitude tests, but only 6 percent of the African Americans passed. The district court and court of appeals ruled for Duke, finding that the purpose of the standards was not to discriminate but to achieve a work force of a certain quality. Griggs appealed to the U.S. Supreme Court.

Case Decision
The Supreme Court reversed, holding that Duke's practices violated Title VII. The Court stated that neutral employment qualifications will be judged by their impact, not by their intent. When such qualifications can be shown to have an adverse impact on members of a protected class, the employer must show that there is a business necessity behind the job qualifications established.

Nothing in the Act precludes the use of testing or measuring procedures; obviously they are useful. What Congress has forbidden is giving these devices and mechanisms controlling force unless they are demonstrably a reasonable measure of job performance. Congress has not commanded that the less qualified be preferred over the better qualified simply because of minority origins. Far from disparaging job qualifications as such, Congress has made such qualifications the controlling factor, so that race, religion, nationality, and sex become irrelevant. What Congress has commanded is that any test used must measure the person for the job and not the person in the abstract.

Managerial Considerations
Qualifications for employment for all positions, including educational achievement and scores on aptitude tests, must be shown by managers to be related in a meaningful way to job performance. Numerous cases have been brought against companies that had job criteria unrelated to ability to perform the job. Many companies use such aptitude tests. Thus, the test developers have become very aware of the need for the tests to be related strictly to the performance of certain tasks that they attempt to predict and to be race and sex neutral as far as possible.

■ DEFENSES UNDER TITLE VII

Employers charged with employment discrimination under Title VII have several defenses. Many employment practices are allowed as a business necessity. Employers are also allowed to give a "professionally developed ability test" and to apply different "terms, conditions, or privileges of employment pursuant to a bona fide seniority or merit system" as long as they are not intended to discriminate on the basis of race, color, religion, sex or national origin. Another statutory defense is the bona fide occupational qualification defense, which applies primarily to charges of intentional discrimination.

Business Necessity.   If employment rules can be shown to have a discriminatory impact on some employees, the 1991 Civil Rights Act makes it clear that the burden is on the employer to establish that the rules are justified as a *business necessity.* Business necessity is evaluated with reference to the ability of the employee to perform a certain job. Written tests, no matter how objective, must meet this business necessity test.

Experience and skill requirements, usually measured in terms of seniority, are often accepted as necessary. For example, to be a skilled bricklayer generally requires experience gained only by performance over a period of time. To require such experience and skill for certain positions is not a violation of Title VII. Similarly, physical requirements may be set if they are job related. If a job requires certain abilities with respect to strength and agility, tests for such ability are legitimate.

Selection criteria for certain professional, managerial, and other white-collar positions must also meet the business necessity test. Insofar as objective criteria often cannot be used in such instances, subjective evaluations such as job interviews, references, and some aspect of job performance evaluation are common and generally recognized as necessary in hiring and promoting professional and managerial personnel. Similarly, such positions may have a strict education requirement. Educational requirements for manual or semiskilled jobs are not likely to be held necessary. However, for such jobs as teachers, police officers, laboratory technicians, airline pilots, and engineers, education requirements are usually determined to be valid.

Professionally Developed Ability Tests.   Tests are often used by employers to determine whether applicants for a job possess the necessary skills and attributes. According to Section 703(h) of the statute:

> [It] shall [not] be an unlawful employment practice for an employer to give and to act upon the results of any professionally developed ability test provided that such test, its administration, or action upon the results is not designed, intended, or used to discriminate because of race, color, religion, sex or national origin.

In general, as stated by the Supreme Court in *Griggs,* such tests must be shown to predict the work ability required for the job. Usually employers are required to supply detailed statistical validation of the tests, and expert testimony from educational and industrial psychologists is often required to interpret the results.

Bona Fide Seniority or Merit Systems.   A third defense involves *bona fide seniority or merit systems.* It is a common employment practice to provide employees with differential treatment based solely on employee seniority. Seniority can be defined as the length of time an employee has been with the company and can be used to determine such things as eligibility for company pension plans, length of vacations, security from layoffs, preference for rehire and promotion, and amount of sick leave. Most collective bargaining agreements contain formalized provisions for the recognition, calculation, and application of seniority. According to Section 703(h) of the statute:

> [I]t shall not be an unlawful employment practice for an employer to apply different . . . terms, conditions, or privileges of employment pursuant to a bona fide seniority or merit system . . . provided that such differences are not the result of an intention to discriminate because of race, color, religion, sex, or national origin. . . .

The Supreme Court has consistently upheld seniority systems even though they have the effect of perpetuating the effects of pre-1964 Civil Rights Act discrimination. That is, the Court will not allow employees who gained seniority when discrimination was in practice to have seniority rights stripped away in favor of workers who previously suffered discrimination.

The effects of seniority systems come under attack most often in cases involving layoffs on the basis of seniority. Many employers hold that in the event of a cutback in the work force, workers with the most seniority have the most job protection—last hired, first fired. This means that minorities may suffer a greater relative share of the layoffs in a cutback because they have less seniority than older white workers who were hired when racial discrimination was practiced. As seen in the *Wygant* case, the Supreme Court recognized this unfortunate fact but held that seniority rights are important.

WYGANT v. JACKSON BOARD OF EDUCATION

United States Supreme Court
476 U.S. 267, 106 S.Ct. 1842 (1986)

Case Background
The Jackson (Michigan) Board of Education agreed with the teachers' union to have a provision in the collective bargaining agreement that in the event of a teacher cutback, the layoffs would be proportional on the basis of race. That way, students would be guaranteed more minority teachers as "role models." When a layoff occurred later, white teachers with more seniority were fired in favor of retaining minority teachers with less seniority. The white teachers with seniority sued the school board, claiming their rights had been violated. The district court and court of appeals ruled for the school board, saying the layoff provision helped to remedy past discrimination. According to the

court, even though no particular discrimination by the school board was shown, minorities have been subject to discrimination by society in general. The teachers appealed to the U.S. Supreme Court.

Case Decision

While hiring goals impose a diffuse burden, often foreclosing only one of several opportunities, layoffs impose the entire burden of achieving racial equality on particular individuals, often resulting in serious disruption of their lives. That burden is too intrusive. We therefore hold that, as a means of accomplishing purposes that otherwise may be legitimate, the Board's layoff plan is not sufficiently narrowly tailored. Other, less intrusive means of accomplishing similar purposes—such as the adoption of hiring goals—are available.

(continued)

The Supreme Court reversed the lower court and reaffirmed the legitimacy of seniority plans. The Court made it clear that it will be unusual when seniority rights may be ignored in favor of correcting past discrimination, especially when no particular discrimination by the employer in question is shown.

Managerial Considerations

The courts recognize that seniority systems lock in place some of the effects of past discrimination. Upsetting the seniority systems would create a very difficult problem of how to reduce seniority benefits without harming those whites who were the innocent beneficiaries of past discriminatory employment practices. As time passes, however, and more older workers retire, the importance of this issue will diminish. Note also that some labor scholars contend that a manager, not caring about the discrimination issue at all, may wish to side with the junior minority employees in favor of firing the employees with seniority to reduce labor costs.

The Bona Fide Occupational Qualification (BFOQ).   Another defense is that of a *bona fide occupational qualification* (BFOQ). Section 703(e) states that discrimination is permitted in instances in which sex, religion, or national origin (but not race) is a BFOQ "reasonably necessary to the normal operation of that particular business." The defense is applicable to hiring and referrals but not to discrimination between classes of current employees.

The EEOC has given this defense a narrow interpretation. For example, just because certain jobs have been traditionally filled by men does not mean that a legitimate defense exists for not hiring women for such positions. There is no BFOQ on the basis of race. For example, an employer cannot assert that the business must have a white person for a particular job.

Generally, the increased cost of hiring members of the opposite sex may not be used to justify discrimination. The fact that separate bathroom facilities will have to be constructed will not be a BFOQ. In one instance, a court held that simply because people were used to seeing and preferred female flight attendants did not mean that the airline could refuse to hire male flight attendants. In 1991, the Supreme Court held that it was not a BFOQ for a company to prevent women of childbearing age from working at certain jobs that could expose their unborn children to possible dangers.

A BFOQ exists where hiring on the basis of a personal characteristic is needed to maintain the "authenticity" of a position. For example, a Playboy club can argue that the cocktail servers should be female, since customers expect that as a part of the service. Male clothing is expected to be modeled by a male model. In some medical care situations, the hospital may restrict the sex of the medical personnel for the comfort of the patients.

DISCRIMINATION AND REMEDIES

Title VII does not list all forms of employment discrimination that are illegal, but it does state some of the remedies available to those who suffer from discrimination. Cases brought before the EEOC and the courts give us ideas about the scope of practices covered by the law.

Examples of Discrimination.   The courts have struck down employment practices that impose *differential standards* on employees on the basis of race or sex. For example, it would be illegal to give male employees positions as traveling sales representatives but not give such positions to women, even though the employer's reason is concern about the possible dangers traveling women face.

While it is obvious that it is illegal to pay women or minorities lower salaries for the same work as performed by white men, when the assignments and the years of service are the same, illegal *compensation differentials* also take into account differences in fringe benefits. It is illegal to base health or retirement benefits on race or sex.

Everyone understands that the most obvious forms of *segregation* in the workplace are illegal. Problems today are more likely to concern such things as segregated social events. It is also illegal to assign employees to customers based on race. That is, it is illegal to send Hispanic employees to serve Hispanic customers and Anglo employees to serve Anglo customers.

Title VII cases have concerned unequal treatment in hiring, promotion, compensation, and discharge decisions. It is also illegal to make life so miserable on the job for an employee in a protected class that the employee is "forced" to quit. To make the working conditions intolerable is illegal *harassment*. If the employee quits because of harassment, it is a *constructive discharge,* which is treated the same as if the employee had been fired illegally.

Remedies.   Title VII states that when the defendant-employer has been found to have intentionally engaged in an unlawful discriminatory employment practice:

> the court may enjoin the . . . practice, and order such affirmative action as may be appropriate, which may include, but is not limited to, reinstatement or hiring of employees, with or without back pay . . . or any other equitable relief as the court deems appropriate.

Courts have used their statutory powers to order offending employers to reinstate employees with back pay, hire new employees with artificial seniority, promote employees, and implement an affirmative action program. Relying on the reference to "equitable relief" in the Act, the courts have also used the broad and flexible powers for courts sitting in equity to provide the most appropriate relief.

The 1991 Civil Rights Act amended Title VII so that the kinds of damages that may be sought by a plaintiff are the same in most discrimination suits. Compensation for discrimination may include back wages and payment for expenses such as psychotherapy or medical treatment related to the discrimination. For example, in one suit prior to the 1991 Act, a woman won a sexual harassment suit against her former employer, for which she was awarded back pay, but she could not recover the expenses she incurred from falling down a flight of stairs trying to get away from her boss. Now, all related expenses may be compensated.

Punitive damages are also authorized by the 1991 Act as a remedy. The amount requested can be unlimited in case of race discrimination. For all other discrimination suits, where punitive damages are requested, companies with fewer than 15 employees are exempt; companies with 15 to 100 employees may be sued for up to $50,000; between 101 and 200 employees,

$100,000; between 201 and 500 employees, $200,000; and more than 500 employees, $300,000.

With regard to seniority, the Supreme Court in *Franks* v. *Bowman Transportation Co.* (1976) held that

> No less than with the denial of the remedy of back pay, the denial of seniority relief to victims of illegal discrimination in hiring is permissible "only for reasons which, if applied generally, would not frustrate the central purposes of eradicating discrimination throughout the economy and making persons whole for injuries suffered through past discrimination."

The Court ordered that employees who had been discriminated against in violation of Title VII should be given *artificial seniority* beginning from the date of the discriminatory act.

In addition, the court is empowered "in such circumstances as [it] may deem just" to appoint an attorney for an impoverished plaintiff. Ordinarily, a plaintiff who wins will be awarded attorney's fees. However, a prevailing employer-defendant may be awarded attorney's fees only if the court determines that the plaintiff's action was frivolous, unreasonable, or without foundation.

INTERNATIONAL ASPECTS | **EMPLOYMENT DISCRIMINATION IN EUROPE AND JAPAN**

With regard to social legislation, Europeans often are portrayed as more sophisticated than Americans. However, in the case of employment, they are years behind the United States in their treatment of minorities and women in the labor force. Most European countries and Japan have antidiscrimination statutes on the books, but the laws are not nearly as strict as the U.S. laws.

Since most of those countries tend to be more racially homogeneous than the United States, they have not gone through the trials of a multiracial society. As a consequence, there is a tendency to treat minority immigrants as second-class citizens. In general, it is much harder for a noncitizen, especially a member of a racial minority, to obtain work and citizenship in Japan and most of Europe than it is in the United States.

Where affirmative action exists, it tends to be trivial or even overtly discriminatory in favor of male-citizen workers who already dominate the labor force. Women are often kept out of many higher level jobs and are not paid as much as men for equal work—especially in Japan.

The first serious sexual harassment case was not decided in Japan until 1992. A woman who was harassed by her boss for two years with lewd remarks was fired for filing a formal complaint with the company. She was awarded $12,500 in damages. While trivial by American standards, the case was a landmark in Japan.

European countries and Japan appear to treat women better in certain respects, such as by statutes mandating generous maternity benefits, but the effect of those laws is to encourage employers not to hire women because of the high cost of the benefits to which women are entitled if they have children. As in the United States, however, attitudes about women in the labor force are changing—but more slowly.

AFFIRMATIVE ACTION PROGRAMS

An *affirmative action program* is a conscious effort by an employer to remedy discriminatory practices in the hiring, training, and promotion of protected class members when a class is underrepresented in the employer's work force.

The implementation of an affirmative action program may be voluntary or involuntary. After finding that members of a protected class are underrepresented in the company's work force, an employer may voluntarily implement an affirmative action program to use best efforts to recruit, train and promote qualified minorities or women. The implementation of an involuntary program may be imposed by the courts as a remedy to correct past discriminatory employment practices by the company or, in the case of government contractors, be imposed by the federal government as a prerequisite to the company's entering into a government contract. In such cases, *quotas* by race or sex may have to be met by certain deadlines.

■ EXECUTIVE ORDER 11246

As the chief executive officer of the United States, the President has the authority to determine certain conditions for government business. Those conditions may be spelled out in *executive orders* issued by the President. Referred to as *government contractors*, businesses must abide by the executive orders when they contract with the government. President Johnson issued Executive Order 11246 in 1965. It has developed into a requirement that government contractors take *affirmative action*.

Monitored and enforced by the Office of Federal Contract Compliance Programs (OFCCP) and the Department of Labor, the law requires all companies with federal contracts totaling $10,000 per year to take affirmative action. Those with $50,000 in contracts and fifty or more employees must have a written affirmative action plan, which requires a contractor to conduct a *work force analysis* for each job within the organization. Jobs are identified and analyzed according to rank, salary, and the percentage of those employed in the job that come from each protected class. A company may find, for example, that lab technicians are submanagerial in rank and 87 percent white, 13 percent African American, and 92 percent male.

The contractor must then undertake an *underutilization analysis*, comparing the percentage of each protected class available in the community in each job category with that percentage actually employed by the contractor. If underutilization is found—say because 8 percent of the lab technicians are women, compared with 17 percent of the lab technicians available in the community—the contractor must establish an affirmative action plan to correct the situation.

The affirmative action program may require that efforts be made to hire more women or to invest in training women to enhance their qualifications for certain jobs. If these efforts fail because it appears the employer was not serious, a quota may be fixed that sets a numerical goal, such as to double the number of female lab technicians in three years. Hiring and promotion quotas that are set are reviewed periodically to determine whether adequate progress is being made. In the event that progress is not being made, the federal contract may be cancelled.

■ AFFIRMATIVE ACTION AS A REMEDY

Title VII provides that in the event an employer is found to have intentionally engaged in illegal discrimination, "the court may . . . order such affirmative action as may be appropriate. . . ." It is not uncommon for the courts to require an offending company or organization to implement an affirmative action program. The court may require the company to reinstate or hire employees in the protected class and can impose quotas to make up for past discriminatory activities. The Supreme Court recently had an opportunity to consider the constitutionality of such affirmative action programs in *United States* v. *Paradise* (1987).

UNITED STATES v. PARADISE

United States Supreme Court
480 U.S. 149, 107 S.Ct. 1053 (1987)

Case Background
In 1972, the federal district court found that the Alabama Department of Public Safety in its thirty-seven year history had never hired an African American trooper or African Americans in any position except as laborers. The court ordered the department to hire one African American trooper for each white trooper hired until African Americans represented about 25 percent of the state trooper jobs. The court also ordered an end to any discriminatory practice on the part of the department. By 1979, not one African American had achieved the rank of corporal, so the court ordered a numerical quota on promotions. Of the sixty African Americans who took the standardized test for promotion to corporal, only five were in the top half of all test takers; the highest ranked eighteenth. The court held the test to be racially biased and ordered that for a certain time period, at least 50 percent of those promoted must be African American if qualified African American applicants were available. The court imposed a goal of 25 percent African American employees at all ranks. The state of Alabama appealed the decision.

Court Decision

In determining whether race-conscious remedies are appropriate, we look to several factors, including the necessity

for the relief and the efficacy of alternative remedies, the flexibility and duration of the relief, including the availability of waiver provisions; the relationship of the numerical goals to the relevant labor market; and the impact of the relief on the rights of third parties. . . . When considered in light of these factors, it was amply established, and we find that the one-for-one promotion requirement was narrowly tailored to serve its several purposes, both as applied to the initial set of promotions to the rank of corporal and as a continuing contingent order with respect to the upper ranks.

The Supreme Court affirmed the quota plan imposed by the district court, stating that strict hiring and promotion quotas may be imposed to overcome discriminatory employment practices.

Managerial Considerations
This unusually strong affirmative action plan was imposed and upheld because of the long history of intentional discriminatory employment practices by the employer. It was clear from the record that the employer kept discriminatory practices in place as long as possible and, when ordered to stop, went no further until the next time there was another court hearing. Such behavior by management will result in a rigid affirmative action program being imposed because of the apparent lack of interest in following the mandates of the law.

■ VOLUNTARY AFFIRMATIVE ACTION PROGRAMS

In addition to implementing an affirmative action program in response to a court order or as a government contractor, a company may voluntarily implement an affirmative action program. As a rule, a company or organization will make such an election after determining that a protected class is underrepresented in its work force. An affirmative action program allows the employer to correct for the underrepresentation. The Supreme Court had an opportunity to examine a voluntary affirmative action program in *Johnson* v. *Transportation Agency, Santa Clara County, California* (1987).

JOHNSON v. TRANSPORTATION AGENCY, SANTA CLARA COUNTY, CALIFORNIA

United States Supreme Court
480 U.S. 616, 107 S.Ct. 1442 (1987)

Case Background
The Transportation Agency voluntarily adopted an affirmative action plan for hiring and promoting employees. Women were significantly underrepresented in some jobs. To achieve a statistically measurable yearly improvement in the hiring and promotion of women, the sex of qualified applicants would be given consideration. No specific goals were set for the number of positions to be occupied by women. The Agency announced a vacancy for the position of road dispatcher, one of 238 positions in the Skilled Craft Worker job category, none of which were held by women. Johnson, a man, and Diane Joyce applied and were rated as the two best qualified for the job. Johnson scored a 75 on the interview test, Joyce a 73. After taking into account Joyce's sex, she was picked over Johnson, who then sued, claiming that he had been discriminated against on the basis of sex.

The district court ruled in favor of Johnson, finding the affirmative action plan illegal. The Court of Appeals for the Ninth Circuit reversed. Johnson appealed to the U.S. Supreme Court.

Case Decision

We reject petitioner's argument that, since only the long-term goal was in place for Skilled Craft positions at the time of Joyce's promotion, it was inappropriate for the Director to take into account affirmative action considerations in filling the road dispatcher position. The Agency's Plan emphasized that the long-term goals were not to be taken as guides for actual hiring decisions, but that supervisors were to consider a host of practical factors in seeking to meet affirmative action objectives, including the fact that in some job categories women were not qualified in numbers comparable to their representation in the labor force.

The Supreme Court upheld the legality of the affirmative action plan. The Court stated that such a flexible, case-by-case approach is consistent with Title VII, since it allows an employer a means to help voluntarily eliminate the vestiges of discrimination. The plan is not a bar to advancement by males; it simply gives extra consideration for sex.

Managerial Considerations
Managers have the option to impose affirmative action plans if they have evidence that women or minorities have been discriminated against in the past. In this case, there was good statistical evidence of discrimination. Management believed this moderate, flexible plan might help reduce the likelihood of a lawsuit by a woman or minority that could result in a less flexible plan's being imposed on the company.

AGE DISCRIMINATION IN EMPLOYMENT ACT

Enacted in 1967, the *Age Discrimination in Employment Act* (ADEA) promotes the employment of older individuals on the basis of their abilities rather than their age. The Act prohibits discrimination in employment against individuals over age forty. All employers, private and public, who have twenty or more employees must comply with this statute. The ADEA essentially is the same as Title VII in its prohibitions, exceptions, and remedies and is enforced by the EEOC.

In determining whether a violation of the ADEA has occurred, the courts use the McDonnell-Douglas test that the Supreme Court devised for plaintiffs bringing a discrimination claim under Title VII. Employees over age forty who meet that test have established a *prima facie* case of age discrimination. The Third Circuit Court of Appeals noted that often there is no "smoking gun," and the court must, as in the case of race or sex discrimination, look to see if age discrimination can be inferred by studying what has actually occurred at the place of employment. The following are examples of typical age discrimination:

- Forcing retirement before seventy only because of age.
- Assigning older workers to duties that restrict their ability to compete for higher level jobs in the organization.
- Advertising for employees to indicate age preference, such as "young, dynamic person wanted."
- Choosing not to promote a younger worker because the older worker being considered may be retiring in several years.
- Cutting health care benefits for workers over age sixty-five because they are eligible for Medicare.

■ BFOQ ON THE BASIS OF AGE

The ADEA specifically states that employers can force high-level executives to retire after age sixty-five. For all other employees, retirement rules or other conditions of employment based on age must be based upon a BFOQ. For example, the New York state police department would not allow any-one over the age of twenty-nine to apply to be a state police officer. The Second Circuit Court of Appeals ruled that this requirement discriminated against potential applicants over age forty. (Since persons between the ages of thirty and thirty-nine are not covered by the ADEA, this decision did not find that the department had discriminated against them.)

The court in this case did not hold that the police department could never discriminate against applicants over age forty. The police department could legally discriminate against individuals over forty if a BFOQ—a le-gitimate reason that persons of certain ages would not likely be capable of performing certain fundamental duties—was involved. For example, some police and fire departments require that officers retire at age sixty. This BFOQ was upheld when it was shown that good health was an essential occupational requirement. Medical evidence indicates that at age sixty, human health begins to deteriorate, making the stress of a police officer's or firefighter's job difficult to manage. In the absence of such a rule, the employer might have to test constantly the health of all officers over sixty—an expensive proposition.

In all cases, BFOQs must be determined for each job and not based on general rules. In addition, they cannot operate to permit age discrimi-nation in other ways. For example, in the 1985 case *Trans World Airlines* v. *Thurston,* the Supreme Court held that the Federal Aviation Administration may require pilots to retire at age sixty because of the statistical evidence of declining health at that age, a situation that could endanger airline pas-sengers. However, since flight engineers could work past age sixty, pilots must be allowed to switch to being flight engineers if they want to and to maintain their seniority. In this way, the BFOQ rule for pilots was restricted to its specific purpose.

Forced Retirement?   As Figure 13–1 indicates, despite the existence of the ADEA, the percentage of men and women who remain in the labor force after age sixty-five continues to decline. Although there is good evidence from various studies that most people prefer to retire before reaching sixty or seventy, the ADEA helps ensure that the choice not to retire will be available.

One practice that the ADEA specifically prohibits is discrimination against older workers, who tend to have the most seniority, and against a reduction in force (RIF) in favor of younger workers with less seniority and lower pay. The Seventh Circuit Court of Appeals held that a forced RIF of older workers created a *prima facie* violation of the ADEA. An employer cannot get around the intent of the law by taking advantage of a cutback in the work force to dismiss senior, higher paid workers. The other circuit courts have agreed and have noted that the ADEA requires fringe benefits, retirement benefits, and severance pay offers to be neutral with respect to age. According to the Fourth Circuit, it is legal for an employer to offer a voluntary RIF program that offers big incentives to older, higher paid workers in an attempt to encourage them to retire. This is legal because it is a voluntary program, not a discriminatory firing of older workers.

A survey by the American Association of Retired Persons showed that most age discrimination suits are brought by professional white males in their fifties who had been dismissed or forced to retire. That violations of the ADEA can be expensive is illustrated by a 16-million-dollar verdict, upheld on appeal in favor of a Sears store manager over age forty who was dismissed and who sued, claiming that he was fired because of age, not performance.

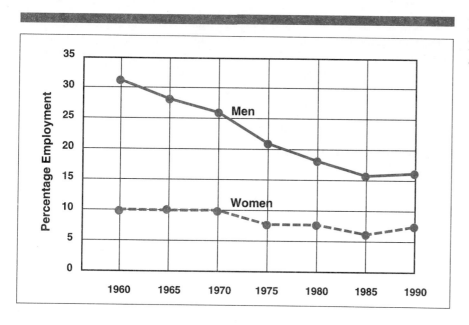

FIGURE 13–1

Percentage of Employed Men and Women Age 65 and Older

DISCRIMINATION AGAINST THE DISABLED

The *Rehabilitation Act* of 1973 provides protection for disabled persons who are seeking employment with or are currently employed by employers that receive federal funds. The Act tends to follow the steps established by the courts in Title VII employment discrimination suits. Section 503 of the Act is most important. It holds that all companies with federal contracts of $2,500 or more—all employers of significant size—have a duty to ensure the disabled an opportunity in the workplace by providing them with reasonable accommodations.

The *Americans with Disabilities Act* (ADA) of 1990 expands the rights of persons with disabilities in employment and supplements access rights to public accommodations, such as hotels, restaurants, theaters, public transportation, telecommunications, and retail stores. The ADA expands the rights of people with mental and physical disabilities beyond those provided by Section 503 of the Rehabilitation Act. Besides encompassing the Rehabilitation Act, the ADA incorporates the remedies and procedures set out in Title VII. The ADA applies to all employers with twenty-five or more employees and, in 1994, to all employers with fifteen or more employees.

DEFINITION OF DISABLED

The Rehabilitation Act and the ADA define a *person with disabilities* as

> any person who (i) has a physical or mental impairment which substantially limits one or more of such person's major life activities, (ii) has a record of such an impairment, or (iii) is regarded as having such an impairment.

The Supreme Court has recognized regulations by the Department of Health and Human Services as a guide to determining what is a disability. The regulations define "major life activities" as "functions such as caring for one's self, performing manual tasks, walking, seeing, hearing, speaking, breathing, learning, and working." The following are examples of disabilities covered by the statutes:

- People with a history of alcohol or other drug abuse.
- People with severe disfigurements.
- People who have had heart attacks.
- People who must use wheelchairs.
- People who are hearing- or vision-impaired.

Even if individuals are not actually impaired, if other people believe them to be impaired, they are disabled. For example, former cancer patients have found that some people are afraid to hire them because they believe that cancer is contagious. As a result, even though no current impairment exists and even though doctors may say there presently is no disease, bias against the person who had the disease may make the person disabled for purposes of this law.

The courts have made it clear that lesser impairments will not constitute a disability for purposes of this law. For example, in a decision of the Fourth Circuit Court of Appeals, a newly hired utility repairman was fired because he had a fear of heights that meant he could not climb ladders to make repairs expected of a person in his position. The fired repairman brought an action under the Rehabilitation Act, alleging that fear of heights caused him to be disabled. The dismissal was upheld by the court because there was no "*substantial* limitation of a *major* life activity." Also in dismissing claims of discrimination against people who are left-handed, the courts note they have no desire to trivialize the statute by allowing it to apply to numerous inconveniences and personal oddities.

■ COMPLIANCE WITH THE STATUTES

The Rehabilitation Act is enforced primarily by complaints to the Department of Labor, which may bring suit on behalf of people with disabilities. An average of twenty-five lawsuits per year have been filed under the Rehabilitation Act. Suits under the ADA will be enforced in the same way that discrimination suits brought under Title VII are enforced.

Reasonable Accommodation. Employers are obliged to make *reasonable accommodations* for persons with disabilities. They are expected to incur expenses in making a position or work station available to qualified disabled applicants and employees. Exactly where the line is drawn is not clear. Ford does not have to redesign its assembly line at high cost so that a worker in a wheelchair could work on the assembly line, because that would impose an *undue hardship* on business operations. However, when a workstation can be redesigned for several thousand dollars to accommodate a person with a disability, it must be done. A Department of Labor study showed that in 80 percent of the cases, the cost of accommodations was under $500. Most problems are likely to arise in the cases where accommodations are more expensive. Firms are expected to provide special equipment and training for the disabled, allow modified work schedules, and provide readers for the blind.

Several firms report that they have had substantial success complying with the law. Marriott has over 6,000 employees with disabilities. The company reports that most can be accommodated at a trivial cost. Sears reports that 5.8 percent of its employees have disabilities, most requiring no or trivial costs. At Southwestern Bell, the consumer-relations manager is blind, so his secretary reads his mail and other messages to him. In the *Arline* case, the Supreme Court discussed the rights of employees with disabilities and how employers must make accommodations.

SCHOOL BOARD OF NASSAU COUNTY, FLORIDA v. ARLINE

United States Supreme Court
480 U.S. 273, 107 S.Ct. 1123 (1987)

Case Background

Gene Arline was hospitalized for tuberculosis in 1957. The disease was not active for the next twenty years, during which time Arline taught elementary school. In 1977 and 1978, medical tests showed the disease to be active again. Because the disease has a small chance of being spread to others, the school board suspended Arline from the classroom with pay for parts of two school years. Arline was then fired in 1979 because the board was worried about the risk of infection. Arline sued, claiming protection under the Rehabilitation Act. The district court ruled that Arline was not disabled under the statute because the law did not apply to contagious diseases. The court of appeals reversed, holding that Arline must either be retained as a teacher or, if the risk of infection is too high, be assigned to nonclassroom duties. The school board appealed to the Supreme Court.

Case Decision

The fact that *some* persons who have contagious diseases may pose a serious health threat to others under certain circumstances does not justify excluding from the coverage of the Act *all* persons with actual or perceived contagious diseases. Such exclusion would mean that those accused of being contagious would never have the opportunity to have their condition evaluated in light of medical evidence and a determination made as to whether they were "otherwise qualified." Rather, they would be vulnerable to discrimination on the basis of mythology—precisely the type of injury Congress sought to prevent. We conclude that the fact that a person with a record of a physical impairment is also contagious does not suffice to remove that person from coverage under [the Act].

The Supreme Court affirmed the decision of the court of appeals. The Court stated that if the risk of infection to the children is trivial, Arline must be reinstated as a teacher; otherwise, she must be given another assignment, such as in administration. She also must be accorded preference in any new hiring over outside applicants.

Managerial Considerations

This decision requires managers to make some difficult choices in such instances. The chance of infection was trivial, but what is trivial for a serious disease? Suppose that despite the trivial odds, a student or coworker contracted the disease from Arline—could the employer be held liable? Suppose that coworkers have irrational fears about the chance of infection, as has been the case of coworkers of cancer and AIDS victims. If that causes the workers to leave the firm or reduces their productivity, what can managers do without violating the rights of the disabled person?

Violations by Employers.   Employers are most likely to violate the Rehabilitation Act or the ADA by failing to make reasonable accommodations for persons with disabilities. Note that as in the case of discrimination based on race, sex, or age, the law is broken if a person is denied an opportunity primarily because of his or her disability. However, in the case of disabilities, besides not discriminating, an employer must make reasonable accommodations—take the extra step to make adjustments for the disabled. In this sense, there is an affirmative action requirement, but it is not tied to goals or quotas, and it works on a case-by-case basis.

Employment situations that are likely to be in violation of the law include the following:

- Using standardized employment tests that tend to screen out people with disabilities.
- Refusing to hire applicants because they have a history of substance abuse rather than because they are currently substance abusers.
- Asking job applicants whether they have disabilities rather than asking whether they have the ability to perform the job.

- Limiting advancement opportunities for employees because of their disabilities.
- Not hiring a person with a disability because the workplace does not have a bathroom that can accommodate wheelchairs.

Hyatt Legal Services ran afoul of the rights of employees with disabilities in 1990 when a federal court awarded $157,000 damages, including $50,000 punitive damages, to a former regional partner of the law firm. The court found that when the plaintiff's employer learned that the plaintiff had AIDS, he was told he could (1) quit and take $12,000 severance pay, (2) take a demotion with a 50 percent pay cut and move to another office, or (3) get treatment at an experimental AIDS treatment program. The court held that this was "a corrupt assault" on the plaintiff's dignity that was unjustified. As employment rights of people with disabilities expand, employers must adjust to the mandated sensitivity.

SUMMARY: A GUIDE FOR MANAGERS

- Title VII of the Civil Rights Act and the Age Discrimination in Employment Act require employers not to discriminate on the basis of sex, race, color, religion, national origin, or age. This applies to all aspects of the employment process—hiring, promotion, discipline, benefits, and firing. The laws are enforced by the EEOC and private party suits.
- Sex discrimination specifically includes discrimination with respect to childbearing plans, pregnancy, and related medical conditions. More recently, the issue of sexual harassment has posed a new legal challenge for managers, who must take steps to inform employees of the seriousness and the consequences of harassment and establish internal procedures to allow claims to be investigated with an assurance of confidentiality.
- Key tests that the courts use to look for discrimination are *disparate treatment*—where, everything else equal, employment decisions are affected by an employee's race, sex, religion, age, etc.; *perpetuating past patterns of intentional discrimination*—where business rules that appear to be neutral have the effect of keeping in place past discriminatory practices; and *disparate impact*—where the effect of hiring or promotion standards is to discriminate, even if unintentional, on the basis of race, sex, etc.
- When employers are sued under the discrimination laws, they must present a preponderance of the evidence that the practices they engage in are not discriminatory. The practices must be shown to be related to business necessity in the way the jobs are structured. Practices that, when properly designed, are allowed to stand include professionally developed ability tests, bona fide seniority and merit systems, and bona fide occupational qualifications that provide a strong reason for discriminating in employee selection.

- An affirmative action plan may be adopted by an employer and a union in a collective bargaining agreement, or it may be adopted voluntarily by an employer. Strategically, doing so voluntarily may reduce the likelihood of a more rigid program being imposed on the company in the event of a lawsuit or government investigation of discrimination charges.

- Employers may have affirmative action plans imposed on them by court order or by the federal government in the case of federal contractors. These plans are designed to increase minority or female representation in certain job categories. In some cases, this is done by setting quotas to be met within certain time frames. Quotas are most likely to be imposed in cases where the employer has failed to take proper steps to be nondiscriminatory in employment policies.

- Section 503 of the Rehabilitation Act and the Americans with Disabilities Act requires employers to take positive steps to make accommodations for disabled workers. Court decisions have broadened the definition of disability to include alcohol and other drug addicts as well as people with serious diseases such as AIDS. Employers must balance the interests and safety of other employees and customers against the rights of the disabled employees to retain meaningful employment.

MANAGER'S ETHICAL DILEMMA

WILL ACCESS REQUIREMENTS ACCOMMODATE BUSINESS REQUIREMENTS?

The Americans with Disabilities Act requires firms to make reasonable accommodations for the disabled. While employers know a fair amount about accommodations for physical disabilities, less is known about what accommodations will be required for persons with mental disabilities, such as drug addiction and retardation.

McDonald's Corporation has been a leader in designing its restaurants to meet access requirements for the physically disabled and, since 1982, has hired and trained over 10,000 mentally and physically disabled workers.

McDonald's was required to pay $210,000 in damages for negligent hiring in a 1991 case. The payment was to a mother and her three-year old son, who was assaulted by a mentally disabled worker at a McDonald's restaurant. The former janitor is now serving a sixteen-year prison sentence for the assault.

McDonald's hired the worker at the recommendation of the Colorado Department of Social Services, which failed to tell the company that the man had a prior conviction for child molestation. The plaintiff argued that McDonald's was negligent for failing to fully investigate the employee's past.

Several employment law specialists noted that this kind of decision will dampen the enthusiasm for this kind of hiring program. In other similar cases, the employers have been faulted for not having known about the criminal background of an employee who is then involved in a criminal act when employed.

QUESTIONS

Background searches are expensive and difficult. There are no central files on every conviction in the United States that can be readily checked. Even a check of every state's records, which would be expensive, would miss some convictions. What sort of criminal background checks should employers make? Is it negligent to hire people who have served a criminal sentence and have "paid their debt to society"? Over two million people in the country have criminal convictions. Should they be excluded from the labor force?

Since some people feel uncomfortable dealing with persons with disabilities, it may hurt the profits of a business to hire the disabled to deal with the public. Should businesses avoid hiring the disabled or, when hiring the disabled, keep them in less visible positions? If there is some uncertainty about the stability of a mentally disabled person, should the person not be hired? How do we balance the rights of employers, the disabled, and the public?

REVIEW AND DISCUSSION QUESTIONS

1. Define the following terms and phrases:

   Discrimination   Artificial seniority
   Protected class   Affirmative action
   Disparate impact   Reasonable accommodations
   Bona fide occupational qualification

2. Compare and contrast the following:

   a. employment-at-will and employment discrimination
   b. Equal Pay Act and Title VII of the Civil Rights Act
   c. discrimination on the basis of race and discrimination on the basis of national origin
   d. seniority systems and merit systems

3. Why were the employee tests given by Duke Power held to be discriminatory? Under what circumstances will such tests be held to be not discriminatory?

4. Would a dress code that required men to wear three-piece suits but stated only that women had to "look professional" be discriminatory against the male employees? What differences would be considered discriminatory?

5. What are the primary defenses used in employee discrimination suits? Do you think these commonly accepted defenses tend to perpetuate the past effects of discrimination? Does not a seniority system mean that those who had been discriminated against will be so forever?

■ CASE QUESTIONS

6. Wise was fired for getting into a fight with another employee during lunch at the company lunchroom. She kicked and scratched the other employee and used abusive language. She claimed sex discrimination under Title VII because male employees who had been in fights had not been fired. Was this sex discrimination? (*Wise* v. *Mead Corp.*, 614 F.Supp. 1131 (M.D. Ga. 1985))

7. A large airline operates a large maintenance and overhaul base in Kansas City, Missouri. Larry was hired by the airline to work as a clerk in the parts department at Kansas City. The department is essential to the airline's operation and must therefore always be open. After working for the airline for a period of time, Larry began to study the religion known as the Worldwide Church of God. One of the tenets of the religion was to refrain from working from sunset on Fridays until sunset on Saturdays. Larry was asked to work Saturdays when a fellow worker went on vacation. Because the airline was unable to accommodate Larry's request not to work on Saturday, Larry refused to report to work. After a hearing, Larry was discharged for insubordination. Was the discharge a religious discrimination in violation of Title VII? What if the company had to shift another employee out of the shift she preferred for similar reasons to fill Larry's position? What if such a shift would have required that the airline circumvent its seniority system?

8. Rawlinson was a twenty-two-year-old college graduate who had majored in correctional psychology. She applied for a position as a correctional counselor— essentially a prison guard—with the Alabama prison system. A correctional counselor's primary duty was to maintain security and control the inmates by continually supervising and observing their activities. The Alabama Board of Corrections rejected Rawlinson's application because Rawlinson failed to meet

the minimum 120-pound weight requirement set by Alabama statute. The statute also imposed a minimum 5-foot, 2-inch height requirement on applicants. Does the Alabama statute violate Title VII? What if the requirements were imposed for the protection of prison guards?

9. Dorr worked at a bank for twenty years. Soon after he was promoted to vice president, he told the bank president that he was gay and that he was the organizer of and president of Integrity, an organization affiliated with the Episcopal Church that advocates equal rights for homosexuals. He said that because of his position with Integrity, he would take public positions on issues affecting the gay community. The bank had a policy that prohibited employees from engaging in outside activities that might undermine public confidence in the bank. The president told Dorr that he would have to resign as president of Integrity and not take public positions on gay issues. Dorr refused and was fired. Dorr sues the bank for discrimination under Title VII. Does he have a suit that could win?

10. The New York City Transit Authority had a policy against hiring people who use narcotics. This included people using methadone, a narcotic given to heroin addicts to break their dependency on heroin. Several people on methadone were refused jobs by the Transit Authority. They sued, claiming the policy was racially discriminatory under Title VII because 80 percent of the methadone users were African American or Hispanic. The district court and court of appeals ruled for the plaintiffs, saying that while they could be excluded from sensitive jobs such as subway car driver, the narcotics users could not be excluded from other jobs. What was the result of the appeal to the Supreme Court? [*New York City Transit Authority* v. *Beazer*, 440 U.S. 568, 99 S.Ct. 1355 (1979)]

■ BUSINESS POLICY QUESTIONS

11. Matt works as one of twenty-six salespeople for a large company. He thinks women belong at home and have no business working, so he insists on insulting women sales representatives when they are around the office together. The women complain about his insults to the supervisor, who warns Matt several times to stop. Matt says it is his right to insult whomever he wants to. Should the company fire Matt for being sexist?

12. The Age Discrimination in Employment Act now holds that starting in 1994, colleges cannot force professors to retire at any age. Colleges are concerned that they will eventually be filled with a large number of very old faculty members and few young ones, so that students will not be able to relate well to the faculty and mental lethargy will set in. Should colleges be allowed to adopt contracts for, say, periods of five or ten years rather than indefinite tenure so that they can get rid of older faculty?

■ ETHICS QUESTIONS

13. You are a supervisor at a company that does not have an affirmative action program. In looking to hire a new person for some position, the person who best fits the job criteria is a white male age thirty. Two other candidates are also well qualified for the position but just slightly less than the top candidate. One of the other candidates is African American; the third is a white woman age sixty-three. You believe that in general there is societal discrimination against minorities and older people. Should you give a little extra credit to the candidates who are in protected classes, given that you can justify whatever choice

you make? How would you decide between the African American man and the older white woman? Should you take into account that the African American man supports a wife and three children, whereas the white woman has an employed husband and no children at home?

14. In response to its concerns about worker safety and health, the Boudreaux Mining Company imposed the following company policy:

> Pregnant females and nonpregnant females capable of bearing children shall hereafter be prohibited from working a job classified as "restricted." Females who cannot bear children may be permitted to work at such a job. A "restricted" job, for purposes of this directive, is one that involves the use of any chemical a female of childbearing age might come into contact with that is extremely hazardous to her well-being.

Is this company policy discriminatory against female employees? What if it is based on sound medical and humane reasons—say, because of the prospects of female workers bearing deformed babies? What if it encouraged women to seek sterilization?

ENVIRONMENTAL REGULATION

CHAPTER 14

MANAGER'S LEGAL CHALLENGE

When a company runs afoul of the environmental laws, the consequences can be expensive: possible fines, legal expenses, compliance costs that must be incurred quickly, and lost sales due to bad publicity. Well-managed companies not only make sure they comply with existing environmental laws but also plan for future environmental controls that, as we will see in this chapter, get even tighter. Compliance with environmental laws requires immediate planning rather than waiting to react to environmental crises.

Herman Miller, Inc., is an office furniture maker in Zeeland, Michigan. Founded by a devout Baptist, the company has a philosophy of strong corporate ethics and participatory management. In 1990, the research manager banned further purchases of two tropical hardwoods from endangered rain forests: rosewood and Honduran mahogany. Some other managers at Herman Miller thought the move was correct, and some were afraid it would kill sales of some of their highest priced items. The change to nonendangered woods was approved, and the company is waiting to see the effect on sales.

Other employees have proposed ideas that have helped the company reduce its adverse effect on the environment—and earn a profit doing so. Almost a million pounds a year of scrap fabric were being dumped into landfills. A buyer in North Carolina was found who shreds the material and uses it for insulation in cars. The result is a savings of $50,000 a year due to reduced dumping fees.

The company built an 11-million-dollar heating and cooling plant that produces most energy by burning company waste. Waste taken to landfills fell 90 percent, saving the company $750,000 a year in disposal costs and utility bills. Similarly, a new toxic solvents incinerator put the company years ahead of what is required by the Clean Air Act but allowed the company to address the problem rationally rather than wait for new regulatory requirements to arrive.

Employees were throwing away 800,000 drink cups a year. The disposable cups were replaced with personal mugs. By redesigning its shipping packages, the company has reduced its use of packing materials and insists that its suppliers do the same—all of which reduces costs. The company also buys back, reconditions, and resells its old furniture. When possible, it makes new furniture with recyclable materials and designs that will come apart easily for recycling when that time comes.

The senior vice president for sales says that the company does not advertise its environmental management when trying to sell its products. He thinks that "green marketing" is a gimmick, aside from the fact that no company can claim to be environmentally perfect.

By encouraging employees to take the initiative and think about the relationship between materials, wastes, productions processes, and the environment in all aspects of operations, the company estimates annual savings of over $3 million a year from the actions it has taken that are not required by law. Such moves have made the company more competitive, and the company is well regarded by environmental regulators and environmental groups in Michigan, reducing the risk of legal problems and bad publicity.

This chapter discusses the federal laws providing for the protection of environmental quality. It begins with a discussion of common law attempts to regulate environmental quality, since much of the present statutory law has been affected by common law principles. Particular attention is paid to the application of nuisance law to environmental pollution problems. The chapter then discusses the creation of the Environmental Protection Agency (EPA) and the major federal environmental quality laws, including the Clean Air Act, the Clean Water Act, and the Resource Conservation and Recovery Act.

Some people claim that the 1990s are the decade of environmentalism for business. Certainly many advertising campaigns emphasize the "green" benefits of various products. Such promotions aside, there is no doubt that business is being forced to devote far more attention to environmental matters than it did in years past. As Figure 14–1 shows, measured in constant dollars, expenditures on pollution control have jumped significantly. In some cases, this is a reflection of costs that were previously being ignored—air, water, and land were often treated as free goods that could be used in the production process without consideration of consequences. In other cases, the increase is a reflection of cleanup costs—paying today for past environmental damage.

POLLUTION AND THE COMMON LAW

Environmental pollution was not subject to serious federal regulation until after 1970. Before then, pollution had been viewed as a problem for state and local governments. Although some state laws were developed to control pollution, citizens had to rely primarily on the common law for relief from environmental pollution.

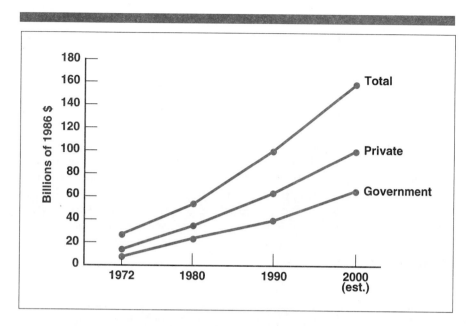

FIGURE 14–1

Pollution Control Costs
Source: Environmental Protection Agency

To resolve disputes involving pollution, judges relied on the laws of nuisance, trespass, negligence, and strict liability for abnormally dangerous activities. Citizens relied mostly on the law of nuisance in actions against business, whether the pollutant was water, air, or land based. According to Professor William Rodgers:

> Nuisance actions . . . challenged virtually every major industrial and municipal activity which is today the subject of comprehensive environmental regulation—the operation of land fills, incinerators, sewage treatment facilities, activities at chemical plants, aluminum, lead and copper smelters, oil refineries, pulp mills, rendering plants, quarries and mines, textile mills and a host of other manufacturing activities.

■ NUISANCE LAW AND POLLUTION

As discussed in the chapter on torts, nuisances are classified as either public or private. A *public nuisance* is defined as an unreasonable interference with a right held in common by the general public. In an environmental pollution case, that right held in common is the community's right to a reasonably clean environment under the circumstances. To be a public nuisance, the pollution affects many people, such as the residents of the community. As a rule, a public nuisance case will be brought against the polluter by the city attorney in the community's name.

A *private nuisance* is defined as a substantial and unreasonable interference with the use and enjoyment of the land of another. It generally involves a polluter who is injuring another person or an identifiable group of people. People suffering from pollution with no commercial activity to protect often find that litigation costs exceed the costs of alternatives, such as selling their property and moving away from the offending polluter or putting up with the problem.

A common law pollution case often involves a company's production process that is offensive or harmful to the company's neighbors. Before requiring a polluter to reduce, clean up, or stop pollution, the court requires the plaintiff to demonstrate evidence of unreasonable interference by the business and the availability of a better means of controlling pollution.

The plaintiff must present evidence that the pollution is an unreasonable interference with the use and enjoyment of the land. In deciding whether the pollution is unreasonable, the court may compare the *social costs* caused by the pollution with the *social benefits* the business provides. In determining the social costs of the pollution, the court will consider the characteristics of the pollution and the degree to which it is permanent or long-lasting. In considering the social benefits, the court will consider the value of the business and the appropriateness of the business's location. If the benefits of the business exceed the harm caused by the pollution, the pollution will be considered reasonable. The *Versailles* case illustrates the court's decision process.

VERSAILLES BOROUGH v. MCKEESPORT COAL & COKE COMPANY

Allegheny County Court
83 Pittsburgh Legal Journal 379 (1935)

Case Background
McKeesport Coal & Coke Company owned 2,500 acres of coal in the borough of Versailles, the city of McKeesport, Pennsylvania. In the process of mining the coal, certain impurities were found. Called "gob," these impurities were removed to the surface because there was no place to store them in the mine. As was the general practice in the industry, the gob was dumped in a pile near the mine. On November 3, 1933, the gob pile caught fire. Because of the smoke and other environmental problems caused by the burning gob pile, Versailles sought an injunction against the coal company as a public nuisance.

Case Decision
The court ruled that the activity of the McKeesport Coal & Coke Company was reasonable under the circumstances and therefore no injunction could be issued based on public nuisance. The court noted that plaintiffs had suffered inconvenience, annoyance, and aesthetic damage from the burning gob pile. The mine, however, was a legitimate business with shareholders who were entitled to a reasonable return on their investment. Furthermore, an injunction would force the mine to close, causing hundreds of men to lose their jobs. Although a number of witnesses complained about irritated throats, asthma, hay fever, headaches, coughs, and eye and nose irritation allegedly caused by the noxious fumes, the effects were not serious. In addition, the court noted that those who seek the employment opportunities and other benefits provided by a large city are aware of the industrial pollution generated by the factories that create the employment. Thus, since the operation of the mine did not create unreasonable health and welfare problems, more injury would be done by an injunction than by allowing the mining operations to continue.

Managerial Considerations
As this case illustrates, the courts were accommodating to industry in early environmental actions. However, the legal environment of pollution control changed dramatically during the 1970s. State and federal legislatures and the agencies they created took primary responsibility for protecting the environment. Despite this shift in responsibility, the common law, particularly the law of nuisance, is still used to resolve many environmental disputes. Now that the courts are considerably less accommodating to industry, environmentalists have found the common law to be an effective tool in controlling pollution.

It is important for managers to understand that although a company may be in compliance with federal statutory requirements, some of its activities could still be judged a nuisance by the courts. Management may want to make the strategic decision to limit or prevent residential growth near existing facilities. As nearby areas become more residential, companies run the risk that their activities will be judged incompatible with the surroundings. In deciding where to locate a new plant, management should determine that the company's operations will be consistent with current and anticipated uses of the land around the proposed site.

Plaintiffs are also required to demonstrate that the business is not doing all it can to control pollution. This may be done by providing evidence on the availability of more stringent pollution control technologies. The business presents evidence about the impractical nature and high cost of proposed pollution control. Courts generally prefer to require superior control technologies instead of requiring the business to close.

▮ TRESPASS AND POLLUTION

Recall that a *trespass* at common law is defined as an unauthorized and direct breach of the boundaries of another's land. The difference between trespass and nuisance is that a trespass occurs when there is an invasion of property. A nuisance requires proof that the interference with the plaintiff's property is substantial and unreasonable.

To establish a trespass in a pollution case, the plaintiff must show that the invasion was more substantial than a mere whiff of smoke, dust, or fumes. In addition, some courts hold that the invasion must be direct. If an intervening force, such as wind or water, carries the pollutants onto the plaintiff's land, the invasion is not direct and therefore is not a trespass. Such restrictions reduce the possible applications of trespass in environmental cases.

▮ NEGLIGENCE, STRICT LIABILITY, AND POLLUTION

Both *negligence* and *strict liability for abnormally dangerous activities* have applications in pollution cases. Tort liability may be due to negligence—failure to use reasonable care to prevent pollution from causing a foreseeable injury. Strict liability for abnormally dangerous activities has a long history, as we saw in the torts chapter. It has a number of applications to businesses emitting toxic pollutants. In imposing strict liability, the courts generally emphasize the risks created by the toxic pollutant and the location of the business relative to population centers. The doctrine is simple, requiring proof only of the fact that the discharge of the toxic pollutant was abnormally dangerous and that the pollutant was the cause of the plaintiff's injury. Courts have found crop dusting, the storing of flammable liquids in quantity in a populated area, and the emitting of noxious gases by factories all to be abnormally dangerous. The following case illustrates the application of strict liability to an environmental pollution problem of growing concern—the contamination of groundwater.

BRANCH v. WESTERN PETROLEUM, INC.

Supreme Court of Utah
657 P.2d 267 (1982)

Case Background
Branch owned property next to the property of Western Petroleum. Western built a pond into which it dumped wastewater from oil wells. The wastewater contained toxic chemicals. It was Western's expectation that the toxic water

in the pond would dissipate by evaporating into the air and percolating into the ground.

The wastewater did percolate into the ground, contaminating the groundwater and Branch's water wells. After water from the wells killed one hundred of his chickens, Branch began trucking in water. Branch brought suit, alleging that since Western's activities created an abnormally

(continued)

dangerous condition, the court should apply a strict liability basis for remedy. The trial court agreed with Branch, holding Western strictly liable for the damages caused by the pollution of the wells. Western appealed the decision to the Supreme Court of Utah.

Case Decision

The Utah high court affirmed the trial court's decision, holding that an industrial polluter who discharges liquid chemical wastes upon the ground is strictly liable for any injuries resulting from the contamination of groundwater. The court noted that many theories, such as public and private nuisance, negligence, negligent trespass, and strict liability, could be used in assessing liability for polluting groundwater through industrial wastes. Since Utah is an arid state, the protection of the purity of its waters is a prime concern. Strict liability will be used when the condition or activity is abnormal and creates a dangerous condition.

Managerial Considerations

Groundwater protection has become an environmental priority for the courts and the environmental protection agencies. Waste storage ponds and underground storage tanks are a source of groundwater pollution. Both are now subject to state and federal regulations, but common law liability can still apply when others are injured by contamination that is allowed to escape.

Management should conduct an environmental assessment of any property it intends to purchase to search out hidden environmental problems. Companies have been stuck with responsibility for pollution caused by a prior owner who left toxic storage tanks buried. In some cases, the cleanup costs have exceeded the cost of the property.

■ COMMON LAW REMEDIES

Parties seeking relief from pollution under the common law generally seek an *injunction* to prohibit the offending business from continuing to pollute and *damages* for their injuries. While willing to award damages, courts also force a business to install pollution controls as a remedy rather than stop production. In most cases, a polluter must meet standard industry techniques for the control of pollution.

In some cases, the courts require the business to improve its pollution control even though it has been meeting industry standards. This is the case when the courts find that the industry is lagging in the development and adoption of new control techniques. Courts can require the business to undertake a research effort to develop better technologies. If the business fails to develop an adequate control technology, a court can issue a permanent injunction so that the operation either has to shut down or move.

FEDERAL REGULATION ■■■■■■■■■■■■

Despite the existence of common law remedies, by the late 1960s, it was generally agreed that environmental pollution control programs were inadequate. The effectiveness of common law remedies was often limited by state statutes and interstate compacts that essentially protected polluters. Major lakes and rivers had become garbage dumps, and air pollution was a health hazard in many cities. Since early federal legislation gave states primary control over pollution, there were few federal standards. The era ended with passage of the *National Environmental Policy Act* (NEPA) and creation of the Environmental Protection Agency in 1970. These were major moves toward substantive federal regulation of the environment.

■ NATIONAL ENVIRONMENTAL POLICY ACT

NEPA was a major policy change by the federal government. After decades of relying on dubious state efforts to control pollution, NEPA proclaimed that pollution was a major federal government concern. According to Congress, the purposes of NEPA are as follows:

> To declare a national policy which will encourage productive and enjoyable harmony between man and his environment; to promote efforts which will prevent or eliminate damage to the environment and biosphere and stimulate the health and welfare of man; [and] to enrich the understanding of the ecological systems and natural resources important to the nation. . . .

Despite being one of the briefest and most general of federal environmental statutes, NEPA has affected virtually every major project—both public and private—since its enactment.

Requirements Imposed on Government.   To implement its objectives, NEPA requires all federal agencies to take into account any environmental impact their programs may create. This purpose of the Act is to reform the decision-making process employed by federal agencies by compelling them to take environmental effects and values into account.

To be assured that federal agencies consider the environmental consequences of their decisions, NEPA requires agency officials to prepare an *environmental impact statement* (EIS) ". . . in every recommendation or report on proposals for legislation and other Federal actions significantly affecting the quality of the human environment." The EIS is intended to assess the environmental effects of an agency's proposal and force the agency to consider the availability of alternatives that might be less damaging to the environment.

NEPA has also had a significant impact at the state government level. The Act inspired enactment of a number of state environmental acts and EIS requirements. While the statutes differ from state to state, they have had a significant impact on the ability of businesses to buy property in a state to construct a production plant or other commercial operation. If the plant can be shown to be expected to cause significant pollution, some state statutes virtually foreclose the possibilities that the business can build in the state.

■ ENVIRONMENTAL PROTECTION AGENCY

After the enactment of NEPA, Congress proceeded to enact a vast body of substantive environmental law. The laws sharply increased federal authority and responsibility to combat virtually every type of pollution. To implement and enforce its environmental mandates, in 1970, Congress created the *Environmental Protection Agency* (EPA). By 1992, the EPA had a six-billion-dollar budget and 17,000 employees.

As Figure 14–2 illustrates, the EPA is responsible for the regulation of pollutants generated by industry (and government agencies) that are transmitted to the external environment. Specifically, the EPA is responsible for four basic types of environmental pollution. The agency is required to control air pollution (through the Clean Air Act), water pollution

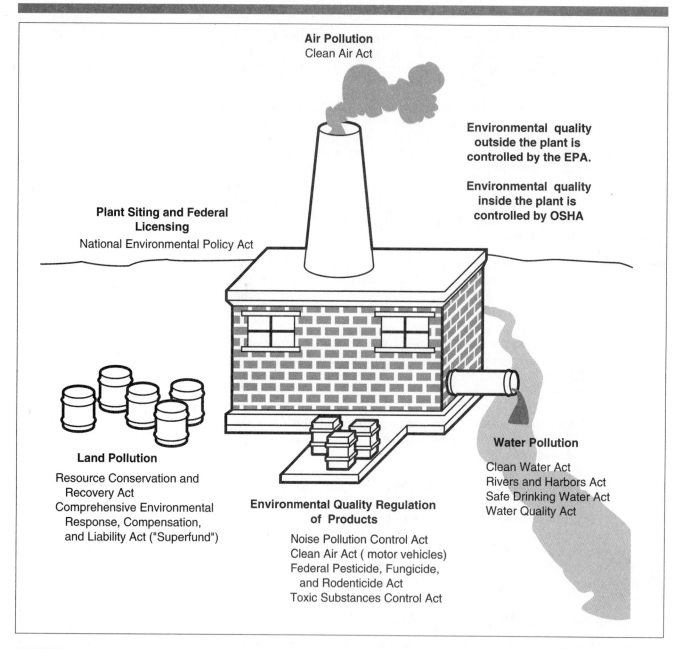

Air Pollution
Clean Air Act

Environmental quality
outside the plant is
controlled by the EPA.

Environmental quality
inside the plant is
controlled by OSHA

**Plant Siting and Federal
Licensing**
National Environmental Policy Act

Land Pollution

Resource Conservation and
Recovery Act
Comprehensive Environmental
Response, Compensation,
and Liability Act ("Superfund")

**Environmental Quality Regulation
of Products**

Noise Pollution Control Act
Clean Air Act (motor vehicles)
Federal Pesticide, Fungicide,
and Rodenticide Act
Toxic Substances Control Act

Water Pollution

Clean Water Act
Rivers and Harbors Act
Safe Drinking Water Act
Water Quality Act

FIGURE 14–2

**Federal Regulation of
Environmental Pollution**

(through the Clean Water Act), land pollution (through the Resource Conservation and Recovery Act and the Superfund), and pollutants resulting
from the use of products by consumers. The following sections provide an
overview of the laws governing the major areas of the environment.

Air Pollution

The federal air quality control program relies on the regulatory approach
embodied in the Clean Air Act of 1970, 1977, and 1990. The Clean Air Act

is without question the most formidable environmental statute in the world. The approach embodied in the Act reflects a rigid, uncompromising goal to reduce air pollution within specified time periods. Other nations have adapted or copied some provisions of the Clean Air Act when developing their own air pollution control statutes.

Early federal regulation, such as the Clean Air Act of 1963, relied heavily on the efforts of state governments. Despite federal intentions to allow state discretion in air and water pollution control, the states demonstrated little desire to be effective. Some blamed the ineffectiveness on the vulnerability of state governments to the interests of local industry. Others considered federal efforts to be lacking in substance and lax in setting and enforcing standards.

■ CLEAN AIR ACT OF 1970

Congress reacted to the shortcomings in state regulatory efforts by enacting the Clean Air Act Amendments of 1970. The *Clean Air Act* sharply increased federal authority and responsibility to control pollution. In the words of the U.S. Supreme Court, Congress intended to "take a stick to the states" with this law. The Act provides a mechanism through which the federal government develops pollution standards and, through the forced cooperation of the states, implements those standards across the country.

The stated purpose of the Act is to "protect and enhance the quality of the nation's air resources." The Act sets forth a comprehensive regulatory program for achieving specified standards of air quality to be uniformly applied across the nation. Those standards are called the *national ambient air quality standards* (NAAQS). The EPA is required to develop standards for every air pollutant emitted by industry that in its judgment "arise[s] or contribute[s] to air pollution which may reasonably be anticipated to endanger public health and welfare." A pollutant's NAAQS are to be based on public health effects. Secondary considerations in the standards are based on the impact on plants, animals, soil, and artificial surfaces. The EPA has developed national standards for major pollutants such as sulfur dioxide, particulates, ozone carbon monoxide, hydrocarbons, nitrogen oxide, and lead. Table 14–1 summarizes the principal characteristics, health effects, and sources of those major air pollutants.

■ CLEAN AIR ACT OF 1977

The 1977 Clean Air Act amendments established specific procedures for the construction of new industrial plants. The requirements imposed on plant owners (and operators) depend on the air quality of the area in which the plant is built. One set of requirements applies if the plant is built in a "clean air area," and another set applies if it is built in a "dirty air area." In either case, the plant owner is required to obtain a preconstruction permit from the EPA.

Clean Air Areas. Areas with clean air—air of better quality than required by the NAAQS—are *attainment areas* or are *prevention of significant deterioration* (PSD) areas. PSD areas include national parks, wilderness areas, and other areas where the air quality is better than the level specified by the national standards. Because of the sensitive nature of those areas, only a

TABLE 14–1
MAJOR AIR POLLUTANTS SUBJECT TO NAAQS

Pollutant	Characteristics	Sources	Health Effects
Sulfur dioxide (SO_2)	Colorless gas with pungent odor; oxidizes to form sulfur trioxide, which forms acid rain.	Power plants and industrial sources that burn sulfur-containing fossil fuels; smelting of sulfur-bearing ores.	Causes and aggravates respiratory ailments, including asthma, chronic bronchitis, emphysema.
Particulates	Any particle dispersed in the atmosphere, such as dust, ash, soot, and various chemicals.	Natural events such as wind erosion; stationary sources that burn solid fuels; agricultural operations.	Chest discomfort; throat and eye irritation.
Ozone (O_3)	A poisonous gas invisible in low concentrations; results from chemical combination of hydrocarbon vapors and nitrogen oxides in the sunlight; smog.	Hydrocarbons and nitrogen oxides mostly from motor vehicle exhaust, refineries, and chemical plants.	Aggravates respiratory ailments; causes eye irritation.
Carbon monoxide (CO)	Colorless, odorless gas.	Motor vehicle exhaust and other carbon-containing materials; natural sources.	Reduces oxygen-carrying capacity of blood; impairs heart functions, visual perception, and alertness.
Nitrogen oxide (NO_x)	Brownish gas with pungent odor; component in photochemical oxidants.	Motor vehicle exhaust; power plants.	Aggravates respiratory ailments.
Lead (Pb)	Heavy metallic chemical element; often occurs as lead oxide aerosol or dust.	Nonferrous metal smelters; motor vehicle exhaust.	High levels of exposure cause lead poisoning.

slight increase in pollution is allowed. That slight increase is called the *maximum allowable increase.* Any activity, including a plant that will cause the maximum allowable increase to be exceeded, is prohibited in a PSD area.

New plants can be built in PSD areas as long as the plant meets two basic requirements. First, the owner must agree to install the *best available control technology* (BACT)—as determined by the EPA—on the new plant to control pollution. Second, the owner must demonstrate that the pollution from the plant will not cause the maximum allowable increase in the area to be exceeded.

The amount of the maximum allowable increase depends upon whether the plant will be located in a Class I, II, or III PSD area. Class I areas have pristine air quality; that is, they are virtually pollution free. Since very little additional pollution would significantly deteriorate the air quality in those areas, only a small maximum increase would be allowed. Once that amount of pollution is added, any economic growth that would result in increased pollution is thereafter foreclosed. Class II and III areas allow progressively more pollution to be added before the maximum allowable increase will be exceeded.

Dirty Air Areas.   Dirty air areas are designated as *nonattainment areas,* signifying that they have not achieved the NAAQS. Businesses wanting to build in nonattainment areas are required to meet even more restrictive and expensive requirements than those in the PSD areas. Through the *emissions offset policy,* the amendments impose three specific requirements on owners of new plants.

First, the owners of the new plant must agree to control the plant's pollution to the maximum degree possible. The plant must use the *lowest achievable emissions rate technology* (LAER). In most cases, LAER will be a more stringent (and more expensive) technology than the BACT requirement in PSD areas. Generally, the EPA will designate the LAER as the most stringent technology in use by any similar plant in the country.

Second, the owners of the new plant must certify that all their other plants in the area are meeting the requirements imposed by the applicable state implementation plan. This provides businesses an incentive to comply with the Clean Air Act's requirements. If the business is unable to verify compliance, the EPA will not allow the new plant to be built.

Third, new plants can be built in nonattainment areas only if the air pollution from the new plant is *offset* by reductions in the same pollutants from other plants in the area. The quantity of the offset from other plants must match the air pollution from the new plant more than one for one. That is, when the new plant is operating, the area must enjoy a *net air quality improvement.* This is to assure that the area will make progress toward achieving the national air quality standards.

To illustrate, suppose that Cavalini Automotive Design has decided to build a new plant in Detroit, a nonattainment area for sulfur dioxide. To build the plant, Cavalini must obtain a preconstruction permit from the EPA. The EPA will require Cavalini to certify that it will apply the LAER technology and that its other plants in the area are currently in compliance with Michigan's state implementation plan. Most importantly, Cavalini will be required to obtain an emissions offset. To obtain this offset, Cavalini must reduce pollution in other plants by buying them and closing them down or by paying for pollution controls in other plants. If Cavalini's new plant will add ten units of pollution to the air, Cavalini must secure a reduction in pollution elsewhere in the area of *more* then ten units. When the plant begins operations, the air quality in the area will have been improved.

The Bubble Concept.   The EPA has a strategy similar to the emissions offset policy, called the *bubble concept,* which treats all facilities that make up an industrial complex as a single pollution source. The industrial complex is considered to be under an imaginary glass bubble that has a single stack emitting pollutants from its top. All emissions from the complex are measured from that smokestack rather than from individual smokestacks. Increases in emissions from changes in the facility have no regulatory consequences so long as decreases from other parts of the facility more than offset the new increases. The net effect—as measured from the smokestack on the bubble—must be a decrease in emissions.

Suppose that Acme Smelting Company decided to add a fourth plant to its three-plant complex. Acme must certify that its other plants are in compliance with the appropriate state implementation plan. Under the offset policy, Acme must agree to apply the LAER technology and obtain an offset. Under the bubble concept, Acme may add any control device it chooses to any of the plants in the complex. The net result—as measured in total from the smokestack of the imaginary bubble—must be a decrease in total pollution emissions.

The bubble concept and the offset policy produce the same net air quality improvement. The bubble concept, however, can be less expensive because the company has greater discretion in selecting pollution control devices. Predictably, the company will develop a strategy that provides the appropriate level of pollution control at the lowest possible cost. Despite its potential cost savings, the bubble concept has been subject to legal challenges. In *Chevron* v. *Natural Resources Defense Council*, the U.S. Supreme Court considered its validity.

CHEVRON, U.S.A., INC. v. NATURAL RESOURCES DEFENSE COUNCIL, INC.

United States Supreme Court
467 U.S. 837, 104 S.Ct. 2778 (1984)

Case Background
To help implement the Clean Air Act the EPA developed the bubble concept, which allows a company to treat all pollution-emitting sources in one industrial complex as if they were under an imaginary glass bubble with a single smokestack—treating the complex as a single source of pollution. The owner of the complex can adjust pollution from individual sources under the bubble as long as the total emissions measured from the single imaginary smokestack meet the requirements of the law. The EPA allowed Chevron to use the bubble concept in meeting the company's air pollution control requirements.

The Natural Resources Defense Council (NRDC) opposed the EPA's use of the bubble concept. It contended that the Act's definition of "source" required each pollution-emitting device to be viewed separately and to meet the law's requirements individually. The NRDC sought review of the bubble concept and its application by Chevron in federal court. The court of appeals agreed with the NRDC and set aside the regulations as contrary to law. Chevron and the EPA appealed to the Supreme Court.

Case Decision
The Supreme Court reversed the decision of the court of appeals, holding that the EPA's definition of the term *source*, which allows the EPA to use the bubble concept, is a permissible construction of a statute that seeks to accommodate progress in reducing air pollution while not discouraging economic growth. The Court noted that neither the Clean Air Act nor the legislative history of the Act refers to the bubble concept or to the definition of "stationary source." When "the statute is silent or ambiguous with respect to the specific issue, the question for the court is whether the agency's answer is based on permissible construction of the statute." Here, the EPA used its expert judgment to carry out the purposes of the Act. In so doing, the EPA rationalized that not using the concept would retard progress in reducing air pollution by "discouraging replacement of older, dirtier processes or equipment with new, cleaner ones." Furthermore, the EPA believed that the concept would encourage investment and modernization, thereby promoting economic growth while implementing the statutory standards. The EPA created a reasonable choice for the implementation of broad legislative directives.

Managerial Considerations
There is little doubt that compliance with environmental standards can be very expensive. As managers have confronted competition from manufacturers located in countries with lax environmental standards, they have sought means by which they could comply and still remain competitive. Innovative managers are challenged to work within the incentive structure provided by the bubble concept in developing techniques and technologies for reducing pollution at costs that are lower than under more traditional regulation, where the technology to be used is dictated by the regulatory agency. The management of a large steel company, for example, estimated that the bubble concept would save the company more than $100,000 per year and allow it to meet compliance deadlines several years sooner than under the offset policy. The EPA is working to develop other concepts that rely on managerial innovation in regulating other kinds of pollution.

■ CLEAN AIR ACT OF 1990

After twenty years of federal regulation of air pollution, as Figure 14–3 shows, some pollutants had dropped substantially, while others remained about the same. Congress addressed several concerns by amending the Clean Air Act of 1970. The 1990 Act had four major parts, which concern the NAAQS, mobile sources of pollution, toxic pollutants, and acid rain.

Ambient Air Quality.   The 1990 Act repeated the requirement for the EPA to set NAAQS for major air pollutants every five years. Every time the EPA issues new NAAQS standards for pollutants, each state must issue a new State Implementation Plan (SIP) that define which areas of the state are nonattainment areas, which are attainment areas, and which cannot be classified for each pollutant. States must also issue SIPs for limiting emissions, prepare schedules for implementing new controls, explain how the controls will be monitored, and note the fees that polluters will be charged to pay for the enforcement program. If a state SIP is rejected, the EPA will force a plan onto the state.

Because of the lack of progress on reducing ozone pollution, tighter controls have been imposed. In areas of high ozone pollution, the SIPs must impose tougher vehicle emissions inspections, have vapor recovery systems at gas stations, force more car pooling, and reduce other ozone-causing pollutants.

Mobile Sources.   Vehicles are a major source of ozone pollution. The level of ozone allowed is determined by the NAAQS, but the law also imposes direct controls on emissions. New tailpipe emissions standards for all cars, trucks, and buses are to be phased in by 1995. Another set of tighter standards can be imposed for model years 2004 or 2007, depending on progress in ozone reduction.

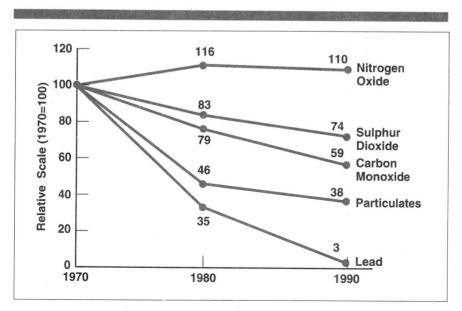

FIGURE 14–3

Results of 20 Years of Air Pollution Controls—U.S. Emissions (increase or decline) Relative to 1970
NOTE: Ozone emissions have changed very little since about 1975.
SOURCE: EPA, National Air Quality and Emissions Trends Report

The 1990 Act also requires more use of alternative fuels, such as methanol, ethanol, natural gas, and reformulated gasoline. These requirements go into effect first in Los Angeles and other nonattainment areas, as does a requirement that fleet vehicles use clean alternative fuels.

The law allows states to impose emissions standards that go beyond the federal requirements. California has set tougher auto emissions standards and requirements for cleaner burning gasoline and has forced use of alternative-fuel and electric-powered cars. The regulations are supposed to cut auto pollution 50 percent more than the federal standards do. In 1991, New York, New Jersey, Pennsylvania, Massachusetts, Virginia, Maryland, Delaware, New Hampshire, Maine, Rhode Island, and Vermont adopted the California standards, which means that California's standards will eventually become the national standard.

Toxic Pollutants.   The 1990 Act lists 191 substances declared to be hazardous air pollutants. The EPA must set *minimum emissions rates* (MERs) for each pollutant. The general goal is a 90 percent reduction in emissions for the pollutants that had been uncontrolled and a 75 percent reduction in cancer caused by air pollution. If the EPA determines that a pollutant is a threat to public health or the environment, tighter control standards are to be imposed without regard to such economic factors as cost or technological feasibility. By the year 2000, very tough standards for many pollutants can be expected, which means that firms must begin to study the problem and react now (as discussed in the Manager's Legal Challenge feature) rather than wait for standards that may close down operations.

Acid Rain.   Two main sources of *acid rain* are sulfur dioxide and nitrous oxides, which mostly come from burning coal or oil to produce electricity. These chemicals become sulfuric and nitric acid, returning to earth in rain or some other form of precipitation. While the extent of the problem caused by acid rain is not established, it is clear that much of it occurs in the northeast, as winds carry acids from 111 electricity plants, mostly in the Midwest and the Appalachian region, especially from those burning soft coal. The law requires that about half of the sulfur dioxide and nitrous oxides emissions that were produced in 1990 be eliminated by 2000.

Enforcement.   The EPA and the state agencies that oversee SIPs have primary responsibility for enforcing the Clean Air Act. Civil penalties up to $25,000 per day may be imposed on violators. Citizens have the right to sue violators of the Clean Air Act, but EPA restrictions have made such suits uncommon. The EPA has broad powers in setting and enforcing regulations under the statute. To get into court, citizens must show that the EPA (or state agency) is failing to enforce pollution control requirements, even after the agency has been notified of the problem. If the EPA shows that it is prosecuting a polluter, citizen suit is prohibited. Unlike other areas of environmental law, especially water pollution, citizen suits under the Clean Air Act are quite rare.

Enforcement of the other environmental statutes discussed in this chapter can be assumed to be similar to the Clean Air Act. Primary responsibility falls on the EPA, which often gives control to state environmental agencies so long as their standards meet EPA approval. If the government agencies fail to enforce the law, most statutes allow citizens to intervene.

Most environmental statutes allow the possibility of criminal convictions for repeated offenses and for wilfull violations that show disregard for the law. Between 1988 and 1991, an average of 100 criminal indictments per year were issued against individuals, and 60 a year were convicted. In 1991, $14 million in criminal fines were imposed, and convicted defendants received average jail time of eight months. Half of all defendants were the president, owner, or a director of the company involved. So the consequences for violating the environmental laws can be severe. Most of the large fines and jail sentences are for managers involved in dumping toxic wastes or otherwise exposing people to hazardous substances in clear violation of the law.

WATER POLLUTION

Federal statutory control over water pollution traces at least as far back as the Rivers and Harbors Act of 1886 and 1899. But like the Federal Water Pollution Control Act of 1948, there was little effective federal control over water pollution. Primary responsibility was left with the states, which did not attack the task with much vigor. By 1970, marine life in Lake Erie was almost gone, and many rivers were unfit for drinking water or recreation. One river in Ohio had so much pollution in it that it caught on fire. Congress began passing water pollution statutes in the 1970s. A substantive set of regulations is now in effect, with more regulations expected in the 1990s.

■ THE CLEAN WATER ACT

The Clean Water Act was passed in 1972 and comprehensively amended in 1977 and again in 1986. The objective of the Clean Water Act is to "restore and maintain the chemical, physical, and biological integrity of the Nation's waters." The Act has five main elements:

1. National effluent (pollution) standards set by the EPA for each industry.
2. Water quality standards set by the states under EPA approval.
3. A discharge permit program that translates water quality standard into enforceable pollution limits.
4. Special provisions for toxic chemicals and oil spills.
5. Construction grants and loans from the federal government for publicly owned treatment works (POTW).

The Act makes it unlawful for any person—defined as an individual, business, or governmental body—to discharge pollutants into navigable waters without a *permit*. Although the Act does not define the phrase *navigable waters*, the following case illustrates that it is broadly interpreted.

QUIVIRA MINING COMPANY v. U.S. ENVIRONMENTAL PROTECTION AGENCY

United States Court of Appeals, Tenth Circuit
765 F.2d 126 (1985)

Case Background
Quivira Mining challenged the authority of the EPA to regulate the discharge of pollutants from the company's uranium mining facilities into gullies or arroyos. Specifically, Quivira contested the pollution control requirements EPA had placed in the company's National Pollution Discharge Elimination System permits. Quivira discharged wastes into Arroyo del Puerto and San Mateo Creek which the company contended were not navigable waterways as required by the Clean Water Act and therefore were beyond the EPA's jurisdiction. The EPA denied Quivira's request for review of its claims, and Quivira appealed to the Tenth Circuit Court of Appeals.

Case Decision
The court of appeals affirmed the EPA decision, holding that the arroyo and the creek are navigable waterways subject to regulation under the Clean Water Act. Even though a waterway may not be navigable by boats, if wastes discharged into it affect interstate commerce, the wastes will fall under the Act. Here, the arroyo and the creek, when filled by rainfall, connect to other streams that are navigable. Furthermore, the wastes discharged into them may flow into underground aquifers and pollute the water supply. Therefore, there is a sufficient connection between the wastes discharged by Quivira and navigable waters to bring the discharge within the reach of the Clean Water Act.

Managerial Considerations
The company may have brought the action merely to delay compliance with the permit requirements. Or management may have understood the permit process and the complexities facing the EPA in assigning pollution control requirements. With thousands of water polluters seeking permits, it was impossible for the agency to visit each plant. In most cases, the EPA assigned control requirements on an industry basis. If a company in an industry had older equipment or used a different process (often the case with small companies), the industry requirements would not work. Those companies sought review by the agency. In a few instances, the agency gave companies an extension or different requirements, giving them a competitive advantage and leading management of other companies to seek review of their requirements.

As *Quivira* makes clear, Congress has the authority to control water pollution in all forms and places. Getting the job done has been much more expensive and has taken longer than was anticipated when the Clean Water Act was passed in 1972. At that time, Congress said that the discharge of pollutants into any waters would be eliminated by 1985. That was an impossible goal. As it stands, discharges have probably dropped to about half of what they were twenty years ago. But since pollutants that are easiest to eliminate have been attacked first, the cost of removing the remaining pollutants will be much higher.

Further, understanding more about the complexity of the environment has made pollution control more difficult, which means that the legal environment is more complex. For example, Figure 14–4 shows that waters treated at *publicly owned treatment works* (POTW) return about half the pollutants to surface waters—oceans, lakes, and rivers. Since metals such as lead and mercury are very toxic, the surface waters are not well protected, and the disposal of *sludge*—the glop from sewage plants not pumped back into surface waters—is another problem. If sludge is dumped into a landfill, the groundwater may be contaminated as the metals leach down into the water supply. The pollutants that evaporate and go into the air may cause violations of the Clean Air Act. Hence, managers must think carefully about all aspects of the disposal process, and one must know today what will be required tomorrow so as to put together the right kind of operation and not have to change everything too often.

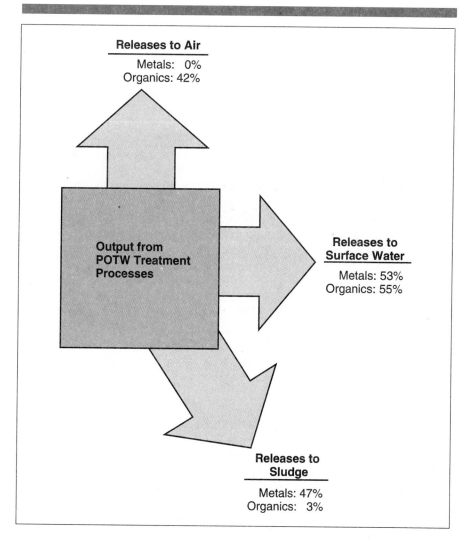

FIGURE 14–4

Percentage of Environmental Releases from POTWs Entering Air, Water, or Sludge
SOURCE: Environmental Protection Agency

▓ POINT SOURCE POLLUTION

Water pollution easiest to identify comes out of a pipe. We can see it, measure it, and, given technical knowledge, treat the discharge. Control of such *point source* water pollution has been the primary goal of federal law the past two decades. Sewage from homes and nonindustrial sources is often treated at POTW. Billions are spent every year to improve existing POTW and put new ones in place in small towns that do not have treatment systems. Since most of effluents treated at POTW are not toxic, the sludge that is removed is often used for fertilizer. The treated water is pumped back into rivers or lakes.

States must designate all surface water as to intended use. If the use is drinking water, treated water dumped into that bay, lake, or river must be quite pure; if the body of water is designated for recreation, the treated water must be clean enough not to contaminate swimmers or fish.

Industrial Permits.   Industrial discharges, which are usually toxic substances from production processes, are subject to a *permit* process. The EPA and state environmental agencies, under the *National Pollutant Discharge Elimination System* (NPDES), require industrial polluters to list the amount and type of their discharges. Industrial polluters are issued permits to pollute certain pollutants in certain quantities. The amount a firm is allowed to pollute depends on the kinds of pollution it produces and the industry of the polluter.

Pollution discharges are regulated industry by industry. Each firm in an industry must meet the effluent limits set by the EPA for each chemical. The list of controlled substances is expanding, and the degree to which the substances must be controlled grows gradually tighter. In general, conventional pollutants, like human waste, must be controlled by the *best conventional technology* (BCT). Congress ordered the EPA to consider cost-effectiveness when setting such standards. Cost considerations are not as important for toxic or unconventional pollutants. These are subject to tighter control, called *best available technology* (BAT)—defined by the EPA as the "very best control and treatment measures that have been or are capable of being achieved." Hence, as better technology is invented to control various pollutants, polluters must use it to reduce their pollution. Regardless of the kind of pollutants, if a polluter is located on a particularly sensitive waterway, even more stringent controls may be ordered, including controls that could force the producer to move operations.

When a new plant is built or a new source of pollution is created by a producer, it is subject to even tighter controls—called *new source performance standards* (NSPS). The law says that the standard is "the greatest degree of effluent reduction . . . achievable through application of the best available demonstrated control technology, processes, operating methods, and other alternatives, including, where practicable, standards permitting no discharge of pollutants." Using BAT controls for the pollution produced is not enough; the entire production process must use technology that exists to minimize pollution output in the entire production process. Before operations may begin, the producer must satisfy the EPA or state agency that this standard has been met so that a pollution permit is issued. If there is a conflict between state standards and those desired by the EPA, the EPA is likely to prevail, as the *Arkansas* v. *Oklahoma* case shows.

ARKANSAS v. OKLAHOMA

United States Supreme Court
____ U.S. ____ , 112 S.Ct. 1046 (1992)

Case Background
In compliance with the NPDES, the City of Fayetteville, Arkansas, received a permit from the EPA for its sewage treatment plant. The permit authorized the City to discharge certain levels of effluents into waters that flow into the upper Illinois River, which flows into Oklahoma. The State of Okla-

homa protested that the water discharged from the plant violated Oklahoma water quality standards for the upper Illinois River that hold that no discharges may be made into the river that degrade its quality. The EPA reviewed the matter and allowed the Arkansas discharge permit to stand. The Court of Appeals reversed the EPA, ruling that the Clean Water Act does not allow a permit to be issued where a source would discharge effluents that would contribute to

(continued)

conditions that violate applicable water quality standards. Since the Arkansas effluents would contribute to the deterioration of the Illinois River in Oklahoma, the permit would have to be revised to require less pollution to be dumped. Arkansas and the EPA appealed.

Case Decision
The Supreme Court reversed the Court of Appeals and allowed the EPA permit to stand. States may not block EPA permits unless the permits are issued in violation of the Clean Water Act. This permit was issued by the EPA under its power to determine NPDES permit standards for effluent discharges. The EPA also has the power to set and approve water quality standards for the states, but Oklahoma may not instruct the EPA on water quality standards. Hence, if the EPA rules that waters flowing from NPDES-approved discharge points in Arkansas into Oklahoma do not violate Oklahoma water quality standards of "no degradation," Oklahoma water standards are not violated no matter what

Oklahoma thinks. Unless the EPA can be shown to have violated the requirements set by Congress for implementing the Clean Water Act, the courts may not override EPA decisions.

Managerial Considerations
State water quality standards must meet EPA approval. In most cases, the state is the enforcement agency. However, when it is uncertain whether an effluent discharge will be allowed, a business should make sure that the discharge will meet EPA standards. Since state officials, in efforts to attract and keep business, can be more forgiving than might the EPA about discharges, a state-issued permit could be overturned by the EPA. In this case, the opposite happened: the EPA allowed more pollution to be discharged into a body of water than a state claimed was proper. Again, this reminds us that federal regulatory authorities are usually supreme in disputes with states about what level of regulation is appropriate.

Enforcement.   Since point source water pollution control is based around a permit system, the system is the key to enforcement. Under the NPDES, the states have primary responsibility for enforcing the permit system, subject to EPA monitoring and approval. Operating without a permit or in violation of the pollution that is allowed under a permit is a clear violation of the law. Firms that have pollution permits must monitor their own performance and file *discharge monitoring reports* (DMRs), available for public inspection. Hence, firms must report violations of the amount they are allowed to pollute under their permits. Lying about violations is more serious than admitting to violations. Penalties run up to $25,000 per day per violation. More serious violations can lead to criminal prosecution.

Citizen suits against polluters are quite common under the Clean Water Act, running at least 200 per year. The citizen, which is usually an environmental organization, must notify the EPA and the alleged permit violator of the "intent to sue." If the EPA takes charge of the situation, the citizen suit is blocked. But if the EPA does not act diligently and the violations continue, the private suit to force enforcement of the law may proceed.

■ NONPOINT SOURCE POLLUTION

About half of all water-borne pollution is from *nonpoint sources*—construction sites, logging and mining operations, runoff from streets, and runoff from agriculture. Various pollutants are washed away by rain into streams and lakes and seep into groundwater. Much of this pollution has only recently come under federal control efforts. The complexity of the problem means that it is being approached from various directions.

Because runoff from streets usually occurs during rainstorms, when sewage treatment plants cannot have the capacity to treat all runoff water, holding tanks may have to be built, allowing the water to be treated later. The City of Chicago spent $4 billion to dig enormous caverns below the city to contain runoff. Since a lot of runoff pollution is due to air pollution, tighter air pollution rules result in less nonpoint source water pollution.

The consequences of groundwater pollution that comes from agricultural fertilizers and sprays is considered by various agencies under statutes in addition to the Clean Water Act, such as the Safe Drinking Water Act, the Federal Insecticide, Fungicide, and Rodenticide Act, the Toxic Substances Control Act, and other laws that deal one way or another with pollution that shows up in water from nonpoint sources. There is no doubt that regulations will be tightened to reduce runoff from construction sites and mining and logging operations.

■ WETLANDS

Until a few years ago, *wetlands* were nuisances to be drained and filled. Wetlands destruction was subsidized by such agencies as the Department of Agriculture and the Army Corps of Engineers. Now that the environmental value of wetlands is better known, there has been a rush to protect them, resulting in developers and others being forced to protect wetlands instead of being encouraged to destroy them.

The EPA defines wetlands as

> Those areas that are inundated or saturated by surface or groundwater at a frequency and duration sufficient to support, and that under normal circumstances do support, a prevalence of vegetation typically adapted for life in saturated soil conditions. Wetlands generally include swamps, marshes, bogs, and similar areas.

This definition includes mangrove swamps of coastal saltwater shrubs in the South; prairie potholes in the Dakotas and Minnesota, where shallow depressions that hold water during part of the year are visited by migrating birds; and playa lakes in the Southwest that are rarely flooded basins. Wetlands can be small holes or large areas and may contain one plant or dozens of important species. What is covered by the law is not yet fixed; the EPA estimates that wetlands cover an area in the lower forty-eight states equal in size to California. As Figure 14–5 shows, over half of the wetlands that existed originally have disappeared.

In general, anyone wanting to change a wetland must receive a permit from the Army Corps of Engineers. The EPA may block a permit, under Section 404 of the Clean Water Act, to prevent environmental damage. About 10,000 permits are issued each year to allow dredging or filling of wetlands. Another 75,000 permits are issued each year for activities that "cause only minimal adverse environmental effects" to wetlands. Hence, businesses involved in construction or other activities that disturb earth must make sure that wetlands requirements have been met.

LAND POLLUTION

Millions of tons of hazardous waste are disposed each year. Much of that waste is not destroyed but is stored in drums and deposited in clay-lined

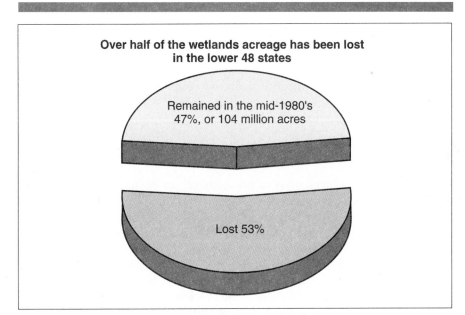

FIGURE 14–5

Loss of Wetlands
SOURCE: Environmental Protection Agency

dumps; injected deep underground between layers of rock; or merely abandoned in vacant lots, lagoons, and landfills. These storage methods fail over time as containers corrode and rain washes the wastes from storage sites. The hazardous wastes then seep into lakes, streams, and groundwater.

To reduce the amount of toxic substances that are dumped into the environment and to limit chemicals that are extremely toxic to people or animals, environmental controls are imposed on the production, distribution, use, and disposal of toxic chemicals. Careless disposal of chemicals in the past means that billions are now being spent to clean up toxic waste sites. Managers must be aware of the liability that can arise from use of chemicals today and from ownership of property that may contain toxic wastes.

■ TOXIC SUBSTANCES CONTROL ACT

Over 68,000 chemicals are in commercial use in the United States. Under the *Toxic Substances Control Act* (TOSCA), passed in 1976, the EPA controls and keeps track of chemicals. Because chemicals can cause such health hazards as birth defects, cancer, and genetic damage, accurate information about their possible effects is vital.

When a producer wants to sell a new chemical, it must notify the EPA, which studies the new substance and its proposed uses to determine environmental hazards. Since companies want to protect new chemical developments, the EPA will not reveal trade secret information. Producers may be required to run tests for toxicity and other effects so that the EPA can determine the restrictions that will be placed on the chemical. EPA restrictions may be nothing more than labeling requirements while some chemicals will be allowed to be used only in restricted cases and others are banned.

A new field of work subject to TOSCA is *biotechnology*—the manipulation of biological processes to produce chemicals or living organisms for commercial use. Since the results may be eligible for patents, this is a field with valuable products expected to be worth tens of billions of dollars. Genetic engineering produces such things as industrial enzymes that can purify water and consume the oil in oil spills. The EPA is monitoring industry efforts to use natural organisms in new ways and to use genetically altered microorganisms.

■ PESTICIDES

Pesticides are substances used to prevent, kill, or disable pests, including undesirable plants, insects, rodents, fungi, and molds. Most pesticides are toxic, and some are extremely toxic to people and the environment. Congress originally passed the *Federal Insecticide, Fungicide, and Rodenticide Act* (FIFRA) in 1947, amending it several times since, most recently in 1988.

The EPA has registered 20,000 products under FIFRA. Registration means that before any pesticide is sold, the EPA has examined scientific data about the product's effects and the label on the product is accurate as to proper usage and precautions. Registration is approved for five years at a time for pesticides that meet these conditions:

1. The product does what the producers claim it will do.
2. The registration materials are accurate, and the label is accurate as to proper usage of the product.
3. The product will do what it is supposed to when used properly without "unreasonable adverse effects on the environment."

FIFRA requires that the economic, social, and environmental costs and benefits of each product be considered. The EPA tries to determine what risk might be posed by a pesticide, such as groundwater contamination or skin irritation, so as to limit how the product is used and who may use it. Since some products pose a danger to certain species, the EPA may restrict use to locations that minimize exposure for those who could be harmed. Working with the FDA, the EPA sets usage requirements to take account of the residues that remain in food products so that consumers are not exposed to unsafe levels of pesticides.

■ RESOURCE CONSERVATION AND RECOVERY ACT

TOSCA and FIFRA are primarily concerned with controlling toxic substances before they get to the market. How toxic substances are handled once they're in the market or when they are being disposed of is the concern of the *Resource Conservation and Recovery Act* (RCRA), passed in 1976 and amended in 1984.

"Out of sight, out of mind" was the "procedure" for the disposal of a lot of hazardous wastes before we came to know about the environmental consequences of improper disposal. RCRA requires that the one-half million generators of about 200 million tons of hazardous wastes each year comply with an EPA regulatory program over the transportation, storage, treatment, and disposal of hazardous wastes that reduces dangers to health and the environment.

Defining a Hazardous Waste. The RCRA requires the EPA to identify and maintain a list of hazardous wastes. The Act defines *hazardous waste* as follows:

> . . . a solid waste . . . which because of its quantity, concentration, or physical, chemical, or infectious characteristics may—
> (a) cause, or significantly contribute to an increase in mortality or an increase in serious irreversible, or incapacitating reversible, illness; or,
> (b) pose a substantial present or potential hazard to human health or the environment when improperly treated, stored, transported, or disposed of, or otherwise managed.

Wastes so identified may be stored or disposed of only at sites whose owners have obtained a permit from the EPA. To get such a permit, the owners of the treatment, storage, and disposal (TSD) sites agree to meet all regulations regarding the treatment and storage of hazardous wastes.

The Manifest System. RCRA forces compliance by generators, transporters, and TSD site owners by a *manifest system.* The generator of a hazardous waste must complete a *manifest*—a detailed form that states the nature of the hazardous waste and identifies its origin, routing, and final destination. In addition, the generator must assure that the waste is packaged in appropriate and properly labeled containers.

Generators must provide transporters of hazardous waste with a copy of the manifest. Transporters must sign the manifest and, upon delivery, provide a copy to the owner of the TSD site who must return a copy of the manifest to the generator, thereby closing the circle. If a generator is not informed of the safe disposal of the waste, it is to notify the EPA. This reporting system provides regulatory authorities with the ability to track hazardous waste through its generation, transportation, and disposal phases. That is, the manifest system provides the EPA with cradle-to-grave control over hazardous waste.

Regulation of TSD Sites. The RCRA requires the EPA to develop regulations for the owners of hazardous waste TSD sites. Over time, fewer hazardous wastes may be legally disposed of, and more and more must be treated. A treatment facility is where any method is used to change the physical, chemical, or biological character of any hazardous waste to make it less hazardous, to recover energy or materials from it, or otherwise process it. A storage facility is where waste is held, such as in storage tanks, until it can be disposed of or treated. A disposal facility is where hazardous wastes are placed into water or land, such as sealed landfills. The EPA and designated state agencies regulate every aspect of TSD operations.

■ SUPERFUND

The RCRA helps prevent improper disposal of hazardous wastes today, but improper dumping practices in the past have left many ground and water sites contaminated with toxic wastes. Cleaning up these dump sites will cost tens of billions of dollars and take decades to accomplish. The EPA has already evaluated 32,000 potential waste sites and has identified over 1,200 that need action—these sites have been placed on the National Priority List. As Figure 14–6 shows, the 1,200 sites that are on the National Priority List are scattered throughout the country. Work on most of these sites has yet to begin. While these are probably the worse dump sites, thousands of more sites have yet to be assessed.

Congress enacted the *Comprehensive Environmental Response, Compensation, and Liability Act* (CERCLA) in 1980. Labeled the *Superfund,* the Act provides the President with the authority to clean up abandoned hazardous sites and to provide necessary remedial actions in the case of spills. Congress amended the Superfund program in 1986 with the *Superfund Amendments and Reauthorization Act* (SARA), which increases federal funding of the hazardous waste cleanup program. SARA imposes a tax on the petroleum and chemical feedstocks industries. The $1 billion to $2 billion

FIGURE 14–6

Hazardous Waste Sites on the National Priority List for the Superfund Program as of 1990.
Source: Environmental Protection Agency.

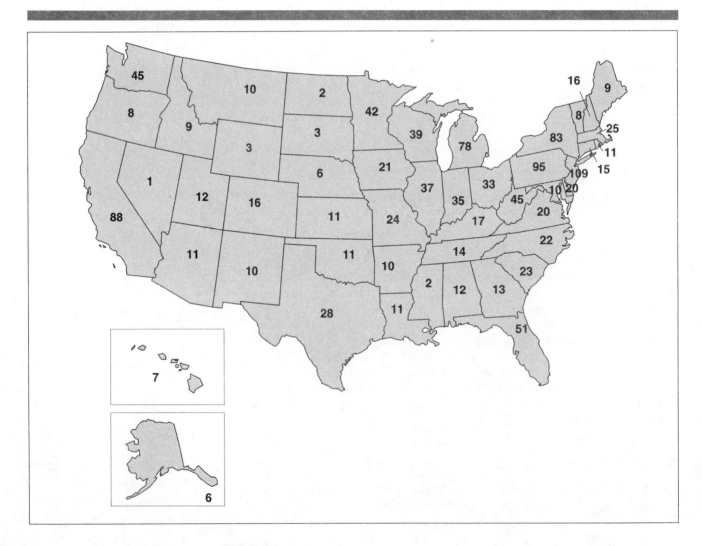

per year in revenues are specifically earmarked for Superfund cleanup efforts and cannot be used by the government for other purposes. However, many private parties are incurring substantial costs.

Responsible Parties. Any given abandoned dump site might contain many kinds of hazardous wastes, which may have been disposed of by many different generators. In addition, the dump site may have been operated by different parties over the years. Thus, it may be impossible to determine one responsible party. Hence, the Act defines who can be held liable for both cleanup costs and damages to natural resources:

1. Current owners of the hazardous waste site.
2. Any prior owner who owned the site at the time of a hazardous waste disposal.
3. Any generator of hazardous waste who arranged for disposal of its wastes at the site.
4. Any transporter of hazardous waste who selected the site for disposal.

Note that the parties may be held *strictly and jointly and severally liable* for these costs; that is, each of the parties could be liable for the entire cost regardless of the size of their contribution to the hazardous waste at the site.

The government has two options for cleaning up hazardous waste sites. If there is a threat of a release of a hazardous substance or a threat of substantial danger to public health, the EPA may undertake the cleanup effort. Later, the government can try to recover expenses by suing responsible parties if the parties can be located. Alternatively, the government can order private parties to pay to clean up the site. This generates a lot of expensive litigation. A study issued in 1992 by the Rand Institute for Civil Justice found that of the $1.3 billion spent on Superfund claims in the late 1980s, 80 percent of the money went for legal bills.

A very difficult problem that managers must consider when purchasing property or another business is whether the property contains toxic wastes that may have been buried years ago or whether the business was involved in handling toxic materials. In such cases, the new owner may be held responsible for cleanup costs of the wastes. Some businesses have been handed cleanup bills for far more than the property itself is worth, even though the new owners were not reponsible for the waste. If they cannot find other responsible parties capable of paying the bill, the new owners are stuck. As a result, many firms have an environmental audit performed for property they intend to purchase. One should also check the history of the company to see whether it might have been involved in dumping toxic wastes in the past at other locations, for which cleanup costs might be imposed.

WILDLIFE PROTECTION

Most environmental laws are written with primary concern for the effect of pollutants on human health. As Table 14-2 shows, a number of federal laws specifically address the problem of environmental protection for wildlife or, more broadly, for all species. The most important of these laws is the

TABLE 14–2
SELECTED FEDERAL WILDLIFE LAWS AFFECTING THE LEGAL ENVIRONMENT OF BUSINESS

Anadromous Fish Conservation Act
Endangered Species Act
Fish and Wildlife Conservation Act
Marine Mammal Protection Act
Migratory Bird Treaty Act
Wild Free-Roaming Horses and Burros Act

Endangered Species Act, originally enacted in 1966 and amended several times since then. In some respects, this act has the potential to be the toughest environmental statute of all.

The Act recognizes the value of habitat and the need to manage on an ecosystem scale. It authorizes designation of critical habitat—areas needed to preserve endangered species—and calls for preparation of recovery plans for listed species. The Department of Interior has estimated that a recovery program for the threatened and endangered species listed in Table 14–3 would cost about $5 billion, but annual funding from the federal government is only in the tens of millions of dollars per year.

The Act authorizes the Secretary of the Interior to declare species of animal or plant life endangered and to establish the "critical habitat" of such species. An *endangered species* is defined by the Act as "any species which is in danger of extinction throughout all or a significant portion of its range. . . ." When a species is listed as endangered, the Act imposes ob-

TABLE 14–3
THREATENED AND ENDANGERED U.S. WILDLIFE AND PLANTS, 1980–1990 (number, cumulative)

	Threatened			Endangered		
Group	*1980*	*1985*	*1990*	*1980*	*1985*	*1990*
Mammals	3	4	8	32	20	53
Birds	3	3	11	66	59	74
Reptiles	10	8	17	13	8	16
Amphibians	3	3	5	5	5	6
Fishes	12	14	33	34	30	54
Snails	5	5	6	2	3	3
Crustaceans	0	1	2	1	3	8
Insects	6	4	9	7	8	11
Arachnids	0	0	0	0	0	3
Clams	0	0	2	23	22	37
Plants	7	10	60	51	67	180
Total	49	52	153	234	225	445

SOURCE: U.S. Department of the Interior, Fish and Wildlife Service, Division of Endangered Species and Habitat Conservation, unpublished data. Washington, D.C.

ligations on both private and public parties. Under the Act, no person may "take, import, or conduct commercial activity with respect to any endangered species." Although in most disputes involving an endangered species, both parties will generally agree that the species is deserving of protection, but the conflict invariably centers on the degree of protection to be afforded.

Despite the lack of federal funds to accomplish the goals of the Endangered Species Act, the Act is used to block or alter development when an endangered species is present. This fact came to attention in the 1978 Supreme Court decision *Tennessee Valley Authority* v. *Hill*. The Court prohibited completion of the Tellico Dam on the Little Tennessee River. Even though the federal government had spent $100 million on the dam, the Court ordered work on the dam stopped because the dam would destroy the habitat of a tiny fish, the snail darter. The Act says that no project may "result in the destruction or modification of habitat of such [endangered] species. . . ." Similarly, in *Seattle Audubon Society*, the Endangered Species Act halted logging in an area equal in size to the states of Massachusetts and Connecticut combined.

SEATTLE AUDUBON SOCIETY v. EVANS

United States Court of Appeals, Ninth Circuit
952 F.2d 297 (1991)

Case Background
The Seattle Audubon Society and other environmental groups sued Evans, Chief of the U.S. Forest Service, and the Washington Contract Loggers Association. The environmentalists sought a permanent injunction against sale of timber in national forests in Washington, Oregon, and California because the logging operations endangered the habitat of the northern spotted owl, which is listed as a threatened species under the Endangered Species Act. The Forest Service contended that it did not have to take into account the viability of species. The district court issued an injunction against logging operations and ordered the Forest Service to devise a plan to ensure the viability of the spotted owl.

Case Decision
The Court of Appeals upheld the decision. The statute is clear that endangered species must be protected. Until a plan to protect the spotted owl is presented and accepted, logging operations must cease.

Managerial Considerations
The Endangered Species Act has been used by numerous environmental groups to stop large developments. Housing subdivisions that were under way, golf course resorts worth over $100 million, and other large projects have been stopped cold when an endangered species was discovered. Since bugs and plants are included, most people would not have any idea that such species may be present. Environmental audits can uncover such potential problems before the property is committed to construction.

GLOBAL ENVIRONMENTAL ISSUES ▬▬▬▬▬

Some of the biggest environmental issues—the ozone layer, global climate change, habitat destruction, and the marine environment—must be dealt with on an international scale. Even if the United States did not contribute to global environmental problems, the consequences would still be borne here, so the United States must work with other countries to decide what to do about such issues. The ozone issue provides a good example of an international legal solution to a potentially serious environmental problem.

■ THE OZONE LAYER

While too much ozone in the air we breathe is a problem caused largely by vehicle exhaust, there is substantial evidence that ozone depletion at high levels in the atmosphere is caused by chemicals called chlorofluorocarbons (CFCs), known popularly by such brand names as Freon. CFCs are widely used as refrigerants in air-conditioning systems, in making computer chips, and in some plastics products. In the stratosphere, CFCs eat away at the ozone, which protects all life on earth from ultraviolet radiation. The effect on humans would be an increase in skin cancer, more cataracts, and suppression of the immune system.

By the early 1980s, there was evidence that CFCs might be a primary reason for the loss of ozone in the upper atmosphere. Evidence of a "hole" in the ozone layer over Antarctica by 1985 convinced industry that this was a serious problem. Since there were estimates that the ozone loss could cause tens of thousands of additional deaths per year due to skin cancer, the possibility of tort liability existed. In the United States, the makers of CFCs—DuPont, Allied Chemical, Pennwalt, Kaiser, and Racon—who produce one-third of the world supply, agreed with the EPA that CFC production had to be eliminated.

The result was that in the United States, other firms were prevented from producing CFCs, and existing producers agreed to support the *Montreal Protocol* of 1987, which the United States signed. Under the protocol, which is an international treaty, most nations that produce CFCs agreed to freeze production levels immediately and cut production by 50 percent by 1998. Later evidence that the problem was worse than thought resulted in the protocol's being revised by the London treaty of 1990, requiring CFCs and halon (the best firefighting chemical) production eliminated by 2000. Then in 1992, given evidence that the problem was getting worse, the Bush administration ordered elimination of CFCs and halon in the United States by 1995.

A solution was achieved that resulted in producers' giving up a multibillion-dollar-per-year market. Producers' cooperation was hastened by the promise from the government that the existing producers would have some monopoly control over the product during its remaining years. The total cost to the world's economy of the CFC phaseout is $200 billion.

■ INTERNATIONAL COOPERATION

CFC production was largely in the hands of the United States, Japan, and European nations, which pretty much had the power to force the decision on this issue. But many of the other international environmental issues will require more cooperation from less developed nations, since these nations will bear more of the effects of changes in policies that would eliminate environmental problems.

The Montreal Protocol provided a fund, set up by wealthy nations, to pay poorer nations to sign the agreement to ban CFCs. That is, the United States bought environmental rights from other nations. Similarly, the United States is helping to pay the cost of water treatment plants in

Mexico located near the U.S. border to reduce pollution of the Rio Grande and the Pacific Ocean.

As we have seen in this chapter, the environmental challenge is massive in the United States. Most of the rest of the world is in far worse condition and does not have the resources necessary to deal with the problem. The German government estimates that it will have to spend $100 billion by 2000 to begin to bring the environment of former East Germany up to the standards expected in West Germany. Yet East Germany was the wealthiest communist nation, with a population of only 20 million. The cost of environmental cleanup in the former communist nations and in the Third World is staggering and is now becoming a real consideration for businesses that used to have no restrictions.

There is little doubt that if the United States and other nations are concerned about species preservation and other environmental issues, they will have to pay less developed nations to protect species and to cover the costs of some pollution controls. This can be expected to be a major issue in the coming decade in which business will play a predominant role.

POLLUTION PREVENTION

Most environmental legislation has been concerned with cleaning up past pollution and setting limits on how much pollution can be dumped into the air, water, and land. The *Pollution Prevention Act* of 1990 provides a framework for thinking about the whole environmental picture as we plan for the future. It focuses on waste management and says that priority should be given to reducing the sources of pollution.

The Act emphasizes the reduction of industrial hazardous wastes and encourages making changes in equipment and technology; redesigning products to minimize environmental damages that arise from the production process and the consequences of the product; substituting raw materials; and improving maintenance, training, and inventory control. The EPA is required to address industrial pollution prevention by the following measures:

- Identify measurable goals.
- Improve measurement, data collection, and access to data.
- Assess existing and proposed programs and identify barriers.
- Offer grants to states for technical assistance programs.
- Require companies to disclose amounts of toxic chemicals they release.
- Use federal procurement to encourage source reduction.

As we saw in the Manager's Legal Challenge feature, managers can integrate pollution prevention into all aspects of the corporate process. Encouraging a companywide commitment to managing pollution control, rather than just respond to specific federal rules on a case-by-case basis as they emerge, companies make environmental management a part of the routine goal of the company. This increases the return to the company on dollars expended for environmental quality, which is a bottom-line concern.

SUMMARY:
A GUIDE FOR MANAGERS

- Businesses face environmental responsibilities imposed by the common law—in the form of private and public nuisance actions, trespass, and strict liability for hazardous activities—and from a host of environmental statutes that may be enforced by state and federal agencies—primarily the Environmental Protection Agency—as well as by citizens.

- The Clean Air Act sets ambient air quality standards for such major pollutants as sulfur dioxide, particulates, ozone, carbon monoxide, nitrogen oxide, and lead. These standards are being constantly tightened, and the toughest standards are applied to new sources of pollution. New polluters must use the best pollution control technology available. In some areas, if a business is to produce any new air pollution, it must buy the right to pollute from existing polluters, who are paid to either quit polluting or install better pollution control equipment.

- Water pollution can be regulated from any source of surface or underground water pollution under the Clean Water Act and other statutes. Most controls have been on point source pollution, which comes out of pipes from factories or sewer systems. Those pollution sources must have permits that allow them to pollute certain amounts that meet water treatment standards according to the use—drinking versus swimming quality—of the body of water the waste is being pumped into. Nonpoint source pollution—runoff from farms, streets, construction sites, mining, and logging—is just beginning to be addressed. Wetlands are protected from being altered without a permit.

- The Toxic Substances Control Act and the Federal Insecticide, Fungicide, and Rodenticide Act require EPA review and approval of toxic substances before they are released to the market. They may also determine restrictions on usage of such products and keep track of evidence of harm from them. The Resource Conservation and Recovery Act requires comprehensive paperwork to follow the production, distribution, and disposal of hazardous substances. Hazardous wastes treatment, storage and disposal facilities are subject to strict licensing and regulatory control.

- The Superfund program provides federal support to clean up abandoned hazardous waste sites, but any private parties who contribute to the disposal of the wastes, even though legal at the time, may be held liable for part or all of the cleanup costs. Land purchasers should consider an environmental audit to check for possibilities of hazardous wastes, wetlands, or endangered species.

- The Endangered Species Act can block any economic activity, without compromise, if the activity can harm the habitat of an endangered species. Compromises that demonstrate habitat protection may allow a project to go forward, but in some cases, the costs have been greater than the value of the project.

- The Pollution Prevention Act of 1990 encourages businesses and government agencies to think about all aspects of pollution reduction by considering environmental concerns in all phases of operations. Integration of environmental concerns into regular managerial controls is becoming a necessity.

MANAGER'S ETHICAL DILEMMA

TREES OR PEOPLE?

Each year, 12,000 American women die of ovarian cancer, a disease with a high mortality rate. By 1989, there was ample evidence that taxol was a promising treatment. Although taxol did not cure the cancer, in a good percentage of patients, it significantly slowed the disease's progress or reversed the cancer's spread. The 30,000 women now diagnosed with ovarian cancer would like to be treated with taxol, but there is not a sufficient amount to treat them all.

The problem is that the only known source of taxol is from the bark of the Pacific yew tree, which grows in the Pacific Northwest. Drug companies need many trees to make taxol. Their desire to cut the trees is opposed by conservationists who argue that the tree is relatively rare, growing in old forests that are refuge to the endangered northern spotted owl and other wildlife.

The National Cancer Institute has appointed Bristol-Myers Squibb Company to carry out development of taxol. To supply its research for one year, Bristol-Myers Squibb needs 40,000 trees cut. Most companies studying taxol have stopped work because not enough trees are being harvested to produce the extract from the bark. If a practical treatment for cancer emerges, hundreds of thousands of yew trees per year would be required to produce the drug. Some research indicates that the drug may be helpful in treating other forms of cancer, which would further increase the demand for the drug, and therefore for the trees.

The Forest Service estimates that 13 million yews grow on private property and more on federal lands. While the tree is not currently endangered, it could be in a few years if needed for cancer treatment. If the Forest Service allows yews in federal forests to be harvested, some environmental groups promise to stall the matter in litigation.

The drug companies guess that substitutes for taxol will be developed in the future. But since there is no substitute now, the issue is clear: either cut more yew trees and treat cancer victims, or let thousands die while waiting for something else to come along.

QUESTIONS

Assume the preceding to be a correct statement of the facts. Can you justify saving trees while people die? What if one of those people was your mother? Do the drug companies have an obligation to slow their work on taxol to try to save the trees while working to develop substitutes? Since slowing the production of taxol means that people will die, is it ethical of the environmental groups to prevent the logging of yew trees by litigation? Are there general principles to guide decisions involving environmental costs versus human welfare?

REVIEW AND DISCUSSION QUESTIONS

1. Define the following terms:
       environmental impact statement
       national ambient air quality standards
       prevention of significant deterioration area
       bubble concept
       point source pollution
       nonpoint source pollution
       wetlands
       manifest system
       Superfund

2. Were common law actions against pollution, such as nuisance, trespass, and strict liability, too weak? That is, was federal statutory intervention needed to prevent serious environmental damage?

■ CASE QUESTIONS

3. For ten years, a company dumped millions of gallons of chemical wastes on its property in Tennessee. The state shut down the site. Residents around the property sued the company, claiming that their drinking water was contaminated. What basis for suit did they have, and could they win? [*Sterling* v. *Velsicol Chemical Corp.*, 647 F. Supp. 303 (W.D. Tenn. 1986)].

4. The EPA set emission standards for vinyl chloride, a toxic substance that is carcinogenic to humans. The Clean Air Act says that such standards must be "at the level which . . . provides an ample margin of safety to protect the public health." The exact threat from vinyl chloride was not known. The EPA said that the proper emissions requirement is the lowest level attainable by best available control technology. The Natural Resources Defense Council sued, contending that since there was uncertainty about the danger, the EPA had to prohibit all emissions. Which position was held correct? [*NRDC* v. *EPA,* 824 F.2d 1146 (D.C. Cir. 1987)]

5. A. B. Little and Company is considering building a new plant. The company engineers know that the plant will produce a sizable quantity of sulfur dioxide. What regulatory requirements will the Clean Air Act bring to bear upon the plant?

6. Litton was operating according to its Clean Water Act discharge permit when certain events within the plant caused the plant's permitted amounts of pollution to be exceeded for three weeks. Stone lived downstream from Litton. He used the stream to irrigate his crops. The pollution by Litton, however, severely damaged Stone's crops. Does Stone have a cause of action against Litton?

7. A South Carolina company ran a hazardous waste disposal and recycling operation. Several companies sent their hazardous wastes to the site. The facility was improperly managed: waste was dumped on the ground, chemicals were mixed, and records were not kept about what was there. The EPA cleaned up the site under Superfund and sued the companies that sent their waste to the site (since the owners of the site could not pay the bill). The companies responded that they were not liable under CERCLA, because there was no evidence that the particular waste they sent had been improperly disposed of. Were they right? [*U.S.* v. *S.C. Recycling and Disposal,* 653 F.Supp. 984 (D.S.C. 1986)]

■ BUSINESS POLICY QUESTIONS

8. It is estimated that two-thirds of the haze over the Arctic regions is due to pollution from Russian smelters that do not have the kinds of pollution controls as required in the United States and Canada. How can we get the Russians to adopt environmental controls similar to ours so that we do not suffer from Russia's environmental abuse?

9. Should pollution control requirements be more or less stringent on pollutants thought to be hazardous but for which little scientific knowledge about their actual health effects exists? Or should the requirements be set according to the existing level of knowledge and then be increased as knowledge of the pollutants' health effects becomes available?

10. Consider the following statement: "Like other environmental laws, the Toxic Substances Control Act's requirements are too strict. They will drive small firms out of business." Should the EPA consider the impacts on small companies when they implement the environmental laws? What if environmental laws cause severe unemployment?

■ ETHICS QUESTIONS

11. You are an executive with a leading manufacturing company. Suppose that one aspect of your business pollutes heavily. You know that you can build a plant in a Third World country to handle that aspect without pollution control. This would mean that for the same amount of production, you would add ten times as much pollution to the world's environment as you do presently, but it would be more profitable for the company. Can you legally move the plant? Should you?

12. Cheezem is a resident of a town in which a large chemical company is located. The chemical company is owned by a family that is very concerned about the impact of industrial pollution on the environment. The family has made every effort to reduce the company's pollution to minimum levels. Recently the family has become concerned about the company's hazardous wastes disposal site. Investigators have determined that the site is located directly over the town's underground water supply. Fortunately, they also determined that the site is posing no current threat to the water supply. Just to be safe, the family would like to move the site. However, because the move would be very expensive, the family would like to share the cost with the town's residents. Cheezem, a very rational man, realizes that even if he doesn't pay his fair share of the cost, he cannot be excluded from enjoying the benefits of a safe and secure water supply. Should he pay?

CONSUMER PROTECTION

CHAPTER 15

MANAGER'S LEGAL CHALLENGE

General Electric (GE) devoted years of research to develop a new generation of compressors—pumps that make cold air—for refrigerators. In 1986, GE began production of the rotary compressor in a new 120-million-dollar factory devoted to the pump's production, putting the company a generation ahead of its Japanese competitors. Over a million compressors were produced the first year, and GE's new line of refrigerators sold very well, capturing 30 percent of the market.

By late 1987, the company was investigating reports of failures of the compressors, which GE had expected to be trouble free and long-lived. A team of engineers worked unsuccessfully for months trying to discover the cause of the failure. Without waiting for a final determination of the cause of the problem, management ordered production of the new compressors to stop and the factory to be closed.

To keep refrigerator production going, GE had to get an old supplier who had closed operations to go back into business making compressors and had to buy more compressors from the Japanese. Later, the problem with the new compressor was discovered, and research was continued to return the compressor to the market.

Since the compressors had a five-year warranty, the failed compressors were replaced. There was no question that GE had a legal obligation to replace failed compressors—either with the same model that failed or with the old reliable model. But the company went further. In 1989 and 1990, it contacted over one million GE refrigerator owners and installed new compressors to replace the dubious rotary model.

GE scrapped the rotary compressor and took a half-billion-dollar loss for replacing the compressors. The company did not have to do that. It could have replaced the compressors that failed within the five-year warranty, and its loss would have been small in comparison.

Looking back, the company admits that it should have tested the new compressor longer before going into production. But at the time, it looked as though GE was giving consumers a superior product at a lower cost. The decision to replace all compressors, even though many would not have failed, illustrates GE's emphasis on assuring the public that GE wants to be known as a quality producer that stands behind its products. The warranty was not only on the compressor but also on the reputation of the company to build long-term customer loyalty for all GE products.

As we will see in this chapter, not only do producers have warranty obligations, which are contractual obligations, but if a regulator determines that a product problem is too widespread, it may order a product recall or other corrective action. This was never threatened in the GE compressor case, since the company took the initiative to go beyond its legal responsibility to its customers.

Most federal agencies are involved with consumer protection in one way or another. Some agencies have mandates to regulate products that significantly affect consumers, such as the Food and Drug Administration (FDA), which is examined in this chapter. Businesses in the food and drug industries come to know FDA regulations very well. Other businesses, such as General Motors, deal with numerous regulatory agencies, including the Federal Trade Commission (FTC), that may examine consumer complaints about defects in cars.

This chapter reviews some major federal regulatory efforts in consumer protection. It begins with a discussion of the FDA and its regulation of food, drink, drugs, and cosmetics. It then reviews the FTC's consumer protection responsibilities in such areas as truthful advertising and consumer fraud. Several agencies regulate consumer credit practices, which the chapter also covers.

In addition to the regulatory agencies considered in this chapter, there are other agencies involved in regulating consumer products. For example, the U.S. Coast Guard regulates boats and boating safety, the Federal Aviation Administration supervises aircraft and air travel, the Consumer Product Safety Commission sets safety standards for some products, the Department of Housing and Urban Development regulates mobile home safety, the National Highway Traffic Safety Administration establishes automobile safety requirements, and the Environmental Protection Agency controls the development of new chemicals. This list is a reminder that there are many different agencies involved in regulating consumer products.

THE FDA: FOOD AND DRUG REGULATION

The *Food and Drug Administration* (FDA) is the federal agency responsible for monitoring food and drug safety. The agency's annual budget is over three-quarters of a billion dollars and supports 7,500 employees. About one-third of the budget is devoted to foods, with food additives, sanitation and processing, and contaminants being the primary areas of concern. One-quarter of the budget is devoted to drugs intended to be used by humans. Smaller portions of the budget are allocated for the study of biological products, veterinary products, medical devices, radiological products, and cosmetics and for the support of the National Center for Toxicological Research. Every year thousands of establishments are inspected and thousands of examinations are made on products as part of the consumer protection function of the FDA.

■ FOOD SAFETY

The control of safety and health in commercial food and drink affects a large sector of the economy. Regulations concerning such products have a longer history than do most product controls. The Pure Food and Drug Act of 1906 was the first major step in developing comprehensive regulations. The primary concern was food safety. This was triggered by several events:

- More soldiers in the American army in the Spanish-American War were thought to have died from impure food than from enemy bullets.
- Upton Sinclair's *The Jungle*, while failing to stir the public to support socialism as Sinclair had hoped, caused much controversy about food safety with its graphic description of food processing.
- The chief chemist of the U.S. Department of Agriculture studied the safety of some food preservatives on human subjects and determined that some were harmful to human health.

    The Bureau of Chemistry of the Department of Agriculture administered the Food and Drug Act until the FDA was created as a separate unit in 1927. Not until the late 1930s did drug regulation become an important concern of the FDA.

Early Sanitation Standards.   The 1906 Act provided protection against adulteration and misbranding of food and drug products. The Bureau of Chemistry performed food analyses for identification of misbranded or adulterated foods. When warranted, the Secretary of Agriculture could ask a U.S. attorney to prosecute a violator of the law and could ask to have the goods seized. The goods could be destroyed or relabeled before sale.

FDA Powers Expanded in the 1930s.   Following a drug disaster in which many people were poisoned by a nonprescription medicine, Congress passed the *Food, Drug, and Cosmetic Act* in 1938. The Act greatly expanded the regulatory reach of the FDA by providing the agency with the power to prohibit false advertising of drugs, classify unsafe food as adulterated, form inspection systems, extend the power to impose standards for foods, and set the safe levels of potentially dangerous additives in foods.

Food Safety Responsibility Placed on Producers.   The burden of responsibility was placed on manufacturers to assure that no damage to health should occur from the substances present in their food. This responsibility was emphasized by the Supreme Court in the *Park* decision, which addressed the responsibilities of corporate executives for compliance with the Food, Drug, and Cosmetic Act.

UNITED STATES v. PARK

United States Supreme Court
421 U.S. 658, 95 S.Ct. 1903 (1975)

Case Background
Park was chief executive officer of Acme Markets, a national food store chain with 874 retail outlets. Acme and Park were charged with violations of the Food, Drug and Cosmetic Act because food in Acme warehouses was found on several inspections to be contaminated by rats. The federal court of appeals ruled that Park could not be held criminally responsible for what happened in the Acme warehouses. The government appealed to the U.S. Supreme Court.

Case Decision
The Supreme Court reversed the lower court, ruling that Park could be held criminally liable for what occurred in his business organization. The Court held that under the Food, Drug and Cosmetic Act, those "who execute the corporate mission . . . [have a] positive duty to seek out and remedy violations when they occur . . . and primarily, a duty to implement measures that will insure that violations will not occur." The standard is demanding, but because the responsibility was assumed voluntarily, and the public interest in pure food is so great, the "highest standard of care" is imposed on distributors.

Managerial Consideration
In the food and drug industries the law imposes duties of care upon managers who have the authority to control the quality of production, storage, or distribution. Although the issue in this case was the criminal liability of a manager who failed to meet his responsibilities, management should also be concerned about the potential impact on the company's reputation caused by a manager's lax quality planning and control. Top management is responsible for establishing the company policy on quality. The company's production engineers must design products according to management's quality requirements. Finally, middle managers must be responsible for maintaining quality during the production, storage, and distribution of the company's products. Maintaining quality involves inspections of the production process and the product—after production, during storage, and when in the hands of the consumer.

As this case illustrates, a manager would not be excused from regulatory responsibilities simply because he or she did not know that some workers were not performing their duties. The courts assume that the manager failed to exercise authority to provide adequate supervision and assure that quality was maintained. The Japanese use quality circles—groups of workers who meet at regular intervals to discuss and resolve quality issues related to the company's product—to maintain quality. This idea is now being employed by some American companies.

Food Additives: The Delaney Clause. A Food Additives Amendment was added to the Food, Drug, and Cosmetic Act in 1958. This amendment, known as the *Delaney Clause,* defines food additives and gives the FDA the authority to license the use and to set the safe-use level of additives. The Delaney Clause—which applies to food additives, color additives, and drugs administered to animals used for food (such as cattle)—says that any substance shall not be approved as an additive if "it is found to induce cancer when ingested by man or animal." The FDA initially interpreted this to mean that the risk of cancer from any of these substances had to be zero—a very difficult standard to meet. After years of deliberation, the FDA in 1985 decided to switch from a zero-risk standard to a *de minimis* standard, which means a very, very small chance of cancer. The FDA says that this allows it to be more reasonable but still to safeguard consumers against real risks.

■ NUTRITION LABELING

The FDA began issuing regulations for *nutrition labeling* in 1973. The Nutrition Labeling and Education Act of 1990 requires the FDA to issue new comprehensive nutrition labeling regulations to take effect in 1993. These requirements apply to over $200 billion worth of food products and about 100,000 labels. The U.S. Department of Agriculture, which regulates meat and poultry, worked with the FDA to have regulations for those foods that are consistent with the FDA rules. The intent is to prevent product claims that can be misleading and to help consumers make informed purchases.

Nutrients by Serving Size.   The FDA regulations list 131 categories of food, from soup to nuts, whose nutrients must be listed by standard serving size. This is intended to list nutrients in realistic serving sizes rather than nutrients by, say, one ounce, which may not be related to a normal eating portion. The following nutrients must be listed per serving portion:

- fat (listing saturated fat separately)
- carbohydrates (sugar and starch separately)
- cholesterol
- calcium
- fiber

Vitamins that are abundant in the American diet—niacin, riboflavin, and thiamine—do not have to be listed, but Vitamins A and C, protein, sodium, iron, and calories do have to be listed. Labels must also list all ingredients in more detail than before.

Standards for Health Claims.   Since the average consumer knows little about nutrition but most consumers express concern about it, labels must conform to standards for words commonly used so that consumers can learn more about what they are buying. For example, "fresh" can refer only to raw food that has not been processed, frozen, or preserved; "low fat" means there are 3 or fewer grams of fat per serving and per 100 grams of the food; "low calorie" means fewer than 40 calories per serving and per 100 grams of food; and "light" may be used on foods that have one-third fewer calories than a comparable product.

Further, health claims that are not sufficiently established, such as the claim that fiber reduces heart disease and cancer, may not be made unless better documented. The food health claims that may be noted on labels are between calcium and osteoporosis, sodium and high blood pressure, fat and heart disease, and fat and cancer.

◼ DRUG SAFETY

Until 1938, drug control seemed a problem of protecting the public against quacks, fraudulent claims, mislabeling, and the sale of dangerous drugs. After the death of about a hundred people who had taken a new drug, the Food, Drug, and Cosmetic Act was enacted in 1938 to provide federal regulators with the new powers. The law prohibits the marketing of any drug until the FDA has approved the application submitted by the manufacturer. The applicant must submit evidence that the drug is safe for its intended use. This control was designed primarily to prevent the sale of untested, potentially harmful drugs in a market that now generates $50 billion per year in sales.

Designation of Prescription Drugs.   Before the 1938 Act, no drugs were designated as *prescription drugs*—that is, drugs that may be used only with the permission of a physician. Drugs were either legal or illegal. Since 1938, the FDA has determined which drugs will be prescription drugs.

Drug Effectiveness.   While earlier regulations were supported by the medical profession, the *Kefauver Amendment* of 1962 has been strongly criticized by physicians and others. Senator Kefauver charged the drug industry with introducing drugs of dubious value that were sold at exorbitant prices. While Kefauver was attacking the drug industry, thalidomide, a sedative sold in Europe, was causing numerous deformities in newborns whose mothers had used the drug during pregnancy. Thalidomide was being studied by the FDA for approval for sale in the United States when the unfortunate results from Europe became known.

Kefauver then successfully introduced legislation requiring the government to approve drugs based on their proven *effectiveness*—not only on their safety, as had been the case before. The FDA must approve human clinical testing of drugs. It has strict regulations concerning testing and adoption of new drugs, so that it now costs an average of over $200 million to develop a new drug over a twelve-year period.

Producer Liability and FDA-Approved Drugs.   The requirements for testing of drugs and for certification by the FDA have led to questions about the liability of drug manufacturers for injuries from FDA-approved drugs. The difficult questions the courts face in such cases are illustrated in the *McDaniel* case.

McDANIEL v. McNEIL LABORATORIES, INC.

Supreme Court of Nebraska
196 Neb. 190, 241 N.W.2d 822 (1976)

Case Background
Innovar is an anesthetic that was tested on 6,000 patients for five years before receiving FDA approval for sale in 1968. The drug was sold with inserts explaining safety evaluations, recommended dosages, and warnings of adverse reactions and their control measures. Before this case, no new adverse reactions had been discovered, nor was the purity of the drug in question.

Marjorie McDaniel, a 47-year-old mother of three, had routine surgery in 1971. Innovar was administered before the operation. During surgery, McDaniel suffered a heart attack. She survived but suffered severe brain damage and was left comatose, with no expectation of recovery. The Nebraska district court refused to allow the case to be submitted to the jury on the theory of strict liability. The issue

before the Nebraska supreme court was whether McNeil Labs could be held strictly liable for physical harm caused to the user of Innovar.

Case Decision
The supreme court of Nebraska upheld the decision of the state district court not to allow the case to go to the jury on the basis of strict liability. The court stated that the FDA had heard virtually the same arguments regarding the drug's safety as those provided by both the plaintiff and the defendant when it initially approved the drug three years prior to this incident. In addition, the FDA had continued to monitor the drug's performance after approving it and had found no reason to recall it. Since there was no evidence presented by the plaintiff indicating that the defendant had withheld or failed to disclose any relevant information about the drug's safety, the court stated that the FDA's approval

(continued)

should not be challenged in a product liability case simply because other experts disagreed with the FDA about the safety of the drug.

Managerial Considerations
This case illustrates the importance of complying with regulatory and statutory requirements when the product the company is producing might cause injury or death. By complying with such requirements, not only can management avoid confrontations with the regulatory agency, it can also present an effective defense against civil actions brought by injured parties. In addition, if management has complied with regulatory requirements, it may be able to avoid the damaging publicity that can accompany a serious accident involving the company's product. As a precautionary measure, management should maintain good records showing that the company has conscientiously met an agency's requirements.

The courts, as in the *McDaniel* decision, tend to give great weight to the protection offered consumers by the regulatory process. This has limited the number of suits plaintiffs can bring under strict liability when they are injured by side effects of a drug that are not preventable given the state of technology. For example, in a 1986 federal court case in which parents brought action against a drug company that made DPT (diphtheria, pertussis, and tetanus) vaccine—which most children receive with no complications but which seriously injured the plaintiffs' child—the court noted that the FDA had extensively regulated the production of the vaccine and knew of the potential dangers. The jury's verdict with respect to the design and production of the drug would not be allowed to stand as a potential obstacle to the accomplishment of the federal objective to have the vaccine widely distributed in the safest manner possible. In similar fact situations, some courts have gone the other way.

What if a drug were improperly administered? Again, the drug companies are not likely to be liable, assuming they have given proper dosage instructions. If a physician ignores the instructions and changes the recommended dosage, resulting in an injury, the drug manufacturer is shielded from liability by the *learned intermediary doctrine*. That is, the learned intermediary—the doctor—would be liable for misuse of the product.

■ ENFORCEMENT ACTIVITIES

Besides deciding when drugs will be allowed to be marketed, the FDA can force existing products, including food, cosmetics, and medical devices, to be removed from the market if their claims appear to be misleading or if new information becomes available that indicates that the product was not as safe as previously thought.

Breast implants were ordered off the market in 1992 by the FDA when questions were raised about the long-term health consequences of the product. The FDA seized $5 million worth of collagen products in 1991, claiming that the producer failed to fully warn doctors that injecting collagen into patients' faces to fill in blemishes could cause serious adverse reactions in patients with connective-tissue diseases. The same year the FDA seized shipments of Citrus Hill Fresh Choice orange juice because the juice was made from concentrate and not fresh from oranges. It also told three vegetable oil manufacturers to wipe "no cholesterol" from the labels of their product or face seizure. The no-cholesterol claim was not false, but the FDA said it was highly misleading, since many consumers think cholesterol is the same as fat, which is not the case.

While enforcement has become tougher, for the first time, the FDA has been allowing quick approval for use of drugs that show some promise in life-threatening diseases, such as AIDS. Rather than require the full, lengthy review process before the drugs are allowed to be sold to informed patients, the FDA is allowing the drugs to be carefully distributed.

INTERNATIONAL ASPECTS | INTERNATIONAL DRUG REGULATION

The FDA has a significant effect on drug production and marketing around the world. Many nations, unable to afford the equivalent of the FDA, simply adopt FDA regulations as a part of their drug standards. In many countries, the domestic market is not regulated—many drugs sold would be illegal in the United States—but the export market is regulated to meet FDA standards. This regulatory scheme is intended to make the domestic pharmaceutical industry competitive in world markets. Since other countries do not want to develop a reputation for producing low-quality or dangerous drugs, they require their exporters to meet U.S. standards.

Another reason countries adopt FDA standards is that the FDA requires foreign drug producers to be licensed and inspected by the FDA to be eligible to export drugs to the United States. FDA inspectors visit foreign plants to check sanitation, production procedures, recordkeeping methods, and other activities to be sure that U.S. standards are met. To have a license to export to the United States, foreign plants must be reinspected periodically. Because FDA approval can take up to two years to obtain, producers must begin that process long before they expect to start shipments.

European nations do not have drug regulations nearly as stringent as those of the FDA. Introducing a new drug to the market often happens years sooner in Europe, where the long testing period prescribed by the FDA for U.S. drugs is frequently not required. Many drugs that require prescriptions in the United States may be bought over the counter in Europe, but some over-the-counter U.S. drugs require a prescription in Europe. Similarly, foreign producers who want to sell drugs in most of Europe do not need to be licensed by each country, since the European Community countries recognize the inspections conducted by each member country. That is, a Ministry of Health inspection and approval in the United Kingdom will make a British producer eligible to export to Germany, France, and the other European Community countries.

The differences between the United States' extensive drug regulation system and that in most other developed nations give rise to considerable discussion about the merits of the two systems. The American system probably reduces risk from defective drugs better, but it also keeps life-saving, pain-reducing, and disease-curing drugs off the market for a much longer time than Europe's system does. As a result, in many areas, drug development is more advanced in Europe than in the United States.

THE FTC AND CONSUMER PROTECTION

The FTC was established by Congress in 1915 to help enforce the antitrust laws. The FTC devotes substantial resources to its Bureau of Consumer Protection, which handles a wide range of matters, including deceptive advertising and marketing practices. Some responsibilities were specifically granted by Congress, such as enforcement of the Magnuson-Moss Warranty Act and various consumer credit statutes. But most consumer protection efforts evolve as the FTC decides what Congress meant in Section 5 of the FTC Act when it said that "unfair and deceptive acts or practices in or affecting commerce are hereby declared unlawful."

■ CONSUMER PROTECTION PROCEDURES

Based on experience, and in response to concerns expressed by or direct orders from Congress, the FTC investigates a wide range of practices suspected to be *unfair and deceptive*. The five commissioners decide by majority vote whether to issue a complaint against individuals or companies engaged in practices the commission would like to see ended or changed.

Settling Complaints by Consent Decree.   Many complaints are settled by a *consent decree* agreed upon by the parties charged in the complaint and by a majority of the commissioners. Consent decrees contain the terms of a settlement and frequently include prohibition of certain practices, redress for consumers, and payment of civil penalties. A small number of cases result in administrative trials at the FTC, the decisions from which may be appealed to a federal court of appeals.

■ REGULATING UNFAIR AND DECEPTIVE ACTS OR PRACTICES

Congress ordered the FTC to attack "unfair and deceptive acts or practices." The lack of legal definition for those terms means that the FTC has considerable leeway in deciding what cases to bring—what advertising is deceptive, what sales practices are unfair, etc. The key word has always been *deceptive*. Essentially, things held to be deceptive are presumed unfair. It is rare for an act to be unfair but not deceptive.

Agency Policy Statement on Deception.   To give the FTC staff guidance in its investigations, the commissioners issued a *deception policy statement* that summarizes a three-part test for deciding whether a particular act or practice is deceptive. There is deception if the following are true:

1. There is representation or omission of information in a communication to consumers.
2. The deception is likely to mislead a reasonable consumer.
3. The deception is material; that is, it is likely to be misleading to the detriment of the consumer.

Some points have been made to help clarify the three elements of deception. First, not all omissions are deceptive. Omissions are not deceptive if there is no affirmative misrepresentation or practice that takes advantage of consumer misimpression. Second, to decide whether a representation or omission is deceptive, the FTC will look at the entire context. For example, the words in an advertisement will be examined in the context of the entire ad, and consideration is given to evidence about what consumers think the ad means. Third, a reasonable consumer is an "ordinary person." Hence, consideration is given to the target audience of the representation. For example, ads directed at children or ill people are held to a tougher standard. Fourth, the misrepresentation must be likely to affect a consumer's product choice. Fifth, no proof of injury to consumers is needed if evidence exists that an injury is likely to occur, given the practice in question.

◼ REGULATING ADVERTISING CLAIMS

The advertising industry generates over $100 billion a year. The *advertising substantiation program* requires advertisers and advertising agencies to have a reasonable basis before they disseminate claims. When advertisers claim that "studies show" or "tests prove," they must have evidence of a reasonable basis for the claims. The FTC considers the following in determining what is a reasonable basis:

- the product
- the type of claim
- the consequences of a false claim and the benefits of a truthful claim
- the cost of developing substantiation for the claim
- the amount of substantiation that experts in the field believe is reasonable

What Advertising is Deceptive? The FTC has considerable leeway in deciding what advertising is deceptive. We look to cases to get a feel for what is deceptive. A number of years ago, the FTC noted in a decision: "Perhaps a few misguided souls believe . . . that all 'Danish pastry' is made in Denmark. Is it therefore an actionable deception to advertise 'Danish pastry' when it is made in this country? Of course not." The point is that some people may misunderstand certain advertisements, but that does not mean that the FTC will be concerned. For example, if a hair dye is advertised as permanent and a person thinks that it means that his or her hair will be the color of the dye for life, rather than that only the existing hair will be the color of the dye, no deception is involved. Most consumers know what the ads mean, and those who don't do not incur significant injury as a result.

The number of people "deceived" by an ad does not necessarily determine whether there is an ad deception case. For instance, car ads will say that the Fireball model got thirty miles per gallon in tests. If that ad is on national television, it may be viewed by tens of millions, of whom several hundred thousand may incorrectly think that all Fireball models will always get thirty miles per gallon. So long as the claim made was true—since most consumers know that miles-per-gallon ratings from tests donot mean that all cars will get exactly the test results—there is no deception that would lead one to believe that the effect injures enough consumers to warrant the ads to be changed.

On the other hand, some ads that reach a small number of people, such as pamphlets distributed door to door, may deceive many consumers who read them, since the claims are false and likely to deceive. Other ads may reach a large number of people, deceive very few, yet be held by the FTC to be deceptive. For instance, if a small number of consumers suffer serious injury (usually wasted money) because they believe a claim made by an advertiser, the FTC may act because of the seriousness of the injury. Note that most states have laws similar to the FTC Act that allow state attorneys general to also file suit in cases of deceptive advertising. North American Philips was sued for false and unsubstantiated advertising claims for its Norelco brand Clean Water Machine. The company claimed that the ''[M]achine helps remove chlorine, sediment, sulfur, detergent, odors, organic chemicals, and other pollutants you may not even be aware of that are in your tap water.'' The FTC charged that the machine's filter actually added a chemical that is potentially hazardous to consumers' health.

The FTC sued the Campbell Soup Company in 1989 for making deceptive and unsubstantiated claims. Campbell's ads linked the low-fat, low-cholesterol content of the soups with a reduced risk of some forms of heart disease but failed to disclose that the soups are high in sodium and that diets high in sodium may increase the risk of heart disease.

Kraft General Foods was ordered in 1991 not to make misrepresentations about any nutrient in any cheese-related product after the FTC found that Kraft ran deceptive ads for Kraft Singles cheese slices that implied that each slice had as much calcium as five ounces of milk, which is not true. The same year, Nestle's Stouffer Food Corporation was sued for falsely claiming that its Lean Cuisine frozen dinners were low in sodium. The ads referred to ''one gram'' of sodium, rather than the common measure of 1,000 milligrams of sodium.

Misleading ''green'' ads will also be attacked. First Brands settled FTC charges by no longer making claims without sufficient proof that Glad trash bags will completely decompose when disposed of as trash. Claims about the environmental advantages of a product must be backed by scientific evidence.

How the powers of the FTC can be used against advertising held to be deceptive is illustrated in the *Warner-Lambert* decision involving Listerine.

WARNER-LAMBERT COMPANY v. FEDERAL TRADE COMMISSION

United States Court of Appeals, District of Columbia Circuit
562 F.2d 749 (1977)

Case Background
Listerine has been marketed since 1879. Beginning in 1921, advertisements for it claimed that it had beneficial effects on sore throats and colds. The FTC found the claims not supported by evidence and issued an order against Warner-Lambert to stop advertising that Listerine could prevent, cure, or alleviate colds. The FTC also ordered corrective advertising. Warner-Lambert challenged the FTC ruling, claiming that even if its ad claims in the past were false, the Commission exceeded its statutory authority. Warner-Lambert petitioned the court of appeals for review of the FTC order.

(continued)

Case Decision

The federal court of appeals upheld the decision of the FTC, noting that " . . . a hundred years of false cold claims have built up a large reservoir of erroneous consumer belief which would persist, unless corrected, long after petitioner ceased making the claims." For one year, all print, television, and radio ads would be required to state: "Listerine will not help prevent colds or sore throats or lessen their severity." Future advertisements had to correct the false impressions made in the past.

Managerial Considerations

As discussed in the antitrust chapters, managers must closely scrutinize pricing and marketing strategies prior to implementing them. Managers must also be concerned about an ad's potential to be deceptive or to misrepresent the company's product. The negative publicity associated with being accused of false and deceptive advertising can seriously damage a company's reputation.

Here, the company had been advertising the product in basically the same way for nearly 100 years. The fact that the basic theme had been used for so many years without incident made management lax in its evaluation of the advertising strategy. This case illustrates the importance of evaluating company and managerial practices on a regular basis—regardless of whether a particular practice appears to be legal or ethical.

In considering its initial response to the FTC's concerns, management may have avoided or at least reduced the harshness of the penalties ultimately imposed if it had abandoned the advertising strategy upon being informed of the FTC's inquiries. The FTC and other federal agencies often terminate such investigations when it becomes apparent that the management of a company is working diligently to police itself.

INTERNATIONAL ASPECTS | FOREIGN ADVERTISING REGULATION

Advertising is subject to very different controls around the world. Except for prohibitions on the advertising of certain products, most countries impose fewer regulations on ads than is the case in the United States. In Europe, ad regulations tend to be tightest in Northern Europe and loosest in the Mediterranean countries.

Britain has an Office of Fair Trading that operates somewhat like the FTC with respect to ad regulation. The general standard is that an ad is illegal if it misrepresents a product, whereas in the United States it may be illegal if it simply misleads. For an ad to misrepresent a product, there must be an estimation that consumers suffer damages because they have not been told the truth in the ad. For example, a soup ad in the United States was held illegal by the FTC because the soup was filmed to look like it had more chunky bits in it than a random bowl of the soup really would have. In most of Europe and Japan, that ad would not be illegal, because although it misleads, it does not injure consumers.

■ FTC ENFORCEMENT ACTIVITIES

The FTC investigates a wide range of business practices that may be unfair and deceptive. Besides being concerned with the advertising cases just discussed and the credit regulations and warranty issues discussed later in the chapter, the Bureau of Consumer Protection may bring cases involving any practice under its jurisdiction that can injure consumers or businesses. The following cases give some idea of the wide range of activities subject to action by the FTC or state attorneys general.

Companies Shipping Unordered Goods.   The FTC obtained a consent decree under which four Florida-based office supply companies agreed to pay $36,000 in civil penalties and to cease certain practices. The companies and the individuals who run them are prohibited from shipping any unordered products, except those clearly marked as free samples, and from seeking payment for unordered merchandise. The FTC claimed that the companies had been shipping large quantities of unordered office supplies to businesses, schools, and other organizations around the United States and then dunning the recipients for payment.

■ TELEMARKETING FRAUD

The FTC obtained an injunction against five telemarketing firms and their owners in 1990 for making misrepresentations in the sale of water purifiers and home security systems. The FTC charged that the companies mailed postcards telling consumers they had won a valuable award, including $5,000 in retail merchandise checks. In fact, the awards consisted only of certificates that required payment of substantial sums of money to obtain the merchandise. The telemarketers also made charges against consumers' credit cards without authorization and billed customers for merchandise never sent.

Oil and Gas Well "Investments".   Several companies were involved in oil and gas well lease scams in the early 1980s. They persuaded over 8,000 people to invest $5,000 to $10,000 each in applications fees to participate in a lottery for mineral (oil and gas) rights on federal lands. The FTC obtained $47 million in refunds in 1991, which was about 90 cents on the dollar lost. Not only were the promoters sued, so were all the companies that worked with them in the scheme, such as insurance companies, banks, and accounting firms.

Art Fraud.   The FTC obtained a consent decree against Austin Galleries, which has art galleries in Chicago, San Francisco, Carmel, and Laguna Beach. Austin bilked consumers by selling fake Salvador Dali, Marc Chagall, Pablo Picasso, and Juan Miro prints as good investments. The company paid $635,000 in consumer refunds and agreed to stop falsely representing the art it sells.

Unfairness and Contract Enforcement.   Section 5 of the FTC Act says "unfair or deceptive acts or practices in or affecting commerce, are declared unlawful." The key word has always been *deceptive*. The word *unfair* is usually tagged on to a charge of deception. The FTC has tried to give operational meaning to unfair acts or practices in business by establishing the following *test for unfairness:*

1. It causes substantial harm to consumers.
2. Consumers cannot reasonably avoid injury.
3. The injury is harmful in its net effects.

The first major consumer unfairness case that did not involve a claim of deception was the *Orkin* case (which was supervised by one of the authors of this text while working for the FTC). The decision to bring the case was based on the perception that the unfairness involved seemed much like fraud and breach of contract, both of which are common-law standards the courts have long enforced.

ORKIN EXTERMINATING COMPANY v. FEDERAL TRADE COMMISSION

United States Court of Appeals, Eleventh Circuit
849 F.2d 1354 (1988)

Case Background
Beginning in 1966, Orkin Exterminating Company offered customers a "continuous guarantee" if they had their houses treated for termites. The contract said that by paying a small annual fee, customers were guaranteed free retreatment if termites reappeared for as long as they owned their house. By 1975, Orkin realized that the promise was a mistake. The annual fee was too low to cover the costs. Orkin then notified over 200,000 customers in their annual bills that the fee was being raised $25 or 40 percent, whichever was greater. If the customers did not pay the fee, the guarantee was lost. The new fee was consistent with current market prices but differed from what the contract had stated. The FTC found the fee increase to be unfair and ordered Orkin to roll back its prices to the original levels. Orkin appealed to the U.S. Court of Appeals.

Case Decision
The court of appeals affirmed the FTC's decision. The court stated that the injury to individual customers was small, but the net effect was to benefit Orkin by about $2 million extra per year in revenues. The court noted that "a practice may be . . . unfair without being deceptive." The FTC's conclusion that breach of 200,000 contracts was unfair is a reasonable application of the FTC Act.

Managerial Considerations
Managers occasionally find themselves burdened with contractual commitments that, contrary to expectations, are losing money. The losses may be due to changes in the company's external environment such as a change in the economy, or to changes in the company's internal environment, such as the loss of key personnel involved in the deal. In either case, the contract may provide management with no alternative but to breach. In most cases where management decides to breach, it does so because the legal damages the courts are likely to order the company to pay because of the breach will be less than the losses the company will incur if it meets its contractual obligations. When breaching, managers must keep in mind other implications of the breach—such as loss of goodwill or injury to the company's reputation—and the possibility that a regulatory agency may respond. Nevertheless, it is legitimate for managers to choose an action that results in the least cost to the company. In this case, the management of Orkin underestimated the impact of its external environment when it implemented a breach by increasing the contract price.

■ TRADE REGULATION RULES

Under Section 18 of the FTC Act, the FTC has the authority to issue certain *trade regulation rules* that set boundaries on acts and practices that the FTC believes are ripe for deception. Such rules tend to be based on FTC experience with problems, although critics charge that the rules can be used to protect existing competitors against innovative entrants by making certain practices the industry standard. Because numerous trade regulation rules are on the books—some dealing with rather narrow areas—only a few of the more important rules are discussed here (the Franchise Rule is discussed in Chapter 17).

When the FTC proposes a rule, the rule must be published in the *Federal Register* so that interested parties may comment on it before it is made final. When the rule is put in place, it gives the FTC solid grounds for charging that violators are committing an unfair and deceptive act, since people in the industry in question are required to know the rule.

The Insulation R-Value Rule.   The FTC's Trade Regulation Rule Concerning the Labeling and Advertising of Home Insulation *(the R-value rule)* was written because of the problems consumers have trying to understand what various insulation claims mean. By standardizing R-values, the FTC requires all insulation manufacturers and installers to use the same terminology and to measure the R-value of their products using specified tests and to disclose the results.

The rule provides consumers with a uniform standard to evaluate home insulation products. Because of the rule, if an insulation company claims that it has provided R-19 value insulation and it has not, there is a standard to measure the R-value that makes the company subject to suit by the FTC in a fairly straightforward manner rather than trying to establish without standards that what was done was deceptive. For example, in 1990, the FTC settled a consent decree with Sears for violating the R-value rule. Sears advertised the thickness and price of an insulation product but failed to disclose the R-value. In the decree, Sears agreed to pay a 100,000-dollar civil penalty, comply with the rule in the future, and pay for advertisements to educate consumers about home insulation and R-values.

The Mail Order Rule.   One of the best known trade regulation rules is that for Undelivered Mail Order Merchandise and Services—the *mail order rule*. Under this rule, if a company offers to sell merchandise by mail, it must have a reasonable basis for expecting to ship the merchandise within the time stated in its ads. Shipping dates must be clearly stated on the offers (such as "Allow five weeks for shipment"), or the merchandise must be shipped within thirty days of receipt of a proper order. If the merchandise cannot be shipped on time, customers must be sent an option notice allowing them to cancel the order and receive a refund or to agree to a new shipping date—which must be reasonable and must be met. There are other provisions to the rule, but its most important effect has been to encourage prompt shipment of mail order merchandise and to provide the FTC with an extra "hook" by which to issue complaints against companies that fail to live up to the terms of their offers.

The Used-Car Rule.   The FTC adopted a *Used-Car Rule* in 1984 that requires dealers to give consumers complete and clear information on who has to pay for repairs after a sale and to have a buyer's guide placed in the side window of each used car offered for sale. The guide will contain the following:

1. A statement of the terms of any warranty offered with the car.
2. A prominent statement of whether the dealer is selling the car "as is" and, if so, that the consumer must pay for any repairs needed after buying the car.
3. A warning that spoken promises are difficult to enforce, with a suggestion to get all promises in writing.
4. A suggestion that the consumer ask for an independent inspection of the car.

The FTC sued a San Francisco car dealer in 1989 for violating the rule by failing to display window stickers on used cars offered for sale. The dealer also failed to provide consumers with copies of the buyer's guide or disclosures concerning warranty. The dealer agreed to comply with the law in the future and paid a civil penalty of $20,000.

■ MAGNUSON-MOSS WARRANTY ACT

A 1975 amendment to the FTC Act gives the FTC power to set guidelines for producers of consumer products for warranty responsibilities. Compliance with the *Magnuson-Moss Warranty Act* does not appear to be costly, but then the benefits of the law are not very clear. Few cases have been brought under the law.

Required Written Warranty Information. The law requires that *written warranties* include information about the following:

- The parts of the product or the types of problems the warranty covers and, if necessary for clarity, the parts or problems it does not cover.
- The period of coverage.
- What will be done to correct problems and, if necessary for clarity, what will not be done.
- How the customer can get warranty service.
- How state law may affect certain provisions of the warranty.

Full or Limited Warranty. Every product that costs more than ten dollars and has a warranty must comply with the provisions of the Magnuson-Moss Warranty Act. The warranty must state clearly and conspicuously whether the warranty is full or limited. A *full warranty* meets the following five standards:

1. Warranty service will be provided to anyone who owns the product during the warranty period.
2. Warranty service will be provided free of charge and include such costs as returning the product or removing and reinstalling the product when necessary.
3. At the consumer's choice, either a replacement or a full refund will be provided if the product cannot be repaired after a reasonable number of tries.
4. Warranty service will be provided without requiring that consumers return a warranty registration card.
5. The implied warranties will not be limited.

If any of these statements is not true, the warranty is a *limited warranty* and must be so stated. A product has a multiple warranty when part of the product is covered by a full warranty and part is covered by a limited warranty. In all events, to comply with the FTC's Rule of Disclosure of Written Consumer Product Warranty Terms and Conditions, warranties must be reasonably clear, simple, and useful. In other words, if a company writes in fine print an unclear warranty that is designed to discourage consumers, the company will be subject to FTC attack, especially if consumers report having difficulties enforcing the warranty. State courts have made similar decisions in cases brought under contract law. Obscure fine print is not looked upon with favor.

CONSUMER CREDIT PROTECTION ACT ▬▬▬

Congress first involved the federal government in the direct regulation of the relationship between consumers and creditors with the *Consumer Credit Protection Act* (CCPA) of 1968. At that time there was about $100 billion worth of consumer credit outstanding; today the figure approaches $1 trillion and is an important part of most consumers' financial organization, as Table 15–1 shows. Credit cards, which were somewhat rare twenty years ago, now carry a huge volume of transactions. CCPA has become an umbrella law containing several credit-related laws. The laws provide certain rights for consumers in credit transactions and place certain requirements on creditors, including the following:

- Creditors are required to disclose all relevant terms in credit transactions.
- Creditors are prohibited from using certain personal characteristics of individual consumers (such as sex or race) in determining an individual's creditworthiness.
- Credit-reporting agencies are required to provide accurate information in consumer reports.
- Abusive debt collection techniques are prohibited.
- Procedures for correcting inaccurate and disputed bills and charges must be provided.

▬ TRUTH-IN-LENDING ACT

As Figure 15–1 shows, the first law to come under the CCPA was the *Truth-in-Lending Act* (TILA), which requires creditors in consumer transactions to *disclose* basic information about the cost and terms of credit to the consumer-borrower. The purpose of the Act is to encourage competition in the financing of consumer credit. By making borrowers aware of specific charges and other relevant information, it encourages them to shop around

TABLE 15–1
GROWTH OF CONSUMER CREDIT OUTSTANDING: 1970 TO 1990

Type of Credit	1970	1975	1980 ($ billion)	1985	1990
All credit	$132	$205	$350	$592	$810
Auto loans	36	57	112	210	285
Revolving (credit cards)	5	15	55	122	218
Consumer credit as percentage of personal income	18.3%	18%	18.3%	21%	21%

SOURCE: *Statistical Abstract of United States* and *Federal Reserve Bulletin*.

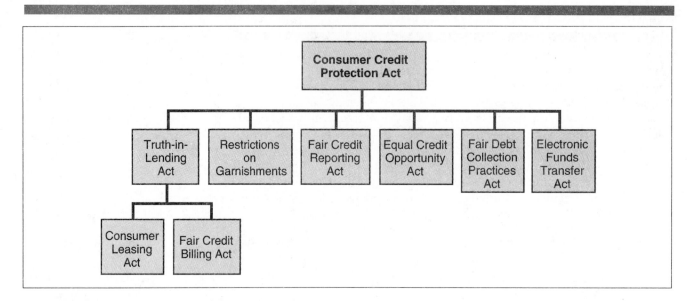

FIGURE 15–1

The Major Elements of Federal Consumer Credit Legislation

for the most favorable credit terms much as they would shop around for the best price for a car.

In addition to requiring that specific costs of credit information be given to consumers, TILA as amended contains the Consumer Leasing Act and the Fair Credit Billing Act. The Consumer Leasing Act establishes standardized terms to be disclosed in consumer leases of personal property, such as automobiles and computers. The Fair Credit Billing Act establishes procedures for consumers to follow when credit cards are lost or stolen or when monthly credit card statements contain billing errors or disputed charges.

Finance Charge Disclosures.   Until TILA was passed, creditors quoted interest in many ways, which caused substantial confusion. For example, an 8 percent add-on interest rate is approximately the same as a 15 percent simple interest rate. This is because an add-on rate calculates interest on the initial amount of the loan regardless of the outstanding principal, whereas the simple interest rate calculates interest only on the outstanding principal. Both methods are legitimate, but standardized terms were adopted under TILA so that consumers could make better comparisons among competing lenders.

TILA requires that consumers be given standardized loan terms before they commit to a credit transaction. It is essentially a disclosure statute—it does not set interest rates. TILA covers only consumer credit transactions since the debtor must be a "natural person," not a business organization, and the creditor must be in the credit business. TILA does not apply to transactions such as loans to friends. The law does not apply if the credit transaction does not include a finance charge, unless the consumer repays the creditor in more than four installments. Finally, the Act does not apply to consumer credit transactions involving more than $25,000, except real estate purchases.

Credit Cost Disclosure Requirement.   Transactions covered by the Act must disclose the credit costs in dollars (the finance charge) and the annual rate of that finance charge (the *annual percentage rate,* or APR). These items must be disclosed more conspicuously than any of the other items in the agreement. The finance charge includes more than interest charges. *Regulation Z,* written by the Federal Reserve Board to implement the Truth-in-Lending Act, specifies items that are part of the finance charge, including the following:

1. Service, activity, carrying, and transaction charges.
2. Loan fees and points.
3. Charges for mandatory credit life and credit accident and health insurance.
4. In non-real estate transactions, the fees for credit reports and appraisals.

Certain other items, such as licenses and fees imposed by law, are not part of the finance charge if they are itemized and disclosed to the consumer in the transaction. In all, there are twelve items related to credit transactions that must be disclosed to the borrower.

TILA Enforcement and Penalties.   TILA provides for both civil and criminal penalties. Penalties do not apply to all violations. The creditor can avoid liability for a violation if the violation is corrected within fifteen days from the time it is discovered by the creditor and before the consumer gives written notification of error. In addition, good faith reliance on official Federal Reserve Board comments about how to follow the law protects creditors from civil liability.

Consumers may sue creditors who violate TILA disclosure rules for twice the amount of the finance charge—up to $1,000—court costs, and attorney's fees. A creditor who willfully or knowingly gives inaccurate information or fails to make proper disclosures is subject to criminal liability, including a fine of up to $5,000, imprisonment of not more than one year, or both, for each violation of the Act.

■ CONSUMER LEASING ACT

The Consumer Leasing Act does for consumer leases, such as for automobiles or electronic equipment, what the Truth-in-Lending Act does for consumer credit. That is, it provides standard terms to help consumers shop around for leases. The Act applies to leases of personal property to be used for personal, family, or household purposes, not for business purposes. The lease must have a term of more than four months and a contractual obligation of less than $25,000. Apartment leases are not covered by the Act, because the property leased is real, not personal, property. Daily car rentals are not covered because the term of the agreement is not long enough.

Disclosure Requirements and Liability.   The Consumer Leasing Act specifies information that must be given before the consumer becomes contractually obligated for the lease. The required disclosures include the following items:

- Number, amount, and period of the payments and the payment total.
- Any express warranties offered by the leasing party or the manufacturer of the leased property.

■ Identification of the party responsible for maintaining or servicing the leased property.

■ Whether the consumer has an option to buy the leased property and, if so, the terms of that option.

■ What happens if the consumer terminates the lease before the lease expires.

The consumer leasing provisions are explained in the Federal Reserve Board's *Regulation M.* The criminal liability for violating the Consumer Leasing Act and Regulation M is the same as the liability for violating the Truth-in-Lending Act and Regulation Z. Civil liability is 25 percent of the total amount of monthly payments under the lease but no more than $1,000, plus court costs and attorney's fees.

■ Fair Credit Billing Act

Congress amended TILA to include the Fair Credit Billing Act (FCBA) in 1974. Before the Act, consumers complained that they were unable to get creditors to correct inaccurate charges or remove unauthorized charges that appeared on billing statements. Consumers who believed that they did not owe the disputed charge would not pay the bill. The nonpayment was reported to credit bureaus, and consumers' credit histories were damaged. Another problem was that credit cards were sent to people who did not request them. Some unsolicited cards were lost or stolen, and consumers who never requested the cards were billed for unauthorized purchases. The FCBA addresses these problems in three ways:

1. It established procedures to dispute *billing errors.* A consumer must notify the creditor in writing within sixty days of the first billing of the disputed charge. The creditor must acknowledge the complaint within thirty days of receipt and has ninety days to resolve the problem and notify the consumer. If the creditor fails to follow the required procedures, it cannot collect the first fifty dollars of the questioned amount.

2. It prohibits the mailing of unsolicited credit cards.

3. It established procedures to report lost or stolen credit cards. If a consumer reports the theft in a timely fashion, maximum liability for unauthorized charges is fifty dollars.

Enforcement.   Most billing disputes are resolved through the procedures established by the FCBA. Dissatisfied consumers can also sue for civil penalties for FCBA violations. In successful actions, creditors are liable for twice the amount of the finance charge, plus attorney's fees and court costs. The FTC is the principal FCBA enforcement agency, with jurisdiction over department stores, gasoline retailers, and non-bank card issuers, such as American Express.

Other federal agencies enforce the credit statutes for other credit-granting institutions. National banks are regulated by the Comptroller of the Currency. State banks that are members of the Federal Reserve system are regulated by the Federal Reserve Board. State banks that are not a part of the Federal Reserve system but are federally insured are regulated by the Federal Deposit Insurance Corporation.

■ FAIR CREDIT REPORTING ACT

Congress added the *Fair Credit Reporting Act* (FCPA) to the CCPA in 1970. The Act regulates *credit bureaus* (consumer reporting agencies). It focuses on confidentiality and accuracy in compiling and distributing *consumer credit reports*. No limit is placed on the kinds of information that consumer reporting agencies may include in their files (such as information on political beliefs or sexual practices), so long as the information is not inaccurate. However, information about most people concerns only credit history.

Agencies may furnish (sell) consumer reports only if the reports are to be used for the purposes stated in the Act. A report may be issued if a business needs to evaluate an applicant for credit, insurance, employment, a government license or other benefit, and other legitimate business needs involving a business transaction with the consumer. Any other use requires either a court order or the consumer's permission.

Consumer Rights with Credit Reports.   The Act gives consumers the right to see negative information reported about them to a creditor that results in their being denied credit. This gives them the chance to correct wrong information. When a consumer tells a reporting agency about incorrect information, the Act holds that the information must be deleted or changed or a statement from the consumer about the problem be placed in the file.

In 1990, the FTC reported more complaints about problems with credit bureaus than any other area of consumer complaint. To settle a lawsuit with the FTC and nineteen states, TRW, one of the big three consumer credit reporting agencies in the billion-dollar-a-year industry, agreed in 1991 to change its practices. TRW will give consumers a copy of their credit report for free (the other big two, Equifax and Trans Union, charge about $15). TRW also agreed to install a toll-free phone line for helping consumers understand their reports and to set up strict rules for handling consumer complaints about errors. All three companies' policies for dealing with consumers are more generous than the rights provided by the statute.

Enforcement and Penalties.   The FTC has responsibility for enforcement of the FCPA. The Act provides a weak civil remedy to injured consumers, who may recover only actual damages when noncompliance is negligent. When the credit agency or the user is in willful noncompliance, the consumer may recover actual damages and a punitive penalty. In a 1991 Wyoming suit, TRW was ordered to pay $290,000 in damages—of which $275,000 were punitive damages—for willfully ignoring a consumer's attempt to correct errors in his credit report.

■ EQUAL CREDIT OPPORTUNITY ACT

Congress enacted the *Equal Credit Opportunity Act* (ECOA) as part of the CCPA in 1974 to prohibit discrimination against applicants for credit. The ECOA prohibits *credit discrimination* on the basis of race, sex, color, religion, national origin, marital status, receipt of public benefits, the good-faith exercise of the applicant's rights under any part of the CCPA, or age (provided the applicant is old enough to sign a contract). Creditors are prohibited from using such criteria (known as *prohibited bases*) in determining creditworthiness.

The ECOA requires a creditor to notify the consumer of its decision to accept, reject, or modify the credit request within thirty days of the completed application. If the credit request is denied or accepted but the terms are unfavorably changed, the creditor must provide specific notice of the reasons for the adverse action and the name and address of the federal agency regulating that creditor.

The Federal Reserve Board was charged with writing a regulation to implement the ECOA; it issued *Regulation B* in response. The Act assigned overall enforcement duties to the FTC.

Unlawful Credit Discrimination.   The guiding law for ECOA compliance is simple:

> A creditor shall not discriminate against an applicant on a prohibited basis regarding any aspect of a credit transaction.

Because this provision is broad, Regulation B provides specific rules explaining what constitutes unlawful discrimination. Some of the rules are as follows:

- A creditor shall not make any written or oral statements to discourage a person from applying for credit on a prohibited basis.

- A creditor shall not use information concerning the likelihood that the applicant may bear or rear children or that the applicant is likely, for that reason, to have reduced or irregular income. The creditor may not ask direct questions about an applicant's birth control practices or his or her plans to have children, nor can the creditor assume that because a female applicant is of childbearing age she will bear children and thus have reduced or interrupted income. Before ECOA, many creditors discounted or considered only a portion of a married woman's income and in some cases required the husband and wife to sign an affidavit that they would not have children.

- If a creditor considers credit history in evaluating creditworthiness, it must, at the applicant's request, consider not only the applicant's direct credit history but also his or her indirect credit history (for example, accounts that the applicant used or was contractually liable for and accounts listed in the name of a spouse or former spouse that the applicant can show reflects his or her own credit history). (This provision is to correct the practices of creditors and credit bureaus when credit history was reported only in the husband's name, but it applies to anyone.)

- A creditor may not request information about a spouse or former spouse of the applicant unless (a) the spouse will use the account or will be contractually liable for the debt; (b) the applicant is relying on the spouse's income or on alimony, child support, or maintenance payments from the former spouse; or (c) the applicant lives in a community property state or community property is involved.

A violation of ECOA exists if it is determined that a creditor used a factor specifically prohibited by the Act. The consumer can sue the creditor for ECOA violations. If the consumer is successful, the creditor is liable for actual damages, punitive damages up to $10,000, attorney's fees, and court costs, whether the discrimination was intentional or not.

ECOA Notice Requirements.   When a consumer's application for credit is denied or accepted at less favorable terms, the creditor must provide *written notification* containing the following information:

1. The basic provisions of ECOA.
2. Name and address of the federal agency regulating compliance by the creditor issuing the notice.
3. Either (a) a statement of the specific reasons for the action taken or (b) a disclosure of the applicant's right to receive a statement of reasons.

The first and second notice requirements tell rejected applicants that it is against the law to discriminate on a prohibited basis and point them to one of the twelve federal agencies designated by ECOA to enforce the Act. By having the name of the appropriate enforcement agency, applicants know where to report suspected acts of discrimination and to ask questions and get answers about ECOA.

The third notification requirement regarding the statement of specific reasons is the most significant. By knowing why they were rejected, applicants can reapply when their situation changes (for example, when the reason for denial is that the time living at the current residence is too short) or they can correct any misinformation used by the creditor. Also, by knowing the reasons for the credit denial, applicants can better understand how decisions concerning creditworthiness are made. This requirement is supposed to help those classes of consumers with a history of credit discrimination and help every rejected credit applicant understand the credit-granting process.

CONSUMER CREDIT PROTECTION ABROAD   INTERNATIONAL ASPECTS

The consumer credit regulatory scheme discussed in this chapter would make little sense to a European or Japanese lender, because very few of the rules that exist in the United States under the CCPA are mandated by legislation in most developed nations.

For example, most of those nations do not have statutes that prevent discrimination in credit markets based on sex, race, or other personal characteristics. The Race Relations Act in the United Kingdom does limit some discrimination based on race or color, but in most countries, minorities have little political clout. Further, women do not have the statutory protection in most countries that is provided by the CCPA in the United States.

Most nations have general laws against misrepresentation and fraud that apply to credit markets. But the kind of standardization that has come about in the United States under the CCPA is not as common in other nations, nor are there as many regulators like the FTC or the various banking authorities who write and enforce credit regulations.

■ FAIR DEBT COLLECTION PRACTICES ACT

Creditors have the right to take steps to collect debts they are owed. If unable to collect, under state law they may go to court and ask for an order to *garnish* (set aside a portion of) the wages of the debtor to pay the debt. If unsuccessful in trying to collect a debt, a creditor can sell the debt to a company that specializes in collecting debts—a *debt collection agency*—or pay the agency a commission for the funds it collects.

Debt collectors do not fare well in the public eye. They are often dunning poor people or people who have gotten themselves into unfortunate financial circumstances for money these people legally owe others. Their image may improve a bit as recently debt collection agencies have been hired by states and by parents to help collect the estimated $20 billion in overdue child-support payments (mostly owed by fathers). The states and mothers report far more success than the state agencies had in trying to collect these legal debts. As Figure 15–2 shows, debt collection agencies handle about $70 billion a year in claims.

To collect delinquent accounts, consumers are advised by telephone or letter of the outstanding debt and are urged to pay. Sometimes, however, delinquent consumers are subjected to phone calls in the middle of the night, obscene language, threats of debtor's prison, and other forms of harassment and abusive tactics. The *Fair Debt Collection Practices Act* (FDCPA) is designed to eliminate unfair, deceptive, and abusive collection techniques used by some debt collectors but permits reasonable collection practices.

FIGURE 15–2

Claims Handled by Collection Agencies ($ billion)
SOURCE: American Collectors Association.

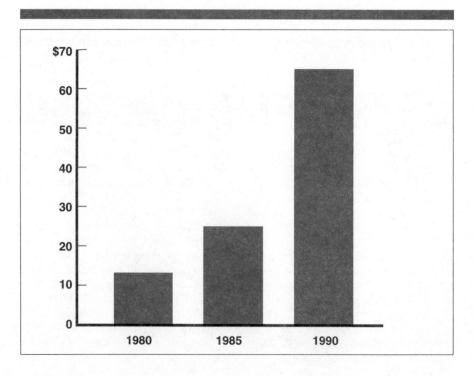

Restrictions Imposed.   The FDCPA regulates the conduct of about 5,000 independent debt collection agencies that collect over $5 billion a year in debts from millions of consumers. It does not apply to creditors attempting to collect their own debts. The Act makes abusive debt collection practices illegal and contains a list of required actions and prohibited conduct by collection agencies. Harassing, deceptive, and unfair debt collection practices—including threats of violence or arrest, obscene language, the publication of a list of delinquent consumers, and harassing or anonymous phone calls—are prohibited. Debt collectors may not discuss the debts with other people, including the debtor's employer. The Act prohibits the use of false or misleading representations in collecting a debt. For example, the collector cannot impersonate an attorney in attempting to collect a debt and cannot misrepresent that papers being sent to the debtor are legal forms.

To illustrate the kinds of collection methods and practices the law is intended to prohibit, consider the collection tactics condemned by the judge in *United States* v. *Central Adjustment Bureau.*

UNITED STATES v. CENTRAL ADJUSTMENT BUREAU, INC.

United States District Court, Northern District of Texas
667 F.Supp. 370 (1986)

Case Background
The Central Adjustment Bureau (CAB) is a debt collection company with its headquarters in Dallas and offices in twenty-five other cities. The government charged CAB with numerous violations of the FDCPA, based on testimony taken from current and former CAB employees and debtors in numerous cities. Testimony established that calls were made to debtors in the early morning and late at night; were made to places of employment after CAB was told not to call there; were harassing and abusive (including making racial slurs and threats and calling people liars, deadbeats, and crooks); were obscene and profane; were made repeatedly to the same person the same day; were made by a person claiming to be an attorney preparing to file suit; were made telling the debtor that he or she would be jailed or that a crime had been committed; and were made telling a debtor that her daughter's college degree would be revoked.

Case Decision
The court found the calls to violate numerous specific sections of the FDCPA. CAB was ordered to stop making such calls and to pay $150,000 in civil penalties. The company also was required to include a notice in every collection letter sent to debtors giving them a brief summary of debtor rights under the FDCPA, including the address of the FTC.

Managerial Considerations
This case illustrates the kind of decision making that can occur once the management of a company decides to consider undertaking an illegal act or practice. In this case, management clearly found that its success rate in collecting delinquent debts was greater when it undertook these illegal acts. It undoubtedly had estimated the probabilities of getting apprehended along with the sanction that would likely be imposed and determined that it was profitable to risk a violation. In addition, the management of CAB was apparently unconcerned about the damage to its reputation if it were caught.

In the vast majority of businesses, management will place considerable weight when making a decision on the potential damage to the company reputation. Even though the probabilities are low that it would be caught doing an illegal activity—and the resulting sanctions would be insignificant—management of such companies is more concerned about the long-term damage to the company reputation and the effect on the company's profitability. However, in the event that the activity is so profitable or the economic environment so depressed that even damage to reputation is not a sufficient deterrent, only the enforcement agency and the courts may be able to deter such activities.

The FDCPA requires the debt collector to send certain information to the consumer within five days of the initial communication:

- Amount of debt.
- Name of the creditor to whom the debt is owed.
- A statement that unless the consumer disputes the validity of the debt or a part of the debt within thirty days, the debt collector will assume that the debt is valid.
- A statement notifying the consumer that the debt collector must show proof of the debt if the consumer advises the debt collector within thirty days of the notification that the consumer disputes the debt.

Contact with the consumer must cease when the collector learns the consumer is represented by an attorney or when the consumer requests in writing that contact end. The debt collector can then either wait for payment or sue to collect the debt.

Enforcement.   The Act is primarily self-enforcing. Consumers subjected to collection abuses will enforce compliance by bringing lawsuits. A collector who violates the Act is liable for actual damages caused as well as any additional damages (not over $1,000) deemed appropriate by the courts. Consumers bringing action in good faith will have their attorney's fees and court costs paid by the collector. The FTC is charged with the administrative enforcement of the Act.

■ ELECTRONIC FUND TRANSFER ACT

Four principal types of electronic fund transfer services are available to consumers:

1. Automated teller machines, also known as 24-hour tellers, that let consumers perform a variety of banking transactions at any time.
2. Pay-by-phone systems, permitting consumers to telephone the bank and order payments to third parties or a transfer of funds between accounts.
3. Direct deposits of wages and other funds into a consumer's bank account or automatic payments that deduct funds from the consumer's account to make regular payments, such as automobile loan payments.
4. Point-of-sale transfers, which allow consumers, through the use of a computer terminal at a retail establishment, to transfer money instantaneously from their bank account to a merchant.

As these electronic innovations developed, Congress became concerned about the rights and liabilities of the consumers, financial institutions, and retailers who use an electronic fund transfer system. The Electronic Fund Transfer Act was passed in 1979 and required the Federal Reserve Board to write *Regulation E* to implement the Act.

Liability for Stolen Cards.   Perhaps the most important protection provided by the Act is the limit on consumer liability in the event a consumer's fund-transfer card is stolen and an unauthorized user drains the account. Unlike the Fair Credit Billing Act's fifty-dollar limit on liability for lost or stolen credit cards, the Electronic Fund Transfer Act's limit on liability is much greater. In some circumstances, the consumer may be liable for an amount equal to all the money in the bank account.

Regulation E provides that the consumer's liability is no more than fifty dollars if the financial institution is notified within two days after the consumer learns of the theft. After that, the consumer's maximum liability becomes $500 as long as the financial institution is notified within sixty days. If the consumer does not report the theft within sixty days after receiving the first statement containing unauthorized transfers, the consumer is liable for all amounts after that. Obviously, the banks have an incentive to provide a secure system.

Liability for Mistakes.   The Act makes the financial institution liable to the consumer for all damages caused by its failure to make an electronic transfer of funds. However, the institution's liability is limited to actual damages proved, such as costs incurred by the consumer when goods are repossessed for failure to make a required payment.

Consumers are to receive a monthly statement from the financial institution. The consumer then has sixty days in which to report any errors. When the consumer reports an error, the institution is required to investigate promptly and to resolve the dispute within forty-five days. If the investigation takes more than ten business days to complete, the institution is required to recredit the disputed amount back to the consumer's account; the consumer has use of the funds after the tenth day until the complaint is resolved. Failure to undertake a good-faith investigation of an alleged error will make the institution liable for triple the consumer's actual damages.

SUMMARY: A GUIDE FOR MANAGERS

- A company's reputation for quality and reliability—particularly in the case of durable goods such as major household appliances, televisions, and automobiles—can significantly affect the long-term viability of the company. Managers will want to have a strategy in the event there is an unforeseen defect or regulatory problem affecting the company's products. The contingency plan would be to resolve consumer concerns and protect the company's reputation. It might include procedures for a product recall or making new information available to consumers.

- Under the Food, Drug and Cosmetic Act, managers who have control over products subject to the Act may be liable for violations. Managers should implement an appropriate quality-control system to assure that they are informed about activities relevant to the quality of a product. By complying with regulatory requirements, managers not only will avoid problems with the regulatory agency but also may have a valid defense in the event of civil suit brought by private parties.

- Food additives must be approved by the FDA before being sold to the public. Nutrition labels on processed foods must list by standard consumer portions, fat, carbohydrates, cholesterol, and other nutrients as well as certain vitamins and minerals and calories.

- The FDA determines when drugs are safe and effective for sale and whether drugs will be sold by prescription only or over the counter. Food, drugs, cosmetics, and medical devices that the FDA determines to be unsafe may be ordered off the market or seized.

- The FTC has broad authority to attack unfair or deceptive business practices. A part of the consumer protection mission includes the advertising substantiation program, which requires advertisers to be able to demonstrate the truth of product claims.

- The FTC issues trade regulation rules to govern business practices that have raised problems. The rules fix standards that businesses must meet, which makes prosecution for rule violations quite simple.

- The Truth-in-Lending-Act, which applies to many consumer loans, requires that lenders meet rigid requirements on how the details of loan amounts, interest charges, and other items are calculated and are stated to the borrower. There is no defense for certain violations of this statute. The Consumer Leasing Act sets similar standards for consumer leases.

- The Fair Credit Billing Act details the rights of consumers to resolve billing errors. Creditors must follow requirements on how long they have to respond to the consumer and what they must do to resolve the dispute. As under other parts of the credit statutes, violations mean double damages, plus attorney's fees, for the plaintiff.

- Credit bureaus are important to lenders for the credit history they provide about those seeking credit. The Fair Credit Reporting Act specifies the rights of consumers to challenge the accuracy of reports issued by these bureaus. Credit bureaus must follow regulatory requirements in responding to inquiries from consumers about errors in their credit reports.

- Under the Equal Credit Opportunity Act, creditors may not consider the following factors in determining who will be granted credit: race, sex, color, religion, national origin, marital status, receipt of public benefits, the exercise of consumer rights under the Consumer Credit Protection Act, or age. Specific regulations govern how lenders must comply with this statute.

- Debt collectors may not abuse the rights of debtors granted by the Fair Debt Collection Practices Act. They may not make abusive phone calls, threats, or claims of legal action not actually under way or use other forms of harassment. A debt collector informed by any debtor that no further contact is desired may not contact the debtor except for notice of legal action.

- Consumer rights and responsibilities for credit or fund-transfer cards that have been stolen are spelled out in detail in the law. To limit liability for unauthorized charges, the consumer must notify the card issuer of the theft of the card.

MANAGER'S ETHICAL DILEMMA

SHOULD ADS AVOID MINORITIES AND YOUNG PEOPLE?

Remember the ads for the Schlitz Malt Liquor bull crashing through a wall or Billy Dee Williams pushing Colt 45 as women flocked to his side? The primary target of malt liquor (beer) ads, are low-income, inner-city blacks, to whom it sells better than regular beer.

Malt is usually 4.5 percent alcohol, compared to 3.5 percent for most beer. The malt producers, whose sales run $500 million per year, recently introduced a higher alcohol malt, including Heileman Brewing's PowerMaster, which is 5.9 percent alcohol, as are several other new entrants. The pitch for the high alcohol malt includes sex and being streetwise and makes known the added punch.

The products and their ads have been under attack by the Bureau of Alcohol, Tobacco and Firearms, which regulates alcohol production and advertising; by groups concerned about alcohol abuse and drunken driving; and by some African American leaders. The Reverend Calvin Butts of the Abyssinian Baptist Church in New York's Harlem says that he is "outraged and frightened" by the new products. Their ad campaigns show "no sense of moral or social responsibility."

Similarly, RJR is criticized for its Joe Camel ads for Camel cigarettes, and Brown & Williamson is under attack for its cartoon penguin who wears shades, a buzzcut, Day-Glo sneakers—and has a Kool cigarette in his mouth. Surveys indicate that a high percentage of children, who may not legally purchase these products, know Joe Camel and the Kool penguin.

Kool "has absolutely no sense of ethical and moral responsibility," says the head of the Advocacy Institute, an antismoking group. The claim is that the companies are trying to get kids addicted to cigarettes, since the median age at which people start smoking is thirteen.

The companies defend their products as legal (which they are), and their ads as necessary in a highly competitive market in appealing to consumers of legal age. Ads do not have to be oriented only to upper income, older whites. Target markets that are mostly black or young adult are just as legitimate. Excluding under-age children, inner-city blacks and young adults have as much right to have producers offer products they find appealing as do other consumer groups.

QUESTIONS

Unless product advertisements that use sex appeal and the like are prohibited (ignoring the constitutional arguments against such restrictions), should marketers use such appeals only to upper income whites and not for lower income blacks? Do marketers have an ethical duty to consider the problems of alcohol abuse among urban blacks, but not quite as much duty to be concerned about better educated, higher income groups? Should advertisements for cigarettes only be designed so they have little appeal to teenagers?

REVIEW AND DISCUSSION QUESTIONS

1. Define the following terms:

   Delaney Clause   trade regulation rules
   Kefauver Amendment   full warranty
   consent decree   limited warranty
   deception   consumer credit reports
   unfairness   debt collection agency

2. If a drug is FDA approved and someone is injured by that drug, is the drug maker immune from a liability suit?

3. What incentives do FDA administrators have to approve new drugs for sale? Do they have an incentive to hurry the process or to be very careful?

4. If consumers believe that agencies like the FTC prevent unfair and deceptive business practices, will they become less careful in watching out for their own interests and thereby encourage more bad business practices?

5. For a year you have owed a local department store $700 for merchandise you charged on one of its store credit cards. Fed up with your lack of payment, the store's collection department calls you late at night, and the caller is abusive. Is this covered by the Fair Debt Collection Practices Act?

6. Laetrile is a drug not approved by the FDA for sale. Some people believe it helps in fighting certain types of cancer. People with cancer will travel to Mexico or Germany to be treated with laetrile and other drugs not available in the United States. Some people dying of cancer sued the FDA, saying that they had a constitutional right to privacy that was being denied by the FDA's refusal to let them have access to laetrile. The federal court of appeals held that it is not reasonable to apply the FDA's drug safety and effectiveness standards to dying cancer patients. The Supreme Court reviewed the case. What was the result? [*United States* v. *Rutherford,* 442 U.S. 544, 99 S.Ct. 2470 (1979)]

7. A store constantly has big signs in its windows and puts ads in the newspapers that take different sales approaches. For a month, the store will advertise "Gigantic Savings of 75%" and similar claims. The next month, it will advertise "Going-Out-of-Business Clearance Sale." The next month, it will advertise "Distress Sale Prices—Everything Must Go." In fact, the store is not going out of business, and most of its prices are always the same. The prices are competitive, but hardly 75 percent off normal retail—or any other great bargain. Is this deceptive advertising?

8. Buckingham Productions sold various diet plans, such as the Rotation Diet and the Freedom Diet. It claimed that dieters could eat almost anything they wanted for four days each week and lose weight if during the other three days they followed a low-calorie diet and took the company's vitamin supplements and other products. The company reported that the average monthly weight loss was eight to twenty pounds for women and twelve to twenty-five pounds for men. What government agency would likely sue the company and on what grounds, and what would be the likely result?

9. A key requirement of the Truth-in-Lending Act and Regulation Z is that each borrower receive two copies of the Notice of Right to Cancel. The lender gave Jacquelyn Elsner and her husband Max each one copy of the notice, along with other materials on the loan document they both signed. The Elsners later moved to tear up the loan agreement because they did not *each* receive two copies of the notice, which was a simple oversight by the lender. Is the loan good, or can they walk away? [*Elsner* v. *Albrecht,* 185 Mich.App. 72, 460 N.W.2d 232 (1990)]

10. Seymour Roseman quit his job as an insurance agent after a company investigation found money missing from his account. The Retail Credit Company credit report on him had this statement in it: "We have handled [the investigation] at the home office in Boston and find that Roseman was employed as a debit agent [for the insurance company]. He resigned due to discovery of discrepancies in his accounts amounting to $314.84. This was all repaid by Roseman. His production in 1970, 1971, and 1972 was above average, and in 1973 and 1974, it was below average. This was the extent of the information available from [the insurance company] due to strict company policy." Roseman asked the credit company to check the accuracy of this information. The

credit company did, confirmed its accuracy, and refused to remove the information from his credit history. He sued under the Fair Credit Reporting Act, claiming his rights had been violated. What was the result? [*Roseman* v. *Retail Credit Company,* 428 F.Supp. 643 (E.D.Pa. 1977)]

11. How could more cooperative private safety efforts be encouraged? Do we want firms in the same industry to act together to work for safer products by using industry safety standards? How about industry standards for deceptive practices?

12. Trade regulation rules exist primarily to make it easier for the FTC to sue companies that are engaging in practices that the FTC does not like. Once a rule is implemented, all firms covered by it are "on notice" of the standard. Some have claimed that such rules are bad because they tend to set the industry practices to protect existing firms, discouraging innovation by would-be competitors. Does this make sense?

13. There has been discussion about forcing credit card issuers (banks that issue cards such as Visa and Mastercard) to charge lower rates of interest on charges that are carried forward. It is claimed that a 19 percent annual rate of interest (or something close to that) is too high, given other interest rates, such as mortgages at, say, 9 percent. It is also claimed that the rate should be kept down because the credit card companies have gotten consumers "addicted" to the cards so they can sting them with high rates for which there are no alternatives. What do you think of these arguments? Since banking is quite competitive, what explains the high rates on credit cards?

■ ETHICS QUESTIONS

14. The FDA, FTC, or some other agency is proposing a regulation that would hurt the sales of one of your company's products. The agency believes that there is a health issue that it should address by the regulation, which you estimate will cost your company $20 million a year in sales and $2 million a year in profits. The three other firms in the industry that make a similar product will similarly be hurt. Your Washington representative tells you that if all four firms are willing to spend $5 million in lobbying efforts and campaign contributions, you will probably get a rider put on the agency annual appropriation bill that will kill the proposed regulation. All other firms agree to help foot the bill. This method of killing proposed regulations has been used by other firms and industries numerous times in the past. Should you pay to help get the regulation killed?

15. Advertisements that would produce a storm of protest in the United States for being sexist are very popular in other countries. For example, in Japan, wall calendars with pictures of nude women are issued by many major corporations, including Japan Air Lines. Similar calendars exist in the United States, but no major U.S. company would think of issuing one. In Japan, women's breasts, covered or not, are featured in ads for numerous products. When women are shown in ads for reasons other than their bodies, they tend to be doe-eyed and complacent. Ads showing women in competent roles are rare. When an American company sells in the Japanese market, does it have a duty to be nonsexist in its ads? If ads with nude women would increase the sales of U.S. computers in Japan compared to other types of ads, should those ads be used? Do American firms have a responsibility not only to avoid sexism but also to combat it by showing women in positive situations?

16. You own a large furniture and appliance store that sells primarily to low-income people. Your store offers credit to customers, including many who have trouble getting credit elsewhere. The prices you charge, credit rates you charge, and profits you earn are determined largely by the default rate of your credit customers. You have a debt collection department in your store instead of using a debt collection agency. You comply with all federal and state credit statutes. However, you have found that by being *very* aggressive in collecting on delinquent debts, you lower your losses. You use tactics that would violate the Fair Debt Collection Practices Act if it applied to your store. Should you use these tactics?

ANTITRUST LAW

CHAPTER 16

MANAGER'S
LEGAL CHALLENGE

The marketing of fashionable clothing is a highly competitive, multibillion-dollar-a-year industry. Brand name clothing companies such as Bill Blass and Liz Claiborne spend substantial sums to design new fashions, choose new fabrics, and put together new wardrobes. After much developmental work, the result is displayed at expensive fashion shows in an effort to attract buyers from department and clothing stores as well as to interest the public.

A problem that clothing marketers face is that the instant they show their new clothing at a show, imitators can copy the style and fabrics and produce knockoffs of the clothing at lower prices. Since the imitators do not incur the high developmental and marketing costs that the originators do, their costs are lower. Their products may use about the same quality of fabric so that product quality is good, or they can cut costs even further and use cheaper fabrics and cheaper production techniques but still produce a fashionable imitation. The imitators even use brand names and labels that play off the originators' names and label designs.

The actions of the imitators are legal. Unlike other inventions, fashions cannot be patented or copyrighted. Hence, fashion originators must find ways to protect their market share from the imitators. Some of these protections involve restraints of trade.

Among the arrangements used are exclusive dealers. Legal questions that managers of fashion producers must be able to answer are, Can we exclude retailers who also stock imitation knockoffs of our clothing lines? Can we require a retailer to carry our men's clothing even if it wants to carry only one line, such as our women's clothing? If a good dealer tells us we must stop selling our clothing to one of its competitors in its city or it will no longer buy from us, can we cut off its competitors? Can we agree with dealers about the retail prices to charge for our products?

In their efforts to protect investments within the limits of the law, managers in the fashion and other industries have been asking the courts to resolve these kinds of questions. As the courts have recognized the competitive benefits of several of these practices in question, antitrust law has become less rigidly applied. Managers have quickly embraced the legal challenge those changes have brought and have moved to implement new and increasingly more innovative strategies to protect their investments. In many instances, those legal strategies would previously have been found illegal by the courts. This chapter looks at some tactics that are legal, some that are illegal, and some that fall in as yet unresolved areas of antitrust.

As far back as the 1500s, the courts in England refused to enforce contracts designed to eliminate competitors. This common law tradition has been maintained in the United States. As was noted in the chapter on contract law, the courts do not enforce contracts that are contrary to public policy. The courts held contracts in restraint of trade to be against public policy long before Congress enacted the antitrust statutes. However, before the statutes were enacted, there were no formal prohibitions on attempts by competitors to work together to *restrain competition* and *injure competitors*. As we will see, the lack of specificity in the antitrust statutes has required the federal courts to determine what really constitutes antitrust law. The Department of Justice and the Federal Trade Commission also play important roles by determining which business activities the government will attack under the antitrust law. Antitrust law, therefore, refers to the antitrust statutes, the interpretation of the statutes by the courts, and the enforcement policies of the administrative agencies. This chapter reviews the antitrust statutes and looks at how antitrust law is applied to both horizontal and vertical business arrangements.

ANTITRUST COMMON LAW

Before the various antitrust statutes were enacted, the U.S. courts had to rely on the common law in dealing with anticompetitive behavior. The principles and rules generally applied by the courts were derived from English legal theory. The American common law disapproved of business practices or agreements that were believed to restrain trade. A practice or agreement restrains trade when it prevents competition.

The common law cases of the nineteenth century did not hold all restraints of trade to be illegal—only those considered to be unreasonable. The courts would refuse to enforce private agreements to restrain trade. Although the courts, as in the *Craft* v. *McConoughy* decision, refused to enforce anticompetitive agreements before passage of the antitrust laws, little could be done to prevent such activities. That is, as long as the parties to an agreement to restrain trade got along, the restraint was not likely to get into the courts.

CRAFT v. McCONOUGHY

Illinois Supreme Court
79 Ill. 346 (1875)

Case Background
The four grain merchants of Rochelle, Illinois, agreed by contract in 1869 to carry on business as usual, except that they would divide up the market and fix prices. One merchant died, and his son who took over the business refused to go along with the other merchants. The others sued him, claiming that he, as the operator of the business, was bound by the contract to which his father had agreed.

Case Decision
The court refused to enforce the contract, ruling in favor of the son. The court stated that the purpose of the contract was restraint of trade, which has long been held to be against public policy. As such, the contract was illegal and void. The court threw the case out, holding that free competition was in the public interest.

Managerial Considerations
Today, no one would risk bringing such a case to court, since it would expose all the parties to public and private antitrust liability. In a case like this, where the parties involved had raised prices by their collusion, they could be held responsible for treble damages to everyone in a class action lawsuit. Besides the legal liability, companies involved in illegal activities suffer from bad publicity that injures their reputations and hurts future business.

THE ANTITRUST STATUTES

The growth of large corporations in the late nineteenth century led to calls for more constraints on business behavior than existed under the common law. The result was the passage of federal antitrust legislation: the Sherman Act, the Clayton Act, and the Federal Trade Commission (FTC) Act (excerpted in Appendix C). These statutes are broadly written. The result has been that except for some actions that are clearly illegal under the statutes, it has been left largely to the federal courts to determine how the laws will be applied in practice.

THE SHERMAN ACT

The *Sherman Antitrust Act* was passed by Congress in 1890 in response to the general unpopularity of the giant industrial organizations that arose out of the Industrial Revolution. The most famous of the time was the Standard Oil Trust, in reference to which the word *antitrust* was coined. Sponsors of the Act regarded it as a way to reduce concerns that Congress was dominated by large business interests.

The major sections of the Sherman Act are so broad that one could find almost any business activity to be illegal. It has fallen to the courts to decide what is in fact illegal under the two major sections of the Act:

Sec. 1: Every contract, combination in the form of trust or otherwise, or conspiracy, in restraint of trade or commerce among the several States, or with foreign nations, is hereby declared to be illegal.

Sec. 2: Every person who shall monopolize, or attempt to monopolize, or combine or conspire with any other person or persons, to monopolize any part of the trade or commerce among the several States, or with foreign nations, shall be deemed guilty of a felony.

■ THE CLAYTON ACT

Enacted in 1914, the *Clayton Act* was intended to supplement the coverage of the Sherman Act. In large measure, the Clayton Act was enacted in response to the Supreme Court's early interpretations of the Sherman Act, which limited its application.

Supporters of the Clayton Act wanted the government to have the ability to attack a business practice early in its use to prevent a firm from becoming a monopoly. The most important sections of the Clayton Act are the following:

> Sec. 2: It shall be unlawful for any person engaged in commerce, . . . either directly or indirectly, to discriminate in price between different purchasers of commodities of like grade and quality, where either or any of the purchases involved in such discrimination are in commerce . . . within the United States . . . and where the effect of such discrimination may be substantially to lessen competition or tend to create a monopoly in any line of commerce, or to injure, destroy, or prevent competition . . . [*This section was added by the Robinson-Patman Act of 1936 and restricts price discrimination.*]
>
> Sec. 3: It shall be unlawful for any person engaged in commerce . . . to lease or make a sale . . . or fix a price charged therefore, or discount from, or rebate upon, such price, on the condition . . . that the lessee or purchaser thereof shall not use or deal in the goods . . . or other commodities of a competitor or competitors of the lessor or seller, where the effect . . . may be to substantially lessen competition or tend to create a monopoly in any line of commerce. [*This is the restriction on tying sales and exclusive dealing.*]
>
> Sec. 7: No corporation engaged in commerce shall acquire, directly or indirectly, the whole or any part of the stock or other share capital and no corporation . . . shall acquire the whole or any part of the assets of another corporation engaged also in commerce, where in any line of commerce in any section of the country, the effect of such acquisition may be substantially to lessen competition, or to tend to create a monopoly. [*This prevents mergers with or acquisitions of competitors.*]
>
> Sec. 8: No person at the same time shall be a director in any two or more corporations . . . if such corporations are or shall have been theretofore, by virtue of their business and location of operation, competitors, so that the elimination of competition by agreement between them would constitute a violation of any of the provisions of the antitrust laws. [*This is the restriction on interlocking directorates.*]

■ THE FEDERAL TRADE COMMISSION ACT

In 1914, Congress also enacted the *Federal Trade Commission Act*, which established the FTC as an agency empowered to investigate and enforce violations of the antitrust laws. Although the majority of the Act provides for the structure, powers, and procedures of the FTC, it does provide a major substantive addition to antitrust law:

> Sec. 5: Unfair methods of competition in or affecting commerce, and unfair or deceptive acts or practices in commerce, are hereby declared unlawful.

The *unfair methods of competition* referred to in the FTC Act have been interpreted by the courts as any business activity that may tend to create a monopoly by unfairly eliminating or excluding competitors from the marketplace.

EXEMPTIONS FROM AND ENFORCEMENT OF THE ANTITRUST LAWS

Not all businesses or business activities are subject to the antitrust laws. In many cases, successful lobbying of Congress resulted in statutory exemptions from antitrust scrutiny. Those who are subject to the antitrust laws face a variety of penalties in cases brought by private parties or by the government.

EXEMPTIONS

The justifications typically provided for exemptions are that the business is regulated by some other government agency or that the business requires protection from competition based on some other public policy rationale. The following activities and businesses are provided exemptions:

- The Clayton Act exempts nonprofit and certain agricultural or horticultural organizations. Extensions have been made to cover agricultural, fishing, and some other cooperatives.
- The Interstate Commerce Act regulates motor, rail, and ship common carriers (means of public transport). Generally, if the Interstate Commerce Commission (ICC) approves the actions of these businesses, the businesses are exempt from the antitrust laws. However, when the activities involved are not or would not be approved by the ICC, the government can take action. One example would be a conspiracy among truck freight carriers to set rates. Similarly, the Shipping Act defers to the Federal Maritime Commission in regulating water carriers of freight. Certain aspects of air transportation are regulated by the Federal Aviation Administration (FAA) and by the Department of Transportation (DOT).
- The Export Trading Company Act allows a seller or group of sellers to receive a certificate from the Department of Commerce and the Department of Justice allowing limited antitrust immunity for the purpose of export trade. For example, a group of domestic producers may be allowed to join together to enhance their ability to sell their products in other countries.
- Subject to approval by the Attorney General, bank mergers are exempt.
- The Parker doctrine allows state governments to restrict competition in industries such as public utilities like cable television, professional services like nursing or dog grooming, and public transportation like taxicabs.

- The McCarran-Ferguson Act exempts the business of insurance from federal antitrust laws, so long as the states adequately regulate insurance.

- Under the Noerr-Pennington doctrine, lobbying to influence a legislature or an agency is not illegal. This is because the First Amendment to the Constitution gives individuals the right to petition their government, even if their purpose in doing so is anticompetitive.

- Certain activities of labor unions are exempt from the antitrust laws because the National Labor Relations Act favors and protects collective bargaining to fix wages and conditions of employment.

■ ENFORCEMENT

The antitrust laws we are about to review in detail may be enforced by various parties. Private parties—individuals and businesses—have the right to sue alleged violators and may seek damages and other remedies discussed below. The majority of antitrust suits are such private actions. The Antitrust Division of the Justice Department brings criminal antitrust prosecutions. For a civil lawsuit under the Sherman Act or Clayton Act, a choice must be made as to whether the Justice Department or the FTC will bring the case. The agencies have agreed to divide jurisdiction by industry but may consult on individual matters to decide which agency will handle a particular case.

Sherman Act.   Violations of the Sherman Act carry the most severe penalties of the antitrust statutes:

- Violations of Sections 1 and 2 of the Sherman Act are *criminal felonies.* Individuals found guilty of violating the Act face up to three years in prison, a fine of $100,000, or both. Corporations found guilty can be fined up to $1 million. Criminal cases are brought by the Antitrust Division of the U.S. Department of Justice.

- Private parties or the government can seek injunctive relief under the Act in a civil proceeding. An *injunction* is an order preventing the defendant (the party who may have violated the Act) from continuing the challenged behavior.

- Private parties who have been harmed by a violation of the Sherman Act can sue for *treble damages;* if they win, they get three times their actual money damages, plus court costs and attorney's fees.

Clayton Act.   Individuals and corporations violating the Clayton Act face penalties different from those provided by the Sherman Act. While the Department of Justice and private parties may initiate civil proceedings, the normal procedure has been for the FTC, which shares jurisdiction with the Justice Department in Clayton Act matters, to issue cease and desist orders, prohibiting further violation of the law by a specific party. The FTC has the authority to investigate suspect business dealings, hold hearings (rather than trials), and issue an administrative order approved in federal court that requires a party to discontinue or modify certain business acts.

Only when these orders are ignored is the firm or individual exposed to criminal sanctions.

FTC Act.   Violation of this statute carries a variety of penalties, ranging from an order preventing a planned merger to substantial civil penalties. The Sherman Act's prohibition of attempts to monopolize can overlap the FTC Act's unfair competition ban. Since, unlike the Justice Department, the FTC is not required to initiate the prosecution of alleged violators through the federal court system, the effect of this overlap is to give the government administrative jurisdiction to proceed against potential Sherman Act violations without the more difficult task of having to prove a criminal violation.

■ REMEDIES AVAILABLE

An action to halt conduct that appears to be an antitrust violation can be brought either by a private plaintiff or by the government. The federal courts can provide a number of remedies including the following:

- Restrain a company or individuals from certain conduct.
- Force a company to divest a subsidiary.
- Use company assets to form another company to compete with the original company.
- Force a company to let others use its patents (licensing).
- Cancel or modify existing business contracts.

Incentives to Sue.   The incentive to bring antitrust suits was increased by the 1989 Supreme Court decision in *California* v. *ARC America Corp.* The Court held that state antitrust statutes can allow collection of treble damages by indirect purchasers. Legal experts expect a rash of class action lawsuits by consumers or on behalf of consumers by private attorneys or by state attorneys general.

The federal antitrust statutes mandate treble damages for direct purchasers. Antitrust statutes in many states allow indirect buyers—which can be a large class of individuals—to sue for treble damages. Hence, class action suits can be brought where each indirect buyer suffers a small loss but the loss suffered by all consumers is large. For example, 100,000 consumers may buy a product at retail that had been involved in price fixing at the wholesale level. Each consumer pays $3 too much at retail because the retailer paid the price-fixing wholesaler $3 too much for each product. The state laws allow the consumers to sue the wholesaler for treble damages ($3 $\times$ 100,000 $\times$ 3 = $900,000). Since the wholesaler is also liable for treble damages to the retailer, the wholesaler could possibly pay sextuple damages.

The Supreme Court gave a boost to efforts by state attorneys general to enforce antitrust statutes in *California* v. *American Stores Co.* (1990). In that decision, the FTC had approved a merger of two grocery store chains in California. After the conclusion of antitrust review by federal officials, California filed suit, claiming that the merger violated the Sherman and

Clayton Acts by damaging actual and potential competition in the grocery market in California. The Supreme Court upheld the right of the state to bring the action despite the completion of the federal review of the merger and upheld the right of the federal district court to block the merger until the challenge to the merger was reviewed. Like *California* v. *ARC America Corp.*, this decision may result in substantially more antitrust suits being brought by state officials, which may change the landscape of antitrust law by the year 2000.

INTERNATIONAL ASPECTS | **ANTITRUST ENFORCEMENT**

All companies are subject to the antitrust laws of the country in which they are located regardless of where the firm has its headquarters. That is, an American firm with an office in Japan is subject to the rules of the Japan Fair Trade Commission, even if all of the company's employees in Japan are U.S. citizens.

Controversy has occurred over the claim by the U.S. Department of Justice and the FTC that they have jurisdiction over antitrust violations that occur overseas and affect U.S. markets, even if the violations do not break the antitrust law of the nation in which they occur. An American company with operations in Germany may be accused of conspiring with German companies, in Germany, to monopolize some aspect of the U.S. market in which the companies operate. The activity does not violate German antitrust laws but may violate U.S. antitrust laws. The American antitrust authorities claim that they can gather documents overseas (enforce subpoenas) and prosecute the American company in U.S. court for the actions that occurred in Germany. European nations do not claim that their antitrust authorities have such an international reach over potential defendants. Hence, managers must be consistently aware not only of the differences in laws in various countries but also of the differences in the laws' enforcement.

THE COURTS AND ANTITRUST ANALYSIS

The Supreme Court has noted explicitly that antitrust law is dynamic—it changes as business and society change and as more is learned about the costs and benefits to society from different business agreements, arrangements, and activities. One question the courts must address is whether, as a matter of policy, a certain business practice will be held to be per se illegal or whether a rule of reason approach can be applied. The courts have also usually classified activities challenged under the antitrust laws as horizontal or vertical restraints of trade.

▪ PER SE RULE

A *per se rule* means that a certain business agreement, arrangement, or activity will automatically be held to be illegal by the courts. The agreement, arrangement, or activity is per se illegal because the courts believe that its use by a business will always result in a substantial restraint of trade. In discussing the notion of per se illegality, the Supreme Court in *Northern Pacific Railway Co.* v. *United States* (1958) stated that there are certain activities that

> . . . because of their pernicious effect on competition and lack of any redeeming virtue are conclusively presumed to be unreasonable and therefore illegal without elaborate inquiry as to the precise harm they have caused or business excuse for their use.

RULE OF REASON

A *rule of reason* approach means that the court will look at the facts surrounding an agreement, arrangement, or other restraint before deciding whether it helps or hurts competition. In reaching its decision, the court will consider such factors as the history of the restraint, the business reasons behind the restraint, the restraining business's position in its industry, and the structure of the industry. In *Chicago Board of Trade* v. *United States* (1918), Supreme Court Justice Louis Brandeis provided the following classic statement on the rule of reason approach:

> [T]he legality of an agreement or regulation cannot be determined by so simple a test, as whether it restrains competition. Every agreement concerning trade, every regulation of trade, restrains. To bind, to restrain, is of their very essence. The true test of legality is whether the restraint imposed is such as merely regulates and perhaps thereby promotes competition or whether it is such as may suppress or even destroy competition. To determine that question the court must ordinarily consider the facts peculiar to the business to which the restraint is applied; its condition before and after the restraint was imposed; the nature of the restraint and its effect, actual and probable. The history of the restraint, the evil believed to exist, the reason for adopting the particular remedy, the purpose or end sought to be attained, are all relevant facts. This is not because a good intention will save an otherwise objectionable regulation or the reverse; but because knowledge of intent may help the court to interpret facts and to predict consequences.

HORIZONTAL RESTRAINTS OF TRADE

When businesses at the same level of operation (such as retailers of a common product or producers of a raw material) come together (integrate) in some manner—through contract, merger, or conspiracy—they run the risk of being accused of creating a restraint of trade. A *horizontal restraint of trade* occurs when the businesses involved are on the same level of the market and generally in the same market. It is easy to visualize a horizontal arrangement among competitors by examining the diagram in Figure 16–1. For example, envision three manufacturers of sixty-watt light bulbs who agree to charge the same price for a bulb or who agree to split the market on a geographical basis.

The diagram could also show an arrangement among wholesalers or among retailers of a certain product. A collection of rival firms that come together by contract or other form of agreement in an attempt to restrain

FIGURE 16–1

Horizontal Business Arrangements

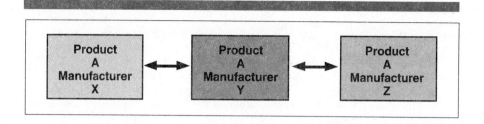

trade by restricting output and raising prices is called a *cartel*. The most famous cartel of our day is the Organization of Petroleum Exporting Countries (OPEC) cartel, the group of oil-producing nations that have banded together for the express purpose of controlling the output and raising the prices of crude oil. Since that cartel consists of sovereign nations, American antitrust laws do not affect it. When private firms in the United States attempt to form an industry cartel, however, they often will be subject to antitrust law.

■ VERTICAL RESTRAINTS OF TRADE

Vertical business arrangements concern relationships in the different stages of the production, distribution, and sale of the same product. It is easy to visualize a *vertical restraint of trade* by examining the diagram in Figure 16–2. For example, envision a manufacturer who imposes resale restrictions on the wholesalers, thereby controlling the wholesaler's resale price, the area of resale, or the wholesaler's customers. Since these arrangements may restrict competition, they may be challenged as being contrary to the goals of antitrust law.

A company that does more than one function internally, such as manufacturing and distribution, is not constrained by the antitrust laws. A

FIGURE 16–2

Vertical Business Relationships

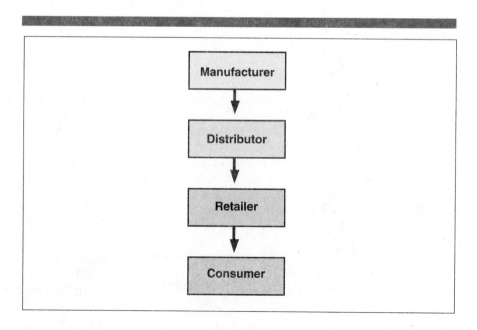

group of firms, however, doing business at different levels in a given product are prohibited from engaging in certain practices. Vertical restraints of trade often pose very subtle questions concerning their effects on consumer welfare and are the subject of vigorous debate.

FOREIGN COMPETITORS FACE JAPANESE DANGO SYSTEM | INTERNATIONAL ASPECTS

The Japan Fair Trade Commission has only recently held that the traditional *dango* system—or prior consultation among bidders on public works jobs—violates Japan's antitrust law. Foreign firms attempting to obtain a share of the construction market in Japan have contended that bid rigging of public works projects remains deeply rooted in Japanese construction. They claim that an alliance of politicians, bureaucrats, and competitors effectively keeps them out of the bidding for multibillion-dollar projects.

The *dango* system has rarely been challenged in Japan, because Japanese antitrust enforcement officials claim that any damage it may create is small. Since the maximum criminal penalty for violating antitrust law was about $37,000 in 1992, violations are of little consequence. In response to complaints, officials have said that there is little evidence of bribery and that the firms involved keep their profit margins small.

Recent evidence of huge payoffs by firms to politicians at the highest level have raised doubts about the claims that *dango* results only in an orderly rotation of contracts rather than a reduction in competition. It has been suggested that foreign firms willing to cooperate with existing competitors could be allowed to enter the system. However, U.S. managers must remember that American firms playing such games could risk prosecution in the United States even if the Japanese accepted the practice.

MERGERS

A *merger* involves two or more firms coming together to form a new firm. The combination can be created by one firm's acquiring all or part of the stock or the assets of another firm. A merger is termed a *horizontal merger* when the two firms were competitors before they merged (e.g., Texaco and Getty Oil). Largely because they frequently involve well-known businesses and thus attract public attention, the general public most often associates the term *antitrust* with merger cases. Merger cases, however, are relatively few in number, since most mergers do not pose antitrust concerns. In one of the most famous merger cases, *Standard Oil Company of New Jersey v. United States* (1911), where the Standard Oil Trust controlled 90 percent of the oil business in the United States, the Supreme Court established the rule of reason as the approach the courts will use in judging merger activities.

■ THE SUPREME COURT'S APPROACH TO MERGERS

Congress did not provide guidance on what would constitute monopolistic behavior in the antitrust statutes. Thus, in using the Sherman and Clayton Acts to control monopolies, the courts must appraise market structures and monopolistic behavior. Measuring monopoly power, however, is not an easy and uncomplicated task. An ideal measure would involve a comparison of prices, outputs, and profits of firms in an industry under competition with those under monopoly control. But such a comparison does not lend itself to measurement. An important decision on mergers is the Supreme Court's *Brown Shoe* decision in 1962, which provided guidance by noting some factors that the courts and antitrust authorities should use in merger cases.

BROWN SHOE COMPANY v. UNITED STATES

United States Supreme Court
370 U.S. 294, 82 S.Ct. 1502 (1962)

Case Background
Brown Shoe, which specialized in children's shoes and was the country's third largest shoe retailer, wanted to merge with Kinney Shoe. Kinney Shoe was the eighth largest shoe company and tended to specialize in adult shoes. Merged, they would have five percent of the footwear market. The Justice Department asked the U.S. Supreme Court to block the merger as a violation of Section 7 of the Clayton Act.

Case Decision
The Court prohibited the merger, holding that it would reduce competition. The Court found that the relevant market was shoes, but it also looked at the market for children's, women's, and men's shoes and examined the market share

the two companies had in a number of small towns. While five percent of the U.S. market was not much of a threat to competition nationally, competition was negatively affected in individual cities where the joint market share was over 20 percent. Further, the Court claimed that this merger would spur other competitors to merge, leading to less competition and limiting the ability of small, less efficient firms to compete with the large firms.

Managerial Considerations
While the mergers of well-known companies get the most press, they often are not subject to antitrust attack. The Court now exhibits less concern about some aspects of mergers, especially mergers that do not show evidence of monopolizing a specific market. Some mergers involving small firms are challenged, however, because they will give a firm a large market share in a specialized market or in a specific city or region.

■ DETERMINING A FIRM'S MARKET POWER

As the Supreme Court noted in *Brown Shoe,* the legality of a merger between two firms in an industry rests on whether "in any line of commerce in any section of the country, the effect of such acquisition may be substantially to lessen competition, or tend to create a monopoly." The phrase "in any line of commerce" refers to a particular *product market*. The phrase "in any section of the country" has reference to a *geographic market*. Therefore, in determining the *relevant market* from which to calculate a firm's market share, the court must take into account the appropriate product and geographic markets.

After determining the relevant market, a firm's market share can then be determined by dividing the firm's total sales by the total sales within that market. In a merger case, the court will often consider whether the combined market share of the two merging firms exceeds some minimum market share and will therefore "substantially . . . lessen competition" within the relevant market. The determination of the relevant market, however, is rarely straightforward. It may even include estimates of the likelihood of future or potential competitors.

Product Market.   In a competitive industry, there are enough producers that a single firm cannot affect the market for the products. One firm will not have sufficient market power to raise the price of its product without having customers purchase the lower priced products of its competitors. That is, in a competitive industry, each firm effectively provides a substitute product for the other firms in the industry. Conversely, a monopoly will exist when there is only one firm producing a product for which there is no reasonable substitute. The monopolist will be able to raise prices because customers will not have lower priced substitute products available.

Geographic Market.   Depending upon the nature of the product, the geographic market could be local, regional, national, or international. In its *Brown Shoe* decision, the Supreme Court looked to a geographic market that included cities "with a population exceeding 10,000 and its immediate contiguous surrounding territory in which both Brown and Kinney sold shoes at retail through stores they either owned or controlled." In its *Standard Oil* decision, the Court determined that the geographic market was the entire nation. As a rule, the geographic market is the area in which the firms involved can be expected to conduct their business activities.

The geographic market is influenced by several factors. For sellers of products, the geographic area is most significantly influenced by transportation costs. Heavy, bulky products, such as cement, tend to compete in local markets; lighter, high-value products, such as tires, can be shipped nationwide. In the case of tires, because shipping costs represent a small percentage of total costs, the product can be shipped to a larger market.

The buyers of a product can also influence the determination of the geographic market. As a rule, the geographic market is limited to the area where consumers can reasonably be expected to make purchases. Consumers are generally more willing to search a larger market if the product being purchased is expensive and purchased infrequently. For example, a corporation is more likely to search the entire nation for the best price on expensive industrial equipment than on general office supplies. Industrial machinery will likely be judged as having a nationwide geographic market, while office supplies will have local markets.

Potential Competition.   Are two firms in competition with each other if they do not offer the same product to the same consumers? Ordinarily one thinks of competitors as offering similar products in the same market area. If the companies do not compete in this sense, should the courts be concerned about a merger? The Supreme Court has stated that the possibility that the two companies are *potential competitors* may be enough to stop a merger.

For example, in *United States* v. *El Paso Natural Gas* (1964), a gas pipeline company with a large share of the natural gas market in California wanted to merge with a pipeline company that operated in the northwest. The Court blocked the merger because the possibility that the northwest company could move into California served as a check on El Paso's operations in California. The Court wanted El Paso to have the threat of strong potential competition that would be eliminated by the merger.

■ Defenses: When Mergers are Allowed

The Court in *Brown Shoe* noted that if one of the firms involved in the merger had been facing bankruptcy or other serious financial circumstances that threatened the firm, the Court might have allowed the merger. The Court was referring to the *failing firm defense*. According to the Court in *International Shoe* v. *Federal Trade Commission* (1930):

> [I]f a corporation with resources so depleted and the prospect of rehabilitation so remote that it face[s] the grave probability of a business failure with resulting loss to its shareholders and injury to the communities where its plants were operated, . . . the purchase of its stock by a competitor (there being no other prospective purchaser), not with a purpose to lessen competition, but to facilitate the accumulated business of the purchaser and with the effect of mitigating seriously injurious consequences otherwise probable, is not in contemplation of law prejudicial to the public and does not substantially lessen competition or restrain commerce within the intent of the Clayton Act.

The failing-firm defense was created by the courts and not provided by statute. To use the defense to avoid violating Section 7 of the Clayton Act, the merging firms must establish that

1. The firm being acquired is not likely to survive without the merger.

2. Either the firm has no other prospective buyers or, if there are other buyers, the acquiring firm will affect competition the least.

3. All other alternatives for saving the firm have been tried and have not succeeded.

Considering Business Realities.   The Court weighs economic evidence and, as a result, has decided that some mergers are not harmful to consumers. In the *General Dynamics* decision, the Court allowed a merger of two coal-producing companies, one of which was a subsidiary of General Dynamics, a large diversified corporation. The fact that one of the merging companies was very large was not decisive, since it did not have monopoly power in the coal industry.

UNITED STATES v. GENERAL DYNAMICS CORPORATION

United States Supreme Court
415 U.S. 486, 94 S.Ct. 1186 (1974)

Case Background
General Dynamics, a large conglomerate firm, owned, among other things, a deep-mining coal operation. It bought a strip-mining coal operation. Together the two operations had 22 percent of the coal sales in Illinois. The government claimed that the acquisition was illegal under Section 7 of the Clayton Act. The district court ruled against the government, which appealed to the Supreme Court.

Case Decision
The Court examined the details of the business in question and found that the coal market was generally declining, most of the coal produced was sold on long-term contracts to utilities for producing electricity, and the two mining methods of operation were very different. The merger was allowed to stand under rule of reason analysis, which found that the effect on competition was too small to prevent the merger.

(continued)

Managerial Considerations

The courts today generally use such a rule of reason analysis in looking at the realities of the market. When markets are declining, mergers are less likely to be opposed. Even if the two companies produce the same product, the use of different methods or sources of production by the two companies may favor the companies merging. Companies may not sell head on in daily competition but rather sell output in long-term agreements to large, sophisticated buyers. The Court also considers the difficulty that potential competitors have getting into an industry—the easier an industry is to enter, the less concern there is about the negative effects of a merger.

HORIZONTAL PRICE FIXING

The Sherman Act prohibits "every contract, combination or conspiracy, in restraint of trade or commerce among the several states, or with foreign nations." Thus, when firms selling the same product agree to fix prices, the agreement will almost certainly violate the Sherman Act. One question the Supreme Court has had to decide, as a matter of policy, is whether price fixing is per se illegal or whether a rule of reason may be applied.

■ PER SE RULE IN PRICE FIXING

The Supreme Court has ruled that horizontal price fixing is per se illegal. One of the classic antitrust cases condemning direct price fixing as an unreasonable per se restraint of trade under the Sherman Act is *United States* v. *Trenton Potteries Company* (1927). In that case, firms that produced 82 percent of the bathroom fixtures in the United States got together to control sales and fix prices. They claimed that since the prices they set were reasonable, their agreement should be left alone. The Supreme Court disagreed and upheld their convictions.

Plain old price fixing—where competitors get together and set prices—is very likely to be per se illegal—there is no defense for it. In *Trenton Potteries,* the Court held that the ability of a firm or a group of firms to fix prices involved the power to control the market. Ultimately, firms with the power to fix even reasonable prices would be able to use that power to fix unreasonable prices.

The Supreme Court again had the opportunity to discuss price fixing in 1982 in the *Arizona* v. *Maricopa County Medical Society* case. Two medical societies formed two foundations for the purpose of promoting fee-for-service medicine and to provide the community with a competitive alternative to existing health insurance plans. Doctors joining the foundations had to agree to not charge more than the maximum fees for medical services set by the foundations. The state of Arizona sued, claiming that the arrangement was a violation of Section 1 of the Sherman Act. The Supreme Court agreed, holding that the maximum-fee arrangements are price-fixing agreements and are per se illegal.

■ THE RULE OF REASON IN PRICE-FIXING CASES

It is undoubtedly true that when competitors collude to fix prices to gain a monopoly, the per se illegal rule is likely to be applied. However, the Supreme Court has used a rule of reason approach in cases involving certain types of price fixing. The door to the application of the rule of reason began to open with the Supreme Court's decision in *Broadcast Music, Inc.* v. *CBS* (1981). CBS sued Broadcast Music, Inc. (BMI), the American Society of Composers, Authors and Publishers (ASCAP), and their members and affiliates, claiming that the blanket license to copyrighted music at fees set by them constitutes illegal price fixing under the antitrust laws.

Tens of thousands of corporations, authors, and composers own copyrights on millions of musical compositions. BMI and ASCAP serve as clearinghouses for the copyright owners. They operate primarily through blanket licenses that give radio stations, television broadcasters, and others the right to perform the compositions owned by the members of ASCAP or BMI as often as they desire for a stated sum. The fees for usage are usually a percentage of the licensees' total revenues or a flat dollar amount. This system emerged because it would be almost impossible for each music copyright owner to contract with each potential user of his or her music and to monitor the use of the music. CBS claimed that ASCAP and BMI are monopolies and that the blanket license is illegal price fixing.

The Supreme Court held that the blanket license issued by ASCAP and BMI does not constitute per se illegal price fixing. Justice White, speaking for an 8–1 majority, held that a rule of reason had to be applied. The Court noted the extensive industry experience in this method of organization and did not find evidence that it hindered trade. Rather, the Court found that this method of organization helped to monitor and enforce proper copyright use, which would be very difficult for individual copyright owners to do. Over the years, it had been demonstrated that other contractual arrangements could exist within the industry, so it did not appear that BMI and ASCAP were excluding possible forms of competition for their services and method of pricing. The Court made it clear that most price-fixing activities would still be per se illegal. Others would be viewed under a rule of reason approach.

The Supreme Court made the sports pages in 1984 when it announced that under a rule of reason analysis, the National Collegiate Athletic Association (NCAA) could not fix prices colleges receive for appearances their football teams make on television.

NATIONAL COLLEGIATE ATHLETIC ASSOCIATION v. BOARD OF REGENTS OF UNIVERSITY OF OKLAHOMA

United States Supreme Court
468 U.S. 85, 104 S.Ct. 2948 (1984)

Case Background
For several decades, the National Collegiate Athletic Association (NCAA) contracted with the television networks for the televising of all college football games involving NCAA members. NCAA-member colleges were paid fixed fees for these broadcasts and were limited in the number of times their games could be televised each year. This limited the appearances and revenues of more popular teams and provided more TV revenues to less popular teams. The universities of Oklahoma and Georgia sued the NCAA. The district court agreed with the universities that the NCAA was a cartel that fixed prices, limited output, and boycotted potential telecasters. The court of appeals agreed, holding that the NCAA television plan was per se illegal price fixing. The NCAA appealed to the U.S. Supreme Court.

(continued)

Case Decision

The Supreme Court agreed with the lower courts that the NCAA had violated the Sherman Act by restraining trade. The NCAA was illegally fixing prices and limiting output. Hence, universities cannot be prevented from making their own contracts for televised games. However, the Court noted that this case was decided under a rule of reason analysis, not by a per se rule. Since the NCAA engages in a number of legitimate activities, courts must study the particular circumstances to determine whether a challenged practice has the net effect of reducing competition.

Managerial Considerations

The courts are more likely to use the rule of reason when the question concerns the activities of a trade association than when it is an agreement between a few competitors. Professional or trade associations can exist for numerous purposes that involve price information, standard setting, and consumer information. Companies can join associations for voluntary industry standards and other benefits, such as some kinds of joint advertising. Thus, in developing and implementing a particular pricing or marketing strategy, managers should consider the advantages offered by cooperating with a professional or trade association—particularly if the strategy has antitrust implications.

The Supreme Court again used a rule of reason analysis in a 1986 decision in *Matsushita Elec. Indus. Co.* v. *Zenith Radio.* The case involved alleged price fixing by Japanese television manufacturers. The Japanese were sued by American television manufacturers for supposedly having conspired for twenty years to sell Japanese televisions in the United States at below-market prices with the intent to drive out the American producers. The Supreme Court agreed with the district court that the case should be dismissed on the basis of a lack of economic evidence. The Court noted that it was not likely that a group of manufacturers would fix prices below market levels and lose money for twenty years. Since that economic assertion made little sense and there was no other acceptable evidence of a conspiracy presented, the Court dismissed the complaint under a rule of reason.

EXCHANGES OF INFORMATION

One problem in antitrust law is deciding whether the trading of information among businesses helps or restrains the competitive process. Some business information is collected and disseminated by the government, but most exchanges are performed by private organizations, such as trade associations composed of firms in the same line of business. If each business knows its competitors' sales, production, planned or actual capacities, cost accounting, quality standards, innovations, and research developments, is competition enhanced, or is the information likely to be used to restrain trade? Does such information encourage better products and reduce waste and inefficiency?

■ PURPOSE OF PRICE INFORMATION CONSIDERED

The *Goldfarb* case hints that exchange of information will be allowed to proceed unless it can be shown that there is injury to consumers. Exchanges of information not used to fix prices or otherwise restrain trade are likely to be allowed.

The *Goldfarb* case is also a landmark antitrust case because of its attack on price setting by such professional groups as lawyers, who for years cloaked price fixing under the mantle of professional ethics and consumer protection. The result of *Goldfarb* and other holdings has been to increase the amount of price and service competition by lawyers and other professionals.

GOLDFARB v. VIRGINIA STATE BAR

United States Supreme Court
421 U.S. 773, 95 S.Ct. 2004 (1975)

Case Background
When the Goldfarbs bought a house in Virginia, they had to have a title search done on the home to obtain a mortgage and title insurance. The title search could be done only by a lawyer licensed in Virginia—a member of the Virginia State Bar. Every lawyer the Goldfarbs contacted charged at least the minimum fee listed in the fee schedule for legal services published and enforced by the bar. The Goldfarbs sued, claiming that the minimum fee schedule was price fixing. The bar claimed it was not subject to antitrust attack because the practice of law is a learned profession, not a trade or commerce covered by the Sherman Act.

The district court held that the bar was liable and enjoined the publication of the fee schedule. The court of appeals reversed, agreeing with the bar that the practice of law was a learned profession and not a trade or commerce as required by the Sherman Act. Goldfarb appealed to the Supreme Court.

Case Decision
The Supreme Court reversed the court of appeal's decision, ruling that the price schedule published by the bar was price fixing under a rule of reason analysis. The Court noted that while publishing price information was acceptable, here the bar was fixing minimum fees and punishing lawyers who did not charge at least those prices.

Managerial Considerations
Professional associations, such as groups of physicians, accountants, and managerial consultants, may not dictate fees. The same is true for trade associations made up of individuals and companies that provide various services. Associations may publish information about prices charged for services, but they may not attempt to use the information to influence the fees that members charge. Managers should be aware that it is clearly illegal to make membership in an organization dependent on following price schedules.

The Supreme Court again considered the issue of the sharing of information by competitors in a 1978 decision, *United States* v. *United States Gypsum Co.* Six major producers of gypsum were charged with conspiracy to fix prices. One alleged action that made the conspiracy effective was that competing manufacturers called each other to determine the price actually being offered on gypsum products to a certain customer. That is, a buyer would tell Company B that Company A had offered to sell a certain quantity of gypsum board at a certain price. Company B would have to beat that price to get the buyer's business. Company B would call Company A to confirm the offer and make sure the buyer was telling the truth. The gypsum companies defended the practice as a good faith effort to meet competition.

On this aspect of the case, the Court said that a rule of reason may be applied. In general, the practice was probably not defensible. The Court said:

As an abstract proposition, resort to interseller verification as a means of checking the buyer's reliability seems a possible solution to the seller's plight [of dealing with inaccurate information from buyers], but careful examination reveals serious problems with the practice.

The Court said that in a concentrated industry, an agreement among competitors to exchange price information would most likely help to stabilize prices and so could not be justified. However, the Court did not apply a per se rule against such price information exchanges. Instead, it warned that the exchanges would be looked at closely and would probably be allowed in only limited circumstances.

CONSPIRACY TO RESTRAIN INFORMATION

Although the courts have indicated that it is legal to share price information in an open manner and it is illegal to share information secretly among competitors or for the purpose of constructing a common price list for competitors, it may also be illegal to band together to restrain certain information.

In the 1986 Supreme Court decision *Federal Trade Commission* v. *Indiana Federation of Dentists*, the Court held that the FTC was justified in attacking the policy of an Indiana dentists' organization that required members to withhold X rays from dental insurance companies. Insurance companies sometimes required dentists to submit patient X rays to help evaluate patients' claims for insurance benefits. The X rays were intended to help eliminate insurance fraud and to make sure dentists did not prescribe unnecessary dental work. The FTC attack on this policy was upheld under a rule of reason analysis that showed the dentists' policy to be a conspiracy in restraint of trade. The Court noted that no procompetitive reason for the rule against providing X rays was found. However, the Court noted that if the state of Indiana were to sanction the action of the dentists, the practice would be legal. State regulations can provide immunity from antitrust attack if the state actively regulates the service in question.

HORIZONTAL MARKET DIVISIONS

A horizontal market division occurs when firms competing at the same level of business reach an agreement to divide the market on geographic or other terms. The effect of such an agreement is to eliminate competition among those firms. Firms that compete on a national market, for example, may reach an agreement to divide the national market into regional markets, with each firm being exclusively assigned to one region. Each firm can then exercise monopoly power within its region.

Agreements intended to provide horizontal customer or territorial allocations are often held to violate antitrust law. When the agreement does not involve price fixing by the firms to the agreement, the case may be considered under a rule of reason; that is, the business agreement will be evaluated in light of its effect on consumer welfare. However, as its decision in *Sealy* reflects, the Supreme Court has tended to be more stringent in those cases involving common pricing by the firms to the agreement.

UNITED STATES v. SEALY, INC.

United States Supreme Court
388 U.S. 350, 87 S.Ct. 1847 (1967)

Case Background

Sealy was in the business of licensing independently owned and operated manufacturers of mattresses to make, according to specifications, and sell bedding products under the Sealy trade name. Sealy was controlled by about thirty manufacturer-licensees who set company policies for all Sealy licensees around the country. Each manufacturer was given an exclusive territory in which to sell Sealy products and was told what prices to charge for various Sealy products. The Justice Department sued, claiming that Sealy could not fix prices or allocate exclusive territories. The district court held that the common pricing practices and territorial divisions were per se illegal. Sealy appealed to the Supreme Court.

Case Decision

The Supreme Court agreed with the lower court that the price-fixing agreements were per se illegal. Because the territorial restrictions were enforced with the price fixing, they also were held to be per se illegal.

Managerial Considerations

There is little doubt that the price-fixing strategy undertaken by Sealy was illegal. To argue that the territorial restrictions were illegal, however, is considerably more difficult in today's antitrust environment. Still, the case illustrates that managers must examine marketing and pricing strategies very carefully—particularly when the two are as intricately tied together as they were in this case. Both the probabilities of an antitrust action being filed and of the company being able to defend itself successfully must be explicitly considered. As in other areas where the law is not clearly defined, the company that monitors its legal environment closely will best assess the probabilities that its strategy will or will not be attacked. Furthermore, if management closely monitors the legal environment, it may be able to alter an innovative marketing or pricing strategy, like that implemented by Sealy, to improve the strategy's acceptability to the antitrust community.

Sealy has been criticized by some observers. In *Sealy,* there is a form of business integration—numerous smaller firms banding together to produce a similar product with national recognition. The price fixing condemned by the Court as detrimental to consumer welfare would not have been illegal had Sealy simply built its own factories around the country or, over time, merged with many smaller mattress makers. That would have resulted in one very large corporation making mattresses nationwide—and selling them at prices fixed by the executives of Sealy. Under the arrangement that existed, there were many small independent firms that could terminate their licenses with Sealy in favor of independent production or to work with another brand name.

As a result of the Court's holding, one way to avoid charges of contractual price fixing is to integrate business operations completely into one company. As the Supreme Court noted in the 1984 decision *Copperweld Corp.* v. *Independence Tube Corp.*, a company and its subsidiaries are incapable of conspiring with one another for purposes of monopolization activities, since there is only one entity.

VERTICAL PRICE FIXING

Vertical price fixing arrangements generally involve an agreement between a manufacturer, its wholesalers, distributors, or other suppliers, and the retailers who sell the product to consumers. As a rule, these arrangements are intended to control the price at which the product is sold to consumers.

In many instances, it is the retailers who approach the manufacturers and request the imposition of such a resale price maintenance agreement. In other instances, the manufacturer requires the wholesaler (supplier) to control the price being charged by the retailer. Agreements can call for the retailer to fix minimum or maximum prices.

■ RESALE PRICE MAINTENANCE

Resale price maintenance (RPM) involves an agreement between a manufacturer, supplier, and retailers of a product whereby the retailers agree to sell the product at not less than a minimum price or at a fixed price. The purpose of such an arrangement is to prevent retailers from cutting the price of a brand name product. Although manufacturers contend such arrangements make product distributions more efficient, antitrust authorities have argued that in most instances they are an illegal restraint of trade. *Dr. Miles Medical Company* (1911) is a leading decision and still provides the legal standard generally followed. In *Dr. Miles,* the Supreme Court ruled that once a manufacturer or supplier has sold a product to the retailer, it cannot fix or otherwise dictate the price the retailer will charge consumers.

DR. MILES MEDICAL COMPANY v. JOHN D. PARK & SONS COMPANY

United States Supreme Court
220 U.S. 373, 31 S.Ct. 376 (1911)

Case Background
Dr. Miles Medical Company made medicines with secret and patented formulas. The medicines were sold to wholesalers who then resold them to drug stores. Dr. Miles set the prices the wholesalers and retailers were to charge at resale. Those companies that refused to comply with the set prices were cut off from further sales. This practice, known as resale price maintenance or vertical price fixing, was challenged by wholesalers and retailers who claimed they had the right to resell the products at any price they wanted. The federal district court and the U.S. Court of Appeals found for the wholesalers and retailers, and Dr. Miles appealed to the U.S. Supreme Court.

Case Decision
The Supreme Court held that under the Sherman Act, resale price maintenance is per se illegal. The Court stated

that the fact that the products were patented did not matter to the result. When a product is sold, the seller cannot attach conditions to the sale concerning the resale of the product that have anticompetitive effects, such as fixing the resale price.

Managerial Considerations
In this case, the management of Dr. Miles implemented a strategic decision to control the retail price of its products. Management's apparent intent in fixing the retail price was to allow the more prestigious drug stores to handle the company's products profitably and keep them from being driven from the market by larger, discount drug stores. Management believed that the integrity of the company's product would be better protected if sold by the prestigious drug stores. Although management very likely understood that such price fixing is illegal, it greatly overestimated the weight the courts would give to the fact that it held patents on its products.

■ VERTICAL MAXIMUM PRICE FIXING

The Court extended its *Dr. Miles* decision in *Albrecht* v. *Herald Company* (1968). In *Albrecht,* the Court held that in addition to the *Dr. Miles* prohibitions against fixing minimum retail prices, a manufacturer or supplier may not fix maximum retail prices. Thus, price fixing in virtually any form will be held per se illegal.

The *Albrecht* decision is consistent with the 1982 Supreme Court decision in the *Arizona* v. *Maricopa County* case cited earlier. These cases make it clear that price fixing in either horizontal or vertical arrangements is likely to meet stiff resistance by the courts. Note, however, that firms that integrate vertically, say from producing through retailing, do not face any constraints on their abilities to fix prices, since all pricing is done within a single firm. That is, a firm such as Sears that is organized from production to retail can control its prices at all levels, unlike independent producers and retailers operating in the same markets.

VERTICAL NONPRICE RESTRAINTS

Manufacturers frequently impose nonprice restraints on their suppliers and retailers. Such vertical agreements and arrangements often take the form of territorial, locational, or customer restrictions on the sale of the manufacturer's products. Coca-Cola, Pepsico, and other soft drink companies, for example, set *territorial restrictions* on their bottlers. Each bottler is permitted to sell and deliver the product within its designated territory. Delivery outside that territory—that is, delivery in competition with another bottler—can bring about the revocation of the franchise agreement.

Locational restraints are a common vertical nonprice restraint among automobile manufacturers. Ford Motor Company, for example, grants dealership authorizations around the country that typically limit the dealer to selling Fords from a specific location. To obtain a dealership, an individual must agree to sell Fords only from that location.

Customer restrictions are typically imposed on suppliers by manufacturers in those situations where the manufacturer has elected to sell directly to a certain customer category. A construction materials manufacturer, for example, may elect to deal directly with large commercial accounts but allow suppliers to deal with smaller and more numerous residential accounts.

Since its first decision on a vertical nonprice restraint in *White Motor Company* v. *United States* (1963), the Supreme Court has generally applied the rule of reason. In *White Motor,* the Court was faced with a vertical territorial limitation on sales. The truck company required its dealers to sell trucks only in an exclusive territory around their dealerships. In addition, White Motor sold trucks directly to certain customers—such as governments—and prevented its dealers from selling to those customers. The Court held that while horizontal territorial restrictions are clearly illegal, vertical territorial restrictions would be weighed on their merits; that is, a rule of reason would be applied to each vertical restriction. After analyzing the territorial restriction under the rule of reason, the Court chose not to strike down the White Motor arrangement.

■ ARE TERRITORIAL RESTRAINTS GENERALLY LEGAL?

In the majority of the territorial restraint cases reaching the courts, the plaintiff will be a retailer or distributor that has been terminated by a manufacturer in the process of implementing a vertical territorial restraint strategy. To successfully implement the strategy, the manufacturer will generally be required to eliminate some distributors so that the remaining distributors have the necessary territorial, location, or customer exclusivity. In retaliation, the distributors adversely affected by the manufacturer's strategy will institute a legal action asserting that the manufacturer is attempting to monopolize the market in violation of the antitrust laws.

The recent history of vertical territorial restraint cases indicates that, absent price fixing, most restraints will be allowed. In *Continental T.V.* v. *GTE Sylvania* (1977), the Supreme Court allowed Sylvania to restrict the locations from which its televisions were sold so as to create more exclusive dealers who would devote more attention to Sylvania products. Then in the 1984 case, *Monsanto* v. *Spray-Rite,* the Court allowed Monsanto to stop doing business with distributors who failed to perform a number of activities that Monsanto said dealers must do in an effort to increase sales.

These cases, combined with the 1988 case, *Business Electronics* v. *Sharp,* indicate that distributors or retailers will have little success bringing suit against manufacturers who terminate business with them. After *Sharp,* several major firms, such as Sony, restricted the distribution of their products to wholesalers and retailers they believe will follow the marketing strategies of the parent company.

BUSINESS ELECTRONICS CORPORATION v. SHARP ELECTRONICS CORPORATION

United States Supreme Court
485 U.S. 717, 108 S.Ct. 1515 (1988)

Case Background
Sharp appointed Business Electronics in 1968 as its exclusive retailer in Houston. Sharp appointed Hartwell as a second retailer in Houston in 1972. Sharp published a list of suggested retail prices, but dealers were not required to adhere to those prices. Business Electronics sold Sharp calculators below Sharp's suggested minimum prices and below Hartwell's prices. Hartwell notified Sharp in 1973 that it would quit selling Sharp products unless Business Electronics was terminated as a Sharp dealer. Sharp terminated Business Electronics, which then sued Sharp for conspiracy under Section 1 of the Sherman Act. Under a per se analysis, the federal district court found for Business Electronics. The Court of Appeals reversed, applying the rule of reason. Business Electronics appealed to the Supreme Court.

Case Decision
The Supreme Court agreed with the court of appeals that this case should not be judged under a per se rule against

Sharp and that the rule of reason must be used to judge vertical restraints. Citing *Sylvania,* the Court noted that interbrand competition can be enhanced by vertical nonprice restraints even if intrabrand competition is reduced. Since there was no evidence of an agreement between Sharp and Hartwell to exclude price cutters, there was no illegal conspiracy.

Managerial Considerations
Dealers and manufacturers are free to discuss ways in which the profitability of both parties will be enhanced by certain business practices so long as there is no intimation of price control by the manufacturers. If a dealer can convince a manufacturer that it should cut off other dealers because the one dealer can provide better sales and service alone under a franchise agreement, that agreement is likely to withstand an antitrust challenge. The courts understand that manufacturers and dealers may be working informally to eliminate price-cutting dealers. But by working with strong dealers only, the elimination of price-cutting dealers who are weak on service may strengthen the long-run position of the manufacturer in the market.

The *Sharp* case clearly indicates that retail dealers and manufacturers are free to discuss ways in which the profitability of both parties will be enhanced by various business practices so long as there is no clear evidence of collusion in determining retail prices. If there are several retailers selling the same brand of product in an area, the manufacturer may work with the retailers to encourage practices that will strengthen consumer satisfaction with their brand relative to other brands. If a manufacturer wants retailers to invest in service departments and other extras, discount dealers, who will not incur the costs of such extras, will likely be dropped from the list of retailers as a consequence. The Court is more concerned with competition among different brands—interbrand competition—than competition among dealers of the same brand—intrabrand competition.

INTERNATIONAL ASPECTS	INTERNATIONAL DISTRIBUTORSHIPS

Managers must be careful in international operations to be sure that a business practice legal in the United States is not a violation of antitrust laws elsewhere. The past decade's worth of cases in the United States involving vertical restrictions in the distribution of products has encouraged firms to establish distributorships with exclusive territories. So long as prices are not controlled by the distributor, there seem to be few limitations on vertical restraints.

However, in Europe, specifically in the twelve nations that are members of the European Economic Community (EC), the European Economic Treaty prohibits exclusive distributorships by territory, since they create intra-EC barriers. Hence, restrictions on the distribution of products that may be legal in the United States may cause legal action in EC nations and elsewhere.

The EC prohibition is not absolute, and a large number of goods and services have been exempted. At the same time, consideration is being given to exempting certain product classes that are subject to the current rule. In any event, legal counsel is needed in each country in which a business operates to ensure antitrust compliance.

VERTICAL EXCLUSIONARY PRACTICES

A principle concern of the antitrust laws is the extent to which firms with market power can exercise that power and control the markets in which they do business. Various business practices, some undertaken by formal contract, are designed to exclude competitors indirectly from a particular market. Those practices are intended to make it more difficult for competitors to challenge the market power of the firm using such tactics. Such practices, which include tying arrangements, exclusive-dealing agreements, and boycotts, can come under antitrust attack if the courts find them to be anticompetitive. Section 3 of the Clayton Act applies to tying arrangements and exclusive-dealing agreements, while Section 1 of the Sherman Act governs the antitrust aspects of group boycotts among vertically related parties.

■ TYING ARRANGEMENTS

In *Northern Pacific Railway Company* v. *United States* (1958), the Supreme Court defined a *tying arrangement* or *tie-in sale* as:

> . . . an agreement by a party to sell one product [the tying product] but only on the condition that the buyer also purchases a different [complementary or tied] product, or at least agrees that he will not purchase that product from any other supplier.

The Supreme Court has consistently held that where there is monopoly power, tying arrangements are a violation of the antitrust laws, finding them to be an extension of the firm's market power over the tying product into the market for the tied product. In reaching its decision, the courts have applied either Section 1 of the Sherman Act—viewing tying arrangements as an unreasonable restraint of trade—or Section 3 of the Clayton Act—viewing tying arrangements as a conditional sales contract that may substantially lessen competition or tend to create a monopoly. Importantly, the Sherman Act applies to both products and services, while the Clayton Act applies only to products.

The practice of tying products together is found in other, generally legal, business practices. A grocery store, for example, that offers a bag of Brand A flour at half price when a buyer purchases a bag of Brand A sugar is conducting a tie-in sale that is legal. It is legal because Brand A has no monopoly power over either product. Since you can buy many different brands of flour and sugar, Brand A sugar has no monopoly power over consumers. In another case, the tie-in sale may be justified if the seller can demonstrate that a new technology in a sensitive machine operates properly only when the seller's replacement parts and service are used.

The Classic Tie-in Case.   A classic tying arrangement was struck down in the 1936 Supreme Court decision *International Business Machines Corp.* v. *United States.* An International Business Machines (IBM) lease required that the user of a leased mechanical tabulating machine use only IBM tabulating cards in the machine—that is, IBM software was tied to IBM hardware. IBM's reason for this requirement was that if cards of the exact quality, size, and thickness of the IBM card were not used, the machine would be damaged, resulting in inaccurate results or malfunction of the machine, either of which could hurt the reputation of the company. The Court struck down the requirement, holding it to be a violation of Section 3 of the Clayton Act. Other companies can make cards of the requisite quality, the court noted, and IBM's claim was rejected. The court also noted that the fact that the IBM machine was patented had no bearing on the holding.

Rule of Reason Applied to Tie-in Cases.   In recent years, the Supreme Court has held that tie-ins meet a rule of reason test so long as competitive alternatives exist. That is, if a tie-in creates a monopoly where there are no or few good alternatives, it is likely illegal. But if products or services are tied together in situations where there are competitors, the tie-in will likely pass the rule of reason test, as we see in the *Fortner* decision.

UNITED STATES STEEL CORPORATION v. FORTNER ENTERPRISES, INC.

United States Supreme Court
429 U.S. 610, 97 S.Ct. 861 (1977)

Case Background

U.S. Steel, a large diversified company, produced prefabricated housing. Fortner needed $2 million to develop land on which to place mobile homes. U.S. Steel's credit division loaned Fortner the entire amount at below-market interest rates. When Fortner's real estate deal failed, Fortner claimed that the contract with U.S. Steel violated antitrust laws because there was a tie-in between the purchase of the homes and the financing. The homes were the product tied to U.S. Steel's alleged power over credit—the tying product. If Fortner was correct, U.S. Steel would be liable for treble damages.

The federal district court held that the evidence justified the conclusion that U.S. Steel did have sufficient economic power in the credit market to make the tying arrangement illegal. The court of appeals affirmed that decision. U.S. Steel appealed to the Supreme Court.

Case Decision

Although the Credit Corp. is owned by one of the nation's largest manufacturing corporations, there is nothing in the record to indicate that this enabled it to borrow funds on terms more favorable than those available to competing lenders, or that it was able to operate more efficiently than other lending institutions. In short, the affiliation between U.S. Steel, Home Division, and Credit Corp. does not appear to have given the Credit Corp. any cost advantage over its competitors in the credit market. Instead, the affiliation was significant only because the Credit Corp. provided a source of funds to customers of the Home Division. That fact tells us nothing about the extent of U.S. Steel's economic power in the credit market.

Fortner won in federal district court, and the verdict was upheld at the court of appeals. The Supreme Court reversed. The high court held that U.S. Steel did not have significant economic power in the market for credit; hence, U.S. Steel could not exploit any monopoly power in that market into another market. The court noted that such matters should be treated with a rule of reason and that the reality of the business situation must be studied.

Managerial Considerations.

This case, which had a very long legal history and cost U.S. Steel huge legal fees, is an example of how selecting your business clients poorly can result in high unanticipated costs. The background of the case indicates that Fortner was a poor credit risk and that the home division, hard pressed for sales, pushed the credit division to finance the scheme. As the Supreme Court noted, it is rather unusual for a business to provide another business with 100-percent financing for such a project, but there is nothing illegal about it. It has not been uncommon in business deals that go bad for one party to consider an antitrust or other legal action to try to make money off a losing proposition. More careful financial analysis and anticipation of legal consequences by management probably would have prevented this case from ever happening.

The Court continued its rule of reason approach in the 1984 decision *Jefferson Parish Hospital District No. 2* v. *Hyde.* In *Jefferson Parish,* the Court considered a suit filed by Hyde, a board-certified anesthesiologist who applied for admission to the medical staff of Jefferson Hospital. Hyde was denied admission because the hospital had a contract with a professional medical corporation requiring all anesthesiological services for the hospital's patients to be performed by that firm. Hyde claimed that the exclusive contract violated Section 1 of the Sherman Act. The federal district court held for the hospital. The court of appeals reversed, finding the contract illegal per se because it created an illegal tying arrangement. The Supreme Court reversed, holding that the contract was not a violation of the Sherman Act.

The Court noted that in such an inquiry, the markets involved and the amount of market power possessed by the providers of the services must be considered. Patients are generally free to choose hospitals other than Jefferson, the Court noted, so that they could obtain other anesthesiological services if they wished. Simply because the two services (e.g., surgery and anesthesia) go together does not make the contract illegal.

Tying arrangements will be condemned if they restrain competition by forcing purchases that would not otherwise be made. Here, there was no evidence that price, quality, or supply or demand for either the tying or the tied product was adversely affected by the exclusive contract.

Vertical Restraint Guidelines.   The Justice Department issued *Vertical Restraint Guidelines* in 1985. Citing the *Jefferson Parish* decision, the guidelines claim that the Supreme Court is likely to impose a per se rule of illegality only when three conditions are met:

1. The seller has market power in the tying product.
2. Tied and tying products are separate.
3. There is evidence of substantial adverse effect in the tied-product market.

In other situations, the rule of reason approach is to be employed. The Justice Department said that in such cases, the following test would hold:

> The use of tying will not be challenged if the party imposing the tie has a market share of thirty percent or less in the market for the tying product. This presumption can be overcome only by a showing that the tying agreement unreasonably restrained competition in the market for the tied product.

■ EXCLUSIVE DEALING

Exclusive dealing involves a contractual arrangement between a manufacturer and a retailer under which the manufacturer agrees to sell the product to the retailer on the condition that the retailer not purchase the products of rival manufacturers. Section 3 of the Clayton Act, as amended, prohibits exclusive dealing contracts when the effect of the contracts would be to "substantially lessen competition or tend to create a monopoly."

In imposing antitrust scrutiny, the courts are concerned that one of the parties to the exclusive dealing agreement may have exerted its superior economic power to gain contract terms and conditions decidedly in its favor. In addition, the courts are concerned about the anticompetitive impacts the contract may have on the markets for the products involved. An exclusive dealing contract that forecloses a substantial share of the market to other suppliers and is long in duration will likely be held to be in violation of Section 3 of the Clayton Act or Section 1 of the Sherman Act. There have been very few of these cases in recent years.

■ BOYCOTTS

A *boycott* occurs when a group conspires to prevent the carrying on of business or to harm a business. It can be executed by any organized group—consumers, union members, retailers, wholesalers, or suppliers—who, acting together, can then inflict economic damage on a business. The boycott is often used to force compliance with a price-fixing scheme or some other restraint of trade. The cases often fall under the per se rule against price fixing.

In an early leading decision, *Eastern States Retail Lumber Dealers Association* v. *United States* (1914), the Court struck down a boycott designed to punish lumber wholesalers who sold directly to the public. A number of lumber retailers would turn in to their association the names of wholesalers who sold to the public. The retailers were obviously trying to limit competition in lumber sales to the public. The association would send out to retailers the names of wholesalers who had sold directly to the public in hopes that the retailers would boycott those wholesalers. Even though there was no enforcement mechanism—retailers were still free to deal with such wholesalers—and there was no evidence that the boycott of the lumber wholesalers who sold to the public caused any loss of business, the Court said that the Sherman Act prohibits such boycotts.

Boycotts and the Per Se Rule.   The Courts have consistently taken a hard line against boycotts, largely because boycotts are efforts by horizontal competitors to restrict vertical competition. That is, unlike other vertical restrictions where one manufacturer negotiates with individual dealers about terms of trade, boycotts involve either all manufacturers getting together to tell dealers what they must do or all dealers getting together to tell manufacturers what they must do. A horizontal restriction on competition is used to force vertical restraints. In 1990, the Supreme Court reiterated that when horizontal competitors use a boycott to force a change in the nature of a vertical relationship, there is a per se violation of the law.

FEDERAL TRADE COMMISSION v. SUPERIOR COURT TRIAL LAWYERS ASSOCIATION

United States Supreme Court
493 U.S. 411, 110 S.Ct. 768 (1990)

Case Background
Operating under the Criminal Justice Act (CJA), a group of about 100 lawyers in private practice regularly acted as court-appointed attorneys for indigent defendants charged in the District of Columbia. The attorneys belonged to the Superior Court Trial Lawyers Association (SCTLA), a private organization. Their fees for legal work ($30 per hour for court time, $20 per hour for out-of-court time) were paid by the District of Columbia on behalf of their clients. The average annual income for the attorneys from this work was $45,000 in 1982. The SCTLA demanded that the government of the District of Columbia double the fees. When this did not happen, the SCTLA organized a boycott. About 90 of the 100 attorneys boycotted the criminal courts of the District; the boycott soon nearly brought the system to a stop. After two weeks, the District raised attorney's fees to $35 per hour for all work and promised to double the fees as demanded as soon as possible. The FTC ruled that the boycott and conspiracy to fix prices was illegal per se under Section 5 of the FTC Act. The court of appeals reversed the FTC, holding that the boycott was a political expression protected by the First Amendment. The Supreme Court reviewed the decision.

Case Decision
The Supreme Court reversed the court of appeals and held the lawyers' boycott of criminal defense work in an effort to force the city to raise the attorney's fees to be illegal per se under the Sherman and FTC Acts.

> SCTLA's boycott "constituted a classic restraint of trade within the meaning of Section 1 of the Sherman Act." As such, it also violated the prohibition against unfair methods of competition of § 5 of the FTC Act. Prior to the boycott CJA lawyers were in competition with one another, each deciding independently whether and how often to offer to provide services to the District at CJA rates. The agreement among the CJA lawyers was designed to obtain higher prices for their services and was implemented by a concerted refusal to serve an important customer in the market for legal services . . . .

Managerial Considerations
No matter how price fixing comes about, the Court takes a hard line against competitors getting together under any guise to rig prices. It is fine for one firm to set whatever prices it likes—buyers can take it or leave it—but when firms get together to rig prices or boycott those who do not toe the line on the prices the sellers want, the consequences can be harsh. Attempts to price fix are not infrequent, since the rewards are high, but since secrecy is hard to maintain, the efforts are usually not successful.

THE ROBINSON-PATMAN ACT ▬▬▬▬

The Robinson-Patman Act, enacted in 1936, amended the Clayton Act. Section 2(a) states that "it shall be unlawful for any person engaged in commerce . . . to discriminate in price between different purchasers of commodities of like grade and quality . . . where the effect of such discrimination may be substantially to lessen competition or tend to create a monopoly in any line of commerce." Thus, a seller is said to engage in *price discrimination* when the same product is sold to different buyers at different prices.

Section 2(a) is perhaps one of the most controversial aspects of antitrust law, since the initial reason for its passage was to limit the ability of chain stores to offer merchandise at a price lower than their single-store competitors. The implication of the Act's application is that consumers will be denied lower prices. As a consequence of this implication, the Justice Department and the FTC have been reluctant to enforce the Act. The vast majority of cases brought under the Robinson-Patman Act are private actions.

■ PRICE DISCRIMINATION

Many of the cases brought under the Robinson-Patman Act concern alleged economic injuries associated either with a firm charging different prices in different markets or with bulk-sale discounts given to larger volume retailers. To illustrate the first type of injury, suppose that two sellers—Allen's Wholesale and Johnston Distributors—sell the same type of product in competition with one another in San Francisco. Allen's also sells the product in Oakland, but Johnston does not. If Allen's reduces its prices in San Francisco but not in Oakland, the price cut is likely to be seen as anticompetitive under the Robinson-Patman Act. Allen's is engaging in price discrimination—charging different prices in different markets to the detriment of its competitors, which in this case is Johnston.

This type of business practice is sometimes seen as *predatory pricing*. That is, Allen's is attempting to undercut Johnston in San Francisco in an effort to drive Johnston from the market. Allen's, however, continues to sell the product for a higher price in other markets in which it does not compete with Johnston. Presumably, the intent of Allen's actions is to drive Johnston from the San Francisco market and then raise prices when Johnston goes out of business. This kind of business practice was illegal under the original Clayton Act but was further strengthened by the Robinson-Patman amendments.

The Robinson-Patman Act is also concerned with sales discounts given to large volume retailers. To illustrate, suppose Allen's and Johnston both buy the same product from Central Distributors for the purpose of selling it at retail. Because Allen's is a larger volume retailer, Central gives Allen's a price discount on its larger bulk purchases. The price discount gives Allen's a competitive advantage over Johnston in the sale of the product to customers in the area. The action that is attacked is the price discount given to Allen's, the larger purchaser. This situation generates numerous cases against producers who discriminate in pricing to wholesalers or retailers.

■ DEFENSES

A key defense that has emerged for firms charged with violating the Robinson-Patman Act is the ability to show a *cost justification* for different prices charged in different markets or to different buyers. An obvious cost-justification defense is a difference in transportation costs—it usually costs more to deliver a refrigerator three hundred miles than fifty miles. The major problem with using the cost-justification defense is that costs usually cannot reasonably be assigned to specific products sold at particular places or to particular buyers—it is virtually an accounting and economic impossibility to assign specific costs of production to individual products. As a consequence, the cost-justification defense is rarely successfully applied by itself.

The other defense that may be used is that of *meeting competition.* That is, a firm cuts its price in response to a competitor cutting its price first. The problem with this defense can be that the original price cut will be held illegal under Robinson-Patman, which will mean that subsequent price cuts may also be illegal, at least at some point. Competitors must try to show that the cutting of prices to meet competition was done in good faith, not in an effort to injure competitors but to stay competitive.

TEXACO v. HASBROUCK

United States Supreme Court
496 U.S. 543, 110 S.Ct. 2535 (1990)

Case Background

Texaco sold gasoline to Hasbrouck (Rick's Texaco) and other independent Texaco gas stations in Spokane, Washington. Texaco also sold its gasoline to Gull and Dompier—but at lower prices. Gull sold the gasoline under the Gull name at its stations. Dompier sold the gasoline under the Texaco brand name at its stations. Because Gull and Dompier paid less for their gasoline, they sold it for less at retail and grew rapidly. Sales at Rick's Texaco and the other independent stations dropped from 76 percent to 49 percent of Texaco retail sales in the area.

The only difference in operations between Dompier's Texaco stations and the independent Texaco stations was that Dompier owned tanker trucks and used them to pick up gasoline from Texaco's plant. The independent dealers asked Texaco if they could hire their own tanker trucks to pick up the gasoline and then pay the same price as Dompier and Gull. Texaco said no.

Hasbrouck and other independent Texaco station owners sued Texaco for violation of Section 2(a) of the Robinson-Patman Act, alleging that Texaco's discounts to Dompier and Gull were illegal. The trial court awarded treble damages to Hasbrouck, and the court of appeals af-

firmed. Texaco appealed, claiming that the lower prices charged to Dompier and Gull were legal functional discounts, that is, "discounts given to a purchaser based on its role in the supplier's distribution system and reflect the cost of the services performed by the purchaser for the supplier."

Case Decision

The Supreme Court affirmed the decision of the courts below.

> In order to establish a violation of the Act, respondents had the burden of proving four facts: (1) that Texaco's sales to Gull and Dompier were made in interstate commerce; (2) that the gasoline sold to them was of the same grade and quality as that sold to respondents; (3) that Texaco discriminated in price as between Gull and Dompier on the one hand and Hasbrouck on the other; and (4) that the discrimination had a prohibited effect on competition. Moreover, for Hasbrouck to recover damages, he had the burden of proving the extent of his actual injuries.

The Court noted that the Robinson-Patman Act allows two reasons for price discounts: (1) those "justified by savings in the seller's cost," and (2) "those that represent a good faith response to the equally low prices of a competitor." Neither of those defenses applied to Texaco. Texaco's costs in dealing with Gull and Dompier were the same as dealing with Hasbrouck. Furthermore, Texaco refused to

(continued)

allow Hasbrouck to haul gasoline in his own tankers, but allowed Dompier to do so. Therefore, the price difference was not based on cost of doing business or because of meeting competition.

Managerial Considerations

The Robinson-Patman Act is clear that it is illegal price discrimination to sell the same good at different prices to different customers unless there are cost differentials in dealing with different customers or prices are cut to meet the competition. The courts are not sympathetic to this law,

because it tends to discourage price discounting, which generally is beneficial to consumers. However, since the law is clear, it is enforced, especially by buyers who have suffered from price discrimination. Suppose that for some reason Texaco wanted to sell all its gasoline through Gull and Dompier and discontinue the independent dealers like Hasbrouck. That would be fine, but Texaco either would have to be a part owner of the stations, so that the pricing action occurred within the firm, or should have established nonprice rules that it knew would drive the independent retailers away.

SUMMARY: A GUIDE FOR MANAGERS

- Business strategies that restrain trade violate the antitrust statutes and expose managers to prosecution by the government or by private parties who have been injured. Contracts in restraint of trade that do not violate the antitrust laws may be unenforceable in court if found to violate public policy. Violations of the antitrust laws can expose defendants to criminal penalties, which can include prison sentences as well as civil penalties. Defendants who lose antitrust suits in which damages are found must automatically pay treble damages.

- Congress has exempted the insurance industry, agricultural cooperatives, labor unions, and others from the antitrust laws. The laws are enforced by the Antitrust Division of the Justice Department, the Federal Trade Commission, and by private parties. Only the Justice Department can bring criminal charges for alleged antitrust violations.

- Most antitrust matters are determined by a rule of reason analysis, where the courts weigh the pros and cons of business practices alleged to be anticompetitive. Some practices, such as price fixing by competitors, are so clearly anticompetitive, that they are declared to be per se illegal.

- Horizontal restraints of trade occur when business competitors at the same level of business, such as producers of similar products, agree to act together. Vertical restraints of trade occur when a firm at one level of business operation controls the practices of a firm at another level of operation, such as a producer telling a retailer what price to charge the public for its products.

- Mergers of competitor companies or companies that could compete with one another are likely to be challenged only if the merger would significantly reduce competition in a market. The market can be a territorial market or a single product line.

- Independent companies in the same industry may not agree, by any means, to segregate the market geographically, by type of customer, or in any other arrangement that reduces competition.

- Horizontal price fixing occurs when competitors agree to act together to set prices for their products or services. This can happen at any level of operation and is usually per se illegal.

- There is no defense for companies in the same industry that get together, by any means, to agree on product prices in the markets in which they operate. Prices may not be fixed at any level by competitors unless there are special circumstances that make the arrangement procompetitive, which is rare.

- Companies in an industry may share price and other market information through a trade association so long as the information is not used to control the market and so long as the information is available to the public.

- Vertical price fixing, or resale price maintenance, where the producer or distributor tells the retailers of its products the minimum or maximum prices at which to sell the products, is per se illegal. Suggested retail prices are legal but may not be enforced by a threat to cut off a retailer who will not adhere to them.

- Vertical nonprice restraints, such as granting exclusive territory to dealers, are viewed under a rule of reason. Recent cases indicate that manufacturers are given wide latitude in picking dealers and deciding the terms under which they will retain them. The producer may not conspire with a dealer against another dealer.

- Tie-in sales, where the sale of one product is tied to the sale of another, are judged under a rule of reason. For such a sale to be illegal, it must be shown that monopoly power in one product existed and was extended to the other product.

- Exclusive dealing contracts are usually allowed but are subject to a rule of reason test to see whether there is evidence of monopoly power being gained in a market through them. An exclusive deal may not be used as a way around a merger that was not allowed to take place.

- When a group of businesses at any one level of business (such as hardware stores) get together to agree to a joint action (such as refusal to deal) against one or more businesses at another level of business (such as a particular hardware supplier), there is usually a boycott that is per se illegal.

- The Robinson-Patman Act holds that price discrimination—selling the same product to different buyers at different prices—must be justified by differences in the cost of selling to the different buyers or because the price difference was required to meet competition. This is one of the most troublesome areas of law for producers, since hundreds of private lawsuits are filed each year by unhappy buyers (usually retailers) claiming that they were discriminated against. The courts are not very sympathetic to such cases, but the cases pose expensive problems that can be avoided by careful planning with legal counsel.

MANAGER'S ETHICAL DILEMMA

BULLYING SMALL COMPETITORS

The Robinson-Patman Act holds that certain forms of price discrimination are illegal. In short, the law says that you may not sell the same product to different people for different prices unless there is a cost justification for the price differential. This law poses a nest of problems for producers and distributors.

Suppose you are a regional manager for Carnation, Borden, or some other large food company. Your products are distributed to almost every grocery store in your region. The grocery market is highly competitive; profit margins are thin. You market a line of frozen pies that have been very successful and are now earning a good rate of return. Your pie sales suddenly drop 40 percent in Chicago, seriously reducing your profits. Investigation reveals that the Center for Disabled Veterans has started a frozen pie operation that produces a fine pie sold to the grocery stores for less than your pies. Their operation is large enough to serve the Chicago market only.

The national manager tells you that you need to work to recoup the market and get your pie profits back up, or you will have a bad mark on your record. The national manager could not care less where the competitor pies come from. "I don't care if my mother makes them," she says. "Get the market back, or the pie will be in your face."

You know that you have several options to try to recapture the Chicago frozen pie market, which shows every sign of getting worse for you. Since you have no control over the pie itself, your efforts must be directed at price and distribution. You discuss with the executives of one large chain of grocery stores how much you would value an exclusive frozen pie freezer in their stores. "Get out all competitors' pies, and I will cut the price to you by 20 percent," you tell them.

Another tactic is to simply slash pie prices in Chicago, perhaps in half, until the Disabled Veterans lose market share and quit production. Later, you expect to be able to raise your prices slowly to their previous levels. The Supreme Court has frowned on this practice in *Utah Pie,* but you think that if carefully done, you can do this without antitrust problems.

QUESTIONS

Is it ethical to try to eliminate a small competitor by using either or both of these practices, which skirt the fringes of antitrust law? Would it be any more ethical if the competitor you were facing were Pillsbury or some other big company? Is it ethical to offer your pies to large grocery chains for less than you offer them to single stores?

REVIEW AND DISCUSSION QUESTIONS

1. Define the following terms:

per se rule	resale price maintenance
rule of reason	territorial restrictions
horizontal business arrangements	tie-in sale
cartel	exclusive dealing
merger	boycott
failing-firm defense	price discrimination
territorial allocation	

2. What are some factors that would seem to make a particular market or industry more likely to be monopolized?

3. Two views exist on allowing firms to trade price and other trade information. One view is that it is anticompetitive because it enhances the ability of competitors to fix prices. The other view is that it helps competition because, so long as the price information is public, it will make both buyers and sellers more knowledgeable. What evidence supports each side?

4. Vertical restraint of trade cases are more likely to be covered by a rule of reason analysis than are horizontal restraint cases, and in general, the antitrust authorities are less critical of vertical restraints than they are of horizontal restraints. Does this distinction seem sensible if you presume that the purpose of antitrust law should be to make the economy more competitive?

5. The courts use a rule of reason in looking at territorial restrictions. Why should there by any concern about territorial restrictions? So long as there is competition between brands, is not that more important than intrabrand competition by the sellers of a product in a given geographic market? That is, can you think of cases in which intrabrand competition might be more important than interbrand competition?

■ CASE QUESTIONS

6. Many professional engineers belong to a trade association called the National Society of Professional Engineers that governs the nontechnical aspects of the practice of engineering. The canon of ethics adopted by the society held that engineers could not bid against one another for a particular job. The society claimed that this rule was to prevent engineers from engaging in price cutting to get engineering jobs, which could then give them incentives to cut corners on the quality of work to save time and resources. Such a practice could lead to inferior work that could endanger the public. The Justice Department sued, claiming that this was a violation of Section 1 of the Sherman Act. The government claimed that the ethical rule reduced price competition and gave an unfair advantage to engineers with well-established reputations. Who wins? [*National Society of Professional Engineers v. United States*, 435 U.S. 679, 98 S.Ct. 1355 (1978)]

7. Several companies operated downhill ski facilities in Aspen, Colorado. They all sold a joint ticket that allowed skiers to ski at all facilities; the receipts were later divided according to various use rates. Eventually, one firm owned all the ski areas but one. This firm stopped issuing the joint ticket and instead issued a ticket good for all of its ski areas. The firm that owned only one ski facility saw its market share fall from 20 percent to 11 percent over a four-year period. It sued, claiming that the larger firm violated Section 2 of the Sherman Act by attempting to monopolize skiing by ending the joint ticket arrangement. Does the smaller firm lose the case, or is the sale of the joint ticket a violation of the antitrust law? [*Aspen Skiing Company v. Aspen Highlands Skiing Corporation*, 472 U.S. 585, 105 S.Ct. 2847 (1985)]

8. In the *NCAA* decision, the Court recognized the importance of a central governing body to make the college football market work. An antitrust issue has been raised with respect to the National Football League (NFL) and the power it has over its member teams. Can the NFL legitimately require teams to stay in the cities to which they were initially assigned, or should the teams be free to move to any city? The Oakland Raiders were allowed by the courts to move to Los Angeles. A franchise for a professional sports team is sold under a contract that keeps the team in a certain city unless the league approves a move. Can

you think of a competitive rationale for not allowing teams to move anywhere they want?

9. Procter & Gamble, a large producer of a variety of household products including laundry detergent, wished to acquire Clorox, which essentially produced only liquid bleach. Procter & Gamble did not produce bleach or any close substitute for bleach. It wanted to buy a high-quality company like Clorox to expand the range of products it had to offer to grocery stores. The government opposed the vertical merger. The claim was that because Clorox was the most successful bleach and because Procter & Gamble was a large, successful household products manufacturer and marketer, Procter & Gamble would be able to injure other bleach competitors because of its outstanding marketing abilities and economic clout in dealing with retailers. Procter & Gamble claimed the merger should be allowed because it was not in the bleach market and consumers would benefit by having a strong, quality company like Procter & Gamble market this product. Can the merger stand? [*Federal Trade Commission v. Procter & Gamble*, 386 U.S. 568, 87 S.Ct. 1224 (1967)]

10. Movie distributors sometimes engage in block booking of movies. That is, they sell movie rentals to theaters and TV stations in packages. For example, a theater or station might not be able to rent *Gone with the Wind* unless it rented a package that included *The Texas Chainsaw Massacre*. This is a sort of tie-in sale, since if the theater or station wants to rent one movie, it must rent the other. Does this provide an example of how monopoly power over one product can be extended over another product? Would this tie-in be likely to be held to be illegal? Remember that the movies are copyrighted, so that there is legally only one source from which theaters and TV stations can rent them.

■ BUSINESS POLICY QUESTIONS

11. Should some practices be per se illegal, or should all actions be judged by a rule of reason? Why might it be efficient to have some per se rules?

12. Nonhorizontal mergers are rarely challenged. The antitrust laws do not attack bigness per se. Should they? Should there be concern when two large firms in different industries merge? These are usually called conglomerate mergers and are rarely attacked, just as vertical mergers are rarely attacked.

13. The Robinson-Patman Act was officially titled the Anti-Chain Store Discrimination Act. Can you see why? The backers of the Act were small store owners who were being hurt by competition in the 1920s and 1930s from the growing chain stores, which now dominate retailing. Is this legislation procompetitive, or does it hurt consumers?

■ ETHICS QUESTIONS

14. You are the head of a company that has only one major competitor in several cities. As in the airline example in the chapter, the president of your competitor calls you to recommend that you both raise prices five percent and promise not to cheat on each other on this agreement. You know that the president is sincere and will stick to the bargain. You know that you will increase your profits by 50 percent if the deal holds. You know that no one is likely to know of the arrangement. What should you do?

15. After the *Albrecht* decision said that newspaper producers cannot control subscription prices if they sell the papers to independent carriers for distribution to the public, many newspapers gradually did away with the independent carriers and hired employees to distribute the papers. By vertically integrating this function within the firm, a newspaper can control the distribution price. Since newspapers rely primarily on advertising revenues, they have an interest in keeping subscription prices low to encourage high circulation, which allows them to charge higher advertising rates. The carriers want higher subscription rates, since they keep all money collected above what they paid the newspaper company for the paper. Is it ethical for the newspaper companies to get rid of the independent carriers in favor of in-house carriers? Does it matter that the public benefits by lower subscription rates?

16. Your firm produces electric blenders. A certain popular model has a suggested retail price of $30. Your firm sells it wholesale for $18. Smaller stores tend to sell the blender at the suggested retail price. One large discount chain begins to sell the blender for $26 and asks you to cut the price of it to $17.50. Because of that chain's large sales, your production and profits are up. You will earn even higher profits if you cut the price to the chain to $17.50 — a possible violation of the Robinson-Patman Act. Should you cut the price for the chain? What if the chain says it will cut its retail price to $25.50 if you cut the price to $17.50?

SECURITIES REGULATION

CHAPTER 17

MANAGER'S LEGAL CHALLENGE

General Electric Company (GE) paid $600 million in 1986 to purchase the New York securities firm of Kidder, Peabody & Company. In February 1987, the SEC and Manhattan U.S. Attorney Rudolph Giuliani informed the company that Kidder was to be indicted on criminal insider trading charges. Guiliani told Kidder it should plead guilty.

The GE executives were shocked by this unexpected development that tied their new company to Ivan Boesky, who had already pleaded guilty to a felony and paid $100 million in settlement. The government complaint charged that Kidder traded securities while in possession of inside information. Kidder also illegally "parked" securities on behalf of Boesky during takeover deals.

GE executives realized that their investment in Kidder could go down the drain. If the charges were upheld in court, Kidder would face, among other penalties, being barred from doing the financial market work that made the company worth $600 million.

GE managers knew that there was a difference between being charged with a crime and being convicted. The major New York law firm that represented Kidder advised GE to fight the charges every step of the way. GE's executives immediately launched their own investigation of Kidder and determined that the government was likely to win the case. Damage control became the primary concern. The senior executives of Kidder and the New York law firm were dismissed. A team from GE moved in to take control and negotiate a settlement with the government.

Meeting with Guiliani and other government prosecutors, the GE team made it clear that Kidder was being swept clean; no moves would be made to protect the old management. GE would cooperate with the government investigation of Kidder, which could help produce evidence pertaining not only to Kidder and its executives but also to others who may have been involved in securities fraud.

In less than three months, this complicated case was settled. Guiliani accepted a settlement of $25 million from Kidder and agreed not to prosecute the company. The SEC would supervise the establishment of new internal controls at Kidder to reduce the likelihood of further illegal insider trading.

The legal issues surrounding the events at Kidder did not end with the termination of the government's case. However, there is no doubt that a major catastrophe for Kidder and its owner, GE, was avoided by decisive, strong managerial control of the legal crisis.

This chapter explains the use of securities in financing business and defines a security from the perspective of the Securities and Exchange Commission (SEC) and the courts. It also reviews the regulatory requirements for new securities—what a corporation must do before selling securities. The Securities Act of 1933 states that if something is a security, it must be registered with the SEC before it can be sold to the public, unless it is sold under an exemption. Certain financial information must be made public for distribution to investors before a security can be offered to the public.

Under the 1934 Securities Exchange Act, continuous disclosure of financial information will occur for as long as the security remains in the hands of the public. Failure to follow these disclosure laws may result in public or private suits for securities fraud. The 1934 Act also ordered the SEC to regulate the markets in which securities are traded, regulate professionals in the securities markets, and control the manner in which other securities transactions take place. These laws have since been followed by various other statutes that regulate the operation of financial markets. The chapter ends with a review of the regulation of the sale of franchises.

CORPORATE FINANCE AND EARLY REGULATION

The sale of securities is a principal means of corporate finance. Thus, the efficient operation of the securities markets is vital to the economy.

■ SECURITIES AND CORPORATE FINANCE

Broadly defined, a *security* is a written instrument that provides evidence of *debt*—such as a corporate note or bond—or of *ownership*—such as a certificate of preferred or common stock. Securities differ from other commodities in that they have no intrinsic value in themselves—corporations could create them virtually without cost. Thus, securities represent value in something else. The value of a corporation's stock depends on the expected future profitability of the corporation as reflected in the price investors are willing to pay for that stock.

Debt.   The capital needs of a corporation can be financed through debt or equity. *Debt financing* involves selling bonds or borrowing money by contract. The debt instrument issued by a corporation usually specifies the following:

1. Amount of the debt.
2. Length of the debt period.
3. Debt repayment method.
4. Rate of interest that will be applied to the sum borrowed.

Thus, debt financing means incurring a liability. A corporation can sell $1 million worth of bonds to the public, promise to redeem the bonds in one year, and pay the creditors or bondholders 10 percent interest on the sum borrowed. In addition, the bondholders can trade those debt instruments in either formal markets—such as the stock market—or informal markets.

Equity. *Equity financing*, on the other hand, involves raising funds through the sale of a corporation's stock. It is called equity financing because purchasers of shares of stock gain ownership, or equitable, interest in the corporation. That is, shareholders have a claim on a specified portion of the future profits of the corporation. The corporation, in contrast to its use of debt financing, has no liability to repay shareholders the amount they have invested. For example, a corporation may issue one million shares of common stock at a price of $10 per share to raise $10 million. Each share sold represents a right to one-millionth of the future annual profits of the corporation.

Investors will be inclined to buy shares in a corporation only if they feel their share in the profits will be sufficient to provide them with a competitive rate of return on their investment. The officers of the corporation are under no obligation beyond making reasonable efforts to make a profit. As in the case of bonds, unless prohibited by contract, corporate stock can also be traded on either formal or informal markets.

More than 50 million people in the United States own stock in corporations. This ownership is evenly divided between women and men. Most investors are investing in securities to provide themselves with retirement income and to fund major expenditures like college education. About $5 trillion worth of securities exist in the United States, about half of which are publicly traded stocks, while the rest are in debt such as government bonds.

ORIGINS OF SECURITIES REGULATION

Public concern with unscrupulous promoters and salesmen led to the enactment of state legislation regulating the sale of securities. The first substantive securities statute was enacted by the state of Kansas in 1911. State securities law became known as *blue sky laws*. Although scholars differ on the exact origin of the title, it is often attributed to an earlier Supreme Court opinion describing the purpose of state securities laws as attempting to prevent the "speculative schemes which would have no more basis than so many feet of blue sky." According to some accounts, promoters had gone door-to-door selling worthless securities to unwitting Kansas farmers. Later, the farmers had discovered—after their money and the promoter were gone—that the securities had nothing more substantial backing them up than the blue sky.

Origins of Federal Regulation.   Federal regulation of securities began during a time of economic catastrophe. The stock market crashed in 1929, and the Great Depression, which lasted until World War II, followed. Over one-quarter of all jobs were lost, and national income fell by one-third. Many people incorrectly blamed the depression on the stock market crash. In fact, the stock market was correctly forecasting the depression and the fall in corporate profits. Nevertheless, there was a common belief that professional manipulators on Wall Street needed to be controlled. Congress responded by enacting six statutes between 1933 and 1940:

1. The Securities Act of 1933.
2. The Securities Exchange Act of 1934.
3. The Public Utility Holding Company Act of 1935.
4. The Trust Indenture Act of 1939.
5. The Investment Company Act of 1940.
6. The Investment Advisors Act of 1940.

Most important are the Securities Act of 1933 and the Securities Exchange Act of 1934. The 1933 Act regulates the initial public offerings of securities. The Act's basic objectives are to require that investors be provided with material information about new securities offered for sale and to prevent misrepresentation and fraud in the sale of those securities.

The 1934 Act extended federal securities regulation to include trading in securities that were already issued. The Act imposes periodic disclosure requirements on corporations with publicly held securities outstanding. The Act also provides for the regulation of securities markets and professionals. Congress hoped that these laws would help maintain confidence in the market.

The Securities and Exchange Commission.   The *Securities and Exchange Commission* (SEC) is the agency charged with the responsibility for the enforcement and administration of the federal securities laws. The Securities Exchange Act of 1934 provides that the SEC has five commissioners appointed by the President for five-year terms. One of these is appointed as chairman. Not more than three may be of the same political party. The SEC's staff is composed of attorneys, accountants, financial analysts and examiners, and other professionals. The staff works in divisions and offices—including thirteen regional and branch offices around the country.

INTERNATIONAL ASPECTS | **INTERNATIONAL STOCK MARKETS**

Equity (stock) financing of corporations is vital in the United States. Over $2 trillion in equities are owned by millions of citizens who share in the good or bad fortune of thousands of corporations. In the past decade, equity markets have grown rapidly in many other nations. The equity markets in Japan, Germany, Switzerland, France, and the United Kingdom are now large and sophisticated. Only in the past decade has it become easy for Americans to own stock in foreign firms and for foreigners to own stock in American firms. Capital funds now flow around the world much more easily than at any other time in history.   *(continued)*

Other countries have developing securities markets, and many more would like to have them. One is struggling to operate in St. Petersburg in Russia. Governments that used to try to control all capital flows have come to understand that it is difficult to stop capital from going to its best opportunities and that if they open their markets, they could benefit from capital inflows. From small nations like Malaysia to large ones like Brazil, stock markets are being developed. Most nations adopt securities laws very similar to U.S. laws because American securities markets have become world models.

Countries have difficulties developing stock markets when they have not had economic or political stability. In many countries of Latin America, where governments seem perpetually unstable, most people are leery of risking their wealth in ventures the government could easily destroy or steal by simply changing the law. The size of a country has little to do with the development of equity markets; Hong Kong and Belgium have healthy markets because of their long-term political stability. The impending takeover of Hong Kong by the People's Republic of China, however, has initiated a capital outflow from Hong Kong. Many current and potential investors do not believe the Beijing government's promise that it will not interfere with Hong Kong's economy.

Stock markets frighten governments because they are a good measure of the wisdom of a government's economic policy. If a government implements policies that investors believe will injure the economy or reduce the rate of return on capital, stock prices will quickly fall as investors react to the news.

DEFINING A SECURITY

Although Congress often provides vague mandates in the laws it passes—allowing the courts and the regulatory agencies to define the terms and the scope of the legislation—this was not the case in defining the term *security* under the 1933 Act. Concerned about the abilities of promoters to devise investment schemes with a variety of names and labels, Congress provided a broad definition of the term *security* that goes well beyond those investment instruments labeled "stocks" and "bonds." According to Section 2(1) of the 1933 Act the term *security* includes

> . . . any note, stock, treasury stock, bond, debenture, evidence of indebtedness, certificate of interest or participation in any profit-sharing agreement, collateral-trust certificate, preorganization certificate or subscription, transferable share, investment contract, voting-trust certificate, certificate of deposit for a security, fractional undivided interest in oil, gas, or other mineral rights, or, in general, any interest or instrument commonly known as a "security," or any certificate of interest of participation in, temporary or interim certificate for, receipt for, guarantee of, or warrant or right to subscribe to or purchase, any of the foregoing.

As a general rule, despite this specific definition of a security, both the courts and the SEC look to the economic realities of an investment instrument in determining whether it is a security. As the Supreme Court noted in *United Housing Foundation* v. *Forman* (1975):

> We reject . . . any suggestion that the present transaction, evidenced by the sale of shares called *stock,* must be considered a security transaction

simply because the statutory definition of a security [under Section 2(1)] includes the words "any . . . stock."

That is, just because something is called a stock does not mean it is a security that falls within the jurisdiction of the federal security laws.

■ SUPREME COURT'S *HOWEY* TEST

Whether an investment instrument is a security determines whether it must comply with the legal requirements imposed on securities issuers. Note that investors have incentives to sue to have the court declare that an investment instrument is a security. If an investment is a security, investors have a greater degree of legal protection than that given to investments that are not securities. In *Howey*, the Supreme Court established a test to determine when an investment instrument is to be considered a security for the purposes of federal regulation.

SECURITIES AND EXCHANGE COMMISSION v. W. J. HOWEY COMPANY

United States Supreme Court
328 U.S. 293, 66 S.Ct. 1100 (1946)

Case Background
Howey owned large tracts of land in central Florida, including a development called Howey-in-the-Hills and hundreds of acres of citrus groves. Half the groves were offered for sale to the public. Prospective buyers were offered title to citrus grove acreage and a service contract under which Howey would cultivate, harvest, and sell the citrus grown on each parcel. Most investors lived outside of Florida and bought the service contract.

The SEC sued Howey, claiming that the sale of the acreage and service contracts was a security that should have been registered with the SEC before being offered for sale to the public. The federal district court and the U.S. Court of Appeals found for Howey. The SEC appealed to the U.S. Supreme Court.

Case Decision
The Supreme Court agreed with the SEC that Howey had violated the Securities Act of 1933 by not registering the sales. More than land was being sold, since management services for the land were also offered and usually taken by the buyers. All the elements of a profit-seeking venture were present. The investors provided the capital and shared in the profits. The promoters managed the enterprise. The fact that land sales were not specified in the 1933 Act did not remove the deal from the kinds of investment contracts covered by the law.

Managerial Considerations
A security is defined by the Court as "a contract, transaction or scheme whereby a person invests his money in a common enterprise and is led to expect profits solely from the efforts of a third party." Since the definition is not concrete, promoters have run afoul of this law and faced serious penalties for selling an unregistered security that they did not know was a security.

When selling a share of a business or some sort of business opportunity, managers need to know in the broadest sense whether a security is involved. The fact that an investment contract is completely legitimate does not affect the requirement of registration. Securities registration is expensive and in some cases can be avoided through the structuring of a transaction. Quality legal counsel is required in such cases.

The test developed by the Court in *Howey* has been applied countless times since the case was decided. The test holds that for an investment instrument to be classified as a security for the purpose of federal regulation, it must contain four basic elements: (1) the investment of money (2) in a common enterprise (3) with an expectation of profits (4) generated solely from the efforts of persons other than the investors.

The first element, *the investment of money*, requires that an investor turn over money to someone else for investment purposes. The second element, *in a common enterprise,* means that the investment is not the personal property of the investor, such as the investor's own warehouse or automobile. Rather, the investor's capital has been pooled with the capital of other investors so that each investor owns an undivided interest in the investment. An investor who buys General Motors Corporation stock, for example, does not have the right to go to a General Motors factory and demand an automobile or other property from the company equal in value to the money the investor has invested in the company. The investor has a claim only to a share of future earnings as set forth in the contract that accompanied the security. Even though stock owners (or shareholders) own a portion of the company, they own an undivided interest in the company. That is, the shareholders cannot divide the property of the company among themselves unless they first agree to liquidate (sell) the company.

The third and fourth elements, *the expectation that profits will be generated by the efforts of persons other than the investor,* require that the investor not have direct control over the work that makes the investment a success or failure. The SEC and the courts have taken a liberal view of the requirement that the profits be generated by other persons, ruling that a security will still be found to exist when most of the efforts to produce the profits will be by other persons. Thus, the president of a corporation who buys shares of the corporation's stock will be found to have purchased a security because most of the profits of the corporation will be generated through the work of others.

■ APPLICATION OF THE SECURITIES DEFINITION

Since many investment opportunities go bad, there are numerous suits claiming securities fraud. For a claim to be tried under the standards imposed by the federal securities laws, the investment instrument must meet the *Howey* test of a security. In various cases, lower courts have broadened the scope of the *Howey* test, but the Supreme Court consistently returns to it.

In *International Brotherhood of Teamsters* v. *Daniel* (1979), the Court considered a case in which a member of the Teamsters Union had been cheated out of his pension by the union. In an effort to get his pension, Daniel sued the union, claiming that the pension fund run by the union, which was invested in securities, should itself have been registered as a security, and it was fraud not to have done so. The lower courts agreed, but the Supreme Court said no. While it sympathized with Daniel's plight, the Court held that pensions are a form of wages, so they are not securities. In *Reves*, a case concerning bonds, or notes, the Court again discussed the *Howey* test.

REVES v. ERNST & YOUNG

United States Supreme Court
494 U.S. 56, 110 S.Ct. 945 (1990)

Case Background
Farmer's Cooperative of Arkansas and Oklahoma (Co-Op) sold promissory notes not backed by collateral or insurance to raise money to support general business operations. The notes paid above-market rates of interest and were called an "investment program." Advertisements for the notes said "YOUR CO-OP has more that $11,000,000 in assets to stand behind your investments. The Investment is not Federal [sic] insured but it is . . . Safe . . . Secure . . . and available when you need it." When the Co-Op filed for bankruptcy in 1984, over 1,600 people held notes worth $10 million.

Reves and other holders of the notes sued Ernst & Young, the firm that audited the Co-Ops's books, claiming that the accounting firm had failed to follow generally accepted accounting procedures in its audit, especially with respect to the value of the Co-Op's assets. They claimed that if Ernst & Young had valued the assets properly, the Co-Op's financial instability would have been obvious and the notes would not have been purchased. Hence, the accounting firm had violated the antifraud provisions of the securities laws. The note holders won a 6.1-million-dollar judgment.

Case Decision
The Supreme Court agreed that the notes issued were securities subject to federal securities law. The Court discussed a four-part test.

> Congress' purpose in enacting the securities laws was to regulate *investments*, in whatever form they are made and by whatever name they are called. . . .
>
> An examination . . . makes clear . . . factors that this Court has held apply in deciding whether a transaction involves a "security." First, we examine the transaction to assess the motivations that would prompt a reasonable seller and buyer to enter into it. If the seller's purpose is to raise money for the general use of a business enterprise or to finance substantial investments and the buyer is interested primarily in the profit the note is expected to generate, the instrument is likely to be a "security." . . .
>
> Second, we examine the "plan of distribution" of the instrument . . . to determine whether it is an instrument in which there is "common trading for speculation or investment,". . . . Third, we examine the reasonable expectations of the investing public: The Court will consider instruments to be "securities" on the basis of such public expectations, even where an economic analysis of the circumstances of the particular transaction might suggest that the instruments are not "securities" as used in that transaction. . . .
>
> Finally, we examine whether some factor such as the existence of another regulatory scheme significantly reduces the risk of the instrument, thereby rendering application of the Securities Acts unnecessary. . . .
>
> . . . we have little difficulty in concluding that the notes at issue here are "securities." . . .
>
> The Co-Op sold the notes in an effort to raise capital for its general business operations, and purchasers bought them in order to earn a profit in the form of interest.

Managerial Considerations
The parties involved in this deal—the people who ran the Co-Op, the accountants, and the investors—may never have had any idea that this was a security that required registration. It is not uncommon for a business investment to be sold without first determining whether it is a security. Since registration is expensive and not registering a security can be a federal crime, one should consult counsel to be sure the investment is either registered as a security or structured so that there is little doubt that it is not a security.

Securities Exempt from Federal Regulation.   Some securities are exempt from regulation. The most important class of securities exempted by both the 1933 and the 1934 Acts is debt issued or guaranteed by a government—federal, state, or local. Since the defaults of New York City and Cleveland on some bond issues, however, Congress has discussed the possibility of removing this privileged status from government debt and making it stand the same tests as private sector securities.

The 1933 Act (but not the 1934 Act) also provides an exemption for securities issued by banks, religious and other charitable organizations, savings and loan associations, motor carriers subject to regulation by the Interstate Commerce Commission (except railroads issuing securities for purposes other than equipment trust certificates), insurance policies, and annuity contracts. Most of these securities are subject to control by other federal agencies, such as the Federal Reserve System.

In general, an exempted security is not subject to the registration and disclosure requirements of the federal statutes. However, the security still may be subject to the Acts' general antifraud and civil liability provisions.

DISCLOSURE REQUIREMENTS

It is generally claimed that the main reason for the securities laws is to assure that investors are provided with adequate and accurate information upon which to base investment decisions. To the extent that managers of a corporation (or any other persons with information about the corporation that is not available to the public) are able to use information about the future profits or losses of the corporation to the disadvantage of investors, confidence in the stock market will be damaged. To alleviate this potential problem, the securities laws require corporations to disclose important information before the sale of securities and after the sale, when securities are traded in the market.

■ DISCLOSURE REQUIREMENTS UNDER THE 1933 ACT

The 1933 Act requires that issuers of securities fully *disclose* all *material information* regarding the security, its backers, and its intended use to prospective investors before the securities are sold. Material information is all key information that an investor would want to know about the background of a company, the company's executives, and the plan of operation. Disclosure is to be accomplished under the Act through the filing of a *registration statement* with the SEC. The registration process is intended to provide investors with sufficient and accurate information on material facts concerning the corporation and the securities it is proposing to sell. With that information, it is expected that investors can make an informed judgment about the merits of the securities being sold in determining whether to purchase them.

The Registration Statement. The registration statement has two parts. The first part is the *prospectus*—a document providing the legal offering of the sale of the security. The second part, which is often referred to as *items-and-answers,* consists of the disclosure of detailed information in response to specific questions asked by the SEC. The items-and-answers disclosure document is not distributed to prospective investors but is available for public inspection at the SEC.

In general, the registration process is intended to provide prospective investors with information on the following:

- Registrant's properties and business.
- Significant provisions of the security to be offered for sale and its relationship to the registrant's other capital securities.
- Information about the management of the registrant.
- Financial statements certified by independent public accountants.

The registration statement becomes effective on the twentieth day after filing is completed. The SEC may, however, advance or delay the date if it deems it appropriate after considering the interests of the investors and the public, the adequacy of the information, and the ease with which the facts about the new offering can be understood. Each year, there are thousands of registrations of hundreds of billions of dollars worth of new stocks and bonds.

The Prospectus.   A prospectus condenses the longer registration statement provided to the SEC and is supposed to help investors evaluate a security before purchase. A preliminary version of the prospectus is called a *red herring* (because of the red ink used on the first page). It is used by securities brokers to interest potential investors in a forthcoming offering. Every prospectus—preliminary or final—provides material information about the security issuer's property and business; the purpose of the offering; the use of the funds collected; the issue's prospects (risks involved); the promoter's managerial experience, history, and remuneration; and financial statements certified by a licensed accountant.

Items-and-Answers.   Unlike the prospectus, which is printed as a pamphlet, the second part of the registration statement consists of formal items-and-answers. More history on the issuers is required, especially about their financial background and past experience with securities. The SEC also may require special information about the proposed business or the issuers. This information may be used by professional investment analysts to study the offering in detail.

Review by the SEC.   The SEC cannot rule on the merits of an offering (that is, the likelihood of success of the proposed business as guessed by the SEC examiner), but it can require issuers to make high-risk factors clear and prominent in the prospectus so as to put buyers on notice. Similarly, if the proposed business involves something that strikes the examiner as strange, such as a peculiar financial arrangement, that fact may need to be highlighted. The SEC can issue a *stop order* to prohibit sale of securities until the registration statement is amended to satisfy the examiners. This power can slow the registration process and quash an offering thought undesirable by the SEC staff.

Shelf Registration.   The SEC allows *shelf registration* of some securities offerings. Shelf registration means that a company can propose a new security offering that meets all registration requirements but all of the security need not be sold at one time. Rather, the securities can be put "on the shelf" to be sold when the time is right. Hence, if a company wishes to sell $200 million of new stock over a two-year period, it need not sell the stock all at once or have separate registrations each time it wishes to sell some of the stock. Instead, it registers the entire offering and sells portions of the stock over time. The rule has reduced the cost of the registration process by eliminating much repetition in registering one security offering after another.

Shelf registration is available only to well-established firms—about 2,000 companies with a track record of obeying SEC requirements and having a minimum of $150 million market value of voting stock held by people not affiliated with the company except for their stock ownership (called a *float*) or a float of $100 million and an annual trading volume of shares of stock of at least three million. Once the registration of the new stock offering has been approved, the stock issuers need only amend the registration statement to reflect changes in any of the information provided.

The Costs of Registration.   Even for small securities offerings, say for $5 million, the registration process is expensive. The prospective issuer must hire such professionals as an experienced securities attorney, a certified public accountant, and a printer for the prospectus. The bill may easily run $100,000, excluding the expense of hiring an *underwriter* (the investment banker who will market the securities). The underwriter's fee may be as high as $500,000 for a 5-million-dollar offering. To avoid some costs of the registration process and other regulations, one may consider selling the security through a transaction that makes the security exempt from registration.

◼ EXEMPTIONS FROM REGISTRATION

Some securities, such as government bonds, are exempt from the jurisdiction of the securities laws. All other securities are subject to SEC jurisdiction, although they may qualify for an *exemption from registration.* If an exemption rule is violated, the securities may become subject to full registration. Only certain transactions involving a security are exempt from registration. That is, the initial *sale* of the securities may be an exempt transaction. The securities are never exempt from the securities laws. Also, it must be remembered that even if a transaction qualifies for an exemption from federal registration, state securities laws must be checked. States often have more stringent rules for exemptions, and registration at the state level may still be required.

Private Placement Exemption.   The 1933 Act provides that registration is not necessary for new securities not sold to the public. In some years, more securities are offered through *private placement* than through public offerings. The big users of the exemption are large blocks of securities sold to institutional investors such as pension funds or insurance companies. In the case of such sophisticated investors, the SEC is less concerned than it might be if the investors were thought to be less able to protect themselves in purchases of unregistered securities.

   Regulation D.   To reduce the uncertainty of what will qualify as a private placement, the SEC adopted Regulation D to spell out the elements of private placement exemptions:

▪ *Accredited investors* are those presumed sophisticated enough to evaluate investment opportunities without the benefit of an SEC-approved prospectus and wealthy enough to bear the risk of loss if an investment goes bad. Accredited investors may buy private placement offerings of securities. Large institutions, like banks, are accredited investors. The general rule for individuals is that they must have an annual income of at least $200,000 and a net worth of at least $1 million. All other investors are classified as unaccredited investors.

- Placements involving up to $5 million in securities can involve up to thirty-five unaccredited investors (and any number of accredited investors). Unaccredited investors must be given information similar to that provided in a registration statement.
- Securities offerings of over $5 million may be made only to accredited investors to keep the private placement exemption.

Rule 144A.   Private placements are most common for large security issues, mostly bonds, that are sold to institutional investors. In 1989, $165 billion was issued in private placements, about one-third of all issues.

This is expected to grow since the SEC adopted Rule 144A in 1990, which exempts U.S. and foreign security issuers from registration requirements for the sale of bonds and stocks to institutions that have at least $100 million in securities. Further, securities issued to such large institutions may be traded among similarly qualified institutions without registration or disclosure requirements.

Intrastate Offering Exemption.   The 1933 Act exempts from registration "any security which is part of an issue offered and sold only to persons resident within a single State . . . where the issuer of such security is . . . a corporation incorporated and doing business within such State." Hence, a security will qualify for the *intrastate exemption* from registration if the business issuing the security (1) is located primarily within the state in which it is selling securities and (2) sells securities only to residents of the state. This is not a commonly used exemption.

■ DISCLOSURE REQUIREMENTS UNDER THE 1934 ACT

While the 1933 Act imposes disclosure requirements on corporations issuing new securities, the 1934 Act imposes *disclosure requirements* on securities that are publicly traded. If a security was originally registered under the 1933 Act, it must be registered with the SEC under the 1934 Act. Even if not registered under the 1933 Act, it must be registered under the 1934 Act if it is traded on a securities exchange (New York Stock Exchange, American Stock Exchange, etc.) or if it is traded *over the counter* (OTC) and the company has $1 million or more in assets and 500 or more shareholders.

This rule applies to over 10,000 companies, most of which have securities traded in the OTC market. These companies must file reports on their securities. The most important report is the *10–K annual report,* an extensive audited document similar in content to the information provided in the registration process under the 1933 Act. Companies must also file *quarterly 10–Q reports* with unaudited financial information and *monthly 8–K reports* if significant developments have occurred. The purpose of these reports is to ensure that comprehensive financial information is disclosed to investors.

SECURITIES FRAUD

The securities registration and disclosure requirements of the 1933 and 1934 Acts do not prevent the sale of stock in risky, poorly managed, or unprofitable companies. Rather, the Acts are intended to help ensure the adequate and accurate disclosure of significant facts concerning the corporation and the securities it is selling. Failure to follow the disclosure requirements imposed by the 1933 and 1934 Acts, say by providing false and misleading statements, may result in SEC prosecution or private suits for securities fraud. Most securities fraud caused by false and misleading information occurs in the registration materials, but it can also be found in information filed during later disclosure, such as a 10–K annual report.

■ SECURITIES FRAUD UNDER THE COMMON LAW

Because contractual obligations and rights are created in the sale of a security, an investor can rely on common law fraud standards for protection. To establish liability under common law fraud, the injured investor must show the following:

1. A misstatement of a material fact—that is, incorrect important information about the security or some aspect of the business has been passed to the buyer.

2. *Scienter*, or intent to defraud—that is, the seller wanted to trick the buyer and intentionally deceived him or her to do so.

3. Knowledge on the part of the seller that a misstatement has been made.

4. Reliance by the recipient on the misstatement in the transaction—that is, the buyer believed what was said and relied on it in buying the stock.

5. Privity between the plaintiff and the defendant—that is, they must have been in a contractual arrangement with each other.

6. Proximate cause—that is, a causal relationship must exist between reliance on the misstatement and the subsequent losses.

7. Damages—that is, money was lost by the buyer.

However, injured investors often have difficulty establishing common law fraud. Thus, in bringing an action against the seller, injured investors generally rely on the antifraud provisions in the 1933 and 1934 Acts which hold that specific actions may result in statutory securities fraud.

■ STATUTORY SECURITIES FRAUD

The 1933 Act established a high standard for truthfulness in securities dealings. Section 11 established civil liabilities for *misleading statements* or *material omissions* in securities registration material. Any person who buys a security covered by a registration statement that contains false or misleading information or that fails to include information that was important to a decision to purchase may sue to recover any losses incurred in that purchase. This liability holds whether or not the security was registered—all securities are covered by the law of securities fraud.

This standard was extended by the 1934 Act to cover misleading information in disclosures required under that statute so that investors have protection during the life of the security. Securities fraud also arises as a result of mismanagement and insider trading.

Rule 10b–5.   Section 10(b) of the 1934 Act holds it unlawful for any person "to use or employ, in connection with the purchase or sale of any security registered on a national securities exchange or any security not so registered, any manipulative or deceptive device or contrivance in contravention of such rules and regulations as the Commission may prescribe. . . ." It provides the broadest base for bringing a securities fraud action and has come to be used in litigation more than any other part of the Act.

The SEC adopted Rule 10b–5 to enforce Section 10(b) of the 1934 Act. The rule is broad in scope:

> It shall be unlawful for any person, directly or indirectly, by the use of any means or instrumentality of interstate commerce, or of the mails, or of any facility of any national securities exchange,
>
> 1. to employ any device, scheme, or artifice to defraud,
> 2. to make any untrue statement of a material fact or to omit to state a material fact necessary in order to make the statements made, in the light of the circumstances under which they were made, not misleading, or
> 3. to engage in any act, practice, or course of business which operates or would operate as a fraud or deceit upon any person, in connection with the purchase or sale of any security.

The rule applies to all securities, registered or not. Although punishment for violations is not prescribed, courts decided decades ago that the usual rules of civil liability would apply for damages inflicted on others. Since the rule does not state specific offenses, it has been left to the SEC and the courts to decide how strict the standards will be and what will constitute offenses.

◼ PENALTIES FOR SECURITIES FRAUD

If an investor buys a security after receiving inaccurate information about the security knowingly provided by the issuer, the investor may institute a private action and sue the issuer to rescind the transaction and recover damages. In addition, Section 11 of the 1933 Act modifies the common law fraud action to make it easier for the injured investor to recover.

Importantly, the privity requirement is relaxed, allowing injured investors to bring an action against all parties connected with the preparation of the securities: every director of the company; the chief executive, financial, and accounting officers of the company; every underwriter involved in the transaction; every accountant, lawyer, and other expert who helped prepare the registration material; and any other person who signed the registration statement. All parties are held to high standards of professional care, which is one reason for the high cost of preparing all disclosure materials. Anyone involved can be responsible for material omissions or misleading statements made in the package by others.

The SEC can also recommend that the Justice Department bring criminal charges against violators. To warrant a criminal action, the offender must have engaged in the perpetration of fraud in any offer or sale of securities. The criminal penalty may involve fines and imprisonment. The rest of this section examines some major areas of securities fraud.

■ LIABILITY FOR MISSTATEMENTS

The 1933 Act imposes liability for omissions and misstatements in securities registration documents before the sale of a security. Under the 1934 Act, liability for *misstatements* or *omissions* about the financial status of a business enterprise that issued securities can be imposed on corporate officials or on those involved in preparing the information containing the misstatements. Securities fraud for misstatements can be based on any relevant business document that contains material omissions or misstatements: accountant reports, SEC disclosure documents, press releases, or public statements by executives.

Misleading information that would reasonably affect investment decisions by current or prospective securities owners includes misinformation about the present financial status or the future prospects of the enterprise that would affect the price of the security. For example, overly optimistic statements made by executives can cause favorable expectations about the future profits of a company, leading investors to bid up the price of the company's stock. When the statements are found to be false, the stock price falls, imposing losses on those who bought the stock on the basis of the positive statements. This is one of the most common grounds for private suits seeking damages based on a claim of *securities fraud*. The *Reves* case earlier in the chapter is an example of a securities fraud suit based on misstatements about material financial information made by an accounting firm about a security issuer.

Directors and senior officers of businesses know they are legally responsible for the consequences of misstatements they make that cause the price of the securities issued by their company to rise or fall. Under the law of securities fraud, if investors lose money because of things not said (omissions) or because of misstatements that investors reasonably rely on, then there was *material misinformation* that caused the loss. The Supreme Court reinforced that point in the *Basic* decision.

BASIC INC. v. LEVINSON

United States Supreme Court
485 U.S. 224,108 S.Ct. 978 (1988)

Case Background
Basic Inc. was a publicly traded company that began talks with Combustion Inc. in 1976 about the possibility of a merger. Basic made three public statements in 1977 and 1978 denying that it was engaged in merger negotiations.

On December 19, 1978, the Basic board endorsed Combustion's offer of $46 per share for Basic's common stock.

Basic and its directors were then sued by shareholders who had sold their stock before the merger announcement but after Basic's first statement in 1977 that there were no merger negotiations. The shareholders received less than $46 per share, claiming that the low price was due to the

(continued)

false and misleading statements by Basic and its directors in violation of Section 10(b) of the 1934 Securities Exchange Act and of Rule 10b–5. The shareholders claimed they were injured because they relied on misleading statements made by Basic. They sold their stock at lower prices than they would have received had the company told the truth about the merger talks. The district court held for Basic, finding that any misstatements were immaterial. The U.S. Court of Appeals reversed. Basic appealed to the U.S. Supreme Court.

Case Decision
Without specifically deciding this case (it was remanded), the Court held that under Rule 10b–5, an omitted fact is material if there is a substantial likelihood that its disclosure would have been considered significant by a reasonable investor. A statement must be misleading as to a material fact. What is material will be determined case-by-case. It is assumed that material misrepresentations affect the market price of a stock. Defendants can rebut that presumption by showing that the alleged misrepresentation or omission was not material and so did not affect the stock price or that the plaintiff did not rely on the information in making the decision to trade the stock.

Managerial Considerations
This decision, which was a close one, seems to have raised the standards of integrity to which managers will be held. Prior to this case, the rule was that unless there was an agreement-in-principle to merge or engage in some other significant act that would affect stock price, the information involved would not be defined as material. Now managers must tread a fine line of not denying that something may or may not happen, such as a merger, while at the same time not raising false expectations about such an event that could cause the stock price to jump when no jump is warranted.

This case illustrates why top executives and directors must be very careful in all statements they make about their company. Since investors listen closely to executives, anything the executives say that misleads investors, causing some to incur losses, will come back in a securities fraud suit. If the statement can be shown to be material—that is, to be a statement that was reasonable for investors to believe and could be expected to affect the stock price—the company and its executives may be responsible for investor losses.

The law of agency holds that corporate officers and directors are expected to perform their duties with the due care and skill expected of persons in such positions. Proving a violation of the duty of care is difficult. It is presumed that directors and officers act honestly and in good faith. So long as decisions reached by corporate officers and directors are "informed" decisions, the corporate officers and directors are protected by the *business judgment rule,* which protects such persons from liability for decisions that turn out, after the fact, to have been ill-advised or just unlucky.

Because of the strong legal protection offered directors and officers, suits for *mismanagement* are not common. The *Revlon* case in Chapter 11 is an example of a successful suit against officers and directors for breach of the duty of loyalty. Liability for mismanagement in securities cases is discussed in the *Santa Fe* case. Since this case, liability for misstatement has been the primary basis for securities fraud suits against executives.

SANTA FE INDUSTRIES, INC. v. GREEN

United States Supreme Court
430 U.S. 462, 97 S.Ct. 1292 (1977)

Case Background
Santa Fe Industries was the majority shareholder in Kirby Lumber. From 1968 to 1973, Santa Fe paid between $65 and $92.50 a share in gathering 95 percent of Kirby Lumber stock. By Delaware state law, since Santa Fe owned over 90 percent of the stock, it could force the remaining minority shareholders to sell their stock to it. Santa Fe obtained an independent appraisal of the value of Kirby from Morgan Stanley, a leading investment banking firm, which valued the remaining shares at $125 each. Santa Fe then offered Green and the other shareholders $150 a share for their stock. Green sued, claiming that the stock was worth $772

(continued)

a share and that Santa Fe had violated Rule 10b–5 by trying to defraud the shareholders of the true value. The district court held for Green, and the U.S. Court of Appeals reversed. Santa Fe appealed to the U.S. Supreme Court. The Court had to decide whether there was securities fraud under Rule 10b–5 because of mismanagement by Santa Fe.

Case Decision

The Court reversed and ruled for Santa Fe, holding that a claim of "unfair" was not sufficient to find liability for mismanagement under the 1934 Act. The plaintiff would have to present more substantial evidence of active manipulation that injured investors than existed here. There was no evidence of an omission or a misstatement of material information that caused manipulation of share prices.

Managerial Considerations

This case and some others like it have given the courts a good sense of when there may be liability imposed on managers for mismanagement that triggers securities fraud. Mismanagement appears to be uncommon, at least as measured by the number of cases that get to court on this basis.

In some cases, managers have not acted intelligently and caused losses to their company and its shareholders. Claims in such cases usually lose to the defense of the "business judgment rule." Mistakes are made, and hindsight is always better. The courts recognize that there is a difference between bad judgment or bad luck and managerial manipulation of a company to cause stock price losses. What would be the consequence of holding managers liable for securities fraud when their bad business judgment can be shown to be the primary cause of a fall in stock prices?

◼ LIABILITY FOR INSIDER TRADING

The most controversial application of Rule 10b–5 concerns the rule's use to prohibit *insider trading*—the buying or selling of stock by persons who have access to information affecting the value of the stock that has not yet been revealed to the public. Corporate executives are the ones most likely to be affected by the rule, as they are most likely to have valuable information concerning the financial well-being of the company that has not been released to the public. Since 1982, prosecutions for insider trading violations have jumped to an all-time high.

Application of the rule has a strange judicial origin, since the law says nothing specific about the issue. Rather, in an administrative ruling in 1961 (*Cady, Roberts & Co.*, 40 SEC 907), the SEC commissioners held insider trading to be illegal. This rule was accepted by the courts in the *Texas Gulf Sulphur* decision in 1968 and has been the subject of controversy ever since.

SEC Prosecution. The SEC will prosecute insiders—those with access to nonpublic information—if the insiders trade to their benefit in the stock in question before the public has a chance to act on the information. For example, if the president of Boeing were to learn that his company had just been awarded a major aircraft construction contract with the airlines, he could call his stockbroker and buy numerous shares of Boeing stock before releasing the good news. Once the word was out, since expectations about the future profits of the company would be good, the stock price would jump, giving a nice profit to the president. If this were discovered, the president could be sued for all the profits he earned in the transaction.

As the Supreme Court noted in the *Texas Gulf Sulphur* decision, the reasoning behind the rule against insider trading is that insiders should not be able to use corporate information for personal gain, since it gives them an unfair advantage in the market over investors who do not have the information. It is illegal for an insider to trade on inside information until the information has been released to the public and the stock price has had time to adjust to the new information. What was not clear was against whom the rule against insider trading applied. If you are riding on the subway in Washington and overhear two executives talking about something big about to happen to their company, you have just learned nonpublic information. Would it be illegal for you to trade on such information? For a while it looked as if that might be the case, but in the early 1980s, the Supreme Court helped clarify the rules.

Supreme Court Interpretation.   A printer at a company that printed financial documents read some confidential information. Trading in the stock of the company involved, the printer made $30,000 in profits because of his access to inside information. The SEC charged the printer, Vincent Chiarella, with securities fraud, but the Supreme Court reversed the lower court conviction.

In the 1980 decision *Chiarella* v. *United States,* the high court said that Chiarella was not a corporate insider who owed a *financial duty* to the shareholders of his company. He was an outsider who was lucky enough to learn about inside information. Only if his position had a requirement that he could not use such information could he be responsible. Chiarella may have had an unfair advantage over other stock traders, but it did not constitute securities fraud, said the Court. "He was not their [the corporation's] agent, he was not a fiduciary, he was not a person in whom the sellers had placed their trust and confidence. He was, in fact, a complete stranger who dealt with the sellers only through impersonal market transactions." The *Dirks* case further clarified liability for insider trading.

DIRKS v. SECURITIES AND EXCHANGE COMMISSION

United States Supreme Court
463 U.S. 646, 103 S.Ct. 3255 (1983)

Case Background
Raymond Dirks worked for a broker/dealer firm in New York. His job was to determine for investors whether they should buy securities in certain insurance firms, including Equity Funding of America. A former officer of Equity Funding told Dirks that Equity officers were engaged in fraud and that the firm's stock was thus overvalued. Dirks investigated the tip and decided that it was probably true. Dirks told some of his clients, who then sold their stock in Equity. The word spread, and in two weeks the price of Equity fell from $26 to $15 per share.

California insurance authorities and then the SEC moved to investigate Equity and uncovered a major investment fraud. The SEC charged Dirks with violating the law against insider trading. Dirks had used knowledge gained in his professional capacity that was not disclosed to the public. The federal court of appeals agreed with the SEC, holding that any person who receives inside information must

divulge the information to the public and not use it in any manner in private trading in securities. Dirks appealed to the U.S. Supreme Court.

Case Decision
The Supreme Court reversed the decision, holding that Dirks was free to use the inside information that he had obtained. Not all trading based on inside information is illegal. To be illegal, the person who uses the information must have a fiduciary duty to the shareholders not to use it and must trade for secret profits. Dirks did neither.

Managerial Considerations
Supreme Court cases and SEC prosecutions indicate that the key to determining the legality or illegality of insider trading is whether a fiduciary duty was violated. Insiders to corporate information—usually top management and directors—have a fiduciary duty not to trade on significant information for their own gain. Neither may insiders give the information to those who know how to trade on it for gain.
(continued)

Those who acquire information by accident or investigation, like Chiarella or Dirks, have no duty to shareholders not to trade on it.

As insider trading has become a major issue in recent years, more companies have taken steps to formalize rules against it. Companies make it a policy that top managers and directors may not trade on inside information and may be required to make their trades on certain schedules to dissuade even the appearance of trading on inside information. That is, the trades of company insiders are watched by market professionals as signs of impending good or bad company news. To prevent such an impression, insiders trade on given dates to reduce speculation.

INSIDER TRADING SANCTIONS ACT

The *Insider Trading Sanctions Act* (ITSA) was passed by Congress in 1984 to give the SEC a statutory basis for prosecuting insider trading. ITSA allows the SEC to bring enforcement actions against violators who buy or sell securities while in possession of material nonpublic information. The courts may order violators to pay treble damages based on a measure of the illegal profit gained or loss avoided by the insider trading. Those convicted of violations may also have to pay back illegal profits to those who suffered the losses, which effectively means quadruple damages. In addition, criminal penalties may be assessed.

MAJOR INSIDER TRADING CASES

Thayer. The SEC filed a complaint in 1984 against the Deputy Secretary of the Department of Defense, Paul Thayer, the former chief executive officer of LTV Corporation. Thayer resigned from his Pentagon post and was convicted in 1985 for obstruction of justice in an SEC investigation of insider trading. He was given a four-year prison sentence and ordered to surrender $555,000 for his insider trading activities. While he was at LTV Corporation, he had divulged inside information to eight friends who gained millions from his knowledge.

Levine. The Thayer case seemed like small potatoes compared with the one involving Dennis Levine which broke in 1986. Levine was sued by the SEC. Cooperating with authorities, he provided information that helped the SEC bring insider trading charges against prominent lawyers and securities traders on Wall Street. Levine agreed to repay almost $13 million in illegal gains. That case led to an even bigger fish—Ivan Boesky.

Boesky. In late 1986, the SEC sued Boesky. The complaint claimed that Boesky purchased securities based on material nonpublic information provided by Dennis Levine as part of an organized trading scheme involving senior officers in prestigious investment firms. It is little wonder that Boesky earned the highest income on Wall Street in 1985. Boesky paid for nonpublic information on tender offers, mergers, and other business deals that greatly affect stock prices.

The SEC claimed that Boesky knew that all such information was confidential and had been obtained through breach of a fiduciary duty. For example, the SEC charged that Boesky paid Levine five percent of his profits earned on securities purchases and sales based on confidential information Levine gave him—some of which was obtained from other investment brokers who were also in on the deal. One firm was handling the forthcoming merger of Nabisco and R.J. Reynolds. That created a fiduciary duty not to reveal that information or act on it for personal gain. However, those in a position of trust sold their valuable information, knowing that when word of the merger was made public, the stock prices of the two companies would rise.

Boesky agreed to pay $100 million in cash and assets. Half of that amount was a civil penalty paid under ITSA to the U.S. Treasury. The other $50 million represented illegal gains and was held for the benefit of investor claims. Boesky also agreed to an order barring him from any association with any broker, dealer, investment adviser, investment company, or municipal securities dealer. That is, one of Wall Street's "most successful" traders is out of the industry for life. Boesky also received a three-year prison sentence. Based on information Levine and Boesky provided, more cases were brought by the SEC in 1987 in a continuing insider trading investigation. As we saw at the beginning of this chapter, Kidder, Peabody & Company agreed to pay $25 million in civil penalties for insider trading in 1987 and to cooperate with the SEC in further investigations.

Drexel.   Drexel Burnham Lambert Inc., one of the most innovative Wall Street firms of the 1980s, increased its business substantially through its junk-bond operations headed by Michael Milken. Milken and Drexel handled the issuance and marketing of about one-half of the nearly $140 billion worth of junk (high-yield) bonds issued through 1988.

In early 1989, Drexel pleaded guilty to six felony counts of securities fraud and agreed to pay $650 million in fines and restitution. Drexel settled the case in part because of concern that if the company lost in court, under the Racketeer Influenced and Corrupt Organizations (RICO) law, it could have been assessed treble damages, plus made subject to other litigation that would follow such a conviction. To help restructure the firm, Drexel then sold its public brokerage offices and hired former SEC Chairman John Shad to be its new chairman. Having been indicted on ninety-eight counts of violations of the securities laws, Michael Milken plead guilty in 1990 to six felony counts. In 1992, Milken agreed to pay $200 million in fines to the government and $900 million in restitution to pay the claims of defrauded investors. Drexel and other parties agreed to pay an additional $400 million. The case against Milken had little to do with his fame for junk bonds, which are perfectly legal, but for his dealings with Boesky and others. Among the crimes he admitted to were

- Cheating Drexel's clients by falsely reporting to them the prices at which securities had been bought and sold, with his junk-bond department keeping the profits.

- Helping a partner evade income taxes by manufacturing losses and gains from apparent stock transactions.

- Conspiring with Boesky to keep secret records to hide the fact that Boesky was the owner of certain securities.

- Secretly agreeing to buy stock from Boesky and hold it at Drexel so that Boesky could appear to have more capital on hand to meet certain SEC capital requirements.

Sentenced to ten years in prison, Milken will be barred from the securities industry for life.

INSIDER TRADING IN EUROPE | INTERNATIONAL ASPECTS

Insider trading cases draw more media attention than any other aspect of SEC law enforcement. The cases involving Milken and Boesky made front-page headlines. In Europe, little attention has been paid until recently to the common practice of insider trading. Most countries have no law against it. In Britain, where insider trading has been illegal since 1980, there has been about one conviction a year, the harshest penalty being a 43,000-dollar fine. Switzerland and Spain passed laws against insider trading in 1988. Germany tightened its law in 1991 so that the EC countries could have an insider-trading standard by 1993.

A major insider trading scandal in France involving people close to France's president was uncovered by the SEC. The result of this scandal was the 1989 passage of a law against insider trading in France. An official of the European Community said, "In America, there is a very important philosophy of shareholder information which is not the same here . . . Some member states do not have a legal definition of the crime and do not give authorities necessary power to pursue it. We are lagging."

One reason for the difference in attitude may be that only about 10 percent of Europeans own stock, compared to a much higher percent of Americans. Since most stock in Europe is owned in large blocks by institutional traders, most citizens have little reason to care about the effects of insider trading.

PROXIES, TENDER OFFERS, AND TAKEOVERS

Securities laws and state corporation laws impose constraints on the way friendly mergers occur and especially on hostile takeovers by one company of another. Any time companies that have issued public securities are involved, the rules of the 1934 Act come into play.

■ PROXIES

A *proxy* is permission given by shareholders for someone else to vote their shares on their behalf in the manner they instruct. Since it is not practical for shareholders to attend corporate meetings at which they vote to approve major decisions, such as to merge with another company or elect the board of directors, shareholders are sent proxy statements to be voted on their behalf. Firms must provide shareholders with proxy statements—information about major proposed changes in the business. SEC regulations spell out the form and timing proxy solicitations must take.

While most proxies are routine, such as voting for boards of directors or amendments to company bylaws, proxy fights can be used in a struggle over the future of the organization. For example, a proxy fight was waged in 1990 to try to force USX to split into two separate companies—U.S. Steel and Marathon Oil. The board of directors was successful in opposing this move, but the vote was close on the issue, which was forced to a proxy vote by dissatisfied USX shareholders.

◼ TENDER OFFERS

When one company attempts to take over another, it often uses a *tender offer*. Shareholders in the target company are offered stock in the acquiring company or cash in exchange for their stock. If successful, the acquiring company obtains enough stock to control the target company. Tender offers must be registered with the SEC, and certain procedures must be followed. These requirements have allowed the SEC to play an active role in the merger and acquisition process and, by raising the costs of takeovers, have reduced the number that have occurred.

Spurred by the wave of merger activities in the 1980s, consideration has been given to revising the 1934 Act to impose more regulations on merger activities, especially hostile takeovers. Some oppose this possible change as legislation designed to protect incumbent management from possibly losing their jobs in a takeover that leads to a shakeup of the managerial structure of the new organization. Supporters of restrictions claim that the takeovers do not increase efficiency.

State Intervention.   There has been a substantial increase in activities at the state level to reduce the ease of takeovers. Corporations chartered in various states petitioned their legislatures to change state laws to help regulate takeovers. The Supreme Court has approved broad authority to the states in this regard, as we see in the *CTS Corporation* case.

CTS CORPORATION v. DYNAMICS CORPORATION OF AMERICA

United States Supreme Court
481 U.S. 69, 107 S.Ct. 1637 (1987)

Case Background
A 1986 Indiana law makes any entity that buys more than 20 percent of the public stock in a corporation chartered and doing business in Indiana subject to special provisions. Such stock acquisitions usually are an attempt to gain voting control of the corporation (a takeover). The law requires tender offers to remain open for at least fifty business days. At the end of that time, the existing board of directors can call a meeting at which the shareholders must vote approval of the takeover, even if the buyer has over 50 percent of the stock. That is, the buyer does not get voting rights with the stock until approved by the board. This is a statutory defense against takeovers.

Dynamics Corporation ran into this law when attempting to buy control of CTS Corporation. Dynamics claimed that the Indiana statute was an unconstitutional interference with federal securities law, which preempt state laws. The federal district court and the U.S. Court of Appeals agreed with Dynamics. CTS appealed to the U.S. Supreme Court.

Case Decision
The Supreme Court upheld the ability of CTS to use the Indiana takeover provisions in defense against Dynamics. The federal securities laws were not held to be a bar against such state laws, since there was no indication that Congress intended to control state corporation law.

(continued)

Managerial Considerations

Within two years of this decision, a majority of the states had enacted similar statutes, passed at the request of corporate managers and directors who claimed that they needed statutory protection against takeovers. Some of the same protection can be provided in "poison pill" provisions of corporate charters which allow corporate directors to take steps to make a company more difficult or less attractive to takeover.

Takeovers mean that shareholders are being given the chance to freely sell their stock, usually at a premium, to the buyer of the company. Several business scholars have questioned whether it is ethical for managers to push for statutory protection for their jobs, which may be eliminated after a takeover. They argue that if the takeover effort fails because of statutory defenses allowed corporate insiders, shareholders will suffer by losing the high price they were offered for their stock.

THE INVESTMENT COMPANY ACT

Congress ordered the SEC to study the behavior of investment companies. The resulting reports led to the *Investment Company Act* (ICA) of 1940, which gives the SEC control over the structure of investment companies. The Act requires investment companies to register with the SEC, which then makes the companies subject to restrictions on their activities and holds them liable to the SEC and to private parties for violations of the ICA.

INVESTMENT COMPANIES

An *investment company* is an entity engaged primarily in the business of investing or trading in securities. The ICA defines three types of investment companies: face-amount certificate companies, which issue debt securities paying a fixed return; unit investment trusts, offering a fixed portfolio of securities; and management companies, the most important type of investment company.

Mutual Funds.   The most common management company is the *open-end company,* generally known as a *mutual fund.* Mutual funds have about $0.5 trillion invested in them. Such companies can expand (keep adding shares) as long as people wish to invest with them. The number of shares can be reduced as investors redeem their shares. The money from these shares is invested in a portfolio of securities. The price of the shares is determined by the value of the portfolio divided by the number of shares sold to the public. This is the most common investment company because of the flexibility it offers to investors and portfolio managers.

There are two kinds of mutual funds: *load* and *no-load.* The former are sold to the public through a securities dealer and have a sales commission (load) of some percentage of the price. No-load funds are sold directly to the public through the mail with no sales commission.

Several organizations are exempt that would otherwise be required to comply with ICA regulations. A company that has fewer than one hundred security holders and does not sell its securities to the public is exempt as a *closely held company.* Similarly, investment companies that do not offer securities to the public but rather are involved in internal investing, such as banks, insurance companies, charitable foundations, tax-exempt pension funds, and other specialized institutions, are exempt.

■ REGULATION OF INVESTMENT COMPANIES

Under the ICA, investment companies must register with the SEC, stating their investment policy and other information. Annual reports and other information must be disclosed on a continuing basis. Capital requirements for operation are set by the SEC, and the debt structure is controlled. Payment of dividends to investors must equal at least 90 percent of the taxable ordinary income of the investment company. A company must invest in only those activities it stated it would in its sales literature and policy statements.

Registration and Disclosure.   Since investment companies sell securities, such as shares in mutual funds, to buy securities for investment purposes, their securities must be registered with the SEC. Hence, companies under the ICA are subject to the *registration and disclosure* requirements of the SEC for publicly traded securities. The sales literature used by mutual fund companies to promote their investment strategies to the public must be filed with the SEC for review. In general, no share of stock in an investment company may be sold for more than the company's current net asset value plus a maximum sales charge (load) of 8.5 percent.

Limiting Conflicts of Interest.   To reduce possible *conflicts of interest*, there are restrictions on who may be on the board of directors of an investment company. At least 40 percent of the members of the board must be outsiders—persons with no direct business relationship with the company or its officers. The outsiders on the board are responsible for approving contracts with the investment advisers who are usually hired to manage the investment fund offered by the company. Further, investment companies may not use the funds invested with them for deals with any persons affiliated with the company. All deals are to be "arm's length," so there is no conflict of interest.

Investment Advisers.   Investment companies usually hire *investment advisers* to manage their operations. Investment advisers have more funds invested in their care than do investment companies. This is because registered investment advisers manage pension funds and the portfolios held by insurance companies and banks. According to the ICA, investment advisers are "deemed to have a fiduciary duty with respect to the receipt of compensation for services" rendered to investment companies. The standard fee paid to advisers to manage an investment company fund is 0.5 percent of the net assets of the funds each year. Investment advisers now manage several trillion dollars worth of investments.

■ ARBITRATION OF DISPUTES

When investors establish accounts with investment firms, they usually sign a standard form that states that in the event of a dispute, the dispute must be arbitrated, not litigated. The SEC issued rules in 1989 to reform the arbitration process that is the primary dispute resolution mechanism for brokers and investors.

Under the regulations, the arbitration requirements must be pointed out to the customer and clearly explained. Arbitration boards appointed to settle disputes usually include one industry professional and two members of the public. Under SEC rules, the arbitrators from the public must provide details of their past ten years' activities, and they may not have worked for the securities industry for at least three years. The new rules also specify that brokers must provide requested documents to investors before arbitration hearings. In general, the rules give parties the right to use procedures that follow the elements of judicial procedure. Further, although arbitration records will be kept secret, the decisions will be made public so that there is better understanding about the process.

About the same time the SEC issued these new regulations, the Supreme Court issued a decision in 1989 that upheld the binding nature of the arbitration agreements. It will be an unusual case in which an investor will be allowed to litigate a dispute with a broker. The Court held that the arbitration agreements apply to security fraud claims against brokers, whether the claim is brought under the 1933 or the 1934 securities law. The Court noted that there is a "strong endorsement of the federal statutes favoring this method of resolving disputes."

Arbitration is generally much less expensive than litigation, and the results tend to be more certain because of the expertise of the arbitrators. Most of the thousands of arbitration cases filed annually are resolved in favor of the client. For example, in 1992 an American Arbitration Association panel ordered Prudential Securities to pay $1.4 million in damages, including $600,000 punitive damages, for allowing its San Diego office to engage in excessive trading in an account of a retired couple. Three officers of the San Diego office were ordered to pay damages from $100,000 to $300,000.

THE INVESTMENT ADVISERS ACT

The *Investment Advisers Act* (IAA) complements the ICA. It defines *investment adviser* as a "person who, for compensation, engages in the business of advising others . . . as to the advisability of investing in, purchasing or selling securities . . . ". The regulations adopted by the SEC under the Act are a part of the regulation of professionals working in the securities industry.

■ BROKERS AND DEALERS

The IAA works with the 1934 Securities Exchange Act to regulate *brokers* (persons engaged in the business of effecting transactions in securities for the account of others) and *dealers* (persons engaged in the business of buying and selling securities for their own account). For simplicity, brokers, dealers, and investment advisers will all be referred to as *securities professionals*. Securities professionals must be registered with the SEC. Violations of SEC rules can lead to suspension or permanent loss of the right to do business in the industry.

■ PROFESSIONAL RESPONSIBILITY TO CLIENTS

One primary concern of the SEC in regulating securities professionals is protection of clients from *conflicts of interest*. The Supreme Court has held that broker/dealers must make known to their customers any possible conflicts or other information material to investment decisions. Professionals violate their duty when they charge excessive markups (commissions) on securities above their market value to unsuspecting customers. Markups over 5 percent are difficult to justify, and those over 10 percent are not allowed under SEC guidelines.

Other practices that have been attacked include *churning*, whereby a broker who has control of a client's account buys and sells an excessive amount of stock to make money from the commissions earned on the transactions. Also illegal is *scalping*, whereby a professional buys stock for personal benefit, then urges investors to buy the stock so that the price will rise to the benefit of the professional.

Another major concern of the SEC in regulating securities professionals focuses on ensuring investors *adequate information* about available securities. Generally, professionals will violate the antifraud provisions of the regulations when they recommend securities without making adequate information available. Registered professionals may not deal in securities not registered under the 1933 or 1934 Securities Act. If the security is exempt from either Act, the professional must have information about the security similar to the information that would be required of a registered security.

■ INVESTMENT NEWSLETTERS

Investment advisers who violate securities laws may be suspended or barred from dispensing investment advice for compensation. While we usually think of an investment adviser who has stolen clients' funds or otherwise abused a fiduciary duty to a client as subject to SEC prosecution, does such regulation extend to the sale of investment advice via an investment newsletter? There are many such newsletters. Annual subscription rates are usually in the hundreds of dollars and some run $1,000 per year. Some publishers of newsletters have made tens of millions of dollars dispensing investment advice in their newsletters. The Supreme Court, in *Lowe* v. *SEC*, addressed SEC regulation of newsletters.

LOWE v. SECURITIES AND EXCHANGE COMMISSION

United States Supreme Court
472 U.S. 181, 105 S.Ct. 2557 (1985)

Case Background
Lowe was a registered investment adviser from 1974 to 1981. After he was convicted for misappropriating client funds, the SEC ordered Lowe not to operate as an investment adviser or to associate with investment advisers.

Lowe then began to publish and sell a semimonthly investment newsletter. The newsletter sold for $900 per year and attracted about 19,000 subscribers in its only year of operation. It contained commentary about securities markets, investment strategies, and specific recommendations for buying, selling, or holding stocks. Subscribers could call a hotline for current market tips.

(continued)

The SEC sued Lowe, claiming that the sale of investment advice by a newsletter violated the IAA because of Lowe's previous conviction. The federal court of appeals agreed with the SEC, holding that the IAA does not distinguish between personal advice and advice given in publications. Hence, the bar to Lowe being an investment adviser extended to selling advice by the newsletter. Lowe appealed to the Supreme Court.

Case Decision
The Supreme Court reversed in Lowe's favor. It held that publishers of investment newsletters are not investment advisers under the IAA; therefore Lowe could not be sued by the SEC. Newsletters are impersonal; the IAA governs personalized investment advice, which is what the law regulates. Further, SEC regulation of publication of investment newsletters, which could include almost any business news publication, would present serious conflicts with the freedom of speech guaranteed by the First Amendment.

Managerial Considerations
Investment newsletters appeal to investors with various perspectives. Some are fundamentalist Christian in orientation, some are politically left, some appeal to "gold bugs." Since there is no evidence in the scholarly finance literature that any investment adviser consistently picks winning investments, the value of investment newsletters is dubious. Nevertheless, in a country that guarantees freedom of the press, investment newsletters, even those that cannot provide the financial insights they claim (at high subscription prices), are free to publish what they want.

STOCK MARKET REGULATION

As Table 17–1 illustrates, the volume and value of stock transactions have grown rapidly in the past decade. As the New York Stock Exchange, which handles about 80 percent of public stock market transactions, heads to round-the-clock trading, this activity can be expected to continue to grow.

■ SELF-REGULATION OF SECURITIES MARKETS

Under the terms of the 1934 Securities Exchange Act, Congress allows private associations of securities professionals to set rules for professionals dealing in securities markets. Congress gave the SEC the power to monitor such self-regulating organizations, including the stock exchanges, such as the New York Stock Exchange (NYSE), the American Stock Exchange (AMEX), the regional exchanges, and the over-the-counter (OTC) market.

Rules for Exchange Members.   The stock exchanges establish and enforce rules of conduct for their members. Some rules govern the operation of the exchange, how securities are listed, obligations of issuers of securities, who may handle certain transactions and in what manner, and how prices are

TABLE 17–1 SALES OF STOCKS ON REGISTERED EXCHANGES				
	1970	1980	1984	1989
Market value of all exchanges ($ billions)	132	522	1,004	2,004
Number of shares exchanged (millions)	4,539	15,488	30,456	54,239

SOURCE: Statistical Abstract of the United States.

set and reported. Other rules concern how member firms and their employees must qualify for membership to be allowed to handle various transactions. These rules include how investors' accounts are to be managed, the qualifications of dealers and brokers, limits on advertising, and other operations of securities firms. Governing the OTC market is the National Association of Securities Dealers (NASD), which sets rules of behavior for traders on the OTC market similar to the rules of the NYSE for its members.

Liability and Penalties. Punishment for violation of rules can include suspension or expulsion from the organization, making transactions by the expelled member impossible. If an exchange knows that a member firm is violating the rules or the law and it ignores such a violation, causing investors to lose money, it can be held liable for the losses. The potential liability and SEC pressure have given the exchanges an incentive to watch securities professionals for violations.

◼ REGULATION OF SECURITIES TRANSACTIONS

The SEC, in cooperation with the NASD, regulates the actions of securities professionals who handle the actual trading of securities. The SEC does not allow professionals to use their position to make transactions for their own benefit. To minimize such problems, floor trading by professionals is strictly limited to registered experts, as is off-floor trading. The difference between these two types of trading is that one is done on the floor of a securities exchange while the other is done elsewhere, such as OTC. In either case, professional securities dealers may not trade for their own advantage ahead of their customers.

Regulations also cover *specialist firms.* These firms generally do not deal directly with the public; rather, they handle transactions for brokers. Brokers may leave their customers' orders with the specialist to be filled when possible. For example, if a stock is currently selling for $21 a share and a stock owner is willing to sell at $22 a share, the order may be left to be filled should the price rise to $22. Specialists also handle transactions that are unusual or difficult for most securities dealers to execute. SEC rules prohibit the specialists from exploiting their special position. Specialists may not deal for their own benefit in the orders left to execute. Since they are first to learn of price changes, they could buy and sell the stock left with them to take advantage of changes in stock prices.

◼ MARGIN REQUIREMENTS

The Federal Reserve Board (the Fed) regulates the amount of credit issued by securities professionals, banks, and other lenders to investors for buying stocks. The Fed establishes a *margin requirement* of the amount of a stock purchase that must be financed by cash. For example, the Fed now rules that only 50 percent of the value may be bought on margin—that is, on credit. The other 50 percent must be paid for in cash by the investor. Should the price of the stock drop drastically, the lender (usually a brokerage house) must make a margin call. That is, the lender must call the customer to cover a portion of the debt (margin) outstanding on the security. The Fed also publishes a list of stocks that may be purchased on margin. Usually the list includes only those stocks traded on major exchanges. Stocks not on the list may not be purchased on margin.

FRANCHISE REGULATION

Sales by *franchise* establishments are approaching $1 trillion per year. While automobile dealerships and gasoline stations have traditionally been franchised, this method of organizing business has spread to many other sales establishments, as Table 17–2 shows. Over 80 percent of franchise establishments are owned and operated by franchisees. The remainder are owned by the parent company, which hires the managers and employees. Franchises employ over seven million people.

While some franchises, like McDonald's, are almost always very successful, as in any business there are failures. Many franchises are sold with little experience in operation. Purchasers of some of those franchises have lost all of their investment, which can be part or all of their life savings. For example, you may agree to pay the Tasty Ant company $10,000 for the exclusive right to distribute Tasty Ant Company-produced chocolate-covered ants in your state. Regardless of how hard you work and how good the product is, you may discover that the market for chocolate-covered ants is smaller than anticipated. The result could be that you are out your $10,000, plus the cost of the inventory you purchased and the value of your time spent promoting the product.

■ FTC FRANCHISE RULE

To try to reduce the number of investors who became involved in dubious franchise operations, the FTC enacted the *Franchise Rule,* which requires the seller of franchise or business opportunities to give prospective buyers a detailed disclosure document at least ten days before any money changes

TABLE 17–2
FRANCHISED BUSINESSES

Kind of Business	Number (in thousands)		Sales (in billions)	
	1970	1990	1970	1990
Total Franchises	396.3	533.0	$119.8	$716.4
Auto/truck dealers	37.2	27.6	58.8	362.3
Gasoline stations	222.0	111.7	29.3	115.1
Restaurants	32.6	102.1	4.6	76.5
Retailing (nonfood)	30.7	54.1	13.1	28.6
Automotive products	20.4	38.6	1.9	13.6
Convenience stores	8.8	17.5	1.7	14.4
Hotels and motels	3.4	11.1	3.5	23.9

SOURCE: U.S. Dept. of Commerce, *Franchising in the U.S. Economy.*

hands or before the buyer is legally committed to a purchase. Much like SEC disclosure documents for new stock offerings, the Franchise Rule's disclosure document includes important information about the business:

- Names, addresses, and telephone numbers of other purchasers.
- An audited financial statement of the seller.
- The background and experience of the business's key executives.
- The responsibilities that the buyer and the seller will have to each other once the purchase is made.

This document enables prospective investors to know about the background of the business and, if the information is not true, allows a legal basis for the buyer to attempt recovery directly or for the FTC to bring an action against the seller. While similar to SEC regulations, this Rule was not implemented by the SEC, because such business opportunities are not securities.

State Regulation.   Many states have recently passed statutes to regulate the sale of franchises. The FTC Franchise Rule sets a minimum national disclosure standard that states may go beyond. Sixteen states have adopted a *Uniform Franchise Offering Circular* (UFOC) that requires financial disclosures by franchisors to prospective franchisees that go beyond the FTC requirements. In particular, the UFOC requires franchise sellers to give details about the earnings history of the company and of franchises in existence. Some franchise sellers give no information about earnings or have exaggerated actual earnings.

Rule Violations.   An example of a Franchise Rule violation is the Tuff-Tire case. The FTC charged the Tuff-Tire Company and its officers with violations of the Franchise Rule. Tuff-Tire misrepresented to potential investors that franchisees could earn from $110,000 to $410,000 annually—amounts that existing franchisees were claimed to have earned. The FTC charged that there was no reasonable basis for these claims and that the company did not provide prospective franchisees with presale information about earnings claims required by the Rule.

INTERNATIONAL ASPECTS | AMERICAN FRANCHISES IN EUROPE

The European Community's move to tear down barriers to trade inside Europe has had many American companies scrambling to get into Europe. The existence of a single market as large as the United States is appealing to firms that could not afford to open operations in Europe on a country-by-country basis. Firms are also concerned that if they do not get a foot in the door right away, they may not be able to get in later if the EC erects trade barriers against the rest of the world.

American franchisers, over 400 of which operate about 40,000 outlets outside the United States, face problems in Europe that make operations more difficult than they are in the United States. In the EC, it is illegal for a franchiser,

(continued)

such as McDonald's, to contract with a single company, say Coca-Cola, to supply all its franchisees with certain products. McDonald's cannot even require its franchisees in Europe to sell Coke. But it can require its franchisees to put a certain amount of catsup on each hamburger.

Such constraints make it difficult to achieve certain economies of scale from the use of standardized operations, quality control, and common advertisements. Further, the details of such regulations are subject to change as EC officials work in Brussels to write new rules. While European franchisers are used to working within these constraints, Japanese and American firms face a set of legal obstacles that strike at the heart of their operations.

The Tuff-Tire Company sold franchises called "Mr. Tuff-Tire" that sold a product for car and truck tires that was to seal punctures and prevent flat tires. Franchisees paid between $2,000 and $98,000 for their franchises. The Justice Department, at the request of the FTC, filed a complaint in federal district court. In 1987, the court ordered the defendants not to violate the Rule in the future and required them to repay $1.4 million in refunds to eighty-seven people who bought franchises based on misrepresentation. The franchisors were also ordered to pay $870,000 in civil penalties. In 1991, the promoter of this scheme was sentenced to three years in prison.

The FTC sued Fax Corp. of America in 1990 for violations of the Franchise Rule. Fax Corp. sold about 500 franchises for an average of $58,000 each. The franchisees would set up public FAX machines that are activated by credit cards. The FTC charged that besides failing to abide by the disclosure requirements of the Rule, the company made false claims about earnings and failed to refund franchise fees paid by franchisees, as it claimed it would. Investors may have lost several million dollars in this case, which was not unique.

SUMMARY: A GUIDE FOR MANAGERS

- Securities includes any (1) investment of money (2) in a common enterprise where there is (3) an expectation of profits (4) from the efforts of persons other than the investors. This definition from the *Howey* case is intended to include any investment device that may be invented that meets these general criteria.

- Registration of new securities requires formal disclosure of financial and managerial information with the SEC. Since the disclosure is complicated and mistakes can lead to serious legal consequences, skilled counsel is required.

- Companies that have securities that are traded publicly must file financial disclosure information monthly, quarterly, and annually with the SEC. Since production of these reports is costly, this must also be considered when weighing the costs and benefits of seeking financing in the securities market compared to private sources.

- While there are some securities not under the federal securities laws, those securities are usually regulated by other authorities. All securities, registered or not with the SEC, are subject to securities fraud law. Securities fraud exposes one to private litigation and to civil and possible criminal prosecution by the government.

- Under the 1934 Securities Exchange Act, liability may be imposed on securities issuers or corporate officials for misstatements in any corporate documents, including statements to the media. Material information that misleads investors about a company and that causes profits in a security to be lost may be the basis of legal action. Hence, corporate executives and directors must address company matters with a high degree of care.

- Liability may also be imposed under Section 10(b) of the 1934 Act on executives and directors for mismanagement of a company that causes investors to lose profits. Suits for this usually require a showing of fraud. Managers are given wide leeway under the business-judgment rule to make decisions that, in hindsight, were wrong.

- Insider trading can lead to criminal and civil prosecution under securities law as well as private liability. Liability is imposed for insider trading when it can be shown that insiders violate a fiduciary duty. That is, if one is in a position of trust that provides access to valuable information, one may not exploit the information for personal gain, since one has a duty to protect the information and use it for the benefit of those to whom the duty is owed—the shareholders.

- All takeover attempts and proxy battles for control of a company must be registered with the SEC when certain levels of stock ownership exist. Most states have adopted statutes that give corporate directors the right to fend off unwanted takeover attempts.

- Securities professionals (brokers and dealers) are regulated by the SEC and must meet certain financial requirements. Those who give investment advice through an investment newsletter are not subject to federal regulation.

- All firms that trade securities for investors (brokerage firms) and firms that make investments for investors (investment companies, such as mutual funds) as well as the stock exchanges are regulated by the SEC. Self-regulatory organizations impose rules on industry members that are subject to SEC approval. Anyone trying to perform these duties without meeting regulatory requirements is subject to civil and criminal penalties.

- Franchised businesses have grown rapidly, and there are many success stories. To reduce the likelihood of an uninformed purchase of a franchise business and to expose the sellers of franchises to federal prosecution for misleading franchise buyers, under the FTC Franchise Rule a prospectus must be given to prospective franchisees that gives the financial and managerial history and plans of a franchise operation.

MANAGER'S ETHICAL DILEMMA

SHOULD BROKERS DEAL WITH "INCOMPETENT" CUSTOMERS?

Stock trading can be a high-risk venture compared to more sedate investments, such as government bonds. Stock prices fluctuate daily, and over a period of months, prices may rise or fall substantially.

Many stocks and options in stock futures are bought for less than full value; that is, they are bought on the margin for perhaps one-half of the purchase price.

Problems arise when there is a drop in the price. The buyer then must cover the difference between the current market price and the original price. There are also broker fees to be paid for each deal made.

Professional dealers trade daily. Some make money, some break even, and some go broke. Some nonprofessionals become intrigued with stock trading because of the price changes and the excitement of the deals. Some make money, some break even, and some go broke.

In a recent case in Seattle, a well-to-do construction company owner became heavily involved in trading. He worked with one broker for seven years, averaging over 1,500 trades per year and losing money every year. His broker, who charged competitive fees for handling the trades, made $400,000 in commissions. The customer lost $1.5 million, ending up bankrupt and losing his construction company.

The customer sued the trading firm, claiming that the broker should have recognized after several years that he was not competent in his trades—in a sense, it was like being addicted to gambling. The federal dis-

trict judge awarded the customer $275,000 in damages for half of the losses he suffered during his last few years of trading. This decision was the first of its kind: a brokerage firm was held liable for losses incurred by a customer when the customer controlled the trades.

QUESTIONS

Assuming that the broker knew that the customer was essentially addicted to trading because of the excitement or because he thought he could make a big profit to cover past losses, should the broker have tried to stop the customer from trading? Suppose the broker closed the customer's account and the customer moved to another brokerage firm to execute trades. Would the broker have a duty to call the new firm and tell it not to accept the customer as a trader? Since prices change when new information becomes available, no one can consistently anticipate the market as to future prices. That is, a professional trader cannot predict the future any better than can nonprofessionals, although the professionals may have more sense about trading strategy. If future prices are unknowable, is there any reason to have different standards for professional and nonprofessional traders? Should a broker treat a rich customer differently than a customer with a modest sum to invest? That is, do brokers have a duty to try to stop less wealthy customers from making big losses (and big gains)?

REVIEW AND DISCUSSION QUESTIONS

1. Define the following terms:

securities	securities fraud
debt	misstatements
equity	insider trading
Howey test	proxy
registration statement	tender offers
exemptions from registration	investment company
disclosure requirements	investment adviser

2. Which of the four elements of the *Howey* test appears to be missing in the *Howey* decision itself?

3. Is a condominium unit a security? What if it were used for vacations and rented out most of the time?

4. What is the difference in the legal protection available to the purchasers of registered versus unregistered securities?

5. More insider trading cases were brought by the SEC during the mid-1980s than were brought in all the years before. Does this indicate that more insider trading must be going on in recent years than before?

6. What could an investment adviser do to profit abnormally at the expense of clients? Would such activities occur more often without SEC controls? Who has an incentive to limit such abuses?

■ CASE QUESTIONS

7. A developer announced that a new apartment building was to be constructed. To have first crack at a unit in the building, you would have to deposit $250 per room. Each room was called a share of stock in the building. If, for example, you wanted a six-room apartment, you had to buy six shares of stock and later pay the sale price or rental rate. The stock price was to be refunded at the time you sold your apartment or quit renting and left the building. You could not sell the stock to another person. Is this stock a security that falls under the 1933 Act?

8. For ten years, a major certified public accounting firm audited the books of an investment company to prepare disclosure documents required by the SEC. The accountants never discovered that there was a big scam going on at the firm and that the head of the firm was stealing investors' funds—he cooked the books, and the accountants never found out. One day the head of the firm disappeared, leaving behind a mess and many unhappy investors. The investors sued the accounting firm to try to recover the money they lost, claiming that the accounting firm is liable for securities fraud. Who won?

9. You go to a party at which you meet a hotshot Wall Street lawyer who advises a famous corporate raider. The lawyer tells you that the raider is about to make a try at getting control of Boring Corporation. The next day you buy stock in Boring. Sure enough, two weeks later the raider tries a takeover, and the stock shoots up. Are you guilty of insider trading? What if you had acquired the same information in a locker room at a tennis club when you overheard the lawyer talking to the raider and they did not know you were listening?

■ BUSINESS POLICY QUESTIONS

10. The Securities Act of 1933 requires that a prospectus be given to all investors in securities before they purchase any security. Evidence is that investors pay little or no attention to these documents. Does the existence of this requirement give investors a false sense of confidence that the investment must be okay because the SEC has reviewed a prospectus? If so, is the prospectus a waste of resources, and does it also perhaps have a negative effect? How about disclosure documents under the FTC Franchise Rule?

11. In the *CTS* v. *Dynamics* decision, the Supreme Court said that states could impose restrictions on takeovers of corporations chartered in their states so long as these regulations essentially furthered federal regulations. A study

published in 1987 by the Bureau of Economics of the FTC estimated that a New York state law passed in 1985 regulating corporate takeovers caused the ninety-four public firms studied to fall in equity value by nearly one percent, which meant that shareholders lost about $1.2 billion dollars in the value of their stock from a law that was supposed to benefit them. Suppose this study is correct—that the main impact of these antitakeover laws is to protect incumbent management against a takeover that would make the company more profitable. Would it be desirable for the Supreme Court to hold such laws as destructive to interstate commerce, or should we, as Justice Scalia said, let economically senseless laws be called constitutional?

■ ETHICS QUESTIONS

12. You started the Triangular Frisbee Company as a small operation. When the product goes over big, you decide to seek outside funding to build a larger company. Your lawyer explains to you the costs of SEC registration and securities disclosure in case of a public stock offering. You can avoid this by organizing as a corporation on the Caribbean island nation of Torlaga and selling stock in the corporation from there. U.S. investors simply buy your stock through a Torlaga stockbroker. This is much cheaper and quicker than U.S. registration. What are the pros and cons of this arrangement? Is it ethical to avoid compliance with American laws in this manner?

Note: Registration only – no manufacturing overseas

13. While at a football game you overhear two corporate executives, whom you recognize, discussing an important announcement that will be made public at 11 A.M. on Monday. The executives say the news will make their company's stock "really shoot up." Obviously, this is inside information that was not intended for your ears. Should you run to a stockbroker first thing Monday morning to buy as much stock in the company as you can? What if you knew the executives personally and they told you "If I were you, I would buy all the stock in our company that you can before 11 A.M. on Monday."? Does it make a difference whether they give the reason you should buy the stock (i.e., the inside information)? Presume that you know that regardless of the legality of such transactions, there is no way you could get caught doing this—it is money in the bank.

14. Some investment newsletters have made multimillionaires out of their authors. Some of these writers become very popular and achieve a cultlike following of mostly middle-class people with modest sums to invest. There is no evidence that any of the newsletter writers have consistently outperformed the market. That is, the advice they sell for a relatively high price is advice that could be had for a very low price from any regular investment firm. The newsletter writers have figured out how to appeal to the biases of particular sets of investors—gold bugs, doomsayers, and so on. It is clearly legal for them to sell their newsletters. Is it ethical? Is it ethical to write a book proclaiming a forthcoming economic calamity or some other unsubstantiated prediction? The authors of some of these books make a small fortune but have no liability for being wrong. In some cases, people take foolish steps with their savings in the belief that there might be something to this year's most popular bit of economic tabloid journalism. Relying on some silly prediction, some people have even quit their jobs, moved, and put their wealth in an unusual form. Should this concern anyone but the investors?

INTERNATIONAL LEGAL ENVIRONMENT OF BUSINESS

CHAPTER 18

MANAGER'S LEGAL CHALLENGE

The U.S. automobile industry suffered heavy losses through the late 1980s and early 1990s. General Motors alone lost more than $3 billion. GM is now in the process of closing several plants and laying off more than 70,000 workers. While several factors contributed to GM's problems, many people blame the Japanese.

The Japanese have maintained a significant trade imbalance with the United States for nearly a decade. Averaging some $45 billion a year (that is, they sell $45 billion more in goods to the United States than they buy), the majority of the deficit is caused by U.S. consumer purchases of cars. Now, the Japanese are selling everything from small cars to luxury cars to trucks. In addition, more and more of those vehicles are being built in the United States.

To solve some of the problems caused by the Japanese car invasion, each of the U.S. car manufacturers has entered into joint venture agreements with Japanese automakers. With one exception, the Japanese/U.S. auto ventures have not produced many successes. That important exception is the joint venture between Ford Motor Company and Mazda.

In the late 1970s, the management of Ford Motor Company made a serious commitment to improving quality and expanding its international operations. In addition to the commitments it made to its European operations, Ford management looked to develop stronger ties with a Japanese automaker. Management was very concerned about the growing costs—now estimated at $2 billion—of developing a new car. A development partner could share those costs. The right partner would also allow Ford to gain access to important new markets and technologies. Management expected that with a Japanese partner, Ford could potentially learn important manufacturing techniques.

In 1979, Ford management elected to acquire 25 percent of Mazda. Management worked to clarify the joint legal and managerial issues. The joint venture was threatened several times by disagreements over projects. In addition, external factors made the arrangement more difficult than a domestic joint venture. The Japanese and U.S. governments argued over trade disputes, and the U.S. government accused Japanese automakers (including Mazda) of dumping (selling at below production cost) minivans.

The joint venture required that special efforts be made to anticipate and overcome cultural and nationality differences. Legal arrangements now dictate how models are to be priced and how development costs are to be shared. In some instances, a preselected mediator had to be brought in to settle disputes and disagreements. Still, Mazda and Ford have maintained some independence—Mazda has kept such models as the Miata to itself, and Ford has kept such models as the Challenger to itself.

The managements of Mazda and Ford now cooperate on new vehicles and share valuable expertise. Mazda is a recognized leader in manufacturing and product development. Ford is recognized in the areas of international marketing and finance. Newly constructed Ford plants in Mexico have used Mazda technology extensively. Through the efforts of Mazda, Ford is the number one selling foreign car in Japan. With the support of Ford, Mazda is now entering the difficult European market. Together, they have developed more than ten models, including the Ford Fiesta, Ford Probe, Ford Explorer, Mazda MX-6, Mazda 323, and Mazda Navajo.

Importantly, the management of Ford is using the legal and managerial methods it has learned from the Ford/Mazda joint venture in other ventures worldwide. Ford is applying the techniques in new relationships with Nissan (Japanese) and Volkswagen (Germany). With Volkswagen, Ford is developing operations in Brazil, Argentina, and Portugal. The efforts undertaken by Ford's management to meet international legal and managerial challenges has made Ford a recognized world leader in the automobile industry.

The difficulties of an international partnership confronting Ford's management is just one of the challenges facing companies operating in international markets. As the discussion serves to illustrate, the risks in international commercial transactions can be far greater than similar activities conducted solely in our domestic market. Commercial activity in the United States, however, is becoming increasingly more international in scope. To be successful, management must be knowledgeable about the technical nuances of international trade and the international legal environment. With experience, managers are quickly learning to reduce the risks associated with international business transactions. In the words of John Adams, president of Meiller Corporation and recipient of the Small Business Administration's *Exporter of the Year* Award:

> Ten years ago, we were not involved in international business. Now it accounts for more than 40 percent of our business. While in the beginning we were terrified of international commerce, I can now say that I have accounts in New York and Arkansas that are more difficult than most of my accounts in Venezuela.

This chapter provides an overview of the international legal environment of business. It begins with a discussion of the nature of international business and the current extent of U.S. involvement in international commerce. The chapter then discusses the major international organizations working to encourage and stimulate international business activity. Next, it considers the various forms of business organization a business may consider before becoming involved in an international commercial venture. Finally, the chapter discusses the nature of international contracting, insurance against loss, and the procedures for the resolution of international disputes.

THE NATURE OF INTERNATIONAL BUSINESS

With the technological improvements in transportation and communications over the past twenty-five years, the nature of general business activity has changed substantially. The percentage of U.S. gross national product involved in direct international trade has tripled during that time. Virtually every business, even domestic businesses, is now affected by events originating in the international business environment. Crop failures in Argentina, political unrest within the Middle Eastern oil-producing countries, and shipping strikes in England can all have a significant impact on both U.S. domestic and international businesses.

■ THE INTERNATIONAL BUSINESS ENVIRONMENT

The term *international business* is often defined to include all business transactions that involve two or more countries. In addition to being involved with the movement of goods across national boundaries, international business involves the movement of services, capital, and personnel. Finally, international business includes the transactions of all multinational enterprises, whether of private, of public, or of mixed ownership.

The *international business environment* involves considerably more than just business transactions across national boundaries. The international business environment also includes business activities that are affected by international business conditions and world events. For example, U.S. businesses that operated solely in the domestic market may now find themselves in direct competition with foreign manufacturers. Initially, their principal source of foreign competition was from imported products. However, in the 1980s, foreign competitors began to build factories in this country to compete more directly with domestic businesses. Direct investments in this country by the Japanese have increased at an unprecedented rate since 1980. The Japanese now compete directly with U.S. businesses in several domestic product markets, and particularly in markets for automobiles.

Many U.S. industries had no intent to enter into international business transactions. As all markets become global markets, those businesses are finding themselves clearly within the international business environment. They must now obtain familiarity with the international legal environment to maintain their competitiveness.

■ RISKS IN INTERNATIONAL BUSINESS TRANSACTIONS

A principal distinction between domestic and international businesses lies in the special risks confronting the international business enterprise. Those risks fall into the general categories of *financial, political,* and *regulatory risks.* They arise from a variety of sources, including differences between countries in currencies, language, business customs, legal and social philosophies, and national economic goals.

International risks can have a considerable effect on profitability. They require a level of managerial supervision not common in domestic operations. The management of financial risks involves consideration of currency exchange rates and of differences in inflation and interest rates among countries. Political risks include the possibility of harsh treatment directed specifically at foreign businesses by the government of the host nation. The potential degree of political risk must be estimated several years in advance if the business is considering building a large plant in another country. The regulatory or legal risks arise from the existence of different legal systems and regulatory policies of the various countries. Taken together, these risks significantly increase the difficulties of operating in international markets.

Several companies specialize in providing the business community with assessments of risks. Those companies very closely monitor economic, political, and financial events in all major countries. Figure 18–1 provides the estimated risks for several companies as of August 1991. The closer the risk assessment is to 100, the less risky the country. For example, Switzerland has a risk assessment of more than ninety (low-risk country), while Cuba's assessment is less than forty (high-risk country). The estimates were made by the *International Country Risk Guide.* Managers will use those estimates and other information before entering into business arrangements in a particular country. It is very likely that Ford Motor Company made a similar risk assessment before entering into its joint venture with Mazda in 1979.

■ CURRENT U.S. INVOLVEMENT IN INTERNATIONAL BUSINESS

Historically, the United States has not participated as heavily in international trade as have other countries. An abundance of natural resources, a large domestic market, and a sense of national independence made international business opportunities a less attractive alternative to domestic business opportunities. Unlike such countries as Japan, Germany, and many other Western European nations, the United States was able to enjoy a strong economy without emphasizing exports.

In the past ten years, both the federal and the state governments have undertaken efforts to encourage U.S. companies to export, since the United States had been running a serious *trade deficit* throughout the 1980s. That is, the value of U.S. consumer purchases of imported foreign goods

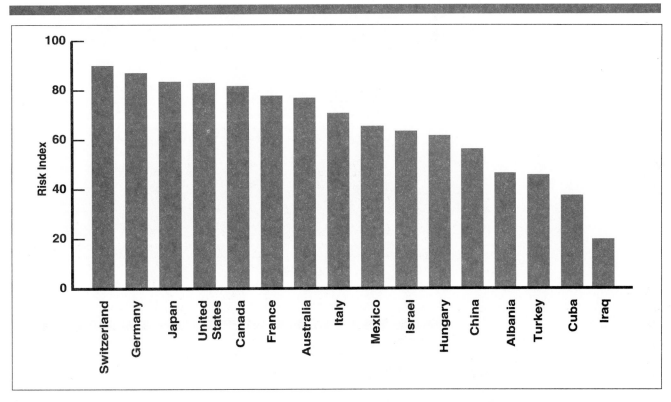

FIGURE 18–1

Measuring Investment Safety: Indexing Country Risk
SOURCE: *International Country Risk Guide,* August 1991.

was far greater than the value of the goods U.S companies were selling to foreign consumers. At one point in the 1980s, the U.S. trade deficit exceeded $140 billion. Recently, that trade deficit has begun to decline. In 1991, the trade deficit fell to just $66.2 billion, its lowest level since 1983. The largest trade deficit is with Japan. Because of U.S. purchases of automobiles made in Japan, the United States experienced a trade deficit with Japan of $43.5 billion in 1991. The United States' largest trading partners are listed in Table 18–1.

While the trade deficit has been a major congressional concern for several years, attention has shifted more recently to the relative decline in U.S. technological development. Technological development, as measured by patents issued, provides a measure of future product development. Countries with an edge in technological development are likely to enjoy a more rapid rate of industrial growth—thereby creating more new jobs and increasing personal income—than countries with a lower rate of development. As Figure 18–2 indicates, only two U.S. companies—General Electric and IBM—were among the top ten companies in terms of U.S. patents issued in 1988. The U.S. decline in technological development has become an increasingly greater concern of Congress as it considers long-term solutions to the trade deficit.

		U.S. Exports	U.S. Imports	
Rank	Country	*(in billions of U.S. dollars)*		Trade Balance
1	Canada	$85.1	$91.1	($6.0)
2	Japan	48.1	91.6	(43.5)
3	Mexico	33.3	31.2	2.1
4	Germany	21.3	26.2	(4.9)
5	United Kingdom	22.1	18.5	3.6
6	Taiwan	13.2	23.0	(9.8)
7	South Korea	15.5	17.0	(1.5)
8	France	15.4	13.4	2.0
9	China	6.3	19.0	(12.7)
10	Italy	8.6	11.8	(3.2)

TABLE 18–1
U.S. TRADING PARTNERS, 1991

SOURCE: U.S. Department of Commerce.

FIGURE 18–2

Leading Winners of U.S. Patents, 1988
SOURCE: Intellectual Property Owners Inc.

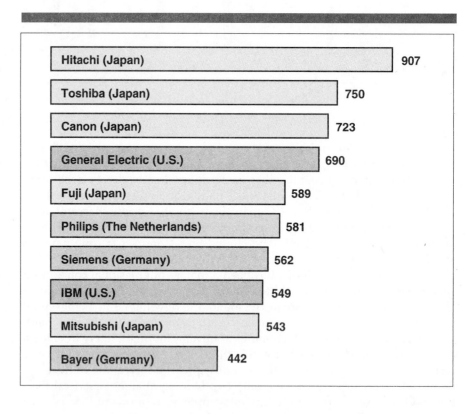

Hitachi (Japan) 907
Toshiba (Japan) 750
Canon (Japan) 723
General Electric (U.S.) 690
Fuji (Japan) 589
Philips (The Netherlands) 581
Siemens (Germany) 562
IBM (U.S.) 549
Mitsubishi (Japan) 543
Bayer (Germany) 442

INTERNATIONAL LAW AND THE REGULATION OF INTERNATIONAL COMMERCE

International businesses function in a unique legal environment. The international legal environment provides no detailed system of laws or regulations for guiding business transactions between two countries. Rather, the legal environment consists of many laws and policies from all countries involved in international commercial activity. As the "International Aspects" features throughout the text have illustrated, countries often differ dramatically in their basic legal philosophies, practices, and procedures. As a consequence, businesses engaging in international business face a variety of legal uncertainties and conflicts.

HISTORY OF INTERNATIONAL LAW

Before the development of the more formal international laws in existence today, nations involved in international commerce established customs upon which trade was to be based. Early trade customs centered around the law of the sea. They provided, among other things, for rights of shipping in foreign ports, salvage rights, fishing rights, and freedom of passage.

International commercial codes date back as far as 1400 B.C. to Egyptian merchants involved in international business and trade. Merchants from other countries developed similar codes and trade customs to provide some degree of legal certainty in international transactions. In 700 B.C., for example, a code of international law had been developed on the island of Rhodes in the Aegean Sea. The Greek and Roman civilizations both had well-developed codes of practice for international trade and diplomacy.

During the Middle Ages, international principles contained in the *lex mercatoria* (or law merchant) governed commercial transactions throughout Europe. These customs and codes of conduct created a workable legal structure for the protection and encouragement of international transactions. The international commerce codes in use today in much of Europe and in the United States are derived from those medieval codes.

OVERVIEW OF CURRENT INTERNATIONAL LAW

The principal sources of international trade law are the laws of individual countries, the laws defined by trade agreements between or among countries, and the rules enacted by a worldwide or regional organization—such as the United Nations or the European Community (EC). There is, however, no international system of courts universally accepted for the purpose of resolving international conflicts between either businesses or countries. International law can be enforced to some degree in (1) the International Court of Justice, (2) through international arbitration, or (3) in the courts of an individual country. However, the decisions of those tribunals can be enforced only if the countries involved agree to be bound by them.

INTERNATIONAL BUSINESS IN THE 1990s

The 1990s decade is witnessing a dramatic change in the world business environment. The opening up of Eastern Europe, the abrupt shift toward open-market policies in the countries making up the former Soviet Union, the resurgence of the Mexican and other Latin American economies, the implementation of 1992 Europe, and significant reductions in domestic market protections in Japan have produced new markets and created incentives for growth in others. Few members of the business community question that the 1990s will be a decade of pronounced international market development and growth.

The enormous business opportunities presented by these changes are not without risk, however. In times of rapid social change like that being experienced in Eastern Europe and the former Soviet Union, political and ethnic upheavals are common. Such upheavals can be very disruptive and expensive to new business ventures. Economic liberalization often begins with an adjustment period characterized by unemployment and inflation—particularly in food prices—that can lead to revolts and sudden changes in governments. In addition, the business community remains concerned about the ability of the outdated legal systems in many of these countries to adequately enforce agreements. An otherwise natural combination of international business opportunities and a desire on the part of Western companies to "go global" has been slowed by uncertainty in the international legal environment.

◼ THE EMERGING EASTERN EUROPEAN ECONOMIES

The sudden and dramatic decline in world communism was perhaps best symbolized by the dramatic fall of the Berlin Wall. Concurrent with that fall, the countries of Eastern Europe were given their economic and political freedom for the first time in more than fifty years. Sweeping economic changes have been introduced in an effort to attract foreign investment, modernize their economies, decrease unemployment, and increase the supply of consumer goods.

As Table 18–2 illustrates, the economies of Germany and Czechoslovakia look to be the most promising for foreign investors. Both Germany and Czechoslovakia are better positioned because of past industrialization efforts, low foreign debt, and a much more favorable legal environment relative to other Eastern European countries. In addition, Germany will benefit economically as a consequence of the reunification of East Germany with West Germany.

While a number of U.S. businesses have operative joint ventures in Eastern Europe, most Western companies remain skeptical about the legal environments in those countries. Constraints on foreign ownership of property, an immature and unsophisticated commercial law, and restrictions on current repatriation are some of the principal concerns voiced by Western entrepreneurs.

TABLE 18–2
FOREIGN INVESTMENT POTENTIAL IN EASTERN EUROPE

	Country— Population GNP per capita	Economic Outlook
Most Promising	(East) Germany 16.6 million $11,240	Union with (West) Germany leads to strong growth after rocky start.
	Czechoslovakia 15.6 million $8,860	Making strong strides toward a market economy; legal system uncertain.
	Hungary 10.6 million $6,780	Reforms have attracted investors including GE, GM, and Levi Strauss.
	Poland 38 million $4,735	Great potential—if worker unhappiness over inflation and unemployment can be contained.
	Bulgaria 9 million $6,004	New leadership encourages investment but little real progress.
	Romania 23 million $5,100	New government not as repressive as old regime and is allowing free trade.
Least Promising	Yugoslavia 23.6 million $2,600	Potential for economic reform may be derailed by ethnic disintegration (figures include Slovenia and Croatia).

Note: Income figures may be too high because conversion into dollars is uncertain.

■ EUROPE 1992

The countries of Western Europe officially began to act as one country for economic purposes on December 31, 1992. The European Community's 1992 directive ends barriers to the free flow of goods, services, and capital, creating a single market of 350 million consumers. The directive includes abolition of currency controls, sweeping deregulation of important markets and industries, standardization of commercial law, and elimination of customs delays. Currently, much of commerce in Europe takes place on a country-by-country basis. Differing standards in everything from electrical plug-ins to telecommunications and significant barriers in financial markets have seriously limited European economic growth. With the unification of Europe and the elimination of those impediments, economic growth is expected to increase, consumer prices are expected to decline, and two million new jobs will be created.

U.S. firms are concerned about the rapid changes in Europe, particularly in the regulatory environment. Most are worried that the regulatory environment could change and shut them out of the European market.

Many U.S. companies are trying to develop European production and distribution facilities. Despite these efforts, however, only 38 percent of the chief executive officers of the largest 350 U.S. companies in Europe believe they are ready to compete in the new unified Europe.

◼ A NORTH AMERICAN UNIFIED MARKET

Canada, Mexico, and the United States are working to create their own unified market. The three countries intend to enter into a North American free trade agreement in the early 1990s. As in Europe 1992, goods and services will flow freely—without tariffs, quotas or duties—across the Canadian, Mexican, and U.S. borders. The agreement will encourage companies to develop continent-wide business strategies. The relative size of the North American unified market in comparison with the Europe 1992 market is provided in Table 18–3.

◼ THE CHANGING U.S.-JAPAN TRADE RELATIONSHIP

Japan became a significant international trading partner with the United States in the 1980s. The U.S. market fueled Japan's dramatic growth but led to the creation of a trade deficit of around $50 billion per year throughout the 1980s (Figure 18–3). Recently, Japan has been severely criticized for making it difficult for U.S. companies to enter its domestic market. U.S. companies need access to Japan's domestic market to reduce the trade deficit.

In an effort to improve trade relations in the 1990s, Japan and the United States entered into an important trade agreement. Under the terms of the agreement, Japan will deregulate its process for approving large department stores, abolish a law that allows the government to restrict foreign investment if it could impact on Japanese domestic businesses, and implement stronger antitrust laws. Prior to the agreement, several U.S. department chains, including Toys R Us, had a difficult time battling Japanese bureaucracy to gain government permission to begin operations. The

TABLE 18–3
COMPARISON OF THE NORTH AMERICAN AND EUROPEAN UNIFIED MARKETS

	Population	Gross National Product	Two-Way Trade
Europe 1992	350 million	$4.8 trillion	$160 billion[1]
North America	360 million	$6.0 trillion	$194 billion[2]

[1]U.S. imports and exports from the EC countries.
[2]U.S. imports and exports from Mexico and Canada.

SOURCE: U.S. Statistical Abstract; Bank of Montreal.

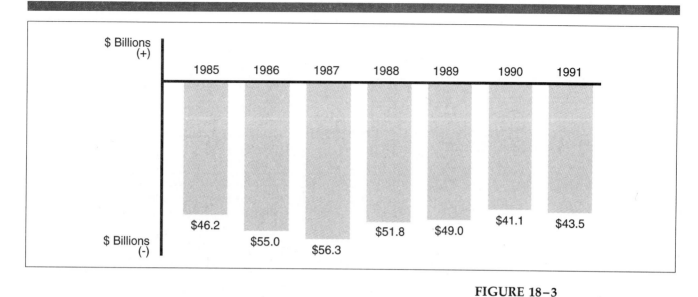

FIGURE 18-3

U.S. Trade Deficits with Japan

agreement also calls for the United States to reduce its budget deficit (which was more than $350 billion in 1992), improve the quality of its education and work force, promote exports by reducing its export licensing requirements, and encourage personal savings. The Japanese view these undertakings as necessary for the United States to become more effective in today's international markets.

INTERNATIONAL ORGANIZATIONS

To encourage international business, a variety of organizations have been developed. Those organizations vary considerably in their activities, size, and sponsorship. The most prominent international organization is the United Nations.

THE UNITED NATIONS

Although created principally as a peace-keeping body, the *United Nations* has enjoyed greater success in its economic and social efforts. The organization's concern for economic development and international trade has led to the development of several departments whose purpose is to facilitate trade. The organizational structure of the United Nations is presented in Figure 18-4.

    The United Nations is most visible in the field of international trade through its *Commission on International Trade Law* (UNCITRAL). The primary purposes of UNCITRAL are to promote uniformity in laws affecting international trade and to encourage the elimination of obstacles to international trade. In addition, the United Nations is involved in efforts to standardize weights and measures and to encourage economic development in less-developed countries.

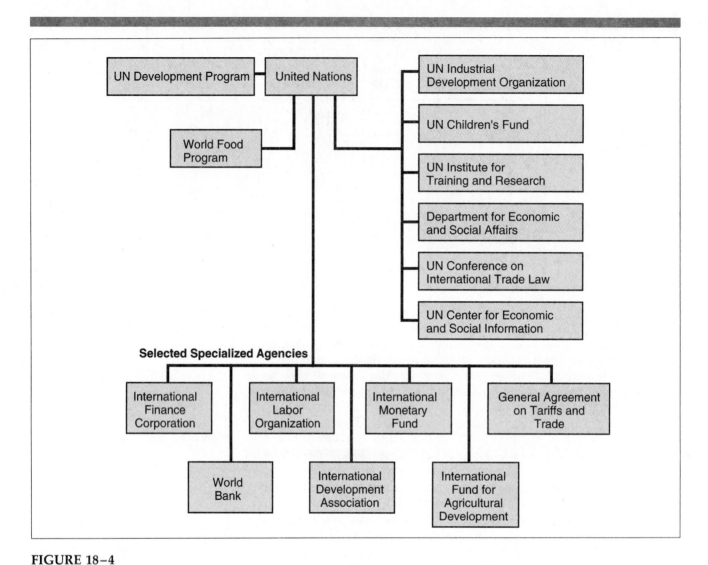

FIGURE 18–4

The Organizational Structure of the United Nations

■ THE WORLD BANK

The *World Bank* is the name given to the *International Bank for Reconstruction and Development.* The bank is located in Washington, D.C. The organization of the World Bank includes the bank itself, the International Finance Corporation (IFC), and the International Development Association (IDA). The current purpose of the World Bank is to "promote private foreign investment by means of guarantees or participation in loans and other investments made by private investors." To accomplish this purpose, the World Bank assists in the financial arrangements of businesses, industries, and agricultural associations of its member countries.

■ INTERNATIONAL MONETARY FUND

The basic purposes of the *International Monetary Fund* (IMF) are to "facilitate the expansion and balanced growth of international trade," to aid in "the elimination of foreign exchange restrictions which hamper the growth of international trade,'' and to ''shorten the duration of and lessen disequilibrium in the international balances of payments of its members.'' These purposes are achieved through the administration of a complex lending system. That system allows a participating country to borrow money either from other IMF members or from the Fund itself. The lending system allows a member country to stabilize its currency in relation to the currencies of other countries. The stability of a country's currency is fundamental to the country's international business viability.

◼ GENERAL AGREEMENT ON TARIFFS AND TRADE (GATT)

Trade barriers imposed by governments, such as import quotas and tariffs, inhibit international trade. *The General Agreement on Tariffs and Trade* (the GATT) was created to reduce such obstacles to trade. The GATT works to achieve its goals by focusing on key trade restrictions. It implements its goals through the publication of tariff schedules that are developed periodically in multinational trade negotiations or ''rounds.'' Over eighty-eight countries have participated as parties to the GATT. Other countries state that the GATT guides them in their international trading policies and conduct.

''Most Favored Nation'' Status.   Each article of the GATT addresses different international trade problems or restrictions. Article I, for example, discusses the commitment by the participants to the practice of ''most favored nation treatment,'' providing that

> [a]ny advantage, favor, privilege or immunity granted by any contracting party to any product originating in or destined for any other country shall be accorded immediately and unconditionally to the like product originating in or destined for the territories of all other contracting parties.

Suppose that the United States agrees to give South Korea certain tariff rates and tells South Korea that those rates are provided to other favored customers. If the United States later provides better rates to Italy, most favored nation treatment under the GATT would require the United States to provide South Korea with the same rates.

Imposition of Antidumping or Countervailing Duties.   The GATT does allow unilateral exceptions to the tariff schedules under certain circumstances. For example, suppose that a country decides to *dump* products on another country at prices below market value. The GATT will allow the imposition of an *antidumping duty* for the purpose of protecting domestic industries. (Recall that this was one of the problems facing Mazda in this chapter's ''Manager's Legal Challenge'' feature.) Also, suppose that an exported product is heavily subsidized by its government and thus enjoys a price lower than the market value of a similar nonsubsidized product in the receiving country. The GATT allows the imposition of a *countervailing duty* by the receiving country (to offset the lower, subsidized price of the imported product).

Nontariff Barriers to Trade.   The GATT addresses approaches to reducing not only tariff barriers but also nontariff barriers. Like tariff barriers, nontariff barriers impose restrictions on free trade. Such nontariff constraints on free trade include import quotas, licensing barriers, administrative delays, and arbitrary classification, labeling, and testing standards imposed on foreign-made products.

Current Round of GATT Talks.   The current round of GATT talks has been stalled for more than a year. The problems arise out of disagreements over farm subsidies. Currently, agricultural exports are heavily subsidized by governments in Europe. The subsidies are intended to protect farm incomes and farm jobs. The U.S. government has asked that Europe reduce its subsidies by 36 percent by the year 1999. The European subsidies create odd market incentives that are disruptive to world markets. For example, the government of Italy provides subsidies on exported pasta. With the subsidies, it is economical for an Italian pasta maker to import wheat from the United States to make pasta. Because of the subsidies, Italy can then export the pasta to the United States and sell it for a lower price than U.S. pasta makers can charge. The subsidy in effective pays for the shipping of the wheat from the United States to Italy and of the pasta from Italy to the United States. Under such conditions, it is difficult for U.S. food manufacturers to compete against European food manufacturers. It is the goal of GATT to eliminate such practices.

■ REGIONAL ORGANIZATIONS

Several regional organizations share the general purpose of facilitating trade and economic development. For example, the *European Community* (EC) was created to eliminate restrictions on the free flow of goods, capital, and persons; harmonize economic policies; and create a common external tariff among its member countries. Member countries of the EC include Belgium, Denmark, France, Greece, Ireland, Italy, Luxembourg, the Netherlands, Portugal, Spain, the United Kingdom, and Germany. Other important regional organizations and their member countries are given in Table 18–4.

U.S. INTERNATIONAL TRADE RESTRICTIONS AND PROMOTIONS

Countries have long imposed restrictions or prohibitions on the importation and exportation of certain products. In addition, export laws and regulations are often enacted to encourage international business activity by domestic industries.

■ IMPORT REGULATION AND PROHIBITIONS

Restrictions on imports take a variety of forms. They are generally imposed for the purpose of generating revenue for the government of the country or to protect the country's domestic industries from lower priced foreign products. Import licensing procedures, import quotas, testing require-

TABLE 18–4
REGIONAL ECONOMIC ORGANIZATIONS

Program	Member Countries
Andean Common Market (ANCOM)	Colombia, Venezuela, Ecuador, Peru, Bolivia
Arab Common Market	Iraq, Jordan, Libya, Mauritania, Syria, South Yemen
Association of Southeast Asian Nations (ASEAN)	Thailand, Malaysia, Singapore, Indonesia, Philippines, Brunei
Caribbean Common Market (CARICOM)	The Bahamas, Belize, Jamaica, Antigua and Barbuda, Montserrat, Dominica, St. Lucia, St. Vincent, Grenada, Barbados, Trinidad and Tobago, Guyana, St. Kitts-Nevis-Anguilla
Central American Common Market (CACM)	Costa Rica, El Salvador, Guatemala, Honduras, Nicaragua
Economic Community of West African States (ECOWAS)	Mauritania, Senegal, Mali, Ivory Coast, Niger, Upper Volta, Benin, The Gambia, Guinea, Ghana, Nigeria, Sierra Leone, Togo, Cape Verde, Guinea-Bissau, Liberia
European Community (EC)	Denmark, United Kingdom, Ireland, the Netherlands, Belgium, Luxembourg, France, Germany, Italy, Greece, Spain, Portugal
European Free Trade Association (EFTA)	Iceland, Sweden, Norway, Austria, Portugal, Switzerland, Finland (associate)
Latin American Integration Association (LAIA)	Bolivia, Brazil, Colombia, Chile, Ecuador, Argentina, Peru, Uruguay, Paraguay, Mexico, Venezuela
West African Economic Community	Ivory Coast, Mali, Mauritania, Syria, South Yemen

ments, safety and manufacturing standards, government procurement policies, and complicated customs procedures are all means of regulating imports. The most common means of regulating imports, however, is through the application of import tariffs.

The Imposition of Import Tariffs. A *tariff* is a duty or tax levied by a government on an imported good. Tariffs can be generally classified into two principal categories: *specific tariffs*, which impose a fixed tax or duty on each unit of the product, and *ad valorem tariffs*, which impose tax based on a percentage of the price of the product. Tariffs are intended to serve either as a revenue-generating device by the government or as a means to provide domestic industries with protection from foreign products. Businesses advocating the imposition of a tariff on a foreign product generally argue that without the tariff, the lower priced foreign product will force them out of the market. Consequently, workers will lose their jobs and the country will grow increasingly more dependent on foreign businesses for supplies of critical products. Those arguing against tariffs assert that only through free trade will the world increase its productive capacity.

In the United States, the duty or tax to be imposed is generally published in the *Tariff Schedules.* These schedules are applicable to all products entering U.S. ports and are applied by customs officials. Customs officials classify the products and determine the tariff rates at the time the products enter the country. Any tariff imposed on a product must be paid before the good may officially enter the country.

The vast majority of business disputes that arise in this area are over the classification of products under the Tariff Schedules. As the following case illustrates, the rate of duty can be significantly affected by a U.S. Customs agent's decision on the classification of a product.

STANDARD BRANDS PAINT COMPANY, INC. v. UNITED STATES

United States Court of Customs and Patent Appeals
511 F.2d 564 (1975)

Case Background
Standard Brands Paint Company imported wooden picture frame moldings in different styles and lengths, each packaged separately. Standard Brands' retail customers would buy these parts and assemble a frame to the needed dimensions. The customs invoice on the imported merchandise read "Wooden Picture Frames." The moldings were classified by U.S Customs agents under the Tariff Schedules of the United States (TSUS) as "wood moldings." Customs then assessed a duty at a rate of 17 percent ad valorem.

Standard Brands claimed that the imported items should have been classified as "picture and mirror frames made of wood." That classification would have resulted in a duty of 12 percent ad valorem. Standard Brands based its claim on the fact that the imported moldings actually constitute unassembled frames. Under the Doctrine of Entireties, these frames should be dutiable as entireties—that is, as "assembled" picture frames made of wood even though they were unassembled.

The U.S. Customs Court ruled against Standard Brands. The court held that the merchandise had been classified properly by customs agents. Standard Brands took its appeal to the U.S. Court of Customs and Patent Appeals (now called the Court of Appeals for the Federal Circuit).

Case Decision
The appellate court reversed the decision of the customs court on the basis of the Doctrine of Entireties. The court held that the imported items should have been classified as requested by Standard Brands and taxed at the lower duty rate. The court stated the Doctrine of Entireties provides that if a merchant imports unattached or separately packaged parts into this country that are intended by the mer-

chant to be joined together as a complete product, the parts will be construed as being assembled—as entireties—for tariff purposes.

Managerial Considerations
An inaccurate assessment of the costs of freight, insurance, or custom duties in an international purchase can mean the difference between a profit and a substantial loss. For example, a medium-sized nut processing company made the strategic decision to expand into an exotic nut that had to be imported from Madagascar. The company was very experienced in wholesaling the finished nut but had no experience with the raw nut. Despite this lack of experience, its buyers purchased 6,000 metric tons of the raw nut and arranged to have it shipped to New York. Given the price at which it was buying the finished nut, the company felt it had a very good deal. However, when the raw nuts arrived at the New York harbor, the duty more than doubled the combined costs of the raw nut, freight, and insurance. The company had failed to determine that the shell on the raw nut was very toxic. The government was imposing a stiff duty to discourage the importation of the nut in the shell. To avoid substantial losses, the company shipped the nuts to India to have the shells removed. The shelled nuts were then shipped back to the United States for processing and distribution. While the company had expectations of making a profit, its lack of understanding of the legal environment led to significant losses.

In contrast, Standard Brands was knowledgeable both about duties and the impact of the higher rate on its business. Management knew that an additional five percent in duty would adversely affect the company's profitability in the long run if Customs continued to charge that rate on subsequent shipments. Management made the strategic decision to pursue a legal resolution to the dispute. The strategy was successful, and Standard Brands' management saved the company a substantial sum of money.

Harmonized Tariff Schedules.   In 1989, the United States replaced its tariff schedules with the *Harmonized Tariff Schedule,* developed by a group of countries for the purpose of standardizing the ways in which goods are classified by customs officials worldwide. Under the system, each country uses the same six-digit codes to classify goods traded. The process greatly streamlines trade by eliminating language and usage differences between countries.

Import Restrictions and Adjustments.   Under the Export Administration Act (discussed later), the government may impose import restrictions when increased imports are a "substantial cause" of injury to a U.S. industry. The industry affected is required to make a request to the International Trade Commission. The Commission then determines whether there is injury. The industry is encouraged to provide a plan outlining the ways in which it can compete with the imports. If the Commission determines that the industry is being injured and that positive adjustments can be made, a temporary restriction can be imposed on the import—from all countries—so that the industry can have time to make the necessary adjustments.

Bans on Certain Designated Products.   The entry of certain products into a country may violate established governmental policies. For example, certain explosives and munitions that raise national security concerns cannot legally be imported into this country. Illegal products, such as narcotics, violate drug safety and other domestic laws and cannot legally be imported. Products made from endangered species are prohibited from importation by environmental laws. Other items may not meet this country's safety regulations or pollution requirements and thus cannot be brought into the country.

   Foreign automobiles that do not comply with U.S. auto safety and pollution regulations will not be cleared for importation into this country. For example, William Gates, the president of Microsoft, tried to import a new Porsche 959 from Germany. The car sold for more than $200,000. Gates's 959 was the first Porsche of that model sold for delivery in the United States. However, upon arrival at the U.S. port, the car was not allowed by customs officials to be imported. According to Customs, that model Porsche had not been crash tested. Since its safety could not be verified, the car could not be imported into the United States.

Duty-Free Importation: Free Trade Zones and Duty-Free Ports.   *Free trade zones* are special territorial areas where goods can be imported without the payment of tariffs. The underlying reason for the use of such zones is to encourage international business and trade. The zone itself is a secured area where goods may be processed, assembled, or warehoused. Tariffs are imposed only on the finished product (generally much less than those imposed on individual parts) and only when the product leaves the zone for sale in the domestic market. Products that are removed from the zone and exported are generally not subject to import fees or tariffs.

   Duty-free ports are those ports of entry that do not assess duties or tariffs on any products. The underlying reason for establishing a duty-free port is to encourage the importation and sale of international goods within the country. Countries such as Hong Kong are well known for such practices. Benefits to a country providing a duty-free port are the general encouragement of trade with other countries and the attraction of businesses and tourists to the country to purchase products free of duties and other fees.

■ EXPORT REGULATION AND PROMOTION

Export regulations or controls are intended to affect the export process. Export regulations may be imposed for any social, political, or financial purpose. Export regulations, however, usually take the form of constraints on products. The sale of a product may be constrained if the product is considered either to be vital to the country's domestic market (usually a raw material, like wood) or, if sold to the wrong country, to have potentially adverse effects on the country's national security (a weapon).

In addition to enacting legislation to discourage certain international activities, it is not uncommon for countries to enact legislation to encourage businesses to engage in international business. In the United States, for example, several laws have been enacted for that purpose. Consider the provisions of the Export Trading Company Act.

Export Trading Company Act of 1982.   The *Export Trading Company Act of 1982* was enacted to provide U.S. businesses with encouragement to export. The Act allows U.S. businesses to form export trading companies to sell either goods or services. The intent of the Act was to allow U.S. businesses to develop trading companies similar to those enjoying such great success in Japan. A typical large Japanese trading company will handle more than 20,000 different products. Japanese trading companies are able to provide customers with better prices and quality control.

Without such a law, U.S. businesses had argued that they were unwilling to establish trading companies. The biggest concern was that a trading company located in the United States would violate antitrust laws. However, although the law does provide an exemption from antitrust laws, the exemption is a very weak one. Unfortunately, the weakness of the exemption has discouraged U.S. businesses from establishing trading companies. To date, there are fewer than forty trading companies operating in the United States under the Act.

Export Controls: The Export Administration Act.   The United States has had formal *export controls* since World War II. Restrictions were imposed during World War II to avert shortages of basic commodities. After the war, political relations with Russia worsened and prompted the enactment of the Export Control Act in 1949. The Act was later amended and renamed the *Export Administration Act.*

Controlling Sensitive Technologies.   The Export Administration Act regulates the export of sensitive goods, technologies, and technical data from the United States. Section 3 of the Act states the underlying U.S. policies in these export controls:

> It is the policy of the United States to use export controls only after full consideration of the impact on the economy of the United States and only to the extent necessary—
> (A) to restrict the export of goods and technology which would make a significant contribution to the military potential of any other country or

combination of countries which would prove detrimental to the national security of the United States.

(B) to restrict the export of goods and technology where necessary to further significantly the foreign policy of the United States or to fulfill its declared international obligations; and

(C) to restrict the export of goods where necessary to protect the domestic economy from the excessive drain of scarce materials and to reduce the serious inflationary impact of foreign demand.

Licensing Requirements.   To perform its regulatory functions, the Act creates three types of export licenses. The first is a *general license,* which essentially authorizes a business to export nonsensitive goods. Its coverage extends to the vast majority of U.S. goods intended for export. The second type of export license is a *qualified general license,* which authorizes the export of multiple products. The third type of license is the *validated license,* which allows for the export of specific products.

The qualified general license and the validated license are used only when the products are being sent to a country that would disqualify the goods from being exported under the general license. Both the qualified general license and the validated license require a written application with the Department of Commerce. The degree of restrictiveness imposed depends upon the product and the countries to which it is to be exported.

Recent Amendments to the Act.   The *Omnibus Trade and Competitiveness Act* of 1988 amends the Export Administration Act in several ways. First, in response to the dramatic changes in world politics, it reduces or eliminates the licensing requirements originally imposed by the Export Administration Act. The Omnibus Trade Act requires the U.S. Department of Commerce to significantly reduce the number of products subject to export control for national security reasons. Several export licensing restrictions have also been eliminated on the communist countries. These changes coupled with the increase in business opportunities in Central and Eastern Europe and the former Soviet Union have brought about an increase of more than 80 percent in the number of licenses issued. Most of the licenses have been for computers and computer accessories.

Second, the Omnibus Trade Act strengthens Section 301 of the Export Administration Act, which provides the government with the ability to "retaliate" against the unfair trade practices of foreign governments. If a foreign government imposes import restrictions against U.S. products, Section 301 allows the U.S. government to impose quotas or duties on products from that country. In most cases, the threat of 301 tariffs is sufficient to bring about a reduction in the foreign government's import restrictions. It has been used, for example, in reaching an agreement with Japan that provides U.S. citrus growers and cattle producers with easier access to Japanese markets. It also was used to bring about greater protection of U.S. intellectual property in South Korea. As the "International Aspects" feature indicates, it is being considered for use against software pirates located in Taiwan.

INTERNATIONAL ASPECTS | CONTROLLING INTERNATIONAL PIRATES

One of the most significant challenges facing a manager is deciding how to react to foreign manufacturers who pirate (copy or clone) a company's products. The pirate generally uses much cheaper materials and then sells the product as authentic at much lower prices than the real thing. The U.S. International Trade Commission estimates that pirates cost U.S. industry more than $40 billion in lost sales every year.

Microsoft Corporation introduced its Windows software in 1989. The software quickly became one of the best selling programs in history. Almost from the beginning, Microsoft was told of the existence of pirates that were making elaborate copies of its Windows software. After a three-month investigation, Microsoft led police to an apartment building in Taipei, Taiwan.

Police uncovered a highly sophisticated software pirating operation. In addition to finding the diskettes, they found flawless copies of the operation and installation manuals. They also found perfect copies of the hologram sticker intended to foil pirates. The number of copies on order represented a lost revenue of $150 million to Microsoft. The management of Microsoft has filed suit against the pirating company. In addition, the U.S. International Trade Commission has issued a warning against Taiwan. Under the warning, Taiwan must undertake efforts to reduce pirating. If it fails to reduce pirating, the United States will impose high tariffs on Taiwanese products entering the United States.

Among industrialized countries, the United States has one of the lowest software piracy rates. As Figure 18–5 shows, in most major European countries, more than 75 percent of all software sold is pirated. Sales of pirated software also exceeds 75 percent of all sales in Japan. Piracy is one of the most serious problems facing the management of U.S. computer and software companies today.

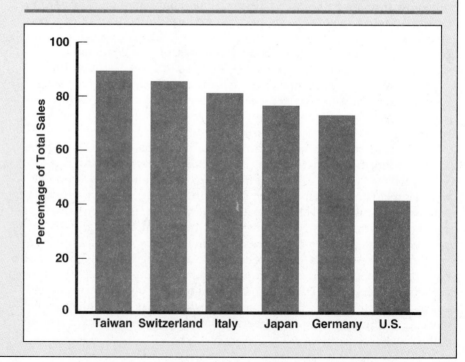

FIGURE 18–5

Sales of Pirated U.S. Software as a Percentage of Total Sales
SOURCE: Business Software Alliance.

Other Laws Controlling Exports.   The Export Administrative Act is not the only legislative mechanism that imposes export controls. The *Arms Export Control Act* of 1976 authorizes the control of commercial arms exports by the Department of State. Export controls are also imposed by the *Nuclear Nonproliferation Act* of 1978, which governs the export of nuclear materials. In addition, the Department of Energy is authorized to control exports of certain technologies. In terms of regulating commercial exports, however, the agencies exerting the greatest influence include the Departments of Defense, Commerce, and State.

ENTERING FOREIGN MARKETS: BUSINESS ORGANIZATIONS

U.S. businesses have sought a variety of means through which to enter foreign markets. In general, there are two basic ways of selling products in foreign markets. A business can either *export* products manufactured in this country to the foreign country or *manufacture* products in the foreign country for distribution there.

■ EXPORTING MANUFACTURED PRODUCTS

Companies initially entering international business (or selling products to countries where political risks are high) generally prefer to export products manufactured domestically. Exporting is preferred because it requires relatively little investment on the part of the business and poses relatively lower risk than foreign manufacturing. Exporting may also be required if the manufacturing of the product requires that the factory be located close to an important natural resource. Clearly, a company selling French spring water would need to locate its factory in France near the spring.

Businesses entering international markets through exporting may choose to do so either directly or indirectly. *Indirect exporting* involves the use of an exporter who sells the product in foreign markets for the U.S. manufacturer. The U.S. manufacturer may also sell to a foreign purchasing agent who is in this country buying products for an overseas customer.

Direct exporting usually involves the development of an organization within the business responsible for export business. Initially, the company may ship directly to its overseas customers. Later, as business expands, the company may elect to develop a marketing organization in its foreign markets and import products from its U.S. factory in its own name.

■ FOREIGN MANUFACTURING OF PRODUCTS

The decision to engage in foreign manufacturing is generally motivated by a business's desire to reduce costs and therefore enhance its ability to compete. Those costs most easily reduced through foreign manufacturing include shipping costs, labor expenses, and raw material costs. In addition, foreign manufacturing may be an effective means to avoid import restrictions or tariffs imposed by the host country.

The management of several leading Japanese companies, for example, have decided to move manufacturing facilities to the United States. They fear that Congress may impose stiff duties on Japanese products in an effort to reduce the U.S. trade deficit. Since products made by a Japanese business located in the United States are legally made in America, they will not be subject to those duties. Managers considering foreign manufacturing have several strategic options available to them, including the following:

1. a wholly owned subsidiary
2. a joint venture
3. a licensing agreement
4. a franchise agreement
5. contract manufacturing

Wholly Owned Subsidiary.   In electing to undertake its foreign manufacturing through a *wholly owned subsidiary,* a business maintains complete ownership in the facilities. In establishing its production facilities, a business may either purchase an existing facility or elect to build a new one. Situations exist, however, where complete ownership is not possible. Several countries impose limits on the percentage of ownership in a manufacturing facility held by foreigners. Until recently, for example, Mexico limited foreign ownership to less than 50 percent.

Joint Venture.   A business may elect to undertake its foreign manufacturing in cooperation with a group of local owners or another foreign group. Through a *joint venture,* virtually any division of ownership is possible. For example, one party may supply the facilities and the other party the technological skills required for the operation. Although a joint venture requires less investment by the company than does a wholly owned subsidiary, a joint venture may also mean loss of managerial control.

Licensing Agreement.   A *licensing agreement* involves a contractual arrangement whereby one business—the licensor—grants another business—the licensee—access to its patents and other technologies. Licenses can be granted to cover the transfer of virtually any kind of expertise. The licensor is usually granted a royalty on net sales, generally from one percent to five percent. Through licensing, the licensor receives income it otherwise would not have received. In addition, allowing the licensee to use the business's trademark could serve to establish a worldwide reputation for the business. However, management of the licensing company will need to take precautions to make sure that the licensing agreement is enforceable in the licensee's country.

Franchising Agreements.   In the past decade, *franchising* has become an extremely popular vehicle for expanding into foreign markets. Franchising is a form of licensing. The franchisor (the supplier) grants the franchisee (the foreign dealer) the right to sell products or services in exchange for a fee. The most visible franchises are fast-food restaurants. McDonald's, Pizza Hut, and Kentucky Fried Chicken have made major inroads as international franchises, particularly in Japan, Canada, and Europe. Other successful franchise operations include hotels (Holiday Inn), car rentals (Hertz and Avis), soft drinks (Coca-Cola), and business services (Muzak). Management of the franchising business must work to make sure that the quality of the company product is maintained at new overseas locations.

Contract Manufacturing.   In some instances, companies may contract for the production of certain products in foreign facilities. U.S. retailers, for example, have found it advantageous to contract for the mass production of clothing and other textile products in Taiwan, Korea, and Hong Kong. In those countries, labor costs are considerably lower than in the United States. The products are then shipped to the United States for sale in retail outlets. Contract manufacturing has the additional advantage of not requiring investment in production facilities.

The management of Nike has made contract manufacturing an important part of its strategic plan. Because the company does not own the manufacturing plants that produce its athletic shoes, all production costs are variable costs rather than fixed costs for the company. When demand for its products slows, management simply does not renew a manufacturing contract. Management does not have to worry about laying off workers or making payments on a plant that is not producing.

INTERNATIONAL CONTRACTS

As in domestic business agreements, the basis for any international agreement is the *international contract* between the parties. Often, however, an international contract will differ significantly from a business's domestic contracts. International contracts often involve parties from differing cultural backgrounds who rarely know each other well at the outset of negotiations. The physical distance between the parties to international agreements often complicates the contract's negotiation, substance, and performance. The differing languages, currencies, legal systems, and business customs of parties will affect the nature of the contract and influence the way the contract is written.

■ CULTURAL ASPECTS OF INTERNATIONAL CONTRACTS

A knowledge of and sensitivity to differences in cultures are important in international contracting. In Japan, for example, *meishi,* or business cards, are exchanged at a first meeting. In the United States, business cards may be exchanged at any time, usually after a meeting is over. In many countries, including China, hours may go by before the subject matter of the business concern is even mentioned. This is quite different from the U.S. approach, where the parties are very forthright as to the purpose and goals of the business meeting.

A major cultural impact on international agreements is the difference in language between the parties. Language itself should not be considered a barrier to an international contract. However, it is important that the terms of the contract are clearly defined in a language that all parties understand. Reliable interpreters can be used as an integral part of both the negotiations and the final draft of the contract where parties are not able to communicate in a common language.

The attitude toward relationships is another cultural difference between countries. Many countries, including Japan and China and many Latin American and Western European nations, have the cultural expectation that the relationship between contracting parties will be long-term. As a result, the negotiation process will be long, since it is necessary for the parties to know one another well before entering into a long-term relationship. Contracts based on trust and long-term expectations are often relatively short in length, with few contingencies expressly provided. The expectation is that contingencies can be worked out as they arise with the parties working to maintain the underlying relationship.

In countries such as the United States, just the opposite is expected. In the United States, a long-term relationship develops after a series of individual short-term business dealings. Therefore, at the onset of any given contract, the negotiation process is expected to be done as quickly and efficiently as possible. The subject matter of the contract is often the only basis of the relationship being considered. Contracts are generally longer and more detailed. The parties are at arm's length from one another and must rely on the written contract to handle contingencies. Both approaches to contractual relationships have their merits, but they are quite different.

INTERNATIONAL ASPECTS | CULTURE AND THE EURO DISNEY INVASION

In May of 1992, the Walt Disney Company opened its Euro Disneyland theme park near Paris, France. In developing the 4.4-billion-dollar project, the management of Disney negotiated with French officials under four different prime ministers and with numerous European trade unions (despite its generally good relations, the park still suffered through a rail strike on its opening day). The company endured a barrage of press criticism that referred to the project as everything from an "imperialist cultural invasion of Europe" to a "cultural Chernobyl." As the park was about to open, local contractors filed a protest with Disney for more than $150 million in costs they assert Disney was trying to avoid paying. Still, Disney expects the project to attract 11 million visitors and generate revenues in excess of $1.5 billion per year.

Euro Disneyland has been a major challenge for Disney management. Clearly, Euro Disneyland will establish a major base for American culture in Europe. But will the American business practices that Disney has so successfully used in the United States transfer to Europe? Will the project ultimately fail from a clash of cultures? For example, in developing the project—from the initial negotiations with the government to the architects to the construction companies to its employees—has Disney been able to use its American experience base? Or has it had to make serious cultural adjustments? If it has not made those adjustments, will it need to do so to survive?

In building hotels for the park, the Disney experience created a problem for European architects. Many architects could not get comfortable with the notion

(continued)

that Disney hotels must be themed. That is, the hotels must carry the park's entertainment concept out of the park itself back to the hotels—so-called story architecture. For example, the Hotel Cheyenne is patterned after an old Western movie set and has a rodeo-themed amusement area. In the beginning, European architects had difficulty with the story or theme concept. As a consequence, many of the initial proposals were rejected. After lengthy discussions, Disney management was able to overcome these cultural impediments. Several of the Disney's European-designed structures have been well received by critics.

Considerable attention was paid to the transfer of Disney's famous dress code to Europe. The dress code makes specific reference to deodorant use—it is mandatory—and to underwear—it must be "natural" in color. However, despite these and other American cultural requirements, more than nine people applied for each of the 12,000 jobs available at the park.

To combat at least some of the "cultural-invasion" criticism, Disney has carefully pointed out that many of its characters are taken from European fables. It also added additional attractions to the park that have a clear European culture orientation. While this show of cultural sensitivity has not convinced the hardcore cultural holdouts, it has shown that the company is concerned about not simply forcing the Disney/American culture on European consumers. In addition, Disney management has also worked to further overcome this problem by encouraging several major European companies to become involved in advertising both the park and other Disney products. In fact, only a very small percentage of the initial $110 million in promotions was paid for by Disney.

Still, many important cultural questions remain that will influence the economic vitality of the project. Will Disney's famous crowd-control techniques work as well in Europe as in the United States and Japan? Several European critics are predicting that it will be a major cultural challenge to persuade short-tempered southern Europeans to stand in line and refrain from smoking. Will Disney be able to change European eating habits in the park so that customers do not crowd into the restaurants all at one time? Disney is banking on the fact that because of multiple nationalities this problem will solve itself. Some nationalities, like the English, eat early, while others, like the Italians, prefer to eat much later. In a culture where beer is available even at McDonald's, will Europeans temporarily give up their alcohol to spend a day at the park, or will Disney eventually make concessions? Currently, Disney is providing an array of soft drinks in its restaurants and has no plans to break from company policy to add alcoholic beverages to its menus.

■ FINANCIAL ASPECTS OF INTERNATIONAL CONTRACTS

Great geographical distance between the parties and differences in the parties' legal systems almost assure that an international contract will require special financial considerations. In managing the financial risks that may arise, care will be required in specifying the method of payment and the currency payment is to be made in. In addition, the parties need to be concerned about the ability to remove their profits from countries in which they conduct their business.

Foreign Exchange Markets.   In an international exchange, a company often receives another country's currency. A business may wish to exchange that currency into its own country's currency. The exchange of money is not always a simple mathematical calculation. Losses in international business sometimes center on exchange risk—the potential loss or profit that occurs between the time the currency is acquired and the time it is sold or exchanged for another currency. Suppose, for example, that U.S Wine Importers Inc. enters into a contract for the purchase of French wines. Suppose further that the contract calls for the payment of 2.8 million French francs in 180 days. When the contract is signed, the exchange rate is 7.00 French francs to the dollar. Thus, if U.S. Wine paid immediately, the 2.8 million French francs would cost $400,000. However, suppose that the management of U.S. Wine has decided to wait the full 180 days before paying. Suppose also that during that time period the exchange rate falls to 6.58 French francs to the dollar. Unless U.S. Wine has undertaken to protect itself from exchange risks, it now must pay $425,000 to satisfy the terms of the agreement. That is, movements in the exchange rate cost the company $25,000.

To avoid such difficulties, the management of U.S. businesses often require payment in dollars rather than in the currency of the other country. The currency of some countries, however, is not recognized by other governments. In such cases, the money is said to be a *nonconvertible* currency. Money that is nonconvertible has value only in the country that issues it. For example, the Russian ruble usually has been nonconvertible. A bank in the United States will not convert rubles to dollars. In most cases, management will be reluctant to do business in a country where the company cannot convert its profits into dollars (or other Western currencies). In some cases, management may be willing to take other goods as payment. The company can then sell those goods in world markets for convertible, or hard, currency. Still other companies are willing to take greater risks. For example, the management of McDonald's opened a restaurant in Moscow knowing that it could not take profits out of the country. However, it was McDonald's strategic plan to be the first major fast-food company operating in the former Soviet Union. McDonald's was willing to take the risk with an appreciation for the potential of the Russian market once the ruble becomes convertible.

Financial Instruments Used in International Contracts.   In many cases, parties to international contracts prefer to use special international financial devices to assure payment for products sold in international commerce. Such devices either assure later payment or allow for the arrangement of credit when buyers are otherwise unable to come up with the cash necessary for the business transaction. A number of credit devices facilitate international transactions. A financial device commonly used is the letter of credit.

A *letter of credit* is an agreement or assurance by the bank of the buyer to pay a specified amount to the seller upon receipt of certain documentation. Those documents will prove that the goods have been shipped and that any other contractual obligations on the seller have been fulfilled. The usual documentation required includes a certificate of origin, an export license, a certificate of inspection, a bill of lading, a commercial invoice, and an insurance policy. Once the bank has received the necessary documents, it will release payment to the seller. Figure 18–6 illustrates the

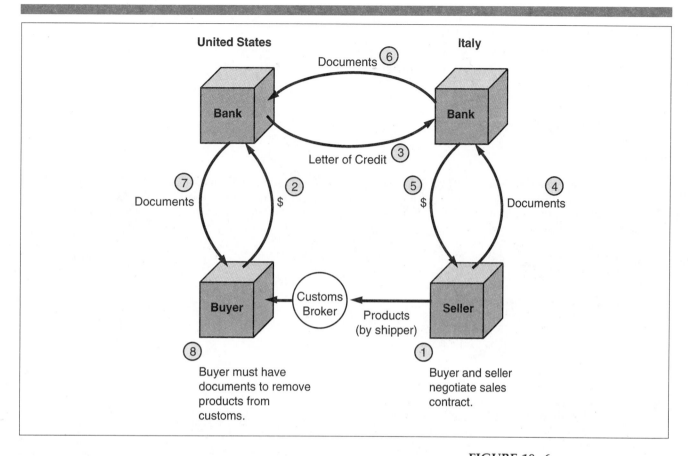

FIGURE 18–6

Letter of Credit in an
International Transaction

route taken by the letter of credit and the documentation in an international business transaction between an Italian seller and an American buyer.

Letters of credit can be either revocable or irrevocable. As the label attached to each implies, a *revocable letter of credit* may be withdrawn, while an *irrevocable letter of credit* may not be withdrawn before the specific date stated on it. Nearly all companies prefer irrevocable letters of credit. Exhibit 18–1 is an example of an irrevocable letter of credit.

Repatriation of Monetary Profits.   Repatriation of monetary profits can sometimes be a concern to a party involved in an international transaction. *Repatriation* in the international business sense refers to the ability of a foreign business or individual to return money earned in the foreign country to its home country. The ability to repatriate is often regulated by a given country's laws. Both Taiwan and the People's Republic of China, for example, have regulations on the amounts of local currencies that can be taken out of their country. The usual reasons for restrictions on repatriation involve concerns about a reserve shortage in foreign currencies and a desire that money earned within the country be reinvested in the local economy. Management should have a thorough understanding of any repatriation restrictions before beginning operations in a foreign country.

EXHIBIT 18–1 ▰▰▰▰▰▰▰▰▰▰▰▰▰▰▰▰▰▰▰▰▰▰▰▰▰▰▰▰▰▰▰▰▰▰▰▰▰

Example of an Irrevocable Letter of Credit

LETTER OF CREDIT — CONFIRMED, IRREVOCABLE

Western Reserve Bank   Letter of Credit #59723
Chicago, Illinois   Issued on August 1, 1992

To: Exotica Company   From Tiramisu Import Company
Dallas, Texas, U.S.A.   Rome, Italy

Gentlemen:

We are instructed by Commercial Bank of Italy, Rome, Italy, to inform you that it has opened its irrevocable credit in favor for account of Tiramisu Import Company, Rome, Italy, for the sum in U.S. dollars not exceeding a total of about $55,000.00 (Fifty-five Thousand and 00/100 Dollars), available by your drafts on us, to be accompanied by:

1. Full Set On Board Negotiable Ocean Bills of Lading, stating "Freight Prepaid" and made out to the order of Commercial Bank of Italy.
2. Insurance Policy or Certificate, covering Marine and War Risk.
3. Packing List.
4. Commercial Invoice in triplicate:
   Covering 200 Pcs. 1025 Electric Espresso Coffee Machines.
           200 Pcs. 750 Stove Top Espresso Coffee Makers
           350 Pcs. 420 Electric Pasta Makers
   Total Value $54,702.75 C.I.F. Rome, Italy
   Import Lic. No. 3792 Expires October 24, 1992
5. Shipper's Export Declaration.
   Partial shipment permitted. Transshipment not permitted.
   Merchandise must be shipped on SS Mercaso.

All documents must indicate Letter of Credit No. 59723, Import License No. 13792, expires October 24, 1992.

All drafts must be marked "Drawn under Letter of Credit No. 59723, issued by Western Reserve Bank. Drafts must be presented to this company not later than October 1, 1992."

This credit is subject to the Uniform Customs and Practices for Documentary Credits (1984 Revision) International Chamber of Commerce Publication No. 400.

We confirm the credit and thereby undertake that all drafts drawn and presented as above specified will be duly honored by us.

                        By
                        International Credit Department

◼ SELECTED CLAUSES IN INTERNATIONAL CONTRACTS

The contract is the foundation of any international business venture. It sets the framework for the relationship between the parties. As with domestic contracts, care should be taken that the intent of the parties is fully represented by the contract. Moreover, any international contract should be written, even if it states merely the positions and goals of the parties. In some cases, standardized contracts may be used by the parties. When such standardized contracts are not available, however, the following clauses are often included in international contracts.

Payment Clauses.   The *payment clause* is an important requirement for any international contract. The method and manner in which payment is to be received as well as the currency in which payment is to be made should be clearly specified. Some nations, such as Hungary, do not allow their currencies to leave the country. If payment is made in currency under such a situation, the payment has special restrictive effects on the receiver of the currency. Those effects should be taken into account when the contract is written. Problems with inflation and currency exchange risks, especially in unstable economies or in long-term agreements, should also be addressed in this contract clause.

Choice of Language Clause.   Parties to international contracts do not always speak the same language. Even when they do, the complex contractual terms may exceed the understanding of one of the parties when the contract is not in that party's native language. Further, a word or phrase in one language may not be readily translatable to another. Therefore, the contract should have a *choice of language clause*. This clause will set out the official language under which the contract is to be interpreted. Although designating an official language may not remedy all language problems, it does aid in notifying the parties of the language that will be used. Examples of a choice of language clause are provided in Exhibit 18–2.

***Force Majeure* Clause.**   *Force majeure* is a French term meaning a "superior or irresistible force." Thus, a *force majeure* clause protects the contracting parties from problems beyond their control. Traditionally, this type of clause was used to protect the parties from the consequences of a natural disaster that interfered with performance. More recently, however, the clause has protected the parties against unprecedented inflation or political upheavals. The conflict in the Persian Gulf in 1990/91 is an example of where the use of such a clause may have assisted parties adversely affected by the event. An example of a typical *force majeure* clause is given in Exhibit 18–3.

EXHIBIT 18–2 ▰▰▰▰▰▰▰▰▰▰▰▰▰▰▰▰▰▰▰▰▰▰

Choice of Language Clauses

Example of Choice of Language Clause with Arbitration Provision
This Agreement is signed in two (2) originals in the English language, which shall be regarded as the authoritative and official text. Any matters referred to arbitration will also be in the English language, which will be the official language used in arbitration.

Example of Choice of Language Clause with Translation Provision
This Agreement is signed in two (2) originals in the French language, which shall be regarded as the authoritative and official text. Parties hereto agree to provide an official translation of this Agreement in the English language. This translation will be ratified by both parties and it may be relied upon as being an accurate representation of the official form.

EXHIBIT 18–3

Example of *Force Majeure* Clause

> The parties hereto shall not be liable for failure of performance hereunder if occasioned by war, declared or undeclared, fire, flood, interruption of transportation, inflation beyond the expected rate, embargo, accident, explosion, inability to procure or shortage of supply of materials, equipment, or production facilities, prohibition of import or export of goods covered hereby, governmental orders, regulations, restrictions, priorities or rationing by strike or lockout or other labor troubles interfering with production or transportation of such goods or with the supplies of raw materials entering into their production or any other cause beyond the control of the parties.

LOSS OF INVESTMENT

International business is rarely undertaken without some risk that the investment will be lost. Political upheavals, unstable monetary systems, dramatic changes in laws and their interpretations, and an array of problems associated with doing business with a developing country are some of the risks management can encounter. In addition, businesses must be concerned about governmental actions that can result in loss of investment. Governments may take private property through nationalization, expropriation, and confiscation. However, foreign investors may reduce their risks of loss through the purchase of insurance.

■ NATIONALIZATION

Nationalization occurs when the government of a country decides to take over, or nationalize, a foreign investment. The compensation provided by the government is often less than the true value of the business. The stated purpose of nationalization is usually related to the public or national welfare. For example, the government may state that the foreign company's product is strategic to the country's national defense. Nationalization has occurred more often than most investors realize—over 260 times in the past two decades. Although such government takeovers usually occur in underdeveloped or developing nations, they are not limited to such countries. A trend to nationalize has been seen in such countries as Iran, Nigeria, Saudi Arabia, and Venezuela. In addition, Canada and England, two highly developed countries, have demonstrated a tendency to nationalize certain industries.

■ EXPROPRIATION AND CONFISCATION

Expropriation is defined as the actions of the government of a country in taking foreign assets or other property rights in accordance with international law. For the expropriation to be valid, there must be public purpose behind the taking and prompt, adequate, and effective compensation must be provided to the investor whose property was taken. The rules of traditional international law recognize a country's right to expropriate the property of foreigners within the country's jurisdiction.

If the takeover is invalid or unlawful, it is called a *confiscation*. The U.S. position has been that takings directed toward a particular nationality are discriminatory and are therefore considered confiscations rather than expropriations. The United States has responded to unlawful takings by denying certain rights under its laws to countries carrying out confiscations.

■ INSURING AGAINST RISK OF LOSS

Managers concerned about the risk of loss of investment may decide to obtain insurance against such possibilities. An all-risk type of insurance policy can provide financial relief in the event of nationalization. Short-term insurance from private insurers usually lasts from three to five years and is readily available for most investments. Outstanding risks such as currency blockages, embargoes, and a government's arbitrary decision to recall letters of credit may be insured by such major insurers as Lloyds of London. In addition, sellers may obtain rejection insurance in the event the buyer rejects the product for reasonable cause, such as spoilage at sea.

Some countries have governmental agencies that assist in insuring their exporters from risk of loss. In the United States, for example, the *Overseas Private Investment Corporation* (OPIC) insures those investors willing to invest in less-developed countries friendly to the United States. OPIC offers investors insurance against expropriation, currency inconvertibility, and damage from wars or revolutions.

INTERNATIONAL DISPUTE RESOLUTION

According to the World Bank, the world now enjoys an annual volume of trade of more than $2 trillion. It is to the credit of the international business community that such a volume of trade exists in spite of the legal uncertainties in international commercial transactions. There are instances, however, when international disputes concerning performance of contracts arise. These may be due to unanticipated events, unforeseen difficulties or expenses in performance, changes in the legal or political climate of a country that affect the contract, or the desire by a party to no longer participate in the contract for any number of reasons. In such instances, parties to international contracts seek institutional assistance to resolve disputes and enforce their rights under the contract.

■ THE INTERNATIONAL COURT OF JUSTICE

Certain disputes may be taken to the *International Court of Justice* (ICJ) for resolution. The ICJ has its headquarters at The Hague, Netherlands. It is a principal organ of the United Nations. The court comprises fifteen judges representing all of the world's major legal systems, with no two judges from the same country. The court is empowered to decide cases in accordance with Article 38 of the Court Statute, which provides the following:

1. The Court, whose function is to decide cases in accordance with international law such disputes as are submitted to it, shall apply:
   a. international conventions, whether general or particular, establishing rules expressly recognized by the contesting parties;
   b. international custom, as evidence of a general practice accepted as law;
   c. the general principles of law recognized by civilized nations;
   d. subject to the provisions of [statutes], judicial decisions and the teachings of the most highly qualified publicists of the various nations, as subsidiary means for the determination of the rules of law.

2. This provision shall not prejudice the power of the Court to decide a case *ex aequo et bono* (according to what is good and just), if the parties agree thereto.

Only countries that are part of the world community have standing to go before the ICJ. Individuals and businesses have no standing themselves to initiate a suit. Further, the countries, and not the parties to the dispute, have complete discretion in deciding whether to pursue the claims. Suppose a country where an international investor does business violates international law to the detriment of that investor. The country of which the investor is a citizen has sole discretion to pursue or not to pursue the investor's claim.

The court's decisions providing for monetary judgments or injunctive relief may be referred to the United Nations Security Council for enforcement. If the judgment is paid, however, the country need not distribute it to the wronged investor unless domestic laws require such a distribution. In the United States, such distributions are handled by the Foreign Claims Settlement Commission.

■ JUDICIAL LITIGATION

A party seeking to resolve an international contract dispute may also seek relief either in the court system within the opposing party's country or within his or her own country. Such litigation, however, is complicated by the fact that evidence, individuals, and documents central to the resolution of the dispute are often located in two or more countries. In some instances, such difficulties may be overcome through treaties or conventions between the two countries. Those treaties or conventions may allow for the proper notice of the suit to the foreign parties involved, appropriate service of process, methods for documentation certification, and procedures for the taking of evidence.

If the action is commenced in a foreign court, the U.S. participant will often encounter a judicial system significantly different from that in this country. Courts in foreign countries are often influenced more significantly by political pressures than are U.S. courts. In addition, foreign courts are often unwilling to enforce provisions in contracts that may be enforceable in this country but are viewed as being against public policy in theirs.

In this country, a fundamental difficulty often arises in attempting to establish proper jurisdiction over both parties to the dispute. U.S. courts will require proof of "minimum contacts" within the United States so that the court can have proper jurisdiction over a foreign defendant. The minimum contacts requirement may be met by a showing of the defendant's presence within U.S. territory; a domicile or residency in the United States; consent to the court's jurisdiction; carrying on of business within the court's jurisdiction; or participation in activities outside the country that have direct, substantial, or foreseeable effects within the country.

◼ Arbitration

Traditional judicial forums have not proved effective in resolving most international commercial disagreements. Costs, jurisdictional problems, barriers to relief, the length of time to litigate, legal uncertainties, and the inability of judicial systems to fashion appropriate relief encouraged the creation of alternative dispute resolution techniques. One of the most popular alternative techniques has been the arbitration process.

Under *arbitration*, the parties agree to submit themselves to a neutral third party to resolve disputes. The third party may be a panel of arbiters or a single arbiter. The arbitration award may or may not be binding. More and more parties to international contracts are choosing arbitration as the mechanism for resolving international commercial disputes.

Attempts by the international business community to standardize arbitral rules and procedures have resulted in the creation of such organizations as the United Nations Commission on International Trade Law, the International Chamber of Commerce, the American Arbitration Association, the Inter-American Commercial Arbitration Commission, and the London Court of Arbitration. These organizations have established rules to address issues concerning arbitral proceedings, tribunals, and awards. In over fifty countries, including the United States, the enforcement of arbitral awards is facilitated by the 1958 United Nations Convention on the Recognition and Enforcement of Foreign Arbitral Awards. The U.S. federal district courts have jurisdiction to entertain motions to confirm or challenge a foreign arbitration award involving a U.S. business.

◼ Doctrine of Sovereign Immunity

A foreign investor who has suffered losses from the expropriation of property may consider suing to recover the losses. The foreign investor may begin this litigation in a country different from the country that expropriated the investment. However, this type of litigation may be prohibited from obtaining relief by the doctrine of sovereign immunity.

In international law, the *doctrine of sovereign immunity* allows a court to give up its right to jurisdiction over a foreign enterprise or country. This doctrine is based on traditional notions that a sovereign should not be subject to litigation in a foreign court. As a result, the foreign investor may not be able to obtain relief in other countries' court systems.

The traditional application of the doctrine can have severe consequences on parties when the suit involves a commercial transaction. The U.S. and several other countries have moved to restrict the doctrine's application in such circumstances. The Foreign Sovereign Immunities Act of 1976 provides a uniform rule for determining sovereign immunity in legal actions in this country's courts. The Act provides the following:

> Under international law, [countries] are not immune from the jurisdiction of foreign courts insofar as their commercial activities are concerned, and their commercial property may be levied upon for the satisfaction of judgments rendered against them in connection with their commercial activities.

■ DOCTRINE OF ACT OF STATE

The *doctrine of act of state* is similar to the sovereign immunity doctrine. It creates a bar to compensation by foreign investors who have sustained losses in host countries. Unlike the sovereign immunity doctrine, however, the doctrine of act of state may create a partial as well as a complete bar to a claim. The act of state doctrine follows the principle that a country must respect the independence of other countries. The courts of one country may not judge the validity of the regulatory acts of another country's government undertaken within its own territory.

U.S. courts have upheld the doctrine, stating that among other things, it ensures international harmony. Although the purpose of the doctrine is to avoid any embarrassment in foreign relations, the practical effect is that a claimant seeking relief may be partially or totally barred from relief in the court where the doctrine applies. The Supreme Court analyzed the doctrine in the following case.

BANCO NACIONAL DE CUBA v. SABBATINO

United States Supreme Court
376 U.S. 398, 84 S.Ct. 923 (1964)

Case Background
Farr, Whitlock & Company, an American commodities broker, contracted to purchase Cuban sugar from C.A.V., a corporation organized under Cuban law. However, the shareholders of C.A.V. were principally American citizens. Farr, Whitlock & Company agreed to pay for the sugar in New York after receiving the appropriate shipping documents. Shortly after the contract was signed, the U.S. Congress imposed a reduction in the sugar quota. The Cuban government viewed the reduction as an act of aggression on the part of the U.S. government. In response, the Cuban government nationalized the Cuban sugar industry, including C.A.V. The nationalization decree imposed the additional requirement that all ships carrying sugar from Cuban ports must have the consent of the Cuban government before leaving Cuban waters. To meet this requirement, Farr, Whitlock & Company was forced to enter into a contract with the bank of the Cuban government, Banco Nacional de Cuba.

Banco Nacional de Cuba presented the shipping documents to Farr, Whitlock & Company in New York and demanded payment. On the same day, C.A.V. (through its American shareholders who stood to lose their investment because of the nationalization) notified Farr, Whitlock & Company that it was still the rightful owner of the sugar and that it was entitled to the payment. Sabbatino was designated as C.A.V.'s representative. Farr, Whitlock & Company gave the payment to Sabbatino.

Banco Nacional de Cuba then brought this action to recover the payment from Farr, Whitlock & Company. The federal district court found that the Cuban nationalization decree violated international law and ruled against Banco Nacional de Cuba. The court of appeals affirmed on similar grounds. Banco Nacional appealed to the U.S. Supreme Court.

Case Decision
The Supreme Court reversed the judgment of the court of appeals. The Court held that the doctrine of act of state prohibits a foreign judicial body from ruling on the validity of the acts of a sovereign that are undertaken within the sovereign's territories. That is, under the doctrine, U.S. courts cannot rule on the validity of Cuba's actions but rather must

(continued)

accept them as valid public acts by a sovereign power recognized by the United States. Thus, under the act of state doctrine, Banco Nacional de Cuba is entitled to the payment for the Cuban sugar originally purchased by Farr, Whitlock & Company from C.A.V.

The Court reasoned that the act of state doctrine was intended to ensure that the judicial branch did not interfere with the practices of the political branch of the government in international dealings. If expropriation occurs, the executive (and not the judicial) branch of the government is empowered to engage in diplomatic talks with the foreign power in the interest of U.S companies adversely affected. The executive branch may submit the problem to the United Nations for possible resolution, engage in bilateral or multilateral talks, or impose economic and political sanctions against the foreign power. If the courts interfered with this diplomatic process, international political negotiations may be undermined. According to the Court, the executive branch, not the courts, is responsible for resolving the issues between Banco Nacional de Cuba and Farr. (Note, however, that Congress was dissatisfied with the Supreme Court's decision and responded by amending the Foreign Assistance Act to direct the courts to disregard the act of state doctrine in cases of expropriation of property.)

Managerial Considerations

Although Congress amended the Foreign Assistance Act to aid U.S. companies when their assets abroad are expropriated, a company's assets are still not absolutely protected from expropriation. In this case, the proceeds from the sugar transaction were physically in the United States. Therefore, the U.S. courts had control and jurisdiction over those assets—an unusual set of circumstances. More commonly, a company's plant, equipment, and other assets are physically located in the foreign country when expropriation occurs. The assets are, therefore, not within the jurisdiction of the U.S. courts. Thus, the executive branch will have to use the traditional responses to expropriation. The typical result is that the assets of the U.S. company are either lost or on hold for a long period of time.

When investing abroad, especially in less stable economies or Third World countries, management must always be acutely aware of the country's political and economic environment. As the Gulf War illustrated, the possibility of an event occurring that can have an adverse impact on the company can be very unpredictable. To protect the company, management may find it less risky to lease equipment or enter into a joint venture than to undertake direct ownership of assets within the foreign country.

SUMMARY:
A GUIDE FOR MANAGERS

- In contrast to the domestic market, the international market is characterized by additional financial, political, and regulatory risks. Those risks arise from differences among countries in currencies, language, business customs, legal and social philosophies, and national economic goals.

- U.S. involvement in international business is increasing. However, the percentage of U.S. businesses involved in international business is still lower than that in Germany and Japan.

- The United States has been running a huge merchandise trade deficit since the late 1970s. With the increased involvement of smaller businesses, the U.S. trade deficit declined to less than $70 billion in 1991. That was its lowest level since 1983. However, despite these improvements, there is still concern about the continued decline in U.S. technological development over the same period.

- The principal sources of international trade law are the laws of the individual countries making up the international business community, the laws contained in trade agreements between or among countries, and the rules enacted by worldwide or regional trade organizations.

- In working to reduce barriers to trade worldwide, many countries have signed the General Agreement on Tariffs and Trade (GATT). GATT's primary function is to reduce obstacles to trade, particularly import tariffs.

- Virtually every country has import and export regulations. Examples of import restrictions include import licensing requirements and procedures, import quotas, safety and manufacturing standards, government procurement policies, and customs procedures. In an effort to standardize tariff schedules and their application, most countries have adopted the Harmonized Tariff Schedule.

- In the past, the United States imposed strict prohibitions on the export of certain technologies that could be used by foreign military. For example, the exportation of computers was heavily monitored by the U.S. government. Now, with the opening up of Central and Eastern Europe, many of those prohibitions have been substantially reduced.

- A company considering entering into international business has a variety of business organizations available to facilitate the venture. The most common business organizations are wholly owned subsidiaries, joint ventures, licensing agreements, franchise agreements, and contract manufacturing. The choice of a particular form of business organization is influenced by the laws of the foreign country, the purposes of the international commercial venture, the financial resources of the parties, and the degree of managerial control desired by the company.

- In international transactions, the basis for any agreement is the international contract between the parties. In creating an effective international contract, a business should consider cultural differences between the contracting parties, including differences in business customs, attitudes toward the contractual relationship, and language. Specific clauses in international contracts worthy of special consideration are the payment, choice of language, and force majeure clauses.

- The decision to participate in business in a foreign country is rarely without risk. Political upheavals, unstable monetary systems, dramatic changes in laws and their interpretations, and an array of problems associated with doing business with a developing country are the kinds of risks international businesspeople may encounter. More importantly, heavy losses may occur through nationalization, expropriation, or confiscation of the foreign investment. Foreign investors concerned with these risks may decide to mitigate their losses by obtaining insurance.

- Although a large volume of international trade is undertaken without incident, there are occasions when disputes arise concerning contract performance. A number of national and international institutions may assist a foreign business in effective dispute resolution. Those institutions include the International Court of Justice, judicial litigation in country court systems, and arbitration. The doctrines of sovereign immunity and act of state may create bars to recovery through the judicial system.

MANAGER'S ETHICAL DILEMMA

SHOULD ITALIAN TAXPAYERS SUBSIDIZE AMERICAN IMPORTERS?

EuroTrade, Inc., is a California-based import-export company. The company had developed from an independent family-run business in the late 1940s to become a well-respected, 40-million-dollar company with fifteen employees in the late 1980s. In the early 1980s, the original founders of the business made the decision to sell the business and retire. After several unsuccessful attempts to sell, the company was finally purchased by a large U.S. food distributor called Fabro Distributors in 1989. Fabro management's strategy was to expand its offerings of international foods. Changes in the U.S. diet had caused consumer demand to increase dramatically for foods such as Italian pasta and olive oil. EuroTrade had exclusive contracts with several leading Italian pasta and olive oil companies. Among other things, it was those contracts that had attracted Fabro to EuroTrade.

As part of the purchase agreement, the key management of EuroTrade had to agree to operate the business for a period of two years. During those two years, EuroTrade was to train Fabro personnel and to introduce them to foreign suppliers. At the end of the two-year period, Fabro was to buy EuroTrade stock at a set price and to provide them with a large severance payment. Fabro would also make the final payment for EuroTrade to the principal shareholder (the owner and founder of EuroTrade who would then retire and take a position on the Fabro board of directors). Because of the nature of the business, this was by far the best deal EuroTrade could expect.

For the first year of the relationship, the two managements worked well together. Then, in late November of 1990, EuroTrade was approached by one of the largest wholesalers of olive oil in the United States—Pure Oil Company. Pure Oil had a proposition for EuroTrade/Fabro, and if EuroTrade/Fabro agreed, Pure Oil would bring its entire business (nearly $55 million) to EuroTrade/Fabro.

Pure Oil had been steadily losing business to foreign suppliers for about three years. This was particularly a problem in sales of low-quality oils. Because of the higher price of its low-quality oils, Pure Oil had lost several major accounts. Through its contacts, it had found a way to reduce the price of its imported olive oil. However, it needed support from a company with olive oil contacts like EuroTrade.

Pure Oil's proposal relied on the fact that in Italy, there are three basic kinds of olive oil: extra virgin (highest quality and used primarily for salads), pure (the second highest quality and used primarily for cooking), and pomace (the lowest quality and generally not used in Italy). Unfortunately, because of its price, pomace is the most widely used olive oil product in U.S. restaurants. To support agriculture, the Italian government was providing subsidies to Italian exporters of olive oil. Both extra virgin and pure olive oil received subsidies of $4 per case. However, there was no subsidy for pomace.

Pure Oil Company's proposal worked like this: Pure Oil Company wanted EuroTrade to buy pomace and a little pure olive oil from its Italian suppliers. Except for the last two rows, the shipping container used to transport the oil to the United States would be filled with pomace. The last two rows would be filled with pure olive oil. When the government people in Italy opened the shipping container to determine the subsidy that would apply, they would see only the last row. If they wanted to inspect further, they almost never checked beyond the second row. In either case, they would only see pure olive oil. With that, they would apply the four-dollar-per-case subsidy to the entire shipment (the container held 2,500 cases). Pure Oil Company was sure that with a company having the good reputation of EuroTrade, the government people probably would not even bother to check the container. Given the volume of trade, Pure Oil and EuroTrade/Fabro would make several million dollars a year (all basically at the expense of the Italian taxpayer). Pure Oil Company summarized the situation by saying that the Italian farmers would benefit because they could sell their pomace, the American consumer would benefit by the lower prices, and Pure Oil and EuroTrade would benefit because they were providing this valuable service. Importantly, no American laws were being broken by the practice.

QUESTIONS

The management of Fabro agreed to the proposal. How should the management of EuroTrade react? Since management is leaving shortly, does it have any reason not to go along with the proposal? Suppose, for a variety of reasons, that the EuroTrade managers refused to go along with the deal. Suppose further that the Fabro people reacted by calling the refusal a breach of their managerial training agreement and threatened to back out of the deal. After having tried to sell the business for several years before the Fabro purchase, the EuroTrade management fully expects that Euro-Trade will not receive anything near the price Fabro has agreed to pay for the business. How should Euro-Trade proceed?

REVIEW AND DISCUSSION QUESTIONS

1. Define the following terms:

   tariff   letter of credit
   free trade zone   repatriation

2. Compare and contrast the following:
   a. specific tariff and ad valorem tariff
   b. licensing agreement and franchising agreement
   c. doctrine of sovereign immunity and doctrine of act of state
   d. nationalization and expropriation

3. Compare the advantages and disadvantages of arbitration and judicial litigation as methods of dispute resolution in international trade.

■ CASE QUESTIONS

4. Consider the following fact situation:

   A Houston-based corporation contracted with a German corporation to tow a drilling rig from Louisiana to an area off Revenna, Italy, where the Houston corporation agreed to drill certain wells. The German company's sea tug was to tow the Houston company's rig to the destination. The contract between the two corporations provided that "Any dispute arising must be treated before the London Court of Justice." While the rig was on its way to Italy in the Gulf of Mexico, a severe storm arose. During the storm, the legs broke off the rig and fell into the sea, damaging the drilling rig. The German sea tug towed the damaged rig to Tampa, Florida, the nearest port of refuge. Ignoring the contract clause to litigate any dispute in the English court, the Houston company initiated a lawsuit in the U.S. District Court at Tampa, seeking $3,500,000 in damages from the German company and its sea tug. [*The Bremen* v. *Zapata Off-Shore Company*, 407 U.S. 1, 59 S.Ct. 687 (1971)]

   Is the use of the American court proper in this situation? Why or why not? What effect would the contract clause have on the lawsuit?

5. Consider this fact situation:

   Liberty Bank issued an irrevocable letter of credit for Anderson-Prichard Oil Corporation. The letter of credit was to be used for the purchase of oilwell casing and tubing from Tegtmeyer, a U.S. importer. The letter of credit was sent to the Bank of America, which then issued its own letter of credit to the Union Bank of Switzerland. Anderson-Prichard and Liberty Bank both refused payment of the two drafts because of allegations of differences between the documents and the letter of credit. One of the allegations was that the bill of lading was "foul" and "not clean"—that is, the printed words in the bill describing that the goods delivered would be "in good order and condition" had been crossed out by the carrier. Immediately below these words was the typewritten insertion "ship not responsible for the kind and condition of merchandise," and in the body of the bill was a stamp stating "ship not responsible for rust." A second allegation was that the letter of credit called for new pipe, but the rail weight certificates described the pipe as secondhand. The pipe in fact did not live up to the expectations that Anderson-Prichard had for it concerning quality. [*Bank of America* v. *Liberty National Bank & Trust Co.*, 116 F.Supp. 233 (W.D. Okl. 1953)]

Should the court require payment by Anderson-Prichard and Liberty Bank? Discuss the letter of credit itself and the expectations of the parties and how they should affect the court's decision.

6. Chisholm & Company and the Bank of Jamaica entered into an agreement. The agreement required Chisholm & Company to arrange lines of credit from a number of banks and to obtain Eximbank credit insurance. As is not unusual in international business, the Bank of Jamaica "went around" Chisholm & Company and dealt with Eximbank directly. It then excluded Chisholm & Company from receiving any benefit from the credit insurance. Chisholm & Company brought an action against the bank. The bank asserted that its actions were protected by sovereign immunity and the act of state doctrine. Was the bank's assertions correct? [*Chisholm & Company* v. *Bank of Jamaica*, 643 F.Supp. 1393 (S.D. Fla. 1986)]

■ BUSINESS POLICY QUESTIONS

7. According to industry statistics, foreign ownership in U.S. properties has jumped dramatically in the past few years. The trade and budget deficits and the weaker dollar are said to be the principal factors causing this. About 64 percent of the real estate in downtown Los Angeles and 40 percent in downtown Houston are now owned by foreigners. One-third of the office space in Minneapolis is owned by Canadians. In addition to owning urban land, foreigners own large tracts of farmland. Foreign investment in the United States is now estimated to be $1.5 trillion. Should we encourage or discourage foreign investments in this country? Are such investments adverse to our national security? Are there other alternatives to controlling foreign investment besides prohibiting or restricting foreign ownership?

8. Why do some countries allow items to enter duty free while other countries may require the same items to be subject to duties? What are the advantages and disadvantages of each approach to international trade?

9. What factors contribute to the decision by a country to regulate or restrict repatriation? What kind of economies tend to use repatriation?

■ ETHICS QUESTIONS

10. In some circumstances, cultural expectations and business customs of a country may run counter to an individual's moral beliefs. What factors should the individual take into consideration if such a conflict arises when he or she is also charged with making a business work within the cultural setting?

11. In some cultures it is expected behavior for businesses to make payoffs to government officials in the process of negotiating an international business transaction. If you find yourself in such a situation, should you provide a payoff? Suppose it makes the difference between getting the contract and not getting the contract? In response to revelations of "questionable" payments by American companies to foreign officials, Congress enacted the Foreign Corrupt Practices Act. Should the U.S. government impose its moral judgments on world business behavior?

FINDING THE LAW

There are several important sources of law in the United States, including the U.S. Constitution; case law established by the written opinions of judges; statutes enacted by legislative bodies; regulatory agency orders, opinions, and regulations; treatises; law reviews; and Restatements of Law. At one time or another, we will reference these sources in explaining the fundamental laws making up the legal environment of business. This section provides a general guide to reading a citation to a source of law. In the event you decide to study an aspect of the legal environment in more detail, this section will provide guidance in locating the appropriate legal material.

■ CASE LAW

The judicial opinions of all federal courts and the appellate state courts are available in court reporters. As a rule, opinions appear in hardback volumes of the *Federal Reporter* about a year after a court has delivered its decision. The opinions are available more quickly, however, in paperback volumes published shortly after the case is decided, through computer research services (such as *Westlaw* and *Lexis*) and in the form of "slip opinions," which are photocopies of decisions made as soon as they are made public by the court.

Supreme Court decisions are published in the *United States Reporter* (U.S.), the *Supreme Court Reporter* (S.Ct.), the *Lawyers' Edition of Supreme Court Reports* (L.Ed.), and the *U.S. Law Week*. Citations read as follows: *Arnett* v. *Kennedy,* 416 U.S. 134, 94 S.Ct. 1633 (1974). This tells us that Arnett appealed a decision of a lower court to the Untied States Supreme Court. In 1974, the Supreme Court decided the case, and its decision is reported in volume 416 of the *United States Reporter* beginning on page 134 and in volume 94 of the *Supreme Court Reporter* beginning on page 1633. A reference to a point cited on a particular page in that opinion might read 416 U.S. 134, 137, which means that the case begins on page 134 and the particular point referenced is on page 137.

Decisions of United States Circuit Courts of Appeals are reported in the *Federal Reporter* (F.), which is now in its second series (F.2d). The following is an example of a citation: *Easton Publishing Co.* v. *Federal Communications Commissions,* 175 F.2d 344 (1949). The decision in this case can be found in volume 175 of the *Federal Reporter* (second series), page 344. The decision was rendered by the court in 1949.

Opinions of U.S. district courts that the judges wish to publish are reported in the *Federal Supplement* (F.Supp.). An example is *Amalgamated Meat Cutters* v. *Connally,* 337 F.Supp. 737 (S.D.N.Y.,1971). The decision can be found in volume 337 of the *Federal Supplement* beginning on page 737. The case was decided by the federal district court in the southern district of New York in 1971.

State appellate court decisions are reported in regional reporters published by West Publishing Company. Decisions of the state supreme courts and courts of appeals for Arkansas, Kentucky, Missouri, Tennessee, and Texas, for example, are reported in the *South Western Reporter* (S.W.). As shown in Figure A–1, other state court opinions are reported in the *Atlantic Reporter* (A.), *North Eastern Reporter* (N.E.), *North Western Reporter* (N.W.), *Pacific Reporter* (P.), *South Eastern Reporter* (S.E.), and *Southern Reporter* (S.), all of which are in the second series (2d). Because they handle so many cases, California and New York have individual reporters—the *New York Supplement* and the *California Reporter*. Some states publish their own reporters in addition to the West series.

STATUTORY LAW

Statutes—laws passed by Congress—are published in the *United States Code* (U.S.C.) and printed by the U.S. Government Printing Office. The U.S.C.

FIGURE A–1

National Reporter System Map—Showing the States included in each Reporter Group

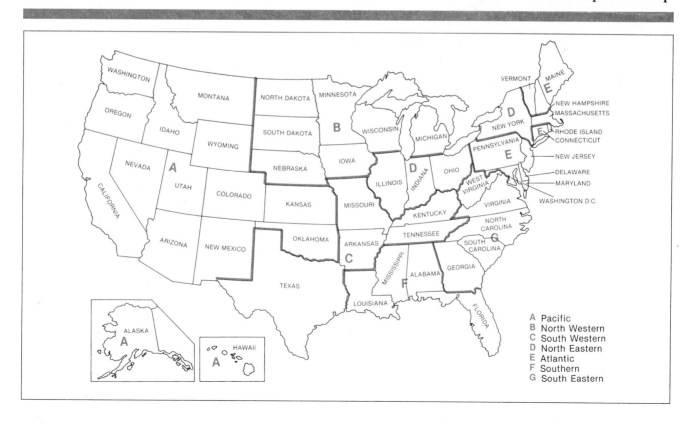

A Pacific
B North Western
C South Western
D North Eastern
E Atlantic
F Southern
G South Eastern

contains the text of all laws passed by Congress and signed by the President. A reference to this source might read 40 U.S.C. § 13.1 (volume 40 of the *United States Code*, section 13.1).

A very popular source of statutory law is the *United States Code Annotated* (U.S.C.A.). In the U.S.C.A., each section of a statute contains helpful annotations that provide references to the legislative history of the section and to court decisions using and interpreting it. A reference to this source might read 14 U.S.C.A. § 45.3 (volume 14, *United States Code Annotated*, section 45.3). In both the U.S.C. and the U.S.C.A., the laws are organized and integrated into a pattern that makes them relatively easy to find and to read.

The U.S. Government Printing Office also publishes *Statutes at Large*, a chronological list of all laws enacted by Congress. This is not often used unless it is necessary to look up a law that has just been passed by Congress but that is not yet reported in the U.S.C. or U.S.C.A. A full citation might read: Voting Rights Act of 1965, Pub.L. No. 89–110, 79 Stat. 437, 42 U.S.C. §§ 1971, 1973. The Voting Rights Act of 1965 was the 110th *Public Law* enacted by the 89th Congress and appears in volume 79 of *Statutes at Large*, section 437. In addition, it appears in volume 42 of the U.S.C., sections 1971 and 1973. Also, remember that there is often a difference between the number of the section in the statute as written by Congress and the number of the section in the Code. For example, the "National Environmental Policy Act of 1969, § 102, 42 U.S.C. § 4332" means that section 102 of the statute as passed by Congress is found in section 4332 of volume 42 of the U.S.C.

■ REGULATORY LAW

Regulations—rules passed by agencies subsequent to a congressional statute—are published in the *Code of Federal Regulations* (C.F.R.). These regulations are intended to implement a particular statute enacted by Congress. The C.F.R., revised annually, is organized by subject matter and contains the text of regulations in effect as of the date of publication. A citation reading 7 C.F.R. § 912.65 refers to Title 7 of the *Code of Federal Regulations*, section 912.65. Different titles refer to different government agencies.

To keep up-to-date on new and proposed regulations, one needs to consult the *Federal Register* (Fed.Reg.). Printed five days a week by the U.S. Government Printing Office, the *Federal Register* lists all proposed regulations and all new and amended regulations. A citation might read 46 Fed. Reg. 26,501 (1981). This refers to volume 46 of the *Federal Register*, published in 1981, page 26,501, which has to do with a new environmental standard.

■ AGENCY ORDERS AND OPINION

Agency orders and opinions are official regulatory materials that go beyond the regulations. Orders may be issued by the top officials (e.g., the commissioners) of a regulatory agency, while opinions are generally issued by an agency's administrative law judge in adjudicatory hearings (discussed in Chapter 6). While agencies usually have official publications, the easiest way to find agency materials is to look in commercial reporters published by private companies such as Commerce Clearing House (CCH), Bureau of National Affairs (BNA), and Prentice-Hall (P-H). Each reporter covers a single topic, such as environmental law or federal tax law. The reporters are up-to-date and contain new regulations, orders, opinions, court decisions, and other materials of interest to anyone following regulations in a certain area. These reporters, which are usually large loose-leaf binders, cover hundreds of topics, such as chemical regulations, hazardous materials, transportation, noise regulations, collective bargaining negotiations, securities regulations, patents, and antitrust laws.

■ TREATISES, LAW REVIEWS, AND RESTATEMENTS OF THE LAW

Important secondary sources of law are legal treatises, law reviews, and Restatements of Law. Treatises generally cover one area or topic of law, summarizing the principles and rules dealing with the topic. An example of a treatise is W. Jaeger, *Williston on Contracts* (3d ed. 1957).

Law reviews, published by law schools and edited by law students, contain articles written by legal scholars, judges, and practitioners on virtually all aspects of the law. An example of a legal citation to a law review is Mark J. Roe, "Corporate Strategic Reaction to Mass Tort," 72 *Virginia Law Review* 1 (1986), which means the article "Corporate Strategic Reaction to Mass Tort" written by Mark J. Roe can be found in volume 72 of the *Virginia Law Review* beginning on page 1.

Like a treatise, a Restatement is limited in its coverage to a single area of law. Restatements are the consequence of intensive study on a specific topic by legal scholars, culminating in a written statement of the law. That statement will include rules stated in bold type—often referred to as "black-letter law"—along with explanatory comments. The rules presented are usually synthesized from opinions of the courts in all jurisdictions. An example is the *Restatement (Second) of Torts.*

THE CONSTITUTION OF THE UNITED STATES OF AMERICA

▓ PREAMBLE

We the People of the United States, in Order to form a more perfect Union, establish Justice, insure domestic Tranquility, provide for the common defence, promote the general Welfare, and secure the Blessings of Liberty to ourselves and our Posterity, do ordain and establish this Constitution for the United States of America.

▓ ARTICLE I

Section 1.   All legislative Powers herein granted shall be vested in a Congress of the United States, which shall consist of a Senate and House of Representatives.

Section 2.   The House of Representatives shall be composed of Members chosen every second Year by the People of the several States, and the Electors in each State shall have the Qualifications requisite for Electors of the most numerous Branch of the State Legislature.

No Person shall be a Representative who shall not have attained to the Age of twenty five Years, and been seven Years a Citizen of the United States, and who shall not, when elected, be an Inhabitant of that State in which he shall be chosen.

Representatives and direct Taxes shall be apportioned among the several States which may be included within this Union, according to their respective Numbers, which shall be determined by adding to the whole Number of free Persons, including those bound to Service for a Term of Years, and excluding Indians not taxed, three fifths of all other Persons. The actual Enumeration shall be made within three Years after the first Meeting of the Congress of the United States, and within every subsequent Term of ten Years, in such Manner as they shall by Law direct. The number of Representatives shall not exceed one for every thirty Thousand, but each State shall have at Least one Representative; and until such enumeration shall be made, the State of New Hampshire shall be entitled to chuse three, Massachusetts eight, Rhode Island and Providence Plantations one, Connecticut five, New York six, New Jersey four, Pennsylvania eight, Delaware one, Maryland six, Virginia ten, North Carolina five, South Carolina five, and Georgia three.

When vacancies happen in the Representation from any State, the Executive Authority thereof shall issue Writs of Election to fill such vacancies.

The House of Representatives shall chuse their Speaker and other Officers; and shall have the sole Power of Impeachment.

Section 3.   The Senate of the United States shall be composed of two Senators from each State, chosen by the Legislature thereof, for six Years; and each Senator shall have one Vote.

Immediately after they shall be assembled in Consequence of the first Election, they shall be divided as equally as may be into three Classes. The Seats of the Senators of the first Class shall be vacated at the Expiration of the second Year, of the second Class at the Expiration of the fourth Year, and of the third Class at the Expiration of the sixth Year so that one third may be chosen every second Year; and if Vacancies happen by Resignation, or otherwise, during the Recess of the Legislature of any State, the Executive thereof may make temporary Appointments until the next Meeting of the Legislature, which shall then fill such Vacancies.

No Person shall be a Senator who shall not have attained to the Age of thirty Years, and been nine Years a Citizen of the United States, and who shall not, when elected, be an Inhabitant of that State for which he shall be chosen.

The Vice President of the United States shall be President of the Senate, but shall have no Vote, unless they be equally divided.

The Senate shall chuse their other Officers, and also a President pro tempore, in the Absence of the Vice President, or when he shall exercise the Office of President of the United States.

The Senate shall have the sole power to try all Impeachments. When sitting for that Purpose, they shall be on Oath or Affirmation. When the President of the United States is tried, the Chief Justice shall preside: And no Person shall be convicted without the Concurrence of two thirds of the Members present.

Judgment in Cases of Impeachment shall not extend further than to removal from Office, and disqualification to hold and enjoy any Office of honor, Trust or Profit under the United States: but the Party convicted shall nevertheless be liable and subject to Indictment, Trial, Judgment and Punishment, according to Law.

Section 4.   The Times, Places and Manner of holding Elections for Senators and Representatives, shall be prescribed in each State by the Legislature thereof: but the Congress may at any time by Law make or alter such Regulations, except as to the Places of chusing Senators.

The Congress shall assemble at least once in every Year, and such Meeting shall be on the first Monday in December, unless they shall by Law appoint a different Day.

Section 5.   Each House shall be the Judge of the Elections, Returns and Qualifications of its own Members, and a Majority of each shall constitute a Quorum to do Business; but a smaller Number may adjourn from day to day, and may be authorized to compel the Attendance of absent Members, in such Manner, and under such Penalties as each House may provide.

Each House may determine the Rules of its Proceedings, punish its Members for disorderly Behaviour, and, with the Concurrence of two thirds, expel a Member.

Each House shall keep a Journal of its Proceedings, and from time to time publish the same, excepting such Parts as may in their Judgment require Secrecy; and the Yeas and Nays of the Members of either House on any question shall, at the Desire of one fifth of those Present, be entered on the Journal.

Neither House, during the Session of Congress, shall, without the Consent of the other, adjourn for more than three days, nor to any other Place than that in which the two Houses shall be sitting.

Section 6.   The Senators and Representatives shall receive a Compensation for their Services, to be ascertained by Law, and paid out of the Treasury of the United States. They shall in all Cases, except Treason, Felony and Breach of the Peace, be privileged from Arrest during their Attendance at the Session of their respective Houses, and in going to and returning from the same; and for any Speech or Debate in either House, they shall not be questioned in any other Place.

No Senator or Representative shall, during the time for which he was elected, be appointed to any civil Office under the Authority of the United States, which shall have been created, or the Emoluments whereof shall have been encreased during such time; and no Person holding any Office under the United States, shall be a Member of either House during his Continuance in Office.

Section 7.   All Bills for raising Revenue shall originate in the House of Representatives; but the Senate may propose or concur with Amendments as on other Bills.

Every Bill which shall have passed the House of Representatives and the Senate, shall, before it become a Law, be presented to the President of the United States; If he approve he shall sign it, but if not he shall return it, with his Objections to that House in which it shall have originated, who shall enter the Objections at large on their Journal, and proceed to reconsider it. If after such Reconsideration two thirds of that House shall agree to pass the Bill, it shall be sent, together with the Objections, to the other House, by which it shall likewise be reconsidered, and if approved by two thirds of that House, it shall become a Law. But in all such Cases the votes of both Houses shall be determined by Yeas and Nays, and the Names of the Persons voting for and against the Bill shall be entered on the Journal of each House respectively. If any Bill shall not be returned by the President within ten Days (Sundays excepted) after it shall have been presented to him, the Same shall be a Law, in like Manner as if he had signed it, unless the Congress by their Adjournment prevent its Return, in which Case it shall not be a Law.

Every Order, Resolution, or Vote to which the Concurrence of the Senate and House of Representatives may be necessary (except on a question of Adjournment) shall be presented to the President of the United States; and before the Same shall take Effect, shall be approved by him, or being disapproved by him, shall be repassed by two thirds of the Senate and House of Representatives, according to the Rules and Limitations prescribed in the Case of a Bill.

Section 8.   The Congress shall have Power to lay and collect Taxes, Duties, Imposts and Excises, to pay the Debts and provide for the common Defence and general Welfare of the United States; but all Duties, Imposts and Excises shall be uniform throughout the United States;

To borrow Money on the credit of the United States;

To regulate Commerce with foreign Nations, and among the several States, and with the Indian Tribes;

To establish an uniform Rule of Naturalization, and uniform Laws on the subject of Bankruptcies throughout the United States;

To coin Money, regulate the Value thereof, and of foreign Coin, and fix the Standard of Weights and Measures;

To provide for the Punishment of counterfeiting the Securities and current Coin of the United States;

To establish Post Offices and post Roads;

To promote the Progress of Science and useful Arts, by securing for limited Times to Authors and Inventors the exclusive Right to their respective Writings and Discoveries;

To constitute Tribunals inferior to the supreme Court;

To define and punish Piracies and Felonies committed on the high Seas, and Offenses against the Law of Nations;

To declare War, grant Letters of Marque and Reprisal, and make Rules concerning Captures on Land and Water;

To raise and support Armies, but no Appropriation of Money to that Use shall be for a longer Term than two Years;

To provide and maintain a Navy;

To make Rules for the Government and Regulation of the land and naval Forces;

To provide for calling forth the Militia to execute the Laws of the Union, suppress Insurrections and repel Invasions;

To provide for organizing, arming, and disciplining, the Militia, and for governing such Part of them as may be employed in the Service of the United States, reserving to the States respectively, the Appointment of the Officers, and the Authority of training the Militia according to the discipline prescribed by Congress;

To exercise exclusive Legislation in all Cases whatsoever, over such District (not exceeding ten Miles square) as may, by Cession of particular States, and the Acceptance of Congress, become the Seat of the Government of the United States, and to exercise like Authority over all Places purchased by the Consent of the Legislature of the State in which the Same shall be, for the Erection of Forts, Magazines, Arsenals, dock-Yards, and other needful Buildings;—And

To make all Laws which shall be necessary and proper for carrying into Execution the foregoing Powers, and all other Powers vested by this Constitution in the Government of the United States, or in any Department or Officer thereof.

Section 9.   The Migration or Importation of such Persons as any of the States now existing shall think proper to admit, shall not be prohibited by the Congress prior to the Year one thousand eight hundred and eight, but a Tax or Duty may be imposed on such Importation, not exceeding ten dollars for each Person.

The Privilege of the Writ of Habeas Corpus shall not be suspended, unless when in Cases of Rebellion or Invasion the public Safety require it.

No Bill of Attainder or ex post facto Law shall be passed.

No Capitation, or other direct, Tax shall be laid, unless in Proportion to the Census or Enumeration herein before directed to be taken.

No Tax or Duty shall be laid on Articles exported from any State.

No Preference shall be given by any Regulation of Commerce or Revenue to the Ports of one State over those of another; nor shall Vessels bound to, or from, one State, be obliged to enter, clear, or pay Duties in another.

No Money shall be drawn from the Treasury, but in Consequence of Appropriations made by Laws; and a regular Statement and Account of the Receipts and Expenditures of all public Money shall be published from time to time.

No Title of Nobility shall be granted by the United States: And no Person holding any Office of Profit or Trust under them, shall, without the Consent of the Congress, accept of any present, Emolument, Office, or Title, or any kind whatever, from any King, Prince, or foreign State.

Section 10.   No State shall enter into any Treaty, Alliance, or Confederation; grant Letters of Marque and Reprisal; coin Money; emit Bills of Credit; make any Thing but gold and silver Coin a Tender in Payment of Debts; pass any Bill of Attainder, ex post facto Law, or Law impairing the Obligation of Contracts, or grant any Title of Nobility.

No State shall, without the Consent of the Congress, lay any Imposts or Duties on Imports or Exports, except what may be absolutely necessary for executing its inspection Laws: and the net Produce of all Duties and Imposts, laid by any State on Imports or Exports, shall be for the Use of the Treasury of the United States; and all such Laws shall be subject to the Revision and Controul of the Congress.

No State shall, without the Consent of Congress, lay and Duty of Tonnage, keep Troops, or Ships of War in time of Peace, enter into any Agreement or Compact with another State, or with a foreign Power, or engage in War, unless actually invaded or in such imminent Danger as will not admit of delay.

▪ ARTICLE II

Section 1.   The executive Power shall be vested in a President of the United States of America. He shall hold his Office during the Term of four Years, and, together with the Vice President, chosen for the same Term, be elected, as follows:

Each State shall appoint, in such Manner as the Legislature thereof may direct, a Number of Electors, equal to the whole Number of Senators and Representatives to which the State may be entitled in the Congress:

but no Senator or Representative, or Person holding an Office of Trust or Profit under the United States, shall be appointed an Elector.

The Electors shall meet in their respective States, and vote by Ballot for two Persons, of whom one at least shall not be an Inhabitant of the same State with themselves. And they shall make a List of all the Persons voted for, and of the Number of Votes for each; which List they shall sign and certify, and transmit sealed to the Seat of the Government of the United States, directed to the President of the Senate. The President of the Senate shall, in the Presence of the Senate and House of Representatives, open all the Certificates, and the Votes shall then be counted. The Person having the greatest Number of Votes shall be the President, if such Number be a Majority of the whole Number of Electors appointed; and if there be more than one who have such Majority, and have an equal Number of Votes, then the House of Representatives shall immediately chuse by Ballot one of them for President; and if no Person have a Majority, then from the five highest on the List the said House shall in like Manner chuse the President. But in chusing the President, the Votes shall be taken by States, the Representation from each State having one Vote; a quorum for this Purpose shall consist of a Member or Members from two thirds of the States, and a Majority of all the States shall be necessary to a Choice. In every Case, after the Choice of the President, the Person having the greatest Number of Votes of the Electors shall be the Vice President. But if there should remain two or more who have equal Votes, the Senate shall chuse from them by Ballot the Vice President.

The Congress may determine the Time of chusing the Electors, and the Day on which they shall give their Votes; which Day shall be the same throughout the United States.

No Person except a natural born Citizen, or a Citizen of the United States, at the time of the Adoption of this Constitution, shall be eligible to the Office of President; neither shall any Person be eligible to that Office who shall not have attained to the Age of thirty five Years, and been fourteen Years a Resident within the United States.

In Case of the Removal of the President from Office, or of his Death, Resignation, or Inability to discharge the Powers and Duties of the said Office, the Same shall devolve on the Vice President, and the Congress may by Law provide for the Case of Removal, Death, Resignation or Inability, both of the President and Vice President, declaring what Officer shall then act as President, and such Officer shall act accordingly, until the Disability be removed, or a President shall be elected.

The President shall, at stated Times, receive for his Services, a Compensation, which shall neither be encreased nor diminished during the Period for which he shall have been elected, and he shall not receive within that Period any other Emolument from the United States, or any of them.

Before he enter on the Execution of his Office, he shall take the following Oath or Affirmation:—"I do solemnly swear (or affirm) that I will faithfully execute the Office of President of the United States, and will to the best of my Ability, preserve, protect and defend the Constitution of the United States."

Section 2.   The President shall be Commander in Chief of the Army and Navy of the United States, and of the Militia of the several States, when called into the actual Service of the United States; he may require the Opinion, in writing, of the principal Officer in each of the executive Departments, upon any Subject relating to the Duties of their respective Offices, and he shall have Power to grant Reprieves and Pardons for Offences against the United States, except in Cases of Impeachment.

He shall have Power, by and with the Advice and Consent of the Senate, to make Treaties, providing two thirds of the Senators present concur; and he shall nominate, and by and with the Advice and Consent of the Senate, shall appoint Ambassadors, other public Ministers and Consuls, Judges of the supreme Court, and all other Officers of the United States, whose Appointments are not herein otherwise provided for, and which shall be established by Law: but the Congress may by Law vest the Appointment of such inferior Officers, as they think proper, in the President alone, in the Courts of Law, or in the Heads of Departments.

The President shall have Power to fill up all Vacancies that may happen during the Recess of the Senate, by granting Commissions which shall expire at the End of their next Session.

Section 3. He shall from time to time give to the Congress Information of the State of the Union, and recommend to their Consideration such Measures as he shall judge necessary and expedient; he may, on extraordinary Occasions, convene both Houses, or either of them, and in Case of Disagreement between them, with Respect to the Time of Adjournment, he may adjourn them to such Time as he shall think proper, he shall receive Ambassadors and other public Ministers; he shall take Care that the Laws be faithfully executed, and shall Commission all the Officers of the United States.

Section 4. The President, Vice President and all civil Officers of the United States, shall be removed from Office on Impeachment for, and Conviction of, Treason, Bribery, or other high Crimes and Misdemeanors.

■ ARTICLE III

Section 1. The judicial Power of the United States, shall be vested in one supreme Court, and in such inferior Courts as the Congress may from time to time ordain and establish. The Judges, both of the supreme and inferior Courts, shall hold their Offices during good Behaviour, and shall, at stated Times, receive for their Services, a Compensation, which shall not be diminished during their Continuance in Office.

Section 2. The judicial Power shall extend to all Cases, in Law and Equity, arising under this Constitution, the Laws of the United States, and Treaties made, or which shall be made, under their Authority;—to all Cases affecting Ambassadors, other public Ministers and Consuls;—to all Cases of admiralty and maritime Jurisdiction;—to Controversies to which the United States shall be a Party; to Controversies between two or more States;—between a State and Citizens of another State;—between Citizens of different States;—between Citizens of the same State claiming Lands under Grants of different States, and between a State, or the Citizens thereof, and foreign States, Citizens or Subjects.

In all Cases affecting Ambassadors, other public Ministers and Consuls, and those in which a State shall be Party, the supreme Court shall have original Jurisdiction. In all the other Cases before mentioned, the supreme Court shall have appellate Jurisdiction, both as to Law and Fact, with such Exceptions, and under such Regulations as the Congress shall make.

The Trial of all Crimes, except in Cases of Impeachment, shall be by Jury; and such Trial shall be held in the State where the said Crimes shall have been committed; but when not committed within any State, the Trial shall be at such Place or Places as the Congress may by Law have directed.

Section 3.   Treason against the United States, shall consist only in levying War against them, or in adhering to their Enemies, giving them Aid and Comfort. No Person shall be convicted of Treason unless on the Testimony of two Witnesses to the same overt Act, or on Confession in open Court.

The Congress shall have Power to declare the Punishment of Treason, but no Attainder of Treason shall work Corruption of Blood, or Forfeiture except during the Life of the Person attainted.

▮ ARTICLE IV

Section 1.   Full Faith and Credit shall be given in each State to the public Acts, Records, and judicial Proceedings of every other State. And the Congress may by general Laws prescribe the Manner in which such Arts, Records and Proceedings shall be proved, and the Effect thereof.

Section 2.   The Citizens of each State shall be entitled to all Privileges and Immunities of Citizens in the several States.

A Person charged in any State with Treason, Felony, or other Crime, who shall flee from Justice, and be found in another State, shall on Demand of the executive Authority of the State from which he fled, be delivered up, to be removed to the State having Jurisdiction of the Crime.

No Person held to Service or Labour in one State, under the Laws thereof, escaping into another, shall, in Consequence of any Law or Regulation therein, be discharged from such Service or Labour, but shall be delivered up on Claim of the Party to whom such Service or Labour may be due.

Section 3.   New States may be admitted by the Congress into this Union; but no new State shall be formed or erected within the Jurisdiction of any other State; nor any State be formed by the Junction of two or more States, or Parts of States, without the Consent of the Legislatures of the States concerned as well as of the Congress.

The Congress shall have Power to dispose of and make all needful Rules and Regulations respecting the Territory or other Property belonging to the United States; and nothing in this Constitution shall be so contrued as to Prejudice any Claims of the United States, or of any particular State.

Section 4.   The United States shall guarantee to every State in this Union a Republican Form of the Government, and shall protect each of them against Invasion; and on Application of the Legislature, or of the Executive (when the Legislature cannot be convened) against domestic Violence.

■ ARTICLE V

The Congress, whenever two thirds of both Houses shall deem it necessary, shall propose Amendments to this Constitution, or, on the Application of the Legislatures of two thirds of the several States, shall call a convention for proposing Amendments, which, in either Case, shall be valid to all Intents and Purposes, as part of this Constitution, when ratified by the Legislatures of three fourths of the several States, or by Conventions in three fourths thereof, as the one or the other Mode of Ratification may be proposed by the Congress; Provided that no Amendment which may be made prior to the Year One thousand eight hundred and eight shall in any Manner affect the first and fourth Clauses in the Ninth Section of the first Article; and that no State, without its Consent, shall be deprived of its equal Suffrage in the Senate.

■ ARTICLE VI

All Debts contracted and Engagements entered into, before the Adoption of this Constitution, shall be as valid against the United States under this Constitution, as under the Confederation.

    This Constitution, and the Laws of the United States which shall be made in Pursuance thereof; and all Treaties made, or which shall be made, under the Authority of the United States, shall be the supreme Law of the Land; and the Judges in every State shall be bound thereby, any Thing in the Constitution or Laws of any State to the Contrary notwithstanding.

    The Senators and Representatives before mentioned, and the Members of the several State Legislatures, and all executive and judicial Officers, both of the United States and of the several States, shall be bound by Oath or Affirmation, to support this Constitution; but no religious Test shall ever be required as a Qualification to any Office or public Trust under the United States.

■ ARTICLE VII

The Ratification of the Conventions of nine States, shall be sufficient for the Establishment of this Constitution between the States so ratifying the Same.

■ AMENDMENT I [1791]

Congress shall make no law respecting an establishment of religion, or prohibiting the free exercise thereof; or abridging the freedom of speech, or the press; or the right of the people peaceably to assemble, and to petition the Government for a redress of grievances.

■ AMENDMENT II [1791]

A well regulated Militia, being necessary to the security for a free State, the right of the people to keep and bear Arms, shall not be infringed.

■ AMENDMENT III [1791]

No Soldier shall, in time of peace be quartered in any house, without the consent of the Owner, nor in time of war, but in a manner to be prescribed by law.

■ AMENDMENT IV [1791]

The right of the people to be secure in their persons, houses, papers, and effects, against unreasonable searches and seizures, shall not be violated, and no Warrants shall issue, but upon probable cause, supported by Oath or affirmation, and particularly describing the place to be searched, and the persons or things to be seized.

■ AMENDMENT V [1791]

No person shall be held to answer for a capital, or otherwise infamous crime, unless on a presentment or indictment of a Grand Jury, except in cases arising in the land or naval forces, or in the Militia, when in actual service in time of War or public danger; nor shall any person be subject for the same offense to be twice put in jeopardy of life or limb; nor shall be compelled in any criminal case to be a witness against himself, nor be deprived of life, liberty, or property, without due process of law; nor shall private property be taken for public use, without just compensation.

■ AMENDMENT VI [1791]

In all criminal prosecutions, the accused shall enjoy the right to a speedy and public trial, by an impartial jury of the State and district wherein the crime shall have been committed, which district shall have been previously ascertained by law, and to be informed of the nature and cause of the accusation; to be confronted with the Witnesses against him; to have compulsory process for obtaining witnesses in his favor, and to have the Assistance of counsel for his defence.

■ AMENDMENT VII [1791]

In Suits at common law, where the value in controversy shall exceed twenty dollars, the right of trial by jury shall be preserved, and no fact tried by a jury, shall be otherwise re-examined in any Court of the United States, than according to the rules of the common law.

■ AMENDMENT VIII [1791]

Excessive bail shall not be required, no excessive fines imposed, nor cruel and unusual punishments inflicted.

■ AMENDMENT IX [1791]

The enumeration in the Constitution, of certain rights, shall not be construed to deny or disparage others retained by the people.

■ AMENDMENT X [1791]

The powers not delegated to the United States by the Constitution, nor prohibited by it to the States, are reserved to the States respectively, or to the people.

■ AMENDMENT XI [1798]

The Judicial power of the United States shall not be construed to extend to any suit in law or equity, commenced or prosecuted against one of the United States by Citizens of another State, or by Citizens or Subjects of any Foreign State.

■ AMENDMENT XII [1804]

The Electors shall meet in their respective states and vote by ballot for President and Vice-President, one of whom, at least, shall not be an inhabitant of the same state with themselves; they shall name in their ballots the person voted for as President, and in distinct ballots the person voted for as Vice-President, and they shall make distinct lists of all persons voted for as President, and of all persons voted for as Vice-President, and of the number of votes for each, which lists they shall sign and certify, and transmit sealed to the seat of the government of the United States, directed to the President of the Senate;—The President of the Senate shall, in the presence of the Senate and House of Representatives, open all the certificates and the votes shall then be counted;—The person having the greatest number of votes for President, shall be the President, if such number be a majority of the whole number of Electors appointed; and if no person have such majority, then from the persons having the highest numbers not exceeding three on the list of those voted for as President, the House of Representatives shall choose immediately, by ballot, the President. But in choosing the President, the votes shall be taken by states, the representation from each state having one vote; a quorum for this purpose shall consist of a member or members from two-thirds of the states, and a majority of all the states shall be necessary to a choice. And if the House of Representatives shall not choose a President whenever the right of choice shall devolve upon them, before the fourth day of March next following, then the Vice–President shall act as President, as in the case of the death or other constitutional disability of the President. The person having the greatest number of votes as Vice–President, shall be the Vice–President, if such number be a majority of the whole number of Electors appointed, and if no person have a majority, then from the two highest numbers on the list, the Senate shall choose the Vice–President; a quorum for the purpose shall consist of two-thirds of the whole number of Senators, and a majority of the whole number shall be necessary to a choice. But no person constitutionally ineligible to the office of President shall be eligible to that of the Vice–President of the United States.

■ Amendment XIII [1865]

Section 1.   Neither slavery nor involuntary servitude, except as a punishment for crime whereof the party shall have been duly convicted, shall exist within the United States, or any place subject to their jurisdiction.

Section 2.   Congress shall have power to enforce this article by appropriate legislation.

■ Amendment XIV [1868]

Section 1.   All persons born or naturalized in the United States, and subject to the jurisdiction thereof, are citizens of the United States and of the State wherein they reside. No State shall make or enforce any law which shall abridge the privileges or immunities of citizens of the United States; nor shall any State deprive any person of life, liberty, or property, without due process of law; nor deny to any person within its jurisdiction the equal protection of the laws.

Section 2.   Representatives shall be appointed among the several States according to their respective numbers, counting the whole number of persons in each State, excluding Indians not taxed. But when the right to vote at any election for the choice of electors for President and Vice President of the United States, Representatives in Congress, the Executive and Judicial officers of a State, or the members of the Legislature thereof, is denied to any of the male inhabitants of such State, being twenty-one years of age, and citizens of the United States, or in any way abridged, except for participation in rebellion, or other crime, the basis of representation therein shall be reduced in the proportion which the number of such male citizens shall bear to the whole number of male citizens twenty-one years of age in such State.

Section 3.   No person shall be a Senator or Representative in Congress, or elector of President and Vice President, or hold any office, civil or military, under the United States, or under any State, who, having previously taken an oath, as a member of Congress, or as an officer of the United States, or as a member of any State legislature, or as an executive or judicial officer of any State, to support the Constitution of the United States, shall have engaged in insurrection or rebellion against the same, or given aid or comfort to the enemies thereof. But Congress may by a vote of two-thirds of each House, remove such disability.

Section 4.   The validity of the public debt of the United States, authorized by law, including debts incurred for payment of pensions and bounties for services in suppressing insurrection or rebellion, shall not be questioned. But neither the United States nor any State shall assume or pay any debt or obligation incurred in aid of instruction or rebellion against the United

States, or any claim for the loss or emancipation of any slave; but all such debts, obligations and claims shall be held illegal and void.

Section 5.   The Congress shall have power to enforce, by appropriate legislation, the provisions of this article.

AMENDMENT XV [1870]

Section 1.   The right of citizens of the United States to vote shall not be denied or abridged by the United States or by any State on account of race, color, or previous condition of servitude.

Section 2.   The Congress shall have power to enforce this article by appropriate legislation.

AMENDMENT XVI [1913]

The Congress shall have power to lay and collect taxes on incomes, from whatever source derived, without apportionment among the several States, and without regard to any census or enumeration.

AMENDMENT XVII [1913]

Section 1.   The Senate of the United States shall be composed of two Senators from each State, elected by the people thereof, for six years; and each Senator shall have one vote. The electors in each State shall have the qualifications requisite for electors of the most numerous branch of the State legislatures.

Section 2.   When vacancies happen in the representation of any State in the Senate, the executive authority of each State shall issue writs of election to fill such vacancies; *Provided*, That the legislature of any State may empower the executive thereof to make temporary appointments until the people fill the vacancies by election as the legislature may direct.

Section 3.   This amendment shall not be so construed as to affect the election or term of any Senator chosen before it becomes valid as part of the Constitution.

AMENDMENT XVIII [1919]

Section 1.   After one year from the ratification of this article the manufacture, sale, or transportation of intoxicating liquors within, the importation thereof into, or the exportation thereof from the United States and all territory subject to the jurisdiction thereof for beverage purposes is hereby prohibited.

Section 2.   The Congress and the several States shall have concurrent power to enforce this article by appropriate legislation.

Section 3.   This article shall be inoperative unless it shall have been ratified as an amendment to the Constitution by the legislatures of the several States, as provided in the Constitution, within seven years from the date of the submission hereof to the States by the Congress.

■ AMENDMENT XIX [1920]

Section 1.   The right of citizens of the United States to vote shall not be denied or abridged by the United States or by any State on account of sex.

Section 2.   Congress shall have power to enforce this article by appropriate legislation.

■ AMENDMENT XX [1933]

Section 1.   The terms of the President and Vice President shall end at noon on the 20th day of January, and the terms of Senators and Representatives at noon on the 3d day of January, of the years in which such terms would have ended if this article had not been ratified; and the terms of their successors shall then begin.

Section 2.   The Congress shall assemble at least once every year, and such meeting shall begin at noon on the 3d day of January, unless they shall by law appoint a different day.

Section 3.   If, at the time fixed for the beginning of the term of the President, the President elect shall have died, the Vice President elect shall become President. If a President shall not have been chosen before the time fixed for the beginning of his term, or if the President elect shall have failed to qualify, then the Vice President elect shall act as President until a President shall have qualified; and the Congress may by law provide for the case wherein neither a President elect nor a Vice President elect shall have qualified, declaring who shall then act as President, or the manner in which one who is to act shall be selected, and such person shall act accordingly until a President or Vice President shall have qualified.

Section 4.   The Congress may by law provide for the case of the death of any of the persons from whom the House of Representatives may choose a President whenever the right of choice shall have devolved upon them, and for the case of the death of any of the persons from whom the Senate may choose a Vice President whenever the right of choice shall have devolved upon them.

Section 5.   Sections 1 and 2 shall take effect on the 15th day of October following the ratification of this article.

Section 6.   This article shall be inoperative unless it shall have been ratified as an amendment to the Constitution by the legislatures of three-fourths of the several States within seven years from the date of its submission.

■ AMENDMENT XXI [1933]

Section 1. The eighteenth article of amendment to the Constitution of the United States is hereby repealed.

Section 2. The transportation or importation into any State, Territory, or possession of the United States for delivery or use therein of intoxicating liquors, in violation of the laws thereof, is hereby prohibited.

Section 3. This article shall be inoperative unless it shall have been ratified as an amendment to the Constitution by conventions in the several States, as provided in the Constitution, within seven years from the date of the submission hereof to the States by the Congress.

■ AMENDMENT XXII [1951]

Section 1. No person shall be elected to the office of the President more than twice, and no person who has held the office of President, or acted as President, for more than two years of a term to which some other person was elected President shall be elected to the office of the President more than once. But this Article shall not apply to any person holding the office of President when this Article was proposed by the Congress, and shall not prevent any person who may be holding the office of President, or acting as President, during the term within which this Article becomes operative from holding the office of President or acting as President during the remainder of such term.

Section 2. This article shall be inoperative unless it shall have been ratified as an amendment to the Constitution by the legislatures of three-fourths of the several States within seven years from the date of its submission to the States by the Congress.

■ AMENDMENT XXIII [1961]

Section 1. The District constituting the seat of Government of the United States shall appoint in such manner as the Congress may direct:
   A number of electors of President and Vice President equal to the whole number of Senators and Representatives in Congress to which the District would be entitled if it were a State, but in no event more than the least populous State; they shall be in addition to those appointed by the States, but they shall be considered, for the purposes of the election of President and Vice President, to be electors appointed by a State; and they shall meet in the District and perform such duties as provided by the twelfth article of amendment.

Section 2. The Congress shall have power to enforce this article by appropriate legislation.

■ AMENDMENT XXIV [1964]

Section 1.   The right of citizens of the United States to vote in any primary or other election for President or Vice President, for electors for President or Vice President, or for Senator or Representative in Congress, shall not be denied or abridged by the United States or any State by reason of failure to pay any poll tax or other tax.

Section 2.   The Congress shall have power to enforce this article by appropriate legislation.

■ AMENDMENT XXV [1967]

Section 1.   In case of the removal of the President from office or of his death or resignation, the Vice President shall become President.

Section 2.   Whenever there is a vacancy in the office of the Vice President, the President shall nominate a Vice President who shall take office upon confirmation by a majority vote of both Houses of Congress.

Section 3.   Whenever the President transmits to the President pro tempore of the Senate and the Speaker of the House of Representatives his written declaration that he is unable to discharge the powers and duties of his office, and until he transmits to them a written declaration to the contrary, such powers and duties shall be discharged by the Vice President as Acting President.

Section 4.   Whenever the Vice President and a majority of either the principal officers of the executive departments or of such other body as Congress may by law provide, transmit to the President pro tempore of the Senate and the Speaker of the House of Representatives their written declaration that the President is unable to discharge the powers and duties of his office, the Vice President shall immediately assume the powers and duties of the office as Acting President.

   Thereafter, when the President transmits to the President pro tempore of the Senate and the Speaker of the House of Representatives his written declaration that no inability exists, he shall resume the powers and duties of his office unless the Vice President and a majority of either the principal officers of the executive department or of such other body as Congress may by law provide, transmit within four days to the President pro tempore of the Senate and the Speaker of the House of Representatives their written declaration that the President is unable to discharge the powers and duties of his office. Thereupon Congress shall decide the issue, assembling within forty-eight hours for that purpose if not in session. If the Congress, within twenty-one days after receipt of the latter written declaration, or, if Congress is not in session, within twenty-one days after Congress is required to assemble, determines by two-thirds vote of both

Houses that the President is unable to discharge the powers and duties of his office, the Vice President shall continue to discharge the same as Acting President; otherwise, the President shall resume the powers and duties of his office.

■ AMENDMENT XXVI [1971]

Section 1.   The right of citizens of the United States, who are eighteen years of age or older, to vote shall not be denied or abridged by the United States or by any State on account of age.

Section 2.   The Congress shall have power to enforce this article by appropriate legislation.

■ AMENDMENT XXVII [1992]

No law varying the compensation for the services of the senators and representatives shall take effect, until an election of representatives shall have intervened.

THE ANTITRUST STATUTES

SHERMAN ACT

■ RESTRAINTS OF TRADE PROHIBITED

Section 1—Trusts, etc., in Restraint of Trade Illegal; Penalty. Every contract, combination in the form of trust or otherwise, or conspiracy, in restraint of trade or commerce among the several States, or with foreign nations, is declared to be illegal. Every person who shall make any contract or engage in any combination or conspiracy declared by sections 1 to 7 of this title to be illegal shall be deemed guilty of a felony, and, on conviction thereof, shall be punished by fine not exceeding one million dollars if a corporation, or if any other person, one hundred thousand dollars, or by imprisonment not exceeding three years, or both said punishments, in the discretion of the court.

Section 2—Monopolizing Trade a Felony; Penalty. Every person who shall monopolize, or attempt to monopolize, or combine or conspire with any other person or persons, to monopolize any part of the trade or commerce among the several States, or with foreign nations, shall be deemed guilty of a felony, and, on conviction thereof, shall be punished by fine not exceeding one million dollars if a corporation, or, if any other person, one hundred thousand dollars, or by imprisonment not exceeding three years, or by both said punishments, in the discretion of the court.

CLAYTON ACT

■ PRICE DISCRIMINATION; COST JUSTIFICATION; CHANGING CONDITIONS

[This section is known as the Robinson-Patman Act]

Section 2—Discrimination in Price, Services, or Facilities.
    (a) Price; selection of customers.
    It shall be unlawful for any person engaged in commerce, in the course of such commerce, either directly or indirectly, to discriminate in

price between different purchases of commodities of like grade and quality, where either or any of the purchasers involved in such discrimination are in commerce, where such commodities are sold for use, consumption, or resale within the United States or any Territory thereof or the District of Columbia or any insular possession or other place under the jurisdiction of the United States, and where the effect of such discrimination may be substantially to lessen competition or tend to create a monopoly in any line of commerce, or to injure, destroy, or prevent competition with any person who either grants or knowingly receives the benefit of such discrimination, or with customers of either of them: *Provided,* That nothing herein contained shall prevent differentials which make only due allowance for differences in the cost of manufacture, sale, or delivery resulting from the differing methods or quantities in which such commodities are to such purchasers sold or delivered: *Provided, however,* That the Federal Trade Commission may, after due investigation and hearing to all interested parties, fix and establish quantity limits, and revise the same as it finds necessary as to particular commodities or classes of commodities, where it finds that available purchasers in greater quantities are so few as to render differentials on account thereof unjustly discriminatory or promotive of monopoly in any line of commerce; and the foregoing shall then not be construed to permit differentials based on differences in quantities greater than those so fixed and established: *And provided further,* That nothing herein contained shall prevent persons engaged in selling goods, wares, or merchandise in commerce from selecting their own customers in bona fide transactions and not in restraint of trade: *And provided further,* That nothing herein contained shall prevent price changes from time to time where in response to changing conditions affecting the market for or the marketability of the goods concerned, such as but not limited to actual or imminent deterioration of perishable goods, obsolescence of seasonal goods, distress sales under court process, or sales in good faith in discontinuance of business in the goods concerned.

■ MEETING COMPETITION

(b) Burden of rebutting prima-facie case of discrimination.

Upon proof being made, at any hearing on a complaint under this section, that there has been discrimination in price or services or facilities furnished, the burden of rebutting the prima-facie case thus made by showing justification shall be upon the person charged with a violation of this section, and unless justification shall be affirmatively shown, the Commission is authorized to issue an order terminating the discrimination: *Providing, however,* That nothing herein contained shall prevent a seller rebutting the prima-facie case thus made by showing that his lower price or the furnishing of services or facilities to any purchaser or purchasers was made in good faith to meet an equally low price of a competitor, or the services or facilities furnished by a competitor.

■ BROKERAGE PAYMENTS ·

(c) Payment or acceptance of commission, brokerage or other compensation.

It shall be unlawful for any person engaged in commerce, in the course of such commerce, to pay or grant, or to receive or accept, anything of value as a commission, brokerage, or other compensation, or any allowance of discount in lieu thereof, except for services rendered in connection with the sale or purchase of goods, wares, or merchandise, either to the other party to such transaction or to an agent, representative, or other intermediary therein where such intermediary is acting in fact for or in behalf, or is subject to the direct or indirect control, of any party to such transaction other than the person by whom such compensation is so granted or paid.

■ PROMOTIONAL ALLOWANCES

(d) Payment for services or facilities for processing or sale.

It shall be unlawful for any person engaged in commerce to pay or contract for the payment of anything of value to or for the benefit of a customer of such person in the course of such commerce as compensation or in consideration for any services or facilities furnished by or through such customer in connection with the processing, handling, sale, or offering for sale of any products or commodities manufactured, sold, or offered for sale by such person, unless such payment of consideration is available on proportionally equal terms to all other customers competing in the distribution of such products or commodities.

■ PROMOTIONAL SERVICES

(e) Furnishing services or facilities for processing, handling, etc.

It shall be unlawful for any person to discriminate in favor of one purchaser against another purchaser or purchasers of a commodity bought for resale, with or without processing, or by contracting to furnish or furnishing, or by contributing to the furnishing of, any services or facilities connected with the processing, handling, sale, or offering for sale of such commodity so purchased upon terms not accorded to all purchasers on proportionally equal terms.

■ BUYER DISCRIMINATION

(f) Knowingly inducing or receiving discriminatory price.

It shall be unlawful for any person engaged in commerce, in the course of such commerce, knowingly to induce or receive a discrimination in price which is prohibited by this section.

■ REFUSALS TO DEAL

Section 3 — Sale, etc., on Agreement Not to Use Goods of Competitor.   It shall be unlawful for any person engaged in commerce, in the course of such commerce, to lease or make a sale or contract for sale of goods, wares, merchandise, machinery, supplies, or other commodities, whether patented or unpatented, for use, consumption, or resale within the United States or any Territory thereof or the District of Columbia or any insular possession or other place under the jurisdiction of the United States, or fix a price charged thereof, or discount from, or rebate upon, such price, on the condition, agreement, or understanding that the lessee or purchaser thereof shall not use or deal in the goods, wares, merchandise, machinery, supplies, or other commodities of a competitor or competitors of the lessor or seller, where the effect of such lease, sale, or contract for sale or such condition, agreement or understanding may be to substantially lessen competition or tend to create a monopoly in any line of commerce.

◼ PRIVATE SUITS

Section 4 — Suits by Persons Injured; Amount of Recovery.   Any person who shall be injured in this business or property by reason of anything forbidden in the antitrust laws may sue therefor in any district court of the United States in the district in which the defendant resides or is found or has an agent, without respect to the amount in controversy, and shall recover threefold the damages by him sustained, and the cost of suit, including a reasonable attorney's fee. . .

◼ MERGERS

Section 7 — Acquisition by One Corporation of Stock of Another.   No corporation engaged in commerce shall acquire, directly or indirectly, the whole or any part of the stock or other share capital and no corporation subject to the jurisdiction of the Federal Trade Commission shall acquire the whole or any part of the assets of another corporation engaged also in commerce, where in any line of commerce in any section of the country, the effect of such acquisition may be substantially to lessen competition, or to tend to create a monopoly.

No corporation shall acquire, directly or indirectly, the whole or any part of the stock or other share capital and no corporation subject to the jurisdiction of the Federal Trade Commission shall acquire the whole or any part of the assets of one or more corporations engaged in commerce, where in any line of commerce in any section of the country, the effect of such acquisition, of such stocks or assets, or of the use of such stock by the voting or granting of proxies or otherwise, may be substantially to lessen competition, or to tend to create a monopoly.

This section shall not apply to corporations purchasing such stock solely for investment and not using the same by voting or otherwise to bring about, or in attempting to bring about, the substantial lessening of competition. Nor shall anything contained in this section prevent a corporation engaged in commerce from causing the formation of subsidiary corporations for the actual carrying on of their immediate lawful business, or the natural and legitimate branches of extensions thereof, or from owning and holding all or part of the stock of such subsidiary corporations, when the effect of such formation is not to substantially lessen competition.

◼ INTERLOCKING DIRECTORATES

Section 8 — Interlocking Directorates and Officers.   No person at the same time shall be a director in any two or more corporations, any one of which has capital, surplus, and undivided profits aggregating more than $1,000,000, engaged in whole or in part in commerce, other than banks, banking associates, trust companies, and common carriers subject to the Act to regulate commerce approved February fourth, eighteen hundred and eighty-seven, if such corporations are or shall have been theretofore, by virtue of their business and location or operation, competitors, so that the elimination of competition by agreement between them would constitute a violation of any of the provisions of any of the antitrust laws. The eligibility of a director under the foregoing provision shall be determined by the aggregate amount of the capital, surplus, and undivided profits, exclusive of dividends declared but not paid to stockholders, at the end of the fiscal year of said corporation next preceding the election of directors, and when a director has been elected in accordance with the provisions of this Act it shall be lawful for him to continue as such for one year thereafter.

FEDERAL TRADE COMMISSION ACT

■ UNFAIR METHODS OF COMPETITION PROHIBITED

Section 5—Unfair Methods of Competition Unlawful; Prevention by Commission—Declaration.   Declaration of unlawfulness; power to prohibit unfair practices.

(a) (1) Unfair methods of competition in or affecting commerce, and unfair or deceptive acts or practices in or affecting commerce, are declared unlawful. . .

(b) Any person, partnership, or corporation who violates an order of the Commission to cease and desist after it has become final, and while such order is in effect, shall forfeit and pay to the United States a civil penalty of not more than $10,000 for each violation, which shall accrue to the United States and may be recovered in a civil action brought by the Attorney General of the United States. Each separate violation of such an order shall be a separate offense, except that in the case of a violation through continuing failure or neglect to obey a final order of the Commission each day of continuance of such failure or neglect shall be deemed a separate offense.

NATIONAL LABOR RELATIONS ACT

■ RIGHTS OF EMPLOYEES

Section 7. Employees shall have the right to self-organization, to form, join, or assist labor organizations, to bargain collectively through representatives of their own choosing, and to engage in other concerted activities for the purpose of collective bargaining or other mutual aid or protection, and shall also have the right to refrain from any or all of such activities requiring membership in a labor organization as a condition of employment as authorized in section 8(a)(3).

■ UNFAIR LABOR PRACTICES

Section 8.

(a) It shall be an unfair labor practice for an employer—

(1) to interfere with, restrain, or coerce employees in the exercise of the rights guaranteed in section 7;

(2) to dominate or interfere with the formation or administration of any labor organization or contribute financial or other support to it: *Provided*, That . . . an employer shall not be prohibited from permitting employees to confer with him during working hours without loss of time or pay;

(3) by discrimination in regard to hire or tenure of employment or any term or condition of employment to encourage or discourage membership in any labor organization. . . .

(4) to discharge or otherwise discriminate against an employee because he has filed charges or given testimony under this Act;

(5) to refuse to bargain collectively with the representatives of his employees, subject to the provisions of section 9(a).

(b) It shall be an unfair labor practice for a labor organization or its agents—

(1) to restrain or coerce (A) employees in the exercise of the rights guaranteed in section 7: *Provided*, That this paragraph shall not impair the right of a labor organization to prescribe its own rules with respect to the acquisition or retention of membership therein; or (B) an employer in the selection of his representatives for the purposes of collective bargaining or the adjustment of grievances;

(2) to cause or attempt to cause an employer to discriminate against an employee in violation of subsection (a)(3) or to discriminate against an employee with respect to whom membership in such organization has been denied or terminated on some ground other than his failure to tender the periodic dues and the initiation fees uniformly required as a condition of acquiring or retaining membership;

(3) to refuse to bargain collectively with an employer, provided it is the representative of his employees subject to the provisions of section 9(a);

(4)(i) to engage in, or to induce or encourage any individual employed by any person engaged in commerce or in an industry affecting commerce to engage in, a strike or a refusal in the course of his employment to use, manufacture, process, transport, or otherwise handle or work on any goods, articles, materials, or commodities or to perform any services; or (ii) to threaten, coerce, or restrain any person engaged in commerce or in an industry affecting commerce, where in either case an object thereof is—

(A) forcing or requiring employer or self-employed person to join any labor or employer organization or to enter into any agreement which is prohibited by section 8(e);

(B) forcing or requiring any person to cease using, selling, handling, transporting, or otherwise dealing in the products of any other producer, processor, or manufacturer, or to cease doing business with any other person, or forcing or requiring any other employer to recognize or bargain with a labor organization as the representative of his employees unless such labor organization has been certified as the representative of such employees under the provisions of section 9: *Provided,* That nothing contained in this clause (B) shall be construed to make unlawful, where not otherwise unlawful, any primary strike or primary picketing;

(C) forcing or requiring any employer to recognize or bargain with a particular labor organization as the representative of his employees if another labor organization has been certified as the representative of such employees under the provisions of section 9;

(D) forcing or requiring any employer to assign particular work to employees in a particular labor organization or in a particular trade, craft, or class rather than to employees in another labor organization or in another trade, craft, or class, unless such employer is failing to conform to an order or certification of the Board determining the bargaining representative for employees performing such work:

Provided, That nothing contained in this subsection (b) shall be construed to make unlawful a refusal by any person to enter upon the premises of any employer (other than his own employer), if the employees of such employer are engaged in a strike ratified or approved by a representative of such employees whom such employer is required to recognize under this Act: *Provided further,* that for the purposes of this paragraph (4) only, nothing contained in such paragraph shall be construed to prohibit publicity, other than picketing, for the purpose of truthfully advising the public, including consumers and members of a labor organization, that a product or products are produced by an employer with whom the labor organization has a primary dispute and are distributed by another employer, as long as such publicity does not have an effect of inducing any individual employed by any person other than the primary employer in the course of his employment to refuse to pick up, deliver, or transport any goods, or not to perform any services, at the establishment of the employer engaged in such distribution:

(5) to require of employees covered by an agreement authorized under subsection (a)(3) the payment, as a condition precedent to becoming a member of such organization, of a fee in an amount which the Board finds excessive or discriminatory under all the circumstances. In making such a finding, the Board shall consider, among other relevant factors, the practices and customs of labor organizations in the particular industry, and the wages currently paid to the employees affected;

(6) to cause or attempt to cause an employer to pay or deliver or agree to pay or deliver any money or other thing of value, in the nature of an exaction, for services which are not performed or not to be performed; and

(7) to picket or cause to be picketed, or threatened to picket or cause to be picketed, any employer where an object thereof is forcing or requiring an employer to recognize or bargain with a labor organization as the representative of his employees, or forcing or requiring the employees of an employer to accept or select such labor organization as their collective bargaining representative, unless such labor organization is currently certified as the representative of such employees:

(A) where the employer has lawfully recognized in accordance with this Act any other labor organization and a question concerning representation may not appropriately be raised under section 9(c) of this Act;

(B) where within the preceding twelve months a valid election under section 9(c) of this Act has been conducted, or

(C) where such picketing has been conducted without a petition under section 9(c) being filed within a reasonable period of time not to exceed thirty days from the commencement of such picketing . . .

Nothing in this paragraph (7) shall be construed to permit any act which would otherwise be an unfair labor practice under this section 8(b).

(c) The expressing of any views, argument, or opinion, or the dissemination thereof, whether in written, printed, graphic, or visual form, shall not constitute or be evidence of an unfair labor practice under any of the provisions of this Act, if such expression contains no threat of reprisal or force or promise of benefit.

(d) For the purposes of this section, to bargain collectively is the performance of the mutual obligation of the employer and the representative of the employees to meet at reasonable times and confer in good faith with respect to wages, hours, and other terms and conditions of employment, or the negotiation of an agreement, or any question arising thereunder, and the execution of a written contract incorporating any agreement reached if requested by either party, but such obligation does not compel either party to agree to a proposal or require the making of a concession . . .

(e) It shall be an unfair labor practice for any labor organization and any employer to enter into any contract or agreement, express or implied, whereby such employer ceases or refrains or agrees to cease or refrain from handling, using, selling, transporting, or otherwise dealing in any of the products of any other employer, or to cease doing business with any other person, and any contract or agreement entered into heretofore or hereafter containing such an agreement shall be to such extent unenforceable and void. . .

■ REPRESENTATIVES AND ELECTIONS

Section 9.

(a) Representatives designated or selected for the purposes of collective bargaining by the majority of the employees in a unit appropriate for such purposes, shall be the exclusive representative of all the employees in such unit for the purposes of collective bargaining in respect to rates of pay, wages, hours of employment, or other conditions of employment: *Provided*, That any individual employee or a group of employees shall have the right at any time to present grievances to their employer and to have such grievances adjusted, without the intervention of the bargaining representative, as long as the adjustment is not inconsistent with the terms of a collective-bargaining contract or agreement then in effect: *Provided further*, That the bargaining representative has been given opportunity to be present at such adjustment.

(b) The Board shall decide in each case whether, in order to assure to employees the fullest freedom in exercising the rights guaranteed by the Act, the unit appropriate for the purposes of collective bargaining shall be the employer unit, craft unit, plant unit, or subdivision thereof. . . .

(c)(1) Whenever a petition shall have been filed, in accordance with such regulations as may be prescribed by the Board—

(A) by an employee or group of employees or an individual or labor organization acting in their behalf, alleging that a substantial number of employees (i) wish to be represented for collective bargaining and that their employer declines to recognize their representative as the representative defined in section 9(a), or (ii) assert that the individual or labor organization, which has been certified or is being currently recognized by their employer as the bargaining representative, is no longer a representative as defined in section 9(a); or

(B) by an employer, alleging that one or more individual or labor organizations have presented to him a claim to be recognized as the representative defined in section 9(a); the Board shall investigate such petition and if it has reasonable cause to believe that a question of representation affecting commerce exists shall provide for an appropriate hearing upon due notice. Such hearing may be conducted by an officer or employee of the regional office, who shall not make any recommendations with respect thereto. If the Board finds upon the record of such hearing that such a question of representation exists, it shall direct an election by secret ballot and shall certify the results thereof.

(2) In determining whether or not a question of representation affecting commerce exists, the same regulations and rules of decision shall apply irrespective of the identity of the persons filing the petition or the kind of relief sought and in no case shall the Board deny a labor

organization a place on the ballot by reason of an order with respect to such labor organization or its predecessor not issued in conformity with section 10(c).

(3) No election shall be directed in any bargaining unit or any subdivision within which, in the preceding twelve-month period, a valid election shall have been held. Employees engaged in an economic strike who are not entitled to reinstatement shall be eligible to vote under such regulations as the Board shall find are consistent with the purposes and provisions of this Act in any election conducted within twelve months after the commencement of the strike. In any election where none of the choices on the ballot receives a majority, a run-off shall be conducted, the ballot providing for a selection between the two choices receiving the largest and second largest number of valid votes cast in the election.

(4) Nothing in this section shall be construed to prohibit the waiving of hearings by stipulation for the purpose of a consent election in conformity with regulations and rules of decision of the Board.

(5) In determining whether a unit is appropriate for the purposes specified in subsection (b) the extent to which the employees have organized shall not be controlling.

(d) Whenever an order of the Board made pursuant to section 10(c) is based in whole or in part upon facts certified following an investigation pursuant to subsection (c) of this section and there is a petition for the enforcement or review of such order, such certification and the record of such investigation shall be included in the transcript of the entire record required to be filed under section 10(e) or 10(f), and thereupon the decree of the court enforcing, modifying, or setting aside in whole or in part the order of the Board shall be made and entered upon the pleadings, testimony, and proceedings set forth in such transcript.

(e)(1) Upon the filing with the Board, by 30 per centrum or more of the employees in a bargaining unit covered by an agreement between their employer and a labor organization made pursuant to section 8(a)(3), of a petition alleging they desire that such authority be rescinded, the Board shall take a secret ballot of the employees in such unit, and shall certify the results thereof to such labor organization and to the employer.

(2) No election shall be conducted pursuant to this subsection in any bargaining unit or any subdivision within which, in the preceding twelve-month period, a valid election shall have been held.

TITLE VII OF THE CIVIL RIGHTS ACT OF 1964

■ DEFINITIONS

Section 701.

(j) The term "religion" includes all aspects of religious observance and practice, as well as belief, unless an employer demonstrates that he is unable to reasonably accommodate to an employee's or prospective employee's religious observance or practice without undue hardship on the conduct of the employer's business.

(k) The terms "because of sex" or "on the basis of sex" include, but are not limited to, because of or on the basis of pregnancy, childbirth or related medical conditions; and women affected by pregnancy, childbirth, or related medical conditions shall be treated the same for all employment-related purposes, including receipt of benefits under fringe benefit programs, as other persons not so affected but similar in their ability or inability to work, and nothing in Section 703(h) of this title shall be interpreted to permit otherwise. This subsection shall not require an employer to pay for health insurance benefits for abortion, except where the life of the mother would be endangered if the fetus were carried to term, or except where medical complications have arisen from an abortion: *Provided,* That nothing herein shall preclude an employer from providing abortion benefits or otherwise effect bargaining agreements in regard to abortion.

■ DISCRIMINATION BECAUSE OF RACE, COLOR, RELIGION, SEX, OR NATIONAL ORIGIN

Section 703.

(a) It shall be unlawful employment practice for an employer—

(1) to fail or refuse to hire or to discharge any individual, or otherwise to discriminate against any individual with respect to his compensation, terms, conditions, or privileges of employment, because of such individual's race, color, religion, sex, or national origin; or

(2) to limit, segregate, or classify his employees or applicants for employment in any way which would deprive or tend to deprive any

individual of employment opportunities or otherwise adversely affect his status as an employee, because of such individual's race, color, religion, sex, or national origin.

(b) It shall be unlawful employment practice for an employment agency to fail or refuse to refer for employment, or otherwise to discriminate against, an individual because of his race, color, religion, sex, or national origin, or to classify or refer for employment any individual on the basis of his race, color, religion, sex, or national origin.

(c) It shall be an unlawful employment practice for a labor organization—

(1) to exclude or to expel from its membership, or otherwise to discriminate against, any individual because of his race, color, religion, sex, or national origin;

(2) to limit, segregate, or classify its membership or applicants for membership or to classify or fail or refuse to refer for employment any individual, in any way which would deprive or tend to deprive any individual of employment opportunities, or would limit such employment opportunities or otherwise adversely affect his status as an employee or as an applicant for employment, because of such individual's race, color, religion, sex, or national origin; or

(3) to cause or attempt to cause an employer to discriminate against an individual in violation of this section.

(d) It shall be an unlawful employment practice for any employer, labor organization or joint labor-management committee controlling apprenticeship or other training or retraining, including on-the-job training programs to discriminate against any individual because of his race, color, religion, sex, or national origin in admission to, or employment in, any program established to provide apprenticeship or other training.

(e) Notwithstanding any other provision of this title, (1) it shall not be an unlawful employment practice for an employer to hire and employ employees, for an employment agency to classify, or refer for employment any individual, or for any employer, labor organization, or joint labor-management committee controlling apprenticeship or other training or retraining programs to admit or employ any individual in any such program, on the basis of his religion, sex, or national origin in those certain instances where religion, sex, or national origin is a bona fide occupational qualification reasonably necessary to the normal operation of that particular business or enterprise, and (2) it shall not be an unlawful employment practice for a school, college, university, or other educational institution or institution of learning to hire and employ employees of a particular religion if such school, college, university, or other educational institution or institution of learning is, in whole or in substantial part, owned, supported, controlled, or managed by a particular religion or by a particular religious corporation, association, or society, or if the curriculum of such school, college, university, or other educational institution or institution of learning is directed toward the propagation of a particular religion.

(f) As used in this title, the phrase "unlawful employment practice" shall not be deemed to include any action or measure taken by an employer, labor organization, joint labor-management of committee, or employment agency with respect to an individual who is a member of the

Communist Party of the United States or of any other organization required to register as a communist-action or Communist-front organization by final order of the Subversive Activities Control Act of 1950.

(g) Notwithstanding any other provision of this title, it shall not be an unlawful employment practice for an employer to fail or refuse to hire and employ any individual for any position, for an employer to discharge an individual from any position, or for any employment agency to fail or refuse to refer any individual for employment in any position, or for a labor organization to fail or refuse any individual for employment in any position, if—

(1) the occupancy of such position, or access to the premises in or upon which any part of the duties of such position is performed or is to be performed, is subject to any requirement imposed in the interest of the national security of the United States under any security program in effect pursuant to or administered under any statute of the United States or any Executive order of the President; and

(2) such individual has not fulfilled or has ceased to fulfill that requirement.

(h) Notwithstanding any other provision of this title, it shall not be an unlawful employment practice for an employer to apply different standards of compensation, or different terms, conditions, or privileges of employment pursuant to a bona fide seniority or merit system, or a system which measures earnings by quantity or quality of production or to employees who work in different locations, provided that such differences are not the results of an intention to discriminate because of race, color, religion, sex, or national origin; nor shall it be an unlawful employment practice for an employer to give and to act upon the results of any professionally developed ability test provided that such test, its administration or action upon the results is not designed, intended, or used to discriminate because of race, color, religion, sex, or national origin. It shall not be an unlawful employment practice under this title for any employer to differentiate upon the basis of sex in determining the amount of wages or compensation paid or to be paid to employees of such employer if such differentiation is authorized by the provision of Section 6(d) of the Fair Labor Standards Act of 1938 as amended (29 U.S.C. 206(d)).

(i) Nothing contained in this title shall apply to any business or enterprise on or near an Indian reservation with respect to any publicly announced employment practice of such business or enterprise under which a preferential treatment is given to any individual because he is an Indian living on or near a reservation.

(j) Nothing contained in this title shall be interpreted to require any employer, employment agency, labor organization, or joint labor-management committee subject to this title to grant preferential treatment to any individual or to any group because of the race, color, religion, sex, or national origin of such individual or group on account of an imbalance which may exist with respect to the total number or percentage of persons of any race, color, religion, sex, or national origin employed by any employer, referred or classified for employment by any employment agency or labor organization, admitted to membership or classified by any labor organization, or admitted to, or employed in, any apprenticeship or other training program, in comparison with the total number or percentage of persons of such race, color, religion, sex, or national origin in any community, State, section, or other area, or in the available work force in any community, State, section, or other area.

◾ OTHER UNLAWFUL EMPLOYMENT PRACTICES

Section 704.

(a) It shall be an unlawful employment practice for an employer to discriminate against any of his employees or applicants for employment, for an employment agency, or joint labor-management committee controlling apprenticeship or other training or retraining, including on-the-job training programs, to discriminate against any individual, or for a labor organization to discriminate against any member thereof or applicant for membership, because he has opposed any practice, made an unlawful employment practice by this title, or because he has made a charge, testified, assisted, or participated in any manner in an investigation, proceeding, or hearing under this title.

(b) It shall be an unlawful employment practice for an employer, labor organization, employment agency, or joint labor-management committee controlling apprenticeship or other training or retraining, including on-the-job training programs, to print or cause to be printed or published any notice or advertisement relating to employment by such an employer or membership in or any classification or referral for employment by such a labor organization, or relating to any classification or referral for employment by such an employment agency, or relating to admission to, or employment in, any program established to provide apprenticeship or other training by such a joint labor-management committee indicating any preference, limitation, specification, or discrimination, based on race, color, religion, sex, or national origin, except that such a notice or advertisement may indicate a preference, limitation, specification, or discrimination based on religion, sex, or national origin when religion, sex, or national origin is a bona fide occupational qualification for employment.

AMERICANS WITH DISABILITIES ACT OF 1990

■ TITLE I—EMPLOYMENT

Sec. 101. Definitions.

(8) **Qualified individual with a disability.** The term "qualified individual with a disability" means an individual with a disability who, with or without reasonable accommodation, can perform the essential functions of the employment position that such individual holds or desires. For the purposes of this title, consideration shall be given to the employer's judgment as to what functions of a job are essential, and if an employer has prepared a written description before advertising or interviewing applicants for the job, this description shall be considered evidence of the essential functions of the job.

(9) **Reasonable accommodation.** The term "reasonable accommodation" may include—

(A) making existing facilities used by employees readily accessible to and usable by individuals with disabilities; and

(B) job restructuring, part-time or modified work schedules, reassignment to a vacant position, acquisition or modification of equipment or devices, appropriate adjustment or modifications of examinations, training materials or policies, the provision of qualified readers or interpreters, and other similar accommodations for individuals with disabilities.

(10) **Undue Hardship.**

(A) In general: The term "undue hardship" means an action requiring significant difficulty or expense, when considered in light of the factors set forth in subparagraph (B).

(B) Factors to be considered: In determining whether an accommodation would impose an undue hardship on a covered entity, factors to be considered include—

(i) the nature and cost of accommodation needed under this Act;

(ii) the overall financial resources of the facility or facilities involved in the provision of the reasonable accommodation; the number of persons employed at such facility; the effect on expenses and resources, or the impact otherwise of such accommodation upon the operation of the facility;

(iii) the overall financial resources of the covered entity; the overall size of the business of a covered entity with respect to the number of its employees; the number, type, and location of its facilities; and

(iv) the type of operation or operations of the covered entity, including the composition, structure, and functions of the workforce of such entity; the geographic separateness, administrative, or fiscal relationship of the facility or facilities in question to the covered entity.

Sec. 102. Discrimination.

(a) General Rule. No covered entity shall discriminate against a qualified individual with a disability because of the disability of such individual in regard to job application procedures, the hiring, advancement, or discharge of employees, employee compensation, job training, and other terms, conditions, and privileges of employment.

(b) Construction. As used in subsection (a), the term "discriminate" includes—

(1) limiting, segregating, or classifying a job applicant or employee in a way that adversely affects the opportunities or status of such applicant or employee because of the disability of such applicant or employee;

(2) participating in a contractual or other arrangement or relationship that has the effect of subjecting a covered entity's qualified applicant or employee with a disability to the discrimination prohibited by this title (such relationship includes a relationship with an employment or referral agency, labor union, an organization providing fringe benefits to an employee of the covered entity, or an organization providing training and apprenticeship programs);

(3) utilizing standards, criteria, or methods of administration—

(A) that have the effect of discrimination on the basis of disability; or

(B) that perpetuate the discrimination of others who are subject to common administrative control;

(4) excluding or otherwise denying equal jobs or benefits to a qualified individual because of the known disability of an individual with whom the qualified individual is known to have a relationship or association;

(5)(A) not making reasonable accommodations to the known physical or mental limitations of an otherwise qualified individual with a disability who is an applicant or employee, unless such covered entity can demonstrate that the accommodation would impose an undue hardship on the operation of the business of such covered entity; or

(B) denying employment opportunities to a job applicant or employee who is an otherwise qualified individual with a disability, if such denial is based on the need of such covered entity to make reasonable accommodation to the physical or mental impairments of the employee or applicant;

(6) using qualification standards, employment tests or other selection criteria that screen out or tend to screen out an individual with a disability or a class of individuals with disabilities unless the standard, test or other selection criteria, as used by the covered entity, is shown to be job-related for the position in question and is consistent with business necessity; and

(7) failing to select and administer tests concerning employment in the most effective manner to ensure that, when such test is administered to a job applicant or employee who has a disability that impairs sensory, manual, or speaking skills, such test results accurately reflect the skills, aptitude, or whatever other factor of such applicant or employee that such test purports to measure, rather than reflecting the impaired sensory, manual, or speaking skills of such employee or applicant (except where such skills are the factors that the test purports to measure). . . .

Sec. 104. Illegal Use of Drugs and Alcohol.

(b) Rules of Construction. Nothing in subsection (a) shall be construed to exclude as a qualified individual with a disability an individual who —

(1) has successfully completed a supervised drug rehabilitation program and is no longer engaging in the illegal use of drugs, or has otherwise been rehabilitated successfully and is no longer engaging in such use;

(2) is participating in a supervised rehabilitation program and is no longer engaging in such use; or

(3) is erroneously regarded as engaging in such use, but is not engaging in such use;

except that it shall not be a violation of this Act for a covered entity to adopt or administer reasonable policies or procedures, including but not limited to drug testing, designed to ensure that an individual described in paragraph (1) or (2) is no longer engaging in the illegal use of drugs. . . .

SECURITIES STATUTES

SECURITIES ACT OF 1933

■ DEFINITIONS

Section 2. When used in this title, unless the context requires—

(1) The term "security" means any note, stock, treasury stock, bond, debenture, evidence of indebtedness, certificate of interest or participation in any profit-sharing agreement, collateral-trust certificate, preorganization certificate or subscription, transferable share, investment contract, voting-trust certificate, certificate of deposit for a security, fractional undivided interest in oil, gas, or other mineral rights, any put, call, straddle, option, or privilege on any security, certificate of deposit, or group or index of securities (including any interest therein or based on the value thereof), or any put, call, straddle, option, or privilege entered into on a national securities exchange relating to foreign currency, or, in general, any interest or participation in, temporary or interim certificate for, receipt for, guarantee of, or warrant or right to subscribe to or purchase, any of the foregoing.

■ EXEMPTED SECURITIES

Section 3.

(a) Except as hereinafter expressly provided the provisions of this title shall not apply to any of the following classes of securities:

(2) Any security issued or guaranteed by the United States or any territory thereof, or by the District of Columbia, or by any State of the United States, or by any political subdivision of a State or Territory, or by any public instrumentality of one or more States or Territories, or by any person controlled or supervised by and acting as an instrumentality of the Government of the United States pursuant to authority granted by the Congress of the United States; or any certificate of deposit for any of the foregoing; or any security issued or guaranteed by any bank; or any security issued by or representing an interest in or a direct obligation of a Federal Reserve Bank. . .

(3) Any note, draft, bill of exchange, or banker's acceptance which arises out of a current transaction or the proceeds of which have been or are

to be used for current transactions, and which has a maturity at the time of issuance of not exceeding nine months, exclusive of days of grace, or any renewal thereof the maturity of which is likewise limited;

(4) Any security issued by a person organized and operated exclusively for religious, educational, benevolent, fraternal, charitable, or reformatory purposes and not for pecuniary profit, and no part of the net earnings of which inures to the benefit of any person, private stockholder, or individual;

■ EXEMPTED TRANSACTIONS

Section 4.   The provisions of section 5 shall not apply to —

(1) transactions by any person other than an issuer, underwriter, or dealer.

(2) transactions by an issuer not involving any public offering.

(3) transactions by a dealer (including an underwriter no longer acting as an underwriter in respect of the security involved in such transactions), except—

(A) transactions taking place prior to the expiration of forty days after the first date upon which the security was bona fide offered to the public by the issuer or by or through an underwriter.

(B) transactions in a security as to which a registration statement has been filed taking place prior to the expiration of forty days after the effective date of such registration statement or prior to the expiration of forty days after the first date upon which the security was bona fide offered to the public by the issuer or by or through an underwriter after such effective date, whichever is later (excluding in the computation of such forty days any time during which a stop order issued under section 8 is in effect as to the security), or such shorter period as the Commission may specify by rules and regulations or order, and

(C) transactions as to the securities constituting the whole or a part of an unsold allotment to or subscription by such dealer as a participant in the distribution of such securities by the issuer or by or through an underwriter.

With respect to transactions referred to in clause (B), if securities of the issuer have not previously been sold pursuant to an earlier effective registration statement the applicable period, instead of forty days, shall be ninety days, or such shorter period as the Commission may specify by rules and regulations or order.

(4) brokers' transactions, executed upon customers' orders on any exchange or in the over-the-counter market but not the solicitation of such orders.

(6) transactions involving offers or sales by an issuer solely to one or more accredited investors, if the aggregate offering price of an issue of securities offered in reliance on this paragraph does not exceed the amount allowed under section 3(b) of this title, if there is no advertising or public solicitation in connection with the transaction by the issuer or anyone acting on the issuer's behalf, and if the issuer files such notice with the Commission as the Commission shall prescribe.

■ PROHIBITIONS RELATING TO INTERSTATE COMMERCE AND THE MAILS

Section 5.

(a) Unless a registration statement is in effect as to a security, it shall be unlawful for any person, directly or indirectly—

(1) to make use of any means or instruments of transportation or communication in interstate commerce or of the mails to sell such security through the use or medium of any prospectus or otherwise; or

(2) to carry or cause to be carried through the mails or in interstate commerce, by any means or instruments of transportation, any such security for the purpose of sale or for delivery after sale.

(b) It shall be unlawful for any person, directly or indirectly—

(1) to make use of any means or instruments of transportation or communication in interstate commerce or of the mails to carry or transmit any prospectus relating to any security with respect to which a registration statement has been filed under this title, unless such prospectus meets the requirements of section 10, or

(2) to carry or to cause to be carried through the mails or in interstate commerce any such security for the purpose of sale or for delivery after sale, unless accompanied or preceded by a prospectus that meets the requirements of subsection (a) of section 10.

(c) It shall be unlawful for any person, directly, or indirectly, to make use of any means or instruments of transportation or communication in interstate commerce or of the mails to offer to sell or offer to buy through the use or medium of any prospectus or otherwise any security, unless a registration statement has been filed as to such security, or while the registration statement is the subject of a refusal order or stop order or (prior to the effective date of the registration statement) any public proceeding of examination under section 8.

SECURITIES EXCHANGE ACT OF 1934

■ DEFINITIONS AND APPLICATION OF TITLE

Section 3.

(a) When used in this title, unless the context otherwise requires—

(4) The term "broker" means any person engaged in the business of effecting transactions in securities for the account of others, but does not include a bank.

(5) The term "dealer" means any person engaged in the business of buying and selling securities for his own account, through a broker or otherwise, but does not include a bank, or any person insofar as he buys or sells securities for his own account, either individually or in some fiduciary capacity, but not as part of a regular business.

(7) The term "director" means any director of a corporation or any person performing similar functions with respect to any organization, whether incorporated or unincorporated.

(8) The term "issuer" means any person who issues or proposes to issue any security; except that with respect to certificates of deposit for securities, voting-trust certificates, or collateral-trust certificates, or with respect to certificates of interest or shares in an unincorporated investment trust not having a board of directors or the fixed, restricted management, or unit type, the term "issuer" means the person or persons performing the acts and assuming the duties of depositor or manager pursuant to the provisions of the trust or other agreement or instrument under which such securities are issued; and except that with respect to equipment-trust certificates or like securities, the term "issuer" means the person by whom the equipment or property is, or is to be, used.

(9) The term "person" means a natural person, company, government, or political subdivision, agency, or instrumentality of a government.

■ REGULATION OF THE USE OF MANIPULATIVE AND DECEPTIVE DEVICES

Section 10.   It shall be unlawful for any person, directly or indirectly, by the use of any means or instrumentality of interstate commerce or of the mails, or of any facility of any national securities exchange—

(b) To use or employ, in connection with the purchase or sale of any security registered on a national securities exchange or any security not so registered, any manipulative or deceptive device or contrivance in contravention of such rules and regulations as the Commission may prescribe as necessary or appropriate in the public interest or for the protection of investors.

GLOSSARY

absolute liability Liability for an act or activity that causes harm or injury even though the alleged wrongdoer was not at fault.

abuse of discretion A judgment or decision by an administrative agency or judge which has no foundation in fact or in law.

acceptance The offeree's notification or expression to the offeror that he or she agrees to be bound by the exact terms of the offeror's proposal. A contract is thereby created. The trend is to allow acceptance by any means that will reasonably notify the offeror of the acceptance.

accord In a debtor/creditor relationship, an agreement between the parties to settle a dispute for some partial payment. It is called an accord because the creditor has a right of action against the debtor.

accord and satisfaction In a debtor/creditor relationship, an agreement between the parties to settle a dispute, and subsequent payment. The agreement is an accord because the creditor has a right of action against the debtor. After the agreement has been reached, the accord and satisfaction is complete when payment has been tendered.

acid rain Pollution that occurs due to the release of acidic chemicals into the atmosphere that then falls elsewhere, changing the acid content of water and the ground and damaging plants.

actual authority Power of an agent to bind a principal where that power is derived from either an express or an implied agreement between principal and the agent.

adjudication The legal process of resolving a dispute.

adjudicatory hearing In administrative law, a formal process involving a regulatory agency and the private parties involved in a complaint; procedures are more informal than a court trial, but protect due process rights.

administrative agency A governmental bureau established by Congress or the President to execute certain functions of Congress or the President; it allows governmental business to be transacted under the authority of Congress or the President by bureaus that specialize in certain tasks.

administrative law The rules and regulations established by administrative agencies to execute the functions given them by Congress or the President to carry out regulatory functions.

adversary system of justice A legal system that is characterized by a process whereby the parties to a dispute present their own arguments and are responsible for asserting their legal rights.

advertising A communication through which a business offers consumers an inducement to purchase with the intent to increase demand (sales) for their product(s).

affirmative action Results-oriented actions that a contractor by virtue of its contracts with the government must take to ensure equal employment opportunity. An affirmative action program may also be imposed by a court as a remedy in a discrimination action. Where appropriate, it includes such goals as correcting underutilization and correction of problem areas. It may also include relief such as back pay, retroactive seniority, makeup goals, and time-tables.

affirmative defense Defendant's response to plaintiff's claim which attacks the plaintiff's legal right to bring the action rather than attacking the truth of the claim. A common example of an affirmative defense is the running of the statute of limitations.

agency A relationship between two persons, by agreement or otherwise, where one (the agent) may act on behalf of the other (the principal) and bind the principal by words and actions.

agency order In administrative law, a statement by a regulatory agency, under its powers granted by Congress and subject to procedural requirements, to inform parties subject to the rules what they must do to comply with a rule they are violating.

agency regulation In administrative law, a rule issued by a regulatory agency, under its powers granted by Congress and subject to procedural requirements, to inform parties subject to the rule what the details of its requirements are.

agency shop In labor law, a unionized workplace where employees who are not union members must pay agency fees to the union for being the sole bargaining agent for all employees; illegal in states that have right-to-work laws.

agent An individual authorized to act for or represent another, called the principal.

agreement A "meeting of two or more minds." An agreement means there is a mutual understanding between the parties as to the substance of a contract.

alternative dispute resolution A process whereby the parties to a dispute resolve it through a mechanism other than the court system. A common alternative dispute resolution process is arbitration.

ambient air Under the Clean Air Act, ambient air is the air outside of buildings or other such enclosures.

amicus curiae A party not directly involved in the litigation but who participates as a friend of the court.

amount in controversy The damages claimed or the relief demanded by the injured party in a dispute.

answer The response of a defendant to the plaintiff's complaint, denying in part or in whole the charges made by the plaintiff.

anticipatory breach The assertion by a party to a contract that he or she will not perform a future obligation as required by the contract.

apparent authority That authority a reasonable person would assume an agent possesses as inferred from the conduct of the principal.

appeal Removal from a court of a decided or an adjudicated case to a court of appellate jurisdiction for the purpose of obtaining review of the decision.

appellant The party, can be either the plaintiff or the defendant, who invokes the appellate jurisdiction of a superior court.

appellate jurisdiction The power of a court to revise or correct the proceedings in a cause already acted upon by a lower court administrative agency.

appellee The party against whom an appeal is taken.

arbiter In an arbitration proceeding, the person to decide the controversy.

arbitrary and capricious A judgment or decision, usually by an administrative agency or judge, which is without basis in fact or in law. Such a decision is often referred to as being without a rational basis.

arbitration A means of settling disputes between two or more parties whereby the parties submit an unresolved issue to a neutral third party empowered by the parties to make a binding decision. It is becoming a popular alternative to the court system for resolving disputes between businesses due to the speed of its decision rendering process.

articles of incorporation Under state law, a document that every new corporation must file providing basic information about the name, address, and purpose of the corporation, as well as a statement about the stock that may be issued and the names of the principal officers.

artificial seniority In employment discrimination law, a remedy that may be granted giving minority or women workers extra years of work credit to make up for past acts of discrimination by their employer.

assault Any word or action intended to cause another to be in fear of immediate physical harm.

assault and battery Intentionally causing another to anticipate immediate physical harm through some threat and then carrying out the threatened activity.

assumption of risk Common law doctrine under which a plaintiff may not recover for injuries or damages as a result of an activity to which the plaintiff assented. The doctrine used by the defendant in negligence when the plaintiff had knowledge of and appreciated the danger, voluntarily exposed himself to the danger, and was injured.

authorization card A card signed by an employee in a union organizing campaign, whereby the employee joins the union and designates the union to be his representative for the purpose of collective bargaining.

back pay Compensation for past economic losses (such as lost wages and fringe benefits) caused by an employer's discriminatory employment practices, including, for example, its failure to remedy the continuing effects of past practices.

balance of payments An official accounting record that follows double-entry bookkeeping practices and records all of a country's foreign transactions. The country's exports are recorded as credits and imports as debits.

bankruptcy A proceeding under the law that is initiated either by an insolvent individual or business (termed a voluntary bankruptcy), or by creditors (termed an involuntary bankruptcy) seeking to either have the insolvent's remaining assets distributed among the creditors and to thereby discharge the insolvent from any further obligation or to untangle and reorganize the insolvent's debt structure.

bankruptcy trustee In bankruptcy proceedings the person given authority to manage the assets of the bankrupt for the benefit of the creditors.

battery The intentional unprivileged touching of another. The "touching" may involve as little as a mere touching that is only offensive, or as much as an act of violence that causes very serious injury.

beyond a reasonable doubt In criminal law, the general rule that for a judge or jury to find a defendant guilty there can be no significant doubt that the defendant wrongfully violated a criminal statute.

bilateral contract A contract formed by the mutual exchange of promises of the parties.

bill of exchange An unconditional order in writing addressed by one person to another, signed by the person giving it, requiring the person to whom it is addressed to pay on demand or at a fixed or determinable future time a sum certain in money.

blue sky laws Name given to state laws that regulate the offer and sale of securities.

bona fide occupational qualification (BFOQ) Employment in particular jobs may not be limited to persons of a particular sex, religion, or national origin unless the employer can show that sex, religion, or national origin is an actual qualification for performing the job. The qualification is called a bona fide occupational qualification.

bond An evidence of debt carrying a specified amount and schedule of interest payments as well as a date for redemption of the face value of the bond.

bondholders Creditors of a business, whose evidence of debt is a bond issued by the business.

boycott An effort to organize a group to not engage in commerce with some party; such as a group of retailers refusing to buy any products from manufacturers who do certain things not liked by the retailers, or a group of labor unions agreeing not to handle any products made by a certain company.

breach of contract Failure, without a legal excuse, of a promisor to perform the terms agreed to in a contract.

bribery The offering, giving, receiving, or soliciting of something of value for the purpose of influencing the action of an official in the discharge of his or her public or legal duties.

brief An appellate brief is a written document, prepared by an attorney to serve as the basis for an argument upon a cause in an appellate court, and usually filed for the information of the court. It contains the points of law the attorney wants to establish, together with the arguments and authorities upon which the attorney rests his contentions. The term is also used to describe a summary or abstract of a case prepared and used by a law student.

bubble concept In environmental law, when a large polluting facility or a geographic area is treated as a single pollution source, in which one may build additional polluting facilities so long as the total pollution produced is lower or no more than before.

business judgment rule A principle of corporate law under which a court will not challenge the business decisions of a corporate officer or director made with due care and in good faith.

business necessity Justification for an otherwise prohibited employment practice based on a contractor's proof that (1) the otherwise prohibited employment practice is essential for the safety and efficiency of the business, and (2) no reasonable alternative with a lesser impact exists.

business tort A noncontractual breach of a legal duty by a business directly resulting in damages or injury to another.

bylaws In corporation law, the rules that regulate and govern the internal operations of a corporation with respect to directors, shareholders, and officers rights and duties.

capacity *See* contractual capacity.

capitalistic economy An economy in which capital is predominantly owned privately rather than by the state.

capital stock The corporation's financial foundation consisting of the money or property contributed by stockholders; the total amount of stock (both common and preferred) representing ownership of a business.

cartel A combination of independent producers within an industry attempting to limit competition by acting together to fix prices, divide markets, or restrict entry into the industry.

cause in fact An act or omission without which an event would not have occurred. Courts express this in the form of a rule commonly referred to as the "but for" rule: the injury to an individual would not have happened but for the conduct of the wrongdoer.

cause of action The fact or facts which give rise to an individual's legal right of redress against another.

caveat emptor Latin for let the buyer beware.

cease and desist order An order issued by an administrative agency or a court prohibiting a business firm from conducting activities that the agency or court has deemed illegal.

ceiling price The maximum price permitted by the governmental authority.

challenge for cause Challenge by an attorney of one of the parties to a prospective juror for which some cause or reason is alleged or asserted.

charter See corporate charter.

citizen-suit provisions In regulatory law, a right provided by Congress for private citizens to bring a suit before a federal court to force compliance with the law passed by Congress; in some instances, the costs of the suit will be borne by the government if the private party wins the case.

civil law (1) Laws, written or unwritten, that specify the duties that exist between and among people, as opposed to criminal matters. (2) Codified or statutory law, used in many Western European countries and Japan, as distinguished from the common or judge-made law used in England and the United States.

closed shop A place of employment where one must be a union member before obtaining work.

closing argument Oral presentation made to the jury by the attorneys after the plaintiff and defendant have rested their cases and before the judge charges the jury.

collective bargaining The process by which unions and employers arrive at and enforce agreements regarding the employment relationship.

commerce clause In general, that part of the U.S. Constitution that gives Congress the power to regulate interstate commerce; the basis of much federal regulation.

commercial speech Expressions made by businesses about commercial matters or about political matters; Supreme Court interpretation of the First Amendment concerns differences between restrictions allowed on such speech.

common law Law developed by American and English courts by decisions in cases; unlike statutes, it is not passed by a legislative body and is not a specific set of rules; rather, it must be interpreted from the many decisions that have been written over the centuries.

common stock The shares of ownership in a corporation having the lowest priority with regard to payment of dividends and distribution of the corporation's assets upon dissolution.

community property Property owned in common by husband and wife.

comparative negligence A defense to negligence whereby the plaintiff's damages are reduced by the proportion his or her fault bears to the total injury he or she has sustained.

compensatory damages A sum of money awarded to the injured party that is equivalent to his or her actual damages or injuries sustained. The rationale behind compensatory damages is to restore the injured party to the position he or she was in prior to the injury.

complaint The initial pleading by the plaintiff in a civil action that informs the defendant of the material facts on which the plaintiff bases the lawsuit.

concentration In antitrust law, the percent of market share (usually sales volume) that one or more firms control in a given product or geographic market; used as a measure of the degree of competition within a market.

concentration ratio Fraction of total market sales made by a specified number of an industry's largest firms. Four-firm and eight-firm concentration ratios are the most frequently used.

concerted activity In labor law, when employees join together for mutual aid and protection; certain rights are protected by the National Labor Relations Act.

concurrent jurisdiction A situation where at least two different courts are each empowered to deal with the subject matter at issue in a dispute.

concurring opinion At the appellate court level, an opinion filed by one or more of the justices (or judges) in which the justice(s) agrees with the majority opinion but decides to state separately his views of the case or his reasoning.

condition A provision in a contract providing that upon the occurrence of some event the obligations of the parties to the contract will be set in motion, suspended, or terminated.

condition precedent In a contract, a condition that must be met before the other party's obligations arise.

condition subsequent In a contract, a condition which, if met, discharges the obligations of the other party.

confiscation The act of a sovereign in a taking without a proper public purpose or just compensation of private property.

conflict of laws Body of law establishing the circumstances in which a state or federal court shall apply the laws of another state rather than the laws of the state in which it is sitting in deciding a case before it.

conglomerate merger A merger between two companies that do not compete with or purchase from each other.

consent A voluntary agreement, implied or expressed, to submit to a proposition or act of another.

consent decree A judgment entered by consent of the parties whereby the defendant agrees to stop alleged illegal activity without admitting guilt or wrongdoing.

consideration In a contract, the thing of value bargained for in exchange for a promise; the inducement or motivation to a contract; the element that keeps the contract from being gratuitous and, therefore, makes it legally binding on the parties.

constructive notice Information or understanding that is equivalent to a formal notice of facts that a person using proper diligence would be expected to know.

consignment The act or process of depositing goods for the purpose of their sale in the custody of a third party who is essentially a bailor.

constitution The fundamental law of a nation; a written document establishing the powers of the government and its basic structure; the controlling authority over all other law.

consumer reports Traditionally called credit reports, these are files maintained by several companies concerning the credit history and evidence of income and debt situation of most adults; these are sold for legitimate business purposes.

contempt of court Any act that is calculated to embarrass, hinder, or obstruct a court in the administration of justice, or that is calculated to lessen the court's authority.

contract A legal relationship consisting of the rights and duties of the contracting parties; a promise or set of promises constituting an agreement between the parties that gives each a legal duty to the other and also the right to seek a remedy for the breach of those duties. The elements of a contract include an agreement, consideration, legal capacity, lawful subject matter, and genuine consent to the contract.

contract clause The statement in the constitution that "No State shall . . . pass any . . . Law impairing the Obligation of Contracts. . . ." Primary applications have been cases in which a state has tried to reduce its obligations previously created by contracts with private parties.

contractual capacity The threshold mental capacity required by law for a party entering into a contract to be bound by that contract. Generally, minors, intoxicated persons, and the insane lack capacity to contract.

contributory negligence As a complete defense to negligence, an act or a failure to act that produces a lack of reasonable care on the part of the plaintiff that is proximate cause of the injury incurred.

conversion The unauthorized taking of property, permanently or temporarily, that deprives its rightful owner of its lawful use.

cooperative A group of two or more individuals or enterprises that act through a common agent or representative to achieve a common objective.

copyright A grant to an author or a publisher of an exclusive right to print, reprint, publish, copy, and sell literary work, musical compositions, works of art, and motion pictures for the life of the author plus an additional fifty years.

corporate charter A certificate issued by a state government recognizing the existence of a corporation as a legal entity; it is issued automatically upon filing the information required by state law and payment of a fee.

corporate social responsibility The belief that businesses have a duty to society that goes beyond obeying the law and maximizing profits.

corporation A business organized under the laws of a state that allow an artificial legal being to exist for purposes of doing business.

cost-benefit analysis A technique by which one computes the costs of implementing a certain activity and compares the estimated monetary value of the benefits from the same activity. Activities where the benefits exceed the costs are undertaken and those where the costs exceed the benefits are rejected.

counterclaim A claim the defendant may assert against the plaintiff.

counteroffer An offeree's response to an offeror that rejects the offeror's original offer and at the same time makes a new offer.

covenant An agreement between two or more parties in which one or more of the parties pledges that some duty or obligation is to be done or not to be done.

craft union A union organized on the basis of a specified set of skills or occupations.

credit rating An opinion as to the reliability of a person in paying debts.

credit report A report made by a credit reporting agency concerning the financial condition, credit character, and reputation of an individual.

creditor A person to whom a debt is owed by another person who is called the debtor.

crime A violation of the law that is punishable by the state or nation. Crimes are classified as treason, felonies, and misdemeanors.

criminal law Governs or defines legal wrongs, or crimes, committed against society. The objective of criminal law is to punish the wrongdoer for violating the rules of society. An individual found guilty of a criminal offense is usually fined or imprisoned.

cross complaint During the pleadings, a claim the defendant may assert against the plaintiff. *See also* counterclaim.

cross-elasticity of demand A measure of the extent to which the quantity of a commodity demanded responds to changes in price of a related commodity. It is used occasionally in antitrust cases to determine the product market for a firm under investigation. If the price of a related product rises and the quantity demanded of the firm's product also rises, the products are substitutes and, therefore, are in the same product market.

cross examination Examination undertaken by the attorney representing the adverse party after the other party has examined his or her witness.

damages Money compensation sought or awarded as a remedy for a breach of contract or for tortious acts.

debt A sum of money due by an express agreement.

debt collection agency A business that buys the right to collect the debts owed by consumers to a business.

debtor A person who owes a debt to another who is called the creditor.

debt securities An obligation of a corporation, usually in the form of a bond, issued for a certain value at a certain rate of interest to be repaid at a certain time.

deception In consumer protection law, a claim, practice, or omission likely to mislead a reasonable consumer and cause the consumer to suffer a loss.

decertification Process through which a group of employees decides it no longer wants a union to be its bargaining unit. The process involves an election conducted by the National Labor Relations Board.

defamation An intentional false communication, either published or publicly spoken, that injures another's reputation or good name.

default judgment Judgment entered against a party who has failed to appear in court to defend against a claim that has been brought by another party.

defendant The party against whom an action or lawsuit is brought.

defense That offered and alleged by the defendant as a reason in law or fact why the plaintiff should not recover, or recover less than what he or she seeks.

Delaney clause The portion of the Food, Drug and Cosmetic Act that holds that any food additive that is found to cause cancer in animals may not be marketed.

delegation The legal transfer of power and authority to another to perform duties.

delegation of powers The right of Congress to authorize government agencies to perform certain legal duties as instructed by Congress under its constitutional authority.

demurrer An older term for a motion to dismiss a claim for failure to state a cause of action. *See* motion to dismiss.

deposition Sworn testimony—either written or oral—of a person taken outside the court.

design defect In products liability litigation, a claim that a consumer suffered an injury because a product was not designed with sufficient concern for safety that could have prevented the injury that occured.

detrimental reliance *See* promissory estoppel.

direct examination The initial examination of a witness by the party on whose behalf the witness has been called.

directed verdict Verdict granted by the court on the grounds that the jury could reasonably reach only one conclusion on the basis of the evidence presented during the trial.

discharge The termination of one's obligation. Under the law of contract, discharge occurs either when the parties have performed their obligations in the contract, or when events, the conduct of the parties, or the operation of law releases the parties from performing.

disclosure requirements In securities law, the revealing of certain financial and other information believed relevant to investors considering buying securities in some venture; the requirement that sufficient information be provided prospective investors so that they can make an intelligent evaluation of a security.

discovery The process by which the parties in a lawsuit may gather information from each other as a part of reducing the scope of what will actually be presented in court; process is determined by rules of procedure and may be limited by the court hearing the case.

discrimination Illegal treatment of a person or group (either intentional or unintentional) based on race, color, national origin, religion, sex, handicap, or veteran's status. The term includes the failure to remedy the effects of past discrimination.

disparagement A false communication that creates injury to an individual in his or her business, profession, or trade.

disparate impact In employment discrimination law, when an apparently neutral rule regarding hiring or treatment of employees works to discriminate against a protected class of employees.

disparate treatment Differential treatment of employees or applicants on the basis of their race, color, religion, sex, national origin, handicap, or veteran's status (including, for example, the situation whereby applicants or employees of a particular race or sex are required to pass tests or meet educational requirements not required of similarly situated contemporary applicants or employees of another race or sex).

dissenting opinion Opinion written by one or more appellate judges or justices explaining why they have disagreement with the decision of the majority of the court.

diversity of citizenship An action in which the plaintiff and the defendant are citizens of different states.

dividend A distribution to corporate shareholders in proportion to the number of shares held.

due care That degree of care that a reasonable person can be expected to exercise to avoid harm reasonably foreseeable if such care is not taken.

due process Constitutional limitation requiring that an individual has a right not to be deprived of life, liberty, or property without a fair and just hearing.

economic efficiency A method of producing some quantity of output is economically efficient when it is the least costly method of producing that output.

effluent charge A fee, fine, or tax on a business for its polluting activity, usually on a per unit basis.

electronic fund transfer The ability to make monetary transactions through electronics (telephone, computer).

embezzlement Statutory offense whereby an individual fraudulently appropriates for his or her own use the property or money intrusted to him by another.

eminent domain The power of the government to take private property for public use for fair compensation.

emotional distress A tort action for damages to compensate for mental injury caused to a person; generally does not require evidence of physical injury.

employee handbooks Manuals issued by employers to inform employees of their duties and rights as employees; often used as evidence of an employment contract that must be followed by both parties.

employment-at-will A doctrine under the common law providing that unless otherwise explicitly stated an employment contract was for an indefinite term and could be terminated at any time by either party without notice.

enabling statute Legislative enactment confering new powers on agencies, allowing them to do things they could not do before.

en banc Legal proceedings before or by the court as a whole rather than before or by a single judge.

endangered species In environmental law, a list of animals and plants declared by the government to be in danger of becoming extinct; violators may be prosecuted for killing the animals or plants or injuring their habitat.

Environmental Impact Statement The statement required by the National Environmental Policy Act to be developed by federal agencies for every recommendation or report on proposals for legislation and other major federal actions significantly affecting the quality of the human environment.

equal protection clause Section 1 of the Fourteenth Amendment to the Constitution, providing that states will treat all persons subject to state laws in a similar manner. "No State shall . . . deny to any person within its jurisdiction the equal protection of the laws."

equity In securities law and with respect to finance, an ownership claim on a business interest; usually a security with no repayment terms.

estoppel A principle that provides that an individual is barred from denying or alleging a certain fact or state facts because of that individual's previous conduct, allegation, or denial.

ethics Moral science that considers the duties which a member of society owes to other members.

evidence In procedural law, the legal matters—oral, written or physical testimony—that may be presented at a trial or at other legal proceeding for use in resolving a dispute.

excise tax A tax on the sale of a particular commodity. A specific tax is a fixed tax per unit of the commodity sold. An ad valorem tax is a fixed percentage of the value of the commodity.

exclusive dealing contract An agreement between two firms to deal only with each other for certain products or services.

exclusive jurisdiction The power of a court over a particular subject matter as provided by statute to the exclusion of all other courts.

exculpatory contract A contract that releases one of the parties from liability for their wrong-doings.

executed contract A contract that has been fully performed by the parties.

executive order Under powers granted by the Constitution or by Congress in legislation, an order by the president to establish a legal requirement or to enforce a legal requirement.

executory contract A contract that has not been performed by the parties.

exemplary damages *See* punitive damages.

exemptions from registration In securities law, provisions that allow certain securities to be sold without meeting the usual registration requirements with the Securities and Exchange Commission; does not exempt the securities from other aspects of securities laws.

exhaustion of administrative remedies Doctrine providing that in those instances where a statute provides an administrative remedy, relief must be sought through the appropriate agency and that remedy exhausted before a court can act to provide other relief.

ex parte By one party.

expert witness Witness with special opportunity for observation, or special or professional training or skill in assessing the facts in a case.

export Products manufactured in one country, and then shipped and sold in another.

express authority In agency law, when an agent has clear authority, verbal or written, to act on behalf of a principal for certain matters.

express contract A contract that is either oral or written, as opposed to being implied from the conduct of the parties (see implied contract).

express warranty A promise, in addition to an underlying sales agreement, that goes beyond the terms of the sales agreement and under which the promisor assures the description, performance, or quality of the goods.

expropriation The taking of a privately-owned business or privately-owned goods by a government for a public purpose and with just compensation.

ex rel (ex relatione) On the relation or information.

externalities Effects, either good or bad, on parties not directly involved in the production or use of a product. Pollution is an example of a bad effect, or negative externality.

failing firm defense In antitrust law, a general rule that firms may be allowed to merge that would not be allowed to do so except for the fact that one of the firms is in danger of going out of business anyway.

failure to warn In products liability cases, where a producer is found liable in tort for not warning consumers of dangers the producer knew existed or should have known to exist.

fair trade laws State statute permitting manufacturers or distributors of name brand products to fix minimum retail resale prices. Fair trade laws are no longer valid.

false imprisonment The intentional detention or restraint of an individual by another.

featherbedding An employee practice, usually under a union rule, in which the number of employees used, or the amount of time taken, to perform a particular job is unnecessarily high. The practice stems from a desire on the part of the employees to insure job security as technology improves.

federal question A question in a case in which one of the parties, usually the plaintiff, is asserting a right based on a federal law.

fellow-servant rule A rule that precludes an injured employee from recovering from his employer when an injury resulted from the negligent conduct of a fellow employee.

felony A serious class of crime (such as rape, murder, or robbery) that may be punishable by death or imprisonment in excess of one year.

fiduciary A person having a duty, generally created by his own undertaking, to act in good faith primarily for the benefit of another in matters related to that undertaking. A fiduciary duty is the highest standard of duty implied by law.

firm offer Under the Uniform Commercial Code, a signed writing by a merchant promising to keep an offer open. In contrast to an option, a firm offer does not require consideration to make the offer irrevocable.

foreign exchange market Institution through which foreign currencies are bought and sold.

foreign exchange rate The price of a particular country's currency stated in terms of the currency of another.

foreseeable dangers In tort law, the duty to have a reasonable anticipation that injury is likely to result from certain acts or from a failure to act to protect others.

forgery The false making or the material altering of a document with the intent to defraud.

franchise With respect to business, a contract between a parent company (franchisor) and an operating company (franchisee) to allow the operating company to run a business with the brand name of the parent company, so long as the terms of the contract concerning methods of operation is followed.

fraud A misrepresentation of an important fact by a person intending to mislead another person interested in some transaction that leads that person to execute the deal and then suffer a loss.

free-market economy An economy in which the decisions of individuals and businesses, as distinct from the government, exert the major influence over the allocation of resources.

free trade A situation where all commodities can be freely imported and exported without special taxes or restrictions being levied.

free trade zone Areas within the United States (or other countries), but outside the customs zone, where foreign merchandise may be brought without formal customs entry and payment of duty for virtually any legal purpose including storage, grading, sampling, manufacturing, cleaning, or packaging. Duties are paid when the products enter the U.S. market.

fringe benefits Medical, hospital, accident, and life insurance; retirement benefits; profit sharing; bonus plans; leave; and other terms and conditions of employment other than wage or salary compensation.

full warranty Defined by the Magnuson-Moss Warranty Act to provide an unlimited warranty for repairs or product replacement for problems that arise with a product within the warranty period.

garnishment A legal process under which a creditor appropriates the debtor's wages, or property in the hands of a third party.

general jurisdiction A power of a court to hear all controversies that may be brought before it.

general partner A partner in a limited partnership or any partner in a general partnership who accepts, or has imposed by law, personal liability for all debts of the partnership.

general verdict Verdict whereby the jury finds either for the plaintiff or the defendant in general terms.

geographic market In antitrust law, the geographic area within the country in which a business is able to exercise market power, or the effects of the business' market power are felt.

golden parachute Severance agreement for which the management of a corporation negotiates in return for the withdrawal of its opposition to a tender offer.

good faith Under the Uniform Commercial Code, "honesty in fact in the conduct or transaction incurred."

government All public officials, agencies, and other organizations under the control of state, local, and federal government.

gratuitous agent An agent who volunteers services without an agreement or expectation of compensation, but a voluntary consent that creates the normal rights and liabilities for parties to the agency relationship.

greenmail A coercive procedure under which an individual or organization who has purchased a large percentage of a corporation's stock pressures management of the corporation to buy back the stock at a premium to protect against the individual or organization using the stock in a hostile takeover attempt.

guardian An individual appointed to act on behalf of another lacking ability to perform legally valid acts, to acquire legal rights, or incur legal liabilities.

hazardous pollutant *See* toxic pollutant.

hearsay Evidence not derived from the personal knowledge of the witness, but from the mere recital of what the witness has heard others say. Hearsay evidence is allowed only in special cases.

hispanic A person of Mexican, Puerto Rican, Cuban, South American, or other Spanish culture or origin, regardless of race.

horizontal business arrangement An explicit or implicit deal among firms operating at the same level of business in the same market.

horizontal merger A merger between two companies that compete in the same product market.

horizontal price fixing Price fixing among competitors; price fixing among businesses on the same level the effect of which is to eliminate competition based on price.

horizontal restraint of trade A restraint of trade involving businesses at the same level of operation. A group of rival firms that come together by contract or some other form of agreement in an attempt to restrain trade by restricting output and raising prices is called a **cartel.**

hot cargo agreement An agreement, express or implied between an employer and a union whereby the employer agrees to cease or refrain from handling, using, selling, transporting or otherwise dealing in any of the products of any other employer the union has labeled as unfair or "hot."

Howey test The rule established by the Supreme Court to determine what is a security under the federal securities law: an investment of money, in a common enterprise, with the expectation that profits will be generated by the efforts of others.

hung jury A jury so divided in opinion that they cannot agree upon a verdict.

identification Under the Uniform Commercial Code, the process of specifying the actual goods that are covered by a contract.

implied authority In agency law, when the right of an agent to act on behalf of a principal is inferred from past actions or from the current position of the agent.

implied contract A contract formed on the basis of the conduct of the parties.

implied warranty A promise or guarantee the court holds to exist that accompanies a good when it is sold even though it was not written or expressed directly.

import A product manufactured in a foreign country, and then shipped to and sold in this country.

impossibility of performance Doctrine used to discharge the obligations of the parties to a contract when an event—such a law being passed that makes the contract illegal or the subject matter of the contract is destroyed (called *objective impossibility*)—makes performance "impossible" for one or both of the parties.

indictment A formal written charge or accusation issued by a grand jury stating that the named individual has committed a crime.

infringement In patent, copyright, and trademark law, the unauthorized use or imitation of another's recognized right to the matter involved.

injunction An order issued by a court that restrains a person or business from doing some act or orders the person to do something.

in personam jurisdiction The power the court has over the person(s) involved in the action.

in rem jurisdiction Refers to an action taken by the court against the property of the defendant.

insider An officer or other person who has information not yet available to the general public concerning the future profits or losses of a corporation.

insider trading The buying or selling of securities of a particular firm by individuals who have information about the firm not yet available to the general public and who have the expectation of making a profit through those transactions.

insolvency The financial state of an individual when his or her debts and liabilities exceed the value of his or her assets.

intellectual property Property recognized at law that arises from creative mental processes, such as inventions and works of art.

intentional tort A wrong committed upon the person or property of another where the actor is expressly or impliedly judged to have intended to commit the injury.

interbrand competition Competition among the various brands of a particular product.

international law Those laws governing the legal relations between nations.

international rules Statements issued by administrative agencies that explain how the agency understands its statutory authority to operate; these may be advisory or binding.

interrogatories In the discovery process, a set of written questions for a witness or a party for which written answers are prepared with the assistance of counsel and signed under oath.

interstate commerce The carrying on of commercial activity between locations in at least two different states.

intraband competition competition among retailers in the sales of a particular brand of product.

invasion of privacy In tort, the encroachment on the right of a person to their solitude, the appropriation of a person's reputation for commercial purposes, or the public disclosure of facts that the person had a legal right to keep private.

investigatory hearing In administrative law, when an agency uses rulemaking authority granted by Congress to gather information, on the public record, needed to determine the desirability of proposed rules.

investment advisers Under securities law, a "person who, for compensation, engages in the business of advising others . . . as to the advisability of investing in, purchasing or selling securities. . . ." This includes securities brokers and dealers.

investment company Any corporation whose business purpose is to own and hold the stock of other corporations.

involuntary bankruptcy A bankruptcy proceeding against an insolvent debtor which is initiated by his or her creditors.

jeopardy An individual is said to be in jeopardy when he or she is officially charged with a crime before a court of law. The constitutional doctrine of *double jeopardy* prohibits an individual from being prosecuted twice in the same tribunal for the same offense.

joint and several liability Liability that an individual or business either shares with other tortfeasors or bears individually without the others.

joint liability Liability that is owed to a third party by two or more other parties together.

joint venture The participation of two companies jointly in a third enterprise. Generally, both companies contribute assets and share risks.

judgment The official decision of a court of law upon the rights and claims of the parties to an action litigated in and submitted to the court for its determination.

judgment notwithstanding the verdict Judgment entered into by the court for a party after there has been a jury verdict for the other party.

judicial review Authority of a court to reexamine a dispute considered and decided previously by a lower court or by an administrative agency.

jurisdiction The right of a court or other body to hear a case and render a judgment.

jurisdiction over the person Power of the court to lawfully bind a party involved in a dispute before it.

jurisdiction over the subject Power of a court to validly affect the thing or issue in dispute.

jurisprudence The science or philosophy of law.

just compensation clause The portion of the Fifth Amendment that "nor shall private property be taken for public use, without just compensation." The requirement that when the government uses its power to force a private party to give up a property interest fair market value should be paid.

Kefauver amendment The portion of the Food, Drug and Cosmetic Act that requires the Food and Drug Administration to approve drugs only after their safety and effectiveness have been established.

laissez faire Literally "let do;" a policy implying the absence of government intervention in a market economy.

law Enforceable rules of social conduct set forth by that society's government to be followed by the citizens of the society.

law merchant In commercial law, the rules devised by merchants in Europe over several centuries to govern their trade; many of these rules were formally adopted into law.

leading question A question by an attorney in a trial that effectively instructs the witness how to answer or provides the desired answer.

legal capacity The right to be able to enter into legal matters that may be restricted by age, mental ability, or other requirements established at common law or by statute.

legal cause *See* proximate cause.

legal ethics Practice and customs among members of the legal profession, involving their moral and professional duties toward one another, clients, and the courts.

legislative history The history of a legislative enactment consisting of the legislative committee reports and transcripts of committee hearings debates on the legislative floor. Legislative history is often used by a court in interpreting the terms and provisions of an enactment.

legislative veto The act by Congress or a state legislature of giving itself or some part of the legislature the power to kill or modify regulations established by a regulatory agency.

letter of credit A written document in which the party issuing the document—usually a bank—promises to pay third parties in accordance with the terms of the document.

liability A general legal term referring to possible or actual responsibility; one is bound by law or equity to be accountable for some act; in product liability, it is in reference to the obligation to pay for damages for which the manufacturer has been held responsible.

libel A defamation that is in the form of a printing, a writing, pictures, or a broadcast on radio or television.

limited liability In corporation law, a concept whereby the shareholders of a corporation are not liable for the debts of the corporation beyond the amount of money they have invested in the corporation.

limited or special jurisdiction Power of a court to hear a particular cause which can be exercised only under the limitations and circumstances prescribed by statute.

limited partner A partner in a limited partnership whose liability for partnership debts is limited to the amount of his or her contribution to the partnership.

limited partnership Business organization consisting of one or more general partners who manage and contribute assets to the business and who are liable to the extent of their personal assets for the debts of the business, and one or more limited partners who contribute assets only and are liable only up to the amount of that contribution.

limited warranty Under the Magnuson-Moss Warranty Act, any product sold with less than a full warranty has what is defined as a limited warranty, the terms of which must be explained in writing.

liquidated damages Those amounts specified in the contract to be paid in the event of a breach by either party. They represent a reasonable estimation by the parties of the damages that will occur in the event of breach.

liquidated debt A debt that is for a known or determinable amount of money and that can not be disputed by either the debtor or the creditor.

liquidation The sale of the assets of a business (or an individual), the proceeds from which are distributed to the creditors of the business (or individual) with any remaining balance to the business (or individual).

lockout Refusal by an employer to provide work for employees.

long-arm statute State statute permitting courts to obtain personal jurisdiction over non-resident individuals and corporations as long as the requirements of the statute are met.

major emitting facility Under the Clean Air Act, a stationary source such as a factory that emits or has the potential to emit 100 tons of any pollutant per year.

mandatory subjects of bargaining Under the National Labor Relations Act, all terms and conditions of employment are subjects that must be discussed by employers and unions or there will be an unfair labor practice.

manifest system In environmental and occupational safety law, the requirement that certain chemicals have documentation concerning their production, distribution, and disposal to ensure proper handling and disposal of toxic substances.

margin requirement The fraction of a price of a stock that must be paid in cash, while putting up the stock as security against a loan for the balance.

market (1) An institution through which buyers and sellers negotiate the exchange of a well-defined product; (2) from the viewpoint of consumers, the companies from which they can buy a well-defined product; (3) from the viewpoint of a company, the buyers to whom it can sell a well-defined product.

market-clearing prices The equilibrium price in a perfectly competitive market. Prices at which the quantity demanded is equal to the quantity supplied, so that there are neither unsatisfied buyers nor unsatisfied sellers.

market failure Failure of the unregulated market system to achieve socially optimal results. The generally recognized sources of market failure include monopolies and externalities. It is often asserted as a justification for government intervention in the marketplace through regulation.

market share liability In the case of a latent injury, in the event the plaintiff is unable to determine which manufacturer of a product within the industry caused his or her injury, the court will assign liability to all industry members on the basis of their shares of the product market. Market share liability has not gained wide acceptance.

maturity The due date of a financial instrument.

mediation Act of a third party who intervenes between parties to a dispute with the intent to reconcile them or persuade them to settle their dispute.

mens rea Latin, the state of mind of the actor.

merchantability In commercial law, the notion that goods are "reasonably fit for the ordinary purposes for which such goods are used."

merger A contractual process through which one corporation acquires the assets and liabilities of another corporation. The acquiring, or surviving, corporation retains its original identity.

merit regulations State securities law provision that in some states allows the securities commissioners to decide if a proposed security offering is "too risky" to be allowed to be sold to the public in that state.

minorities All persons classified as black (not of Hispanic origin), Hispanic, Asian, Pacific Islander, American Indian, or Alaskan native.

misdemeanors A lessor crime, that is neither a felony nor treason, punishable by a fine and/or imprisonment in other than state or federal penitentiaries.

misstatements In securities law, liability may be imposed on those responsible for issuing information about new or existing securities who produce misleading information to investors that would reasonably affect their investment decisions.

mistrial A trial that cannot stand in law because the court lacks jurisdiction, due to juror misconduct, or because of disregard for some other procedural requirement.

mitigation of damages Doctrine that imposes a duty upon the injured party to exercise reasonable diligence in attempting to minimize damages after being injured.

mobil source Under the Clean Air Act, a mobil source of pollution refers to moving polluters such as automobiles, trucks, and airplanes.

monopoly A market structure in which the output of an industry is controlled by a single seller or a group of sellers making joint decisions regarding production and price.

moral agent A person capable of deciding and carrying out actions on their own and accepting responsibility for the actions.

moral principles Rules that categorize different actions as right or wrong.

morals Generally accepted standards of right and wrong in a society.

motion The formal mode in which an attorney submits a proposed measure for the consideration and action of the court.

motion to dismiss A motion requesting that a complaint be dismissed because it does not state a claim for which the law provides a remedy, or is in some other way legally insufficient.

national ambient air quality standards Federal standards under the Clean Air Act that set the maximum concentration levels in the ambient air for several air pollutants. There are two types: a primary standard and a secondary standard. The primary standard for each air pollutant is calculated to protect the public health. The secondary standard is calculated to protect the public welfare.

national uniform effluent standards Federal standards under the Clean Water Act that set the water pollution effluent standards for every industry that discharges liquid wastes into the nation's waterways.

natural monopoly An industry characterized by economies of scale sufficiently large that one business can supply the entire market most efficiently.

necessary and proper clause In general, that part of the U.S. Constitution that gives Congress the authority to use various powers to execute its functions under the Constitution.

negligence The failure to do something that a reasonable person, guided by the ordinary considerations that regulate human affairs, would do, or the doing of something that a reasonable person would not do.

negotiation The deliberation over the terms and conditions of a proposed agreement or business transaction, or over the terms and conditions to an agreement resolving a dispute arising from a business transaction.

nominal damages A damage award whereby the courts recognize that plaintiff has suffered a technical breach of duty, but has not suffered any actual financial loss or injury as a result. Plaintiff's recovery for such technical breaches is often as little as a dollar.

nonattainment area An area under the Clean Air Act in which the air quality for a given pollutant fails to meet the national ambient air quality standards.

nonpoint sources Under the Clean Water Act, nonpoint sources of water pollution are sources of pollution that are diverse and difficult to identify. Examples are urban and agricultural runoff from rainstorms.

novation An agreement between the parties to a contract to discharge one of the parties and create a new contract with another party responsible for the discharged party's performance.

nuisance An unreasonable and substantial interference with the use and enjoyment of another's land (*private nuisance*); an unreasonable or substantial interference with a right held in common by members of the general public (*public nuisance*).

occupational licensure Requirements usually at the state level that for one to be allowed to practice a certain profession one must meet certain educational or experience guidelines, pass an entry examination, and often must show evidence of continuing education accomplishments.

offer A proposal to do or refrain from doing some specified thing by an individual called the offeror to another called the offeree. The proposal creates in the offeree a legal power to bind the offeror to the terms of the proposal by accepting the offer.

offeree The party to whom an offer is made.

offeror The party making an offer to another party to enter into a contract.

opening argument Oral presentation made to the jury by the attorneys before the parties have presented their cases.

original jurisdiction Power of a court to take cognizance of a lawsuit at its beginning, try it, and pass judgment upon the law and facts.

out-of-court settlement An agreement by the parties in a case to resolve the matter before a determination by the court.

over-the-counter market A stock market for securities generally not sold in large daily volumes so that they are not listed on a major stock exchange, such as the New York Stock Exchange; a securities market made by stockbrokers calling information to a central place about desires to buy or sell certain amounts of a stock.

parol In French and Latin, spoken or oral.

parol evidence rule A substantive rule of contract law that prohibits the introduction into a lawsuit of oral evidence that is contradictory to the terms of a written contract intended to be the final and complete expression of the agreement between the parties.

partnership A business owned by two or more persons that is not organized as a corporation.

par value stock Stock that has been assigned a specific value by the corporation's board of directors.

patent A grant from the government conveying and securing for an inventor the exclusive right to make, use, and sell an invention for seventeen years.

per curiam opinion Latin, by the court. A Per Curiam opinion expresses the view of the court as a whole in contrast to an opinion authored by an individual member of the court.

per se In itself or taken alone; as in per se rule in antitrust, whereby the facts alone are enough to lead to conviction of the defendants.

perfect tender rule At common law, seller's offer of delivery must conform to every detail in terms of contract with buyer; under the Uniform Commercial Code, parties may agree to limit the operation of this rule or the seller may cure a defective tender if the time for performance has not ended, the seller notifies the buyer quickly of intent to cure defect, or the seller repairs or replaces defective goods within performance time limits.

performance In contract law, the fulfilling of obligations or promises according to the terms agreed to or specified by parties to a contract. The complete performance of those obligations or promises by both parties discharges the contract.

periodic disclosure In securities law, requirements that issuers of most publicly held securities must file monthly, quarterly, and annual reports with the Securities and Exchange Commission.

personal property Physical, moveable property other than real estate.

personal service In the pleadings stage, personal service of the complaint is made by delivering it physically to the defendant.

piercing the corporate veil A court's act of ignoring the legal existence of a corporation and then holding the corporation's officers personally liable for their wrongful acts done in the name of the corporation.

plaintiff The party who initiates the lawsuit.

pleadings Statements of the plaintiff and the defendant that detail their facts, allegations, and defenses, thereby creating the issues of the lawsuit.

point source Under the clean Water Act, a point source is any definitive place of discharge of a water pollutant such as pipes, ditches, or channels.

political speech In constitutional law, speech that concerns political, as opposed to commercial, matters given a high level of protection by the First Amendment.

pollution The release of substances into the air, water, or land that cause physical change.

power of attorney A document authorizing another person to act as one's agent or attorney with respect to the matters stated in the document.

precedent A decision in a case that is used to guide decisions in later cases with similar fact situations.

preferred stock Class of stock that has priority over common stock both as to payment of dividends and to distribution of the corporation's assets upon dissolutionment.

preponderance of the evidence In civil trials, the burden of persuasion to win a verdict requires that the plaintiff prove its claims by having the majority or bulk of the evidence on its side.

prevention of significant deterioration area An area as defined under the Clean Air Act whereby the air quality is better than required by the national ambient air standards.

price discrimination In antitrust law, charging different prices to different customers for the same product without a cost justification for the price difference.

prima facie Latin, at first sight. Something presumed to be true until disproved by contrary evidence.

principal In an agency relationship, an individual who by explicit or implicit agreement authorizes an agent to act on his or her behalf and perform such acts that will become binding on the principal.

private law An artificial classification of law, but generally one denoting laws that affect relationships between people.

private nuisance In tort law, when an activity reduces the right of one person, or a small number of persons, to enjoy his or her property without unreasonable interference.

private property right An individual economic interest supported by the law.

privilege In tort law, the ability to act contrary to another individual's legal right without that individual having legal redress for the consequences of that act; usually raised by the actor as a defense.

privity A legal relationship between parties, such as the relationship between parties to a contract.

privity of contract The immediate relationship that exists between the parties to a contract.

probable cause Reasonable ground to believe the existence of facts warranting the undertaking of certain actions such as the arrest or search of an individual.

procedural law The rules of the court system that deal with the manner in which to initiate and go forward with an action. Court systems generally have rules regarding pleadings, process, evidence, and practice.

product market In antitrust law, the product market includes all other products that can be reasonably substituted by consumers for the product of the business under investigation. The determination of the product market is important in the assessment of the market power of the business.

program trading The trading of stock on the large exchanges through the use of computers programmed to trade at prespecified prices and other conditions.

promise A statement or declaration that binds the individual making it (the promisor) to do or refrain from doing a particular act or thing. The individual to whom the declaration is made (the promisee) has a right to demand or expect the performance of the act or thing.

promissee Individual to whom a promise is made.

promisor Individual who makes a promise.

promotion Any personnel action resulting in movement to a position affording higher pay or greater rank and provides for greater skill or responsibility or the opportunity to attain such.

promulgation An administrative order that is given to cause an agency law or regulation to become known and obligatory.

promissory estoppel Doctrine under which promises can be enforced in the absence of consideration in the event a promise is made which the promisor should reasonably expect to induce action or forbearance on the part of the promisee and, in fact, does cause such action or forbearance to the detriment of the promisee.

proprietorship A business owned by a person that is not organized as a corporation.

prospectus Under securities law, a pamphlet required to be produced for distribution to prospective buyers of securities that contains information about the background of the security being offered.

protected class Under Title VII of the Civil Rights Act of 1964, one of the groups the law sought to protect, including groups based on race, sex, national origin, and religion.

proximate cause In tort law, the act of a defendant that was the reason or main reason for the occurrence of injuries suffered by the plaintiff; without the cause, the injury or damage in question would not have existed.

proxy Giving another person the right to vote one's vote on one's behalf; in stock votes when a person gives another the right to vote in a certain manner, such as for a certain list of candidates for board of directors.

public law An artificial classification of law, but generally one denoting laws that affect relationships between people and their governments.

public nuisance In tort law, when an activity reduces the right of the public in general to enjoy property without unreasonable interference.

punitive damages Compensation awarded to a plaintiff beyond actual damages (awarded to punish the defendant for doing a particularly offensive act).

quasi in rem jurisdiction Proceeding brought against the defendant personally, but where the defendant's interest in property serves as the basis of the court's jurisdiction.

quasi-contract A contract imposed by law, in the absence of such an agreement, to prevent unjust enrichment. A contract implied in law.

ratification In contract law, the act of accepting the responsibilities for a previous act that without the ratification would not constitute an enforceable contractual obligation. The act of ratification causes the obligation to be binding as if it were valid and enforceable in the first place.

real property Land, the products of land (such as timber), and property that cannot be moved (such as houses).

reasonable accommodation In employment discrimination law, the requirement that employers take steps that are not extremely costly to make the workplace open to persons with disabilities.

rebuttal During the trial stage where evidence is given by one party to refute evidence introduced by the other party.

recission In contract law, the cancellation of a contract without performance by the agreement of the parties; as a remedy, the cancellation of a contract by a court, the effect being as if the contract had never been made.

red herring See also prospectus. In securities law, a prospectus that has not yet been approved by the Securities Exchange Commission or state securities commissioners. It has a red border on its front to signal to interested parties that it is not yet approved for final distribution to encourage securities sales; used as an advertising device.

refuse matter Materials such as garbage or sewage that are discarded.

registration statements In securities law, the financial information that must be filed with the Securities and Exchange Commission for review prior to the sale of securities to the public.

Regulation Z Rule issued by the Federal Reserve Board to implement the Truth-in-Lending Act that requires systematic disclosure of the costs associated with credit transactions.

rejoinder During the trial stage where the defendant answers the plaintiff's rebuttal.

remand The act of an appellate court in sending a case back to trial court ordering it to take action according to its decision. The order usually requires an entire new trial or limited new hearings on specified subject matter.

remedy The legal means by which a right is enforced or the violation of a right is prevented or compensated.

removal jurisdiction The power to remove a case from a court system to another.

repatriation The process a company follows in transfering assets or earnings from a host nation to another nation.

reply During the pleading stage, plaintiff's response to the defendant's answer to the plaintiff's original complaint.

repudiation A rejection, disclaimer, or renunciation of a contract before performance is due that does not operate as an anticipatory breach unless the promisee elects to treat the rejection as a breach and brings a suit for damages.

res Latin, a thing or things.

res ispa loquitor Latin for "the thing speaks for itself;" given the facts presented, it is clear that the defendant's actions were negligent and the proximate cause of the injury incurred.

res judicata A rule that prohibits the same dispute between two parties from being relitigated by a court after final judgment has been entered and all appeals exhausted.

resale price maintenance When the manufacturer or wholesaler of a good sets the price of the good at the next level, such as at the retail level; if the price set is not followed by the retailer, the manufacturer or wholesaler will no longer sell the good to the retailer.

respondeat superior Doctrine of vicarious liability under which an employer is held liable for the wrongful acts of his employees committed within the scope of their employment.

respondent The party, plaintiff, or defendant that won in a lower court but must now respond to the appeal of the case by the losing party, the appellant.

restraint of trade Any contract, agreement, or combination that eliminates or restricts competition.

reverse A decision by an appellate court that overturns or vacates the judgment of a lower court.

revocation The recall of some power, authority, or thing granted; in contract law, the withdrawal by the offeree of an offer that had been valid until withdrawn.

right-to-work law State laws that limit or prohibit labor agreements from making union membership a condition of retaining or receiving employment.

rule of reason In antitrust law, as opposed to the per se rule, it means that the court will consider all the facts and decide whether what was done was reasonable and did not harm competition in net.

rulemaking In administrative law, the procedures that agencies must follow in the issuance of rules to interpret or enforce the statutory authority they were granted by Congress.

sales contract Under the Uniform Commercial Code, "the passing of title from the seller to the buyer for a price."

sanction A penalty used to provide incentives for obedience with the law or with rules and regulations.

satisfaction The performance of a substituted obligation in return for the discharge of the original obligation.

scienter Latin for "knowingly;" usually meaning that the defendant knew that the act in question was illegal.

secondary boycott A union's refusal to handle, purchase, or work for a secondary company with whom the union has no dispute with the intent of forcing that company to stop doing business with the union's employer with whom the union has a dispute.

secured creditors A person who has loaned money to another and has a legally recognized interest in the property of the debtor until fulfillment of the terms of the debt agreement.

securities Debt or equity instruments that, in securities law, are evidence of a contribution of money by a group of investors into a common enterprise that will be operated for profit by professional managers.

securities fraud In securities law, the statutory basis for charging anyone involved in the issuance or trading of securities with fraud, which is usually due to misleading information or failure to state material information that causes investors to suffer losses.

self-incrimination The rule that a witness is not bound to give testimony that would incriminate the person with respect to a criminal act.

service of process In the pleadings stage, the delivery of the complaint to the defendant either to him personally or, in most jurisdictions, by leaving it with a responsible person at his place of residence.

shareholder The owner of one or more shares of stock in a corporation.

shelf registration A rule by the Securities and Exchange Commission that allows a company to file a single registration statement for the future sale of securities. This type of registration allows the company to react quickly to favorable market conditions.

short-swing profits Profits made by an insider on the purchase and sale of stock of a corporation within a six-month period.

sight draft A draft payable upon proper presentment.

slander An oral defamation of one's reputation or good name.

sole proprietorship *See* proprietorship.

sovereign A person, body, or nation in which independent and supreme authority is vested.

sovereign immunity Doctrine under which a nonsovereign party is precluded from engaging a legal action against a sovereign party, unless the sovereign gives its consent.

special damages In contract law, damages not contemplated by the parties at the time of the making of the contract. To be recoverable, they must flow directly and immediately from the breach of contract, and must be reasonably foreseeable.

specific performance An equitable remedy, whereby the court orders a party to a contract to perform his duties under the contract. This remedy is usually granted when money damages are inadequate as a remedy and the subject matter of the contract is unique.

standing The right to sue.

stare decisis The use of precedent by courts; the use of prior decisions to guide decision making in cases before the courts.

stationary sources Under the Clean Air Act, a nonmoving source of pollution such as a factory or an electrical power plant.

statute Law enacted by a legislative body.

Statute of Frauds A statutory requirement that certain types of contracts be in writing to be enforceable.

statute of limitations A statute setting maximum time periods, from the occurrence of an event, during which certain actions can be brought or rights enforced. If an action is not filed before the expiration of that time period, the statute bars the use of the courts for recovery.

statutory law Laws enacted by a legislative body.

stock Equity securities that evidence an ownership interest in a corporation.

strict liability The case whereby responsibility for damages is assigned regardless of the existence of negligence; in tort law, any good sold that has a defect that causes injury leads to the imposition of responsibility.

strike A work stoppage by employees for the purpose of coercing their employer to give in to their demands.

subsidy A government monetary grant to a favored industry.

substantial performance A doctrine which recognizes that an individual who performs his contract, but with a slight deviation from the contract's terms, is entitled to the contract price less any damages caused by that slight deviation.

substantive law Law that defines the rights and duties of individuals with regard to each other, as opposed to procedural law, which is law that defines the manner in which those rights and duties may be enforced.

substantive rules Administrative rulings based on statutory authority granted an agency by Congress; the rules have the same legal force as statutes passed by Congress.

substituted service Form of service other than personal service, such as service by mail or by publication in a newspaper.

summary judgment A judgment entered by a trial court as a matter of law when no genuine issue of law is found to exist.

summons Process through which a court notifies and compels a defendant to a lawsuit to appear and answer a complaint.

sunset laws A statute that requires periodic review of the rationale for the continued existence of an administrative agency or other governmental function; the legislature must take positive steps to allow the functions to continue in existence by a certain date or it ceases to exist.

superfund In environmental law, the Comprehensive Environmental Response, Compensation, and Liability Act (CERCLA) is commonly called Superfund; which concerns requirements about when hazardous waste sites must be cleaned up and who is liable for the costs of the clean up.

syndicates Business association made of persons or business firms for the purpose of carrying out some particular business transaction in which the members are mutually interested.

takings clause *See* just compensation clause.

tariff Tax imposed on imported goods by the government for the purpose of encouraging or maintaining domestic industry, or raising revenues.

tax incentive Government taxing policy intended to encourage a particular activity.

tender offer An offer to buy a stock at a certain price open to all current stockholders; offer may be contingent upon receiving a certain amount of stock before any buys will be completed or may be an open offer; a method used to obtain enough stock to control a corporation.

termination In contract law, the ending of an offer or contract, usually without liability.

territorial allocation In antitrust law, the boundaries specified by contract or other agreement in which a wholesaler or retailer may sell a product.

territorial jurisdiction Territory over which a court has jurisdiction. The authority of any court is generally limited to its territorial boundaries. *See* long-arm statute.

tie-in sale In antitrust law, the requirement that if one product or service is purchased then another product or service must also be bought even if it is not desired by the customer.

title Generally, the legal right of ownership; under the Uniform Commercial Code title is determined by rules regarding identification of goods, the risk of loss of goods, and insurable interest in the goods.

tort An injury or wrong committed with or without force to another person or his or her property; a civil wrong that is a breach of a legal duty owed by the person who commits the tort to the victim of the tort.

tortfeasor An individual or business that commits a tort.

toxic pollutants A pollutant that may cause an increase in mortality or very serious illness.

trademark A distinctive design, logo, mark, or word that a business can register with a government agency for its exclusive use in identifying its product or itself in the marketplace.

trade name A word or symbol that has become sufficiently associated with a product over a period of time that it has lost its primary meaning and acquired a secondary meaning; once so established, the company has a right to bring a legal action against those who infringe on the protection provided the trade name.

trade regulation rules Administrative rulings by the Federal Trade Commission or other agencies that hold certain practices to be illegal or create standards that must be met by sellers of certain products or services.

trade secret Valuable, confidential data, usually in the form of formulas, processes, and other forms of information not patented, or not patentable that are developed and owned by a business.

treason A breach of allegiance to one's government, usually committed through levying war against such government or by giving aid or comfort to the enemy.

treble damages A money damage award allowable under some statutes that is determined by multiplying the jury's actual damage award by three.

trespass An unauthorized intrusion on the property rights of another.

trial A judicial examination of a dispute between two or more parties under the appropriate laws by a court or other appropriate tribunal that has jurisdiction.

trial de novo A new trial or retrial at an appellate court in which the entire case is examined as though no trial had been undertaken previously.

trustee A person who has legal title in some property (such as the property of a bankrupt business) held in trust for the benefit of another person (the beneficiary).

tying arrangements Any agreement between a buyer and a seller in which the buyer of a specific product is obligated to purchase another good.

unconscionable contract A contract, or a clause in a contract, that is so grossly unfair to one of the parties because of stronger bargaining powers of the other party; usually held to be void as against public policy.

underutilization employment of members of a racial, ethnic, or sex group in a job or job group at a rate below their availability.

underwriter A professional firm that handles the marketing of a security to the public; it either buys all of a new security offering and then sells it to the public, or takes a commission on the securities it actually sells.

undue influence The misuse of one's position of confidence or relationship with another individual by overcoming that person's free will, thereby taking advantage of that person to affect decisions.

unenforceable contract A contract that was once valid but, because of a subsequent illegality, will not be enforced by the courts.

unfairness In consumer protection law, a charge under Section 5 of the Federal Trade Commission Act that a business practice causes harm to consumers that they cannot reasonably avoid.

Uniform Commercial Code A statute passed in similar form by all states that sets many rules of sales agreements and negotiable debt instruments.

unilateral contract An offer or promise of the offeror that is binding only after the completed performance by the offeree. The offeree's completed performance serves as both the acceptance of the offer and the full performance of the contract.

union An association of workers that is authorized to represent them in bargaining with their employers.

union certification In labor law, when a majority of the workers at a workplace vote to have a union be their collective bargaining agent, the National Labor Relations Board certifies the legal standing of the union for that purpose.

union shop A place of employment where one must be a union member before obtaining employment or must become a union member after obtaining employment.

unknown hazard In products liability, a claim that tort liability should be assigned to a producer for injuries suffered by a consumer due to a defect or hazard in a product that was not known by the producer at the time the product was made.

unliquidated debt A disputed debt; a debt that has not been reduced to some specific amount.

upset A situation wherein a business's normal pollution control functions are disturbed by malfunctions or accidents causing environmental pollution beyond the control of the business.

usury laws Statutes that prohibit finance charges (interest and other forms of compensation for loaning money) above a certain level for debt.

valid contract A contract in which all of the elements of a contract are present and, therefore, is enforceable at law by the parties.

venue The geographic area in which an action is tried and from which the jury is selected.

vertical merger A merger of two business firms, one of which is the supplier of the other.

vertical price-fixing An agreement between a supplier and a distributor, relating to the price at which the distributor will resell the supplier's product.

vesting Under the Employee Retirement Income Security Act, the requirement that pension benefits become the property of workers after a specific number of years of service to an employer.

vicarious liability Liability that arises from the actions of another person who is in a legal relationship with the party upon whom liability is being imposed.

void contract A contract that does not exist at law; a contract having no legal force or binding effect.

voidable contract A contract that is valid, but which may be legally voided at the option of one of the parties.

voidable preference A preference given to one creditor over another by a bankrupt, usually manifested by a payment to that creditor just prior to the bankruptcy declaration, that may be set aside by the trustee in bankruptcy.

voir dire Literally, to "speak the truth." In the trial stage, preliminary examination of a juror in which the attorneys and the court attempt to determine bias, incompetency, and interest.

voluntary bankruptcy A bankruptcy proceeding that is initiated by the debtor.

waiver An express or implied relinquishment of a legal right.

warrant A judicial authorization for the performance of an act that would otherwise be illegal.

warranty An assurance or guaranty, either express in the form of a statement by a seller of goods, or implied by law, having reference to and ensuring the character, quality, or fitness of purpose of the goods.

warranty of title In general, the duty of a seller to provide good title or legal right of ownership of goods to the buyer; under the Uniform Commercial Code, specific warranty rights are provided when title to goods pass.

wetlands In environmental law, land covered by water at least a part of the year; exact coverage by various environmental statutes is still unresolved.

whistleblower An employee who alerts the proper authorities to the fact that his or her employer is undertaking an activity that is contrary to the law.

winding up Process of settling the accounts and liquidating the assets of a partnership or corporation for the purpose of dissolving the concern.

workers' compensation laws State statutes that provide for fixed awards to workers or their dependents in the event that the worker incurs an injury or an illness in the course of his or her employment. Under such compensation laws, the worker is freed from the responsibility of bringing a legal action and proving negligence on the part of the employer.

writ A mandatory precept issued by a court of justice.

writ of certiorari An order by an appellate court that is used by that court when it has discretion on whether or not to hear an appeal from a lower court. If the appeal is granted, the writ has the effect of ordering the lower court to certify the record and send it up to the higher court which then has the discretion to hear the appeal. If the writ is denied, the judgment of the lower court is allowed to stand.

writ of execution A writ to put into force the judgment of a court.

yellow-dog contract An agreement between an employer and an employee under which the employee agrees not to join a union and that discharge will occur if he or she later breaches the agreement by joining the union.

INDEX

Absolute privilege, 178
Acceptance
   buyer's duty of, 275
   of offer, 235–237
   in sales contract, 267
Accord, 239, 250
Accord and satisfaction, 239, 250
Account, agent's duty to, 299
Accredited investors, 509–510
Acid rain, 410
Act of state, doctrine of, 568
Actual authority, 300
Actual malice, 178
Adjudication, 150
Adjudicatory hearings, 152–153
Adjudicatory power, of
         administrative agencies, 150
Administrative agencies
   budget for, 161
   congressional restrictions on power
         of, 160–163
   creation of, 142–143
   definition of, 142
   direct observation by, 149
   in Japan, 156–157
   judicial review of decisions,
         157–160
   orders and opinion, 576–577
   process and procedures, 151
      formal, 152–157
      informal, 151–152
   purpose of, 143
   regulatory powers of, 145
      adjudicatory, 150
      enforcement of, 150–151
      investigative, 148–150
      legislative or rulemaking,
         145–148
   as source of law, 60
   subpoena power of, 150
Administrative law, 143
   and New Deal agencies,
         144–145
   and social reform, 145
Administrative Procedures Act (APA)
      (1946), 143–144
Ad valorem tariffs, 549

Adversary system of justice, 88–92
   appellate stage, 106
   discovery stage, 99–100
      depositions and interrogatories, 99
      impact on business, 100–101
      mental and physical
            examinations, 100
      orders for the production of
            documents, 99
      requests for admissions, 99–100
      sanctions for failing to respond
            to a discovery request, 100
   enforcement stage, 106
   pleadings stage, 95–97
      affirmative defenses, 98
      answer, 98
      counterclaim, 98
      motion to dismiss, 98
      reply, 98
      responses to the complaint and
            summons, 98
   pretrial stage, 101–102
   trial stage
      jury, 102
      Seventh Amendment, 102
      trial, 102–105
Advertising
   deceptive, 440–441
   and free speech, 127–128
   regulation of foreign, 442
Advertising substantiation program,
      440–441
Affirmative action programs, 373,
      383
   executive order 11246, 383
   as remedy, 384
   voluntary programs, 384–385
Affirmative defenses, 98
Age, BFOQ on the basis of, 386–387
Age Discrimination in Employment
      Act, 368, 385–386
Agency, law of, 514
Agency relationship
   agent's authority to act for the
         principal, 300
      actual authority, 300
      apparent authority, 300

agent's duties to the principal,
      298–299
creating an agency, 298
definition of, 297
liability for contracts and torts,
      300–301
   contract liability of disclosed and
         partially disclosed
         principals, 301
   liability for torts of the agent,
         301–303
principal's duties to an agent, 298
termination of an agency, 303–304
Agency shops, 338
Agent, 297
   authority to act for principal, 300
   duties to principal, 298–299
   liability for torts of, 301–303
   principal's duties to, 298
Agreement, 233–237. *See also*
      Contract(s)
   effect of illegal, 244
Airline Deregulation Act (1978),
      145
Airline industry, deregulation of, 21
Air pollution, 404
   legislation on, 405–408
Ally doctrine, 346
Alternate dispute resolution, 107–108
   advantages of, 110
   arbitration, 108, 343, 522–523, 567
   minitrials, 109
   negotiation, 109–110
American Arbitration Association,
      567
Americans with Disabilities Act
      (1990), 350, 368, 388, 609–611
Andean Common Market (ANCOM),
      549
Annual percentage rate, or APR,
      449
Answer, 98
Anticipatory breach, 247
Antidumping duty, 547
Antitrust legislation
   Clayton Act, 466, 595–599
   common law provisions, 464

635

court interpretation, 470
   horizontal restraints of trade,
      471–472
   per se rule, 470–471
   rule of reason, 471
   vertical restraints of trade,
      472–473
enforcement of, 468–469
exchanges of information, 479
   conspiracy to restrain
      information, 481
   purpose of price information
      considered, 479–481
exemptions, 467
Federal Trade Commission Act,
   466–467, 599
horizontal market divisions,
   481–482
horizontal price fixing, 477
   per se rule in price fixing, 477
   rule of reason in price-fixing
      cases, 477–479
international distributorships, 486
international enforcement of, 470
in Japan, 473
mergers, 473
   defenses, 476
   determining a firm's market
      power, 474–475
   Supreme Court's approach to,
      473–474
remedies available, 469
   incentives to sue, 469–470
Robinson-Patman Act, 491
   defenses to, 492
   price discrimination, 491
Sherman Act, 465, 595
vertical exclusionary practices, 486
   boycotts, 489–490
   exclusive dealing, 489
   tying arrangements, 487–489
vertical nonprice restraints, 484
   territorial restraints, 484–486
vertical price fixing, 482–483
   resale price maintenance, 483
   vertical maximum price fixing,
      483–484
Apparent authority, 300
Appellate jurisdiction, 67
   state courts of, 69
Appellate stage, 106
Apportionment of state tax burden,
   124
Arab Common Market, 549

Arbiter, 108
Arbitration
   and collective bargaining, 343
   court-annexed arbitration, 108
   of international disputes, 567
   of securities disputes, 522–523
Arms Export Control Act (1976), 555
Army Corps of Engineers, 416
Artificial person, corporation as, 74
Assault, 175
Association of Southeast Asian
   Nations (ASEAN), 549
Assumption of risk, 186, 212
Attainment areas, 405
Authority, of agent to act for
   principal, 300
Automobiles
   crashworthiness of, 203–204
   trade bans on, 551
   and used-car rule, 445

Bailment contract, 263
Bank mergers, antitrust exempt, 467
Battery, 175
Beech Nut Nutrition Company, case
   study in, 141–142
Best available control technology
   (BACT), 406
Best available technology (BAT), 414
Best conventional technology (BCT),
   414
Bilateral contract, 231
Biomet, legal environment at, 14
Biotechnology, 418
Blass, Bill, 463
Blue sky laws, 501
Board of directors of corporation,
   314–315
Boesky, Ivan, 519–520
Bona fide occupational qualification
   (BFOQ), 380, 386–387
Bona fide seniority or merit systems,
   379
Boycotts, 489–490
   and the per se rule, 490
   primary, 345
   secondary, 345–346
Breach, anticipatory, 247
Breach of contract, 246
Breast implants, 437
Briefs, 106
Bubble concept, 407–408
Budget, for administrative agencies, 161

Business. See also International
   business
   damage awards imposed on, 95
   as defendant, 90–92
   external environment in, 10–14
   impacts of discovery on, 100–101
   internal environment in, 8–9
   judgments against, 94–95
   legal environment within, 18
   location of, 17
   markets served by, 17
   size of, 16–17
      and interstate commerce, 119
   and tort law, 173
Business communications, and
   defamation, 191
Business debts, settlement of,
   239–240
Business dispute, 92
   complexity in resolving, 92–94
Business environment
   American, 5
   international, 537
Business judgment rule, 315, 514
Business litigation, growing
   significance of, 94
Business necessity, 378
Business organization, 16, 304
   characteristics of major forms of,
      317
   cooperatives, 322–323
   corporations, 311–312
      creation of, 312, 314
      as legal entity, 312
      management, 316
         relationship of the parties,
            314–316
      termination of, 316
   factors in the choice of, 316–317
      capital requirements, 320–321
      duration, 320
      liability, 318
      taxation considerations, 321
      transferability of ownership
         interests, 319–320
   foreign manufacturing of products,
      555
      contract manufacturing, 557
      exporting manufactured
         products, 555
      franchising agreements, 556–557
      joint venture, 556
      licensing agreement, 556
      wholly owned subsidiary, 556

general partnerships, 305–308
    definition of, 305
    formation, 306, 307–308
    relationship of the parties, 306
    termination, 306
joint stock companies, 322
joint ventures, 322
limited partnership, 309
    definition of, 309
    formation, 309, 310
    relationship of the parties, 309,
        311
    termination of, 311
sole proprietorships, 305
statistical overview, 304–305
syndicates, 323
Business relationship
    importance of, and litigation, 90–91
    interference with, 193
Business torts, 173, 190–191
    disparagement, 191
        business communications and
            defamation, 191
        interference with a business
            relationship, 193
        interference with contractual
            relations, 192–193
Buyer
    obligations of, under UCC,
        275–276
    rights and remedies under UCC,
        284–287

Capacity, 241
    definition of, 242
    of insane, 242–243
    of intoxicated persons, 242–243
    of minors, 241–242
Capitalistic economic system, 5
Capital requirements, and choice of
        business organization, 320–321
Caribbean Common Market
        (CARICOM), 549
Cartel, 472
Case law, 574–575
Causation, 184
Cause in fact, 184
Caveat emptor, 201
Central American Common Market
        (CACM), 549
Certificate of incorporation, 312–314
Certificate of limited partnership,
        309, 310

Chamberlain contractors, drug
        testing at, 331
Chlorofluorocarbons (CFCs), 424
Churning, 524
Civil Aeronautics Board (CAB), 144
Civil law, 62
Civil litigation, 65
    remedies in, 79–81
Civil procedure, rules of, 65
Civil Rights Act (1991), 381–382
Civil Rights Act (1964), 17
    coverage and enforcement of,
        370–371
    defenses under, 378–380
    discrimination and remedies,
        380–382
    protected classes under, 372–376
    theories of discrimination under,
        376–377
    Title VII, 368, 370, 605–608
Civil Rights Acts of 1866 and 1871,
        368
Civil rights movement, 369
Claiborne, Liz, 463
Clayton Act, 333, 466, 595–599
    antitrust exemptions in, 467
    enforcement of, 468
    and exclusive dealing, 489
    and tying arrangements, 487
Clean Air Act, 143, 150, 157–158
    enforcement of, 150–151
Clean Air Act (1970), 405
Clean Air Act (1977), 405–408
    bubble concept, 407–408
    clean air areas, 405–407
    dirty air areas, 407
Clean Air Act (1990), 409–411
    and acid rain, 410
    ambient air quality, 409
    enforcement of, 410–411
    mobile sources, 409–410
    toxic pollutants, 410
Clean Water Act (1972, 1977, 1986),
        411–412, 415, 416
    nonpoint source pollution, 415–416
    point source pollution, 413–415
    wetlands, 416
Closed shops, 338
Closely held company, 521
Closing arguments, 104
Collective bargaining, 341
    and arbitration, 343
    concerted activities, 343–344
    employer economic responses, 344

good faith bargaining, 341–342
mandatory subjects of bargaining,
    342–343
Color, discrimination based on,
    372–373
Columbia Organic Chemical
    Company (COCC), case study
    of, 295–296
Commerce
    interstate, 118
    limits on congressional powers to
        regulate, 118–119
Commercial speech, 126–128
Common law, 56
    and antitrust, 464
    and pollution, 398–402
    relationship between UCC Article 2
        and, 261–262
    securities fraud under, 511
Communication
    of contract, 236–237
    of offer, 234
Comparative economic statistics, 6
Comparative negligence, 187
Compensation differentials, 381
Compensatory damages, 80, 251
Competition, 5, 10
    strategic responses to, 4–5
Complaint, 95, 97
    response to, 98
Complete defense, 187
Comprehensive Environmental
    Response, Compensation, and
    Liability Act (CERCLA) (1980),
    420
Concerted activities, 343–344
Concurring opinions, 106
Condition
    concurrent, 248
    precedent, 248
    subsequent, 248
Conditional privilege, 178
Condition concurrent, 248
Confiscation, 565
Conflict-of-law rules, 79
Conflict resolution, as function of
    law, 54–55
Congress, U.S., restrictions on
    administrative agency powers,
    160–163
Consent, 176
    reality and genuineness of, 244
Consent decree, settling complaints
    by, 439

Consideration, 237–240
    adequacy of, 238
    definition of, 237
    enforceable promises without, 240
    preexisting obligations and past,
        238–239
    and settlement of business debts,
        239–240
Constitutional privilege, 178
Constitutions. *See also* U.S.
        Constitution
    as source of law, 57–60
    in United Kingdom, 129–130
Constructive discharge, 381
Consumer credit. *See also* Consumer
        protection
Consumer Credit Protection Act, 447
    Consumer Leasing Act, 449
        disclosure requirements and
            liability, 449–450
    Electronic Fund Transfer Act, 456
        liability for mistakes, 457
        liability for stolen cards, 456–457
    Equal Credit Opportunity Act,
            451–452
        notice requirements, 453
        unlawful credit discrimination,
            452–453
    Fair Credit Billing Act, 450
    Fair Credit Reporting Act, 451
        consumer rights with credit
            reports, 451
        enforcement and penalties of,
            451
    Fair Debt Collection Practices Act,
            454–456
        enforcement of, 456
        restrictions imposed, 455–456
    international aspects of, 453
    Truth-in-Lending Act, 447
        credit cost disclosure
            requirement, 449
        enforcement and penalties of,
            449
        finance charge disclosures, 448
Consumer Leasing Act, 449
    disclosure requirements and
            liability, 449–450
Consumer products, 200
    current applications of negligence,
        202–204
    negligence standard, 202
    rise of negligence in tort, 201–202
    rule of *caveat emptor*, 201
    strict liability in tort, 206–207

Consumer Product Safety
        Commission (CPSC), 145
Consumer protection. *See also*
        Consumer credit
    and Magnuson-Moss Warranty Act,
        446
    role of Federal Trade Commission
        in, 439–445
    role of Food and Drug
        Administration in, 432–438
Contempt of court, 100
Contract(s). *See also* Sales contract
    bailment, 263
    bilateral, 231
    capacity to, 241
        insane and intoxicated persons,
            242–243
        minors, 241
    classifications of, 230–232
    contrary to public policy, 243
    definition of, 230
    destination, 269
    discharge of, 246
        agreement of the parties,
            249–250
        anticipatory breach, 247
        failure of condition precedent
            and occurrence of express
            condition subsequent,
            247–248
        impossibility, 248
        operation of law, 249
        performance, 246
    elements of
        agreement, 233–237
        consideration, 237–240
    executed, 231
    executory, 231
    express, 230–232
    freedom of, 228–229
    implied, 230–232
    installment, 276–277
    international, 557
        choice of language clause in, 563
        cultural aspects of, 557–559
        financial aspects of, 559–561
        financial instruments used in,
            560
        payment clauses in, 563
    with Japanese, 245–246
    legality
        contracts contrary to public
            policy, 243
        contracts in restraint of trade,
            244

    contracts with public servants,
            243
    effect of illegal agreements, 244
    exculpatory agreements, 243
    unconscionable contracts, 243
    liability for, in agency relationship,
        300–301
    outside the coverage of the UCC,
        262
    with public servants, 243
    quasi-, 232
    reality and genuineness of consent,
        244
    remedies, 250–251
        mitigation of damages, 252
        monetary damages, 251–252
    in restraint of trade, 244
    shipment, 269
    unconscionable, 243
    unenforceable, 232
    unilateral, 231, 237
    valid, 231
    void, 231
    voidable, 232
    in writing and the statute of
            frauds, 244–245
    yellow-dog, 334
Contract law
    sources of, 229
    strict liability under, 204–206
Contract manufacturing, 557
    Contract rights, developing in
            central and Eastern Europe,
            232–233
Contractual capacity, 241
Contractual relations, interference
        with, 192–193
Contributory negligence, 187, 213
Conversion, 182
Cooperatives, 322–323
Copyrights, 217–219
Corning Glass Works, and
        employment discrimination,
        367–368
Corporate charters, 312
Corporate finance. *See also* Securities
        regulation
    debt financing, 500–501
    equity financing, 501
Corporate responsibility, 38
    broad view, 42
    conceptual issue debate, 39–41
    narrow view, 41–42
    RP perspective, 43
    utilitarian perspective, 43–44

Corporations, 311–312
  as legal entity, 312
  liability of, 318
  capital requirements of, 321
  debate over as moral agents, 39–41
  duration of, 320
  liability of directors and senior
      officers, 513–514
  making more morally responsive, 44
  management of, 316
  method of creation, 312, 314
  political speech by, 124–126
  relationship of the parties, 314–316
  self-interest motivation of, 41–42
  taxation of, 321
  termination of, 316
Counterclaim, 98
Counterfeiting of trademarks,
    215–216
Counteroffer, 235
Countervailing duty, 547
Court-annexed arbitration, 108
Courts
  federal, 69–71
  in France, 72
  state, 67–69
Cover
  buyer's right to, 286
  damages when the buyer elects not
      to, 287
Credit. *See* Consumer credit
Credit bureaus, regulation of, 451
Creditors, rights of, to goods, 271
Criminal law, 62–63
Criticism, rights in, 127–128
Cross-examination, 103
Culture, 8
Curia Regis, 56
Customer restrictions, 484

Damages
  compensatory, 80, 251
  consequential, 288
  exemplary, 80
  expectancy, 251
  incidental, 284, 287
  liquidated, 252
  mitigation of, 252
  monetary, 80, 251–252
  nominal, 80, 252
  punitive, 80, 252
  special, 252
Death, and termination of contract,
    235

Debt
  liquidated, 239
  unliquidated, 239–240
Debt collection, 179
Debt collection agency, 454
Debt financing, 321, 500–501
Deception policy statement, 439
Decertification of union, 338
Defamation, 177–178, 191
  defenses to, 177–178
Defamation per se, 177
Default judgment, 73
Defendant, 65
Defenses to defamation, 177–178
Delaney Clause, 434
Deliveries, withholding or stopping
    under UCC, 283–284
Delivery terms, in sales contract, 266
Demographic factors, 11
Deposition, 99, 100
Design defects, 209
Destination contract, 269
Detrimental reliance, 240
Direct examination, 103
Direct exporting, 555
Direct testimony, presentation of, 103
Disabled discrimination
  and compliance, 389–391
  and definition of disabled, 388–389
  legislation prohibiting, 350, 368,
      388, 609–611
Discharge monitoring reports
    (DMRs), 415
Discovery stage in litigation, 99–100
Discrimination. *See also* Employment
    discrimination
  credit, 451–453
Dismiss, motion to, 98
Disney, Walt, Company, 6
Disparagement, 191
Disparate impact, 377
Disparate treatment, 376
Dissenting opinions, 106
Dissolution
  of a corporation, 316
  of a partnership, 306
Distress, emotional, 179
Diversity of citizenship jurisdiction,
    69
Dow Chemical
  case study of, 25–26
  external environment at, 10
  legal environment at, 13
Drexel Burnham Lambert Inc.,
    518–519

Drug-Free Workplace Act (1988),
    350–351
Drug regulation, international, 438
Drug safety, 435
  designation of prescription drugs,
      436
  drug effectiveness, 436
  producer liability and
      FDA-approved drugs,
      436–437
Drug testing, legal issues in, 350–352
Due care, 183
Due process, 133–135
Duration, and choice of business
    organization, 320
Duty-free ports, 551
Duty of care of board of directors, 315

Economic Community of West
    African States (ECOWAS), 549
Economic environment, 10
8-K reports, 510
Eighth Amendment, on excessive
    fines, 133
Electronic Fund Transfer Act (1979),
    456
  liability for mistakes, 457
  liability for stolen cards, 456–457
Electro-Wire Products Inc., case
    study of, 3–4
Emissions offset policy, 407
Emotional distress, 179
Employee assistance programs, and
    substance abuse, 350
Employee handbooks, 348
  and punitive damages, 348–349
Employee Retirement Income
    Security Act (1974) (ERISA),
    361–362
Employees, duties of, under OSHA,
    354–355
Employer
  economic responses of, to
      collective bargaining, 344
  responses to union organizing,
      339–340
  substance abuse policy of, 352–353
Employment-at-will, 347–348
  public policy exceptions, 348
Employment discrimination
  affirmative action programs, 383
    executive order 11246, 383
    as remedy, 384
    voluntary programs, 384–385

against the disabled, 388
   compliance with the statutes, 389–391
   definition of disabled, 388–389
Age Discrimination in Employment Act, 385–386
   BFOQ on the basis of age, 386–387
civil rights movement, 369
Equal Pay Act, 369–370
   enforcement provisions of, 370
   scope and coverage of, 370
   in Europe and Japan, 382
Title VII of the 1964 Civil Rights Act, 370
   coverage and enforcement of, 370–371
   defenses under, 378–380
   discrimination and remedies, 380–382
   protected classes under, 372–376
   theories of discrimination under, 376–377
Enabling statute, 143
Endangered Species Act, 422–423
Enforcement, 450
Enforcement power of administrative agencies, 150–151
Enforcement stage, 106
Enlistment contracts, 242
Environmental fit, definition of, 20
Environmental impact statement (EIS), 403
Environmental Protection Agency (EPA), 143, 145, 403–404, 416. *See also* Pollution
   creation of, 402, 403
   and enforcement of clean air acts, 405, 409, 410–411
   and pesticides, 418
   and point source pollution, 414–415
   and Resource Conservation and Recovery Act, 418–419
   responsibilities of, 403–404
   and Superfund enforcement of, 420–421
   and Toxic Substances Control Act, 417–418
Environmental regulation. *See* Pollution
Equal Credit Opportunity Act (1970), 451–452
   notice requirements, 453
   unlawful credit discrimination, 452–453

Equal Employment Opportunity Act (1972), 367, 370
Equal Employment Opportunity Commission (EEOC), 145, 369, 370
Equal Pay Act (1963), 368, 369–370
   enforcement provisions of, 370
   scope and coverage of, 370
Equal protection, 135–136
Equitable remedies, 80–81, 253–254
Equity financing, 321, 501
Erie doctrine, 78
Error of law, 106
Ethics
   comparison with etiquette, 29
   comparison with the law, 29–30
   conceptual tools in, 30–33
   corporate social responsibility, 38
      broad view, 42
      conceptual issue debate, 39–41
      narrow view, 41–42
   definition of, 29
   moral theories, 33
      ethics of respect for persons, 35–37, 42, 43
      nature of, 33–34
      utilitarianism, 34–35, 42–44
   nature of, 33–34
   surveys and perceptions of, 26–29
Ethics of respect for persons (RP morality), 35–37
   applying, 36–37
   and corporate responsibility, 42, 43
   doctrine of rights, 36
   hierarchy of rights, 36
   shortcomings in, 37
Etiquette, comparison with ethics, 29
Euro Disneyland, 558–559
Europe
   American franchises in, 528–529
   drug regulation in, 438
   employment discrimination in, 382
   insider trading in, 519
   products liability in, 213
European Community (EC), 549
   1992 directive, 543–544
European Free Trade Association (EFTA), 549
Evidence
   documents and exhibits used as, in business dispute, 93
   restrictions on use of collected, 129
Ex aequo et bono, 566
Excessive fines, 133
Exclusive dealing, 489

Exclusive jurisdiction, 71
Exculpatory agreements, 243
Executed contracts, 231
Executive branch, as source of law, 61
Executive order 11246, 383
Executory contracts, 231
Exemplary damages, 80
Exhaustion doctrine, 159
Expectancy damages, 251
Expert testimony, reliance on, in business dispute, 93
Export
   of manufactured products, 555
   regulation and promotion, 552–553, 555
Export Administration Act, 552–553
Export Control Act (1949), 552
Export Trading Company Act (1982), 552
   antitrust exemptions in, 467
Express condition subsequent, 248
Express contract, 230
Express warranties
   disclaiming, 281
   of quality, 277–278
   strict liability based on, 205–206
Expropriation, 564–565
External environment, 7, 10–14
   in Europe, 14–15
Extortion, definition of, 31
Exxon *Valdez*, 349–350, 353

Failing-firm defense, 476
Failure of a condition precedent, 248
Failure to warn, 208–209
Fair Credit Billing Act (1974), 450
Fair Credit Reporting Act (1970), 451
   consumer rights with credit reports, 451
   enforcement and penalties of, 451
Fair Debt Collection Practices Act, 454–456
   enforcement of, 456
   restrictions imposed, 455–456
Fair Labor Standards Act (1938), 360
False imprisonment, 176
Federal Aviation Administration (FAA), 467
Federal Communications Commission (FCC), 144
Federal court system, 69–70
Federal Express, social environment at, 11

Federal Insecticide, Fungicide, and Rodenticide Act (1947), 416, 418
Federal Maritime Commission, 467
Federal Mediation and Conciliation Service, 343
Federal minimum wage requirements, 360
Federal Register, 155–158, 354, 444
Federal Reserve Board, margin requirements of, 526–527
Federal Rules for Civil Procedure, 65
Federal Trade Commission, 144, 439
    consumer protection procedures under, 439
    creation of, 466
    enforcement activities of, 442–443
    and regulation of advertising claims, 440–441
    and regulation of credit bureaus, 451
    and regulation of unfair and deceptive acts or practices, 439–440
    and telemarketing fraud, 443
        art fraud, 443
        oil and gas well "investments," 443
        unfairness and contract enforcement of, 443
    trade regulation rules, 444
        insulation r-value rule, 444–445
        mail order rule, 445
        used-car rule, 445
Federal Trade Commission Act (1914), 466–467, 599
    enforcement of, 469
Fiduciary duty in partnership, 306
Fiduciary duty of loyalty of board of directors, 315
Fifth Amendment
    on just compensation, 130–132
    and self-incrimination, 130, 148
Finance charge, disclosure of, 448
Fines, excessive, 132
First Amendment
    and free press, 115–116
    and free speech, 124–128
Fitness for a particular purpose, implied warranty of, 280
Float, 509
Food, Drug, and Cosmetic Act (1938), 433
    Delaney Clause, 434
    Kefauver Amendment to, 436

Food and Drug Administration (FDA), 144, 432–433
    budget of, 432–433
    and drug safety, 435–437
    enforcement activities of, 437–438
    and food safety, 433–434
    and nutrition labeling, 434–435
Food safety, 433
    and food additives, 434
    and nutrition labeling, 434–435
    and sanitation standards, 433
Force majeure clause, 563, 564
Foreign Claims Settlement Commission, 566
Foreign Corrupt Practices Act (FCPA) (1977), 31
Foreign exchange markets, 559–560
Foreign Sovereign Immunities Act (1976), 568
Fourteenth Amendment
    due process, 133–135
    equal protection, 135–136
Fourth Amendment, and search and seizure, 128–130, 148
France
    court systems in, 72
    tort liability in, 188
Franchise regulation
    in Europe, 528–529
    under FTC, 444, 527–529
Franchise Rule, 444, 527–529
Franchising agreements, 556–557
Fraudulent transfer, 271
Freedom, 34
Freedom of Information Act, 143
Freedom of Information Act (1966), 162
Freedom of Information Act (1974), 162
Free trade zones, 551
Full warranty, 446
Fungible goods, and implied warranties of quality, 278

Garnishment, 454
General Agreement on Tariffs and Trade (GATT), 547
    current round of talks, 548
    imposition of antidumping or countervailing duties, 547
    "most favored nation" status, 547
    nontariff barriers to trade, 547–548
General Electric Company
    and consumer protection, 431–432
    and securities regulation, 499–500

General jurisdiction, 67
General Mills, legal environment at, 13
General Motors
    case study of, 87–88
    and legal environment at, 13
General partnerships, 305–308
    definition of, 305
    formation of, 306, 307–308
    liability of, 318
    relationship of the parties, 306
    termination, 306
Geographic market, 475
Golden Rule, 35–36
Good(s)
    buyer's disposition of rejected, 285
    delivery by moving, 269
    delivery without moving, 269
    disposition of rejected, 286
    identification of, in sales contract, 268–269
    international sales of, 268
    resale of rejected, 285–286
    reselling, 284
    rights of creditors to, 271
    sale of, by nonowners, 271
    title to
        identification, 268–269
        passage of title, 269
        special problems regarding title, 270–271
        statute of frauds, 272
    under the UCC, 263
Good faith bargaining, 341–342
Good faith dealing
    definition of, 263
    UCC's test of, 267
Good faith purchaser, 271
Government in the Sunshine Act (1976), 143, 162–163
Grievance arbitration, 343
Gross domestic product (GDP), 6

Handicapped. *See* Disabled
Harmonized tariff schedules, 550–551
Hazard communication standard, 356–357
Hazardous waste, definition of, 419
Hearings
    adjudicatory, 152–153
    investigatory, 153–156
Horizontal market divisions, 481–482
Horizontal merger, 473

Horizontal price fixing, 477
    per se rule in price fixing, 477
    rule of reason in price-fixing cases,
        477–479
Horizontal restraints of trade,
    471–472
Howey test, 504–505

Illegal agreements, effect of, 244
Image, 8
Immigration, restrictions on,
    359–360, 376
Immigration Reform and Control Act
    (1986), 359–360, 376
Implied contract, 230
Implied warranties
    disclaiming, 281–282
    of quality, 278–280
    strict liability based on, 204–205
Import
    bans on certain designated
        products, 551
    duty free, 551
    harmonized tariff schedules,
        550–551
    imposition of tariffs, 549–550
    regulation and prohibitions,
        548–549
    restrictions and adjustments, 551
Impossibility, discharge of contract
    by, 248
Imprisonment, false, 176
Incidental damages, 287
Indirect exporting, 555
Industry, legal environment of
    business in, 16
Infringement, 215
    of copyrighted material, 218–219
Injunction, 254
    definition of, 81, 254, 468
    prohibition of, in nonviolent labor
        disputes, 334
    as remedy for pollution, 402
In personam jurisdiction, 72
Insane persons, 242
    and capacity to contract, 242–243
    and termination of contract, 235
Insider trading
    in Europe, 519
    liability for, 515–516
    major cases in, 517–519
Insider Trading Sanctions Act (1984),
    517

Inspection
    buyer's right of, 275
    of OSHA workplace, 354
Installment contracts, 276–277
Insulation r-value rule, 444–445
Insuring against risk of loss, 565
Intangible property, 214
Intellectual property, 214–215
    copyrights, 217–219
    trademarks, 215–216
    trade names, 216–217
    trade secrets, 220
Intent in sales contract, 264
Intentional torts, 173–174
    interference with personal rights,
        174–175
        assault, 175
        battery, 175
        consent, 176
        defamation, 177–178
        emotional distress, 179
        false imprisonment, 176
        invasion of privacy, 179
        privilege, 176
    interference with property rights,
        180
        conversion, 182
        nuisance, 180–181
        trespass to land, 180
        trespass to personal property, 182
Inter-American Commercial
    Arbitration Commission, 567
Internal environment, 7, 8–9
International business, 537
    current U.S. involvement in,
        538–540
    environment of, 537
    loss of investment, 564
        expropriation, 564–565
        insuring against risk of loss, 565
        nationalization, 564
    in the 1990s, 542
        changing U.S.–Japan trade
            relationship, 544–545
        emerging Eastern European
            economies, 542
        European Community's 1992
            directive, 543–544
        North American unified market,
            544
    risks in transactions, 538
    and state taxes, 122–123
International Chamber of Commerce,
    567

International contracts
    choice of language clause in, 563
    cultural aspects of, 557–559
    financial aspects of, 559–561
    financial instruments used in, 560
    payment clauses in, 563
International Country Risk Guide, 538
International Court of Justice,
    565–566
International Development
    Association (IDA), 546
International dispute resolution, 565
    arbitration, 567
    doctrine of act of state, 568
    doctrine of sovereign immunity,
        567–568
    International Court of Justice,
        565–566
    judicial litigation, 566–567
International distributorships, 486
International Finance Corporation
    (IFC), 546
International law
    history of, 541
    overview of current, 541
International Monetary Fund,
    546–547
International organizations
    General Agreement on Tariffs and
        Trade (GATT), 547
        current round of talks, 548
        imposition of antidumping or
            countervailing duties, 547
        "most favored nation" status,
            547
        nontariff barriers to trade,
            547–548
    International Monetary Fund,
        546–547
    regional organizations, 548, 549
    United Nations Commission on
        International Trade Law
        (UNCITRAL), 545
    World Bank, 546
International pirates, controlling,
    554
Interpretative rules, 147
Interrogatories, written, 99
Interstate commerce
    definition of, 118
    state law impediment of, 120–121
    and state taxation, 123–124
Interstate Commerce Act (1887),
    antitrust exemptions in, 467

Interstate Commerce Commission (ICC), 144, 467, 506–507
creation of, 145
Intervening conduct, 186
Intoxicated persons, 242
and capacity to contract, 242–243
and termination of contract, 235
Intrastate offering exemption, 510
Invasion of privacy, 179
Investigative powers of administrative agencies, 148–150
Investigatory hearings, 153–156
Investment advisers, 522
Investment Advisers Act (1940), 521, 523
arbitration of disputes, 522–523
brokers and dealers, 523
investment companies, 521
mutual funds, 521
investment newsletters, 524
professional responsibility to clients, 524
regulation of, 522
investment advisers, 522
limiting conflicts of interest, 522
registration and disclosure, 522
Involuntary dissolution of a corporation, 316
Italy, trials in, 107

Japan
administrative agencies in, 156–157
dango system in, 473
employment discrimination in, 382
labor relations in, 347
management style in, 20–21
tort litigation in, 182–183
U.S. trade relationship with, 544–545
Japan Fair Trade Commission, 470, 473
Joint stock companies, 322
Joint ventures, 322, 535–536, 556
Judgment notwithstanding the verdict, 104
Judgments, size of, against businesses, 94–95
Judicial litigation, 566–567
Judicial review
function of, 61
right to, 157–159
scope of, 159–160

Judiciary, as source of law, 61
Jurisdiction. *See* Subject matter jurisdiction; Territorial jurisdiction
Jurisdiction in *rem*, 76
Jury, 102
instructions to the, 104
selection process, 102
Jury trial, right to a, 152
Just compensation, 130–132

Kefauver Amendment of 1962, 436

Labeling, adequacy of, and implied warranties, 279
Labor-Management Relations Act (1959), 335–336
Labor-Management Reporting and Disclosure Act (1947), 335
Labor relations
Clayton Act, 333
collective bargaining, 341
and arbitration, 343
concerted activities, 343–344
employer economic responses, 344
good faith bargaining, 341–342
mandatory subjects of bargaining, 342–343
duty of employees, 355
employee handbooks, 348
punitive damages, 348–349
employee rights, 354–355
employer responses to union organizing, 339–340
employment-at-will, 347–348
public policy exceptions, 348
establishing safety and health standards, 354
federal minimum wage requirements, 360
general regulation of labor markets, 359
restrictions on immigration, 359–360
in Japan, 347
Landrum-Griffin Act, 335–336
National Labor Relations Board, 336–337
Norris-La Guardia Act, 333–334
occupational licensure and regulation, 360–361

protection of worker safety and health, 353
Occupational Safety and Health Act, 354–355
and toxic substances, 355–357
regulation of private employee retirement plans, 361–362
vesting requirements, 361–362
Sherman Act, 333
substance abuse
employer substance abuse policy, 352–353
legal issues in drug testing, 350–352
as practical problem for business, 349–350
Taft-Hartley Act, 335
unionization, 337
agency shops, 338
movement to, 337
representation elections, 337–338
right-to-work laws, 339
union certification, 338
unlawful labor activities, 345
secondary boycotts, 345–346
Wagner Act, 334–335
workers' compensation, 357
basis for a claim, 358–359
compensation provided, 357–358
flaws in, 359
incentives for safety, 358
workplace inspections, 354
Lamon Brothers Plastic Fabricators, case study of, 259–260
Land, trespass to, 180
Land pollution, 416–417
pesticides, 418
Resource Conservation and Recovery Act, 418–419
Toxic Substances Control Act, 417–418
Landrum-Griffin Act (1959), 335–336
Last clear chance, 188
Latin American Integration Association (LAIA), 549
Law. *See also* Litigation
administrative, 143
case, 574–575
classifications of, 61–62
civil or criminal law, 62–63
public or private law, 62
substantive or procedural law, 64
comparison with ethics, 29–30
definition of, 52–53

functions of, 53–55
origin of, in the United States
  administrative agencies, 60
  common law, 56
  constitutions, 57–60
  doctrine of *stare decisis*, 56–57
  executive, 61
  judiciary, 61
  statutory law, 60
  regulatory, 576
  statutory, 575–576
  subject-matter jurisdiction, 65–71
  territorial jurisdiction, 72–77
Law reviews, 577
Lawsuit, as aspect of strategic plan,
    91–92
Legal benefit, 237
Legal capacity, 241
Legal detriment, 237
Legal environment, 11–14
  characteristics of, 15–18
  definition of, 11
  impact of judicial review on, 61
  lost opportunities as threats in, 21
  and management process, 18–19
  strategic planning and, 20
Legislative delegation, 143
Legislative power of administrative
    agencies, 145–148
Legislative rule, 147
Legislative veto, 161
Letter of credit, 560–561
Levine, Dennis, 517
Lex mercatoria, 541
Liability, as factor in choice of
    business organization, 318
Libel, 177
  in foreign courts, 178–179
Licensing agreement, 556
Limited jurisdiction, 67
Limited partnership, 309
  definition of, 309
  formation of, 309, 310
  liability of, 318
  relationship of the parties, 309, 311
  termination of, 311
Limited warranty, 446
Liquidated damages, 252
Liquidated debt, 239
Litigation
  effect of, on goodwill, 90
  functions of, 65
  process of, 65
Locational restraints, 484
Lockout, 344

London Court of Arbitration, 567
Long-arm statute, 74
Lowest achievable emissions rate
    technology (LAER), 407
Loyalty, agent's duty of, 298–299

Magna Charta, 58
Magnuson-Moss Warranty Act (1975),
    446
Mailbox rule, 236
Mail order rule, 445
Management, definition of, 7
Management process, and legal
    environment, 18–19
Management style in Japan, 20–21
Managerial environment, 7
Managerial process, 7
Manifest, 419
Manifest system, 419
Manville Corporation, case study of,
    51–52
Market power, determination of,
    474–475
Market share liability, 211–212
Marriage contracts, 242
Material breach, 246
Maximum allowable increase, 406
McCarran-Ferguson Act, 468
Mediation, 109–110
Merchant
  firm offer of, in sales contract,
      266–267
  sales by and between, 263
Merchantability, implied warranty of,
    278–279
Mergers
  defenses, 476
  determining firm's market power,
      474–475
  Supreme Court's approach to,
      473–474
  and tender offers, 520
Milken, Michael, 518
Miller, Herman, Inc., 397
Minimum emissions rates (MERs), 410
Minitrials, 109
Minors, 241
  and capacity to contract, 241–242
Misstatements, liability for, 513–514
Mitigation of damages, 252
Mixed economic system, 5
Mixed transaction, 262
Monetary damages, 80, 251–252
Monetary profits, repatriation of, 561

Montreal Protocol, 424
Moral agent, 35
  debate over corporations as, 39–41
Moral judgments, 33–34
Moral principles, disagreements over
    genuine, 33
Moral responsiveness, of
    corporations, 44
Morals, definition of, 29
Moral standard, 33
Moral theories, 33
  ethics of respect for persons,
      35–37, 42, 43
  nature of, 33–34
  utilitarianism, 34–35, 42–44
Moral thinking, conceptual tools for,
    30–33
Motorola
  drug testing at, 332
  and legal environment at, 13
Mutual funds, 521

National Ambient Air Quality
    Standards (NAAQS), 405
  major air pollutants subject to, 406
National Association of Securities
    Dealers (NASD), 526
National Environmental Policy Act
    (NEPA) (1070), 402, 403
National Institute of Occupational
    Safety and Health (NIOSH), 354
Nationalization, 564
National Labor Relations Act (1935),
    334–335, 600–604
  and discrimination, 369
National Labor Relations Board
    (NLRB), 336
  complaint procedure, 336–337
  creation of, 334
  and discrimination, 369
  jurisdiction of, 336
National origin, discrimination based
    on, 376
National Pollutant Discharge
    Elimination System (NPDES),
    414
National Priority List, 420
Negative moral obligations, 41
Negligence
  causation, 184
    cause in fact, 184
    intervening conduct, 186
    proximate cause, 184–186
  comparative, 187

contributory, 187, 213
current applications of, 202–204
defenses to a negligence action, 186
    assumption of risk, 186
    comparative negligence, 187
    contributory negligence, 187
    last clear chance, 188
and pollution, 401
reasonable person standard, 183–184
rise of, in tort, 201
standard, 202
Negotiation, 109–110
Net air quality improvement, 407
New Source Performance Standards (NSPS), 414
Nicotine, employer policy on, 353
Noerr-Pennington doctrine, 468
Nominal damages, 80, 252
Nonattainment areas, 407
Nonowners, sale of goods by, 271
Nonpoint source pollution, 415–416
Norris-La Guardia Act (1932), 333–334
North American Free Trade Agreement, 4, 544
Notification limitations, 77
Notify, agent's duty to, 299
Novation, 250
Nuclear Nonproliferation Act (1978), 555
Nuisance, 180–181
Nuisance actions, 91
Nuisance law, and pollution, 399–401
Nutrition labeling, 434–435
Nutrition Labeling and Education Act (1990), 434–435

Obedience, agent's duty of, 299
Occupational licensure and regulation, 360–361
Occupational Safety and Health Act (1970) (OSHAct), 354–355
    cost benefit analysis, 356
    hazard communication standard, 356–357
    significant health risk requirement, 356
    toxic substance standards, 356
Occupational Safety and Health Administration (OSHA), 145
    and warrantless searches, 129

Offer, 233
    acceptance, 235–237
    communication of the, 234
    definite terms and conditions, 234
    manifestation of intent, 233–234
    in sales contract, 265–266, 266–267
    terminating, 234–235
Offeree, 231, 233
Offeror, 231, 233
Office of Federal Contract Compliance Programs (OFCCP), 383
Omnibus Trade and Competitiveness Act (1988), 553
Opening statements, 102
Operation of law, termination of contract by, 235
Oral arguments, 106
Ordinary care, 183
Organization of Petroleum Exporting Countries (OPEC) cartel, 472
Original jurisdiction, 67, 71
    state courts of, 67–68
Overseas Private Investment Corporation (OPIC), 565
Ownership interests, transferability of, 319–320
Ozone layer, 424

Packaging, adequacy of, and implied warranties, 279
Parker doctrine, 467
Parol evidence rule, 245
Partial capacity, 241
Parties, termination of contract by, 235
Partnership. See also General partnership; Limited partnerships
Partnership agreement
    basic, 307–308
    capital requirements of, 320–321
    duration of, 320
    taxation of, 321
Patents, 219
    Japanese and American, 219
Payment, buyer's obligation of, 275–276
Payment terms, in sales contract, 266
Pennzoil, 227–228
Pension Benefit Guaranty Corporation, 362
Perfect tender rule doctrine, 273
Performance, discharge of contract by, 246

Per se rule, 470–471
    boycotts and the, 490
    in price fixing, 477
Personal property, trespass to, 182
Personal service, 73
Persons, ethics of respect for, 35–37
Pesticides, 418
Plaintiff, 65
Pleadings, 98
Pleadings stage, in litigation, 95–97
Point source pollution, 413–415
Political speech by corporations, 124–126
Pollution
    air pollution, 404, 405–411
    and the common law, 398–402
    Environmental Protection Agency, 403–404
    federal regulation, 402
    global environmental issues, 423
        international cooperation, 424–425
        ozone layer, 424
    land pollution, 416–417
        pesticides, 418
        Resource Conservation and Recovery Act, 418–419
        Toxic Substances Control Act, 417–418
    National Environmental Policy Act, 403
    and nuisance law, 399–401
    prevention of, 425
    Superfund, 419–421
    and trespass, 401
    water pollution, 411
        Clean Water Act, 411–412
        nonpoint source pollution, 415–416
        point source pollution, 413–415
        wetlands, 416
        wildlife protection, 421–423
Pollution Prevention Act (1990), 425
Positive moral obligations, 41
Post-trial motions, 104
Predatory behavior, 193
Predatory pricing, 491
Preference utilitarianism, 34
Pregnancy, and sex discrimination, 374
Pregnancy Discrimination Act (1978), 370, 374
Preponderance of the evidence, 104
Press, freedom of the, 115–116
Pretrial stage, 101–102

Prevention of significant deterioration
(PSD) areas, 405
Price, in sales contract, 265
Price discrimination, 491
Price fixing
horizontal, 477
per se rule in, 477
rule of reason in, 477–479
vertical, 482–483
Primary boycott, 345
Principal, 297
agent's authority to act for, 300
agent's duties to, 298–299
contract liability of disclosed and
partially disclosed, 301
duties to agent, 298
liability of, for torts of agent,
301–303
Privacy, invasion of, 179
Privacy Act (1974), 162
Private employee retirement plans,
regulation of, 361–362
Private law, 62
Private nuisance, 180
definition of, 399
Private placement exemption, 509
Privilege, 176
Privity of contract, 200
Procedural law, 64
Procedural requirements, review of
agency's, 160
Procedural rules, 148
Product abuse, 212
Product liability cases, standards
applied in, 17
Product market, 475
Products liability, 190
in Europe, 213
market share, 211–212
need for reform, 213–214
and negligence, 200–204
strict defenses, 212–213
strict liability, 204
based on express warranty,
205–206
based on implied warranty,
204–205
extensions of, 207–211
in tort, 206–207
Professionally developed ability tests,
378
Prohibited bases, 452
Promissory estoppel, 240
Prospectus, 507
Proximate cause, 184–186

Proxy, 314, 519–520
Public law, 62
Publicly owned treatment works
(POTW), 412, 413
Public nuisance, 180–181
definition of, 399
Public policy, contracts contrary to, 243
Public servants, contracts with, 243
Public utility industry, legal
environment in, 16
Punitive damages, 80, 252
Pure Food and Drug Act (1906), 433

Quality
express warranties of, 277–278
implied warranties of, 278–280
Quantity, in sales contract, 265
Quarterly 10-Q reports, 510
Quasi-contract, 132
Quasi in rem jurisdiction, 77

Race, discrimination based on,
372–373
Racketeer Influenced and Corrupt
Organizations (RICO) law, 518
Reasonable accommodation, and
disabled workers, 389
Reasonable care and performance,
agent's duty of, 299
Reasonable person standard, 183–184
Recession, 10
Red herring, 508
Reduction in force (RIF), 387
Regional organizations, 548, 549
Registration statement, 507–508
Regulation B, 452
Regulation D, 509–510
Regulation E, 456, 457
Regulation M, 450
Regulation Z, 449, 450
Regulatory law, 576
Rehabilitation Act (1973), 350, 368
enforcement of, 389
Rejection, buyer's right of, 275
Religion, discrimination based on, 373
Repatriation of monetary profits, 561
Reply, 98
Resale price maintenance, 483
Rescission, 249–250
Res judicata, 106
Resolutions, 314
Resource Conservation and Recovery
Act (1976, 1984), 418–419

Resources, 8–9
Respondent superior, 301, 303
Restatement, 577
Restatement of Contracts, 229
Restatement of Torts, 220
Restraint of trade
contracts in, 244
horizontal, 471–472
vertical, 472–473
Reverse discrimination, 373
Revocation, 235
Right, definition of, 36
Right-to-sue letter, 371
Right-to-work laws, 339
Ripeness, 159
Risk, assumption of, 186
Robinson-Patman Act (1936), 491
defenses to, 492
price discrimination, 491
RP morality. See Ethics of respect for
persons
Rule 10b-5, 512
Rule 144A, 510
Rulemaking by administrative
agencies, 145–148
Rule of reason, 471
applied to tie-in cases, 487–489
in price-fixing cases, 477–479

Safe Drinking Water Act, 416
Sale(s)
by and between merchants, 263
under the UCC, 262–263
Sales contract. See also Contract(s)
acceptance, 267
contract modification and
consideration requirements,
267
formation of a, 263–268
indefinite offer, 265
open delivery term, 266
open payment term, 266
open price term, 265
open quantity terms, 265
intent to contract, 264–265
merchant's firm offer, 266–267
under UCC, 262–263
Sales warranties. See also Warranties
conflicting, 280–281
disclaimers, 281–282
express, of quality, 277–278
implied, of quality, 278–280
third-party beneficiaries of, 282
of title, 276–277

Sanctions, 11
Satisfaction, 239, 250
Scalping, 524
Search and seizure, 128
    due process, 133–135
    equal protection, 135–136
    excessive fines, 133
    limitations on, 128–129
    restrictions on use of evidence
        collected, 129
Search warrant, 149
Secondary boycotts, 345–346
Second restatement of torts, 207
Securities
    definition of, 500, 503–504
    franchise regulation, 527
        in Europe, 528–529
        FTC franchise rule, 527–529
    proxies, 519–520
    tender offers, 520
Securities Act (1933), 500, 502,
        507–509, 612–614
    disclosure requirements under
        costs of registration, 509
        items-and-answers, 507
        prospectus, 507
        registration statement, 507–508
        review by the SEC, 507
        shelf registration, 507–508
    exempt securities under, 506
    intrastate offering exemption, 510
    liability for misstatements, 513–514
    and securities fraud, 511
Securities and Exchange Act (1934),
        500, 502, 614–615
    disclosure requirements under,
        510
    exempt securities under, 506
    and regulation of brokers and
        dealers, 523
    Rule 10b-5, 512
    and securities fraud, 512
    and tender offers, 520
Securities and Exchange Commission
        (SEC), 144, 500, 502
    arbitration requirements of,
        522–523
    filing of registration statement
        with, 507–508
    and prosecution of inside traders,
        515–516
    and protection of clients from
        conflicts of interests, 524
    registration and disclosure
        requirements of, 522

registration of securities
        professionals with, 523
    regulation D, 509–510
    regulation of newsletters by, 524
    and regulation of securities
        professionals, 526
    Rule 10b-5, 512
    Rule 144A, 510
    securities review of, 508
    and shelf registration, 507–508
Securities fraud, 511
    under common law, 511
    and liability for insider trading,
        515–519
    and liability for misstatements,
        513–514
    penalties for, 512–513
    statutory securities fraud, 511–512
Securities regulation. *See also* Stock
        market regulation
    corporate finance and early
        regulation, 500
        origins of securities regulation,
            501–502
        securities and corporate finance,
            500–501
    defining a security, 503–504
        application of, 505–507
        exemptions from registration,
            509–510
        Howey test, 504–505
Self-incrimination, 130
Self-interest motivation, of
        corporation, 41–42
Seller
    cure by, 273–274
    incidental damages under UCC,
        284
    obligations of, under UCC,
        272–275
    rights and remedies of, under
        UCC, 282–284
Service of process, 72
Settlement agreement, 239
Seventh Amendment, and trial
        rights, 102, 132
Sex discrimination, 373–374
    and pregnancy, 374
Sexual harassment, 374
Shareholders
    of corporation, 314
    liability of, 318
Shelf registration, 507–508
Sherman Act (1890), 333, 465, 595
    enforcement of, 468

and exclusive dealing, 489
    and tying arrangements, 487
Shipment contract, 269
Shipping Act, 467
Shoplifting, and false imprisonment,
        176
Sine qua non rule, 184
Sixth Amendment, and trial rights,
        132
Slander, 177
Sludge, disposal of, 412
Small claims courts, 68
Social environment, 10–11
Socialist economic systems, 5
Sole proprietorship, 305
    capital requirements of, 320
    duration of, 320
    liability of, 318
    taxation of, 321
Sovereign immunity, doctrine of,
        567–568
Special damages, 252
Special jurisdiction, 67
Specialist firms, 526
Specific performance, 81, 253–254
Specific tariffs, 549
Speech
    commercial, 126–128
    political, by corporations, 124–126
Standing, 158–159
Stare decisis, doctrine of, 56–57
State constitutions, 60
State court
    of appellate jurisdiction, 69
    of original jurisdiction, 67–68
    substantive law in, 79
State Implementation Plan (SIP), 409
State law
    and federal law, 120
    and interstate commerce, 120–121
State regulation
    of franchises, 528
    of takeovers, 520
Statute of Frauds, 244–245
    under UCC, 272
Statutory interpretation, review of
        agency's, 160
Statutory law, 575–576
    as source of law, 60
Statutory reporting requirements, 161
Stock market, international, 502–503
Stock market regulation, 525
    margin requirements, 526–527
    regulation of securities
        transactions, 526

self-regulation of securities
markets, 525
liability and penalties, 526
rules for exchange members,
525–526
Stop order, 508
Strategic decision, definition of, 20
Strategic plan, law suit as aspect of,
91–92
Strategic planning, and the legal
environment, 20
Strict liability, 204, 206–207
abnormally dangerous activities,
189
under contract law, 204–206
extensions of, 207–208
design defects, 209
failure to warn, 208–209
unknown hazards, 209–211
and pollution, 401
and products liability, 190
Strike, 345
Subject-matter jurisdiction, 65–66
federal appellate courts, 70
federal district courts, 70
organization of the American court
system, 67
specialized federal courts, 70
and the federal court system, 69
and the state court systems, 67–69
U.S. Supreme Court, 70–71
Subpoena, 150
Substance abuse, 349. *See also* Drug
safety
employer substance abuse policy,
352–353
legal issues in drug testing, 350–352
as practical problem for business,
349–350
Substantial factor test, 185–186
Substantial performance, 246
Substantive determinations, review
of agency's, 159–160
Substantive law, 64
in federal courts, 78
in state court, 79
Substantive rules, 146–147
Summary judgment, 101–102
Summons, 72
response to, 98
Sunset laws, 161
Superfund, 419–421
Superfund Amendments and
Reauthorization Act (SARA),
420

Superseding cause, 186
Supreme Court Selections Act (1988),
71
Syndicates, 323

Taft-Hartley Act (1947), 335, 343
Takings clause, 130–132
Tariff, 549
harmonized schedule of, 550–551
imposition of import, 549–550
Taxation
federal, 122
state
apportionment of burden, 124
and international commerce,
122–123
and interstate commerce,
123–124
Technologies, export control of,
552–553
Telemarketing fraud
art fraud, 445
oil and gas well "investments," 445
unfairness and contract
enforcement of, 445
10-K annual report, 510
Tender offers, 520
Termination
of agency, 303–304
of corporation, 316
of general partnership, 306
of limited partnership, 311
of offer, 234–235
Territorial jurisdiction, 72
based upon power over property,
76–77
over out-of-state corporate
defendants, 74–75
over out-of-state defendants, 74
over the person, 72
Territorial restraints, 484–486
Texaco, 227–228
Thayer, Paul, 517
Third-party beneficiaries of
warranties, 282
Title
to goods
identification, 268–269
passage of title, 269
special problems regarding title,
270–271
statute of frauds, 272
warranties of, 276–277
disclaiming, 281

Tort(s)
abnormally dangerous activities,
189
business, 190–191
disparagement, 191
interference with business
relationship, 193
interference with contractual
relations, 192–193
intentional
assault and battery, 175–176
conversion, 182
defamation, 177–178
emotional distress, 179
false imprisonment, 176
invasion of privacy, 179
nuisance, 180–181
trespass to land, 180
trespass to personal property,
182
liability for, in agency relationship,
300–301
products liability, 190
rise of negligence in, 201–202
strict liability in, 189, 206–207
Tort law
and business, 173
purposes of, 172–173
Tort liability
causation, 184–186
defenses to, 186–188
in France, 188
negligence, 183
reasonable person standard,
183–184
Tort litigation
costs of, 173
in Japan, 182–183
Toxic pollutants, 410
Toxic substances, and workers,
355–357
Toxic Substances Control Act (1976),
416, 417–418
Toxic substance standards, 356
Trade deficit, 538–539
Trade disparagement, 191
Trademarks, 215–216
Trade names, 216–217
Trade regulation rules, 444
insulation r-value rule, 444–445
mail order rule, 445
used-car rule, 445
Trade secrets, 220
Trade usage, implied warranties
arising under, 280

Transportation, U.S. Department of (DOT), 467
Treatises, 577
Treatment, storage, and disposal (TSD) sites, 419
regulation of, 419
Treble damages, 468, 469
Trespass
to land, 180
to personal property, 182
and pollution, 401
Trial, 102–105
closing arguments in, 104
instructions to jury in, 104
in Italy, 107
length of in business dispute, 93–94
motions after verdict, 104–105
opening statements at, 102
presentation of direct testimony, 103, 104
right to, 102, 132
Trial de novo, 68
Truth-in-Lending Act, 447
credit cost disclosure requirement, 449
enforcement and penalties of, 449
finance charge disclosures, 448
Twenty-sixth Amendment, 117

Unconscionable contracts, 243
Underwriter, 509
Unenforceable contracts, 132
Uniform Commercial Code (UCC), 205, 229, 234
contracts outside coverage of the, 262
foundation of sales contract under, 263–268
goods under, 263
impact of, on business, 260
and mixed transactions, 262
origin of, 260–262
perfect tender rule doctrine, 273
performance and obligations under, 272–276
principal articles of, 261
relationship between Article 2 and the common law, 261–262
rights and remedies, 282–288
of buyer, 284–287
of seller, 282–284
sales by and between merchants, 263
sales contracts under, 262–263

sales under the, 262–263
sales warranties under, 276–282
title to goods under, 268–272
Uniform Limited Partnership Act, 309
Uniform Partnership Act (UPA), 305
Unilateral contract, 231, 237
Unionization, 337
agency shops, 338
and discrimination, 376–377
employer responses to union organizing, 339–340
movement to, 337
representation elections, 337–338
right-to-work laws, 339
union certification, 338
Union leadership, monitoring, 335
Union member bill of rights, 335–336
Union shops, 338
United Kingdom
constitutional law in, 129–130
libel in, 178–179
Race Relations Act in, 453
United Nations, 545
United Nations Commission on International Trade Law, 545, 567
United Nations Convention on the International Sale of Goods, 268
United Nations Convention on the Recognition and Enforcement of Foreign Arbitral Awards, 567
U.S. Constitution, 58, 578–594. *See also specific amendments*
amending, 116–117
background on, 116–117
commerce clause in, 117–118
contract clause in, 121–122
and free speech, 124–128
intellectual property in, 214–215
limits on congressional powers to regulate commerce, 118–119
necessary and proper clause in, 118
protection against search and seizure, 128–130
taxing power in, 122–124
U.S. international trade restrictions and promotions, 548
Arms Export Control Act, 555
export regulation and promotion, 552
Export Administration Act, 552–553
Export Trading Company Act, 552

import regulation and prohibitions, 548–549
bans on certain designated products, 551
duty-free importation: free trade zones and duty-free ports, 551
harmonized tariff schedules, 550–551
import restrictions and adjustments, 551
imposition of import tariffs, 549–550
Nuclear Nonproliferation Act, 555
U.S. Supreme Court, 70–71
Unknown hazards, 209–211
Unliquidated debt, 239–240
Used-car rule, 445
Utilitarianism, 34–35
application of, 34
on corporate responsibility, 43–44
justifications for narrow view of corporate responsibility, 42
necessary conditions for the implementation of, 34
preference, 34
shortcomings in, 35

Valid contract, 231
Venue, 77–78
Verdict, motions after, 104–105
Vertical exclusionary practices, 486
boycotts, 489–490
exclusive dealing, 489
tying arrangements, 487–489
Vertical maximum price fixing, 483–484
Vertical nonprice restraints, 484
territorial restraints, 484–486
Vertical price fixing, 482–483
resale price maintenance, 483
vertical maximum price fixing, 483–484
Vertical Restraint Guidelines (1985), 489
Vertical restraints of trade, 472–473
Vicarious liability, 301
Voidable contract, 132
Voidable preference, 271
Void contract, 231
Voir dire, 102
Voluntary dissolution of a corporation, 316

Wage
    and compensation differentials, 381
    and Equal Pay Act, 369–370
    minimum requirements, 360
Wagner Act (1935), 334–335, 600–604
    and discrimination, 369
Warranties. *See also* Sales warranties
    under Magnuson-Moss Warranty
        Act, 446
    strict liability based on express,
        205–206
    strict liability based on implied,
        204–205
Water pollution, 411
    Clean Water Act, 411–412
    nonpoint source pollution, 415–416

point source pollution, 413–415
    wetlands, 416
West African Economic Community, 549
Wetlands, 416
White-collar crime, 63
Wholly owned subsidiary, 556
Wildlife protection, 421–423
Winding up
    of a corporation, 316
    of the partnership, 306
Women
    and affirmative action, 383–385
    and compensation differentials, 381
    and Equal Pay Act, 369–370
    and sex discrimination, 373–374
    and sexual harassment, 374

Worker safety and health, 353
    and Occupational Safety and
        Health Act, 354–355
    and toxic substances, 355–357
Workers' compensation, 357
    basis for a claim, 358–359
    compensation provided, 357–358
    flaws in, 359
    incentives for safety, 358
World Bank, 546
Writ of certiorari, 71
Writ of execution, 106
Written interrogatories, 99

Yellow-dog contracts, 334